I0554914

THE STARS SHONE ON PHILADELPHIA:

THE 1934 NEGRO NATIONAL LEAGUE CHAMPIONS

EDITED BY FREDERICK C. BUSH AND BILL NOWLIN

ASSOCIATE EDITORS LEN LEVIN AND CARL RIECHERS

Society for American Baseball Research, Inc.
Phoenix, AZ

The Stars Shone on Philadelphia: The 1934 Negro National League Champions
Edited by Frederick C. Bush and Bill Nowlin
Associate editors Len Levin and Carl Riechers

Front cover design: Rachael Sullivan
Cover photograph: Philadelphia Stars © 2005 City of Philadelphia Mural Arts Program / David McShane,
Belmont & Parkside Avenues. Photo by Rob Westle.
Design: Rachael Sullivan

978-1-960819-04-8 ebook
978-1-960819-05-5 paper
Library of Congress Control Number: 2023910135

CONTENTS

PREFACE & ACKNOWLEDGMENTS

The current volume is the sixth in a series of SABR books about great Negro League teams.

Ed Bolden made his mark on Philadelphia baseball with the Hilldale team, which played in the first two Negro League World Series (1924 and 1925) and won the title in '25. Then in 1933 he returned to professional Negro League baseball with a new team, the Philadelphia Stars. The Stars played their inaugural season as an independent team, then joined the new Negro National League II (NNL2) for the 1934 season. After fending off the intrastate-rival Pittsburgh Crawfords, the Stars claimed the NNL2's second-half championship and triumphed over the first-half-champion Chicago American Giants to claim the NNL2 title. As fate would have it, however, the 1934 team's rapid ascent to championship status was tainted by controversies between Stars players and umpires in the title tilt, and the team never won a second crown before it went out of business in 1953.

Provided here are an overview of the Stars franchise history and a detailed account of the 1934 championship team. Majority owner Ed Bolden, a vital figure in the history of Philadelphia baseball, and minority owner/booking agent Eddie Gottlieb – who is better known to basketball fans – are both featured. Passon Field, named after another prominent local baseball entrepreneur, was the Stars' home ballpark in 1934, and its history is also presented.

As always, we have endeavored to include as many of the team's players as possible, even those who only participated in a single game. The Stars featured future Hall of Famers Raleigh "Biz" Mackey and Jud Wilson; stalwarts like Phil Cockrell, Webster McDonald, and Chaney White; shooting star Stewart "Slim" Jones; and temporary fill-ins like Frederick Coleman and Clifford "Whip" Irons. A complete season timeline, articles about select games such as the epic September 9 Satchel Paige-Slim Jones pitching duel at Yankee Stadium, and a complete write-up of the NNL2 championship series round out the book.

As has been the case in each of the previous five books in the series, we have encountered several players who either did not play for the 1934 squad – though there may be sources that list them on the team's roster – or for whom inadequate information is currently available. The following players fall under one of these categories:

1. **? Bolt.** The Seamheads Negro League Database lists a player by this name as having made a single plate appearance in one of the championship series games. Between the fact that our researchers were unable to find a player with that last name and that he had a single plate appearance, it is highly likely that this was a name error made by the press.

2. **Alex Brooks.** SABR author Margaret M. "Peggy" Gripshover determined that Ameal Brooks and Alex Brooks were the same person.

3. **Tom Finley.** Per Seamheads, Finley, who had played third base for the Stars the previous season, died on September 5, 1933.

4. **Richard Harris or James "Sonny" Harris?** SABR researcher/author Rich Bogovich summarized his findings as follows:

The Stars employed an infielder named Harris in a few games toward the end of August. For a time, his first name was entered in Seamheads as Richard, but that is no longer the case. As of this writing, Seamheads assigns this Harris's three Stars games to James "Sonny" Harris, who also played two games with the Baltimore Black Sox in 1934.[1] However, Sonny Harris was with the Black Sox on at least two of the days on which there was also a Harris in the lineup of the Philadelphia Stars.

On the night of August 23, 1934, the Stars had a first baseman named Harris in a game against the Newark Dodgers at Trenton, New Jersey. On that same night, the Baltimore Black Sox had a Harris at second base, presumably Sonny, in a game at Chester, Pennsylvania (albeit only 45 miles away).[2]

On August 24 the Stars reportedly played night games against local teams at two different Philadelphia ballparks, and Harris was at first base for the Stars in both.[3] He was also at the same position in both games of a doubleheader against the Birmingham Black Barons on August 25.[4]

On August 26 a player named Harris was in the Black Sox lineup against a team called the Birmingham Black Crackers (which had a lineup very different from that of the Black Barons).[5] Meanwhile, the Stars deployed their Harris at second base, instead of first, on August 26 in both games of a doubleheader against the Nashville Elite Giants.[6]

If the infielder on the Stars was named Richard Harris, then there is precious little information about a Black athlete by that name – especially in the Philadelphia area, where he most likely lived. One of the few leads is the fact that a Richard Harris played on a Black basketball team called the Philadelphia Panthers in late 1932.[7] No conclusive information is currently available, but it appears possible, or likely, that there may have been two different players named Harris, who played for the Stars and Black Sox respectively.

5. **? Johnson.** This pitcher, who won the first game of a July 10 doubleheader, turned out to be Slim Jones. (See the season timeline in this volume.)

6. **? Jones.** Seamheads lists this player as having played right field and credits him with a single plate appearance during the NNL2 regular season. It is entirely possible that this was pitcher Slim Jones, as no other player with that last name has been identified as a member of the 1934 Stars.

7. **James "Jimmy" Miles.** A right fielder who played in 14 NNL2 regular-season games and had one pinch-hit appearance in the championship series, but for whom no personal information is currently available, including the often-used starting points of birth or death data. A few individuals by that name in the Philadelphia area were considered as possibilities, but it was impossible to confirm any of them as having been this player.

8. **Tom Richardson.** This pitcher, misidentified as Jim Richardson in older sources, pitched in a June 25 exhibition game against the Germantown Artisans. Seamheads credits Richardson with one mound appearance for the Stars in 1933 as well as a lone appearance for the Philadelphia Bacharach Giants in 1934; since Seamheads currently does not include exhibition game statistics, Richardson is not listed as a member of the 1934 Stars on that site. Researcher Rich Bogovich, who attempted to find additional material, noted that, outside of game accounts from his career, "surprisingly little information exists about Tom Richardson's life."

This book represents the collaborative effort of 25 SABR members, who all did due diligence to uncover as much information as possible about their subjects. While the information presented is ample, it is a fact that the 1934 Stars had numerous cup-of-coffee and other short-time players; that made the search for photos a more challenging task than for some of the past volumes. The fact that we have as many photos and graphics as we do, and in a variety of visual representations, is due to the efforts and generosity of numerous individuals. Thanks are due to artists Graig Kreindler and David McShane, Dr. Layton Revel and the Center for Negro League Baseball Research, Gary Ashwill, and Brian Michael.

Thanks also are due to the associate editors on our team, fact-checker Carl Riechers and final-copy editor Len Levin. It has been such a pleasure to work with them, along with all of the other SABR members, that the next book – which will feature the 1939 Baltimore Elite Giants – is already in progress. In the meantime, enjoy reading and learning about the year 1934, when *The Stars Shone on Philadelphia*.

Frederick C. Bush
Bill Nowlin
April 2023

Notes

1   For an example of Sonny Harris being identified as a member of the Baltimore Black Sox by early August, see "Among Our Colored Citizens," *Chester* (Pennsylvania) *Times*, August 4, 1934: 3. This article noted that he had been "purchased from the Cincinnati Tigers and has been going great until he suffered a slight injury several games ago." See also "Double Bill," *Cincinnati Enquirer*, October 21, 1934: 29.

2   "Newark Dodgers Win Over All-Stars, 4-3," *Trenton* (New Jersey) *Evening Times*, August 24, 1934: 17. "Black Sox Meet Bacharach Today," *Chester Times*, August 25, 1934: 13. The date of Baltimore's night game against the Miami Giants was confirmed in "Among Our Colored Citizens," *Chester Times*, August 25, 1934: 3. See also "Black Sox Meet Miami Tonight," *Chester Times*, August 23, 1934: 16.

3   "Phila. Stars Blanks [*sic*] Passon A.A. Sluggers," *Philadelphia Inquirer*, August 25, 1934: 14. "Phila. Stars Trip Holmesburg Nine," *Philadelphia Inquirer*, August 25, 1934: 24.

4   "Phila. Stars Land Twin Bill Victory," *Philadelphia Inquirer*, August 26, 1934: S7.

5   "Black Sox Win Pair on Local Diamond," *Chester Times*, August 27, 1934: 11.

6   "Phila. Stars Twice Down Nashville Foes," *Philadelphia Inquirer*, August 27, 1934: 16.

7   "Panthers All Set for Big Season," *Philadelphia Tribune*, December 8, 1932: 9.

BACKGROUND

ED BOLDEN'S PHILADELPHIA STARS: A FRANCHISE IN THE SHADOWS OF ITS PEERS

By Courtney Michelle Smith

Ed Bolden's Philadelphia Stars existed for almost exactly 20 years. They were formed in February 1933, in the middle of the Great Depression and the transition from Herbert Hoover to Franklin Delano Roosevelt. The Stars formally ceased operations in the spring of 1953, in the middle of the National and American Leagues' imperfect yet steady progress toward integration. During those intervening 20 years, the Stars experienced the highs and lows common to all Negro League teams in the 1930s and 1940s. They offered Black baseball players opportunities denied to them in the two leagues then deemed "major." Ironically, once those leagues welcomed Black players, the Stars no longer had a place within the American sports world. They represented a relic of a segregated world that started to disappear in the late 1940s. The Stars' death happened quietly; no one seemed to mourn their passing in 1953 because the sports world had moved on from the Negro Leagues. However, the Stars' existence mattered, and the franchise's history tells a tale about the triumphs and obstacles Negro League teams faced in the middle of the twentieth century.

The February 9, 1933, edition of the *Philadelphia Tribune* carried the news of the birth of Bolden's Philadelphia Stars. A headline announced the franchise's creation, and the accompanying article shared a few interesting details as to how it came into existence.[1] Formally, the franchise was born during a meeting of Black baseball leaders in Ed Gottlieb's office. Gottlieb was a (White) Jewish booking agent and sports promoter who worked in Philadelphia, and he was to provide financial support both to the Stars and to the Negro National League II (NNL2). The NNL2 was looking to build an Eastern division, and the Stars were projected to be one of the teams to populate it. Gottlieb worked behind the scenes in scheduling games and managing finances, while Bolden served as the franchise's public face. Bolden, whose name remained part of the franchise's official name throughout its existence, was a Black resident

of nearby Darby, Pennsylvania, who had already made a name for himself in Negro League baseball. He had steered the Darby-based Hilldale Daisies to prominence in the 1910s and 1920s before an ugly falling-out ended his tenure with Hilldale a few years before that franchise folded. Hilldale's demise opened the Philadelphia market and gave Bolden the opportunity to return to Black professional baseball as well as to reestablish himself as one of the top Black baseball moguls in the country.

Under Bolden's guidance, the Stars enjoyed a successful inaugural season that saw them win every series and earn praise as the "[b]est balanced Colored attraction in baseball."[2] Bolden skillfully used his connections within the Black baseball world to sign established and talented players like Dick Lundy,

Ed Bolden was owner of the 1925 Negro World Series champion Hilldale team and the 1934 NNL2-champion Philadelphia Stars.

Webster McDonald, Biz Mackey, Jud Wilson, Jake Stephens, Porter Charleston, Dick Seay, and Cliff Carter. With their talented roster, the Stars amassed a winning record by defeating local semipro and professional all-White baseball teams. The Stars also defeated Negro League clubs like the Pittsburgh Crawfords and semipro Black teams like Passon Club, owned by Philadelphia businessman Harry Passon. Bolden's Stars also developed a rivalry with Passon's other club, the Bacharach Giants. The Stars fared well against their rivals and cemented their status as the city's next great Black baseball team.[3]

In addition to relying upon his connections within the sports world, Bolden also used his connections to columnists in Black newspapers, particularly the *Pittsburgh Courier* and the *Philadelphia Tribune,* to help build a fan base for his new franchise. Bolden had honed those connections during his years with Hilldale, and his team's success helped to ensure favorable coverage in the city's largest Black newspaper. Prior to the season, columnist W. Rollo Wilson, who had hinted at Bolden's comeback in a column published on February 4, 1933, declared that "[u]niform makers, sporting goods houses [and] similar concerns" had entered into a bidding war for the Stars' business.[4] In the *Philadelphia Tribune,* Randy Dixon lauded Bolden's roster as a "choice coterie of diamond laborers whose past exploits and present records insure [*sic*] [Bolden] of fielding an aggregation that will doff the sombrero to no rival cast."[5] As the Stars accumulated victories, Dixon continued his praise for Bolden and declared that the team had "stepped in the front rank of eastern Negro baseball teams."[6] Throughout the 1933 season, the *Philadelphia Tribune* provided regular, and laudatory, coverage of the Stars as they faced well-known teams like the Pittsburgh Crawfords and local teams like the Bacharach Giants. With that coverage, the Stars built a fan base, and Bolden renewed his connections with a newspaper that provided a critical link to the fans who attended Stars games.[7]

Perhaps the wisest decision Bolden made during the Stars' inaugural season was to keep the franchise out of the new NNL2. Bolden had bad experiences operating within league structures when he owned the Hilldale team, and he correctly saw that an independent status was the best option for his new club. Gus Greenlee, who operated both legal and illegal businesses in Pittsburgh, steered the creation of the NNL2 and envisioned a "national" league with franchises stretching from Chicago eastward to Philadelphia. His legal businesses included the Pittsburgh Crawfords, an entry in the NNL2, and the Crawford Grill nightclub. Greenlee's illegal businesses included the numbers lottery and selling alcohol during the Prohibition Era. His launch of the new league came at the same time as he stood trial in Pittsburgh for charges stemming from his illegal gambling business. Though the jury found Greenlee not guilty, his court case foreshadowed continued legal troubles for himself and an unsettled inaugural season for the NNL2. The NNL2 seemed to fall apart in the middle of the season when Cumberland Posey of the Homestead Grays, another Pittsburgh-based franchise, allegedly signed two players claimed by the Detroit Stars. As a result, the NNL2 dismissed the Grays from the league. Disputes between Posey and John Clark, one of Greenlee's associates, spilled over into the pages of the *Pittsburgh Courier* and painted the picture of a league in disarray.[8]

Greenlee's efforts to build the NNL2 were not a total failure, and the league he founded did manage to survive for the next 15 seasons. His best decision came when he oversaw the first East-West Game, an event that became the annual All-Star Game for the Negro leagues and a premier showcase for some of the best Black baseball players in the country. To help generate interest for the game, Greenlee had ballots printed in the *Pittsburgh Courier,* the *Philadelphia Tribune,* and other Black newspapers. The East-West Game was a huge success; the game was played in Comiskey Park, the home of the Chicago White Sox. Notable players at the first East-West Game included Oscar Charleston, Satchel Paige, Norman "Turkey" Stearnes, Judy Johnson, and James "Cool Papa" Bell. Even though the Stars did not belong to the NNL2, the East roster included four members of the squad – Biz Mackey, Jud Wilson, Dick Lundy, and Rap Dixon. Greenlee, furthermore, did not give up on his determination to include the Stars in the NNL2, and his determination paid off when Bolden and Gottlieb added the franchise to the league prior to the 1934 season.

The Stars' 1934 season, the best campaign in their history, began with their ungraceful entry into the NNL2. At a meeting in Philadelphia in February 1934, the NNL2 owners seemed poised to welcome two Philadelphia teams into the league, the Stars and the Bacharach Giants. Bolden, however, objected to the Bacharach Giants' entry, and Harry Passon withdrew his team's application. As Bolden explained, he did not believe that Philadelphia could successfully support two league franchises, so the Stars would not join the NNL2 if the other owners accepted the Bacharach Giants into the fold. Bolden made further waves at the meeting by arguing against a stipulation that each league franchise make financial deposits. The other owners insisted on those deposits because the money could help protect them against fines and defaults in players' earnings. Bolden did receive some good news when the other NNL2 owners elected the newspaper columnist W. Rollo Wilson, with whom he had a close working relationship, as the league's commissioner. That decision, along with Gottlieb's continued status as a scheduler for many NNL2 games and as an overseer for the league's finances, helped cement Philadelphia's special status within the league. Such as status came in handy at the end of the season when the commissioner needed to make key decisions involving the championship series.[9]

For the 1934 season, the NNL2 had both full and associate members. The full members included the Stars, Pittsburgh Crawfords, Cleveland Red Sox, Nashville Elite Giants, Newark Dodgers, and Chicago American Giants. After withdrawing his franchise's application as a full NNL2 member, Passon brought the Bacharach Giants into the league to join the Homestead Grays, Memphis Red Sox, and Birmingham Black Barons as associate members. To help determine the league champion, the owners divided the 1934 regular season into two halves. After the regular season ended, the winners of the two half-seasons would meet to determine the NNL2 champion. As it had during the previous season, the league again experienced some instability in the 1934 season. The Cleveland Buckeyes withdrew from the circuit during the second half of the season, and the Nashville Elite Giants did not have any home games on the second-half schedule. Similarly, the league's attempt to expand into the Baltimore market with the Baltimore Black Sox failed when other league teams refused, for financial reasons, to travel to Baltimore for games.[10]

Due to the Stars' ability to consistently draw large crowds to home games and to their talented roster, the franchise remained insulated from the troubles plaguing other league teams. The Stars played many of their home games at Passon Field, at 48th and Spruce Streets in West Philadelphia. Passon Field underwent renovations in preparation for the Stars' games; the improvements included the installation of 4,000 new seats. Five thousand fans greeted the Stars at their home opener, a 12-0 victory over the Newark Dodgers. In addition to watching their team shut out the Dodgers, the Stars' fans enjoyed pregame festivities featuring the O.V. Catto Elks Band. With the exception of starting pitcher Stuart "Slim" Jones,

every player in the Stars lineup notched at least one hit, and the team's offense prowess drove the Dodgers' starting pitcher from the game in the fifth inning. The Stars' home opener set the tone for the rest of the season. Most importantly, it introduced Slim Jones to Philadelphia's Black baseball fans and to the rest of the NNL2.[11]

Born in Baltimore in 1913, Jones emerged as one of the best pitchers in the NNL2 and as one of the best players ever to don a Stars jersey. Slim earned his nickname because he stood 6-feet-6 inches and weighed only 185 pounds. Prior to joining the Stars in 1934, Jones spent the 1932 and 1933 seasons with the Baltimore Black Sox and the 1933-34 winter season with a team in Puerto Rico.[12] Despite his youth and inexperience, Jones often started important games for the Stars during the 1934 season. As an example, the rivalry between the Stars and the Bacharach Giants carried over from the 1933 season, and Jones started the first and fourth games of a five-game series between the two foes. Jones pitched a shutout in both games; he allowed a total of seven hits and posted double-digit strikeouts in each. Not surprisingly, Jones was one of the pitchers chosen to represent the East team at the second annual the East-West Game. Jones combined with two other pitchers on the East team, including Leroy "Satchel" Paige, on a 1-0 shutout of the West team. Jones's and Paige's paths crossed again a short time later, this time as opponents during a new feature in the NNL2 schedule that exposed Black baseball players to a wider audience.[13]

In the 1930s and 1940s, Negro League franchises occasionally faced off in four-team doubleheaders at Yankee Stadium. These doubleheaders typically served as benefits for people or organizations and attracted crowds with both White and Black fans. A few weeks after the East-West Game, the NNL2 held the season's first doubleheader at Yankee Stadium. Held to benefit Sergeant George W. Curley and John W. Duncan, it featured the American Giants and the Black Yankees in the first game and the Stars and Crawfords in the second.[14] The Stars-Crawfords game, a 1-1 pitching duel between Jones and Paige, was called after nine innings because of darkness. Both pitchers completed similar performances. Paige allowed six hits and notched 12 strikeouts while Jones allowed three hits and struck out nine batters. The *Tribune's* Ed Harris praised Paige and Jones and noted that the event attracted many White spectators. Harris also wrote that both games featured playing "fit for the big leagues" and that the high attendance disproved the notion "that

Negro baseball isn't worth a dime."[15] Three weeks later Paige and the Crawfords triumphed over Jones and the Stars in a rematch at another Yankee Stadium four-team doubleheader. The second doubleheader attracted another large crowd to Yankee Stadium, and the crowd cheered for Jones in the losing effort.[16]

Overall, Jones's performance reflected the team's performance throughout the 1934 season – they held their own against the top teams and top players in the NNL2. Jones led the Stars' pitching staff with a 20-4 record and a 1.29 ERA. Webster McDonald, Rocky Ellis, and Lefty Holmes joined Jones in the starting rotation and all posted sub-3.00 ERAs. McDonald also served as the team's field manager. Among the Stars' offensive players, infielder Jud Wilson led the team with a .358 batting average and a .931 OPS. Outfielder Chaney White had the second-highest batting average on the team, .302, and an OPS of .760. Other top performers on the team included Jake Dunn, Jake Stevens, and Biz Mackey. The Stars finished with a league record of 39-18-10 and captured the second-half title of the NNL2 season. They faced the Chicago American Giants, winners of the first half, in a controversy-marred championship series that undermined the Stars' achievements.[17]

The controversies in the championship series revolved around the actions of the umpires and of the NNL2 commissioner, Rollo Wilson. In Game Six, two Stars players, Jud Wilson and Ameal Brooks, physically attacked umpires in two separate incidents. Despite those outbursts, the umpires did not eject either Wilson or Brooks from the game. The Stars won Game Six, prompting American Giants manager Dave Malarcher to formally protest the game to the commissioner. Rollo Wilson considered suspending Jud Wilson and Brooks from Game Seven, the last scheduled game in the series. Both Bolden and Gottlieb met with Wilson prior to Game Seven and pressured Wilson to avoid suspending either player. Bolden added to the tense atmosphere and to the American Giants' justified anger by threatening to pull the Stars from the series if Wilson suspended the two players. The threat worked, and Wilson both denied the American Giants' protest of Game Six and permitted all players to participate in Game Seven.[18]

Due to the lack of any consequences for bad behavior in Game Six, the on-field disruptions continued for the rest of the series. Game Seven featured another player-led attack on an umpire. This time, the American Giants' left fielder, Mule Suttles, protested a called third strike by hitting the umpire in the head with his bat. Unlike the previous game, the umpire promptly ejected Suttles, and a riot nearly erupted on the field. To compound those on-field problems, the game ended in a tie because it was played on a Sunday in Philadelphia and the state of Pennsylvania still enforced blue laws in 1934. Those laws put a 6:00 P.M. curfew on the game, and the on-field disruptions prevented the game from being completed by the curfew. The tie game resulted in a hastily scheduled Game Eight on Monday, a game that brought more protests from both the Stars and the American Giants. The American Giants disputed an umpire's call at home plate. The Stars argued that the American Giants used a player who was under contract with another NNL2 franchise.[19]

Not surprisingly, coverage of the championship series spent little time praising the Stars and much time lamenting the sorry spectacles that played out over the series' final games. Columnist Ed Harris asserted that Wilson's and Brooks' "illegal" and unfair" actions in Game Six set "[u]nhappy precedents" and fomented "out-and-out diamond lawlessness."[20] Harris further criticized Wilson and Brooks for forgetting "it was a championship game, that their services were valuable to the teams, [and] that spectators had paid to see a baseball game and not a court-room debate or a prize fight."[21] He both expressed sympathy for and criticized the umpires in Game Six. While acknowledging that umpires' decisions almost always attract criticism, Harris chastised them for not ejecting Wilson and Brooks. According to Harris, their actions set "unfortunate precedents" and gave Malarcher ammunition for filing a protest with the league commissioner.[22] Harris also correctly predicted that the controversy-filled resolution to the 1934 NNL2 season would spill over into plans for 1935. Robert Cole, the American Giants' owner, refused to sign paychecks unless all NNL2 members showed up at a meeting scheduled for Pittsburgh. Only Greenlee and Cumberland Posey of the Homestead Grays showed up, leading Cole to act upon his threat. One of the unsigned paychecks belonged to the commissioner, and that led Wilson to allege publicly that Cole was engaged in spiteful behavior in retaliation for his rulings during the championship series.[23]

The messy 1934 NNL2 championship series closed a chapter in the Stars' history, one marked with power and success. With the Stars' triumph, Bolden earned the distinction of taking his second franchise to the pinnacle of its league. He built the new franchise from scratch by relying on key veterans he knew from his

Center for Negro League Baseball Research

Penmar Park, also known as the 44th and Parkside ballpark, served as the Stars' home field from 1936 to 1947.

days with Hilldale and by finding key younger players with promising futures. Bolden furthermore flexed his power by relegating another franchise in Philadelphia to a secondary status within the NNL2 and, in collaboration with Gottlieb, by pressuring the commissioner to avoid suspending players for bad on-field conduct. After the 1934 season, the Stars never again reached the pinnacle of the Negro Leagues, and the franchise spent the much of remainder of the decade flirting with obscurity. The Stars and their fan base never truly savored their 1934 title, and the rest of the league quickly moved on from the controversy-plagued series.

During the remainder of the 1930s, four key events exemplified the fallout from the Stars' 1934 victory and the obstacles that prevented the franchise from rebounding and contending for another title. The first of those events happened early in 1935 as NNL2 owners gathered in Philadelphia to plan for the coming season. Wilson lost his job as league commissioner to Ferdinand Q. Morton, a New York City civil service commissioner who had no experience in professional baseball. The press speculated that Morton likely earned his new job because of a shift in power within the NNL2 to New York City. For the 1935 season, the league said farewell to the Bacharach Giants and hello to three franchises based in New York City region, the New York Cubans, Brooklyn Eagles, and Newark Dodgers. The introduction of the Brooklyn Eagles brought Abe and Effa Manley into the NNL2. The Manleys combined the Dodgers and Eagles franchises and moved the new team to Newark; Effa was to emerge as one of the league's most influential officials. Overall, the election of a new commissioner and the welcoming of three new franchises marked a new

chapter for both the Stars and the rest of the NNL2. The league now had a foothold in the New York City market and a decreased presence in the Philadelphia region. Additionally, by selecting a new commissioner, the team owners also delivered a rebuke to Wilson and demonstrated a desire to move on quickly from the Stars' victory.[24]

The second key event came later in the 1935 season, a frustrating season for Bolden and the Stars, when Bolden lashed out at his players and the NNL2's overall management. While the Stars mounted a challenge for the second-half title, they also endured a prolonged losing streak during the first half of the season and missed out on a chance to defend their crown. In response to that losing streak, Bolden used the pages of the *Philadelphia Independent* to detail extensive roster overhaul through in-season trades. Those trades never materialized, but Bolden's frustration with his players persisted. Bolden suspended Slim Jones and stripped him of his salary for his "failure to attain proper physical condition."[25] Two other pitchers, Paul Carter and Rocky Ellis, faced fines of $5.00 and $10.00 respectively for "absence from the club during working hours without permission."[26] Bolden's disdain for his players ran so deep that he asked Greenlee, the NNL2's president, to limit the number of Stars players on the East team at the annual East-West Game. Greenlee did not take that action, and seven Stars players appeared on the East's roster. Those players included the suspended Slim Jones; Webster McDonald, the Stars' manager, managed the East squad. Undeterred, Bolden maintained his tough posture against his players and again threatened a roster overhaul before the next season. Bolden also used a spokesperson to vent about the league's management and the unfair position he saw for the Stars within the NNL2. Through the spokesperson, Bolden complained about the amount of money the Stars lost on their road trips while other teams made money playing in Philadelphia due to the presence of more semipro teams whose contests filled gaps in the teams' league schedules. Ultimately, Bolden wanted the NNL2 to cover less territory, wanted to expose a small group of owners who controlled all league affairs at the Stars' expense, and wanted Philadelphia to host the next East-West Game.[27]

Bolden's frustrations with his fellow owners seeped into the next season and led to the third key event

Center for Negro League Baseball Research

As a player/manager, Webster McDonald worked on all phases of his game.

that characterized the Stars' post-1934 existence – the confusion over the first-half winner and ultimate cancellation of the 1936 league championship series. Prior to the 1936 season, Greenlee needed to resign his position as the NNL2's president, and Bolden won the election to replace him. Bolden balanced his role as the league's president with his role in building the Stars' roster, making good on his threats from the previous season to complete a roster overhaul. Through his efforts, the Stars' 1936 roster featured new players like Norman "Turkey" Stearnes, Larry Brown, Roy Parnell, and Bill Yancey. The revamped Stars held their spring training exercises at a YMCA in southwest Philadelphia, near the site of their home ballpark at 44th and Parkside Avenue. On the eve of the 1936 season opener, Bolden invited reporters to the YMCA and used the opportunity to deliver a stern lecture to his players. Through his lecture, Bolden established his high expectations for the Stars' players both on and off of the field and his determination to release under-producing players.[28] For most of the first half of the season, the Stars fulfilled Bolden's high expectations and appeared poised to clinch the first-half title. Officially, however, the NNL2 did not recognize a first-half champion because neither the Stars nor the Baltimore Elite Giants, the other team claiming the first-half title, had followed the league's rules. Those rules required NNL2 teams to play each other at least five times in each half of the season, so both the Stars and the Elite Giants needed to play additional games before the league would recognize a first-half champion.[29]

In July the controversy deepened when the league's secretary, John Clark, who was affiliated with the Pittsburgh Crawfords, published official standings that awarded the first-half title to the Elite Giants. Bolden correctly noted that those standings were incomplete since the two teams still needed to face each other in two games as mandated by the league's rules. His reasonable, and correct, objections created fissures among the NNL2 owners as some sided with Bolden while others sided with Tom Wilson, the Elite Giants' owner who also served as the NNL2's treasurer. Ultimately, the controversy proved to be moot. The Stars and Elite Giants played the two missing games later in the season, and the Elite Giants won both of them to officially capture the first-half title. The NNL2, however, never officially crowned a champion since neither the Elite Giants nor the Crawfords, the second-half winners, played the championship series. Most of the players from both teams opted to participate in the annual *Denver Post* Tournament; rather than carry on a sham of the championship series, the NNL2 simply canceled it and left the championship vacant for the 1936 season.[30]

Two years later came the fourth and final key event that characterized the Stars' post-1934 existence and their inability to win another title – the premature death of Slim Jones. According to a story that appeared in November 1938, Jones died in his hometown of Baltimore after suffering a bout of double pneumonia. Later information, however, indicated that Jones died from kidney failure and other ailments. Jones never lived up to the promise he showed in the Stars' championship season when he held his own in pitching duels against future Hall of Famer Satchel Paige. He suffered injuries to his left shoulder, a career-interrupting or career-ending development for a left-handed pitcher. To cope with his injuries, Jones turned to alcohol, and his alcoholism likely contributed to his death and to the clashes he had with Bolden over his physical conditioning. Jones's death served as a tragic and apt example of the precarious life many players experienced in the Negro Leagues. They lacked the support systems modern-day baseball players have to recover from injuries and to prolong their careers. Jones' death, furthermore, also tragically and aptly captured how the Stars paid a heavy price for their lone championship and never returned to the vaunted place within the NNL2 that they occupied in the 1934 season.[31]

Those four key events – the change in NNL2 commissioner and admission of three New York City area franchises; Bolden lashing out against his fellow NNL2 owners; the messy resolution of the first-half winner in 1936; and Jones' untimely death – came against a backdrop of continued problems for the NNL2. Teams in the league regularly failed to play all the games on their published schedules, and players habitually "jumped" their contracts for more lucrative deals with teams outside of the league and outside of the United States.[32] While owners threatened to ban contract jumpers, they never followed through with those threats since the contract jumpers ranked among the top players in Black professional baseball. The NNL2 also faced a competitor when the Negro American League (NAL) was launched in 1937 with teams scattered across Midwestern and Southern cities. Starting in 1939, a more ominous challenge to the existence of both the NNL2 and the NAL appeared in the pages of the *Pittsburgh Courier*, one of the most prominent Black newspapers in the country.

On those pages, Wendell Smith wrote a series of articles that investigated whether the "major leagues" would welcome Black players. Those articles foreshadowed the intensive effort by Smith and others to pressure National and American League franchises to sign Black players and to end the segregation era in professional baseball.[33]

For the Stars and the rest of the Negro Leagues, the possibility of Black players in the segregated "major leagues" seemed remote in the early 1940s. Both the NNL2 and the NAL suffered many of the same problems that had plagued them in the 1930s – financial instability, incomplete schedules, and internal divisions among team owners. Additionally, both the NNL2 and NAL owners faced the continued prospect of contract jumpers and, once the United States entered World War II, the loss of players to the armed forces. The Stars remained mired in the middle-to-lower tier of teams in the NNL2 and toiled in the shadows of top-tier Black teams like the Homestead Grays, Newark Eagles, and Kansas City Monarchs. Behind the scenes, Bolden used his connections with members of the Philadelphia community to generate interest in the Stars and to try to make the team a part of the city's culture. Gottlieb maintained a prominent role in scheduling games, and he worked closely with Effa Manley on managing the NNL2's finances.[34]

During the World War II era, the most interesting development for the Stars came in 1943 when they started using Shibe Park to stage some home contests. Since their inception, the Stars had used two small ballparks for their home games – Passon Field at 48th and Spruce Street and the PRR YMCA Park at 44th and Parkside Avenue. The latter field, dubbed "Bolden Bowl" by Black sportswriters, was owned by the Pennsylvania Railroad and sat near a roundhouse in West Philadelphia. Due to that location, the 44th and Parkside ballpark presented some challenging playing conditions. Smoke from passing trains caused some game delays, and fans had to navigate the accumulated soot and ashes that covered parts of the ballpark, including the screen behind home plate. Shibe Park offered much better amenities as well as the potential for larger crowds. Since both the Philadelphia Phillies and Philadelphia Athletics used Shibe Park for their home games, the Stars faced a limit on the number of games they could play at the larger and nicer ballpark. The use of Shibe Park became a double-edged sword for the Stars and portended a troubled future for the franchise, particularly as the effort to get Black players into the White major leagues gained momentum during the wartime years.[35]

World War II provided a boost to the effort started and sustained by Wendell Smith in the pages of the *Pittsburgh Courier*. America's global fight against fascism resonated with civil-rights activists on the home front and led to a movement call the Double Victory campaign that promised victory over racism at home and abroad. In 1944, the death of longtime Commissioner Kenesaw Mountain Landis, who did not appear to favor integration, provided some hope that at least one franchise would soon sign Black players. Landis's replacement, Albert "Happy" Chandler, expressed more openness toward integration, and New York City's government got involved as a way to pressure the Yankees, Giants, and Dodgers to open their franchises to Black players. Meanwhile, Wendell Smith and other Black sportswriters intensified their own campaigns. Prior to the end of World War II, Smith arranged for tryouts involving several Negro League players and major-league franchises. More importantly, Smith indirectly introduced Jackie Robinson to Branch Rickey, the general manager of the Brooklyn Dodgers who was secretly planning to sign Black players. Rickey threw his support behind a new Negro league, the United States League, as a way to send his scouts to review Black players and to hide his true intentions. Robinson and Rickey had their famous meeting in Brooklyn in August 1945, and the formal announcement of Robinson's signing came in October 1945 shortly after the conclusion of the baseball season.[36]

Robinson's signing with the Brooklyn Dodgers organization initiated the final and most challenging era for the Stars and the rest of the Negro Leagues. In 1946, as Robinson played for the Montreal Royals, the Negro Leagues benefited from the attention devoted to him. The Stars and other teams enjoyed large crowds at their games, and those large crowds generated bountiful gate receipts for the Negro League franchises; for example, a game featuring the Stars and the Homestead Grays at Shibe Park attracted over 10,000 fans. The Stars even flirted with a first-place finish in the NNL2, but they lost steam and again finished the season out of contention for the championship. In the midst of the good news, the Stars and other franchises faced some ominous signs about their future. Stories about Robinson and a few other Black players who had signed with White major-league franchises dominated sports pages in Black newspapers. Additionally, Rickey and other officials who signed Black players

did not always honor those players' contracts with Negro League teams and offered little to no compensation. The decline in attention combined with the lack of respect foretold a bad future for both the NNL2 and the NAL in spite of an otherwise successful 1946 season.[37]

While the Stars and other Black teams prepared for the 1947 season, the Brooklyn Dodgers selected Robinson's contract, and all attention in the baseball world went to the rookie who finally broke the color barrier. A few months into the 1947 season, Larry Doby joined the Cleveland Indians, meaning that both the American League and the National League featured integrated teams. Stories about Robinson and Doby appeared prominently in the sports pages of Black newspapers. The Stars felt this problem acutely as the *Philadelphia Tribune* carried advertisements for the Dodgers' games against the Phillies and for the Cleveland Indians' games against the Athletics. Those advertisements crowded out stories about the Stars and led to attendance problems felt around both the NNL2 and NAL. At the end of the season, when the Brooklyn Dodgers secured a World Series berth, the *Philadelphia Independent*'s editorial board devoted a lengthy editorial to Robinson's presence in the World Series. The editorial praised Robinson for establishing a good example for other Black players and compared him to previous African American leaders like Frederick Douglass, Mary McLeod Bethune, and W.E.B. Du Bois. The Stars and other Negro League teams received scant attention, a sign that the Black press and baseball had largely moved on from those teams.[38]

The 1948 season featured even more Black players in the NL and AL and brought the Negro Leagues to the brink of irrelevancy. Bolden tried to reverse his franchise's fortunes by hiring Oscar Charleston to be the field manager and also attempted to restructure the roster with younger talent. That revamped roster, however, lacked its own home ballpark since the Stars lost use of the field at 44th and Parkside and had to use Shibe Park to stage home contests in Philadelphia. Shibe Park offered only limited opportunities for the Stars to stage home games since both the Phillies and Athletics used the ballpark on most days of the baseball season. The Stars' problems represented a microcosm of the problems facing both the NNL2 and the NAL. Major-league officials rejected all attempts by the Negro Leagues for consideration as minor leagues, and Negro League games drew sparse crowds. The NNL2 and NAL staged a final World Series between the two circuits in which the Homestead Grays defeated the NAL's Birmingham Black Barons to emerge as champions. Soon after the series ended, the Grays left the NNL2 and decided to operate as an independent franchise. The Manleys sold the Eagles franchise, and the new owners took the team to Houston for two years and New Orleans for one final season before ceasing operations. The New York Black Yankees disbanded; the NNL2 also disbanded, leaving remaining teams like the Stars with few options to continue operations.[39]

For the next four seasons, the Stars endured an odd existence that merely delayed the franchise's inevitable dissolution. In 1949, they joined a revamped NAL, but league-organized play had effectively ceased with the end of the NNL2. The Stars and other remaining teams had little to support themselves other than the shrinking gate receipts they collected from their games. Additionally, the Stars continued to lose players to the major-league franchises and to see other players jump their contracts to join teams in the Mexican League. Bolden tried to minimize the damage from those developments by not publicly speaking about the losses and trying to focus attention on the players who remained on the Stars' roster. In September 1950 the Stars suffered their biggest loss when Bolden died at the age of 68. He suffered a stroke at his home in Darby; he died on September 27 at Darby's Mercy-Fitzgerald Hospital. Bolden's wife, Nellie, had died in 1948; he was survived by their daughter, Hilda, the director of a medical health center in Washington, D.C., and his two brothers. His funeral at Darby's Mount Union Zion Church attracted many prominent members of the Philadelphia community and testified to the respect Bolden had earned throughout his lifetime.[40]

After Bolden's death, the Stars continued to operate under the guidance of Gottlieb and Charleston. Charleston served as the team's field manager and took control over personnel decisions. He built rosters full of young players and emphasized the Stars as a stepping stone to careers in major-league organizations. Through Charleston's scouting efforts, the Stars attracted many local high-school and sandlot players and, for the 1952 season, carried a youthful roster whose players averaged 21 years old. Those young players faced grueling schedules that kept them on the road for long periods of time; to compound those problems, the Stars posted losing records and financial losses. Due to schedule conflicts with the Phillies and Athletics, the Stars also gradually delayed their debuts at Shibe Park. From 1948 until 1950, the team

Jud Wilson was a career .357 hitter in 1,155 major Negro Leagues games.

held its opener at Shibe Park in May, but rain washed out the scheduled opener in May 1950, and the Stars did not play in Philadelphia until early July. In their 1951 Shibe Park debut, the Stars lost a doubleheader to the Indianapolis Clowns and attracted a woeful crowd of 3,000 fans; at the same time, the last-place Phillies and the Dodgers drew 85,000 fans to a three-game series. The Stars' 1952 "home" season again did not begin until July, and they attracted a meager 4,000 fans to their home opener.[41]

With those conditions facing the Stars, and with few prospects for a rebound in future seasons, Gottlieb in March 1953 made the sudden, yet not unexpected, announcement of the franchise's dissolution. A few weeks later, Gottlieb retracted his earlier announcement and said that he would look for a buyer for the franchise. When no buyers came forward, Gottlieb put the Stars out of business; he granted all players free-agent status and focused his attention toward his basketball team, the Philadelphia Warriors. The Stars had played their final game. Their passing came without any retrospectives or mournful articles in the Black newspapers.[42]

In their 20 years of existence, Ed Bolden's Philadelphia Stars reflected the highs and lows, as well as the triumphs and tribulations, common to teams in the Negro Leagues in the 1930s, 1940s, and 1950s. Their lone championship season came with a string of controversies that revealed the ugly side of the Negro Leagues and that ultimately prevented them from joining the register of top teams in the NNL2. Similar to other Negro League teams, the Stars struggled to remain relevant after Jackie Robinson's debut with the Brooklyn Dodgers. The Stars were a product of a segregated sports world and no longer had a place once franchises like the Dodgers, Cleveland Indians, and others carried integrated team rosters. The Stars' story, though, remains relevant since it offers a fascinating and at times frustrating window into the challenges facing Negro League teams as they navigated racism, economic deprivation, and a world war.

Notes

1   Dick Sun, "Lundy To Lead Phila. Nine In Diamond Loop; Mogules Meet Here and Map Out Campaign for 1933 Season," *Philadelphia Tribune*, February 9, 1933.

2   "Philadelphia Stars, Greatest Defensive Club in the East," *Colored Baseball and Sports Monthly* 1, no. 4 (October 1934): 18. Edward Bolden Papers, Box 186-1, Folder 21; Manuscript Division, Moorland-Spingarn Research Center, Howard University.

3   Courtney Michelle Smith, *Ed Bolden and Black Baseball in Philadelphia* (Jefferson, North Carolina: McFarland, 2017), 68-74.

4   W. Rollo Wilson, "Sport Shots," *Pittsburgh Courier*, February 25, 1933.

5   Randy Dixon, "Galaxy of Baseball Aces to Play for Ed Bolden's Phila. Stars this Season," *Philadelphia Tribune*, March 16, 1933.

6   Dixon, "Stars Subdue Crawfords on Wilson's Blow," *Philadelphia Tribune*, May 18, 1933.

7   "5 Game Series Between Stars and Bacharachs," *Philadelphia Tribune*, June 22, 1933; "Boldenmen and Passons Under Arclights Fri," *Philadelphia Tribune*, July 20, 1933; "Crawfords Drub Boldenmen Three Times to Even Series," *Philadelphia Tribune*, August 17, 1933.

8   "Greenlee Cleared in Lottery Case," *Pittsburgh Courier*, March 18, 1933; Smith, *Ed Bolden and Black Baseball in Philadelphia*, 68; Leslie Heaphy, *The Negro Leagues 1869-1960* (Jefferson, North Carolina: McFarland, 2003), 93.

9   Dixon, "Newspaperman Accepts Job as Baseball Commissioner; Sweeping Reforms Are Made," *Philadelphia Tribune*, March 15, 1934; Smith, *Ed Bolden and Black Baseball in Philadelphia*, 76-78; "Baseball Owners Enroute to Philly Pow Wow," *Pittsburgh Courier*, February 10, 1934.

10   Dixon, "Wide Representation as Baseball Moguls Launch Plans for a Real League," *Philadelphia Tribune*, February 15, 1934; Smith, *Ed Bolden and Black Baseball in Philadelphia*, 76-78; Neil Lanctot, *Negro League Baseball: The Rise and Ruin of a Black Institution* (Philadelphia: University of Pennsylvania Press, 2004), 35-39.

11   "Stars Topple Newark 12-0 for Initial League Win," *Philadelphia Tribune*, April 19, 1934.

12   There is contradictory information about Jones's career before he joined the Stars. Part of the confusion lies in the name of the franchise that played in Baltimore in 1932 and 1933. According to historian Gary Ashwill, the owners of the Baltimore Black Sox Baseball Club Inc. sought an injunction to prevent Joe Cambria, the owner of the NNL2 club, from using the name "Black Sox." Newspapers referred to the franchise as both the Baltimore Sox and Baltimore Black Sox. "Black Sox Not to Disband; Locals Will Have Strong Team Says Cambria," *Baltimore Afro-American*, February 18, 1933; "Seek to Enjoin Team from Use of 'Black Sox,'" *Baltimore Afro-American*, May 27, 1933; "Sound Second Call for Baseball Meet," *Baltimore Afro-American*, January 27, 1934; "Jack Farrell Let Go Upon Larceny Count," *Baltimore Afro-American*, July 14, 1934.

13   "Stars Down Passon," *Philadelphia Tribune*, August 16, 1934; "25,000 See East Down West 1-0," *Philadelphia Tribune*, August 30, 1934; Smith, *Ed Bolden and Black Baseball in Philadelphia*, 80-83; Jack Pace, "Slim Jones," *Colored Baseball and Sports Monthly*, v1 n2 (October 1934) in Edward Bolden Papers Box 186-1 Folder 21; Manuscript Division Moorland-Spingarn Research Center, Howard University; "Slim Jones," *Seamheads Negro Leagues Database*, https://www.seamheads.com/NegroLgs/player.php?playerID=jones01sli.; "Slim Jones," *Baseball Reference*, https://www.baseball-reference.com/players/j/jonessl01.shtml; "1934 East-West Game," *Seamheads Negro Leagues Database*, https://www.seamheads.com/NegroLgs/year.php?yearID=1934&lgID=EWA.

14   Ed Harris, "Jones and Paige Duel to 1-1 Tie," *Philadelphia Tribune*, September 13, 1934.

15   Harris, "Points and Errors," *Philadelphia Tribune*, September 13, 1934.

16   Harris, "Paige Tops Jones Before 25,000," *Philadelphia Tribune*, October 4, 1934.

17   "1934 Philadelphia Stars," *Seamheads Negro Leagues Database*. https://www.seamheads.com/NegroLgs/team.php?yearID=1934&teamID=PS&lgOrd=1.

18   Ed Harris, "and Bright Stars," *Philadelphia Tribune*, October 11, 1934.

19   Smith, *Ed Bolden and Black Baseball in Philadelphia*, 84-85.

20   Harris, "To Be or Not to Be," *Philadelphia Tribune*, October 4, 1934.

21   "To Be or Not to Be."

22   "To Be or Not to Be."

23   Harris, "Second the Motion," *Philadelphia Tribune*, November 15, 1934; see also December 20, 1934.

24   Smith, *Ed Bolden and Black Baseball in Philadelphia*, 87-90.

25   "Slim Jones Suspended, Two Others are Fined," *Philadelphia Independent*, August 11, 1935.

26   "Slim Jones Suspended, Two Others are Fined."

27   "Bolden Will Quit," *Philadelphia Tribune*, August 29, 1935.

28   Dixon, "Stearns, Suttles, Brown Head Here, Stevens Jumps," *Philadelphia Tribune*, April 5, 1936; "Stars Fail to Land Chicago Aces; Slim Jones Ailing," *Philadelphia Tribune*, April 12, 1936; Dixon, "The Sports Bugle," and "Bolden Faces Problem with Gaps in Infield," *Philadelphia Tribune*, April 19, 1936; Dixon, "Bolden Cracks Whip as Campaign Nears," *Philadelphia Tribune*, May 3, 1936; "Ed Bolden Will Actively Manage Stars in Title Dash; Cockrells Ready," *Philadelphia Tribune*, March 26, 1936; Ed Harris, "Ed Bolden Expects to be Strong Contender in 1936 Nat's Assn. Race," *Philadelphia Tribune*, April 16, 1936.

29   "Local Fans Acclaim Phila. Stars' Feat," *Philadelphia Independent*, May 17, 1936; Dixon, "The Sports Bugle," *Philadelphia Tribune*, June 14, 1936; Dick Sun, "Stars Lose League Lead; Drop Three in Row to Elites," *Philadelphia Tribune*, June 28, 1936; "Stars-Elites Tied, League Title Decided This Week," *Philadelphia Tribune*, July 5, 1936; "First Half Ends with Title Undecided," and Dixon, "Sports Bugle," *Philadelphia Tribune*, July 12, 1936.

30   Ed Bolden, "Bolden Says League Secretary Guilty of Misusing Office," *Philadelphia Tribune* August 23, 1936. Bolden, "Bolden Gives Views on 1st Half Title," *Pittsburgh Courier*, August 22, 1936; Cumberland Posey, "Posey's Points," *Pittsburgh Courier*, July 25, 1936; August 1, 1936, and August 29, 1936; Harris, "Empty Barrels," *Philadelphia Tribune*, October 8, 1936; "Elites Okay Title Frays," *Philadelphia Independent*, September

6, 1936; Dixon, "Loyal Roots Go Broke When Greenlee's Serfs Form Link with Gamblers," *Philadelphia Independent,* September 13, 1936; Dixon, "Craws-Elites Give Fans Bum's Rush," *Philadelphia Independent,* October 4, 1936.

31 ""Stars' Southpaw Dies in Baltimore," *Philadelphia Tribune,* November 27, 1938; Frederick C. Bush, "Stewart Jones," Society for American Baseball Research Biography Project, Accessed January 17, 2023, https://sabr.org/bioproj/person/slim-jones/.

32 In the Negro Leagues, rainouts often resulted in canceled games because the venue would no longer be available to the teams. Additionally, owners who wanted the extra revenue of postseason games would intervene to make league games exhibition games in order to ensure postseason berths.

33 Wendell Smith, "Brooklyn Dodgers Admit Negro Players Rate Place in Majors" *Pittsburgh Courier,* August 5, 1939; Wendell Smith, "Would Be a Mad Scramble for Negro Players if Okayed," *Pittsburgh Courier,* August 12, 1939; Wendell Smith, "Owners Will Admit Negro Players if Fans Demand Them – Cards' Pilot," *Pittsburgh Courier,* August 19, 1939; Wendell Smith, "Owners Must Solve Color Problem in Majors – Stengel," *Pittsburgh Courier,* August 26, 1939.

34 Smith, *Ed Bolden and Black Baseball in Philadelphia,* 109-119.

35 *Ed Bolden and Black Baseball in Philadelphia,* 130-132.

36 *Ed Bolden and Black Baseball in Philadelphia,* 134-137.

37 *Ed Bolden and Black Baseball in Philadelphia,* 139-144.

38 "R. Partlow Rejoins Phila. Stars in Ala.," *Philadelphia Independent,* April 26, 1947; "Phila. Stars Tripped by Elites in Opener," *Philadelphia Independent,* May 10, 1947; "Dodgers' Manager Bert Shotten Says ... Jackie Robinson Will Make Grade in Majors," *Philadelphia Independent,* May 31, 1947; "Cleveland Indians Buy Larry Doby from Eagles," *Philadelphia Independent,* July 12, 1947; "Jackie Robinson in the World Series," *Philadelphia Independent,* October 4, 1947.

39 Smith, *Ed Bolden and Black Baseball in Philadelphia,* 144-148.

40 W. Rollo Wilson, "Through the Eyes of W. Rollo Wilson"; "Notables to Attend Rites for Bolden," Edward Bolden Papers Box 186-1 Folder 1; Manuscript Division, Moorland-Spingarn Research Center, Howard University; Funeral Program for Ed Bolden, Edward Bolden Papers Box 186-1 Folder 1; Manuscript Division, Moorland-Spingarn Research Center, Howard University; Western Union telegram, George B. Stevenson to Doctor Hilda Bolden, September 30, 1950; Condolences from Harriet Wright Lemon to Hilda Bolden; Condolence from Russell F. Minton, M.D., to Hilda Bolden; Western Union telegram, Dr. J.B. Martins, President of the NAL, to Hilda Bolden, October 2, 1950; Western Union telegram, Ambassador & Mrs. King, Liberian Embassy, to Hilda Bolden; Western Union telegram, Memphis Red Sox to Family of Edward Bolden, October 2, 1950; Western Union telegram Wayne L. Hopking to Hilda Bolden, October 2, 1950, Edward Bolden Papers Box 186-1 Folder 1; Manuscript Division, Moorland-Spingarn Research Center, Howard University.

41 Smith, *Ed Bolden and Black Baseball in Philadelphia,* 148-152.

42 Smith, *Ed Bolden and Black Baseball in Philadelphia,* 154-156.

A SECOND ACT IN BLACK PROFESSIONAL BASEBALL: ED BOLDEN, HILLDALE, AND THE PHILADELPHIA STARS

By Courtney Michelle Smith

Ed Bolden's Philadelphia Stars represented a part of the greater Philadelphia area's civic and social fabric for two decades. For most of that time, Bolden himself represented the heart of the franchise. His name formed part of the franchise's official name, and his home address in Darby, Pennsylvania, adorned the franchise's official stationery. While he worked with a partner, Ed Gottlieb, Bolden served as the franchise's public face and touchstone. Headlines and stories in the *Philadelphia Tribune* occasionally called the team the "Boldenmen" and nicknamed the team's home ballpark in West Philadelphia the Bolden Bowl. Although there were many roster changes over the years, Bolden remained the franchise's constant through the Great Depression, World War II, and the new challenges presented by the reintegration of the National and American Leagues in what was then known as major-league baseball. Through his work with the Stars, Bolden cemented his place as a valued member of the greater Philadelphia community. He made connections with civic leaders and often welcomed them to attend Stars games. When Bolden died in September 1950, the dignitaries who gathered at his funeral served as a testament to the respect he had garnered throughout his lifetime.[1]

For Bolden, though, the Stars represented his second act in Black professional baseball. Bolden's baseball career began in 1911, 22 years before he founded the franchise that bore his name. In that year, Bolden joined a franchise called the Hilldale Daisies that was based near his home in Darby. At the time, Hilldale was a sandlot team full of teenagers; they turned to the then 29-year-old Bolden to keep score for one of their games. Bolden remained with the youngsters and, within a decade, transformed the franchise into one of the most fearsome Black professional baseball teams in the Eastern United States.[2]

To support the professional Hilldale club, Bolden spearheaded the Hilldale Base Ball and Expedition Company, an all-Black corporation formed in 1917 with other Darby leaders. With Hilldale, Bolden won his first championship, a World Series over the Kansas City Monarchs in 1925. That series marked a rematch between the two teams from the previous season; Kansas City had won the first contest. Alongside highs like the World Series title, Bolden also endured some lows with Hilldale. Most of those down times stemmed from his longtime rivalry with Andrew "Rube" Foster, a Black baseball mogul from Chicago who operated the Chicago American Giants and led the formation of the first Negro National League (NNL) in 1920. Hilldale briefly joined the NNL as an associate-member franchise, but Bolden pulled them out to form his own league, the Eastern Colored League (ECL), in 1923 because he bristled under Foster's management. The accumulated stresses of running a league and a team led Bolden to have a nervous breakdown in September 1927, but he returned in time for the 1928 season and led the Hilldale franchise for a few more years.

The era from 1928 to 1933 marked the end of Bolden's first baseball life with Hilldale and the start of his second one with the Stars. During that period, Bolden faced a barrage of criticism as he endured both a very ugly separation from Hilldale and an imperfect return with the Stars. The criticism he faced nearly ended Bolden's career in Black professional baseball and was a far cry from the praise bestowed upon his death in 1950. The events of that era help to contextualize Bolden's actions during his career with the Stars and showcase some of the ugly racial issues present within Black professional baseball. Additionally, the events reveal a facet of Bolden's persona not always evident in his leadership of the Stars. Most importantly, the events that pushed Bolden out of Hilldale help to make the Stars' quick rise to a title in 1934 all the more remarkable. Bolden had truly faced the depths of life in Black professional baseball and, for a while, a triumphant return with another franchise seemed unlikely. He made the unlikely happen, though not without incurring some sharp criticism and going back on some promises he seemingly had made to a different group of young men in Darby.

In 1928 Bolden's return to Hilldale after his nervous breakdown came on the heels of a tumultuous year for himself and the league he had formed. Hilldale's World Series championship in 1925 marked the apex of his time leading both Hilldale and the ECL. Soon, both his team and his league suffered from acute financial problems due to declining attendance. As those financial problems grew, Bolden faced near-constant criticism for decisions he made as the ECL's leader. In January 1927, the other ECL owners ousted Bolden from his role as the league's president and replaced him with Isaac Nutter, an attorney from Atlantic City. Bolden continued to serve as the ECL's secretary-treasurer, but his authority over league affairs had effectively ended. Once Bolden suffered his nervous breakdown in September 1927, he spent a short amount of time receiving treatment from a local hospital. Newspaper columnist W. Rollo Wilson reported that he spoke with Bolden at a football game in the fall of 1927 and correctly predicted that the mogul would return to Hilldale with a fighting attitude. Members of the Hilldale Company, however, did not act as if Bolden would definitely return to the franchise. They chose Charlie Freeman, a former Hilldale player and vice president of the corporation, as the new leader.

Freeman made plans for the 1928 season without Bolden's involvement.[3]

As Wilson had predicted, Bolden returned to Hilldale in 1928 and was spoiling for a fight since he had no intention of ceding control over the franchise. In March three members of the Hilldale Company, Freeman, Lloyd Thompson, and James Byrd, tendered their resignations. With those resignations, Bolden regained his position as Hilldale's president, and he hired allies to round out the rest of the franchise's and company's leadership. Once he made those moves, Bolden turned his attention to the ECL and withdrew Hilldale from the league. In retaliation, ECL President Nutter accepted a new franchise from the Philadelphia area, the Tigers, and predicted that Bolden would return Hilldale to the organization. Bolden used the pages of both the *Pittsburgh Courier* and *Philadelphia Tribune* to explain his actions and to outline the financial losses incurred by Hilldale while it operated as a member of the ECL. His actions seemed prescient; the ECL disbanded in June 1928, and Hilldale made it through the season. Hilldale's future still seemed precarious since the team continued to struggle to attract large crowds, a symptom of an economic downturn that hit the team's Black baseball fans and made an outing to the ballpark an unaffordable luxury.[4]

In early 1929, Bolden tried to repeat his success with the ECL by forming the six-team American

Ed Bolden (in suit) with his 1911 Hilldale team.

Negro League (ANL) with several franchises that also had belonged to the ECL. Bolden served as the ANL's president and immediately sought to assert his authority over the other league owners and to enact strict laws governing player behavior. While the ANL teams managed to play almost all the games on their schedules, the owners, including Bolden, seemed uninterested in enforcing the league's laws. The lack of discipline exhibited by ANL players brought Bolden a fresh round of criticism, this time from Syd Pollock, a Jewish booking agent who owned an independent all-Black team called the Havana Red Sox. Pollock wrote an article that ran in the *Pittsburgh Courier* in which he demanded answers from Bolden and the ANL about why they forbade any ANL team to face his Red Sox. Additionally, Pollock used the opportunity to highlight the ANL's shortcomings and to argue that the league needed a better leader.[5]

Overall, 1929 brought a series of challenges, and few successes, for Bolden. Since he failed to uphold his own rules regarding player discipline, on-field fights disrupted many Hilldale games. Bolden also faced biting criticism from the *Philadelphia Tribune* about his determination to use White umpires. The newspaper implied that Bolden's use of White umpires fed into ugly racial stereotypes about Black Americans. On top of those issues, Hilldale and other ANL teams, along with teams in the NNL, continued to face financial challenges and low attendance at games. Soon after the 1929 season ended, the stock market crashed and ushered in a prolonged era of financial anxiety. Bolden had tried, and failed, to gather ANL owners for a meeting earlier in October. In February 1930 Bolden and the ANL owners finally gathered at the Republican Club in Philadelphia. They met not to plan for a 1930 season but to formally dissolve the ANL. Hilldale once again faced the prospect of operating independently of a league structure, but Bolden had other plans for his franchise that would ultimately push him out of the sport.[6]

Prior to the ANL's dissolution, Randy Dixon reported on rumors of big changes coming to Hilldale. A few months later, Bolden seemed to confirm Dixon's rumors by announcing that Hilldale had lost its long-time playing field in Darby. In truth, Bolden did not renew the lease at Hilldale Park because he intended to dissolve the Hilldale Company and build a new franchise, Ed Bolden's Hillsdale Club, with the financial backing of Harry Passon. Passon, a White sports promoter, owned Passon Field at 48th and Spruce Streets in West Philadelphia. The new club would use Passon Field as its home ballpark, and Bolden intended for his Hilldale team to make its debut in the 1930 season. Bolden's plans never materialized because other members of the Hilldale Company fought back and stopped him from dissolving the franchise. Lloyd Thompson and Charles Freeman, both of whom had resigned after Bolden had returned from his nervous breakdown, came back to save Hilldale. They removed Bolden as the organization's president; Thompson replaced Bolden and promptly renewed the lease that Bolden had allowed to lapse. Bolden's baseball career appeared to be over.[7]

In the eyes of the *Tribune's* Dixon, Bolden's baseball career had permanently ended. Dixon delivered a harsh assessment of Bolden, an assessment that touched upon issues of leadership and race:

> At last it looks as if Ed Bolden is fading from the picture. Once an omnipotent figure in Negro baseball. Once the czar of the East. Once the dictator. Once feared and respected. Bolden is through, readers, make no mistake.

> The history of the erstwhile postal clerk reads like a dime store bestseller. ... It is all history now how Bolden wrecked his team when he went hog wild and administered the oft mentioned boot in the buttocks to several stalwarts, hiring them away from Darby loam with the info that their batting eyes were becoming dulled or their joints were beginning to annoy him with their frequent creaking as the case might have been.

> But as if this wouldn't suffice, Bolden proved himself a traditional cullud [*sic*] man by playing 'Uncle Tom' and taking his advantages to the Nordic faction. ... When the American League folded up, Bolden came through with a subsequent statement that Hilldale had dissolved. The Dynasty had ended. He got Nordic backing. Made arrangements to take something that had been nurtured by colored people and was a colored institution and bend it in such a manner to as to fill the coffers of the Nordic. Not maliciously or intentionally perhaps, but such was the case or almost the case.

> Lloyd Thompson has stepped in and thwarted Bolden at every turn and now the man who was once a king is now a piker and Ed Bolden is through. We mean THROUGH![8]

While Bolden's career had not ended, he faced several obstacles in any attempt to return to Black professional baseball. One major obstacle was finances – Bolden lacked the capital to build a new team on his own, and the ongoing Great Depression limited the amount of capital available to anyone who wanted to build a new baseball franchise. The bad economy contributed to the demise of the original NNL and a new league, the East-West League, that had attempted to replace it in 1932 and did not last the season. Another major obstacle complicating Bolden's return to Black professional baseball was Hilldale's continued existence. Bolden tried to launch a new team with the support of former Hilldale star John Henry "Pop" Lloyd and Harry Passon, the co-owner of a company that had supplied Hilldale's equipment.[9] John Drew, a wealthy African American from Darby, had assumed control of the Hilldale franchise. Drew decided to take command of the team after several members of the financially insolvent Hilldale Company approached him for aid. Lloyd declared that had he "known Hilldale was to have a team [he] surely would not have considered Mr. Bolden's offers" because he did not want to associate with a new team that challenged an established team.[10] Bolden, therefore, suspended his plans to launch a new franchise and spent the 1931 season in the wilderness while plotting his next move.

Although Hilldale fielded a team in 1932, Bolden decided to make his move back into Black professional baseball through the Darby Phantoms. Bolden's plans for the Phantoms seemed to echo the plans he had executed for Hilldale 20 years earlier and foreshadowed his future ideas for the Stars. He rebranded them Ed Bolden's Darby Phantoms, received absolute control, and sought to transform them into the region's next great professional baseball team. The Phantoms struggled under Bolden's single-minded leadership; nearby, Bolden's former franchise endured its own set of struggles in what turned out to be its final season. By the middle of June, Drew could no longer pay Hilldale's players or coaches their salaries, and he raised ticket prices at Hilldale Park in a vain attempt to substitute the gate receipts for the salaries. Drew formally dissolved the Hilldale franchise at the end of July, thereby removing an obstacle to Bolden's return. The Philadelphia region still appeared to offer fertile ground for a Black professional baseball team, but the Darby Phantoms had thus far failed to give Bolden the entry back into the game he loved.[11]

In February 1933, Bolden completed his return to Black professional baseball when he attended a meeting at Ed Gottlieb's office in Philadelphia. Gottlieb, a Jewish booking agent, hosted the meeting to help announce the formation of a new, second iteration of the Negro National League (NNL2). Gus Greenlee, a Black sports promoter from Pittsburgh, was the main force behind the NNL2's launch, and his Pittsburgh Crawfords represented one of the new league's franchises. Bolden attended the meeting not as a representative of the Darby Phantoms, but as a representative of a new franchise he had formed with Gottlieb's support. The new franchise, Ed Bolden's Philadelphia Stars, aspired to fill the void left by Hilldale's dissolution and showed that Bolden had given up on the Phantoms. Ironically, the Phantoms still bore Bolden's name on their official stationery and baseball uniforms. Bolden's move to a new franchise came as a surprise to the Phantoms' management and displayed the same edge of ruthlessness evident in Bolden's behavior since the late 1920s.[12]

While most of the Philadelphia sports world praised Bolden's return to Black professional baseball, the Phantoms' Ray Macey made sure that people did not forget about the promises made to the young team. In a scathing column in the *Tribune,* Macey hinted that Bolden had engaged in some subterfuge regarding his involvement with the Phantoms. Macey alleged that Bolden had recently asked for his name to remain associated with the Phantoms through his role as an honorary member of the organization. Bolden, however, had not attended any recent meetings, and he sent a letter to a Philadelphia sporting-goods company in which he denied any involvement with the Phantoms baseball team. Macey lamented that many of the young Phantoms players idolized Bolden because he too lived in Darby and had achieved astounding success with Hilldale. The players had fallen under Bolden's spell and had sacrificed their amateur status to pursue the dream of becoming the next Hilldale. Macey's comments implied that the Phantoms players could not revert to amateurs, but he wasn't clear as to the reasons why they could no longer play as amateur ballplayers. Macey furthermore accused Bolden of obfuscation since the players found out through newspaper stories, not through direct communication from Bolden, that he had abandoned them to form a new team.[13]

Macey's article got Bolden's second act with the Philadelphia Stars off to a rough beginning. In addition to abandoning the Phantoms, Bolden butted heads with Greenlee and resisted overtures for the Stars to join the NNL2 in 1933. While the animosity did not reach the levels seen between Bolden and Foster in the 1920s, the stubbornness Bolden displayed showed that he carried the scars of the battles he had fought when he had led Hilldale. Bolden and the Stars joined the NNL2 in 1934 and famously enjoyed their best season while also stirring controversy for the ugly incidents that marred the championship series. The seemingly unfair resolutions of those incidents appeared to favor Bolden and the Stars and cost newspaper columnist W. Rollo Wilson his job as NNL2 commissioner. Bolden often had contentious relationships with other NNL2 owners and officials; he occasionally held leadership positions within the league, but he never recaptured the total control he had enjoyed with the ECL in the 1920s. Bolden often found himself at the mercy of other NNL2 officials who exerted more influence within the league and who operated more successful franchises. Ironically, the Stars outlived many of those more successful franchises, giving Bolden a longer foothold within Black professional baseball than most of his peers.

Bolden lived long enough to move past the issues that forced him out of Hilldale and to witness the demise of the Black baseball world of the twentieth century. His death came in September 1950, more three years after Jackie Robinson debuted with the Brooklyn Dodgers and heralded the beginning of the end of racial segregation in professional baseball. As Robinson and other Black players joined franchises like the Dodgers, Cleveland Indians, and New York Giants, all-Black teams like the Stars ceased to serve a purpose within the American sports world. Bolden initially seemed oblivious to this reality, believing that the Stars and other all-Black teams would continue to serve as steppingstones for Black baseball players on their way to successful careers. Like other franchises, however, the Stars struggled to stay relevant, and Bolden saw the team's best players move on to retirement or to franchises in the formerly all-White minor and major leagues. Bolden's death not only marked the end of his second act in Black professional baseball, but it also symbolized the end of an era within the Philadelphia sports world. Dignitaries from the region's sports, political, and cultural world served as Bolden's pallbearers, and memorials praised his lifetime of achievements with two franchises. The Stars plodded ahead for two more largely forgettable seasons before folding and joining their founder as part of the city's history.[14]

Ed Bolden spent most of his life in Black professional baseball and lived through two separate acts in that career, each act punctuated with great heights and depths. In both acts of his baseball career, Bolden displayed a single-minded focus that occasionally escalated into ruthlessness toward players and other officials. Bolden's decisions in the late 1920s nearly ended his baseball career and marked a period of transition for Black professional baseball. By adapting to a new reality for Black professional baseball, Bolden rebounded and enjoyed a second act with a franchise that bore his name beyond his death.

NOTES

1   Michael Haupert, "Ed Bolden." Biography Project, Society for American Baseball Research, accessed January 17, 2023, https://sabr.org/bioproj/person/ed-bolden/.

2   Haupert, "Ed Bolden."

3   Lloyd Thompson, "Keenan Goes West with Rest of League Moguls; May Have Changed His Mind," *Philadelphia Tribune*, January 15, 1927; Wilson, "Eastern League Elects Nutter Pres. to Succeed Bolden," *Pittsburgh Courier*, January 22, 1927; "Ed Bolden, Hilldale Mentor, Suffers Nervous Breakdown," *Philadelphia Tribune*, September 29, 1927; "Bill Francis Signs as Manager of Hilldale for 1928," *Philadelphia Tribune*, December 15, 1927; "Charlie Freeman Succeeds Bolden as Hilldale Head," *Chicago Defender*, November 26, 1927; "Bill Francis Will Manage Daisies," *Chicago Defender*, December 17, 1927; "Ed Bolden Suffers Nervous Breakdown," *Pittsburgh Courier*, October 1, 1927; Wilson, "Sport Shots," *Pittsburgh Courier*, October 29, 1927; "Bolden 'Let Out' as Head of Hilldale Baseball Club," *Pittsburgh Courier*, December 10, 1927; Wilson, "Sport Shots," *Pittsburgh Courier*, December 10, 1927.

4   Edward Bolden, "Bolden Back in Perfect Health, Proffers Views," *Philadelphia Tribune* February 2, 1928; Randy Dixon, "Hilldale and Giants Quit Eastern Loop," *Philadelphia Tribune*, March 15, 1928; "Freeman Out as Hilldale Quits Eastern League," *Chicago Defender*, March 17, 1928; "Nutter Backed by Magnates Defies Bolden," *Philadelphia Tribune*, March 15, 1928.

5   "Eastern League, Punctured Already, Gets Flat Tire," *Chicago Defender*, April 21, 1928; Wilson, "Eastern League Will Continue," *Chicago Defender*, April 28, 1928; "Eastern League Bubble Bursts as Moguls Disagree," *Chicago Defender*, May 5, 1928; "Eastern League Disbands," *Pittsburgh Courier* April 21, 1928; "Jap Champs to Play Hilldale," *Pittsburgh Courier*, May 12, 1928; "Eastern League Disbands; Fate Long Predicted," *Philadelphia Tribune*, April 18, 1928; Randy Dixon, "Sport Sidelights," *Philadelphia Tribune*, April 18, 1928; "Veteran Outfielder and Star Pitcher Will Play for Daisies; Report Soon," *Philadelphia Tribune*, March 29, 1928; "Hilldale Club Battles House of David Sat.," *Philadelphia Tribune*, June 28, 1928; "Bolden's Pets Wreck House of David; Divide with the Bacharachs at the Seashore," *Philadelphia Tribune*, July 5, 1928; "12,000 Watch Hilldale and Rivals Split," *Philadelphia Tribune*, July 19, 1928; "Fandom Eagerly Awaits Initial Fray of Series to Determine Supremacy," *Philadelphia Tribune*, September 13, 1928; Dixon, "Sport Sidelights," *Philadelphia Tribune*, September 20, 1928; Courtney Michelle Smith, *Ed Bolden and Black Baseball in Philadelphia* (Jefferson, North Carolina: McFarland, 2017), 46-53; "Eastern League Formed, Grays Join," *Pittsburgh Courier*, January 19, 1929; Wilson, "American Negro League Flays Barnstorming; Reserves Named," *Pittsburgh Courier*, March 2, 1929; "A.N. League Makes Laws," *Pittsburgh Courier*, June 8, 1929; "Possibility of New Baseball League to Replace Defunct Eastern Circuit Looms in Conclave Here Next Month," *Philadelphia Tribune*, January 3, 1929; "System of Rotating Umps Agreed by Baseball Magnates at Parley Here," *Philadelphia Tribune*, February 28, 1929; "A.N. League Makes Laws," *Pittsburgh Courier*, June 8, 1929; "Baseball War Looms as East Raids Western Clubs," *Chicago Tribune*, July

13, 1929; Dixon, "Sport Sidelights," *Philadelphia Tribune*, April 25, 1929; "Baseball War Between American and National Negro Leagues Looming," *Philadelphia Tribune*, July 15, 1929; Dubbia Ardee, "Antics of Cum Posey Are Likely to Harm Future of Organized Baseball," *Philadelphia Tribune*, August 1, 1929; Syd Pollock, "Syd Pollock Calls New League 'Joke,' Makes Grave Charges," *Pittsburgh Courier*, August 3, 1929; "Baseball War Between American and National Negro Leagues Looming," *Philadelphia Tribune*, July 15, 1929.

6   "Negro Umps at Hilldale," *Pittsburgh Courier*, August 3, 1929; "Hilldale Again," *Philadelphia Tribune*, August 8, 1929; Wilson, "Sport Shots," *Pittsburgh Courier*, October 12, 1929; Wilson, "Sport Shots," *Pittsburgh Courier*, November 30, 1929; "American Negro League Votes to Disband," *Pittsburgh Courier*, February 22, 1930; "American Negro League Disbands; Teams Enter Independent Field," *Philadelphia Tribune*, February 20, 1930.

7   Wilson, "Sport Shots," *Pittsburgh Courier*, October 12, 1929; Wilson, "Sport Shots," *Pittsburgh Courier*, November 30, 1929; "American Negro League Votes to Disband," *Pittsburgh Courier*, February 22, 1930; "American Negro League Disbands; Teams Enter Independent Field," *Philadelphia Tribune*, February 20, 1930; "Clan Darby Status in Doubt," *Pittsburgh Courier*, April 5, 1930; Wilson, "Sport Shots," *Pittsburgh Courier*, April 19, 1930; Wilson, "Sport Shots," *Pittsburgh Courier*, April

26, 1930; "Bolden Loses in Effort to Bust Daisies," *Philadelphia Tribune*, April 3, 1930; Smith, 53-59; "Ed Bolden to Head Up New 'Hillsdale' Club," *Pittsburgh Courier*, April 19, 1930; "Ed Bolden to Organize New Ball Outfit," *Philadelphia Tribune*, April 10, 1930; Dixon, "Sport Sidelights," *Philadelphia Tribune*, April 10, 1930; "Lincoln Giants, Hilldale and Bolden's Latest Club to Furnish Pastime," *Philadelphia Tribune*, April 17, 1930; Dick Sun, "Original Hilldale Club to Open Home Season on May 3 with Camden Nine," *Philadelphia Tribune*, April 24, 1930.

8   Dixon, "Sport Sidelights," *Philadelphia Tribune*, April 24, 1930.

9   Mark Ribowsky, *A Complete History of the Negro Leagues 1884 to 1955* (New York: Carol Publishing Group, 1995), 139-156; Dixon, "Sports Sidelights," *Philadelphia Tribune*, January 29, 1931.

10   Dixon, "Sports Sidelights," *Philadelphia Tribune*, March 5, 1931.

11   Smith, 60-65.

12   Smith, 66-69.

13   Ray Macey, "Phantoms Ride Bolden for Quitting Team," *Philadelphia Tribune*, March 23, 1933; Smith, 70.

14   Haupert, "Ed Bolden"; Smith, 148-153.

PLAYERS

BERNARD BLACKWELL

BY MARGARET M. GRIPSHOVER

During the Philadelphia Stars' 1934 championship season, a pitcher named "Blackwell" poured himself a cup of coffee but didn't stick around for a refill. Blackwell has been described as a "fringe player" who "pitched briefly" with the Stars that year, but that "his playing time was severely restricted."[1] His only documented appearance with the Stars took place in Philadelphia on July 6, 1934.[2] Blackwell was described as a "Holmesburg high lad," and he shared pitching duties with another prep athlete named Clifford Irons, who was a "first-rate twirler" from suburban Bryn Mawr.[3] On that day, the Stars and their two rookie hurlers defeated the Mitchell Athletic Association of Philadelphia in a nonleague tilt by a score of 6-2.[4] Neither Blackwell nor Irons was ever seen in a Stars' uniform again.

Who was this mysterious Blackwell whose given name never appeared in newspaper accounts of his games? There was only one person who lived in Philadelphia who fit Blackwell's description in terms of age, location, and baseball participation. That person was Bernard Harvey Blackwell. He was born in Philadelphia in 1916. When he pitched for the Stars in 1934, he was 18 years old and fresh out of high school. Blackwell attended a high school in Philadelphia, but the name of the school is unknown. Although one newspaper described him as a "Holmesburg high" student, no such school existed. Holmesburg is a community located approximately 10 miles northeast of Philadelphia, but Blackwell did not live there. He spent nearly his entire life closer to the northeast Philadelphia neighborhood of Frankford, roughly six miles from downtown. Frankford was home to several amateur baseball teams that provided Blackwell with an opportunity to play. Blackwell's World War II draft card supplies some additional evidence to support the theory that he was the same "Blackwell" who had a fleeting career with the Stars. His draft card described him as nearly 6 feet tall and weighing 150 pounds, a suitable conformation for a pitcher.

After his one-game performance for the Stars, Blackwell's baseball career continued for two more years. He played for the Frankford Giants, a well-respected local team that shared its name with its neighborhood. Blackwell's results were mixed. In May 1935 he "twirled for the fast-stepping Frankford Giants" in a 5-3 victory over the Philadelphia Ukrainians.[5] A few weeks later, however, he was pummeled by Lou Kirner's North Phillies, 12-2.[6] In the next game, the Frankford Arrows belittled the Giants, 8-3, using Blackwell's pitches for target practice, a circumstance that resulted in his demotion to relief and utility duties.[7] Blackwell's baseball career ended on a sour note on July 19, 1936, when his Frankford Giants were cut down to size by the Mt. Holly Relief Athletic Association, 16-3.[8] After the loss to Mt. Holly, Blackwell's name did not appear in any additional game reports for the Frankford Giants or any other Philadelphia area team.

After his brief foray into amateur and professional baseball, Blackwell married and served in the US Navy during World War II. He followed in his father's footsteps as a postal clerk and mail carrier, a similar career path that once was taken by the Philadelphia Stars' owner, Ed Bolden.[9] Bernard Blackwell married Mary E. Ruffin about the time when he played his final games for the Frankford Giants. The Blackwells had no children. Bernard Blackwell died in Philadelphia in 1985 and was buried in the Beverly National Cemetery in Burlington, New Jersey.

SOURCES

Unless otherwise indicated, all Negro League statistics and records were sourced from Seamheads.com.

Ancestry.com was used to access census, birth, death, marriage, military, immigration, and other genealogical and public records.

NOTES

1   James A. Riley, *The Biographical Encyclopedia of the Negro Baseball Leagues* (New York: Carroll & Graf Publishers, Inc., 1994), 88.

2   "Philly Stars Garner Two During Week," *Baltimore Afro American*, July 14, 1934: 19.

3   "Philly Stars Garner Two During Week."

4   "Philly Stars Garner Two During Week."

5   "Frankford Giants Win," *Philadelphia Inquirer*, May 28, 1935: 25.

6   "North Phils Top Frankford Giants," *Philadelphia Inquirer*, June 16, 1935: 42.

7   "Frankford Arrows Win Series Opener," *Philadelphia Inquirer*, July 28, 1935: 36; "Beth-Allens to Close Their Season Today," *Allentown* (Pennsylvania) *Morning Call*, September 16, 1936: 16.

8   "Relief A.A. Nine Laces Frankford Giants, 16-3," *Camden* (New Jersey) *Courier-Post*, July 20, 1936: 18.

9   Neil Lanctot, *Fair Dealing & Clean Playing: The Hilldale Club and the Development of Black Professional Baseball, 1910-1932* (Syracuse: Syracuse University Press, 2007), 17.

AMEAL BROOKS

By Margaret M. Gripshover

Ameal Brooks played for semipro and Negro League teams from the late 1920s to 1950. He was known primarily for his work as a versatile catcher and out-fielder, his clouting abilities at the plate, and an affinity for alcohol, which may explain his habit of jumping from team to team, sometimes in midseason. For more than 20 years, he was known by many names, suited up for numerous teams, and was adept at multiple defensive positions. His life on and off the field is often difficult to document in part because of the many spelling variations for his given name, "Ameal." In some cases, Brooks was mistakenly identified as one of three different persons. "Ameal Brooks," "Alex Brooks," and "Alvin Brooks" were once thought to be three separate individuals, when in truth, they were all the same person – Ameal Brooks.[1] Brooks's given name took many other forms including Arnold, Eamel, Emil, Emanuel, and Emmanuel.[2] On more than one occasion, his name appeared in print in a form that bore no relation at all to "Ameal," such as Clarence, Frank, John, Joseph, Manny, and Ralph.[3] In addition to his shapeshifting first name, he was also bestowed with various nicknames including Ardi-Milla (or Ardmilla), Macon, and Bucket Brooks.[4] With more than a dozen variations of his given name, and the relative common occurrence of his sur-name, it is not surprising that research-ers and record-keepers have frequently confused Brooks with other players or believed that Alex and Ameal Brooks were two different persons. They were not. They were one-and-the-same.

Over the course of his long career, Brooks wore the uniforms of at least 19 semipro and/or Negro League nines including the Chicago Union Giants, Chicago Royal Giants, Chicago American Giants, Texas Colored Giants, Chicago Colored Athletics, Foster's Cleveland Cubs, Columbus Blue Birds, Homestead Grays, Philadelphia Stars, Cleveland Red Sox, Brooklyn Royal Giants, New York Black Yankees, Cincinnati Ethiopian Clowns, New York Cubans, North All Stars, Jacksonville Eagles, Newark Eagles, Milwaukee Tigers, and the Harlem Globetrotters baseball team. He also played winter league ball in Venezuela and Puerto Rico.[5] Of the many teams on his résumé, he was most frequently in the lineups for the New York Black Yankees, Brooklyn Royal Giants, and the New York Cubans. Of these three, he stepped up to the plate most often for the New York Cubans.

Brooks batted left-handed and threw right. He had early success as a catcher but was just as adept at patrolling the outfield or defending the infield, most frequently at third base. On a few rare occasions, at the beginning and end of his career, he could even be pressed into service on the pitcher's mound.[6] Brooks was known for being fleet of foot as an outfielder and on the basepaths, and for his power at the plate. During his time in the Negro Leagues, Brooks accrued a respectable .259 career batting average and banged out 54 extra-base hits, 14 of which were home runs. And he likely clouted even more extra-base hits in nonleague games.

Ameal Brooks was born on June 3, 1907, in New Orleans.[7] His father, Joseph Horace "Joe" Brooks, was born in Mississippi in 1884, and his mother, Sarah Williams Brooks, was from Louisiana. Brooks had six siblings, only two of whom lived to adulthood. Three of his siblings were born in Louisiana. His eldest sibling, John Westley Brooks, was born in 1905 in Wilson, Louisiana. Two other brothers were born in Shreveport, Louisiana; both died in infancy. By 1918, the Brooks family had left Shreveport for Chicago, joining the "Great Migration" of African Americans who moved from the South to Northern cities in the early twentieth century.[8] Brooks's three youngest siblings

Catcher Ameal Brooks

Gary Ashwill

were born in Chicago, including his only sister, Gladys Irene Brooks, who was born in 1918. In 1923 tragedy struck twice in the Brooks household. Ameal Brooks's mother, Sarah, gave birth to a stillborn son, and within five months his mother was also dead.

Little is known about the circumstances of Brooks's childhood, but the available evidence suggests that it was a difficult one. The Brooks family lived in the South Side of Chicago, where his father worked as a hostler at the nearby New York Central Railroad yards. By 1920, Brooks's parents took two foster children into the family's home. During that same time, Ameal Brooks was living at the Chicago Parental School, a residential facility for "troubled" and truant children.[9] By mid-1923, his father, Joseph, had buried three children and his wife. In 1933 Joseph married Eva Tracy Russell, with whom he had one son, Brooks's half-brother, Richard Brooks, who was born in Chicago in 1934. Although some genealogical sources and researchers claim that John Christopher Beckwith was Ameal Brooks's half-brother, no verifiable evidence of such a familial relationship exists.[10] When Beckwith was born, in Louisville, Kentucky, in 1900, the Brooks family was living in Louisiana. But by the time his father remarried, Ameal Brooks was long gone from the family household and had embarked on what would become a nearly 25-year-long career in baseball.

Brooks likely began his baseball career in the late 1920s with various iterations of the Chicago Royal Giants, Union Giants, and Chicago American Giants. As early as 1926, a pitcher named Brooks was a member of the barnstorming Chicago Royal Giants.[11] Given that he lived in Chicago and played for the Royal Giants in subsequent years, it is reasonable to assume the pitcher was Ameal Brooks. He did not appear in any game reports for the Chicago Royal Giants in 1927, but he resurfaced in the summer of 1928 as a catcher described as a former member of the Chicago Union Giants.[12] In the spring of 1929, Brooks made his Negro League debut as a backstop for the Chicago American Giants. Early in the season, he had the distinction of claiming the second-highest batting average in the Negro National League (NNL), a sizzling .667.[13] As impressive as that may sound, consider that in 1929, Brooks had just three plate appearances in two games with the Chicago American Giants.

Brooks's brief tenure with the American Giants ended in early June. Within a few weeks, he was signed as a catcher for the Texas Colored Giants, a barnstorming team composed mainly of players from Chicago

and owned by a Canadian promoter, Rod Whitman of Lafleche, Saskatchewan, who lived nowhere near Texas.[14] The team was billed as "real ball players" and "natural comedians" who were "recruited from the pick of players in the Chicago colored league."[15] They also made the far-fetched claim that they were the "1928 champions of the Southern States," but it made for good promotional copy.[16] Brooks spent most of the summer of 1929 traveling with the Texas Colored Giants to Canadian cities including Edmonton, Regina, Moose Jaw, and Saskatoon, and gaining valuable experience along the way.[17] Brooks, described as the team's "peppy center fielder and catcher," was one of the stars of the show and lit up scoreboards by stealing bases and clouting extra-base hits, including some thunderous home runs.[18] In a sense, the summer of 1929 was Brooks's apprenticeship, and it prepared him for what was to become his peripatetic life as a Negro League ballplayer.

The Texas Colored Giants took the road again in 1930 but without Brooks on their roster. Although Brooks and the Texas Colored Giants crossed paths during their travels, during the summer of 1930, he wore the uniform of the Chicago Colored Athletics. The Athletics' booking agent was Abe Saperstein, who promised potential opponents that "these dusky boys, with their comical ways natural to their race, will provide you with an excellent game of entertainment for your fans."[19] The Athletics toured the Midwest before heading for Canada, following a path blazed for them by the Texas Colored Giants, and staged contests with local nines in Regina, Edmonton, and Calgary, and, on occasion, with the Texas Colored Giants themselves.[20] Brooks had a terrific summer with the Athletics – behind and at the plate. In early June, he went on a home-run tear, knocking the horsehide out of the park on a regular basis. On June 9, the Athletics "lost the valuable services of Brooks, their catcher, in the seventh when he caught his foot on the bag at second and sprained his ankle."[21] He was out of the lineup for more than three weeks, but upon his return, Brooks picked up where he left off and hit two home runs in a losing effort against the Texas Colored Giants in Edmonton.[22] But Brooks, "who was nursing an injured leg," was eventually replaced behind the plate by the end of July.[23] In late August, after 120 games in less than three months, the Texas Colored Giants headed back to the Midwest for their final games of the season, without Brooks in the lineup.[24] He did not appear in another semipro or Negro League game until 1932.

After a year off from baseball, Brooks regained his form. He started the 1932 season with the short-lived barnstorming Rube Foster's Chicago Memorial Giants, a team that was reconstituted as Foster's Cleveland Cubs.[25] During their tour of the South in the spring of 1932, Brooks was noted as one of Cleveland's top performers and home-run hitters.[26] By early June, he was signed by the Chicago American Giants (also known as "Cole's American Giants") as the backup for starting catcher John Hines. Brooks was one of six catchers used by Chicago that year.[27] Despite their inability to decide on a starting backstop, the American Giants were the Southern Negro League champions in 1932. Brooks played in at least 11 games for Chicago and batted .281. William "Dizzy" Dismukes, in the *Pittsburgh Courier*, named Brooks and his Chicago teammate Kermit Dial as hot prospects for 1933, having "flashed signs of becoming stars" during the 1932 season.[28] Dismukes' prediction held somewhat true for Brooks, but not for Dial, who played only two more seasons for Negro League teams. Perhaps Dismukes' focus on Brooks and Dial in his newspaper column had more to do with self-promotion than for his enthusiasm for specific players. In the spring of 1933, Dismukes became the manager of the Columbus Blue Birds, that featured many former Chicago players, including Brooks and Dial.

Brooks began the 1933 season with the Columbus Blue Birds but finished it with a different team, the Homestead Grays. When he was with the Blue Birds, Brooks was the starting catcher and an occasional outfielder. He was having a good year before Columbus collapsed in late July and was repackaged as the Cleveland Giants and Akron Grays, two independent traveling squads that were thought to be a more lucrative alternative for the teams' owners.[29] In his final game with the Blue Birds, on July 23, 1933, Brooks capped off his tenure with Columbus with a triple and homer in a doubleheader defeat of the Detroit Stars.[30] Although the Blue Birds dispersed their flock and flew the Negro National League coop in the summer of 1933, Brooks made the most of his scrambled season in the form of long friendship with teammate Leroy Morney. After the Columbus team folded, Brooks and Morney migrated to the Homestead Grays to finish out the 1933 season, playing three and eight games respectively for the Grays. They later reunited as members of the 1938 New York Black Yankees, and in the summer of 1938 Morney served as one of the witnesses for Brooks's marriage to Mary Myers.

In the minds of the Homestead Grays' management, Brooks and Morney were set to return to the club in the spring of 1934. Much to Cum Posey's consternation, however, the two men, along with the Grays' outstanding left fielder, Vic Harris, jumped to other teams.[31] Brooks signed with the Cleveland Red Sox while Morney and Harris joined up with the Grays' crosstown rivals, the Pittsburgh Crawfords. It was an interesting season for Brooks. He started the year with a team that finished in last place in the NNL2 and ended it with the Philadelphia Stars, the 1934 Negro League champions. Brooks was Cleveland's backup catcher to starter Dennis Gilchrist, who played with Brooks on the 1933 Columbus Blue Birds. But the Red Sox, like the Blue Birds, did not last a full season in the NNL2.[32] Cleveland's record of 3-22 in league play placed them deep in the cellar. Brooks had more RBIs (5) than the team had total wins (4) in 1934. And Brooks had an equally abysmal record in Cleveland with a paltry .189 batting average, although three of his seven hits in 12 games he played for Cleveland were for extra bases.

When the Cleveland Red Sox disbanded in July, Brooks was quickly picked up by the league-leading Philadelphia Stars. Brooks was added to catchers on the Stars' roster who included starter William "Mickey" Casey and future Hall of Famer Biz Mackey. Although Brooks appeared in only 14 games for the Stars and batted .263, six of his 10 hits were for extra bases, including two home runs. Certainly, the highlight of his year and career to date was his appearances in the 1934 NNL2 championship series between the Philadelphia Stars and the Chicago American Giants, albeit with one exception. The Negro League championship was not played in consecutive games and was interrupted by the Stars' and Giants' participation in two lucrative four-team exhibitions at Yankee Stadium in September that also involved the Pittsburgh Crawfords and the New York Black Yankees.[33] Brooks participated in the first of the exhibitions as a pinch-hitter for Dick Seay and had the ignoble distinction of being dramatically fanned for the last out in the ninth inning by Satchel Paige, an event that was floridly described by *New York Age* sportswriter Jocko Maxwell and included in his "Sports Biggest Thrill in 1934."[34] Maxwell recounted the event vividly:

"… Brooks batting for the weak hitting Seay. Paige winds up, strike one – called no siree. Brooks swung and how, but he hit that ozone out of the park. Again that dark-skinned sinewy arm takes that cranklike [*sic*] windup, here she comes, it's in there! Umpire Forbes hawkes [*sic*] out strike two and Brooks unwinds himself, he's swung again, and gotten humiliation as his reward! Boy, oh boy, what is this, can Paige do it again, can he? Brooks calls time out, he talks to himself, no one ever will know the exact words that's not important. He tightens his belt, he's ready and so is Satchell [*sic*] Paige. The wind up, slow, now fast, 30,000 eyes on one man in the dark shadows of Yankee Stadium, that man is Paige! That ball has left his hand, it's speeding through the ozone. Silence! All eyes are on Brooks's [*sic*], there is the swing. HE MISSED IT. Umpire Forbes turns his back – thousands of baseball fans jam the playing field. There is the crowd literally ripping the uniform of Satchell [*sic*] Paige from his back."[35]

No doubt this same moment was not a thrill for Brooks. If he was hoping for redemption in the championship series games, his wish was only partially granted. Brooks had had three hits in nine at-bats for the series and scored at least one run.[36] However, the only newspaper column-inches he garnered for his efforts were for an incident during Game Six in which he shoved umpire Johnnie Craig not long after umpire Bert Gholston was on the receiving end of a punch thrown by Brooks's teammate, future Hall of Famer Jud Wilson.[37] Chicago manager Dave Malarcher vehemently protested the game but to no avail.[38] Brooks did not appear in the final and deciding Game Eight, in which the Stars defeated the Giants, 2-0, and were crowned the 1934 National Negro League II champions.[39] Wilson, who generated so much controversy for his violent outburst in Game Six, was named the series' Most Valuable Player.[40] Wilson returned to the Stars lineup in the spring of 1935. Brooks never wore a Philadelphia Stars uniform again.

As in previous years, Brooks began the 1935 season with one team but finished on the roster of another. In the spring he was with the Brooklyn Royal Giants. He made a few appearances with the New York Black Yankees before hopping aboard the Pennsylvania Red Caps of New York as his last stop for the 1935 season. Brooks, with his defensive versatility and offensive firepower, proved to be an asset for all three teams. He was the Royal Giants' primary catcher but also saw action at third base, shortstop, and outfield. Brooks was in the Black Yankees' lineup by late June and quickly demonstrated his aggressive offensive style in one game by scoring two runs and badly spiking the Brooklyn Bushwicks' shortstop, Dutch Woerner.[41] This was the first of five seasons Brooks spent with

the Black Yankees, but it also was his briefest tenure with the team.

After a few weeks with the Black Yankees, Brooks jumped to the independent Penn Red Caps. The Red Caps were named for the porters who worked at Pennsylvania Station in Manhattan, some of whom were African American baseball players who worked for the railroad during the offseason.[42] The 1935 edition of the Red Caps was described as being able to "hold their own with the best semi-pro teams in the metropolitan district including … the Bushwicks, Farmers, and Philadelphia teams."[43] By the time Brooks joined the Red Caps, he was known as "one of the hardest hitters in the game," and that "[if] he gets the range of the right field fence at the stadium the fans are likely to see some home runs."[44] And there was some extra inducement for Brooks to swing for the fences because his manager, George Brooks (no relation), paid his Red Caps players a $2 bonus for every home run they hit.[45] Brooks probably did not cash in on that offer too often that season. His extra-base hits were mainly doubles, but he did hit an inside-the-park home run in late August, albeit during one of his dalliances with the New York Black Yankees.[46] There was no word on whether or not Black Yankees manager Bob Clarke offered Brooks a $2 bonus.

From the mid- to late 1930s, Brooks played primarily for two teams: the Brooklyn Royal Giants, a well-established independent team, and the New York Black Yankees of the NNL2. In 1937, for the first time in his career, he spent the entire season in the uniform of one team – the Brooklyn Royal Giants. He was the Royal Giants' go-to outfielder and dependable infielder, stationed mainly at third or second base. Royal Giants' manager John Beckwith occasionally called upon Brooks for backstop duties, but that responsibility mainly fell to Joe Lewis. Brooks had a good offensive year with the Royal Giants but the team itself was dreadful. Most of its losses were to veteran independent clubs in the Northeast region such as the Bushwicks and Bay Ridge.[47] The few wins that Brooklyn enjoyed in 1937 were mainly the results of contests against weaker local nines like the Stroudsburg Poconos.[48]

Even as the Royal Giants were dethroned by their opponents, more often than not newspaper accounts of their games were peppered with reports of Brooks's talent for extra-base hits and his RBI production. For example, in his first start for Brooklyn, he hit a triple in a doubleheader loss to Bay Ridge.[49] In a late May win over the Belmar Braves, Brooks hit three doubles, and he repeated the feat two days later against the Cuban All-Stars.[50] In early July, the Royal Giants fell to the Red Bank Pirates despite Brooks's grand slam.[51] In the first week of August, in a game against the Scarlets of Mount Vernon, New York, Brooks hit another grand slam, described as a, "four-ply wallop [that] cleared the centerfield fence … in one hop, the first time any fence in this field has ever been cleared."[52] Brooks's exploits with the Brooklyn Royal Giants in 1937 did not go unnoticed. In his end-of-the-year column in the *Pittsburgh Courier*, Cum Posey named Brooks as the Giants' best outfielder and in the company of those whose defensive and offensive skills represented the elite of Negro League baseball, including Oscar Charleston, Rap Dixon, Vic Harris, and Cool Papa Bell.[53]

If 1937 was a season of stability for Brooks, 1938 was a year of inconsistency and major life changes. Unlike in the previous year, Brooks played for multiple teams in 1938. He debuted with the New York Black Yankees and ended the regular season with the independent Cuban Stars, after which he sailed off for a brief winter stint with the Indios de Mayagüez of the Puerto Rico Winter League. The 1938 edition of the Black Yankees gave fans little to cheer about and the only team that kept them from the depths of the NNL2 cellar was the even more pitiful Washington Black Senators, who won just two league games in 1938. As the Black Yankees' losses piled up, Brooks's bat fell silent. While his defensive skills in the outfield and at third base continued to draw praise, thanks to his speed and "sparkling catches," he had no homers and just three RBIs.[54]

But it was the intersections between Brooks's baseball career and his personal life that took the most unusual turns in 1938. At the end of June, Brooks played his last game of the year with the New York Black Yankees – an 11-6 loss to the Newark Eagles.[55] Brooks then left the Black Yankees for the Cuban Stars. He made his first start for the Cuban Stars on July 4 in a doubleheader against his old team, the Brooklyn Royal Giants, in which he made three errors as a second baseman and right fielder; a disappointing performance given his usually sharp defensive skills.[56] Perhaps it was an omen. That same day, he married Mary Myers before a judge in Manhattan. One of the witnesses to the ceremony was Brooks's longtime friend and former teammate, Leroy Morney. Brooks, the groom, was 31 years old. His new bride was 16 years old and more than likely pregnant with their first child. The marriage license listed Brooks's occupation

as a "physical instructor," but perhaps "professional ballplayer" was not an option on the form. Myers' occupation was listed as "servant." The marriage had a similar outcome as the Cubans' games against the Royal Giants – it was a split decision. By 1940, the couple had at least two children, but Ameal Brooks was not living in the same household and the marriage crumbled.

In the winter of 1938-1939, Brooks left his expectant wife behind and headed to Puerto Rico to participate in a newly formed winter league. He signed with the Indios de Mayagüez, but this partnership also was not destined to last. One of his Indios teammates described him as "an interesting character who spent almost twenty years in the Negro leagues ... [but] did not last long with the Indians due to, according to some, an exaggerated fondness for the nightlife of the Sultana club."[57] Brooks's reputation for drinking and carousing at the expense of his career was well-known among his fellow players and may account for his tendency to switch teams multiple times during a season, his offensive ups and downs, and his failed marriage. Frazier Robinson, who played against Brooks in Negro League games in the 1940s, remembered him as one of the few players who could "go yard" on Satchel Paige but noted that Brooks's superhero feats were neutralized by his kryptonite – alcohol:

"Another was a boy by the name of Ameal Brooks, who used to catch for the New York Black Yankees and the Brooklyn Royal Giants. Brooks was an alcoholic – he'd drink all the time – but he could hit Satchel. This guy Brooks could even take Satchel over the fence. [Jim] West and Brooks just seemed to know what Satchel was going to throw, and they'd sit on his fastball. Then they wouldn't take a vicious cut, just swing at it and make contact."[58]

In January 1939 Brooks returned from his Puerto Rican misadventures, along with Indios and New York Black Yankees teammate Ralph Burgin, aboard the *SS Borinquen*. Brooks spent the entire 1939 season with the Black Yankees, playing most of the time in the outfield. He finished the year batting .280 but had just one extra-base hit and a meager eight RBIs. That was less than half of the runs generated by Black Yankees' third baseman Walter Cannady, who played in the same number of games as Brooks. It was a mediocre year for both Brooks and the Black Yankees. The team finished in third place in the NNL2 with a record of 19-18. Brooks did not appear on their roster again for seven years.

Brooks signed with the Brooklyn Royal Giants for the 1940 and 1941 seasons. It was like déjà vu all over again. The Royal Giants were no better than they had been when Brooks played for them in 1937. In fact, they may have been worse. It was not unusual for Brooklyn to lose by a 10-run margin to seemingly inferior squads, despite Brooks's doubles and home runs.[59] The season ended with a thud in mid-September, when the Royal Giants were embarrassed by a twin-bill sweep at the hands of Queens Club, 13-3, and 10-9.[60] In October, with baseball season over, Brooks registered for the US Army draft. He was described on his draft card as 5-feet-8 tall, 165 pounds, and with a scar behind his left ear and a mark near his left eye. Brooks was unemployed and lived in an apartment on West 138th Street in New York City. When asked to name a "person who will always know your address," he chose his father, Joseph Brooks of Chicago, rather than Mary Brooks, his wife of two years in New York.

Brooks returned to the hapless Brooklyn Royal Giants for the first half of the 1941 season. With the 1940 season and his failed marriage behind him, things were looking up; in fact, 1941 turned out to be a great year for Brooks. His lumber awoke from its slumber, and Brooks once more was described in newspapers as "Home Run Brooks" and as "one of the most feared players" in the league.[61] In August he was picked up by the Homestead Grays, who used him mainly in left field and as a catcher, and he lived up to his billing. In September, he went on a home-run tear along with teammate and future Hall of Famer Buck Leonard.[62] The highlight of his 1941 season was the role he played in the Grays' NNL2 championship run. Brooks helped clinch the title by hitting home runs in both games of the doubleheader before a crowd of 12,000 at Yankee Stadium.[63] It was a thrill he likely had not experienced since hitting a home run off Satchel Paige in that same ballpark in 1934. It may have also served as his atonement to Cum Posey for jumping from Homestead to Cleveland that same year.

Brooks never replicated the success he enjoyed in 1941. Then again, by the time the 1942 season started, the United States and the much of the world were at war and things would never be the same again. During the World War II years, Brooks experienced more career lows than highs. In 1942 he started the season with the Cincinnati Ethiopian Clowns. The team marketed him as "Wahoo Brooks," someone "who can play any position, [is] the 'Babe Ruth' of colored baseball, [was] last season's Homestead Gray's leading hitter, [and] who walloped two long home runs in one

afternoon out of the park" at Yankee Stadium.[64] The statistics shared by the Clowns with the press included inflated and unreliable promotional claims such as Brooks being the Homestead Grays' leading home-run hitter in 1942 (that honor went to Buck Leonard), and that as a member of the Cincinnati aggregation, Brooks had hit 14 home runs in the spring alone and had batted .419.[65] Both of those achievements are dubious at best, but the Clowns were more interested in generating turnstile clicks than accurate statistics. Brooks's ride in the Clowns' car ended in July when he signed with the New York Cubans.

Of the four seasons that Brooks spent with the New York Cubans, 1943 was his best. That year, he hit a career-high number of extra-base hits, including 7 doubles and 4 home runs, and generated 26 RBIs. In 1943 Brooks was 36 years old. He played in at least 33 NNL2 games for the Cubans and batted a respectable .265. The Cubans finished the year in second place behind the champion Homestead Grays. Brooks had two memorable games with the Cubans in 1943, both in late September. First, and most notably, was a game at Yankee Stadium between the Cubans and the Kansas City Monarchs in which, before 20,000 riveted fans, Brooks hit a towering home run off Satchel Paige.[66] For that game, "'Bucket' Brooks … was the slugging sensation of the day by hitting one of Satchell [sic] Paige's high fast ones 325 feet into the right field bleachers," and "sewed things up with his first and longest wallop of the day, a 375-foot drive into Ruthville."[67] It was also noted that these two rockets were among the six home runs that Brooks hit at Yankee Stadium that year, and that Brooks "hit twice as many home runs [there] as any Negro player."[68] Brooks faced Paige once more, at the end of the season, this time in the North-South All-Star Game in New Orleans. Brooks only managed to cop two singles off Paige in the Crescent City as the South All-Stars got the best of the North All-Stars, 5-2.[69] Perhaps more important was the fact that the game netted over $100,000 in War Bond sales.[70]

Brooks reupped with the Cubans for the 1944 season, but it was the beginning of the end for his professional baseball career. As in 1943, the Cubans ended the year as the second-best team in the NNL2 to the champion Homestead Grays. Brooks played in 24 league games but did little to light up the scoreboard. Newspapers described him as "Ameal 'Home Run' Brooks," but that turned out to be mostly false advertising.[71] He did manage to hit one home run in an exhibition game in Dayton, Ohio, against the Birmingham

Black Barons.[72] However, even that highlight was spoiled by Brooks's instigation of a bench-clearing brawl when he accused the opposing pitcher, John Huber, of "altering the ball in order to better control."[73] He batted a meager .176 in league games with just one extra-base hit, a double, and racked up just four RBIs. His duties were mainly in the outfield, but he sometimes was called upon as a pinch-hitter; more often than not, he was demoted to batting near the bottom of the order.[74] Brooks ended his season as a participant in the North-South All Star Game in New Orleans.[75] He went hitless in one at-bat in relief of the North's starting catcher and Brooks's Cubans teammate, Lou Louden.

After 1944 Brooks played three more years in the NNL2, each year for a different team. In 1945 he had three official appearances with the second-place New York Cubans, but he also played in several games against independent teams, either as a catcher or pinch-hitter.[76] He went hitless in all three attempts in NNL2 games for the Cubans, and if started in the field, he was frequently pulled for a pinch-hitter late in the game.[77] Brooks spent the first half of the 1946 season in the outfield for his former team, the cellar-dwelling New York Black Yankees, mustering just 4 hits in 20 at-bats. In late June, Brooks jumped to the Jacksonville Eagles, remaining with the Florida-based team through the end of the season.[78]

In early May of 1947, Brooks made his final appearances in the Negro Leagues when he played in two games for the Newark Eagles. Retrosheet shows that his only hit for the Eagles was a solo home run in a losing effort against the Baltimore Elite Giants.[79] By the end of May, Brooks had flown the Eagles' coop for the barnstorming Milwaukee Tigers, a team whose record would be better suited for a litter box than for the annals of baseball glory. It was initially announced that Brooks would be the team's manager, but ultimately those duties fell upon Alex Radcliffe, the brother of Ted "Double Duty" Radcliffe. The nadir of Brooks's summer with the Tigers likely came when he found himself playing against such local amateur nines as the Waterloo, Iowa, "Chicken Basket," or during Milwaukee's 22-7 loss to the "Clark Tructractors" of Battle Creek, Michigan.[80] The Tigers were toothless and an embarrassment. In Battle Creek they were described as "the most miserable conglomeration of misfits ever to get a place on the local schedule," and the game was considered a "farce."[81] The Tigers were billed as having a record of 27 wins against just 5 losses, a claim that was unsubstantiated by newspaper

accounts of their games and was most certainly a fiction conjured up purely to generate ticket sales.[82] In the game between the Tigers and the Tructractors, one indignant sportswriter reported that "[u]mpire Bill Price mercifully called time after six and one-half innings of play. To have detained the fans longer under the guise of a baseball game would have been unadulterated mayhem, no less."[83]

Things did not improve for Brooks and the Tigers. In a mid-July game against an amateur aggregation from Winona, Minnesota, local fans seeing the Milwaukee squad for the first time, "witnessed a spectacle in which a 'semi-professional' baseball team conducted itself like a group of sandlotters."[84] It was a forgettable game for Brooks as well. For the first time in decades, he was tapped as the starting pitcher, and after contesting an umpire's call, Brooks initially "stalked off the field in a display of childish pouting and gesturing and proceeded to pack up the Tigers' equipment."[85] Brooks returned to the mound but his "pitches consisted of leisurely tosses, until darkness finally forced the umpires to call the game in the seventh."[86] For the remainder of the summer, Brooks and the Tigers slogged their way from the Midwest to the East Coast, finishing out the year with a game against a local nine in Washington, Pennsylvania. After an abysmal season with the Tigers, Brooks went out on a high note as he belted a three-run homer to decide the game.[87]

After the demoralizing summer spent with the Milwaukee Tigers in 1947, Brooks appears to have taken a baseball sabbatical in 1948. No records or newspaper accounts of his play have been located for that year. It is possible that he played for a team outside of the United States, but at age 41, and with the demise of Negro League baseball, there were few professional outlets for his diminishing talents. All of that changed for Brooks in 1949 when he was signed by Abe Saperstein to play for the Harlem Globetrotters baseball team.[88] Brooks was tapped as a "utility player" and backup catcher for the Trotters' player-manager Paul Hardy.[89] Brooks appeared in a handful of games for the Globetrotters in the summer of 1949, but he did little to garner any headlines and the paucity of box scores for the team's games makes it difficult to determine his contributions. The following spring, Brooks was named as one of the "topnotch" players on the Globetrotters' 1950 roster and was described as having "formerly caught for the New York Cuban Giants."[90] However, after this initial announcement in May, Brooks was not mentioned again as a member of the team. In fact, he vanished from the Globetrotters' lineup after May 14, 1950.[91]

Brooks's baseball career came to a grinding halt in 1950. After more than 20 years and untold miles spent traveling with a multitude of teams, Brooks ended his career in the Negro Leagues with a .259 batting average. He had played his best baseball with the New York Black Yankees and New York Cubans, and had been effective with the bat well into his 30s. His personal demons of a quick temper and alcohol abuse likely robbed him of a more notable career. The final two decades of Brooks's life were filled with as much mystery and uncertainly as were the first few decades of his life. Details of his activities after baseball are scarce and offer few insights into his private life. What is known is that he spent his remaining years in the Bronx, where he died in 1971 at the age of 64. No obituary or record of his death was published, and the location of his final resting place is unknown.

Sources

Unless otherwise indicated, all Negro League statistics and records were sourced from Seamheads.com.

Ancestry.com was used to access census, birth, death, marriage, military, immigration, and other genealogical and public records.

Acknowledgment: Special thanks to Dr. David J. Keeling for providing Spanish-language translation of documents used for this research.

Notes

1   James A. Riley, *The Biographical Encyclopedia of the Negro Baseball Leagues* (New York: Carroll & Graf Publishers, Inc., 1994), 112.

2   "Milwaukee Tigers Here for Twilight Battle Wednesday," *Battle Creek* (Michigan) *Enquirer*, July 6, 1947: 16; "Cuban Star Threat," *Detroit Michigan Chronicle*, June 10, 1944: 15; "Powerful New York Cubans to Play Savitt Gems Here Tonight at 8:30," *Hartford Courant*, August 30, 1944: 12; "New York Cubans to Meet Memphis Red Sox at Stadium," *Springfield* (Ohio) *Daily News*, June 16, 1943: 11; "League Players and New York Cubans to Tangle," *Sandusky* (Ohio) *Register*, September 7, 1943: 9.

3   "Royal Giants Now Boasting Strong Lineup," *Brooklyn Citizen*, April 12, 1935: 6; "Brooklynites to Play Here Tonight," *Ithaca* (New York) *Journal*, August 5, 1937: 12; "New York Cubans Down Lafayette Team in Fine Exhibition Struggle, 11 to 7," *Lafayette* (Indiana) *Journal and Courier*, August 5, 1943: 18; "New York Cubans Have Classy Club," *Dayton* (Ohio) *Journal Herald*, August 8, 1945: 9; "Milwaukee Tigers Play Double Header Sunday," *Milwaukee* (Wisconsin) *Journal*, June 29, 1947: 39; "Manheim Barons Meet New York Black Yankees Tonight," *Lancaster* (Pennsylvania) *Intelligencer Journal*, June 15, 1939: 13.

4   "Negro National Leaguers Will Play Here Today," *Paterson* (New Jersey) *Morning Call*, June 25, 1938: 22; "Negro Leaguers Clash at Hinchliffe Stadium Tonight," *Paterson Morning Call*, July 2, 1938: 22; "Satchell [sic] Paige Shut Out by Cubans," *New York Age*, September 18, 1943: 11.

5   William F. McNeil, *Black Baseball Out of Season: Pay for Play Outside of the Negro Leagues* (Jefferson, North Carolina: McFarland & Co.), 217.

6   "Chicago Royal Giants Defeat Florence 3 to 2," *Denver Post*, September 21, 1926: 24; "Milwaukee Tigers Play Like Sandlotters Against PNA's," *Winona* (Minnesota) *Republican-Herald*, July 18, 1947: 11.

7   Ameal Brooks's birth date was determined from his World War II draft card and a 1938 marriage license. Other documents state that Brooks was born in either 1904 or 1906.

8   Brian McCammack, *Landscapes of Hope: Nature and the Great Migration in Chicago* (Cambridge: Harvard University Press, 2017), 159, 250.

9   Cynthia K. Barron, *History of the Chicago Parental School, 1902-1975*. Dissertation, Loyola University of Chicago (1993).

10   Gary Ashwill, *Agate Type: Irvin Brooks, PR Man*, March 30, 2009, https://agatetype.typepad.com/agate_type/irvin-brooks/, accessed September 1, 2022.

11   "Chicago Royal Giants Defeat Florence 3 to 2," *Denver Post*, September 21, 1926: 24; "Wichita Leaguers Tossers Triumph," *Wichita Eagle*, October 18, 1926: 10.

12   "Bendix Slate Royal Giants," *South Bend Tribune*, August 28, 1928: 16; "Royal Giants to Tackle Bendixers at Playland To-Day," *South Bend Tribune*, September 2, 1928: 13.

13   "Batting Average of Natl. Negro League," *Indianapolis Recorder*, June 8, 1929: 6.

14   "Texas Colored Giants to Play Here Saturday Afternoon," *Edmonton* (Alberta) *Journal*, June 19, 1929: 9; *Western Canada Baseball, Texas Colored Giants*, http://www.attheplate.com/wcbl/1929_1g.html, accessed June 30, 2022.

15   "Texas Colored Giants to Play Here Saturday Afternoon"; "Baseball," *Saskatoon* (Saskatchewan) *Star-Phoenix*, July 20, 1929: 15.

16   "Texas Colored Giants to Play Here Saturday Afternoon."

17   "Colored Giants, Mill City Team Divide Honors," *Regina* (Saskatchewan) *Leader-Post*, July 15, 1929: 10; "Giants Take Final Brace," *Saskatoon Star-Phoenix*, July 22, 1929: 11; "Colored Giants Trim Transcona," *Winnipeg* (Manitoba) *Tribune*, August 28, 1929: 15.

18   "Ruthilda Drops Second Game of Series," *Saskatoon Star-Phoenix*, August 14, 1929: 10.

19   "Bears to Meet Chicago Team on Local Lot," *Davenport* (Iowa) *Quad-City Times*, May 9, 1930: 32.

20   "Moosomin Nine Lose Twice to Chicago Team," *Regina Leader-Post*, June 5, 1930: 13; "Texas Giants Win by 16-11 Against Chicago Athletics," *Edmonton Journal*, July 14, 1930: 7; "Colored Nines Each Win Game," *Calgary* (Alberta) *Herald*, July 21, 1930: 6.

21   "Dusky Baseballers Defeat Local Select," *Regina Leader-Post*, June 10, 1930: 13.

22   "Texas Giants Win by 16-11 Against Chicago Athletics."

23   Colored Nines Each Win Game."

24   "Chicago Colored Athletics Will Play Bettendorf," *Davenport* (Iowa) *Daily Times*, September 16, 1930: 12.

25   Paul Debono, *The Chicago American Giants* (Jefferson, North Carolina: McFarland & Co., 2011), 129-130.

26   "Grey Sox Upset by Giants, 8 to 3," *Montgomery* (Alabama) *Advertiser*, March 27, 1932: 8; "Memphis Takes 3 Straight from Cleveland," *Chicago Defender*, May 21, 1932: 9.

27   Delbono, 132.

28   William Dismukes, "Retrospective and Perspective," *Pittsburgh Courier*, December 24, 1932: 15.

29 Riley, 188; "Blue Birds Reorganize," *Columbus* (Ohio) *Journal Dispatch*, July 16, 1933: 37; Russell J. Cowans, "Thru the Sports Mirror, *Detroit Tribune*, July 29, 1933: 8.

30 "Detroit Stars Drop 2 Games to Blue Birds," *Detroit Tribune*, July 29, 1933: 8.

31 Cum Posey, "Pointed Paragraphs," *Pittsburgh Courier*, December 22, 1934: 14; James E. Overmeyer, *Cum Posey of the Homestead Grays* (Jefferson, North Carolina: McFarland & Co., 2020), 143.

32 Riley, 180.

33 William E. Clark, "30,000 Attend Four-Team Double Header at Yankee Stadium; Black Yanks Lose; Stars-Crawfords Tie," *New York Age*, September 15, 1934: 5.

34 Jocko Maxwell, "Sports Biggest Thrill in 1934," *New York Age*, December 29, 1934: 7.

35 Maxwell.

36 John Holway, *The Complete Book of Baseball's Negro Leagues: The Other Half of Baseball History* (Fern Park, Florida: Hastings House Publishers, 2001), 313.

37 Holway, 312; Neil Lanctot, *Negro League Baseball: The Rise and Ruin of a Black Institution* (Philadelphia: University of Pennsylvania Press, 2004), 36, 37.

38 "Chi Manager Protests Game with Philly," *Pittsburgh Courier*, October 13, 1934: 14; Debono, 137.

39 Stars Upset Giants Win National Title," *Philadelphia Inquirer*, October 3, 1934: 22.

40 Holway, 313.

41 "Bushwicks Rout Black Yankees in First Game, Throw Away Second; Bill Woerner Is Badly Spiked," *Brooklyn Citizen*, July 1, 1935: 6; "Dutch Woerner Out of Bushwick's Lineup Due to an Injured Leg," *Brooklyn Daily Eagle*, July 1, 1935: 17.

42 Neil Lanctot, *Fair Dealing and Clean Playing: The Hilldale Club and the Development of Black Professional Baseball, 1910-1932* (Syracuse: Syracuse University Press, 1994), 151; Leslie A. Heaphy, *The Negro Leagues, 1869-1960* (Jefferson, North Carolina: McFarland & Co. Inc., 2003), 152.

43 "Penn Red Caps to Meet Black Yankees Here Saturday," *Paterson Morning Call*, August 1, 1935: 22.

44 "Penn Red Caps Will Face Black Yankees Here Today," *Paterson Morning Call*, August 3, 1935: 19.

45 "Penn Red Caps Will Face Black Yankees Here Today."

46 "Enzmann Hurls Dexters to Victory," *Brooklyn Daily Eagle*, August 22, 1935: 20.

47 "Parkways, Bay Ridge in Auspicious Starts with Double Victories," *Brooklyn Daily Eagle*, April 26, 1937: 20; "Curvers Clicking, Bushwicks Brace and Win Twin Bill," *Brooklyn Times-Union*, May 17, 1937: 12.

48 "Mack Wagner Stars in Relief Role but Poconos Lose to Brooklyn Giants," *Middletown* (New York) *Times Herald*, June 15, 1937: 8.

49 "Parkways, Bay Ridge in Auspicious Starts with Double Victories."

50 "Brooklyn Giants Take Braves in Opener," *Long Beach* (New Jersey) *Daily Record*, May 29, 1937: 5; "Royal Giants Win Twice," *Brooklyn Times-Union*, June 1, 1937: 14.

51 "Pirates Win Ninth; Beat Royal Giants, by 6 to 5," *Long Branch Daily Record*, July 7, 1937: 7.

52 "O'Brien Wins Second After Scarlets Lose," *Mamaroneck* (New York) *Daily Times*, August 2, 1937: 7.

53 Cum Posey, "Posey's Points," *Pittsburgh Courier*, December 4, 1937: 16.

54 "12,000 See Black Yankees Take Two Games from Bushwicks, 5-1, 1-0," *Brooklyn Citizen*, April 25, 1938: 6.

55 "Newark Eagles Are Victors in National Negro League," *Paterson Morning Call*, June 27, 1938: 18

56 "McDuffie Pulls Iron-man Feat," *Brooklyn Daily Eagle*, July 5, 1938: 16.

57 Jaime Cordova, *Beisbol de Corazon* (San Juan, Puerto Rico: Ediciones Callejón, 2007), 202.

58 Frazier Robinson, *Catching Dreams: My Life in the Negro Baseball Leagues* (Syracuse: Syracuse University Press, 1999), 85.

59 "Double Win Over Brooklyn Royal Giants Entrenches Scarlets in First Place," *Mount Vernon* (New York) *Argus*, June 17, 1940: 12; "Bay Parkways Win Two Games; Gray Stars," *Brooklyn Citizen*, July 1, 1940: 6.

60 "Ferrick Now Dexter Top Man," *Brooklyn Daily Eagle*, September 16, 1940: 17.

61 "Dahn Sees Club 'Holding' Brooklyn Royal Giants," *Poughkeepsie* (New York) *Eagle-News*, July 2, 1941: 10.

62 "Grays Defeat Cubans 11 to 8," *Kane* (Pennsylvania) *Republican*, September 2, 1941: 5; "Homestead Grays Take Decision Over Cubans," *Washington* (Pennsylvania) *Reporter*, September 3, 1941: 10.

63 Buster Miller, "Homestead Grays Win 1941 Negro Nat'l League Pennant," *New York Age*, September 27, 1941: 11.

64 "Semi-Pro Champions to Play Here," *Tampa Bay* (Florida) *Times*, April 12, 1942: 25.

65 "Clowns Here for Four-Game Series," *Detroit Tribune*, May 30, 1942: 7.

66 "Satchell [*sic*] Paige Shut Out by Cubans," *New York Age*, September 18, 1943: 11.

67 "Satchell Paige Shut Out by Cubans."

68 "Satchell Paige Shut Out by Cubans."

69 "18,000 See Satchel Paige Win with South All-Stars," *New Orleans Item*, September 27, 1943: 10.

70 "18,000 See Satchel Paige Win with South All-Stars."

71 "New York Cubans at Park Tonight," *Lafayette* (Indiana) *Journal and Courier*, June 8, 1944: 20.

72 "Black Barons Edge Cubans," *Dayton* (Ohio) *Journal Herald*, September 7, 1944: 6.

73 "Black Barons Edge Cubans."

74 "Eagles Plan More Contests as They Split," *Brooklyn Daily Eagle*, July 5, 1944: 15; "Josh Hits 2 Homers in N.Y.," *Pittsburgh Courier*, July 22, 1944: 12; Sam Gunst, "Taylor Pitches Well but Savitt Gems Lose, 6-3," *Hartford Courant*, August 31, 1944: 13.

75 "North-South Title Battle Saturday," *Nashville Tennessean*, September 18, 1944: 10; "Cubans Will Play Here Tomorrow," *Atlanta Constitution*, September 23, 1944: 5.

76 "Moscowitz Too Slick on Hill for N.Y. Cubans," *Brooklyn Daily Eagle*, July 19, 1945: 16; "Bushwicks Lose 2 After 13 Victories," *New York Daily News*, July 30, 1945: 38.

77 "Bushwicks Lose 2 After 13 Victories."

78 "Jacksonville Noses Out Lloyd in 10th, 5-4," *Chester* (Pennsylvania) *Times*, June 27, 1946.

79 Retrosheet, "The 1947 Batting Log for Ameal Brooks," https://www.retrosheet.org/NegroLeagues/boxesetc/1947/Bbrooa1011947.htm, accessed November 1, 2022.

80 "Basket to Meet Milwaukee Negro Nine Friday Night," *Waterloo* (Iowa) *Courier*, June 17, 1947: 13; "Clarkmen Slay Milwaukee Club," *Battle Creek* (Michigan) *Enquirer*, July 10, 1947: 23.

81   "Clarkmen Slay Milwaukee Club."

82   "Tructractors Out to Prove Amateur Supremacy Tonight," *Battle Creek Enquirer*, July 9, 1947: 18; "Clarkmen Slay Milwaukee Club."

83   "Clarkmen Slay Milwaukee Club."

84   "Milwaukee Tigers Play Like Sandlotters Against PNA's," *Winona* (Minnesota) *Republican-Herald*, July 18, 1947: 11.

85   "Milwaukee Tigers Play Like Sandlotters Against PNA's."

86   "Milwaukee Tigers Play Like Sandlotters Against PNA's."

87   "Myer Nine Goes Through Tough Weekend," *Washington* (Pennsylvania) *Reporter*, August 18, 1947: 8.

88   "Brooklyn Royal Giants to Play Famous 'Trotters Here Monday," *Indianapolis Recorder*, May 29, 1949: 11.

89   "Royal Giants and Globetrotters to Play Here Tonight," *Owensboro* (Kentucky) *Messenger*, June 2, 1949: 12; "Trotters, House of David Meet Here Tonight at 8:15," *Pocatello* (Idaho) *Tribune*, June 29, 1949: 7.

90   "Harlem Nine to Play Here Saturday," *Austin* (Texas) *American*, May 9, 1950: 18.

91   "Negro Nines Play Twin-Bill Next Sunday," *Louisville Courier Journal*, May 14, 1950: 32.

GEORGE "TANK" CARR

By Mike Whiteman

"It is very doubtful if colored baseball has known a more dangerous hitter than George Carr," wrote Cum Posey in 1937.[1] Posey certainly knew a dangerous hitter when he saw one since, as the longtime owner of the Homestead Grays, he had employed Negro League legends Josh Gibson and Buck Leonard. Given the nickname "Tank" because of his stocky 5-foot-11, 200-pound frame, the switch-hitting Carr, a natural right-hander,[2] added speed to his powerful build, consistently ranking among the league leaders in stolen bases. A versatile player, he made most of his appearances at first base, but by the end of his career had taken the field at every position but pitcher. Carr's exploits on the East and West Coasts gained him admirers and acclaim as well as recognition from the influential *Pittsburgh Courier,* which included him on its all-time team of Negro League players in 1952.[3] Although he never reached Cooperstown despite a career .311 batting average, he was a vital cog on some of the greatest baseball teams of all time.

George Henry Carr was born on September 2, 1893 (or possibly 1894 or 1895) in Atlanta, the son of Stephen and Idella Carr,[4] Per the 1910 US Census, Stephen was a janitor and Idella was a dressmaker. The mystery regarding George's birth year lies in the facts that his headstone states he was born in 1893, while Carr reported his birth year as 1894 in his World War I draft card and 1895 in his World War II draft card. Carr made his way to California at an early age, and attended Pasadena High School.[5] However, according to census records, he attended high school for only about a year. On his World War I draft card, he listed himself as a "movie actor" at Universal City, California.[6]

Carr's earliest documented baseball experience was in the winter of 1915-1916, when he played for a semipro team, the Los Angeles White Sox, in the winter months. The team occasionally participated in the California Winter League, which allowed African American baseball players the opportunity to compete against White major leaguers. He was recognized for his skill, with the *California Eagle* describing him as "what we might call an all-star player, and adding, "Carr hits like Tris Speaker, fields like 'Stuffy' McInnis, and despite the fact that he tips the beam around the 200-mark, he runs bases like Ty Cobb. Again we say, he's some player."[7] With the exception of 1918-1919, when they did not play, the White Sox continued to exist as a semipro team over the winters, until they joined the California Winter League as a full professional team in 1920-21. Carr was the team's manager in 1919-20.

Carr traveled east in the spring of 1920 to suit up for the Kansas City Monarchs of Rube Foster's newly formed Negro National League. The Monarchs' first NNL game took place on May 29, 1920. According to the *Kansas City Sun,* Carr was slated to "probably" start the contest in right field.[8] In the next game, on the 31st, his versatility was on display: The *Sun* reported

First baseman George "Tank" Carr

43

that "Carr, the Monarchs second baseman, made one of those impossible catches in the sixth inning to the electrification of all fans."[9]

For that initial NNL season, Carr served as the Monarchs' primary first baseman, and he turned in a fine .315/.355/.435 effort with a 132 OPS+, and finished fifth in the circuit with 18 stolen bases. In 1921 he played even better, slashing at .323/.389/.518, improving his OPS+ to 158, and ranking among the league leaders in home runs, RBIs, walks, stolen bases, and OPS. The Monarchs finished in second place behind Foster's Chicago American Giants in both seasons.

After the 1921 season, Carr took his hot bat back home, batting .336 for the "Colored All Stars" of the California Winter League, a team that also included future Hall of Famers Oscar Charleston, Biz Mackey, and José Méndez

The 1922 NNL season brought a change of position for Carr; he moved off first base to roam the outfield,

First baseman "Tank" Carr looked dapper off the field and played outstanding ball on it.

primarily center field. He struggled at the plate, perhaps due to the greater physical demands of playing the outfield, slumping to .265/.342/.378. His cold bat followed him to California in the winter as he struggled to a .214 average.

The 1923 season brought a newcomer to the Black baseball scene – the Eastern Colored League. As Foster had done with Midwestern teams, Ed Bolden led the organization of the ECL, which served to bring organized Black baseball to the East Coast and provided a new competitor to the NNL. ECL teams raided NNL teams for star players like Mackey, George Scales, Heavy Johnson, Pop Lloyd, and Charleston.[10] Carr joined Bolden's Hilldale Club, located in Darby, Pennsylvania (in the Philadelphia area), which became one of the great Negro League teams of the 1920s. The "Darby Daisies" took the first three ECL flags and, after losing the inaugural Negro League World Series to the Kansas City Monarchs in 1924, defeated them in 1925 to win the title as champions of all of Black baseball. Carr was back at first base, and was solid in the 1923 and 1924 seasons, posting 109 and 114 OPS+. In 1924 he batted .295 as Hilldale came up short in the first Negro League World Series.

After the 1924 season, Carr again went to California and had perhaps his best winter season, batting .383 with 11 home runs in 32 games.

Carr's torrid play carried over to the 1925 ECL season. He was arguably the best first baseman in the league, ranking in the top five in slugging percentage, OPS, and offensive WAR while leading the league with 24 stolen bases. The *Pittsburgh Courier* referred to Carr as "the most improved player of the league" and "without a doubt the sensation of the Eastern circuit this season."[11] His efforts helped Hilldale to the Negro League World Series rematch in which they whipped the Monarchs, winning five of six games. Carr batted .308 with one homer and six RBIs in the World Series. In California in the winter, he claimed another title by leading the Philadelphia Royal Giants to the Winter League championship with a league-leading 8 home runs and a .342 batting average.

Carr was at his peak, both in the ECL and CWL, from 1924 through 1926. In a total of 563 at-bats, he hit .355 with 50 doubles, 15 triples, 30 home runs, and at least 24 stolen bases (though likely more, as stolen-base statistics from the CWL are unavailable).

The Daisies again had the best record in the ECL in 1926, although the Atlantic City Bacharach Giants represented the circuit in the Negro League World Series that year. Carr contributed a .315/.412/.441 slash line and a 132 OPS+ as Hilldale finished 53-33-2 (a .616 winning percentage). In the offseason, he opted for a change of scenery and spent his winter in Cuba. Carr did not play in the Cuban Winter League but in the "independent league known as Triangular – because 3 teams were in competition – [that] conducted its games at the University of Havana Stadium, showcasing the best Cuban and imported players of the time, lured from the official league by higher compensation."[12] Carr batted .416 playing for Alacranes, which finished in first place with a 22-15 record.[13]

In 1927 Hilldale fell to fifth place in the ECL. Carr held up his end on the field, leading the team with a .323 batting average, but all was not well. He was suspended, along with pitcher Nip Winters and outfielder Namon Washington, "for lack of discipline and indifferent playing."[14] After his rough time with Hilldale that season, Carr returned to California, where he batted .377 for the California Winter League champion Philadelphia Royal Giants.

The next April, Carr was traded to the New York Lincoln Giants with Winters because it was "Hilldale's policy ... to get rid of dissatisfied players, and men who won't stay in condition."[15] Shortly after the season started, the Giants dropped out of the ECL, and Carr moved on to the Atlantic City Bacharach Giants. The ECL folded in June, but the Giants continued to play an independent schedule.[16] In 1929 the American Negro League was formed, with many of the same players and teams from the ECL. Carr stayed on with Atlantic City, batting .370 in limited duty before returning to Hilldale for one game.

After 1929, Carr appears to have dropped out of league ball until 1934. In 1930 he reportedly played for the independent Milwaukee Colored Giants.[17] In the summer of 1931, he joined the Royal Giants on a tour of Hawaii. During the winter of 1932-1933, Carr played first base and batted .355 for Lonnie Goodwin's Philadelphia Royal Giants tour of Hawaii, Japan, China, and the Philippines, during which the team won 50 of the 52 games played.[18] Among his teammates on the tour were Hall of Famers Mackey and Andy Cooper.[19]

In the summer of 1933, Carr caught on with the independent Philadelphia Bacharach Giants. Another trip overseas to the Orient was planned for the next winter, but Carr ended up going to Puerto Rico instead, playing in exhibition games.

Carr's last season in the Negro major leagues was 1934. He began the season with Ed Bolden's Philadelphia Stars; he had a longtime connection to

Bolden that went back to his days with the Hilldale team. But Carr's tenure in Philadelphia encompassed only a doubleheader on June 8.[20] He played first base in both games and collected three hits. It is not known why he left the team, but about a week later he was playing third base for the independent Washington Pilots.[21] The players on the Pilots became the primary participants for the Baltimore Black Sox, who entered the Negro National League II in the second half of the season but shut down after limited action. Carr played three games at third base and wielded a still potent bat even though he was approaching age 40 – 6-for-11 with a home run and two stolen bases. His known playing career concluded with player-manager stints for the independent Philadelphia Black Meteors in 1935 and the Philadelphia Colored Giants in 1941.[22]

Little is known of Carr's personal life after baseball. Census records from 1940 indicate that he lived in Los Angeles with his wife, Sarah; his son, Ernest; his daughter-in-law, Celia; and two grandsons.[23] He was employed as a cook in a café.[24]

George Carr died suddenly on January 14, 1948, in McPherson, Kansas, of a heart attack while working for the Rock Island Railroad Company.[25] He had just recently come into the area for the work.[26] He left behind his wife, two children, and four grandchildren.[27] Carr was buried in Evergreen Cemetery in Los Angeles. Among the pallbearers at his funeral service were former teammates Mackey, Dobie Moore, Jess Hubbard, and Carlisle Perry.

Despite his showing on the *Pittsburgh Courier's* list of all-time Negro League players, Carr has not been mentioned as a Hall of Fame candidate. He was not among those players considered for enshrinement by the 2006 Special Committee on the Negro Leagues. A look at his stats, however, indicates that he may have been worthier of inclusion in Cooperstown than many thought. Carr's lifetime 129 OPS+ is higher than that of Cool Papa Bell among primarily Negro League players. It's also higher than the career marks of Hall of Fame first basemen and contemporaries George Sisler and Jim Bottomley. Most winters he traveled home to play in the California Winter League, where he was one of the more accomplished players in the history of the circuit. His .336 lifetime batting average is ninth all-time, and he ranks high on the career lists in doubles, triples, and home runs. Should one downplay the quality of competition in Carr's Winter League play, it's important to note that among his contemporaries over 13 seasons were 20 Hall of Famers, both from the Negro Leagues and the White major leagues. If one combines his Negro League and California Winter League appearances, he batted .320 over more than 3,500 plate appearances.

While the numbers demonstrate Carr's all-around skills, the "intangibles" are a bit mixed. His leadership skills were displayed at a young age when he managed the White Sox in his 20s. He was well liked, and affectionately called "Native Son" in the media and managed local teams after he left league play. His perceived attitude problems at the end of his tenure in Hilldale and rumors of alcoholism and possible effects on play[28] may take away from his on-field exploits.

Carr's ultimate baseball legacy probably lies in the years when he played for Hilldale. He slashed .316/.380/.473 with a 127 OPS+ over his five years with the team, among the greatest of all time. The headliners of those teams were a group of Hall of Famers – shortstop Lloyd, catcher-infielder Mackey, and third baseman Judy Johnson. Like any baseball dynasty, after that first tier of star power, there was another group of very good players who were crucial to their team's success. Think of players like Bob Meusel with the 1920s Yankees. Charlie Keller with the 1930s Bronx Bombers, and Hank Bauer of Casey Stengel's 1950s clubs. Carr's contributions to the Daisies look similar in context to those of these talented players.

The more one digs into Carr's career, the more one is impressed by his all-around skills. His place on the *Courier* list is indeed well deserved.

Sources

In addition to the sources cited in the Notes, the author consulted baseball-reference.com and Seamheads.com for player statistics and team records. He also consulted the following:

McNeil, William. *The California Winter League: America's First Integrated Baseball League* (Jefferson, North Carolina: McFarland, 2002).

Notes

1   Cum Posey, "Posey's Points," *Pittsburgh Courier* November 27, 1937: 16.

2   Email exchange with Scott Simkus, January 23, 2023.

3   "Power, Speed, Skill Make All-American Team Excel," *Pittsburgh Courier*, April 19, 1952: 16.

4   George H. Carr in the 1910 United States Federal Census (https://www.ancestry.com).

5   George H. Carr obituary (https://www.findagrave.com/memorial/99620094/george-henry-carr).

6   George Henry Carr World War II Draft Registration Card (https://www.ancestry.com). Universal City is an unincorporated enclave within Los Angeles.

7   Hilberte L. Rozier, "Thoughts Wise and Otherwise," *California Eagle*, October 14, 1916: 8.

8   "Base Ball," *Kansas City* (Missouri) *Sun*, May 29, 1920: 8.

9   "Monday's (Decoration Day) Game," *Kansas City Sun*, June 5, 1920: 8.

10 Lawrence Hogan, *Shades of Glory: The Negro Leagues and the Story of African American Baseball* (Washington: National Geographic, 2006), 166; John B. Holway, *Blackball Stars: Negro League Pioneers* (Westport, Connecticut: Meckler Books, 1988), 221, 332.

11 W. Rollo Wilson. "Eastern Snapshots," *Pittsburgh Courier*, September 12, 1925: 13.

12 Jorge S. Figueredo, *Cuban Baseball: A Statistical History, 1878-1961* (Jefferson, North Carolina: McFarland, 2003), 171.

13 Figueredo, 171-72.

14 Neil Lanctot, *Fair Dealing and Clean Playing: The Hilldale Club and the Development of Black Professional Baseball, 1910-1932* (Syracuse, New York: Syracuse University Press, 2007), 157.

15 "Lincolns and Hilldales in Big Trade: Nip Winters and George Carr Leave the Clan of Darby," *Pittsburgh Courier*, April 21, 1928: 17.

16 Center for Negro League Research, www.cnlbr.org.

17 "New Pitcher Added," *California Eagle* (Los Angeles), November 21, 1930: 9.

18 Center for Negro League Research.

19 Ancestry.com, accessed January 4, 2023.

20 "Giants Take Twin Bill From Philly: Foster and Trent Hurl Coles to Win," *Chicago Defender*, June 9, 1934: 17.

21 "Pilots Beat All-Phillies," *Pittsburgh Courier*, June 16, 1934: 15.

22 Center for Negro League Research.

23 Ancestry.com, accessed January 4, 2023.

24 Ancestry.com, accessed January 4, 2023.

25 "Check Death of Negro Man Here," *McPherson* (Kansas) *Daily Republican*, January 15, 1948: 1.

26 "May Hold Autopsy in Negro's Death," *McPherson Daily Republican*, January 16, 1948: 2.

27 George H. Carr obituary (https://www.findagrave.com/memorial/99620094/george-henry-carr.

28 James A. Riley, *The Biographical Encyclopedia of the Negro Leagues* (New York: Carroll and Graf, 1994), 154.

PAUL CARTER

BY RICHARD BOGOVICH

Paul Carter was a late bloomer as a professional pitcher with a career ERA+ of 85, a statistic that appears to denote him as a below-average pitcher. Nevertheless, across the 54 games he pitched for teams of Negro major-league quality, he had a record of 22 wins and 15 losses that resulted in an impressive .595 win percentage. Three victories were likely his personal high points. He put an exclamation point on his first full season on a top Black club by hurling a no-hitter at the age of 31. Three years later he was dominant in one of the most important games in the history of the Philadelphia Stars, when he saved them from elimination in the 1934 Negro National League II (NNL2) Championship Series. He hurled another no-hitter the following summer, in what turned out to be his final full season in the Negro Leagues.

Paul Carter and his twin, Andrew, were born on May 24, 1900, in Kennett Square, Chester County, Pennsylvania, to William Daniel Carter and Martha (Washington) Carter.[1] The Carters were visited for the 1900 census about three weeks later, at which point they owned their home on East State Street. The couple had been married for eight years, and Martha had given birth to six children by then. The newborns had two brothers and two sisters ranging in age from 2 to 8. William's occupation was simply entered as laborer.

Kennett Square is called the Mushroom Capital of the World. Its first such business started in 1896, so the Carter children grew alongside that local industry – and at around age 20, Paul was a farm laborer.[2] In the Civil War era, Chester County had been important to the Underground Railroad that helped escaped slaves to freedom because of the two states it bordered in Pennsylvania's southeastern corner. "Both Delaware and Maryland were slave states, so self-liberators from those states, or from the lower South, needed to keep moving north to reach freedom," states the Kennett Underground

Pitcher Paul Carter

Gary Ashwill

Railroad Center. "This combination of factors – proximity, the presence of a large Quaker population opposed to slavery, organized abolitionist societies, and a relatively large number of free African American communities – made Chester County an important stop on the way north."[3] Still, Kennett Square itself had a population of only 606 in the 1860 census, on the eve of the Civil War.[4]

Presumably those traits were ingrained enough to make Kennett Square a relatively pleasant place for the Carters to live in. However, when Paul and Andrew were 4 years old, a local Black man named John Taylor lost a pioneering lawsuit against the school board for segregating his four children, and others of their race, from the White pupils. Professor Walter E. Dengler, the principal, said students had been grouped based on the pace at which they completed schoolwork, and mentioned that one Black student was in a classroom with White children. Despite such a rationale, Judge William Butler doubted the practice was legal. Ultimately, though, the jury ruled against Taylor.[5] In 1900 one or two of the older Carter children were of school age but weren't identified as students in that census, so it is unknown whether any of them were classmates of the Taylor children at the time of the jury's verdict. In any event, the 1940 census indicated that Paul Carter had completed through the sixth grade.

By the 1910 census, the Carter family had moved to Walnut Street. Not only did they own that home as well, but it was free of a mortgage. William worked at a greenhouse, and Martha worked as a laundress out of their residence. The family had grown by two more boys and a girl, and all nine offspring were still living. (And all were members of the household.) The twins and two

47

older siblings had attended school during the previous 12 months.

Quite possibly the first mention in a newspaper of Paul Carter on a baseball team occurred in mid-1917. "Kennett is about to be favored with a new base ball team, under the management of Geo. Harris," reported the *Philadelphia Tribune* (today the nation's oldest continuously published African American newspaper). "It is to be known as the Young Athletes." Presumably the Paul Carter named among the nine additional men was the future Philadelphia Stars pitcher.[6] In mid-1919 there was a Black team called the Kennett Square All-Stars, but the two known box scores did not include any player named Carter.[7]

When Carter completed a military registration card in 1918, he worked as a hod carrier for Lynch Construction of Wilmington, Delaware, little more than 10 miles from Kennett Square. (That job involved carrying bricks, mortar, and the like at construction sites in a distinct three-sided box.) He was still living at home, at 138 North Walnut in Kennett Square. That was also true at the time of the 1920 census, in which the twin brothers and their father were all identified as farm laborers. The youngest boy and girl in the family had been attending school.

Documenting Paul's baseball career during the 1920s is complicated by two factors. One is other pitchers named Carter on Black teams in and near eastern Pennsylvania, particularly Cliff Carter (no known relation). It seems a necessity to report regularly on both Carters' – Paul's and Cliff's – whereabouts over that decade. The other factor is the common practice on sports pages then of not using players' first names. It may be there was no instance before 1926 of any newspaper outside of Chester County using Paul Carter's first name, or at least a helpful identifier like his hometown. Paul's earliest season with a top Black team in a Negro major league did not occur until 1931, when he pitched for the independent Hilldale club of Philadelphia and Yeadon, Pennsylvania.

Cliff Carter, who was a little older than Paul, lived roughly halfway between Philadelphia and Pittsburgh at least through the 1920 census and had a Negro League career that overlapped with Paul Carter's in the 1930s. However, it is known where Cliff pitched for almost all seasons from 1923 through 1934. What's more, after Paul and Cliff were both established professionals, they had at least three teams in common and were even teammates sometimes.

It remains murky whether either, or neither, was the Black pitcher nicknamed Cannonball Carter – sometimes spelled "Cannon Ball" – who was active in 1921 on a couple of teams in Wilmington.[8] As was mentioned previously, that city was a short trip from home for Paul Carter. Of course, it is possible the nickname Cannonball was applied to both Paul and Cliff, and even some other Carter(s) at times. In fact, in mid-1922 a Cannon Ball Carter "jumped the Buffalo Stars" and joined the Harrisburg Giants, and that was very likely Cliff.[9]

Compounding the confusion is Black pitcher Nick Carter of the 1920s. In 1994 Negro League historian James A. Riley identified Nick as Paul Carter's nickname, and not also one for Cliff; however, Cliff was indeed called Nick as well.[10] Furthermore, from 1916 through 1920 the National League's Chicago Cubs had a pitcher named Paul Carter, whose nickname was likewise Nick. It is entirely possible that Cliff and the pair of Paul Carters shared this nickname because of a popular and long-running fictional detective by that name.[11]

In June of 1920, there was a pitcher named Carter on a team called the Harlan Giants, the "premier colored aggregation" of Wilmington, Delaware.[12] That could certainly have been the Cannonball Carter who was active there during 1921. If this Carter was indeed Paul, then one of his early teammates was none other than future Hall of Famer Judy Johnson.[13] The two were definitely teammates toward the end of Carter's career, in 1937.

In 1922 there were not many signs of the Carter who had been active on Wilmington teams the two previous years. One exception was the pitcher who teamed with a catcher named Faulkner on the Sun Co. team in July. The chances of that Carter being Paul seem good, partly because there was a Black catcher named Faulkner on Wilmington teams who was also from Kennett Square.[14] Additionally, in May of 1922 there was a pitcher named Carter on a Baltimore team called the Pennsylvania Eagles. (Baltimore is about 70 miles from Kennett Square.) That club also had a pitcher by the same name in 1921 and 1925, at a minimum.[15] A player named Carter also pitched for the Pittsburgh Keystones on June 10, though nobody with that last name currently is listed as having been on that club's roster. The Keystones had a pitcher named Carter in at least four games in 1923, but a complete roster for that season's club was unavailable as of 2023.[16]

For 1923, Cliff Carter hurled for top clubs like the Baltimore Black Sox and the Atlantic City Bacharach Giants, but apparently he was also the Carter on a

Philadelphia team called the Madison Stars, from which he moved to the Richmond Giants.[17] Meanwhile, Paul Carter might not have played with any prominent team that season. Of course, it is possible that for some or even many seasons from his late teens to age 30. Paul did not play much or any baseball at all.

Cliff Carter pitched in two games for the Bacharachs in 1924; however, in March, he reportedly signed with the Brooklyn Cuban Giants.[18] He also spent parts of 1924 with the Baltimore Black Sox, Chappie Johnson's Colored Stars, Ed Bolden's Hilldale club, and the Harrisburg Giants. On at least two of those teams, he was sometimes called Nick Carter.[19] Beyond that batch of clubs, it remains uncertain whether it was Paul, Cliff, or some other Carter(s) who spent time in 1924 with the Wilmington Black Sox, Newark Black Sox, and Anchor Giants.[20]

Cliff Carter's 1925 season has not been documented as well as some of his other campaigns. Shortly before the start of the season he was reported to be with the Harrisburg Giants, and late that year he was with Chappie Johnson's team.[21] Unclear is the identity of the pitcher named Carter who played for the Anchor Giants and Pennsylvania Eagles that year.[22]

In 1926 there was a Carter on the spring-training roster of the Donora Athletics, "one of the leading Negro semi-pro baseball clubs" of Pennsylvania, headquartered in or near Pittsburgh. As they prepared to open their season, it was stated that "Paul Carter, Kennett Square pitcher," was being considered to start their first game. During the second half of May, he hurled a four-hitter to win a 3-2 game for Donora.[23]

Paul Carter was almost certainly the leader of "Carter's A.B.C. Giants, of Kennett Square," in the summer of 1927. That club had a "Falkner" at shortstop atop one batting order. It is also likely that Paul Carter was part of the battery with Richard Faulkner for Faulkner's Biltmore Stars a few weeks earlier.[24] Cliff Carter played in at least 27 games for the Harrisburg Giants that year, so it is unclear who the Carter was who pitched for a team called the Broncos, led by Hall of Famer Louis Santop.[25] Santop's club had a Carter hurl for it in 1928 as well, and late that year he was called Nick Carter, the team's pitching ace.[26]

Paul Carter was definitely with the Kennett Square Gray Sox, under the leadership of Richard "Dick" Faulkner, during the early weeks of the 1928 season. However, Carter's place of residence was identified in one article as Philadelphia rather than Kennett Square itself. A few weeks later, a report implied that Carter had played with teams in Toledo and Cleveland (though searches for any Carter on Black teams in those two Ohio cities earlier that decade turned up no such information).[27] At the end of May, Faulkner and Carter were the winning battery in one game. By then, it had been announced that the team was being sponsored by future Hall of Famer Herb Pennock, a Kennett Square native.[28]

In July of 1929, "Carter, Kennett Square pitching ace," hurled at least once for the Wilmington Blue Sox, but later that same month, a Carter was again pitching for Kennett Square's club. Another five weeks later, Carter was back with the Blue Sox, and he remained with the team until at least mid-September.[29]

In the 1930 census, Paul Carter was living at the same address as in 1918 and 1920. The Carter household was a large one and included sons-in-law and grandchildren. Paul worked as a landscape laborer, and he married Martha Brown in 1931.

During the second half of 1930, both Paul and Cliff Carter apparently had stints with Hilldale, less than a month apart. Cliff had pitched in seven American Negro League (ANL) games for Hilldale in 1929, but his 1930 return engagement encompassed only two games for the team, which now played as an independent franchise. Cliff lost a seven-inning complete game to the Lincoln Giants on July 17. As for Paul Carter, on August 6 "the recently acquired chukker from Kennett Square" won a game easily for Hilldale.[30]

Before and after Cliff Carter's complete game for Hilldale, he pitched for a barnstorming team called the Havana Red Sox.[31] A second team for Paul Carter in 1930 was reportedly the New York Lincoln Giants. In fact, the day before Cliff and Hilldale lost to the Lincoln Giants, the latter had a pitcher named Carter who started against a Wilmington team.[32] It is difficult to identify any other teams for whom Paul also pitched during 1930. However, it is possible to rule out his participation on two teams based on identifying details, specifically the Pittsburgh Monarchs and a Baltimore-area team called the Silver Moons.[33]

As of early 2023, Paul Carter's first confirmed season with a Negro League team of major-league quality was 1931, with Hilldale, which was again an independent club that year. In eight games, he won five and lost two. However, in May and the first half of June he had been with the Wilmington Hornets.[34] It was toward the end of June that he was identified as a new pitcher on Hilldale's staff. On Labor Day (September 7), he threw a no-hitter against the Baltimore Black Sox in which he allowed one walk and struck out four batters in a 6-0 triumph. However,

Pittsburgh Courier columnist W. Rollo Wilson wrote that everyone in the press box had disagreed with official scorer Frank Caulk's error rulings on two plays in the same inning.[35]

Given that dissent, Carter's shutout about a month later may have been almost as significant. He scattered seven hits as Hilldale beat a team of "Major League All-Stars," 2-0, on October 10. One player he held hitless was Chick Fullis, whose batting average across eight National League seasons was .295.[36]

In 1932 Paul Carter again spent time with Hilldale, which was a member club of the short-lived East-West League (EWL) that season. He also spent time with another EWL squad, the Baltimore Black Sox. After pitching to a 5-2 record for Hilldale in 1931, he was a combined 2-8 in 1932 (1-7 with Hilldale and 1-1 with the Black Sox). Carter apparently left the Hilldale club by mid-July, at which point he was with Kennett Square's team in the Chester County League. About a week into August, he was again with the Wilmington Hornets, and by mid-September he was pitching for the Black Sox.[37]

Meanwhile, Cliff Carter's pitching line for 1932 shows him to have been a member of the Philadelphia Bacharach Giants and, like Paul, the Hilldale team. At the end of August, the Brooklyn Royal Giants had a pitcher named Carter, but it is uncertain which of the two Carters that was.[38] In any case, Cliff's 1933 season shows that he split time between the Philadelphia Stars and the Bacharach Giants, and he spent time with only the latter team in 1934, which was his final season.

In 1933 Paul Carter played the first of three seasons with the Philadelphia Stars; thus, he and Cliff were teammates for a time in 1933. Philadelphia was an independent club in 1933 but belonged to the Negro National League II in 1934 and 1935. Paul's record for the Stars in 1933 was 6-1. His subsequent records were also good, 4-2 (including 1-0 in the postseason) in 1934 and 5-2 in 1935, for a composite league record of 15-5. There were indications that Paul Carter spent all of 1933 with the Stars, though in mid-October a paper in Wilmington said he might pitch for the Kennett Square Gray Sox in the deciding game for the championship of the Southern Chester County Twilight League. (But either the paper did not report the outcome or the game was not played.)[39]

In March of 1934, Paul Carter's father died. Readers of his obituary learned he was son of a Civil War veteran, Joseph Carter. William D. Carter had lived his entire life in or near Kennett Square.[40]

On June 28, a preview of a Bacharach Giants game that day said their starting pitcher would be "Paul Carter, righthand ace, who last year performed with Ed Bolden's Philadelphia All Stars." Presumably, that was actually Cliff. Two days earlier, the Stars had a pitcher named Carter, presumably Paul, who competed against the Scanlon C.C. nine.[41] A little insight into Paul Carter's time away from the diamond was provided by the *Philadelphia Tribune* on July 12. On a previous Tuesday evening, either July 3 or 10, he and Stars teammate Phil Cockrell were socializing back in Kennett Square.[42]

In September the Stars and the Chicago American Giants began a seven-game playoff to determine the NNL champion. By September 29, Chicago led the series, three games to two. That day, at Philadelphia's Passon Field, Paul Carter drew the starting assignment in front of 3,000 fans. Turkey Stearnes homered off Carter in the third inning, but the Stars soon used six hits to push across pairs of runs in consecutive innings. Chicago threatened in the fifth frame, in part due to a walk by Carter, but the Stars escaped unscathed. "At no other time was Carter in trouble," the *Philadelphia Tribune* noted. Carter yielded only four hits that afternoon, and the 4-1 result pushed the series to a decisive seventh game. The *Philadelphia Inquirer* called Carter's pitching "brilliant," and the *Tribune* called it "effortless."[43] The Stars won the championship at the same park on October 2.[44]

In the wake of that performance, it was no surprise that Carter was back with the Stars in April of 1935 as they conducted their spring training in Philadelphia. His best game that season was his pitching gem on August 17, as the Stars hosted the Brooklyn Eagles at PRR YMCA Field. It was the second game of a doubleheader and thus was limited to seven innings. Carter's single in the second inning drove in the game's first run. On the mound he issued two walks, but no runner reached second base against him that afternoon. He struck out five Eagles on his way to a 4-0 no-hitter. The *Philadelphia Tribune* said "he kept the Stars in the race for the second half honors" in the NNL2.[45]

In April of 1936, Paul Carter was among the pitchers on a team led by Cockrell called the Yeadon Yuccas. In mid-May, he was identified as a starting pitcher in a game for the Brooklyn Royal Giants; he had been formally released by the Philadelphia Stars around that time.[46]

By early July, Carter was plying his trade with the New York Black Yankees of the NNL2. He pitched in a few nonleague games for them that month.[47] Carter threw in just one NNL game in 1936, a start for the Black Yankees in which he pitched into the seventh inning but was neither the winning nor losing pitcher. He gave up six runs, five of which were earned, in that August 4 game against the Pittsburgh Crawfords in Akron, Ohio. A late rally, after Carter had exited the contest, gave the Black Yankees a 9-6 victory.[48] Carter won a rematch less than a week later, by a score of 9-3, but the lack of an available box score has kept this game out of his official stat line for the time being.[49] Coincidentally, pitching for the Crawfords was "E. Carter," according to the batteries printed beneath the available line score; this Carter was longtime Negro League pitcher Ernest "Spoon" Carter.[50]

In April and May of 1937, Paul Carter was said to be on the pitching staff of the Brooklyn Royal Giants,[51] but he was also said to be on the Wilmington Red Caps with Judy Johnson, and an R. Faulkner at third base. Carter appeared in multiple box scores with the latter club in May and June.[52] In at least two box scores during June, catching for the Red Caps was a J. Carter, and once their pitcher was identified as C. Carter. Nevertheless, two articles shortly thereafter were explicit about Paul Carter being the ace of the Red Caps.[53] That appears to have been the extent of Carter playing with any baseball team of note.[54]

At the time of the 1940 census, Paul and his wife, Martha, were living with her mother, Sallie Brown, in Kennett Square. The only other person in the household was Martha's brother, Walter. Carter worked for a nursery. When he completed a military registration card two years later, his employer was specified as Longwood Nurseries, owned by Ben J. Myers. Sallie died in 1943, and Martha in 1949.[55] A shared gravestone indicates that Carter's mother died in 1953 and his twin brother in 1958.

In 1955, around Labor Day, the celebration of Kennett Square's centennial included "two Old Timers' baseball games," and "on hand, but not playing will be Paul Carter, one-time pitcher for the famous Hilldale Philadelphia team." The backgrounds of several White players were described, but none seemed as accomplished as Carter. However, a younger Old Timer was Joe Pennock, quite possibly Herb's son by that name.[56]

Paul Carter died almost 20 years later, on May 9, 1975, close to his 75th birthday, after having been hospitalized for a brief illness. He had continued to work for the Myers landscaping and nursery business until his retirement a decade earlier. Carter was survived by three siblings, and he was buried at Kennett

Square's Union Hill Cemetery. His obituary said he had pitched "with the Baltimore Black Sox, Black Yankees, Nashville Giants, Homestead Greys [sic] and Chicago American Giants," but some of those were presumably incorrect. Conversely, the Philadelphia Stars were omitted.[57]

Carter was occasionally remembered publicly over the remainder of the century. In a 1982 newspaper article, Webster McDonald took credit for developing him. Carter was also recalled a decade later in a brief history of Kennett Square's Gray Sox. Before the invention of radar guns, teammate Bob Jackson assumed Carter threw fastballs at 90 miles per hour. In a mid-1998 article, the Gray Sox were cited in passing, and Paul Carter was mentioned foremost among "the local Negro League legends" who had been on that club.[58] Not bad for someone who was essentially a rookie at age 31.

SOURCE

The Seamheads.com Negro League Database was consulted for player statistics, rosters, and team records.

NOTES

1   The 1900 census page on which the Carter family is listed is dated June 13, and it states that the twins were born in May of that year. The date of the 24th is from https://www.chesco.org/DocumentCenter/View/48797/Birth-Registers-1893-1907-A-I on page 127, while twin brother Andrew is listed on the previous page. In sporting databases, May 10 has been commonly identified as his date of birth, based on his military registrations around the two World Wars. Their father's middle name was identified on Paul's military registration card in 1918. Their mother's maiden name was identified on their sister Hattie's marriage application in 1929, along with the obituary of "Paul Carter," Kennett (Square, Pennsylvania) News & Advertiser, May 15, 1975: 3. Special thanks to Debbie Kellar of the Chester County Library System for providing that obituary.

2   Joseph A. Lordi, Kennett Square (Charleston, South Carolina: Arcadia Publishing, 2006), 8. See also Paul Carter's occupation in the 1920 federal census.

3   See https://www.kennettundergroundrr.org/kennett-and-the-ugrr.

4   Lordi, 7.

5   "Negro Loses in Suit against School Board," Philadelphia Inquirer, October 21, 1904: 3.

6   "Kennett Square," Philadelphia Tribune, June 2, 1917: 8.

7   "Another for the Giants," Chester (Pennsylvania) Times, July 14, 1919: 8. "Wilmington Giants Win," Every Evening (Wilmington, Delaware), July 28, 1919: 9.

8   For an example of the nickname being spelled "Cannon Ball," i.e., as two words, see "Flashes of Local Sport," Wilmington (Delaware) Morning News, July 8, 1921: 7.

9   For much of the 1921 season, Cliff Carter pitched for a team based in Buffalo, New York, called the Pittsburgh Colored Stars, managed by the famous Grant "Home Run" Johnson. For example, see "Semi-Pro Baseball," Buffalo Enquirer, October 6, 1921: 7. It seems probable that this was the "Buffalo" team mentioned in "This Is the Day Set for Start of Harrisburg

Giants' Series – West End Game," *Harrisburg* (Pennsylvania) *Telegraph*, June 6, 1922: 15.

10   James A. Riley, *The Biographical Encyclopedia of the Negro Baseball Leagues* (New York: Carroll & Graf Publishers, Inc., 1994), 156, 158. The Seamheads.com entry for Cliff Carter puts him on the Harrisburg Giants in 1926 and 1927, and that pitcher was called "Nick" at least once each season. See "Hilldale Clubs Three Harrisburg Hurlers for a 12 to 5 Victory," *New York Amsterdam News*, August 4, 1926: 12. See also "Bolden Lifts Suspension on Nip Winters and Washington," *Baltimore Afro-American*, June 18, 1927: 15.

11   Confirmation of the White Paul Carter's nickname is provided at https://www.baseball-reference.com/players/c/cartepa01.shtml. Regarding the fictional character who was created in 1886 and whose 12-year radio drama ended in 1955, see https://www.britannica.com/topic/Nick-Carter.

12   "Harlan Giants Drop Twilight Game to Fast St. Mary Crew," *Wilmington Morning News*, June 15, 1920: 8.

13   In mid-1920, the Harlan Giants had a "J. Johnson" at shortstop and a Carter sometimes pitching in box scores, such as the one that accompanied "Harlan Giants Battle Nine Innings to Tie With K.F.C.," *Wilmington Morning News*, July 20, 1920: 8. The following spring it was specified that their shortstop was *Judy* Johnson, in "Careful Now, 11th Ward," *Wilmington Evening Journal*, May 4, 1921: 11. He grew up in Wilmington, and played his earliest baseball there, according to Thomas Kern, "Judy Johnson," https://sabr.org/bioproj/person/judy-johnson/.

14   See Note 7 for two 1919 box scores in which the Kennett Square All-Stars had a catcher named Faulkner. The Sun Co. team had a battery of Carter and Faulkner in the box score that accompanied "Overlook Keeps One Run Ahead," *Wilmington Evening Journal*, July 17, 1922: 11. This team also had a shortstop named Stokes, who was likely the frequent Harlan Giant by that name. In 1928, Richard "Dick" Faulkner's Biltmore Stars became the Kennett Square Gray Sox, according to "Kennett Gray Sox Seek Ball Games," *Wilmington Evening Journal*, April 19, 1928: 20.

15   "Penna Eagles, 5; Lincoln A. C., 4," *Baltimore Afro-American*, May 12, 1922: 12. "Eagles Divide with Wilkins A. C.," *Baltimore Afro-American*, September 2, 1921: 7. "Eagles To Meet Locust Point Decoration Day," *Baltimore Afro-American*, May 30, 1925: 7.

16   "Careys Beat Keystones," *Pittsburgh Press*, June 11, 1922: 18. For an example of a Carter pitching for the Keystones the following season, see "Garfield Ahead," *Pittsburgh Daily Post*, April 22, 1923: 27.

17   "Logan Opens Season with Big Victory," *Philadelphia Inquirer*, April 29, 1923: 20. The Madison Colored Stars had absorbed the Richmond Giants, according to "Madison Stars at Doherty Oval," *Paterson* (New Jersey) *Morning Call*, May 17, 1923: 16. The Carter on the Baltimore Black Sox, who was Cliff, was a former Richmond Giant, according to "Eastern Colored League Baseball Clubs Staging Pretty Fight for the Pennant," *Richmond* (Virginia) *Planet*, June 30, 1923: 2.

18   "Brooklyn Cuban Giants to Have Fast Club This Season," *Philadelphia Tribune*, March 15, 1924: 11. This article noted that Cliff had pitched for the Richmond Giants and Baltimore Black "Socks." See also "Cuban Giants Invade League to Get Players," *Pittsburgh Courier*, April 19, 1924: 10.

19   W. Rollo Wilson, "Eastern Snapshots," *Pittsburgh Courier*, August 9, 1924: 7; Ben Taylor, "Ben Taylor Calls Oscar Charleston Of Harrisburg World's Greatest Fielder," *Baltimore Afro-American*, February 7, 1925: 6.

20   "To Trounce SPHA's," *Wilmington Evening Journal*, June 2, 1924: 14. "Lit Nine Swamps Newark Black Sox," *Philadelphia Inquirer*, June 15, 1924: 23. "Anchor Giants Blanked," *Philadelphia Inquirer*, August 1, 1924: 20.

21   "Rotating Umpires in Eastern League," *Baltimore Afro-American*, March 28, 1925: 8. "Record Crowd Expected for 'Malin's Night'," *Glens Falls* (New York) *Post-Star*, September 22, 1925: 6.

22   "Moorlyn's 3 Runs at Start Enough," *Philadelphia Inquirer*, June 12, 1925: 22. See also Note 15.

23   "Donora Athletics Drill," *Pittsburgh Post-Gazette*, April 4, 1926: 28. "Donora Will Open Season on Saturday," *Pittsburgh Courier*, April 24, 1926: 14. "Donora Beats Elizabeth, 3-2," *Pittsburgh Courier*, May 29, 1926: 15. The Richmond Colored Giants had a player named Carter later that season, but in a June game he only played left field and in a July box score he started at second base before going in to pitch: "Springfield Senators Drop Close Contest," *Brooklyn Standard-Union*, June 18, 1926: 11. "Jamaica Cardinals Win Tenth Straight," *Brooklyn Standard-Union*, July 7, 1926: 10.

24   "West Chester on Top," *Lancaster* (Pennsylvania) *New Era*, August 18, 1927: 11; "Colored Nines Clash," *Wilmington Evening Journal*, July 28, 1927: 17. For a bit more about Faulkner, see also "Colored Teams Battle on Pennsy Ball Field," *Wilmington Morning News*, June 30, 1927: 21.

25   "Jacobson-Werner Heavy Artillery for Springfield," *Brooklyn Standard-Union*, June 13, 1927: 13. "Montalvo's 2 Homers Give Lincoln Giants Two Victories Sunday," *New York Age*, July 2, 1927: 6.

26   "Santop's Broncos Are to Play Two Games with Bay Parkways," *Brooklyn Citizen*, September 7, 1928: 8.

27   "Kennett Gray Sox Seek Ball Games," *Wilmington Evening Journal*, April 19, 1928: 20. "Seek Ball Games," *Wilmington Evening Journal*, May 7, 1928. The latter article said Faulkner had spent time with "Memphis and Salem teams," and identified the manager as C.J. Miles, 221 South Union Street, Kennett Square.

28   "Brownson Divides; Harrington Loses Two to Laurel," *Wilmington News-Journal*, May 31, 1928: 15; "Holiday Twin Bill for Pennsy Field," *Wilmington Evening Journal*, May 29, 1928: 13.

29   "Monarchs Deliver Lacing to Blue Sox," *Wilmington Evening Journal*, July 8, 1929: 17; "Kennett Square Halted by Gap in Fast Battle," *Lancaster* (Pennsylvania) *Sunday News,* July 21, 1929: 9; "Home Helps Tox Trim Hornets, 4-2," *Wilmington Evening Journal*, August 24, 1929: 15; "Hornets Play Blue Sox," *Wilmington News-Journal*, September 14, 1929: 15.

30   "Clan Returns Home to Trounce Mayfair Team after Upstate Sojourn," *Philadelphia Tribune*, August 14, 1930: 10. For a box score, see "Bunker Hill Bows to Hilldale Club," *Shamokin* (Pennsylvania) *News-Dispatch*, August 7, 1930: 8.

31   "East Rockaway Team Beats Havana Sox," *Brooklyn Times Union,* June 6, 1930: 9; "Red Sox Play in Canada Sunday," *New York Amsterdam News*, July 30, 1930: 13; "Red Sox Score Four Shutouts in 6 Days," *Baltimore Afro-American*, August 9, 1930: A14; "Bill Sisler Turns Down Cuban Red Sox," *Rochester* (New York) *Democrat and Chronicle,* September 15, 1930: 19.

32   "Wilmington Chicks Defeat Lincoln Giants at Pennsy Field, 6 to 3," *Wilmington Morning News*, July 17, 1930: 8. Paul Carter was identified as having "had a successful season" in 1930 with the Lincoln Giants in "Manlove Will Hurl for Pros," *Wilmington Morning News*, May 23, 1931: 10.

33   The pitcher named Carter on the Pittsburgh Monarchs was called "Al" and was from Lawrenceville, according to "Pgh. Monarchs To Be Strong," *Pittsburgh Courier*, April 12, 1930: 2. From 1929 through 1932, at a minimum, the Silver Moons had a pitcher named Carter, but one article called him Lefty. Seamheads.com identifies both Paul and Cliff Carter as righties. See "Silver Moons Take Two from Lockes," *Baltimore Afro-American*, August 31, 1929: 14. Another Baltimore-area team that had a pitcher named Carter was the Oval Blue Monarchs; see "Home Run Wins Game for Oval Blue Monarchs, 4-3," *Baltimore Afro-American*, July 21, 1928: 12.

34   "Wilmington Pros Oppose Hornets," *Wilmington Morning News*, May 22, 1931: 10. This article noted that he hailed from Kennett Square and "played with the Hilldale Daisies two years ago." See also "Pros-Hornets in Second Battle," *Wilmington Morning News*, June 6, 1931: 10. The latter article said Paul Carter "had Eastern Colored League experience," and affirmed that the Lincoln Giants and Hilldale club were previous teams of his.

35 "Bill Robinson's Stars Again Beaten by Hilldale Club," *New York Age*, June 27, 1931: 6; "Black Sox Lose Two Games to Darby Daisies," *Baltimore Afro-American*, September 12, 1931: 3; W. Rollo Wilson, "Sport Shots," *Pittsburgh Courier*, September 19, 1931: 4. Wilson wrote, "In one inning Lundy 'dragged' a ball towards first base. Carter ran over to pick it up but fell, and Lundy was safe and nobody had touched the ball. Then Jackson, following Thomas' infield out, hit through Dallard to right field. Dallard was given an error on a ball which was hit so hard that Dihigo picked it up in deep right and was able to throw Lundy out at the plate!"

36 "Hilldale Defeats Major Stars Twice," *Philadelphia Inquirer*, October 11, 1931: Sports, 2. See also https://www.retrosheet.org/NegroLeagues/ boxesetc/1931/B10101HIL1931.htm.

37 "Kennett Tackles Colored Davids*," Wilmington Evening Journal*, July 20, 1932: 14; "Bacharach Giants Lose to Wilmington Hornets," *Wilmington News-Journal*, August 9, 1932: 24; "Black Sox Win Series from Black Yankees," *Baltimore Afro-American*, September 17, 1932: 22. The latter includes a box score of a game in which Carter was the losing pitcher.

38 "Wings Set to Resume Hit Spree Against Royals Tomorrow," *Bergen Evening Record* (Hackensack, New Jersey), August 31, 1932: 16.

39 "Kennett Square," *Philadelphia Tribune*, September 7, 1933: 13; "Bolden Stars Top Loop Picked Squad," *Philadelphia Inquirer*, September 13, 1933; "Legion Favors Sewer Project," *Wilmington News-Journal*, October 14, 1933: 20.

40 "W. Harry Le Fevre Dies; 74 Years Old," *Wilmington News-Journal*, March 7, 1934: 12.

41 "Bacharach Giants Under the Lights at Metuchen," *Daily Home News* (New Brunswick, New Jersey), June 28, 1934: 20; "Bolden Stars Win," *Philadelphia Inquirer*, June 27, 1934: 19.

42 "Kennett Square," *Philadelphia Tribune*, July 12, 1934: 15. The two ballplayers were guests at the residence of a Mr. Everett Glasco. Carter had also spent "several days" back home during the second half of June, according to "Kennett Square," *Philadelphia Tribune*, June 28, 1934: 8.

43 "Stars Jolt Giants and Tie Up Series," *Philadelphia Inquirer*, September 30, 1934: 51; "Stars Tie Series in Stiff Tiff," *Philadelphia Tribune*, October 4, 1934: 14. The *Inquirer* said the Stars scored "in the fifth and sixth frames," and the *Tribune* concurred, but both papers' line scores showed those pairs in the fourth and fifth innings.

44 "Stars Upset Giants[,] Win National Title," *Philadelphia Inquirer*, October 3, 1934: 22. For insights into the controversy toward the end of the series, see David M. Jordan, "Another Quaker City Champion: The 1934 Philadelphia Stars," *Black Ball*, Spring 2012: 30-31.

45 "Bolden's Stars Won't Go South; Prep in Philly," *Baltimore Afro-American*, April 13, 1935: 17; "No-hit Tilt as Stars Win Two," *Philadelphia Inquirer*, August 18, 1935: 35; "Stars Lose 1, Win 3 From Brooklyn 9," *Philadelphia Tribune*, August 22, 1935: 9. The latter article, which was accompanied by box scores for all four games, noted that Carter was right-handed.

46 "Yeadon Yuccas Open," *Chester* (Pennsylvania) *Times*, April 10, 1936: 16; Irwin N. Rosee, "Bushwicks, Farmers Win Two – Bay Ridge and Parkways Split Twin Bills," *Brooklyn Times Union*, May 18, 1936: 3A; "Giants Not in Association," *Kansas American* (Topeka), May 22, 1936: 7.

47 For example, see "Bearded Tossers Lose Two Games," *Brooklyn Times Union*, July 5, 1936: 14.

48 "Black Yanks Defeat Crawfords with Eighth Inning Rally, 9-6," *Akron Beacon Journal*, August 5, 1936: 15. Carter's seamheads.com entry shows him with no decision and having retired one batter in the seventh inning.

49 "Three in One Day for Black Yanks," *Brooklyn Times Union*, August 10, 1936: 11.

50 Ernest "Spoon" Carter was presumably the pitcher Carter traded from the Crawfords to the Stars before the 1938 season, giving the latter team its third hurler with that surname in less than a decade. See "NNL Reinstates 'Jumpers'; New D.C. Club Is Admitted," *Baltimore Afro-American*, March 12, 1938: 18.

51 "Bay Parkways Play Royal Giants Twice for Regular Opening," *Brooklyn Citizen*, April 24, 1937: 6; "Royal Gts. Vs Carltons," *New York Age*, May 1, 1937: 8.

52 "Red Caps Start with Nicetown Giants," *Philadelphia Tribune*, April 29, 1937: 12; "Red Caps Open Baseball Season With Nicetown," *Wilmington Morning News*, May 13, 1937: 13; "Wilmington Red Caps Beat Coatesville Tossers, 6-3," *Wilmington Morning News*, May 17, 1937: 12; "Washington Nine Ekes Out Win Over Red Caps," *Wilmington News-Journal*, May 24, 1937: 18. The latter two games were played in Kennett Square.

53 "Pennsy Tossers Score 4-0 Win Over Red Caps Team," *Wilmington Morning News*, June 9, 1937: 17; "Red Caps to Play Zulus," *Wilmington News-Journal*, June 12, 1937: 17; "Red Caps vs. Elkton Stars," *Wilmington News-Journal*, June 19, 1937: 17.

54 Casting just a little doubt on whether Paul Carter's career ended very close to home is the fact that in the following offseason, a Cannonball Carter was reportedly pitching for the Detroit Colored Giants in the vicinity of Los Angeles. For example, see "Darkness Ends Baseball Clash," *Bakersfield Californian*, November 8, 1937: 13.

55 "Mrs. Sallie Brown Dies," *Wilmington News-Journal*, September 14, 1943: 19. His wife's Certificate of Death is accessible online via genealogical websites. In between, those, the death of his brother Joseph, a roofing contractor, received some media attention due to the uncommon cause: "Stung by Hornet, Man Dies on Roof," *Philadelphia Inquirer*, July 22, 1945: 13.

56 "2 Old-Timers Baseball Games on Kennett Centennial Card," *Wilmington News-Journal*, September 3, 1955: 15.

57 "Paul Carter," *Kennett News & Advertiser*, May 15, 1975: 3.

58 Gene Seymour, "In a League by Himself," *Philadelphia Daily News*, August 23, 1982: 8, 16, 17; Don Beideman, "Teammates Recall Pride and Success of Kennett Gray Sox," *Philadelphia Inquirer*, November 1, 1992: CC-3, CC-32; "Old-timer's Statue Sparks New Debate on Race," *Bedford* (Pennsylvania) *Gazette*, July 12, 1998: 4. The latter was about an unsuccessful proposal to erect a statue of Herb Pennock in Kennett Square. Opponents pointed to the hostility to Jackie Robinson in 1947 by the Phillies, for whom Pennock was GM. Pennock biographer Keith Craig has taken issue with such accusations. For example, see Chris Barber, "New Book Asserts Pennock Was No Racist," *West Chester* (Pennsylvania) *Daily Local News*, July 11, 2016, accessible at https://www.dailylocal. com/2016/07/11/new-book-asserts-pennock-was-no-racist-2/.

MICKEY CASEY

By Paul Hofmann

Mickey Casey was a stout, 5-foot-7½-inch, 200-pound journeyman catcher who had a 12-year professional career in the Negro Leagues. Known for his strong work ethic, the well-traveled backstop was characterized as "a mediocre hitter, not noted for either consistency, contact ability, or power."[1] Though accurate from an offensive perspective, it understates Casey's value to the teams he played for. He was a serviceable catcher and versatile enough to play other positions, particularly third base and the outfield.[2]

Casey played for the Brooklyn Royal Giants, Baltimore Black Sox, Philadelphia Stars, Washington Black Senators, Newark Eagles, Pittsburgh Crawfords, New York Cuban Giants, and Baltimore Elite Giants. Along the way his career intersected with greatness. He was an integral member of the 1934 Negro National League II (NNL2) champion Philadelphia Stars, driving in the series-clinching run, and was teammates with 10 future Hall of Famers: Turkey Stearnes, Monte Irvin, Willie Wells, Roy Campanella, Leon Day, Biz Mackey, Ray Dandridge, Oscar Charleston, Mule Suttles, and Jud Wilson.

William Cofer Casey was born on May 5, 1905, in Newport News, Virginia.[3] He was the youngest child and only son of the four known children of William and Eleanor (Roberts) Casey. William had three older sisters: Lattie, Ruth, and Peachy. His father was a laborer in the shipyards of Newport News. His mother, Eleanor, died when William was young.[4]

Little is known about Mickey Casey's childhood. He went by his middle name as a child and is listed as "Coffer" [sic] in both the 1910 and 1920 censuses, perhaps to distinguish him from his father. While most sources identify Casey as Black, the 1920 census identified him as a 15-year-old mulatto. His light complexion and a noticeable scar above his left eyebrow later were noted on his World War II draft card. By 1920, he was already working as a laborer and presumably starring on the local sandlots of Newport News.

Casey played baseball at Johnson C. Smith University (JCSU) in Charlotte, North Carolina.[5] His path to JCSU is unclear and like many university athletes at that time, there is no record of Casey having attended classes at JCSU. In addition to Casey, JCSU produced three other Negro League players: "Steel Arm" Johnny Taylor, Burnalle "Bun" Hayes, and William "Red" Lindsay.[6] One source indicates Casey finished three years of high school.[7]

By the age of 21, Casey had two sons, William (b. 1924) and Cofer (b. 1926). While there is no record of Casey being married at this time, the two boys were consistently identified as his children in public records.

Gary Ashwill

Catcher Mickey Casey

Cofer, the younger of the two, died of tuberculosis just before his 19th birthday in 1945.

Casey began his professional career in 1930, a season in which he played first for the Brooklyn Royal Giants and later for the Baltimore Black Sox.[8] Currently available statistics suggest Casey had a feast-or-famine type of rookie season at the plate in games against other major Eastern Independent clubs. He played in eight games for the Royal Giants, sharing catching duties with Willie Creek, and hit only .037 (1-for-27) with one RBI. By July, Casey had moved to Baltimore and in 12 games with the Black Sox he hit .370 (10-for-27), with 4 RBIs and an .859 OPS. For the year, he batted a cumulative .204 and drove in five runs. He also made his only professional pitching appearance with the Black Sox, throwing one inning and giving up four runs (three earned) on two hits and two walks.

In 1931 Casey returned to the Black Sox, who were still playing as one of the major independent clubs along the Eastern Seaboard. He was primarily used behind the plate, sharing the catching duties with Bob Clarke, but also saw some action in the outfield, and he hit .306 and drove in 15 runs in 36 games against other top Black teams. That year the *Pittsburgh Courier* identified the chunky catcher and first baseman Dave Thomas as "two of the best youngsters who have broke in around here in many moons."[9]

There is some evidence that Casey may have toyed with the idea of playing for the Detroit Wolves in 1932. After Detroit signed Cool Papa Bell and Tom Young, the *Pittsburgh Courier* assessed the Wolves' potential catching duo as formidable. Said an article in the *Courier:* "Young is a great receiver and dependable hitter and teaming with Casey in back of the plate will give the Motor City Club just about the greatest catching staff in the league."[10]

Ultimately, Casey continued to play for the Black Sox, now managed by Dick Lundy, after the franchise joined the East-West League (EWL) in 1932. He played a utility role for Baltimore as he appeared in 31 games as a catcher, 17 at third base, 9 at second base, and 4 in the outfield. He batted .258 with one home run, the only known major-league home run he hit, and 16 RBIs. The Black Sox finished in third place behind the runaway champion Detroit Wolves, the team Casey was linked to during the offseason. The East-West League folded in June, but there is no evidence that Casey played elsewhere for the remainder of the season.

Casey moved to Philadelphia in 1933 when he was signed by the independent Philadelphia Stars as a reserve catcher to back up veteran receiver Biz Mackey. W. Rollo Wilson wrote in his season preview of the Stars that "Mackey and Casey left nothing to be desired in the way of catchers," emphasizing their strong arms and ability to manage the pitching staff.[11]

Mackey undoubtedly played an integral part in development of Casey and other young catchers. The consensus among Negro Leagues scholars is that Josh Gibson was the better hitter, but that Mackey was by far his defensive superior.[12] Negro League historian James A. Riley may have stated it best when he wrote, "Considered the master of defense, (Mackey) possessed all the tools necessary behind the plate. ... An expert handler of pitchers, he studied people. ... [H]e was a master at ... framing and funneling pitches. Pitchers recognized his generalship and liked to pitch" to Mackey.[13] His defensive prowess, understanding of people, and level-headedness made him an ideal tutor for Casey.

A personal highlight of Casey's 1933 season came toward the end of the season. On September 28 the Stars beat the Pittsburgh Crawfords 4-3 in a five-inning rain-shortened affair. Pinch-hitting for pitcher Cliff Carter, Casey drove in the tying and winning runs off Satchel Paige with a single to right-center in the bottom of the fifth.[14] For the year, Casey played in 21 games including 11 at catcher, in which he did not commit an error behind the plate, while hitting .222 with 10 RBIs. The Stars finished with a record of 22-13 and had the most victories of all the independent clubs in the East.

The Philadelphia Stars joined the NNL2 in 1934, and Casey became the team's starting catcher when the aging Mackey went down with an injury. In addition to handling the bulk of the catching duties (52 games), he played third base twice, two games in the outfield, and one game at second base. He batted .250 with 24 RBIs, helping the Stars capture the league's second-half title, which secured a spot in the NNL2 Championship Series against the first-half-champion Chicago American Giants.

W. Rollo Wilson, commissioner of the Negro National League, named Gibson and Larry "Iron Man" Brown as the best catchers, but singled out Casey of the Stars as the "hardest-working mask man in the league and deserving honorable mention."[15] The recognition was earned in large part because Mackey had not been able to perform and Casey had been forced to take on extra work without a reliable backup. Casey finished sixth among catchers in fan voting for the East-West All-Star Game, receiving just under 4,000 votes.[16]

Casey played in six games in the 1934 Negro League Championship series, two behind the plate and three games in left field. Although he hit only a meager 1-for-15 with two walks in 18 plate appearances, his fourth-inning RBI single that plated Mackey in Game Eight proved to be the series-winning RBI as the Stars won the series over the American Giants, 4-3-1.[17]

Casey returned to a backup role with the Stars in 1935. He played in 31 games, which included 25 appearances behind the plate and two games in left field. He enjoyed his best season offensively, hitting .383 with 23 RBIs and a .932 OPS. The increased offensive production was in part due to a decreased workload behind the plate. Fans continued to take notice of Casey; he finished fourth in the East in fan voting (Mackey was second) with 5,940 votes.[18] The Stars finished in fourth place, behind the first-half and eventual league champion Pittsburgh Crawfords, the New York Cubans, and the Columbus Elite Giants. Casey filled a similar role with the Stars in 1936, this time backing up starting catcher Larry Brown. In 30 games he hit .278 with 11 RBIs as the Stars fell to last place in the NNL.

In 1937, his last full season with the Stars, Casey married Ophelia Mack. She was the youngest of the three children of Thomas and Gertrude (Gatling) Mack of Philadelphia. He was 32 years old at the time and Ophelia was 23. The couple eventually had nine children together, five boys (William, Johnny, Michael, Thomas Richard, and James) and four girls (Bonnie, Geneva, Eleanor, and Maureen). Ophelia, commonly known as Mother Casey,[19] worked at St. Vincent DePaul Hospital as a nurse.[20] At the time of her death in 2005, the family included "27 grandchildren and a host of great-grand and great-great-grandchildren."[21]

Casey was steady behind the plate in 1937, but his offensive production dropped off to a .206 batting average, 8 RBIs and a .471 OPS. The Stars did better that year but still finished in third place, behind the league champion Homestead Grays and second-place Newark Eagles.

Casey traveled throughout the Northeast in 1938, playing for four teams, the Philadelphia Stars, Pittsburgh Crawfords, Newark Eagles, and Washington Black Senators. As he probably had trouble remembering his address from one day to the next, he hit a combined .225 (16-for-82 with 9 walks) with only 6 RBIs.

After the collapse of the Black Senators, Casey signed with the New York Cubans for 1939. He appeared in 14 NNL2 games at catcher and enjoyed one of his better seasons at the plate. In 14 games he hit .320. The Cubans finished in last place.

Casey played a second season with the Cubans in 1940, and the now 35-year-old backstop shared the team's catching duties with his 44-year-old player-manager José María Fernández. Casey slumped to a .192 batting average in 19 league games as the Cubans finished tied for last with the New York Black Yankees. On his World War II draft registration card, dated October 16, 1940, Casey indicated that he had no employer. Wherever he may have found employment in 1941, it was not with a team in professional Black baseball.

In 1942 Casey played one final game in the NNL2 with the Baltimore Elite Giants, which featured a 20-year-old catcher named Roy Campanella. Whether Casey was a player-coach is unclear, but he made just one appearance, as a pinch-hitter, and was hitless.

According to Riley's *The Biographical Encyclopedia of the Negro Baseball Leagues*, Casey's playing career extended into the 1950s. Casey's entry in the encyclopedia states:

> In 1950, twenty years after he started his professional career, he finally played in organized ball, playing at Eau Claire in the Northern League, where he registered a .282 average. In 1953 the veteran receiver was with Jacksonville in the Sally League, where he hit .253. the next season he split time between Jacksonville and Dallas in the Texas League, hitting an aggregate .184. His last season was split between Charlotte in the South Atlantic League (.214) and Atlanta in the Southern Association (.250), where he was used sparingly.[22]

However, this is not the same William Casey. Baseball-reference.com identifies the William Casey who played in Eau Claire, Jacksonville, Dallas, Charlotte, and Atlanta as William Carl Casey, born on July 14, 1930, in Parkin, Arkansas, not Mickey Casey. In 1950 Mickey was residing on Saybrook Avenue in an African American community in Philadelphia with Ophelia, six of their children, two nephews, and a niece.

The additional account that Casey took "a turn in the latter stages of his career as a manager"[23] is unsubstantiated. While he had a baseball pedigree that suggests he would have had the opportunity to manage, there is no evidence that he managed in the Negro Leagues or any other league in Organized Baseball. Any managerial position he had would have been at the amateur or semipro level.

Casey finished his 12-year Negro League career with a .259 batting average, 1 home run, and 128 RBIs. While his offensive numbers, albeit incomplete, may seem relatively modest, he obviously brought value to the teams he played for, or he would not have had a career of such length.

Little is known about Casey's post-baseball life. He and Mother Casey were active in the church and helped others in the local community. Casey died of stomach cancer on January 23, 1968, in Philadelphia. He and Ophelia are buried in Rolling Green Memorial Park in West Goshen, Pennsylvania, just outside of Philadelphia.

Sources

In addition to the sources cited in the Notes, the author also consulted Baseball-reference.com.

Negro League player statistics, team records, and league standings were taken from Seamheads.com.

The author would like to acknowledge the contributions of Frederick C. Bush and Bill Nowlin, whose research contributed to this piece.

Notes

1   James A. Riley, *The Biographical Encyclopedia of the Negro Baseball Leagues* (New York: Carroll & Graf Publishers, Inc., 1994), 159.

2   Riley, 159.

3   While there are conflicting dates of his birth, ranging anywhere from 1905-1906, May 5, 1905, is the most commonly cited date and the only date cited more than once.

4   The 1910 US Census lists the 5-year-old boy's father (William Casey) as a widower.

5   Johnson C. Smith University is a private liberal arts university with proud Historically Black College and University (HBCU) traditions.

6   JCSU was founded as Biddle Memorial Institute in 1867. In 1876 it became Biddle University. Biddle University changed its name to JCSU in 1923. Taylor played there prior to 1923 when it was still Biddle University.

7   Casey's World War II draft registration card dated October 16, 1940.

8   James Riley's work states that Casey played for famed Hilldale Daisies of Philadelphia in 1930. However, there are no sources to support that.

9   "Baltimore-Daisy Tilt Saturday Interests," *Pittsburgh Courier*, May 2, 1931: 15.

10   Dizzy Dizmukes, "Dizzy's Dope on Baseball," *Pittsburgh Courier*, March 19. 1932: 14.

11   W. Rollo Wilson, "Sports Shots: Bolden's Philly Stars Have That Thing Called Class," *Pittsburgh Courier*, May 13, 1933: 14.

12   Chris Rainey, "Biz Mackey," SABR BioProject. Retrieved on February 13, 2023 from sabr.org/bioproj/person/biz-mackey/.

13   Riley, 502-03.

14   "Phillies Rally Tops Crawfords," *Pittsburgh Courier*, September 30, 1933: 14.

15   W. Rollo Wilson, "Baseball's Curtain Falling on Season," *Pittsburgh Courier*, September 15, 1934: A4.

16   "Voting for East-West Stars," *Pittsburgh Courier*, August 25, 1934: 15. Josh Gibson won the fan voting for catcher with 5,496 votes.

17   The two half-season champions of the 1934 NNL were the Philadelphia Stars and the Chicago American Giants, who met in a best-of-seven series, which went eight games because of a Game Seven tie.

18   "The East," *Pittsburgh Courier*, August 10, 1935: 15.

19   Perhaps in recognition of how she was commonly referred to, Mickey Casey listed Ophelia as his mother on his 1940 World War II draft registration card.

20   Ophelia M. Casey obituary. Retrieved from www.terryfuneralhome.com/obituaries/Ophelia-M-Casey?obid+2056973#/celebrationWall.

21   Ophelia M. Casey obituary.

22   Riley, 159.

23   Riley, 159.

PORTER CHARLESTON

By Jay Hurd

Porter Riley Charleston was born in Mexia, Limestone County, Texas, on January 8, 1904. Charleston's life story is filled with gaps. His parentage remains obscure; whether or not he played in one of the Negro/Colored Leagues in Texas is not known.[1] When Charleston first traveled to Pennsylvania, where his Negro League career began with the Hilldale Daisies in 1927, is uncertain. However, it appears that he called Chester, Pennsylvania, in Delaware County, his home during his Negro League career and until his death on June 11, 1986.

Porter began his professional Negro League career with the Daisies in 1927. At 23 years of age, he provided a bright spot in Hilldale's pitching rotation. The 1927 Hilldale Daisies – also known as Clan Darby (or Darbie) – were managed by Frank Warfield for the first 17 games, and later by Otto Briggs for the final 70 games. The team, owned by Ed Bolden, featured greats Biz Mackey and Judy Johnson. That first season, Charleston, who stood 6-feet-1 and weighed 181 pounds, appeared in four games, completed three, and owned a 1-2 record. His performance earned praise from the press; and he was dubbed the "Swarthmore Rookie,"[2] perhaps due to Chester's proximity to Swarthmore College. From the outset of his playing days, the gaps in Charleston's life story were acknowledged. One reporter wrote, "The Rookie Twirler of the Clan Darbie, Porter Charleston, seems to know what it is all about. He has pitched several splendid games for Ed Bolden and he looks like a real find. How they caught him, found him, came by him, I know not. And it matters not, if he continues to deliver the goods."[3] The 1927 Daisies finished the Eastern Colored League (ECL) season with a 38-48 record.

The 1928 Daisies fared much better under manager Otto Briggs, and with the addition of 31-year-old center fielder and future Hall of Famer Oscar Charleston. Porter Charleston played in 15 games,

pitching to a 4-6 record, with five complete games. The right-handed hurler also hit .222 that year.[4]

In 1929 Charleston pitched a career-high 120⅓ innings, with 12 games started, and produced a 9-5 record. Managers for the Daisies were Oscar Charleston (0-4) and Phil Cockrell (44-32-4); the team's overall record was 44-36-4, and in the American Negro League, 43-35-3. The *Pittsburgh Courier* wrote that Charleston "has been touted as one of the [Daisies'] newest stars."[5] He also was identified that year as a utility player.[6] He showed great promise, and it was noted that "Charleston has developed into one of the best hurlers on the strong staff of Clan Darbie and is most effective against tough competition."[7]

The 1930 season was unusual in that Charleston received little attention, except for a note by W. Rollo Wilson that identified strengths and weaknesses in his game: "I consider Charleston was [one] of the best pitching prospects in the country, and only his own conduct off the field can keep him from stardom."[8] The "conduct off the field" statement is notable and indicates that Charleston may have run afoul of Bolden, the Hilldale owner, or worse. Charleston does not appear to have pitched for Hilldale that season; if he did, he was not involved in games against any of the other major Black clubs in the East. Hilldale finished with only the fifth-best record among the Eastern Independent clubs under manager Phil Cockrell and had a miserable 8-30-1 record.

In 1931 the 27-year-old Charleston was back with Hilldale and appeared in 11 games, finishing with an 8-2 record and nine complete games. Managed by Judy Johnson, the Hilldale Club – the team's name that year –finished as the top squad among the East's Independent Clubs with a 38-14-1 record. Of note is an article that addressed Charleston's

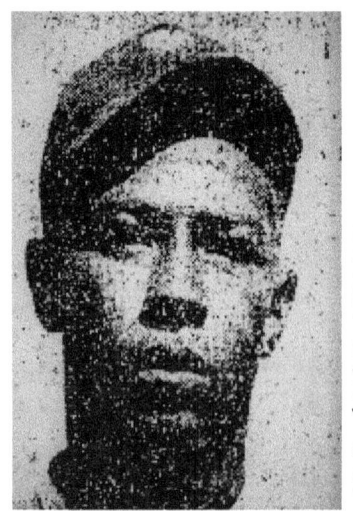

Pitcher Porter Charleston

Afro-American, *July 25, 1931*

off-the-field reputation: "Porter Charleston is home again. The bad boy of the suburbs is back from the Pacific slope."[9]

In 1932, his final year with the Hilldale Club, Charleston delivered a 5-3 record, completing each of the eight games he started. That same year, the Baltimore Black Sox acquired Charleston, who appeared in one game as a relief pitcher. The Baltimore club, managed by Dick Lundy, had a record of 33-33 in the East-West League that year.

Charleston became a Philadelphia Star in 1933. He started four games and compiled a 3-0 record, completing three of the four games. He married Cora Robinson on July 20, 1933.[10] They had at least one child, a son named Porter Charleston Jr., who achieved some repute as a boxer.[11]

The Philadelphia Stars of 1934, managed by Webster McDonald, accumulated an overall record of 49-24-3 and a Negro National League II (NNL2) record of 39-18-2. After winning the NNL2's second-half title, the Stars captured the league championship by defeating the Chicago American Giants, winners of the first-half title. Charleston's role on the team is not clear, but his name does appear in some press clippings. In June a columnist reported, "The Boldeners have had a run of hard luck. ... Porter Charleston reported with a sore arm and it gets no better right along."[12] Apparently Charleston sat out the year with an injury, but it is possible that he played in exhibition games later in the season.[13]

Charleston was 31 in 1935, which was his last in the Negro Leagues. But it certainly was not his final year in baseball. Playing for the Philadelphia Stars, he had a record of 2-1 in five league games. The press still praised Charleston as "a great natural pitcher, who may start the [season] opener against the Grays."[14] Indeed, the 1935 season looked bright for him; a newspaper commented, "Local sports fans who looked askance at the weak performance of Porter Charleston during the '34 season are in for a surprise. Exhibiting a contract from Ed Bolden's Philadelphia Stars, Charleston, for several years, the ace of the Negro pitchers, is signed for comeback."[15]

After his final season with the Stars, Charleston continued to play with semipro teams, including Ed Billstein's Congoleum Crescents. (Billstein was "one of the prominent members of the Congoleum-Nairn office."[16]) Other teams for whom he played were the Chester Elks, the Swarthmore Giants, the Lincoln Giants, and Stan Jackson's Chester Clippers. (Stan Jackson was a Chester High School baseball and football player.[17])

Charleston's appearance with the Baltimore Black Sox in 1939 was noteworthy. The *Delaware County Daily Times* reported, "Porter Charleston, famous Negro League pitcher, leads the Baltimore Black Sox into town tonight to battle the Lloyd A.C. Tossers. ... Charleston is one of the most popular pitchers ever to appear in Chester and is quite well known around the local diamonds."[18]

With World War II raging, Charleston registered for the military draft. His draft card notes his age as 35, but as most records indicate he was born in 1904, he was more likely 36. He listed his wife, Cora Robinson, as his contact person and gave his employer as L.M. Supplee, possibly a hardware supplier. Charleston was not called to service, so he was able to continue to play baseball, and he garnered positive press coverage. In 1941 his name headlined a story: "Charleston Stars as Clippers Win." In this game, pitching for Stan Jackson's Chester Clippers, Charleston allowed the Eveready A.C. team, of Leesburg, Virginia, "2 hits in the first inning," then "faced only 25 men in the last eight frames. He had four hits in four times and batted in the only two runs of the game."[19]

In a 1942 reflection on decades of Negro League baseball, sportswriter Randy Dixon included Charleston as one of many Negro Leaguers who had the talent to play in what were then termed the (White) major leagues.[20]

As the years passed, Charleston received attention for his baseball play and for non-baseball-related events. In 1948 a newspaper reported that "police are investigating the shooting of Porter Charleston,"[21] adding, "... According to the story he told police, the shot was fired by William Johnson, his next door neighbor." Charleston said the Johnsons were in his home that evening, and that Johnson aimed his pistol at Mrs. Johnson. After the gun failed to fire, Johnson fired again and "Mrs. Johnson is said to have ducked. Charleston who was in the line of fire received the bullet."[22]

More details came out in December 1948: William Johnson was sent to the county jail for three to 23 months. Porter Charleston testified that "Mrs. Johnson ducked into my room" when she saw her husband coming up the stairs. Johnson fired one shot, the bullet going through Charleston's right side without damaging any vital organs. ..."[23] As troubling as this story was, Charleston still garnered attention for his baseball prowess as well. The article stated that "At one time

[Charleston] was rated the equal of the famed 'Satchel' Paige, according to Arnold (Lefty) Vann, manager of the Lloyd A.C. who has played against both men."[24]

Ten years later, Charleston was seriously injured in an automobile accident. According to a newspaper report, "Charleston, 54, of 114 Flower St., considered one of the [greatest] Negro baseball stars of all time, was injured when the car he was driving collided with one operated by Dolores J. Chandler. … He was treated at Chester Hospital for cuts of the arm, face, leg and back. …"[25]

In another reflective piece that considered Negro League players who could have played major-league baseball, the *Delaware County Daily Times* asserted, "Porter Charleston, as a pitcher of note, who appeared at Smedley Field to play ball against Chester usually belted the ball out of the park over the centerfield flag pole with plenty to spare."[26]

A 1968 article in the *Daily Times* noted that Charleston was to be included, for the first time, on the Delaware County Hall of Fame ballot and mentioned that he had played winter ball in Arizona and California. The article said, "Porter called himself primarily a fast ball pitcher – but I had a little bit of everything, he adds with a grin."[27] The writer quoted former Pittsburgh Pirates manager Danny Murtaugh, who said that Charleston "had everything necessary to make it to the big leagues. He just came along a little too soon."[28] Charleston was finally inducted into the Delaware County Hall of Fame in 1970, at which time he was described as "the man called a fit rival for the legendary Satchel Paige."[29]

Porter Charleston died at the age of 82 on June 11, 1986, and reportedly was buried at the Haven Memorial Cemetery in Chester, Pennsylvania. The uncertainties of his life remain. He was indeed a very good baseball player – he played in the Negro Leagues from 1927 to 1935, and his baseball talent brought him numerous appearances on semipro teams. In newspaper articles, he was described as a quiet man who worked for the city of Chester. While these reports are incomplete, he is remembered for his baseball play and for the reality that he, among others, did not play in the National or American Leagues simply because he was a Black man.

SOURCE

Unless otherwise noted, all Negro League statistics and records were taken from Seamheads.com's Negro League Database.

NOTES

1   Mexia, Texas, near the Fort Worth area, featured the Texas Negro League, the Colored Texas League, the South Texas Negro League, and the West Texas Colored League.

2   "Cubans Are Beaten in 2 Contests," *Pittsburgh Courier*, September 10, 1927: 18.

3   W. Rollo Wilson, "Sports Shots," *Pittsburgh Courier*, September 3, 1927: 18.

4   It is not clear whether Porter Charleston batted right or left.

5   "Baltimore Bows Before Grays in 4 Close Tilts; Hilldale Here Friday," *Pittsburgh Courier*, June 22, 1929: 16.

6   "Daisies to Show on Forbes Field," *Pittsburgh Courier*, June 22, 1929: 16.

7   W. Rollo Wilson, "Sports Shots," *Pittsburgh Courier*, August 31, 1929: 5.

8   W. Rollo Wilson, "Sports Shots," *Pittsburgh Courier*, April 19, 1930: 16.

9   "Charl'ton Holds Sox to 3 Hits in Classic," *Pittsburgh Courier*, May 9, 1931: 5.

10 Delaware County Records Center, Marriage Records 1885-1950, http://archives.co.delaware.pa.us/Archives/Marriage1885.aspx.

11 Frank Johnson, "Local Boxers Win All Lloyd AC Contests," *Delaware County Daily Times* (Chester, Pennsylvania), August 3, 1949: 14.

12 W. Rollo Wilson, "Sports Shots," *Pittsburgh Courier*, June 9, 1934: 14.

13 "Among Our Colored Citizens," *Delaware County Daily Times*, August 9, 1934: 18.

14 "Local Sports," *Pittsburgh Courier*, April 27, 1935: 16.

15 "Among Our Colored Citizens," *Delaware County Daily Times*, February 13, 1935: 7.

16 "Crescents to Meet Boldens," *Delaware County Daily Times*, August 4, 1936: 10.

17 *Delaware County Daily Times*, September 20, 1937: 30.

18 "Charleston to Pitch in Clash at Lloyd Field," *Delaware County Daily Times*, August 11, 1939: 12.

19 "Charleston Stars as Clippers Win," *Delaware County Daily Times*, July 2, 1941: 20.

20 Randy Dixon, "The Sports Bugle," *Pittsburgh Courier*, August 15, 1942: 16.

21 The Editors, "How It Looks to Us," *Delaware County Daily Times*, October 23, 1948. 1

22 "Former Negro Baseball Star Shot in Side," *Delaware County Daily Times*, October 23, 1948: 1.

23 Chester Youth Pleads Guilty in Assault Case," *Delaware County Daily Times*, December 31, 1948. 2.

24 "Former Negro Baseball Star Shot in Side."

25 "7 Injured in County Accidents," *Delaware County Daily Times*, June 16, 1958: 46.

26 "Old Timers Hall of Fame Rapped for Omitting Greats," *Delaware County Daily Times*, January 12, 1967: 23.

27 John Plaisant, "Porter Charleston Fired Fast Ball 25 Years Too Soon," *Delaware County Daily Times*, January 16, 1968: 32.

28 Plaisant.

29 "Tunnell, Walker Lead Greats into Hall of Fame," *Delaware County Daily Times*, January 6, 1970: 15.

PHIL COCKRELL

By Thomas Kern

*"If you were to ask me who is the
smartest hurler in our league, there could be
but one answer, and that is 'Cockrell.'"*
– W. Rollo Wilson[1]

Phil Cockrell's arrival in the North is one person's story of the Great Migration, the movement of millions of African Americans from the South as they sought jobs and hoped to avoid inequality in the early 1900s. According to the US National Archives:

> The Great Migration was one of the largest movements of people in United States history. Approximately six million Black people moved from the American South to Northern, Midwestern, and Western states roughly from the 1910s until the 1970s. The driving force behind the mass movement was to escape racial violence, pursue economic and educational opportunities, and obtain freedom from the oppression of Jim Crow.[2]

For Cockrell, it was baseball that drew him to upstate New York and then Pennsylvania. And, in so doing, he made a name for himself in the annals of the Negro League game.

Phillip Cockrell Williams was reputedly born in Augusta, Georgia, on June 29, 1895. However, as is the case with many Black ballplayers born before the turn of the twentieth century, records are spotty and not much is known about his origins. A 1900 Census record might be of his family and him as a 5-year-old, residing in the Burke Militia District (30 miles from Augusta) with father Phillips, mother Francis, and three siblings. The 1910 Census records potentially tie then 15-year-old Philip to a Williams family that included 55-year-old father William and three siblings residing in Augusta. His grave records indicate a July 9, 1895, birthdate. Yet Cockrell's own draft registration card from the early 1940s identifies Philip Cockrew (so spelled even though his own scrawling signature shows Cockrell ending in two l's, not a w) Williams born in Augusta, Georgia, on June 29, 1898. It must

suffice to say that Cockrell was born in the latter half of the final decade of the nineteenth century.

Little is known of Cockrell's youth except for his Augusta roots, which is where, in his teens, Pop Watkins discovered him. Baseball lifer Watkins occasionally coached Paine College's baseball team and likely recruited Cockrell or spotted him on the team. In the mid-1920s, once Cockrell reached stardom, the *Augusta Chronicle* happily laid claim to him, writing "Have you ever heard of Phil Cockrell? Well, he is an Augusta colored professional baseball player who hurls at will a no-hit, no-run game. … Out in the East, Cockrell is good advertising for Augusta."[3] A year later, the *Chronicle* announced Cockrell's March appearance in Augusta: "Phil Cockrell is a product of

Pitcher Phil Cockrell

Gary Ashwill

61

Paine College and will help to work out the team while he is in the city."[4]

The man who discovered him, John McCreary "Pop" Watkins, was a Black baseball icon who played most of career with the Cuban Giants. In 1907 Watkins broke his leg in a game, and although he recovered enough to play in the field again, his career took a turn.[5] By then in his 40s, Pop shifted his baseball talents toward assembling Black teams in the South that he then took North to compete against amateur, semipro, and other Black and White squads. Born in the South (some records show North Carolina, others Georgia), he gravitated toward Augusta where, according to newspaper accounts of the day, he recruited young ballplayers, aided by his coaching the local Black school team at Paine College, a Historically Black College. Watkins' business acumen and his skill in finding talented ballplayers came to define his career and offered a proving ground for players like Cockrell to find a place in Black baseball.

Watkins most famously organized and managed the Havana Red Sox, an itinerant team based in Norfolk, Virginia, and Buffalo, New York, prior to its relocation to Watertown, New York. In 1913 the *Buffalo Evening News* provided one of the first sightings of Watkins' team noting that "the Havana Red Sox, known the country over as one of the greatest colored baseball teams ever organized, will be seen in Buffalo for the first time next Sunday. ... [T]his famous club is under the management of Pop Watkins, who is the oldest player manager today in baseball."[6] No mention was made of Cockrell being in the lineup, and other 1913 articles offer no indication of whether an 18-year-old Cockrell was yet on the team.

However, over the next four seasons, 1914 to 1917, Cockrell featured prominently for the Havana Red Sox in its Watertown home. One of the first references to Cockrell on the Red Sox appeared when the team played in Kingston, Ontario, in July 1914. "On Monday, at Lake Ontario Park, the fastest ball players that have been in Kingston in a long while will play the winners of the Ponies-Victoria game. These fellows are all students in negro colleges and call themselves the Havana Red Sox. The lineup [includes] Cockrell, from Paine College, Augusta, Ga."[7] An article in the *New York Age, an* African American newspaper, further substantiated Cockrell's presence on the Red Sox roster.[8] And the *Watertown Daily Times* regularly reported on games that he pitched or played the outfield in, noting by the end of September that he was "one of Pop's best."[9]

In 1916, a reference to Cockrell's unique pitching style made the news. In a July 29 game against the Gouverneur Collegians, "Cockrell twirled a splendid [complete] game, striking out eleven of his opponents with the spitter" for a 3-1 win. Also noteworthy was the article's allusion to what was common practice for many Black teams at the time: "The Watkins club kept the spectators amused throughout the game with the comedy stuff, besides showing some clever fielding."[10]

Cockrell began the 1917 season with the Red Sox and on one of Havana's road trips to New York City apparently drew the attention of the New York Lincoln Giants team that was managed by Smokey Joe Williams. In the autumn of that year, Cockrell made his debut in the top tier of Black baseball.[11] The *Watertown Daily Times* noted his move to New York in an October 1917 article:

> Phil Cockrell, who was the star-colored twirler of the Havana Red Sox, the former part of this season, is now doing mound duty for the Lincoln Giants, one of the fastest colored aggregations in New York city. Cockrell played with the Pittsburgh Stars up to two weeks ago when he made a shift to the colored nine of the metropolis. Phil pitched his second game for the Lincoln Giants on Sunday afternoon at the Olympic field in New York city, [winning] 4 to 2.[12]

His brief stint with the Pittsburgh Stars, before moving to the Giants, was also captured by the *Watertown Daily Times*:

> The Pittsburgh Stars, star colored team of Buffalo captained by Home Run Johnson, a former member of Pop Watkins' aggregation, is composed mainly Red Sox players who have either been released by the venerable Watkins or have left the team of their own accord. ... Phil Cockrell, who left Pop's crew of colored baseball tossers in August to join the Buffalo aggregation, twirled in [the Sunday, September 23 game against the Buffalo Internationals] and allowed the Bisons but three hits.[13]

Statistics record one appearance against another major-league-quality Black ballclub in 1917 for the 22-year-old with the Lincoln Giants, a six-hit shutout.[14] Managed by Smokey Joe Williams, the Lincoln Giants finished with the best record among the Eastern clubs. Williams led the way with pitching support from Gifford McDonald and Lee Wade. Doc Wiley, Judy Gans, Ted Kimbro, Jules Thomas, and Spottswood Poles featured prominently in the field and at bat.

In the winter of 1917-1918, Cockrell made the first of several appearances in the Florida Hotel League, possibly initiated by his newfound connection to Smokey Joe Williams, who managed the Breakers Hotel team on which Cockrell played. Cockrell made further appearances for the Breakers in 1921, 1925, and 1926.[15]

Cockrell's winter ballplaying was not confined to Florida. He was with the Bacharach Giants in 1920-1921, on which team he joined future Hall of Famers Louis Santop and Oscar Charleston, for the squad's losing tour (4-12) of Cuba against Almendares and Habana.[16] Cockrell's stats show him playing mainly as an outfielder in six games, going hitless, with two innings in relief in one pitching appearance.

Cockrell started the 1918 season with the Lincoln Giants, but it was that year that Ed Bolden, the Hilldale entrepreneur and president, decided to pursue the right-hander,[17] most likely based on his pitching performance for his New York team in a May 12 game against the Brooklyn Royal Giants at Olympic Field. The game is worth noting, given its pivotal role in Cockrell's long-term career with Hilldale and later with Bolden's Philadelphia Stars.

> Tom Williams and Phil Cockrell, two colored twirlers who have seen service in Watertown with Pop Watkins' dusky squad, participated in a pitching duel at the Olympic Field in New York city Sunday afternoon. Both twirlers were relieved at the close of the 11th inning with the score two all. Both received rounds of applause from the biggest crowd that has ever been at the park. The Lincoln Giants, of which Cockrell is a twirler, were, however, defeated in the 12th inning by the Royal Giants 4-2. In eleven innings Cockrell struck out eight men, gave two bases on balls and allowed a wild pitch.[18]

The rise of Hilldale as a national Black baseball power coincided with moves like the signing of Cockrell. Bolden had already brought Otto Briggs and Doc Sykes into the fold in 1917. In 1918, along with Cockrell, Bolden signed Louis Santop, Arthur Dilworth, Tom Williams, Judy Johnson, Dick Lundy, Pearl Webster, and George Johnson to the club for the start of a decade of excellence.[19]

In the period 1918 to 1920, Hilldale established itself as both a quality team and a sound organization. It was competitive, finishing second, fourth, third, and first among Eastern Independent Clubs from 1918 to 1921. The team foundered somewhat at 20-26 in 1922, eighth among Independent Clubs. Thereafter, Hilldale hit its stride. In the five years of existence of the Eastern Colored League (1923-1927), the team came in second, first, first, first, first, and fifth, appearing in the first two Negro League World Series in 1924 and 1925. Its 53-33 aggregate record against all Negro League teams in 1926 was not enough to surpass the Atlantic City Bacharach Giants in games won within the ECL for a fourth consecutive Eastern title.

By 1921, Cockrell was known well outside Philadelphia. A Chicago paper wrote, "Cockrell is one of the many pitchers who long ago demonstrated the fact that the Southland is full of worthy baseball talent. Phil Cockrell is one of the Hilldales great staff of pitchers and is rated one of the best right handers in the business."[20]

In early 1923, Cockrell's pitching talents were confirmed by Black baseball's preeminent personage himself, Rube Foster. The Associated Negro Press ran a story in March, stating:

> Phil Cockrell, 'the pitching wonder' who is wintering in Palm Beach, Florida, received a flattering letter from Rube Foster. The letter is in Edward Bolden's hands and Phil declares he will stick with the Hilldale team and support his present manager. …[21]

Cockrell was very much a part of Hilldale's winning formula. In his 15 years with the franchise, through 1932 when the team collapsed financially, he pitched 202 games, starting 165 and finishing 133 of them. He went 96-67 with a 3.88 ERA. Pitching alongside Nip Winters, Red Ryan, Rube Curry, Script Lee, Bullet Campbell, and later, Darltie Cooper, Oscar Levis, and Webster McDonald, the Hilldale rotation was solid and dependable. As Cockrell aged into his 30s, he no longer figured as the main attraction for Hilldale, but Bolden remained loyal to him.

There was one hiccup, though. Foreshadowing the irony of his post-playing career, Cockrell became embroiled in something more than a dust-up with an umpire:

> On August 8, 1926, at Atlantic City … [he] attacked an umpire for reversing a decision. While many observers were angered by the

harsh response of white park security, who hauled Cockrell from the field and struck him with a blackjack, Bolden insisted that Cockrell was at fault for assaulting the umpire. … Cockrell received a five-day suspension and a $100 fine.[22]

In spite of this unfortunate episode, Cockrell was still known as one of the best and smartest hurlers in Negro League baseball. The *Pittsburgh Courier's* W. Rollo Wilson captured Cockrell's pitching repertoire perfectly:

The sterling pitcher of Clan Darbie is still winning ball games. And how? His head and control. If you were to ask me who is the smartest hurler in our league, there could be but one answer, and that is "Cockrell." … [He] is a veteran of the game and he knows all the questions and their solutions. He can find the weak spot of a batter more quickly than any moundsman hereabouts. His spitball is more deception than reality, his curve is a curve by courtesy only. He can flash a speed ball on occasion. But his brain works constantly, and his control is good or better most of the time. … Other eastern pitchers have more mechanical ability, but none ties him in brain power.[23]

Cockrell's spitball was considered by many to be his signature pitch. The American and National Leagues banned the spitball after 1920 (allowing the 17 pitchers already using it to continue until they were out of the game).[24] However, "The Negro Leagues, on the other hand, did no such thing. While Negro League officials claimed that their games adhered to Major League rules, NNL players, managers, and umpires accepted ball doctoring as a part of their sport."[25] This state of play welcomed a range of styles for Negro Leaguers to doctor the ball. For Cockrell, it was a "moist ball" rather than a heavily saliva-covered pitch.[26]

Teammate Paul "Jake" Stephens had an insider's view of Cockrell's spitter:

Phil Cockrell was a great pitcher, but you hated to play behind him because he threw that spitball, and you'd get ahold of the goddamn spit sometimes. You just couldn't throw true. I never will forget this no-hit no-run game on Sunday against the Paterson Silk Sox in New Jersey. They really had a good ball club. And

I made a play out this world. The following week they had a return bout, and we went along about the seventh or eighth inning 0-0, and with two men out and a man on second base, he threw a spitball. I grabbed ahold of the spitty side and threw it into the dugout. The man scored and beat us 1-0. Cockrell wouldn't talk to me for two weeks.[27]

Perhaps the most prominent display of Cockrell's spitter came in the first game of the 1924 Colored World Series between the Kansas City Monarchs and Hilldale on Friday, October 3, in Philadelphia. Bolden elected to start Cockrell rather than Nip Winters, despite the latter's stellar season. On a 1-and-2 count to the Monarchs' first batter, Lem Hawkins, Cockrell threw a spitball that led to the home-plate umpire stopping play. The umpire was a White official from the International League who was ready to enforce the ban, but Bolden appealed to Rube Foster, commissioner for the Negro National League, to allow the game to continue without prohibiting the pitch. Foster agreed. Cockrell completed the game but lost to Bullet Joe Rogan, 6-2, giving up five runs in the sixth in large part due to his three errors.[28]

The 1924 Colored World Series between the Negro National League and the Eastern Colored League was the first of two that the Hilldale squad and Cockrell played against the Kansas City Monarchs. Cockrell started two games. In addition to his Game One loss, he started Game Six in Kansas City on October 12, going only two-thirds of an inning and giving up four runs. He did not take the loss, as Hilldale later came back to tie the game before Script Lee, who relieved Cockrell, allowed two more runs in a 6-5 defeat.[29] Despite better hitting and a lower ERA, Hilldale eventually dropped the Series 4-5-1.

Redemption was on the way with a 1925 rematch between the two teams. In the second game of the series, Cockrell pitched a complete game in Kansas City on October 2, losing to Nelson Dean 5 5-3. Cockrell gave up 10 hits, struck out four, walked four, and was hurt by two untimely errors. However, on a blustery, freezing October 10 at the Baker Bowl in Philadelphia, he made up for his earlier loss by defeating William Bell and the Monarchs, 5-2, winning the series 5-1. Over the course of his nine-inning complete game, Cockrell surrendered eight hits, struck out six, and walked four.[30]

Cockrell's ascendency to Hilldale also placed him in a postseason barnstorming world in which teams like Bolden's often participated. In October 1926 Cockrell starred in the first game of a two-game series against Earl Mack's All-Stars. "On October 1, Phil Cockrell, a tiny right-handed spitballer, edged the Macks 3-2 on John Beckwith's long two-run homer in the eighth."[31] Records do not identify Cockrell's mound opponent, but the following day Hilldale again defeated the Mack team and its pitcher, a young Lefty Grove.

After the 1927 season, Ed Bolden pulled Hilldale from the struggling Eastern Colored League that eventually collapsed in June 1928. Hilldale played an independent schedule for the remainder of 1927 and, in 1928, loosely affiliated with other Eastern teams including the Homestead Grays, New York Lincoln Giants, and Baltimore Black Sox.

Throughout all of the upheaval in the late 1920s and early 1930s, Cockrell remained loyal to Bolden and the city of Philadelphia. The 1928 Hilldale team finished first among Eastern Independent clubs and included such stalwarts as Biz Mackey, Judy Johnson, Oscar Charleston, Frank Warfield, Clint Thomas, Darltie Cooper, and Walter Cannady.

In 1929 Hilldale joined the American Negro League that Bolden himself helped to organize. It was made up of many of the core Eastern teams that had formed the Eastern Colored League. By that time, Cockrell was past his prime. He appeared on an independent team led by Danny McClellan in addition to being on the Hilldale roster. Early in the season, he replaced Oscar Charleston as Hilldale's manager. The team struggled, primarily due to Bolden's conflict with other officials in the ANL; public-relations issues, such as his insistence on using White umpires, that aggravated the Black community; and, ultimately, the economy. Prior to the 1930 season, Bolden was forced to relinquish ownership of the team to Lloyd Thomson, who ran the team for one year before the franchise was bought and overseen by John Drew until its demise in mid-1932.

During the unstable 1929 ANL season with Hilldale, Cockrell tied for the second-most wins, and the third-highest innings pitched for a squad that, while finishing over .500, was 11 games back of the pennant-winning Baltimore Black Sox. Cockrell managed Hilldale again in 1930 and, for a time, in 1932. After Hilldale folded in midseason, he jumped to the Bacharach Giants, now located in Philadelphia under the ownership of Harry Passon. In addition to the Bacharachs, he played for some other teams in 1933.[32]

That same year, Bolden resurfaced on the scene, launching the Philadelphia Stars, an independent team that played mostly a local schedule. In 1934, the Stars joined the year-old Negro National League II and, in February of that year, Bolden signed Cockrell once more.[33]

Cockrell appeared in seven league games for the Stars, starting four and winning one. At 39, he did not have much left in the tank. His season stats for Philadelphia showed him starting the fewest number of games of the Stars starters, behind 20-game winner Slim Jones, player-manager Webster McDonald, Rocky Ellis, Lefty Holmes, and Paul Carter. McDonald managed the team to its only NNL2 pennant during its 15 years in the league. (The team ceased play at the conclusion of the 1948 season.)

Cockrell did not rejoin the Stars in 1935. Instead, he moved to the Bacharach Giants as manager and sometimes pitched or played the outfield. The May 3, 1935, *Delaware County Daily Times* announced that the "Bacharach Giants will introduce their new team under the management of Phil Cockrell, former member of Bolden's Stars. Phil will most likely pitch in Sunday's game."[34] Box scores from the season recorded his occasional appearances in the field.

In 1936 Cockrell organized his own squad. A news article explained, "Phil Cockrell, veteran spitball pitcher, has made arrangements with John M. Drew, owner of Hilldale Park, whereby he will place a club in the field the coming season."[35] For better or worse, he named the team after himself: the Cockrells.[36]

Eventually, after his playing career was over, he became an umpire. According to Negro League historian James Riley:

> Cockrell began a second baseball career, as an umpire in the Negro National League that lasted through the 1946 season. Umpiring in the Negro Leagues could be hazardous, and Cockrell once made a call on a close play that infuriated Jud Wilson. In the locker room after the game, the enraged Wilson grabbed him by the skin of his chest and lifted him off the floor. Fortunately, cooler heads prevailed, and Cockrell was rescued.[37]

Fortunately for Cockrell, he is far better remembered for his pitching acumen than for his run-ins with his former peers as a Negro League umpire. In fact, one of the more impressive aspects of his career is that it was punctuated by six no-hitters. Chronologically, they were against the All Nationals of New York (1919), the Detroit Stars (1921), Chicago American Giants and Patterson Silk Sox (1922), the South

Phillies (six innings, 1923), and Cape May (1930).[38] The home game against the Stars on Labor Day exhibited Cockrell in his prime: no hits, 6 strikeouts and 16 infield outs, suggestive of a masterful spitball that Detroit batters could not command.[39]

Cockrell's other no-hitter against a Negro League side was equally compelling. Hilldale traveled to Chicago at the end of the Eastern season for a five-game series with the American Giants. Despite Cockrell's herculean efforts – he won two of the games himself – Hilldale lost the series three games to two. The hometown *Chicago Defender* wrote of Cockrell's Game One no-hitter: "Spitballer Phil Cockrell … [tossed] a no-hitter while walking only three batters during the Easterners' 5-0 triumph [in Game One].[40] The *Chicago Tribune* cited his seven strikeouts and mentioned that "not a local man reached third."[41] The American Giants won the next two contests before Cockrell's four-hit, three-strikeout game bested Chicago 5-3 in Game Four. Cockrell helped his own cause with two hits and a run scored."[42] However, the American Giants won Game Five and the series, 7-6 in 12 innings.[43]

The no-hitter against the Silk Sox that same year showed Cockrell to be firing on all cylinders:

> Hilldale defeated the fast Paterson Silk Sox here [Clifton, New Jersey] in a red-hot game. Score, 1 to 0. Phil Cockrell, Manager Bolden's ace, pitched the greatest game of his career, having a no-hit, no-run game to his credit. … Cockrell also had a perfect day at bat, with two singles and a sacrifice. The winning run was scored in the third on Downs' single, Cockrell's sacrifice, Briggs' out and Francis' pop fly to right. Three thousand fans saw the game.[44]

After so much success on the playing field, the last inning of Cockrell's life turned out to be a tragic one. He settled in Philadelphia after his long career and lived at 322 North 55th Street. Cockrell worked as a bartender at a taproom at 55th and Summer Streets, just blocks from his home. He was stabbed to death early Saturday morning, March 31, apparently the victim of a robbery, according to his obituary in the *Philadelphia Inquirer*.[45] The online notation from Mount Lawn Cemetery in Sharon Hill, Pennsylvania, where he was buried, stated "he was shot by a jealous husband in a case of mistaken identity."[46]

Phil Cockrell's career statistics show a durable, dependable pitcher: 10th in complete games, 14th in games started, 19th in wins, 24th in shutouts, and 27th in strikeouts. In 1952 the *Pittsburgh Courier* polled the "top baseball men" in the country to choose the All Time, All America [Black] Baseball Team from ballplayers between 1910 and 1952. Although not on the first or second team, Phil Cockrell made the "Roll of Honor" and was called the "greatest spit-ball pitcher of all time."[47]

SOURCES

Unless otherwise noted, all cited statistics are from Seamheads.com.

NOTES

1   "Sports Shots," W. Rollo Wilson, *Pittsburgh Courier*, August 27, 1927: 16.

2   https://www.archives.gov/research/african-americans/migrations/great-migration. Accessed October 12, 2022.

3   "Notes Among the Colored People," *Augusta* (Georgia) *Chronicle*, September 20, 1925: 3.

4   "Famous Negro League Pitcher," J.C. Mardenborough, *Augusta Chronicle*, March 18, 1926: 11.

5   "Pop Watkins' 45th Year in Baseball: Red Sox Pilot 12 Years," *Watertown* (New York) *Daily Times*, July 30, 1919: 8.

6   "Havana Red Sox Here Next Sunday," *Buffalo Evening News*, June 5, 1913: 18.

7   "The Havana Red Sox," *Kingston* (New York) *Whig-Standard*, July 21, 1914: 3.

8   "The Havana Red Sox," *New York Age*, August 27, 1914: 6.

9   "Utica Leaguers Here for Games," *Watertown Daily Times*, September 26, 1914: 8.

10   "Errors Lose Game for Gouverneur: Red Sox Score Three Runs in First Inning," *Watertown Daily Times*, July 29, 1916: 8.

11   Even after Cockrell's ascendency to the top tier, he did not sever his Havana Red Sox connection. The *Watertown Daily Times* carried sightings of him with the Red Sox. This movement was not uncommon and was likely done with the understanding of Cockrell's managers. "Prospects Play Red Sox Sunday," *Watertown Daily Times*, July 28, 1919: 8.

12   "Phil Cockrell with the Lincoln Giants: Former Havana Red Sox Twirler Has Shifted to the Metropolis," *Watertown Daily Times*, October 10, 1917: 11.

13   "Sox Players with Pittsburgh Stars: Cockrell the Star Hurler," *Watertown Daily Times,* September 9, 1917: 8.

14   Box scores are not available (or have not yet been discovered) for many games. The stats that Seamheads has for Cockrell for that year are against other Eastern Independent teams.

15   William F. McNeil, *Black Baseball Out of Season: Pay for Play Outside the Negro Leagues* (Jefferson, North Carolina: McFarland & Co., 2007), 23.

16   Jorge S. Figueredo, *Cuban Baseball: A Statistical History, 1878-1961* (Jefferson, North Carolina: McFarland & Co., 2003), 137, 139.

17   Neil Lanctot, *Fair Dealing and Clean Playing: The Hilldale Club and the Development of Black Professional Baseball, 1910-1932* (Syracuse, New York: Syracuse University Press, 2007), 52.

18   "Colored Hurlers in Pitching Duel: Former Red Sox Slabsters Twirl Eleven Innings to a Tie in New York," *Watertown Daily Times*, May 15, 1918: 6.

19   Courtney Michelle Smith, *Ed Bolden and Black Baseball in Philadelphia* (Jefferson, North Carolina: McFarland & Co., 2017), 19.

20   "An Eastern Cracker," *Chicago Whip*, July 23, 1921: 8.

21   "Philadelphia the Birthplace of Colored Eastern Organized Baseball," *Richmond* (Virginia) *Planet*, March 7, 1923: 3.

22   Lanctot, 145-6.

23   W. Rollo Wilson, "Sports Shots," *Pittsburgh Courier*, August 27, 1927: 19.

24   https://sabr.org/research/article/the-spitball-and-the-end-of-the-deadball-era/.

25   https://www.downthedrive.com/2020/8/22/21396997/pitching-from-the-shoulders-up-spitball-pitching-in-the-negro-leagues.

26   *Chicago Defender*, August 20, 1927: 10.

27   John B. Holway, *Black Diamonds: Life in the Negro Leagues from the Men Who Lived It* (New York: Stadium Books, 1991), 9.

28   Larry Lester, *Baseball's First Colored World Series: The 1924 Meeting of the Hilldale Giants and the Kansas City Monarchs* (Jefferson, North Carolina: McFarland & Co., 2006), 107.

29   Lester, 148-152.

30   "World Series Play by Play," *Chicago Defender*, October 17, 1925: 8.

31   McNeil, 92.

32   Newspaper references also place Cockrell with the Gouldtown Frogs in southern New Jersey: *Bridgetown Evening News*, August 17, 1933: 5, and August 31, 1933: 8.

33   W. Ardee, "Phil Cockrell to Twirl for Phila. Stars," *Philadelphia Tribune*, February 22, 1934.

34   "Chester Team Plays Tomorrow: Meets Charlotte Hornets at A.A. Field; Bacharach Sunday," *Delaware County Daily Times* (Chester, Pennsylvania), May 3, 1935: 17.

35   "Cockrell Returns to Darby," *Delaware County Daily Times*, February 3, 1936: 12.

36   "Phil Cockrell's Baseball Club to Be Tough," *Kansas City* (Kansas) *Plain Dealer,* March 6, 1936: 3.

37   James A. Riley, *The Biographical Encyclopedia of the Negro Baseball Leagues* (New York: Carroll & Graf Publishers, 1994), 182-3.

38   Lanctot, 147.

39   https://sabr.org/gamesproj/game/september-5-1921-hilldales-phil-cockrell-tosses-no-hitter-against-detroit-stars/#:~:text=Phil%20Cockrell%2C%20raved%20the%20Philadelphia%20Inquirer%2C%20%E2%80%9Cdrew%20transportation,career%20as%20pitcher%20has%20been%20largely%20overlooked.%202.

40   "Phil Cockrell Throws a Mean-Mean Baseball: Pitches No-Hit, No-Run Game Against American Giants for Hilldale Team," *Chicago Defender*, August 26, 1922: 10.

41   "Hilldale Lad Pitched No-Hit, No-Run Victory," *Chicago Defender*, August 20, 1922: 8.

42   "American Giants Beaten," *Chicago Tribune*, August 23, 1922: 15.

43   "Rube Foster Takes Final of Series," *Philadelphia Inquirer*, August 24, 1922: 17.

44   "Additional Sports News: Cockrell Enters 'Hall of Fame,'" *Cleveland Gazette*, July 1, 1922: 2.

45   "Baseball Hurler Stabbed to Death," *Philadelphia Inquirer*, April 1, 1951: 48. The *Arizona Sun* and other papers carried a slightly longer obituary from the NNPA Black Press of America elaborating on his career. "Former Pitcher Stabbed to Death," *Arizona Sun*, April 13, 1951: 5.

46   https://www.findagrave.com/memorial/98761973/phillip-cockrell. Newspapers stated that Cockrell was stabbed, conflicting with the Cemetery notation.

47   "Power, Speed, Skill, Make All-America Team Excel," *Pittsburgh Courier*, April 19, 1952: 14, 16.

FREDERICK COLEMAN

By Margaret M. Gripshover

Frederick Davis "Fred" Coleman began his baseball career as a pitcher for his high-school team and later with several amateur and semipro nines in suburban Philadelphia. However, on one occasion, Coleman had a brief taste of life in Negro League professional baseball when he took the mound for the Philadelphia Stars on July 2, 1934.[1]

Coleman was born in Phoenixville, Pennsylvania, on November 30, 1906. He was one of six children born to Charles and Minnie Davis Coleman. His father was a crane operator at a Phoenixville steel foundry and his mother was a music teacher. Around 1920, Coleman's family left Phoenixville and moved about 50 miles southeast to Darby, five miles west of South Philadelphia. By 1924, Coleman was a student at the Ridge Avenue Junior High in Darby and was active in extracurricular sports activities; a renaissance man of sorts, he also co-authored a class play.[2] Among his classmates were brothers Raymond and Thomas Macey, with whom Coleman played high-school baseball, and later all three were teammates with the Darby Phantoms.[3]

After his prep career ended in 1928, Coleman made his debut in amateur baseball in 1929 with the Darby Phantoms, an African American team in the mixed-race Interurban League in suburban Philadelphia.[4] The Phantoms were managed by Lloyd P. Thompson, who began his long association with baseball in 1910 as a player for the Hilldale club along with Ed Bolden.[5] Thompson later served as an executive in the Hilldale organization and as a press agent for the Eastern Colored League.[6] Thompson's Darby Phantoms, which had the unfortunate nickname of "the Spooks," were one of the Interurban League's top teams, and Coleman and the Macey brothers were among the squad's best players.[7] Coleman was fortunate to make his amateur debut with the league-leading Phantoms.[8] Thanks to his "brilliant pitching," young "Lefty Coleman" helped the Phantoms earn the first of three Interurban League titles.[9] Coleman, who was touted as the "former ace left-hander of Darby High School," also saw action in the Phantoms' outfield

along with John Coleman, who was not a member of Fred Coleman's immediate family.[10]

Fred Coleman returned to the Darby Phantoms for the 1930 season but was used primarily as an outfielder rather than as a pitcher.[11] That season, the Phantoms claimed the Interurban League crown for a second time and the future looked bright for the Delaware County aggregation.[12] The 1931 season saw the return of Thompson as the manager of the Phantoms. He was assisted by player-manager John Burgin, former player Raymond Macey as the team's business manager, and by Coleman's brother, Burgess A. Coleman, who was the president of the executive committee.[13] As in 1930, Coleman proved to be a versatile player, taking the mound as their "invincible" southpaw, and tending to Darby's outer garden as needed.[14] The 1931 season ended as it had for the previous two years – another Interurban League championship season for Coleman and the Phantoms.[15] What Coleman did not know at the time was that 1931 would mark the last hurrah for the Phantoms.

Prior to the start of Interurban League play in 1932, the Darby Phantoms announced a change in management. Lloyd Thompson was out, and Ed Bolden was "at the helm."[16] But some things remained the same. Coleman's brother Burgess A. Coleman remained as a member of the "board of athletic directors," and Raymond Macey continued as the business manager.[17] Bolden's attempt to turn the Phantoms into a revenue-generating enterprise was a disaster. After three straight championship seasons, the Bolden's Phantoms left the Interurban League to become a traveling team.[18] Despite Bolden's marketing efforts, the Darby club was "consistently overmatched" by their opponents and posted a lackluster record.[19]

In 1933 Bolden abruptly abandoned the Phantoms and shifted his attention to the Philadelphia Stars.[20] The blame for Darby's implosion was placed squarely on Bolden by the Phantoms' business manager, Raymond Macey. Macey was especially bitter and enraged by "Bolden's abrupt withdrawal" from the Phantoms.[21] He accused Bolden of using "flowery words" on a group of "young amateurs" and leading them into "a premature and near fatal leap into professionalism."[22] Macey's sharp criticisms of Bolden were echoed by the local press. The *Chester Times* noted that the Phantoms' attempt to "break into 'fast company' under the leadership of Ed [Bolden], former Hilldale pilot," was a misstep, and that it failed because the team "tired of independent competition."[23]

In 1934 the Darby Phantoms and Coleman hit the reset button. They rejoined the Interurban League and were "back to prove to the fans of Delaware County and surrounding territory that they still retain mastery" over the local nines.[24] The Phantoms named Bob Clark as their manager and went to work reestablishing their dominance over the other six league teams.[25] The Phantoms were one of four "Negro clubs" in the loop along with three White teams.[26] But Coleman did not play for the Phantoms in 1934 because they became literal apparitions and vanished without playing a single league game. He signed with a different Interurban team, the Darby Cubs, who were Interurban League contenders at the beginning of the season.[27] Coleman, along with his former Phantoms bullpen mate Tom Macey, helped the Cubs remain in the championship hunt for much of the first half of the season, second only to Clearview, the eventual league champion.[28] By the end of the 1934, however, Coleman and the Cubs found themselves hibernating near the bottom of the standings and out of the playoffs.[29] Coleman's tenure with the Darby Cubs lasted just one year. The Cubs jumped to the Suburban Colored League in 1935 but folded before the season ended.[30]

Coleman's 1934 season with the one-and-done Darby Cubs was punctuated by one high note – his only known appearance with a professional baseball team. On July 2, 1934, Coleman was tapped as the starting pitcher in one game for Ed Bolden's Philadelphia Stars.[31] Bolden knew Coleman from his days with the Darby Phantoms and was likely the one who gave the southpaw a shot at the big time. The game was staged in Philadelphia before 3,500 fans and pitted the Stars against the semipro Bartram nine of the Philadelphia League.[32] It was a rough initiation for Coleman. The Stars fell to Bartram 11-10, in an eight-inning affair.[33] Coleman was roughed up by Bartram and was eventually relieved of his mound duties by the Stars' regular pitchers, Paul Carter and Stewart "Slim" Jones.[34] It may have been a memorable experience for Coleman, but it was not exactly a command performance. A star was not born that day, and he was not invited back for an encore.

In 1935 Coleman played for at least two Suburban Colored League teams; Paschall A.C. and the Morton Republican Club.[35] He spent the bulk of the year with the Morton Republican Club as a pitcher, outfielder, and pinch-hitter.[36] The Morton Republican Club of Delaware County sponsored a baseball team as early as 1912, when it was known as the Morton Colored Republican Club.[37] Coleman had some sparkling moments with Morton. He swatted a game-winning triple to topple the league-leading Oakeola nine and tossed a three-hitter against the Swarthmore Hornets.[38] In what was likely his final appearance for Morton, Coleman was on the losing end of a "heart-breaking mound duel" against Oakeola, by a score of 4-3.[39] The Morton Republicans were mediocre and were never a threat to take the league title. By the close of the 1935 season, the Suburban Colored League bureaucracy was falling apart, the Morton team disbanded, and Fred Coleman's baseball career was over.[40]

In December 1935, after his retirement from baseball, Coleman married Sylvia G. Rue in Darby. By 1940, he was the father of three children and working as a gardener for a private estate in suburban Philadelphia. In the 1940s he followed in his father's footsteps and went to work at a steel mill in Darby. By the 1950s, the Coleman family expanded to include six children. Although he was no longer involved in baseball, Coleman participated in local African American community organizations in Chester County. He served as a district lecturer and member of the Rose of Sharon Masonic Lodge.[41] In 1955 he was a guest at a speech given by Thurgood Marshall on the topic of Jim Crow and housing segregation.[42] He was also an outspoken supporter of programs that addressed local poverty and housing issues.[43]

Frederick D. Coleman died in Chester County on September 30, 1986. He was buried in Eden Cemetery, a historic African American cemetery in Collingdale, Pennsylvania. It is the same cemetery where Ed Bolden was laid to rest in 1950.

SOURCES

Unless otherwise indicated, all Negro League statistics and records were sourced from Seamheads.com.

Ancestry.com was used to access census, birth, death, marriage, military, immigration, and other genealogical and public records.

NOTES

1   "Bartram Topples Philadelphia Stars," *Philadelphia Inquirer*, July 3, 1934: 16.

2   "Darby," *Chester* (Pennsylvania) *Times*, June 18, 1924: 4.

3 "Darby Defeats Media in Tenth," *Chester Times*, May 23, 1928: 15; "Darby High Defeats Ridley Park in Tenth Inning, Score 3-2," *Chester Times*, June 6, 1928: 11.

4 Neil Lanctot, *Fair Dealing & Clean Playing: The Hilldale Club and the Development of Black Professional Baseball, 1910-1932* (Syracuse: Syracuse University Press, 2007), 203; "Twelve Teams Proposed for New League," *Chester Times*, March 29, 1929: 26; "Phantoms Win First from Rival Foes," *Philadelphia Inquirer*, July 10, 1929: 18.

5 Lanctot, 17.

6 Lanctot, 205.

7 "Phantoms Win Interurban Title," *Pittsburgh Courier*, July 20, 1929: 18.

8 "Darby Phantoms Win Over Colwyn Team," *Chester Times*, July 17, 1929: 14.

9 "Phantoms Win First from Rival Foes," *Philadelphia Inquirer*, July 10, 1929: 18.

10 "Phantoms Capture Interurban Title," *Philadelphia Inquirer*, September 16, 1929: 18.

11 "Darby Phantoms Win from Colored Elks," *Chester Times*, August 4, 1930: 13; "Lester Wins Another Game," *Chester Times*, September 9, 1930: 13.

12 "Darby Phantoms Win Interurban Title," *Chester Times*, September 22, 1930: 12.

13 "Darby Phantoms Elect," *Baltimore Afro-American*, March 14, 1931: 15.

14 "Interurban League," *Philadelphia Inquirer*, August 5, 1931: 16; "Game Ends in Tie," *Chester Times*, August 20, 1931: 15; "Darby Phantoms Win League Title," *Chester Times*, August 29, 1931: 11.

15 "Another Title for the Darby Phantoms," *Chester Times*, September 23, 1931: 12.

16 "Darby Clubs Names Aides for Bolden," Baltimore Afro-American, February 27, 1932: 14.

17 "Darby Clubs Names Aides for Bolden."

18 "Interurban Title Series to Start," *Chester Times*, September 1, 1933: 13.

19 Lanctot, 222.

20 Lanctot, 222.

21 Lanctot, 222.

22 Lanctot, 222.

23 "Phantoms Return to the Interurban," *Chester Times*, March 22, 1934: 19.

24 "Phantoms Return to the Interurban."

25 "Phantoms in PA. League," *Baltimore Afro-American*, March 31, 1931: 17.

26 "Amateur Baseball," *Chester Times*, April 24, 1934: 12.

27 "Interurban League," *Chester Times*, June 1, 1934: 17.

28 "Clearview Nears First Half Crown," *Chester Times*, June 27, 1934: 15; "Delco Teams Play," *Chester Times*, June 30, 1934: 11; "Clearview Takes Interurban Title," *Chester Times*, September 24, 1934: 10.

29 "Southwest Phils Lead League," *Baltimore Afro-American*, September 8, 1934: 15.

30 "County Leagues Ready for Grind," *Chester Times*, April 13, 1935: 12.

31 "Bartram Topples Philadelphia Stars."

32 "Bartram Topples Philadelphia Stars."

33 "Bartram Topples Philadelphia Stars."

34 "Bartram Topples Philadelphia Stars."

35 "Paschall Nips Columbia," *Philadelphia Inquirer*, June 25, 1935: 20; "A Hectic Duel," *Chester Times*, July 31, 1935: 10.

36 "Paschall Nips Columbia"; "A Hectic Duel"; "Morton Captures Pair Over Week-End," *Chester Times*, August 5, 1935: 11.

37 "Stars Are Dimmed," *Chester Times*, July 6, 1912: 3; Kristi Nelson, "End May Be Near for GOP Club," *Philadelphia Inquirer*, June 6, 1995: W1.

38 "Morton Blanks Oakeola Champs," *Chester Times*, August 9, 1935: 14; "Morton Defeats Swarthmore, 4-2," *Chester Times*, August 10, 1935: 12.

39 "Paschall Nears Lead in S.C. Loop," *Chester Times*, August 14, 1935: 12.

40 "Sports Shorts," *Chester Times*, May 28, 1936: 22.

41 "Rochester is Re-Elected Masonic District Chairman," *Chester Times*, January 14, 1955: 12.

42 "Anti-Segregationists Point Efforts at Bans in Housing," *Chester Times*, March 5, 1955: 2.

43 Frederick D. Coleman, "People Are Skeptical," *Delaware County Daily Times* (Norristown, Pennsylvania), May 22, 1969: 6.

DEWEY CREACY

BY BILL NOWLIN

In 13 of his 15 seasons in Negro Leagues baseball, Dewey Creacy played for teams called the Stars. He was a third baseman who played on four championship teams, including three for the St. Louis Stars (1928, 1930, and 1931) and one with the Philadelphia Stars (1934). In 1925 St. Louis was the second-half champion but lost the league championship to the Kansas City Monarchs in a playoff series that went the full seven games.

Creacy played in the original Negro National League from 1924 to 1931 with the St. Louis Stars, and then after two years (1932 and 1933) when there was not a solid league established, he played for a few other clubs. From 1934 onward, he played his final five seasons with the Philadelphia Stars.

In his 20s, he had hit for higher batting averages and hit for more power than he did in his 30s, wrapping up his career when he was near 40. Over the course of the 983 games for which statistics are currently available, he hit for a .291 batting average with a .355 on-base percentage.[1]

There are some uncertainties regarding Creacy's upbringing. He first shows up in the 1910 US census, at which time he was part of a large household on South Austin Street in Dallas. The head of the household was 50-year-old Mary Lewis, a native of Tennessee who worked from her home as a laundress. She lived with two sons (George Stone, 34, a teamster involved in excavating, and Eugene Page, 28, a laborer in an automobile factory) and a daughter (Lissie Goldwaite, 32, who also worked as a laundress from home). One can't help but note that all three of her children had different surnames, and none of them were Lewis; She also had suffered the loss of another child. Two nieces of Lewis lived in the household – Mamie Winfrey, 23, and Emile Winfrey, 21 – who both also worked as laundresses at home. The census reflects that Mary Lewis was widowed, as were both her sons and Emile Winfrey. There is an "S" next to Lessie Goldwaite's name, suggesting she was single.[2] Rounding out the large, extended family were three granddaughters

– Exaline Benjamin (13 years old), Ida Creasy (7), and Irene Page (5), and two grandsons – Dewey Creasy (9) and Thomas Creasy (5).[3]

All sources seem to agree that Dewey was born Albert Dewey Creacy on April 13. His draft cards for World War I and World War II both say he was born on April 13, 1900, in Dallas.[4] On his death certificate, his mother's maiden name was given as "Golothwaite," which is more likely than not the Lessie (or Lissie) Goldwaite from the 1910 census. However, matters are further confused by the fact that both his World War II draft card and that of Thomas Creacy provide their mother's name as Alberta Duncan of Dallas.

Gary Ashwill

Third baseman Dewey Creacy

FURTHER GENEALOGY

Looking at Mary Lewis more thoroughly, the 1900 census shows her as married to day laborer Rip Lewis. They had two sons – George Stone and Eugene Page – and a daughter, Milissie, who was born in 1878 and was doing washing for a living. Her given name may have been Melissa and her surname Goldthwaite, with her father having the name Tommy Creasy, as indicated by daughter Ida's 1975 Texas death certificate. She was Ida C. Bacon at the time.

The 1910 census, conducted on April 15, 1910, says Dewey was 9 – indicating a 1901 birth. A Missouri marriage certificate from December 1923 – a few months before he began playing for the St. Louis Stars – says he was 23 when he married Mary Simpson. The 1930 census lists him as a ballplayer named Cresy in St Louis; he was shown as age 30 on April 11 that year (which would mean he had been born in 1899). He was living in a hotel with 64 others, one of whom was also listed as a ballplayer – Henry Williams, a catcher on the St. Louis Stars.

The World War I draft card shows him as married to Ophelia Creacy and living in Dallas. He was working at the time as a laborer for Shipper's Compress Co. of Dallas. A 1933 death certificate from Texas shows the death at Parkland Hospital, Dallas, of a 16-year-old boy Albert McCoy Creacy, born to Ophelia Walton and Dewey Creacy. Born in July 1917, he died of meningitis.

Ophelia and Albert Creacy are found in the 1921 Dallas city directory. The 1922 directory has Dewey living with Thomas, a shine boy, and Ollie Creacy, a bootblack. In 1923 it was only Dewey and Thomas. No occupation is shown for Dewey in any of the years, and only those three years are currently to be found online. Thomas (born in 1904) died the year before Dewey, in Los Angeles on July 22, 1983. The spelling "Creacy" will be used throughout this biography.

CREACY'S BASEBALL DAYS

Following Creacy's baseball career is much easier. Standing 5-feet-10 and listed at 171 pounds, he was right-handed. He first turns up in 1924 – age 24 or 25 – with the St. Louis Stars, managed by Candy Jim Taylor. Negro Leagues researcher James A. Riley reports, "Before joining the Monarchs in 1924, he had served in the 25th Infantry."[5] Creacy had reported to spring training with the Kansas City Monarchs, but by the time the regular season began he was with the Stars.[6]

Creacy's debut was at second base on May 13, but it was not until late May that he cracked the starting lineup. The 40-year-old Taylor played third base in the beginning of the season, but beginning on July 7, he played Creacy at third.[7] Creacy played 55 of 84 known games, 41 of them at third base. Taylor himself played most of the other games at third. Among his teammates were future Hall of Famers Willie Wells at shortstop and Cool Papa Bell in center field. Creacy hit .254 (the team average was .277) with a .304 on-base percentage. He hit one home run and drove in 24 runs, and he fielded his position at a .950 clip. The team's record was 43-41, which put it in fourth place in the nine-team Negro National League.

After the season, the Stars went west to California and played as the St. Louis All-Stars in the California Winter League. An October 31 story in the *St. Louis Argus* noted that "Creacy at third has the best arm in the eastern league."[8] In a game against Glendale, Creacy drove in five runs in a 10-run second inning of a 13-7 win.[9] More frequently billed as the St. Louis Giants, the team played in November, December, and all the way into mid-March 1925, closing things out with a five-game series in Sacramento. A November 14 article by umpire Billy Donaldson, previewing the Stars' 1925 season, said, "One thing that I noted carefully was when Jim Taylor pulled himself out of the lineup and placed Creacy at third base, the infield became faster and the club had more defense at the hot corner. ... Creacy is not a flashy player, but ... he is a much better player than the fans think he is. If played all through next season he will be able to show his ware as a third baseman."[10] In the December 26 *Argus*, reviewing season-end statistics of the All-Stars, it was noted, "Third baseman Creacy is also a long distance hitter. Six of his fourteen safeties have been for extra bases, four being triples and two doubles." He was reported as having batted .269; for context, teammates Cool Papa Bell hit .377 and catcher Mitchell Murray .375.[11]

In 1925, after some local exhibition games in April, and still playing their home games at Stars Park in St. Louis, the 59-30 team won the second-half title. The first-half champions were the Kansas City Monarchs. Creacy played in almost every game and had a .323 batting average with 14 homers and 73 RBIs in 83 games. He stole 17 bases, though in no other year did he steal as many as half that number. There was a "little World Series" between the two teams, the Monarchs winning four games to three. Creacy was 6-for-23 (.261), with one homer and three RBIs.

The 1926 season saw the Stars finish in third place behind the Monarchs and the second-half and league champion Chicago American Giants. The Stars had three successive managers during the course of the season: Branch Russell, Dizzy Dismukes, and John Reese. Even with a .340 batting average, Creacy only finished in fourth place on the team. Future Hall of Famer Mule Suttles joined the Stars and led with .425, 32 homers, and 130 runs batted in. Creacy homered 23 times and drove in 107 runs in the 92 games he played – along with his batting average, he achieved career highs in all three categories.

Candy Jim Taylor took over again as manager in 1927 and specialized in pinch-hitting, batting .420 in 50 at-bats. The Stars (62-37) finished second in the league in winning percentage but won neither the first-half nor second-half title, and were thus left out at playoff time. Creacy had another good year, batting .316 with 13 homers and 84 RBIs, second only to Willie Wells on the Stars.

The 63-26 St. Louis Stars dominated in 1928, winning the first half and then the league championship over the Chicago American Giants, five games to four. Creacy was .329/10/54 in the regular season games. He helped the Stars even things up at three games apiece, going 2-for-3 with a home run in Game Six at Stars Park in St. Louis on September 30, a 12-7 win.

The 1929 Stars were second only to the Monarchs, but since the Monarchs won both the first half and second half, there was no championship series. Creacy had an off year, batting only .258. He drove in 60 runs, ranking fifth on the team.

The 1930 Stars played 94 games for new manager John Reese, who had taken over from Taylor. They put up a record of 69-25-1 and were the first-half champions, playing the Detroit Stars in the championship series, Creacy rebounded, hitting .301 and knocking in 73 runs. They beat Bingo DeMoss's Detroit team, four games to three in the championship series. In California that winter, he played third base for the Nashville Elite Colored Giants.

The first, Rube Foster-founded incarnation of the Negro National League played its final season in 1931. It was Creacy's eighth year with St. Louis. In 35 games, he hit .303, without a homer, and drove in 19 runs. The Stars finished well ahead of the other teams – down to just six from the nine the league had fielded the year before. In the overall standings, they had been 13½ games ahead of second-place Kansas City in 1930. They finished 13 games ahead of the second-place Cleveland Cubs in 1931, league champions

for the second year in a row. With the 1928 season included, Creacy was a three-time champion.

Immediately after the regular season, the Stars played against a team that featured a number of major leaguers, including Lloyd and Paul Waner, Babe Herman, Bill Terry, and others, beating them 18-1.[12] Creacy returned to California with a team billed as the Philadelphia Colored Giants, with Satchel Paige, Bill Foster, Biz Mackey, Cool Papa Bell, Willie Wells, and others.[13]

Creacy played for two different teams in 1932. He initially played 29 games for the first-place (28-9) Detroit Wolves of the East-West League (EWL), managed by Dizzy Dismukes and featuring five future Hall of Famers, for whom he hit .255 with only 10 RBIs. In mid-June, the Wolves merged with the Homestead Grays, but Creacy was among those who were not included on the Grays.[14] He then signed with the EWL's Washington Pilots and played 34 games for the 17-30 sixth-place squad under Frank Warfield and then Webster McDonald. Creacy batted .310 with 25 RBIs for the Pilots.

His 1933 season saw Creacy with two teams again; this time they were member franchises of the second iteration of the Negro National League (NNL2). He got into 27 games for the Columbus Blue Birds (16-28 on the season), hitting just .236 with 6 RBIs. Later in the season, he hit .250 (hitting a double in four at-bats) for the Cleveland Giants, who finished the season with a record of 0-1.

Creacy had led Cleveland ownership to believe that he was going to become their manager in 1934. However, as the season approached, he signed a contract with the Philadelphia Stars. Resolution of the conflict between the two franchises required a ruling from the new Negro National League's commissioner, W. Rollo Wilson. He placed Creacy with the Stars but wrote, "The player deserves nothing but centure [sic] for his double dealings with the Cleveland club, and is warned that any similar conduct in the future will result in his suspension from organized baseball."[15]

Creacy became a champion again with the 1934 Philadelphia Stars, but his .217 batting average was second-lowest among the starting position players. Still, manager Webster McDonald played Creacy in 68 games, a fact that is rather surprising since it was far from his best fielding season either, with Creacy posting a .923 fielding percentage, the worst of any year to date in which he had played 25 or more games. The Stars, though, were 39-18, second-half champions and ultimately league champions after beating the Chicago

American Giants, four games to three, in Creacy's first of five years with Philadelphia.

The team played fewer games in 1935, and Creacy appeared in 57 of them, batting .298 and driving in 27 runs. The Stars were 37-31-4 and finished in fourth place. The "snappy Philly third baseman" was expected to work the hot corner for the East team in the 1935 East-West All-Star Game but ended up not appearing in the game.[16]

After the season, he joined a team that Frank Duncan put together to play winter ball in Puerto Rico.

The Philadelphia Stars sank to last pace in a seven-team league in 1936, with their first losing record. Creacy held his own, batting .301, but drove in only 29 runs – though there were only three players on the team who drove in more.

The Homestead Grays dominated the NNL2 in 1937, and the Stars – now piloted by Jud Wilson – again lost more games than they won. Creacy played in only 22 games and hit only .261 while driving in 12 runs. Remarkably, only one player on the team drove in more than 15: Curtis Harris, who led the Stars with 18.

Creacy appeared in 46 games in 1938. His .213 average was the lowest among regular position players, more than 30 points below the next man. The Stars, however, finished in second place, in Creacy's final year of NNL2 play.

Still playing third base, Creacy joined Dave "Showboat" Thomas and the Brooklyn Royal Giants in 1938, 1939, 1940, and 1941. There had been rumors in early 1940 that Creacy was going to become manager of the Philadelphia Stars.[17] That did not come to pass, and he played out the season with the Royal Giants and at least into the first part of the 1941 season.

Subsequent to the end of Creacy's professional baseball career, almost nothing can be found about him for the last 43 years of his life.

After baseball, per his World War II draft card (dated April 15, 1942), he was living in New York City and working at 2424 Seventh Avenue for Daniel Woods. The address is in Harlem, between 141st and 142nd Streets. The nature of the work is not indicated.

Dewey Creacy appears to have lived his later years in California, and he died on November 17, 1984, in Los Angeles. Interestingly, he turned up in 1956 on a list of supporters of US presidential candidate Estes Kefauver.[18]

SOURCES

In addition to the sources cited in the Notes, the author made extensive use of Seamheads.com and Ancestry.com. Thanks to Clem Hamilton for supplying much of the information regarding Creacy's time with the St. Louis Stars.

NOTES

1   For summary statistics, this biography relies on Seamheads.com. Data presented is as of August 2021.

2   The 1908 Dallas City Directory lists her alone, with the differing spelling of her first name.

3   We will use the more frequent "Creacy" as the spelling of Creacy's last name.

4   There is a death certificate, from Los Angeles, saying that he was born Albert Dewey Creacy on April 13, 1901, with his birthplace noted only as "Texas," but the preponderance of evidence from when he was alive indicates that he was born in 1900.

5   James A. Riley, *The Biographical Encyclopedia of the Negro Baseball Leagues* (New York: Carroll & Graf, 1994), 198.

6   "Monarchs to Start Training," *Kansas City Times*, April 2, 1924: 14.

7   "St. Louis Stars Capture Final with Memphis, 8-2," *St. Louis Globe-Democrat*, July 8, 1924: 18.

8   "St. Louis Stars Now in Their Winter Home," *St. Louis Argus*, October 31, 1924: 7.

9   "St. Louis Knocks Sox Off of White Socks," *California Eagle*, November 14, 2021: 7. Creacy followed a bases-clearing triple with a two-run single.

10   "Donaldson Says Stars Can Win Pennant," *St. Louis Argus*, November 14, 1924: 7.

11   "J. Bell Leading Hitter on St. Louis All-Stars," *St. Louis Argus*, December 26, 1924: 7.

12   "Stars Slam Walker and Trim Careyites," *St, Louis Globe-Democrat*, October 3, 1931: 7.

13   See, for instance, a game against the White Kings that the Giants won, 8-4, in Los Angeles. James Newton, "Homers Win for Giants," *Pittsburgh Courier*, December 12, 1931: 16.

14   "Greys, Detroit to Merge; League Shifts Loom," *Pittsburgh Courier*, June 11, 1932: 15. See also Lewis Dial, "The Sport Dial," *New York Age*, June 18, 1932: 6. On his signing with the Pilots, see "Pilots Get a Clouter," *Washington Evening Star*, June 9, 1932: 43.

15   "Creacy Awarded to Philadelphia Stars by Judge Wilson," *Pittsburgh Courier*, March 24, 1934: 14. Creacy was also required to settle any financial obligations due Cleveland.

16   The phrase came from Chester L. Washington, "East, West Cross Bats," *Pittsburgh Courier*, August 10, 1935: A4. In 1933 Creacy had led in the voting for the West team right up until near the end, but did not appear in that game, either. In 1935 Creacy was listed as the likely starter in the August 10 editions of both the *Courier* and the *Chicago Defender*. On the morning of the game, the August 11 *Chicago Tribune* had Ray Dandridge listed to start at third base. In the actual game, Jud Wilson played third, rather than at first base, where he had been the leading vote-getter, while the Brooklyn Eagles' George Giles played first. Why Creacy did not play is unclear.

17   Randy Dixon, "The Sports Bugle," *Pittsburgh Courier*, January 20, 1940: 17.

18   See advertisement on page 12 of the May 31, 1956, *California Eagle*.

JAKE DUNN

By Jeb Stewart

Jake Dunn was a versatile middle infielder and out-fielder who played in the Negro leagues for parts of 11 seasons, from 1930 to 1943. He was a right-handed-hitting contact hitter who stood 5-feet-11 and weighed a solid 190 pounds.[1] He also served as a player-manager late in his career.

Joseph Phillip Dunn Jr. was born on November 5, 1909, in Luther, Oklahoma. A 1910 Census record covering the city listed "mulatto" as the race for both of his parents, Joseph Phillip Sr. and Annie, both of whom were born in Tennessee.[2] His father worked as a farmer and his mother was a farm laborer. Dunn had six older siblings including four sisters (Ethel, Lydia, Zelia Aster, and Vern Christina) and two brothers (Clyde and Kermitt).

By 1930, the family had relocated to Los Angeles, where his father found work as a night watchman in a cotton oil mill[3] before later returning to farming.[4] While details regarding the family's decision to leave Oklahoma have been lost to history, they did so several years before the Dust Bowl forced thousands of others to abandon the Great Plains in search of new opportunities in the West.

Little is known about Dunn's upbringing, education, or how he got interested in baseball. An April 1930 Census record from Los Angeles County noted that he had attended school within the previous year and was working as a laborer at an oil mill.[5]

Dunn probably got his start in professional baseball as a left fielder and shortstop with the Philadelphia (sometimes identified as hailing from Nashville) Royal Giants in 1930 in the California Winter League as a player named Dunn was mentioned in box scores.[6] Whether the player was Jake Dunn is uncertain, but it would have made sense. First, the Giants often played home games at White Sox Park in the Boyle Heights section of Los Angeles, which was not far from his home.[7] Second, there is a record of a Jake Dunn who played the following winter for Nashville, hitting .322 with five home runs.[8]

By early May of 1930, the 20-year-old had impressed the Detroit Stars enough to join the team in the Negro National League (NNL). In his first appearance in a box score, Dunn immediately had an impact as he had a home run and a double as the Stars' starting shortstop.[9] The next month he had four hits in five trips to the plate, including a double and a triple, against the St. Louis Stars.[10] According to the same report, "[h]is play in the field was sparkling."[11]

In August Dunn led the Stars to four straight wins over the visiting Birmingham Black Barons at Hamtramck Stadium. In one of the games, which the Stars won 14-3, Dunn pounded out three hits, including a triple.[12] In another contest in the series, "Dunn got three hits in four trips, a double, triple, and home run, and helped to drive most of Detroit's tallies across the plate" in a 10-1 win.[13] Although newspapers did not report most of Detroit's games, Dunn's strong hitting was evident in the box scores that did appear.[14]

Gary Ashwill

Rightfielder Jake Dunn

75

Dunn batted .283 for Detroit and tied Crush Holloway for the team lead in games played with 71.[15] He finished second on the team in RBIs (39) and stolen bases (8) and hit three home runs as the Stars finished 52-37 and won the NNL second-half title.

In the playoffs, Detroit fell to St. Louis in an exciting series, four games to three. Based on the available box scores and game accounts, Dunn batted .308 for the series. In three of the games his performance was notable. In Game One, he had a double in two at-bats in a 5-4 loss.[16] The next day he contributed a hit and helped turn a triple play to end the game in a wild 11-7 win.[17] In Game Five, "[a]lthough [Willie] Wells and [Mule] Suttles hit home runs, Dunn, the Detroit shortstop, was the batting star of the afternoon with three safeties in four trips to the plate."[18]

The St. Louis Stars repeated as champions of the NNL in 1931, while Detroit slipped into the second division with a disappointing losing record.[19] Dunn returned to play right field for the Philadelphia Royal Giants in the California Winter League,[20] but there is no record of his playing in the NNL in 1931. He may have spent the year barnstorming with the Los Angeles Colored Giants. One report noted that "Dunn was a shortstop for the Nashville Giants, but because of his heavy hitting and lightning speed the L.A. Giants made him over to a center-fielder."[21]

Dunn also returned to the California Winter League in 1931-32 as a left fielder with the Royal Giants.[22] He then signed with the Washington Pilots of the East-West League as a shortstop for the 1932 campaign.[23] With the Pilots, Dunn was regularly described as being flashy with his glove at shortstop.[24] He batted .302 for Washington and tied for second in the league with four home runs. Despite his efforts, the Pilots foundered and finished in sixth place with a disappointing 17-30 record.

The following year, Dunn played for two teams in the new Negro National League II (NNL2), the Baltimore Black Sox and the Nashville Elite Giants.[25] He appeared in 25 games for Baltimore, where he led the club with a .392 batting average and a 154 OPS+,[26] but played in only six games with Nashville.[27] His combined .367 batting average was good for fifth in the NNL2 and was the highest for his career.

In May a report stated that the Black Sox had signed Dunn to play shortstop.[28] However, in the same month, his name also appeared in game stories as being a member of the Elite Giants.[29] With Nashville, he showed off his versatility, playing second and third base as well as center field.[30] It is unclear how the Elite

Giants obtained Dunn, but, by mid-June, he rejoined Baltimore after he had "deserted the club earlier in the season."[31] It appears Dunn stayed with the Black Sox for the rest of 1933.[32] However, Baltimore's owner, Joe Cambria, apparently wanted Dunn to integrate another team he owned, the Albany Senators of the International League. Jesse "Mountain" Hubbard recalled:

> Joe Cambria owned the Baltimore Black Sox, and he also owned the white team in Albany, New York. Hack Wilson played for him in Albany.
>
> The Black Sox that year had a shortstop named Jake Dunn, a great hitter and an arm out of this world. Best looking young boy you've seen in a long time playing short. Jake was lighter than you are, and Joe Cambria wanted him to go up there to Albany and play for the white team. But Jake wouldn't go, said he wouldn't leave his wife. His wife was black.
>
> I said, 'Leave your wife, you'll be coming here every now and then to play. Shoot man, go up there and play with that white team.'
>
> But he said, 'Aw, I want my wife to be with me, and they'll find out I'm colored.' Instead he went to Puerto Rico, him and Slim Jones, and he won medals for being the best shortstop and Slim Jones for pitching the most scoreless innings and striking out the most men.[33]

Dunn played well enough to appear on the all-star ballot as a member of the Black Sox.[34] He finished second in fan voting for shortstop behind Dick Lundy on the East squad in the East-West All-Star Game, which was played at Comiskey Park in Chicago.[35] Columnist W. Rollo Wilson rated Dunn as his top choice at shortstop for the East squad.[36]

By February of 1934, Ed Bolden's Philadelphia Stars agreed to join the NNL2.[37] Dunn, now 24, was listed among the players being targeted to join the Stars.[38] His signing was confirmed by the *Philadelphia Tribune* on February 15, 1934.[39]

In April Philadelphia opened the 1934 campaign with an integrated game against Wentz-Olney in front of 3,000 fans on a Sunday, thanks to the repeal of a blue law. Dunn, playing right field for the Stars, went 2-for-5 with an RBI in the 10-4 win.[40] On the field, he completed a double play by throwing out a runner at home to prevent another run.[41]

For the season, Dunn batted .278 and led the Stars with 43 runs batted in and 7 triples. Among Dunn's highlights for 1934 were the following:

- On April 25, he had two hits, including a homer, in the Stars' sweep of Meadowbrook.[42]
- He had two hits, including a double and triple, in a 12-0 win over Meadowbrook in May.[43]
- Dunn had three hits and scored three runs in a doubleheader against Meadowbrook in June.[44]
- He had four hits and scored twice in a 16-6 win over the Germantown Artisans in an exhibition game in June.[45]
- He pounded out another four hits in a 10-9 win over the Homestead Grays on July 1.[46]
- He had three hits and scored two runs in a doubleheader sweep of the Nashville Giants on July 13.[47]
- A week later, he doubled off Satchel Paige to break up a scoreless tie in the fifth inning against the Pittsburgh Crawfords, and added another hit in the Stars' 2-1 win.[48]
- He had three hits in a doubleheader split with the New York Black Yankees on July 22.[49]
- He added three hits against the Bacharach Giants on July 29 in the first game of Philadelphia's City Championship series.[50]
- On August 4, he had three more hits in a wild 19-14 win over the Baltimore Black Sox.[51]
- On September 7, he again had three hits and scored a run in the Stars' 2-1 win over Chicago.[52]

The Stars finished 39-18 in league play, which was the best winning percentage in the NNL2 (.684) and captured the second-half flag. They faced the first-half champions, the Chicago American Giants, in the NNL2 championship series. Before the series, columnist W. Rollo Wilson selected his "all-league" players at each position and was sufficiently impressed by Dunn's performance to name him as his starting right fielder, writing:

Right Field: Dunn, Stars. A sure fielder, a fast man and the best arm in the outfield, he was a consistent hitter in the second half and draws the assignment over [Jimmie] Crutchfield, Crawfords; [Ted] Page, Crawfords, and Rap

Dixon, Baltimore Sox, whose early-season illness kept him from the regular ranks most of the year.[53]

The Stars won an exciting eight-game series over the American Giants for the championship of the NNL2, four games to three with one tie. Dunn hit a triple in the Stars' loss in Game Two,[54] but his biggest hit of the series came in Game Three. With the Stars trailing 3-1 in the fourth inning, and facing the prospects of a three-games-to-none series deficit, he hit a double, sparking a two-run rally.[55] The Stars went on to win the game, 5-3, which probably saved the series.[56]

However, the American Giants won Game Four, 2-1, forcing the Stars to win the final three games to win the series, which they did, 1-0, 4-1, and 2-0. In Game Eight, Dunn caught Dave Malarcher's fly ball to right to complete the Stars' comeback and clinch the NNL2 championship.

The next year, Dunn was cited as one of the players expected to return for the Stars, who were favored to repeat as NNL2 champions.[57] The *Pittsburgh Courier* repeated the boastful assessment of one Stars fan who had proclaimed "that Ed Bolden's Philadelphia Stars of 1935 is the greatest colored combination ever to represent Philly."[58] The paper also cited Dunn's hitting and versatility in the field as being one of the keys to the Stars' expected success, writing:

It is doubtful if any Bolden-owned club has been better prepared for infield and outfield emergencies. The Stars are fortunate in having two men like Jud Wilson and Jake Dunn on the squad. Both can play around the inner cordon or man the outer walls. And both lug hefty willows to the platter.[59]

In the early spring the Stars lived up to their billing as the team raced to an 8-0 record in exhibition games.[60] For his part, Dunn went 5-for-11 with a double in a two-game sweep of the Bay Parkways.[61]

Just as the NNL2 schedule was getting underway, Dunn was mentioned as the postscript to a bizarre murder-suicide story. Dorothy Dunn was living with her mother, Murial Robinson, and her new stepfather, Henry Clare, in Los Angeles.[62] Clare suspected his wife was being unfaithful and, in a fit of rage, shot her with his pistol before shooting himself in the head.[63] According to the *California Eagle,* "Mrs. Dorothy Dunn, the married daughter, is the wife of the famous ball player, Jake Dunn, who usually played shortstop for the Royal Giants winter league team for several seasons past at White Sox park."[64]

On the other side of the country, Philadelphia failed to live up to the lofty expectations of sportswriters. The Stars fell to fourth place in the NNL2 with a disappointing 37-34-4 record.

However, Dunn, who was now 25, had an exceptionally good year at the plate, batting .321 with an OPS+ of 124. He also posted the highest on-base and slugging percentages of his career. He tied Ted Page for most runs scored on the club with 41, and led the Stars with 30 walks. In a 9-0 win over the Pittsburgh Crawfords in May, he collected four hits.[65] Late in the summer, in a doubleheader against the House of David, Dunn had eight hits in 10 at-bats and reportedly played outstanding defense as a shortstop.[66] Fans noticed his performance and he finished second behind only Martín Dihigo in voting for right field in the 1935 East-West Game.[67]

By 1936, Dunn, who had a lifetime batting average of .302 entering the season and was just 26 years old, should have been in the prime of his career. Once again, expectations were high for him and the Stars. Cum Posey observed that "[the] Philadelphia Stars will again have a strong club. ... Any club which has Wilson, [Roy] Parnell, [Lloyd] Davenport and Dunn must be reckoned as hard to beat."[68] *Brooklyn Times Union* columnist Irwin Rosee was even more effusive with his praise, writing:

> The Philly Stars will come to Dexter Park Sunday with their strongest team in history. For pitchers they have Stuart (Slim) Jones, Satchell Paige's closest rival; Willie Hunter, Tommy Thompson, Ellis Yokely and Manager Webster MacDonald. They also have one of the greatest colored infielders in Jake Dunn and two top-flight outfielders in Turkey Stearns, the Babe Ruth of colored baseball, and Roy Parnell.[69]

Despite Dunn's two hits in the opening game in Brooklyn, the Bushwicks rallied from a 5-4 deficit in the bottom of the ninth to defeat the Stars, 6-5.[70] The Stars brushed off the defeat and started the season 12-5; they were leading the NNL2 standings on June 13.[71] However, they eventually collapsed and finished in last place.

Dunn, who played mostly as a shortstop and second baseman, was one of the few bright spots for Philadelphia in 1936. On July 18 he had three hits, including two doubles, in a 10-9 win over the Homestead Grays.[72] He stayed hot for two months from July 11 to September 12, batting .303.[73] He finished with a respectable batting average of .287, but his decline had begun.

Dunn's fortunes mirrored Philadelphia's performance as the Stars failed to win an NNL title from 1936 to 1940 and finished above .500 only once. Based on the available statistics, which may not tell the complete story, Dunn's offensive skills also sagged significantly over the same time frame. His batting average plummeted to .255 and his OPS+ fell well below the league average every year from 1936 to 1940.

Even so, there were still some bright spots as Dunn's career began to wind down. He was chosen to play as a reserve in the East-West Game in 1937 and 1938. In 1937 Dunn finished fourth in the fan voting as a center fielder,[74] but he appeared in the game at second base for the East, drawing a walk in two plate appearances in the East's 7-2 win in Comiskey Park.[75]

In 1938 Dunn he finished seventh in voting as a shortstop[76] but was added to the East team as a utility infielder, reportedly batting .317 with 9 home runs.[77] Two weeks before the game, Dunn homered off Jonas Gaines of the Baltimore Elite Giants in the Stars' 7-3 win at the dedication of Randall's Island Stadium.[78] In the East-West Game, the East trailed 5-4 in the ninth inning. Dunn nearly sparked a rally with his one-out single. However, Double Duty Radcliffe was able to pitch out of trouble to complete the West's triumph.[79]

For Dunn, 1938 was a disappointment as he batted only .251 with an 83 OPS+. While Philadelphia managed to finish in second place with a 41-32-3 record, the Stars were a distant 9½ games behind Homestead. There were no NNL2 playoffs that year.

Through the first half of the 1939 campaign, the Stars limped to an 11-17-1 record. Hoping a change might spark his team, Bolden named Dunn as his new player-manager in place of Jud Wilson.[80] Russ J. Cowans reported the news in his column:

> In an effort to keep alive the interest in baseball, it has been very low recently, Ed Bolden, owner of the Hillsdale Stars, has demoted Jud Wilson as manager of the Philadelphia team, and elevated Jake Dunn to that exalted position.
>
> Jake, a mild-mannered young chap, has been alternating in the infield and outfield for the Stars for the past six or seven years. He came out of the west by the way of Detroit.

Dunn came to Detroit in 1923, an eighteen-year-old short stop who had made a remarkable record in California. Steve Pierce, then owner of the Detroit Stars, had seen Jake scoop up hot grounders and tear the hide off the ball, before leaving California to take over the Detroit team.

Jake was unable to displace Arvil [sic] Riggins, then in the short field position for the Stars, and the following year joined with the teams in the East.

A little erratic in his field, Dunn made himself a favorite with the Detroit fans with his heavy hitting. Add to this Jake's fine sportsmanship, both on and off the field, and it can be readily understood why he was so well liked by the Detroit fans.[81]

With Dunn at the helm, Philadelphia fared better. The Stars won nine out of 11 games and newspapers cited the "… improved style of play under Jake Dunn,"[82] as being "responsible for the climb of the Stars since he took over the managerial duties."[83] Dunn also contributed as a hitter. In a win over the New York Black Yankees, he homered twice in the seventh inning, tying an NNL2 record set by Josh Gibson.[84] Despite the improvement, Philadelphia finished the second half with a 13-12 record and an overall fifth-place finish.

That winter, Dunn sharpened his managerial skills as the skipper of the Philadelphia Royal Giants in the California Winter League. Early in the season, "he read the 'riot act' to his [players]" and "threatened to send any weak hitter home if he did not improve his batting eye."[85] The Giants won the league title and Dunn led the league in hitting with a .350 average and tied for the league lead in homers.[86]

Entering 1940, Dunn agreed to return and manage the Stars but was "luke warm to retaining the post," according to columnist Randy Dixon of the *Pittsburgh Courier*.[87] By April, both Chester L. Washington and Cum Posey reported that Bolden had to find a new manager to replace Dunn, who had suddenly abandoned his post and signed to play in Mexico.[88] Dunn played in 16 games for the Diablos Rojos del México in the Mexican League, hitting just .188, and also appeared in one game for La Junta de Nuevo Laredo.

Back in Philadelphia, Roy Parnell soon replaced Dunn as the manager, although newspapers continued to include Dunn's name on the Stars' roster.[89] By June,

Dunn returned to manage the Stars. Columnist Russ J. Cowans reflected on the development, but did not attempt to reconcile whether Dunn had deserted the club as Posey had reported:

> Roy Parnell, who was placed in the driver's seat at the beginning of the current season, had not been able to inject an aggressive spirit among the players, and, consequently, the club is down in the league standing. So Jake is back as manager.
>
> Jake Dunn is a credit to baseball. He had always displayed the type of clean sportsmanship which makes him a model for the young ball players to pattern after.[90]

The Stars were 5-7 (.417) under Parnell and 26-33 (.441) under Dunn, finishing a forgettable fifth in the NNL2 standings in 1940. Dunn's managing duties were soon behind him for good. Baseball historian James A. Riley noted, "Dunn was not comfortable in the manager's seat, and he asked to be relieved of the responsibility after the season."[91]

There is no record of Dunn appearing in any games with the Stars in 1941. The only evidence that he may have played for Philadelphia was a handful of newspaper stories in spring previews that listed him as an outfielder.[92] However, his name did not appear in any of the Stars' box scores that year.[93]

It appears that Dunn spent the entire NNL2 season in the Army.[94] Sometime in 1939, Dunn had registered for military service, listing "baseball player" as his usual occupation on his registration card. He noted that his place of employment was in Philadelphia, but listed an address in Los Angeles as his home. He identified his sister, Mrs. Verna Smith, as someone who would always know his address. Whether or not he was still married to Dorothy Dunn at this point is unknown, but they did get divorced at some point before his military service.[95]

An October newspaper article reported that Dunn had been inducted into the Army sometime in 1941 but had been released from duty due to his age; he returned to play in the California Winter League in October.[96] However, the league's schedule was cut short by the United States' entry into World War II,[97] and his professional baseball career was suddenly over at only 31.

In the spring of 1942 several newspapers reported that the New York Cubans had acquired Dunn.[98] On May 31 Yankee Stadium hosted a doubleheader showcasing four Negro League teams.[99] The Cubans faced the Newark Eagles in the second game. According to the box score, the center fielder for the Stars was "Dunn," who went 0-for-3 at the plate in the 8-3 defeat. However, the earlier newspaper reports citing "Jake Dunn" on the Cubans' roster were probably wrong. More than likely, the player was Alphonse Dunn, who was an outfielder with New York in 1942.

Instead of playing baseball in 1942, Dunn had returned to the Army, as "[he] was one of the first players from the Negro Leagues to enter military service after the bombing of Pearl Harbor."[100] He enlisted on April 25, 1941.[101] According to the Center for Negro League Baseball Research, he served in the Army from 1942 to 1945, as a private[102] However, he appeared in two games for the Stars in 1943, once at first base and another as a relief pitcher, perhaps while on leave. Additional details regarding his military career have not been uncovered.

After the war, Dunn may have attempted a brief comeback. On July 4, 1946, an advertisement appeared in the *California Eagle* for a game between the Oakland Larks and the Los Angeles White Sox that was scheduled for July 8 at Wrigley Field in the short-lived West Coast Colored Association.[103] The advertisement highlighted Dunn as one of the star players for the White Sox. Neither a box score nor a story of that game has been located. Notably, the teams had played a doubleheader in Oakland the day before the scheduled game in Los Angeles. Dunn did not appear in either box score.[104] Whether he ever appeared in a game with the White Sox will likely remain an unanswered question.

Dunn is not forgotten, but his contributions to the history of the Negro leagues have largely been overlooked. He does not have a player file with the National Baseball Hall of Fame Library.[105] He may not have been soft-spoken, but he was probably quiet around sportswriters; none of the newspaper sources in this biography include any direct quotes from him. While there have been many retrospective articles about the Negro Leagues, it does not appear he was ever featured in any stories while he was still alive. The details about his career in most books about the Negro Leagues are also sparse.

What is known about Dunn is that he was a solid if unspectacular .275 hitter and a reliable defensive player during his career in the Negro Leagues. He was also indefatigable as he continued to play baseball each winter (truly his "usual occupation") rather than taking a break.[106]

Dunn lived another 41 years after his playing days but his life after baseball is mostly a mystery. According to the 1950 Census, he married Jessie L. Dunn, and the couple resided in Los Angeles with his sister Verna.[107] He worked as a truck driver for a paper box company and his wife made rubber balls in a factory.[108] Dunn died on July 24, 1984, in Los Angeles at the age of 74, and is buried in Lincoln Memorial Park Cemetery in nearby Carson.[109]

In 2020, Major League Baseball announced that seven professional Negro Leagues that operated from 1920 to 1948 have been designated as major leagues.[110] Thus, Dunn has finally been recognized as a major leaguer for his decade in professional baseball.

Sources and Acknowledgments

All player statistics and team records were taken from Seamheads.com, except where otherwise indicated.

The author is grateful to James Tate, a member of the Historical Negro League Baseball Site, for responding to questions about Dunn. Rick Bush provided important details about Dunn's military service and wives. In addition, Gary Ashwill of Seamheads was generous to provide information regarding Dunn's 1933 season and his life after baseball. The author also appreciates editor Bill Nowlin's patience and helpful suggestions.

Notes

1   https://www.seamheads.com/NegroLgs/player.php?playerID=dunn-01jak.

2   Oklahoma. Logan County. 1910 U.S. Census.

3   California. Los Angeles County. 1930 US Census.

4   California. Los Angeles County. 1940 US Census.

5   California. Los Angeles County. 1930 US Census.

6   Hal Cwain, "Shells Win Over Royal Giants 5-2, Will Play Again Today," *Long Beach* (California) *Sun*, February 2, 1930: 11; "Crowded White Sox Park Sees The Nashville Royal Giants In Action," *California Eagle* (Los Angeles), October 24, 1930: 9.

7   "Shell Oils Nose Out Pirrone All-Stars, 6-5," *Long Beach Sun*, November 11, 1929: 11.

8   William F. McNeil, *The California Winter League: America's First Integrated Professional Baseball League* (Jefferson, North Carolina: McFarland Publishing, 2002), 148.

9   "St. Louis Stars Beat Detroit Team, 18 To 8, Then Lose, 10 To 1," *St. Louis Post-Dispatch*, May 5, 1930: 16.

10   "Stars Drop First To St. Louis Nine," *Detroit Free Press*, June 22, 1930: 18.

11   "Stars Drop First To St. Louis Nine."

12   "Stars Triumph And Retain Lead," *Detroit Free Press*, August 24, 1930: 19.

13   "Dunn's Slugging Helps Stars Win," *Detroit Free Press*, August 26, 1930: 17.

14   "Stars Drop Pair to Cuban Team, *Detroit Free Press*, May 14, 1930: 22 (two hits in the first game; and one hit in the second); "Stars Win First From Birmingham," *Detroit Free Press*, August 11, 1930: 15 (a double); "Stars Continue Winning Streak," *Detroit Free Press*, June 15, 1930: 19 (one hit); "Detroit Stars Win In Overtime Game," *Detroit Free Press*, August 31, 1930: 20 (three hits).

15 https://seamheads.com/NegroLgs/team. php?yearID=1930&teamID=DS&LGOrd=1&tab=bat&sort=SB_a. All statistics in this biography are from Seamheads or Retrosheet.org.

16 "Stars Win First Game of Negro World Series," *St. Louis Post-Dispatch*, September 14, 1930: 24.

17 "Triple Play End Stars' Rally And Detroit Wins, 11-7, Stars Continue Winning Streak," *St. Louis Star and Times*, September 16, 1930: 17.

18 "Stars take Lead In Title Series, *Detroit Free Press*, September 21, 1930: 52.

19 https://seamheads.com/NegroLgs/year.php?yearID=1931.

20 "Giants To Play Asahis Sunday In Stadium Mix," *Honolulu Star-Bulletin*, May 30, 1931: 11.

21 "L.A. Colored Giants Bringing up Good Outfit." *Ventura County Star* (Camarillo, California), August 21, 1931: 9.

22 "Colored Ball Club Billed for Sunday At Seaside Park," *Ventura County Star*, February 19, 1932: 7.

23 "Wolves To Meet Revamped Pilots," *Detroit Free Press*, June 30, 1932: 17; "Pilots Add Evans, Suttles, Eggleston; Balto. Going Strong," *Pittsburgh Courier*, June 19, 1932: 15.

24 "Fast Negro Clubs In Title Clashes," *Richmond Times Dispatch*, June 23, 1932: 8; "Suttles Stocks Up With New Bats As Pilots Prep For Craws Here," *Pittsburgh Courier*, July 2, 1932: 15.

25 James A. Riley, *The Biographical Encyclopedia of the Negro Baseball Leagues* (New York: Carroll & Graf Publishers, 1994), 257. Adding to the confusion, Riley noted that Dunn also played for the independent Philadelphia Stars in 1933 and Baseball Reference's Bullpen also makes this claim. Riley, 257; also see https://www.baseball-reference.com/bullpen/ Jake_Dunn. The author was unable to confirm this in news reports. However, Dunn does not appear on the Stars roster in Dick Clark and Larry Lester, *The Negro Leagues Book* (Cleveland: SABR, 1994), 113. Seamheads. com does not list Dunn as a member of the Stars in 1933 either. https:// seamheads.com/NegroLgs/team.php?yearID=1933&teamID=PS&LGOrd=2.

26 https://www.seamheads.com/NegroLgs/team. php?yearID=1933&teamID=SOX&LGOrd=1.

27 https://www.seamheads.com/NegroLgs/team. php?yearID=1933&teamID=NEG&LGOrd=1.

28 "Black Sox To Open Season Here Sunday with Pittsburghers," *Baltimore Evening Sun*, May 15, 1933: 21.

29 "Stars Shut Out Nashville Nine," *Detroit Free Press*, May 21, 1933: 18; "Nashville Loses To Stars Again," *Detroit Free Press*, May 23, 1933: 20; "Detroit Takes Nashville Series," *Pittsburgh Courier*, May 27, 1933: 15; "Elites Win First Tilt From Grays, 7-1," *Pittsburgh Courier*, June 10, 1933: 15.

30 "Stars Shut Out Nashville Nine"; "Detroit Takes Nashville Series"; "Elites Win First Tilt From Grays, 7-1."

31 "Sox Return Home Sunday; Hubbard After 2 Quakers," *Baltimore Evening Sun*, June 15, 1933: 29.

32 "Baltimore Sox Bow To Giants By 14-3," *Akron Beacon Journal*, July 7, 1933: 26; "Black Sox To Face Philadelphia Stars In Twin Attraction," *Baltimore Evening Sun*, July 28, 1933: 26; "No-hit Game Spoiled by Walt Rogers' Bat," *Central New Jersey Home News* (New Brunswick), August 17, 1933: 16; "Grays Top BlackSox, 10 To 6," *Pittsburgh Courier*, August 26, 1933: 14; "Baltimore Sox Beaten In 16-Inning Thriller," *Baltimore Sun*, September 4, 1933: 8.

33 John B. Holway, *Black Giants* (Springfield, Virginia: Lord Fairfax Press, 2010), 33.

34 "Here You Are, Fans! Take Your Pick Of The All-Star Teams For The Chicago Classic," *Pittsburgh Courier*, August 5, 1933: 15.

35 "The East-West Game Player Vote," *Pittsburgh Courier*, September 9, 1933: 15.

36 W. Rollo Wilson, "Sport Shots," *Pittsburgh Courier*, August 12, 1933: 14.

37 "Baseball Men Meet In Philly; Favor League," *Baltimore Afro-American*, February 17, 1934: 19.

38 "Blacksox, Grays Not Included, Seek 7th Club," *Pittsburgh Courier*, February 17, 1934: 14.

39 "Baseball Magnates Convene In Parley Here," *Philadelphia Tribune*, February 15, 1934: 1.

40 "Bolden's Stars Swamp W. Olney In First Game," *Pittsburgh Courier*, April 14, 1934: 12.

41 "Bolden's Nine Wins Sunday's Ball Opening," *Chicago Defender*, April 14, 1934: 17.

42 "Bolden's Stars Win 2 From Newark," *Philadelphia Tribune*, April 26, 1934: 12.

43 "Stars Topple Newark 12-0 For Initial Win," *Philadelphia Tribune*, May 17, 1934: 12

44 "Stars Divide Twin Bill After Losing Four In Row," *Philadelphia Tribune*, June 7, 1934: 12.

45 "Stars Trip Artisians In Frantic Fuss," *Philadelphia Tribune*, June 28, 1934: 12.

46 "Bolden Boys Trip Grays, 10-9, 6-2; Tie 1," *Philadelphia Tribune*, July 1934.

47 "Boldens Whip Nashville," *Chicago Defender*, July 14, 1934: 16.

48 W. Rollo Wilson, "Boldenmen Trip 'Craws' Twice to Take Top Run Of League Flag Ladder," *Pittsburgh Courier*, July 21, 1934: A4.

49 "Stars Win Five, Drop 2; Player Breaks Leg," *Philadelphia Tribune*, July 26, 1934: 12.

50 "Stars Drub Bees in City Series Start: Boldenboys Take Two Games," *Philadelphia Tribune*, August 2, 1934: 12.

51 "Balto. Black Sox Lose To Stars," *Philadelphia Tribune*, August 9, 1934: 12.

52 "Giants Lose To Philly; Then Tie 1-1," *Chicago Defender*, September 8, 1934: 17.

53 W. Rollo Wilson, "Baseball's Curtain Falling On Season," *Pittsburgh Courier*, September 15, 1934: A4.

54 "Giants, Stars Break Even In DoubleHeader," *Chicago Tribune*, September 17, 1934: 23.

55 "Giants Split With Philly Stars in Chicago Clash," *Baltimore Afro-American*, September 22, 1934: 21.

56 "Giants Split With Philly Stars in Chicago Clash."

57 Chester Washington, "Sez 'Ches,'" *Pittsburgh Courier*, January 19, 1935: 15.

58 "Better Than The Hilldale Club?," *Pittsburgh Courier*, June 8, 1935: 17.

59 "Philly Preps For Brooklyn Series," *Pittsburgh Courier*, May 11, 1935: 15.

60 "Philly Stars Thump Dukes In Twin Bill," *Brooklyn Times Union*, April 29, 1935: 13.

61 "Philly Stars Thump Dukes In Twin Bill."

62 "Kills Wife, Commits Suicide," *California Eagle*, May 10, 1935: 1-2.

63 "Kills Wife, Commits Suicide."

64 "Kills Wife, Commits Suicide." Details regarding Dunn's marriage to Dorothy have not been uncovered.

65 "Philadelphia All-Stars Shut Out Pittsburg Crawfords, 9-0," *York* (Pennsylvania) *Daily Record*, May 29, 1935: 10.

66   "Philadelphia Stars Carry Off Both Ends Of Doubleheader To Win Series," *York Daily Record*, September 21, 1935: 10.

67   "Shifts Seen Leaders as E-W Game Vote Spurts," *Pittsburgh Courier*, August 3, 1935: 14.

68   "Cum Posey's Painted Paragraphs," *Pittsburgh Courier*, April 25, 1936: 14.

69   Irwin N. Rosee, "Philly Star Nine Menaces Dexters," *Brooklyn Times Union*, April 29, 1936: 10.

70   Irwin N. Rosee, "Dexters Shine As Late Rally Tops Star Nine," *Brooklyn Times Union*, May 4, 1936: 11.

71   "League Standings," *Pittsburgh Courier*, June 13, 1936: 16.

72   "Grays Divide with Stars," *Pittsburgh Sun-Telegraph*, July 19, 1936: 16.

73   "Individual Batting Averages, Negro National League July 11-Sept. 12," *New York Age*, September 26, 1936: 9.

74   "Final East-West Game Vote," *Pittsburgh Courier*, Aug. 7, 1937: 18.

75   "Come East Young Man," *Pittsburgh Courier*, Aug. 14, 1937: 17.

76   Larry Lester, *Black Baseball's National Showcase, The East-West All-Star Game, 1933-1953* (Lincoln: University of Nebraska Press, 2001), 119.

77   "Here's The East's Line-Up For Dream Game," *Pittsburgh Courier*, August 20, 1938: 16.

78   "Many Organizations To Participate In Dedication of Randalls Island Stadium," *New York Age*, July 16, 1938: 8; "Byrd and Scales Hit First Home-Runs at Randalls Island Stadium – Philly Stars Win," *New York Age*, August 20, 1938: 8.

79   Lester, 114.

80   Russ J. Cowans, "Thru The Sports Mirror," *Detroit Tribune*, July 1, 1939: 7.

81   "Thru The Sports Mirror."

82   "Phila. Stars Aim To Win Two Tilts," *Philadelphia Inquirer*, July 8, 1939: 25.

83   "Tonight's Rival Has Been Tough Foe For Locals," *Delaware County Daily Times* (Chester, Pennsylvania), August 18, 1939: 13.

84   Chester L. Washington Jr. "Sez Ches," *Pittsburgh Courier*, September 9, 1939: 16.

85   "Roofers In Ball Bow Tomorrow," *Los Angeles Evening Citizen News,* October 21, 1939: 14.

86   McNeil, 199.

87   Randy Dixon, "The Sports B-U-G-L-E," *Pittsburgh Courier*, January 20, 1940: 17.

88   Cum Posey, "Newark Eagles Count on Rookies," *Pittsburgh Courier*, April 27, 1940: 16; Chester L. Washington, Jr. "Sez Ches," *Pittsburgh Courier*, Apr. 27, 1940: 16.

89   Cum Posey, "Posey's Points," *Pittsburgh Courier*, May 4, 1940: 16; "Braves Open Friday," *Long Branch* (New Jersey) *Daily Record,* May 27, 1940: 7; "Homestead Replaces Black Yankees On Belmar Schedule," *Red Bank* (New Jersey) *Daily Standard,* May 28, 1940: 16; "Braves Pitted Against Stars," *Asbury Park* (New Jersey) *Press,* June 4, 1940: 10; "Twin Bill Here Sunday," *Harrisburg* (Pennsylvania) *Telegraph,* June 8, 1940: 8.

90   Russ J. Cowans, "Thru The Sports Mirror," *Detroit Tribune*, June 15, 1940: 7.

91   Riley, 257.

92   "Bay Parkways Now To Battle Philly Stars," *Brooklyn Citizen*, May 1, 1941: 6; "Bay Parkways, Philly Stars To Play 2 Games," *Brooklyn Citizen*, May 3, 1941: 6; "Teams Well Matched," *York Observer*, May 27, 1941: 16; "Bushwicks, Parkways In Bulb Battle," *Brooklyn Daily Eagle*, June 20, 1941: 17; "Philly Stars Parkway Foes in 2 Tomorrow," *Brooklyn Daily Eagle*, June 21, 1941: 11.

93   "Cuban Stars Win Opener," *Philadelphia Inquirer*, May 11, 1941: 64; "Baltimore Beats Phila. Stars, 9-4," *Philadelphia Inquirer*, May 18, 1941: 40; "Stars Divide With Yanks," *Philadelphia Inquirer*, May 25, 1941: 40; "Roy Nassau, Memphis Nine Jolts Quaker City Rivals," *Harrisburg Telegraph*, August 13, 1941: 15; "Phila. Stars Jolt N.Y. Yanks, 6-0," *Philadelphia Inquirer*, September 1, 1941: 20.

94   Smith, 119.

95   California. Los Angeles County. 1950 US Census; United States World War II Army Enlistment Records, 1938-1946.

96   Cullen J. Fentress, "Down in Front," *California Eagle*, October 16, 1941: 13.

97   McNeil, 15.

98   "Negro Stars Fill Cubans Roster," *Chambersburg* (Pennsylvania) *Public Opinion,* May 22, 1942: 4; "Cuban Stars In Doubleheader," *Harrisburg Telegraph,* May 22, 1942: 14; "Present Judgment On Teams Of Coming Game," *Michigan Chronicle* (Detroit), May 30, 1942: 14; "Large Crowd Expected To See Two Games," *Michigan Chronicle*, June 6, 1942: 17.

99   "17,000 See Elite Giants And Newark Eagles Win At Stadium," *New York Age*, June 6, 1942: 11.

100   Riley, 257.

101   United States World War II Army Enlistment Records, 1938-1946.

102   http://www.cnlbr.org/Portals/0/RL/Served_in_WWII.htm; United States World War II Army Enlistment Records, 1938-1946.

103   "League Baseball," *California Eagle*, July 4, 1946: 14. The league was more commonly referred to as the West Coast Negro Baseball League.

104   "Larks In Double Win Over Sox," *Oakland Tribune*, July 8, 1946: 7.

105   Cassidy Lent, director, Library at the National Baseball Hall of Fame and Museum, email correspondence with author, May 16, 2022.

106   Against big-league teams in four exhibition games, Dunn batted .188 in 16 at bats. Todd Peterson, ed., *The Negro Leagues Were Major Leagues: Historians Reappraise Black Baseball* (Jefferson, North Carolina: McFarland & Company, Inc., 2020), 232.

107   California. Los Angeles County. 1950 US Census.

108   California. Los Angeles County. 1950 US Census.

109   Email from Gary Ashwill, April 7, 2022.

110   https://www.mlb.com/news/negro-leagues-given-major-league-status-for-baseball-records-stats.

ROCKY ELLIS

BY DAVE WILKIE

Rocky Ellis is one of the many Negro League players whose statistics tell only a fraction of the full story. Sandwiched between official league contests were the numerous battles against teams of varying skill. These games made up the meat of a player's diet but usually are not taken into consideration when the breadth of a career is examined. Nonetheless, it was in these games that a player's reputation, fan base, and livelihood often were built.

Ellis is best known for his tenure with Ed Bolden's Philadelphia Stars, and he made a name for himself pitching for the 1934 squad in the Negro National League II Championship Series. The diminutive, scrappy right-hander was described by his submarining teammate, Webster McDonald, as "a little guy with a big heart." McDonald also praised Ellis as one of the few pitchers who could get the mighty Josh Gibson out on a regular basis.[1]

Raymond Charles Ellis was born on January 26, 1911, in Darby, Pennsylvania. His father, Washington Ellis, was born in either 1871 or 1873 in Virginia as recorded by the 1910 and 1920 censuses respectively. His mother, Mary Hudson, was born in October of 1874, also in Virginia. The two were married on April 11, 1894, in Nottoway, Virginia, and had nine children together, including seven daughters – Mattie, Edna, Hannah, Lillie, Marion, Dorothy, and Jewcella – and two sons, George and Raymond. Raymond was born eighth of the nine children and a full 20 years separates the birth of their second child, Edna, and their last, George. Mysteriously, their first child, listed as Mattie Hill, was born in 1886, meaning that Mary, her mother, would have been 12 at the time of her birth. Mattie died in 1918 at the age of 32, and Washington and Mary Ellis are listed as her parents, but she is not mentioned in the 1900 or 1910 censuses as living with the couple.[2]

The *Philadelphia Tribune* described Ellis as "the peppy mascot" and "the youngster scurrying about the field" when Ellis toted bats for the legendary Hilldale clubs of the mid 1920s.[3] The 13-year-old Ellis had a front-row seat as the Hilldale Club, or Daisies as they were often called, played in the first two Negro League World Series, winning on their second try in 1925. As a 16-year-old in 1927, Ellis was inserted into left field in the seventh inning of an 11-3 blowout in a game against the Judy Gans All-Stars.[4] It was Ellis's first Negro League appearance. The following season, in 1928, he was given a chance to compete for a spot in the outfield, but opportunities were slim as stalwarts Oscar Charleston, Otto Briggs, Clint Thomas, and Bill Johnson all stood in his path.[5] Ellis was seldom used, as his two error-free innings in center field and a base hit in his lone plate appearance attest. The *Philadelphia Tribune* lauded Ellis as "roaming far and wide to show that he can play ball as well as perform mascot duties."[6] Ellis and two teammates were released by the club in late July for refusing to take their jobs seriously. Perhaps this is not too surprising, since Ellis was just 17 at the time.[7]

Pitcher Rocky Ellis

In May of 1928 Ellis signed on with one of the top Black semipro teams in Philadelphia, the Emerald Colts, but his time with the Colts was short-lived and by July he was a regular with the Inter-Urban Twilight League powerhouse Darby Phantoms.[8] Ellis found his footing with the Phantoms as evidenced by a two-game set played on October 6 in which he twirled a four-hit, 6-0 shutout against Colwyn in the early match and showed up in the second game in right field, smacking two hits in a surprise 6-6 tie with the far superior Hilldale Club.[9] Ellis was the team's vital cog and led it them to consecutive championships in 1929 and 1930. In the 1929 finale, he toed the rubber for the clincher against Sandy Conway's Colwyn team, coming through with a 3-2 complete-game victory in which he limited Colwyn to just three hits.[10] The following season's playoff performance was even more spectacular as Ellis took the hill for both games of a two-game sweep, once again against the Colwyn club, team, taking the first game, 7-3, and the clincher, 4-1, in the best-of-three series. Ellis allowed just six hits in the winner, chipped in with an RBI triple, and scored the winning run in the second inning of the contest.[11]

Showing off his athleticism, Ellis also spent some time on the gridiron in 1930 as he finished out the year with the Philadelphia-based Progressive Tornadoes. In a losing effort against a much better Mauch Chunk team, Ellis was praised for his effort at right halfback and punter.[12] Ellis returned his Phantoms baseball contract unsigned in 1931, but was back with his comrades by early summer. He played left field in a June 4 contest against Daugherty C.C. and rapped two hits in the matchup.[13]

White sports promoter, sporting goods owner, and Philadelphia native Harry Passon built Passon Field at 48th and Spruce Streets in Philadelphia to support his Philadelphia Bacharach Giants team in 1931; and, after his brief reunion with the Phantoms, Ellis signed on with the team. Passon Field was a state-of-the-art diamond that featured seats for 6,000 spectators and lights to support night baseball.[14] Ellis was in fine form on June 21 as he spun a complete-game seven-hitter in a 4-3 victory over a team from Camden, New Jersey.[15] Philadelphia Stars owner Ed Bolden, stating that the City of Brotherly Love could not support two Black teams, helped to block Passon's team from gaining admission to the Negro National League in 1931. Bolden's interference did not deter Passon, and his Bacharach Giants trudged forward during the 1931 season.[16] The Giants were finally granted admission into the NNL in 1934 but withdrew from the league the following season, citing violence at Passon Field as the cause. The team pressed on as a semipro squad until it finally disbanded subsequent to Passon's death in 1942.[17]

Ed Bolden took control of the Darby Phantoms prior to before the 1932 season in hopes of repeating the success he had experienced with Hilldale, which he had molded during the previous decade from a group of young amateurs into a high-class professional championship team.[18] Ellis rejoined the Phantoms for the third time as it was announced on April 5 that he was expected to report for the team's practice and begin the season on May 7.[19] The versatile Ellis shined early in the season, banging out two hits and playing left field in a loss to Chester. In a doubleheader vs. the Lancaster Red Sox, Ellis had two more safeties and recorded eight putouts at first base in the opener and played a flawless third base in the nightcap with three assists, although the Phantoms lost both games.[20] The Phantoms never lived up to Bolden's high hopes and struggled to compete with the semipro teams they lined up against.[21] Bolden abandoned the Phantoms after the season, leaving them in the lurch and without direction. By early 1933, he was openly advertising his newly formed Philadelphia Stars team. Bolden asserted that he would "land a team which will make the city forget its baseball headaches of recent seasons."[22]

Ellis was not prepared to rejoin a Bolden-owned team just yet. Instead, he suited up for the Brooklyn Cuban Giants, playing out of Reading, Pennsylvania, in 1933.[23] After an August 16 game against the Waterville All-Stars, the *Waterville* (Maine) *Morning Sentinel* praised Ellis, declaring, "[T]his Ellis is just about as classy a pitcher as ever invaded this fair town. The smoke artist had a barrel of speed, he was rifling 'em up like cannonfire, the pellet looked like a pea, and he had control aplenty." Ellis completed the game, surrendering just two hits in a lopsided 11-1 victory.[24] Ellis finished out the year in style, traveling to Puerto Rico to play for the eventual championship team, Estrellas de Ramirez. The loaded team featured Josh Gibson, Rap Dixon, Ted Page, Jim Williams, and Bill Holland.[25] W. Rollo Wilson of the *Pittsburgh Courier* declared that "the two best pitchers in Porto Rico last winter were Slim Jones and Rocky Ellis."[26] Both pitchers joined Ed Bolden and his Philadelphia Stars for the 1934 campaign in the Negro National League II (NNL2).

Ed Bolden, ever the marketing genius, used the Black press to help promote his newly minted Philadelphia Stars in their inaugural season of 1933.

Players came from far and wide to join his new club, including veterans Biz Mackey, Jud Wilson, Dick Lundy, Rap Dixon, and Webster McDonald.[27] The Stars began as an independent team that maiden season but were granted admission into the NNL2 in 1934, to compete against such legendary teams as the Pittsburgh Crawfords and Chicago American Giants. Thanks to Ellis's penchant for never straying far from Philadelphia, his first season in the NNL2 coincided with the Stars' magical championship ride of 1934.

In what may have been Ellis's first appearance for the Stars, he started and pitched the first three innings of an April 15, 1934, victory over the Raphael team that had won the previous year's Philadelphia League championship. The Stars won the game, 9-3, and Ellis struck out three batters in his three innings of work.[28] The grand opening of the NNL2 season took place on May 13 in Newark, New Jersey, with a doubleheader matchup against Dick Lundy's Newark Dodgers. Ellis was in fine form in the nightcap, restricting Newark to three hits in a 4-1 complete-game victory after hurler Lefty Holmes had taken the first game, 5-4, with Slim Jones finishing out the ninth inning.[29] Holmes and Ellis traded places in a June 24 double bill against the Cleveland Red Sox. Ellis won the first game, 2-1, limiting Cleveland to six hits and outdueling eight-time all-star Bill Byrd, while Holmes captured the second game in a 9-0 laugher.[30]

The Stars' biggest rival in 1934 was the Pittsburgh Crawfords, a team that featured five future Hall of Famers and whose spectacular 47-27-3 record was just barely eclipsed by the Philadelphia squad. On July 12 Ellis was on the winning side of a gutsy 7-6 contest against the Craws in which he went the distance while surrendering 10 hits and outlasting Pittsburgh starter Sam Streeter to salvage a split of that day's doubleheader.[31] Ellis' dominance continued on July 18 in a 7-1 drubbing of the NNL2 rival Nashville Elite Giants, led by Candy Jim Taylor.[32]

In what turned out to be a Championship Series preview, the Stars took on the Chicago American Giants on July 28 and Ellis limited the Windy City gang to seven hits in a 9-3 victory.[33] Dave Malarcher's Chicago American Giants, led by future Hall of Famers Turkey Stearnes, Willie Wells, Willie Foster, and Mule Suttles, secured a spot in the championship series by winning the first half of the NNL2 campaign. The hard-luck Pittsburgh Crawfords had a far superior overall record than Chicago but could not manage to capture either half of the season as the Stars took the league's second-half title.

When manager and pitcher Webster McDonald credited Ellis as the guy who "won the championship for us" in 1934, he was probably referring to Ellis's masterful Game Five performance.[34] Down three games to one to the American Giants and facing elimination against Rube Foster's brother, future Hall of Famer Willie Foster, Ellis twirled the game of his life, going the distance with nine strikeouts in a 1-0 masterpiece. The Stars took Games Six and Eight (Game Seven ended in a tie) and finished off the Giants to take home the championship.

The 23-year-old Ellis threw 18⅔ innings in the series, giving up 14 hits with 16 strikeouts and a 2.41 ERA. Notably, he was also the recipient of a fair amount of luck as he also allowed 10 free passes.

The team celebrated its victory at the O.V. Catto Elks Lodge, an all-Black fraternal order in South Philadelphia that also served as a dance hall and boxing and wrestling club. The *Philadelphia Tribune* singled out Ellis and teammate Jake Stephens, observing that "the boys were so happy that their smiles never left their faces till after two in the morning."[35]

The following season was a letdown for the Stars, who could not quite keep up with the powerful Crawfords. Ellis remained in fine form, though, and was praised early in the season by the *Chicago Defender*, which wrote that he had "profited much by last year's experience and will be one of the best curve ball throwers in the loop."[36] It was not the only time Ellis's curve drew attention that season as the *Norfolk (Virginia) New Journal and Guide* noted in early June that "Rocky Ellis has a sharp-breaking curve and speed a'plenty."[37] Ellis got the nod on Opening Day and pitched seven strong innings in securing a 7-5 win against the Brooklyn Eagles. He also socked one over the left-field fence for a third-inning home run for the victors.[38]

The Stars were never able to recapture the glory of their 1934 championship season, and the 1936 squad tumbled all the way to last place in the NNL2. The juxtaposition between Ellis's official records and what was reported by the newspapers at the time is difficult to sort out. In early July the *Delaware County Daily Times* said of Ellis: "He is recognized as one of the aces of the National Negro League and has been defeated only twice this season."[39] This seems to suggest that Ellis performed much better against nonleague teams, although he did enjoy some success against top clubs. In a career highlight on May 17, Ellis outdueled Satchel Paige and the defending champion Pittsburgh Crawfords by a score of 6-2. It is also noted that the Stars took sole possession of first place on this date.[40] A seven-inning, two-hit triumph vs. the New York Black Yankees on September 17, followed by a 10-strikeout, six-hit, 5-3 win over the Nashville Elite Giants more than solidified Ellis's worth to the team.[41]

In a tough loss to the Pittsburgh Crawfords on September 26, 1936, Ellis was literally knocked out of the game by Crawfords shortstop Chester Williams. *Pittsburgh Courier* writer W.B. Wilson painted the picture:

> Now Rocky has been one pitcher whom Ches has always had trouble hitting but Saturday he hit him – several ways. Taking an extra tug on his pants the Louisiana boy slammed one of Rocky's fast ones back at him and almost tore his right foot off, the batted ball bounding across the foul line at third base. The next time up Ches hit another one which nearly amputated Ellis' left pedal, this time the ball rebounding towards first base. That was enough for Rocky. After being given first aid by the club trainer, he limped from the field, absolutely through for the day.[42]

Ellis was also married in 1936, to 26-year-old Ophelia Sparrow in Philadelphia.[43]

The remainder of the decade provided few highlights for the Stars and a distant second-place finish to the powerful Homestead Grays in 1938 was the closest they came to a return to the playoffs. Ellis was still a respected pitcher as was evidenced by the fact that the *Philadelphia Tribune* exclaimed in early 1938 that he was a "mighty powerhouse despite his slight stature."[44] White sportswriter Jimmy Powers campaigned for Ellis by name – as well as for other Negro League players – in a column in July, his *New York Daily News* column titled "The Powerhouse," stating that they were baseball stars who could help the struggling Brooklyn Dodgers.[45]

At some point during the 1939 season, Ellis was banned from baseball for his refusal to accept a trade to the Homestead Grays. He eventually relented and reported to the Grays for the 1940 season after having taken another winter trip to Puerto Rico to play for the Caguas Criollos.[46]

The Homestead Grays were league champions of the NNL2 in 1940, but unfortunately Ellis was not with the team at the end of the season to enjoy the spoils. The *Pittsburgh Courier* had called him "one of the best right-handers in Negro baseball" during his stint with the Grays and he had been firmly entrenched in

the starting rotation throughout most of the summer.[47] In a game on June 1, Ellis made his presence known from the coaching box, rather than the mound, in a game against his former team, the Philadelphia Stars. On a heads-up play while coaching first base for the Grays in the fifth inning, Ellis yelled to first baseman Buck Leonard, "[T]hrow the ball to second, Buck," after noticing that baserunner Bill Cooper had failed to touch second base on his return trip to first after a long fly out. Cooper was called out on the play and the Grays won the game, 5-2.[48] Ellis was back with the Stars by late August. In a doubleheader against the Memphis Red Sox on September 7, he struggled but managed to pull out a 10-5 victory while scattering 10 hits. In the nightcap he played left field and batted ninth.[49]

Ellis began the 1941 season with the Brooklyn Royal Giants, a team without a home that traveled across the country in style in their special deluxe bus. The team had journeyed over 30,000 miles the previous season, and Ellis was now along for the ride.[50] By all accounts, he held his own and was pitching well in July with complete-game victories over the Collingswood All-Stars and the Red Bank Pirates.[51] It was also reported that Ellis defeated the Candy Jim Taylor-led Chicago American Giants that summer.[52]

Dr. Joseph Henry Thomas had created a paradise for Black entertainment just eight miles out of Baltimore in Turner Station, Maryland, in 1929. It featured an amusement park, a concert pavilion, restaurants, and a beach, but what probably landed Rocky Ellis in 1942 was the 5,000-seat covered grandstand with all the modern conveniences not usually available to Black ballplayers. His team, the Baltimore Grays, sprang up in 1935 and in 1942 the squad was part of the Negro Major League, a short-lived rival of the Negro American and National Leagues.[53] The Grays, managed by standout catcher Mickey Casey, demolished the Richmond Hilldales 12-3 on June 7 thanks to a 5-hit complete game victory by Ellis.[54] The unstoppable Grays later defeated the Cincinnati Ethiopian Clowns on July 6 for their 16th victory in 17 games.[55]

Rocky Ellis enlisted in the US Army on June 15, 1942, effectively ending his baseball career. He served in both World War II and in Korea and rose to the rank of master sergeant during his 20 years of service. He was discharged on July 31, 1962, and was living in Richmond, Virginia, by 1985, a city that his parents no doubt had been familiar with.[56] His wife, Ophelia Sparrow, passed away in 1985 in Philadelphia. Ellis is listed as widowed on his death certificate, but his wife's name is mentioned as Evelyn Ellis. It is unknown if he remarried or if this was another name for Ophelia. Rocky Ellis died from aspiration pneumonia due to sepsis on November 15, 1989, at the Metropolitan Hospital in Richmond. He is buried at Evergreen Cemetery, a historical African American cemetery in Richmond.[57]

Rocky Ellis sports a meager 24-24 record in Negro major-league games for his baseball career, but it is obvious that his stamp on the game was much more indelible than that. At the very least, his six years with the storied Philadelphia Stars, when he was often ranked as one of the top pitchers in the league, and his short stints with acclaimed teams like the Homestead Grays and Brooklyn Royal Giants hint at his greatness. Ellis was only 31 when he left baseball in 1942 to join the war, but from his humble beginnings as a 13-year-old Hilldale batboy to his final pitch for the Baltimore Grays, his almost 20 years in the game should ensure that he will always be remembered.

SOURCES

All statistics, unless otherwise noted, are from Seamheads.com.

NOTES

1   John Holway, *Voices From the Great Black Baseball Leagues* (New York: Da Capo Press, Inc., 1992), 83.

2   Ancestry.com.

3   *Philadelphia Tribune*, December 29, 1927: 10.

4   "Stars Beaten as Hilldalers Slug the Ball," *Philadelphia Tribune*, September 22, 1927: 11.

5   "Charleston and Dalty Cooper Sign With Hilldale," *Pittsburgh Courier*, March 31, 1928: 16.

6   "Bolden's Pets Wreck House of David," *Philadelphia Tribune*, July 5, 1928: 11.

7   "Hilldale Players Released," *Pittsburgh* Courier, July 28, 1928: A4.

8   "Ellis and Thorpe on Elmwood Nine," *Philadelphia Tribune*, May 9, 1929: 10; "Phantoms Tie For Lead in League Race," *Philadelphia Tribune*, July 11, 1929: 10.

9   "Phantoms Win and Tie," *Philadelphia Inquirer*, October 6, 1929: 6.

10   "Darby Phantoms Win League Flag," *Baltimore Afro American*, September 21, 1929: 15.

11   "Rocky Ellis Bright Star as Darby Boys Clout Way to Suburban Loop Crown," *Philadelphia Tribune*, September 25, 1930: 10; "Darby Phantoms Win Interurban Title," *Delaware County Daily Times* (Chester, Pennsylvania), September 22, 1930: 12.

12   "Progressives Bend Knee at Mauch Chunk," *Philadelphia Tribune*, October 30, 1930: 10; "Colored Pro team Defeated by 38-6," *Baltimore Afro-American*, November 1, 1930: 16.

13   "Interurban League," *Philadelphia Inquirer*, June 5, 1931: 20.

14   Euell A. Nielsen, "The Bacharach Giants (1916-1929) (1931-1941)," December 1, 2020 https://www.blackpast.org/african-american-history/the-bacharach-giants-1916-1929-1931-1941/. Accessed February 22, 2023.

15   "Steele, Woodington Share Pitching Honors," *Camden* (New Jersey) *Morning Post*, June 22, 1931: 13.

16   Nielsen, "The Bacharach Giants (1916-1929) (1931-1941)."

17   Nielsen.

18   Courtney Michelle Smith, *Ed Bolden and Black Baseball in Philadelphia* (Jefferson, North Carolina: McFarland & Company, Inc., 2017), 64.

19   "Brice to Captain Darby Phantoms," *Delaware County Daily Times*, April 5, 1932: 11.

20   "Chester Tops Darby Phantoms," *Delaware County Daily Times*, May 9, 1932: 13; "2 Local Boys Play With Sox," *Lancaster* (Pennsylvania) *New Era*, May 9, 1932: 1.

21   Smith, 64.

22   Smith, 70.

23   "Rady Says: Editor," *Philadelphia Tribune*, May 25, 1933: 11.

24   "Cubans Win Easily, 11-1," *Waterville* (Maine) *Morning Sentinel*, August 17, 1933: 3.

25   "Rady Says: Baseball in Puerta Rica," *Philadelphia Tribune*, April 12, 1934: 10.

26   "Sports Shots: Press Box and Ring Side Here's Your Old Col Again," *Pittsburgh Courier*, May 5, 1934: A4.

27   Smith, 69-70.

28   "Philly Stars Crush Raphael," *Baltimore Afro-American*, April 21, 1934: 18.

29   "Philadelphia Stars Win 2 From Newark," *Philadelphia Tribune*, May 17, 1934: 12.

30   "'Rocky' Ellis Allows 6 Hits in Sunday Tilt," *Philadelphia Tribune*, June 28, 1934: 12.

31   "Crawfords and All-Stars Split," *York* (Pennsylvania) *Gazette and Daily*, July 13, 1934: 11.

32   "Philly Stars in Win Over Elites," *Chicago Defender*, July 21, 1934: 16.

33   "Stars Drub Bees in City Series Start," *Philadelphia Tribune*, August 2, 1934: 12.

34   Holway, 85.

35   "O.V. Catto Elk News," *Philadelphia Tribune*, October 25, 1934: 8.

36   "Champion Philly Stars to Open with the Grays," *Chicago Defender*, April 27, 1935: 16.

37   "Philadelphians Debating Class of 1935 Stars," *Norfolk* (Virginia) *New Journal and Guide*, June 8, 1935: 14.

38   "Phila. Stars Subdue Brooklyn Eagles, 7-5," *Philadelphia Inquirer*, May 12, 1935: 43.

39   *Delaware County Daily Times*, July 8, 1936: 10.

40   "Phila. Stars in Loop Lead," *Philadelphia Tribune*, May 21, 1936: 12.

41   "Phila. Stars Beat Black Yanks, 3-2," *Philadelphia Tribune*, September 17, 1936: 15; "Philly Stars Grab Three: Bolden Nine Beats Yanks Twice and Elite Giants," *Baltimore Afro-American*, September 19, 1936: 22.

42   "National Sport Shots," *Pittsburgh Courier*, September 26, 1936: A5.

43   Ancestry.com.

44   "Bolden Predicts Pennant," *Philadelphia Tribune*, April 28, 1938: 12.

45   "The Powerhouse by Jimmy Powers," *New York Daily News*, July 11, 1938: 83.

46 "Outfielder Sends Word He Wants More Money," *Philadelphia Tribune*, March 14, 1940: 11; "Posey's Points," *Pittsburgh Courier*, December 23, 1939: 16.

47 "Posey's Points," *Pittsburgh Courier*, May 4, 1940: 16; "Grays Will Gun for Pennant With This Group," *Pittsburgh Courier*, May 11, 1940: 16; "Homestead Grays Tied By Meteors," *Pittsburgh Courier*, August 3, 1940: 16.

48 "Dunn Renamed Manager of Stars, *Philadelphia Tribune*, June 6, 1940: 11.

49 "Stars Sweep Memphis Series," *Philadelphia Tribune*, September 12, 1940: 11.

50 "Brooklyn Royals Tangle with Black Barons in Muny Stadium," *Davenport* (Iowa) *Daily Times*, July 23, 1941: 17.

51 "Royal Giants Rally in Sixth Inning to Nose Out Suburbanites, 3-2," *Camden Morning Post*, July 15, 1941: 14; "Pirates Beaten by Royals, 8-4," *Asbury Park* (New Jersey) *Press*, July 19, 1941: 10.

52 "Turner Field Tilt Features Hunter, Ellis," *Munster* (Indiana) *Times*, July 30, 1941: 19.

53 "Dr. Thomas' Experiment Might Be Salvation of Negro Baseball," *Pittsburgh Courier*, May 30, 1942: 16; J.K. O'Neill, "What's Up with Dr. Thomas? Part 1," *Dundalk* (Maryland) *Eagle*, April 7, 2016, https://www.pressreader.com/usa/the-dundalk-eagle/20160407/281792808180231. Accessed February 22, 2023.

54 "Baltimore Grays Twice Trip Richmond Hilldales," *Baltimore Afro-American*, June 13, 1942: 23.

55 "Clowns Downed, 8-2, By Baltimore Grays," *Cincinnati Enquirer*, July 7, 1942: 2.

56 Ancestry.com.

57 Ancestry.com.

JOHNNY HAYES

BY JAY HURD

From 1934 to 1951, the name Johnny Hayes appeared in newspaper sports pages and box scores for seven Negro baseball teams. His career, interrupted by service with the US Army during World War II, was split between the second Negro National League (NNL2), the Negro American League (NAL), and the short-lived United States League (USL). He appeared in two East-West All-Star games,1947 and 1951; and he saw playing time, with the NNL2 champion Philadelphia Stars in 1934. He played baseball in Puerto Rico and Cuba, sharing the fields with Monte Irvin, Josh Gibson, Howard Easterling, Frank Duncan, and others.[1]

John William Hayes, born on April 17, 1910, in Independence, Missouri, was the youngest of five children. He had two sisters, Virgie and Mary Ella, and two brothers, Ray and Cecil. His parents, John William Hayes Sr. (b.1868) and Martha "Mattie" Wood Hayes (b.1871), were born in Missouri and married in 1892 in Chariton County, Missouri. (The 1910 Census indicates that Mattie gave birth to six children and notes that four had survived. Johnny, born the fifth surviving child, would arrive that same year.) According to the 1910 Census, John and Mattie could read and write, owned their home, and engaged in the "eating house" industry. (They operated a restaurant.)

The 1920 U.S. Federal Census notes that John Sr., widowed, was head of his household in St. Joseph Ward 5, Buchanan, Missouri. Mattie had died on May 8, 1918. Remaining in the household were Virgia, 23, Mary Ella, 20, Cecil 15, and Johnny, 9. Ray, age 27, the oldest of the Hayes children, at this time worked as a railroad laborer and lodged in Salisbury, Chariton County. John Sr. worked as a butcher. Johnny's siblings who were still in the household were employed – the young men as butchers or laborers in a local packing house, and the young women as cooks – either with a private family or in a hotel setting.

Unfortunately, as with many Negro League players, records of Johnny Hayes' early life and his baseball career are few. One of the earliest records of his playing baseball is a 1933 Arriving Passenger and Crew List for the passenger ship *Carabobo*, which sailed

from New York City to San Juan, Puerto Rico. Along with other ballplayers, including Paul Dixon of the 1933 New York Black Yankees and Herb Smith of the 1933 Philadelphia Stars, Hayes arrived in San Juan on October 16, 1933. It is quite likely that this was the first of his visits to the islands – namely, Puerto Rico and Cuba – to play winter baseball. Whether he had been playing baseball in Missouri or elsewhere, it is certain that he had achieved, by 1933, a level of talent and notoriety that qualified him for travel to Puerto Rico. Official records for winter baseball in Puerto Rico were not available until the 1938-1939 season.[2]

Catcher Johnny Hayes

Hayes, at 5-feet-10 and 195 pounds, batted left-handed and threw right. In 1934 he began his professional career in the Negro Leagues with the Newark Dodgers, managed by Dick Lundy. He shared catching duties with Frank McCoy and appeared in 26 games. Hayes batted .308 with 24 hits, including three doubles, one triple, and one home run, and had 16 RBIs. After the Newark Dodgers completed the season with an overall 19-18-1 record, Hayes joined the Philadelphia Stars, owned by Ed Bolden and managed by Webster McDonald. The Stars won the NNL2 championship over the Chicago American Giants that year, but Hayes did not play in any of the eight championship games. However, he played three "Out of Season"[3] games: as catcher, two were for Ed Bolden's Stars.[4] In one of those games, Hall of Famer Biz Mackey, who shared catching duties with Mickey Casey during the regular season, played first base.[5] Next, Hayes caught game one of a doubleheader while Mickey Casey caught the second game.[6] In the third game the team, identified as the Philadelphia Stars, faced a "handpicked team of the Philadelphia League," including Dizzy and Paul Dean and Pepper Martin.[7]

In 1935 Hayes returned to the Newark Dodgers, managed by Lundy for two games and William Bell for the remaining 60 games. That season Hayes, age 25, shared backstop duties with Frank McCoy. Hayes appeared in 32 games and amassed 29 hits, 12 RBIs, and a .266 batting average.

In 1936 two teams, the Brooklyn Eagles and the Newark Dodgers, "were consolidated into a single team by co-owners Abe and Effa Manley,"[8] the Newark Eagles. In addition to Hayes, the team included Leon Ruffin, Mule Suttles, Ray Dandridge, and Wille Wells. William Bell managed the team for 34 games and Abe Manley for 25 games. That year, Hayes compiled 10 hits, 6 RBIs, and a .192 average in 17 games. He remained with the Newark Eagles for two more seasons.

The 1937 season saw the Eagles managed by Tex Burnett and Dick Lundy. Hayes shared catching with Joe Brown, and hit a mere .158 in 26 games, with 12 hits and 8 RBIs.

In 1938, under managers Abe Manley and Dick Lundy, he appeared in 21 games, had 13 hits, 11 RBIs and a .232 average.

Dick Lundy managed the 1939 team for the entire season. Hayes played in 24 games, had 19 hits, 7 RBIs, and a .250 average.

Throughout his career, Hayes traveled via ship or airline, to and from Puerto Rico and Cuba. He was a year-round ballplayer. His name appears on passenger and crew lists, or in photograph captions.[9] His wife, Alice, appears on at least two passenger lists – one shipboard in 1942 and the second as airline passenger with Illis [sic] Air Services in 1946.[10] Teams he played for in Puerto Rico include the Mayagüez Indios, the Crillos de Caguas, the San Juan Senators, the Santurce Crabbers, and the Tiburones de Aguadilla. Hayes joined Josh Gibson, Quincy Trouppe, and Robert Clarke as catcher-manager for Puerto Rican teams. While he played more often in Puerto Rico than in Cuba, he did play with the Leopardos de Santa Clara.[11]

The New York Black Yankees added Hayes to their roster in 1940. Managed by Tex Burnett, Hayes and Bob Clarke shared the backstop duties for the team. In 18 games, Hayes had eight hits, two RBIs and a .200 average. In 1941, again under manager Tex Burnett, Hayes, now 31 years old, had one of his finest seasons. In 26 games, he had 24 hits, 11 RBIs, and a .293 average. Hayes continued his fine play into the 1942 season with the Black Yankees, hitting .283 with 28 hits and 13 RBIs in 33 games.

With World War II intensifying, Hayes registered for the military draft on October 16, 1940, at Local Board No. 24, Essex County, New Jersey. Three questionable items appear on his draft card that warrant attention: first, while most records indicate that Hayes was born in Independence, Missouri, the card notes Kansas City, Missouri, as place of birth; second, his baseball résumé consistently shows him at 5-feet-10 and 195 pounds but on the card his "Approx." height and weight are 5-feet-7 and 138 pounds; and third, his employer's surname was misspelled – his employer was James Semler, owner of the New York Black Yankees, not James Simnley.

As Hayes continued to play ball through the 1942 season, two other noteworthy events occurred in his life. First, on December 13, 1942, he and Alice Parms (or Parmes) from New Orleans were married.[12] Their marriage license indicates his occupation as "Ball Player" while census records identify Alice as a "houseworker." He was 32, she 39, and they lived at 142 West 139th Street, New York City. The second event was Hayes' enlistment in the US Army on December 15, 1942. Unlike his marriage license, his enlistment record shows his "civil occupation" under the category "Athletes, Sports instructors, and sports officials." He served in the European Theater of Operations from 1944 to 1945 and was discharged, at the rank of sergeant, on November 25, 1945.[13]

After the war, and before he returned to the Black Yankees for the 1946 season in August, Hayes played for the Boston Blue Sox of the USL.[14] When that league folded, also in 1946, manager Tom Parker "had the Boston Squad in First place."[15] In addition to his time with the Boston Blues, he may have played briefly with the USL's Pittsburgh Crawfords

In 1947 Hayes appeared in 31 games and batted .278 with 25 hits and 13 RBIs for the New York Black Yankees, now managed by Marvin Barker. His play that year earned him a spot on the East All-Star team, managed by Biz Mackey. Due to the "popularity of the East-West game among Negro League fans,"[16] the 1947 contest offered two games – the first at Comiskey Park, Chicago, on July 27 (won by the West, 5-2) and the second on July 29 at the Polo Grounds, New York City (also won by the West, 8-2).[17] Hayes played in both games but was hitless.

The following season marked the final year of the NNL2 and Hayes' final year with the Black Yankees. The team was again managed by Marvin Barker and had an overall record of 13-45. Hayes, now 38, played in 14 games, had 11 hits, 3 RBIs, and a .262 average. In 1949 Hayes moved to the Baltimore Elite Giants of the Negro American League.[18] In 1951, his final season, he was once again selected for the East-West All-Star Game. He and his Elite Giants teammate Kelly Searcy helped the East All-Stars defeat the West All-Stars, 3-1, at Comiskey Park on August 12. Hayes had two hits and Searcy was the winning pitcher.[19] Ben Littles of the Philadelphia Stars pinch-hit for Hayes in the ninth.[20] The Elite Giants "club was sold … in 1951 for $11,000. After returning the team to Nashville [the team's city of origin] for a final season, the team was dissolved. …"[21] Perhaps this was a fitting conclusion to Hayes' baseball career.

As of 1950, Hayes and his wife, Alice, still lived in New York City; the 1950 Census identified his occupation as "other," and Alice's as "keeping house." Alice Hayes died at the age of 75 on September 8, 1977. She was interred on September 12 in Long Island National Cemetery in Farmingdale, New York. Her grave marker indicates that her marriage to US Army veteran Sergeant John W. Hayes sanctioned her burial in a National Cemetery.[22] Hayes lived another 11 years until he died of natural causes on November 16, 1988, in Cook County, Illinois, where he had been working as a clerk in his later years. There is discrepancy regarding which village outside of Chicago Hayes had claimed as residence when he died: Most records indicate Auburn Park while others list Evergreen Park.

Hayes was buried in Cook County, Illinois, although his exact place of burial was not recorded and has been lost to history.[23]

Negro Leaguer Gordon "Hoppy" Hopkins of the Indianapolis Clowns noted that "[t]here was a lot of other guys that helped me out: Buck O'Neil, Buck Leonard, and Leon Day [and] Johnny Hayes up in New York. …"[24] Johnny Hayes was not a Hall of Famer, but he was a competitive, All-Star ballplayer.

SOURCES

In addition to the sources cited in the Notes, the author consulted Ancestry.com, Baseball-Reference.com, Family Search.com, GenealogyBank.com, Google Books, the SABR Biography Project, and Seamheads.com (the source for all Negro League statistics, unless otherwise indicated).

| DNOTES

1   Johnny Hayes has been confused with John Hayes, born in 1931, who played with the Hartford Chiefs in 1952, and with Frankie Hayes, who happened to be a catcher in the same era, with the Philadelphia Athletics.

2   Larry Lester, *Black Baseball's National Showcase: The East-West All-Star Game, 1933-1953* (Lincoln: University of Nebraska Press, 2001), 67.

3   James C. Isaminger, "J Dean Twirls 3 Frames; Paul Plays Afield," *Philadelphia Inquirer*, October 17, 1934: 17.

4   "Satchell Paige's Fireball Hurling Fells Stars by 4-2 Count," *Pittsburgh Courier*, October 13, 1934: 4.

5   "Satchell Paige's Fireball Hurling Fells Stars by 4-2 Count."

6   Isaminger.

7   "Dean Brothers and Martin to Play in Philadelphia," *Scranton Times Tribune*, October 13, 1934: 13.

8   "Newark Eagles," The Negro Leagues, Powered by the Negro Leagues Museum, https://www.mlb.com/history/negro-leagues/teams/newark-eagles.

9   Lester, 67.

10   "John Hayes in the Puerto Rico, U.S., Arriving Passengers and Crew Lists, 1901-1962, Ancestry.com, https://www.ancestry.com/discoveryui-content/view/1286624:2257?tid=&pid=&queryId=3f8b999e1960c2387a6fa42d3c3b-deb2&_phsrc=Zla48&_phstart=successSource.

11   Jorge S. Figueredo, *Who's Who in Cuban Baseball, 1878-1961* (Jefferson, North Carolina: McFarland Publishers, Inc., 2007), 378.

12   "Marriage Licenses Issued," *New York Age*, January 2, 1943: 5

13   Gary Bedingfield's Baseball in Wartime, https://www.baseballinwartime.com/negro.htm.

14   Center for Negro League Baseball Research, http://cnlbr.org/MuseumGallery/Programs/tabid/83/mid/402/ProjectId/62/wildRC/1/Default.aspx.

15   Bill Johnson, "Tom Parker," SABR Baseball Biography Project, https://sabr.org/bioproj/person/tom-parker/.

16   Jim Overmyer, "July 29, 1947: The West Wins Another Negro League East-West Game at Polo Grounds," SABR Baseball Games Project, https://sabr.org/gamesproj/game/july-29-1947-the-west-wins-another-negro-league-east-west-game/two.

17   "East-West All Star Summaries," Center for Negro League Baseball Research, http://www.cnlbr.org/Portals/0/RL/East-West%20All%20Star%20Game%20Summaries.pdf.

18   Dr. Layton Revel, "Forgotten Heroes: Henry Kimbro," Center for Negro League Baseball Research, http://www.cnlbr.org/Portals/0/Hero/Henry_Kimbro%202019-10.pdf. (Photo Page 2).

19   "East Negro League All-Stars Beat West, 3-1," *Chicago Tribune*, August 13, 1951: 51.

20   Lester, 67.

21   "Baltimore Elite Giants," Negro Leagues Baseball Museum eMuseum, https://nlbemuseum.com/history/teams/baltegiants.html.

22   "Alice Hayes," Find-a-Grave, https://www.findagrave.com/memorial/82594090/alice-hayes.

23   "Illinois, Cook County Deaths, 1871-1998," database, FamilySearch (https://familysearch.org/ark:/61903/1:1:Q23W-NJDD: 18 March 2018), John Hayes, 16 Nov 1988; citing Evergreen Park, Cook, Illinois, United States, source reference, record number, Cook County Courthouse, Chicago; FHL microfilm.

24   Brent Kelley, *The Negro Leagues Revisited: Conversations with 66 More Baseball Heroes* (Jefferson, North Carolina: McFarland, 2010), 301.

FRANK "LEFTY" HOLMES

By Frederick C. Bush

The 1934 Philadelphia Stars, champions of the second iteration of the Negro National League (NNL2), used a balanced four-man rotation that consisted of two righties and two lefties for most of their league games. Slim Jones, a 21-year-old southpaw, emerged as the team's ace as he pitched to a 20-4 record and a 1.29 ERA in league games during what was to be his lone season as a top-flight player. The Stars' other portsider, Lefty Holmes, also had his finest season as he contributed seven victories in league play while posting a 2.61 ERA that was second on the team only to Jones's otherworldly mark.

Holmes had been pitching professionally in New York, Baltimore, and Philadelphia since 1929, but fans may well have thought he was several different players due to both the various first names (Frank, Eddie, and Sam) and nicknames (Lefty, Sonny, Ducky) that the press used for him. Holmes had his greatest success in the 1932 and 1934 seasons. He continued to play ball into at least the 1942 season, at which time his name conundrum still had not been settled, with one season preview article referring to him as "Sonny 'Lefty' Holmes."[1] After his baseball career ended, he resided in Philadelphia another four decades before returning to his native Georgia a few years before his death.

Frank Holmes was born on February 28, 1907, in Brunswick, Georgia, to George and Phoebe (Hall) Holmes. The couple had married on January 28, 1892, and George worked as a day laborer at such jobs as he could find, while Phoebe tended to their family that grew to include nine children. Frank had five older siblings (three brothers and two sisters) and three younger (two brothers and a sister). Leroy (also known as Phillie), who was almost six years younger than Frank, played second base and joined his older brother as a member of the Harlem Black Sox in 1930.

Philadelphia Tribune, August 27, 1931

Pitcher Frank "Lefty" Holmes

Frank moved from his southeastern Georgia home to Philadelphia at some point in his late teens, though the exact age is unknown; he had still been living at home at age 13 when the 1920 US Census was taken. A maternal uncle, Felix Hall, originally from Darien, Georgia, resided in the City of Brotherly Love, so he had a family member to help him get acclimated to the area. Holmes and Hall maintained a close relationship and often worked together until Hall's untimely death of tuberculosis on May 1, 1954. Holmes made the most of the opportunities available to him in Philadelphia, which were likely greater than any in the Jim Crow South. In fact, at the outset of his professional baseball career, the *Brooklyn Times Union* reported that Holmes had "recently graduated from high school."[2] However, since Holmes was already 22 years old by this time, it is more likely that he had been attending a college or professional school.[3]

Whatever his exact educational status may have been, Holmes's debut for the New York Lincoln Giants appears to have taken place on June 30, 1929, in a doubleheader against Hilldale at the Protectory Oval in the Bronx. The *New York Amsterdam News* raved, "A youngster by the name of Holmes came through with some good relief pitching last Sunday [June 30] in the first game of a doubleheader," a 9-6 victory for the Lincoln Giants.[4] Holmes also pitched 5⅓ innings in the nightcap after starter Herb Thomas surrendered nine runs (including seven in the top of the fourth inning). Holmes gave up one more run in a 10-6 loss.

Holmes had made a big enough impression on his manager, future Hall of Famer John Henry "Pop" Lloyd, that he started the first game of a July 4 doubleheader against the Cuban Stars at Dexter Park in Queens. Holmes went the distance in a 21-3 thrashing of the Cubans. He also went 3-for-6 at the plate and scored four runs in support of his three-hit pitching effort.[5]

Despite Holmes's impressive showing, he was used sparingly in league games the rest of the season and finished with a 2-1 record and a 4.24 ERA over 17 innings pitched in four games (one start). The Lincoln Giants finished at 40-26-2 in American Negro League (ANL) play, which was only good enough for second place, eight games behind the Baltimore Black Sox.

In 1930 Holmes joined the independent Harlem Black Sox for which "[b]ookings [had] been made for the whole summer in and around New York State by Nat Strong, owner of the Royal Giants."[6] The team trained in Florida and Georgia, where it picked up additional team members, before barnstorming its way north. The *New York Amsterdam News* observed, "Phillie Holmes, younger brother of Sonny Holmes, is the only rookie of the crop, but to date he has been playing and batting on a par with the big guns and he has every qualification for a star infielder, taking care of the keystone cushion in a fitting manner."[7]

The Holmes brothers were joined by twin brothers Herbert "Ruff" and Willie "Lock" Gay, who both had played briefly with the Chicago American Giants the previous year. Apparently, the two sets of brothers were to function as more than just ballplayers: The *Amsterdam News* concluded its preview by noting, "Sonny Holmes, the elder, is very much like Stepin Fetchit in looks and acts and is very amusing with his brother and the Gay twins. Entertainments of dance, song, and cracks will be put on in each city they play."[8] Extremely few press accounts of the team's games can be located and most involve exhibition games in Florida before and after the summer; thus, little is known about the 1930 Harlem Black Sox.

In 1931 Holmes pitched briefly for the Cuban House of David squad, an independent team without a home ballpark that received as little news coverage as the Harlem Black Sox had. Holmes started and was the winning pitcher in an 8-5 triumph over the Winsted (Connecticut) Town Team on June 19.[9]

At some point during the season, Holmes joined the Philadelphia Bacharach Giants – not to be confused with the famous Atlantic City Bacharach Giants – as was evidenced by his appearance in a team photo in the August 27 edition of the *Philadelphia Tribune*.[10] Teammate Halley Harding, who played third base, provided a glimpse of Holmes's personality in a humorous article for the *Chicago Defender*, in which he wrote:

Frank Holmes of the Bacharach Giants has a droll sense of humor. For many years his only comment on an error by one of his mates, a strikeout by himself or another player has been, "I didn't thought you'd notice it." This phrase has become an institution around the bench and clubhouse wherever the B's are playing and always draws a laugh.[11]

Harding also played seven games for the Baltimore Black Sox in 1931, for whom he was to pitch the next season.

At the outset of the 1932 season, Holmes was still pitching for the Philadelphia Bacharach Giants. On April 24 he entered a game against the Lancaster Red Sox in relief of Red Ellis as the Bacharachs triumphed, 13-3.[12] Shortly thereafter, he joined the Baltimore squad and made an immediate impact with a 5-0 shutout of the Washington Pilots in the second game of a doubleheader at Maryland Baseball Park on May 8.[13]

A late-May *Pittsburgh Courier* article about the East-West League that extolled Holmes's initial prowess with the Black Sox also created some of the confusion surrounding his identity. The unnamed columnist wrote:

Dick Lundy has uncovered a young lefthander who appears destined to go places. Eddie Holmes is the youngster's name and in two starts he has blanked the Washington Pilots and lost a hairline decision to the Hilldale club. What makes the feats stand out is that the rookie was pitted against Webster McDonald and Porter Charleston. Holmes is a product of the Philadelphia sandlots and has been passed up by at least two of the East-West Clubs before Dick Lundy gave him a chance.[14]

"Eddie" Holmes was Frank Holmes and, although he had been discovered in his adopted hometown of Philadelphia, he was no rookie. The error became rampant throughout the press for a time as even the *New York Amsterdam News*, which had covered Holmes when he truly had been a rookie with the Lincoln Giants in 1929, reported that "Eddie Holmes, Lefty Allen and Jay Cook, enjoying their first fling at big time baseball, have been blazing a trail through the ranks of the Eastern clubs."[15]

On June 26 Holmes lost a tough 1-0 rematch of his Baltimore debut at Maryland Baseball Park. The hometown newspaper waxed poetic in its recap, recounting, "In the opener, McDonald, star pilot twirler, bested Holmes in a neat hill duel."[16] Holmes continued to pitch well and threw a 9-4 complete-game victory over a team of all-stars from Philadelphia on July 23. The *Philadelphia Inquirer*, in its coverage of the game, finally set the record straight about Holmes's identity as it reported, "Frank Holmes, Black Sox hurler, was the master of the homebred sluggers."[17]

In all, Holmes made 18 appearances (10 starts) for Baltimore in league play during the 1932 season. He fashioned a 5-6 record in those games with a 3.65 ERA (113 ERA+) over 116 innings pitched. The Black Sox finished at 29-26 in EWL games, which put them in third place, nine games behind the first-place Detroit Wolves and 2½ behind the Homestead Grays; the team finished at 33-33 against all Negro major-league-caliber competition. The 1932 season also marked the first time that Holmes was teammates with Slim Jones, who was to catapult to superstardom with the 1934 Philadelphia Stars but was 0-3 with Baltimore as a 19-year-old.

After the EWL season ended, Holmes had the opportunity to test his mettle against White major- and minor-league players as the Black Sox played a seven-game series of weekend games against an all-star team at Baltimore's Bugle Field from September through October. Holmes won the second game of the October 9 doubleheader, which was shortened to "the usual five innings," by a 9-6 score.[18] He allowed at least one home run to Hack Wilson, "Brooklyn slugger, imported from Martinsburg, W.Va., to give the All-Stars more power."[19] Holmes started the finale of the series on October 30, but was rocked for seven runs in the seventh inning and surrendered a total of nine runs in a 13-9 defeat.[20]

On the heels of his most successful season with a team of major-league caliber to that point, Holmes disappeared off the baseball map in 1933. He does not appear to have played ball that year; no mention of his name in game articles or box scores has been found. Additionally, no records have been unearthed to indicate whether Holmes had either a positive or negative life event that interrupted his career. After his mysterious 1933, Holmes resurfaced as a member of the Philadelphia Stars in 1934.

Pitcher Webster McDonald was then the manager of the Stars. He had faced Holmes in some tough pitching battles in 1932, so he knew that he was getting a proven commodity; even though Holmes had been away from baseball for a year, he was still only 27 years old. On May 13 McDonald sent Holmes to the mound as the starter in the first game of a doubleheader against the

Newark Dodgers and Holmes' former manager, Dick Lundy, at General Electric Field in Bloomfield, New Jersey. It was Opening Day for the Dodgers and, as "[f]ive thousand fans turned out ... with two bands furnishing the music, a flag-raising preceding the game and Rollo Wilson, the Judge Landis of Negro baseball, tossing out the opening ball," Holmes garnered the victory.[21] He hurled eight innings of Philadelphia's 5-4 triumph before giving way to Jones when he got into a jam in the ninth.

As the weather became hotter, so did Holmes. On June 15, at Eagle Park in York, Pennsylvania, he struck out 15 batters in a 5-4 complete-game victory over the NNL2 rival Nashville Elite Giants.[22] Nine days later, back home at Passon Field in Philadelphia, Holmes fired a 9-0 shutout in the second game of a doubleheader against another league opponent, the Cleveland Red Sox.[23]

Philadelphia's primary starters – Jones, Rocky Ellis, McDonald, and Holmes – all had seasons in which they were well above the league average in ERA+, and the Stars were locked in a three-way battle with the Chicago American Giants and the intrastate rival Pittsburgh Crawfords for supremacy in the NNL2. Chicago claimed the league's first-half title, but the Stars prevailed in the second half.

Although Holmes continued to pitch well, he did not throw a single inning in any of the eight games (Game Seven ended in a tie) of the NNL2 championship series that pitted Philadelphia vs. Chicago. Manager McDonald opted to use a rotation that included Jones, Ellis, Paul Carter, and himself.

However, Holmes did pitch for the Stars during that time. Philadelphia played several exhibition games during the championship series and, after the American Giants had taken a three-games-to-one lead with a 2-1 victory on September 17, the first of these contests took place on September 20. Holmes took the mound against the Newark Dodgers at Windsor Airport Field in Trenton, New Jersey, and went the distance in a 2-1 walk-off triumph.[24]

On October 2 at Passon Field, Jones threw a 2-0 shutout in the eighth game of the championship series that completed Philadelphia's epic comeback to claim the NNL2 title. Four days later, Holmes made what appears to have been his last appearance for the Stars in 1934 when he opposed Satchel Paige and the Pittsburgh Crawfords at the same venue on October 6 in a game that ended as a 4-2 loss for Philadelphia. The *Pittsburgh Courier* commented that Holmes "had too much difficulty with his control" as he issued five walks and that he "also was the victim of weak support from the rest of the cast. No fewer than six errors were charged against Philadelphia."[25]

Although it surely was not the way Holmes wanted his season to end, it did not detract from the fact that he had been a key cog in Philadelphia's 1934 championship machine. He had appeared in 14 league games (12 starts) and pitched to a 7-6 record with a 2.61 ERA (149 ERA+) over 107 innings. It appeared that Holmes was now on his way to a successful stint in the Negro major leagues, but the 1934 season turned out to be the high point of his professional baseball career.

Holmes returned to the Stars in 1935, and the team was expected to contend for a second consecutive championship. An article in the *Chicago Defender* declared that the Stars' pitching staff – Holmes, Ellis, McDonald, Porter Charleston, Carter, and Jones – was "rated with the best in baseball."[26] However, the vaunted staff's ERA climbed from 2.61 in 1934 to 5.28 in 1935 and the team finished in fourth place in the NNL2 with a 37-31-4 record. Jones fell from 20-4 with a 1.29 ERA to 4-5 with a 5.88 ERA while Holmes's record fell to an almost identical 4-6 mark as his ERA skyrocketed to 6.84 (a 74 ERA+ that indicates his pitching was well under average that year).

Homestead Grays owner Cum Posey, in his *Pittsburgh Courier* column of April 25, 1936, predicted that the Stars would be a strong club and that "Holmes, who was ill in 1935, will be much better in 1936."[27] Instead, the Stars finished in last place while Holmes pitched sparingly for two different NNL2 squads, appearing in five games with the Washington Elite Giants and one with the New York Cubans. He had no decisions in his six games while posting a 6.05 ERA in 19⅓ innings pitched.

The 1937 season found Holmes back with the semipro Philadelphia Bacharach Giants for the first time in five years. Prior to a mid-May game against the Allentown nine, the local press touted "Sonny Holmes, formerly of the Phila. Stars and a sensational hurler" as a member of the Bacharachs.[28] In June, a Lancaster paper referred to him as "Ducky Holmes, another former Phila. Star performer."[29] Whichever name newspapers used, it was Frank Holmes who was doing the pitching, and he seemed to have recovered some of his acumen. After Philadelphia whipped the All-Lancaster team, 7-1, on September 9, a game recap proclaimed, "'Sonny' Holmes, who served them up for the Bacharachs, pitched good ball. He limited the locals to five hits during the seven inning [sic] contest and whiffed seven of the All Lancaster stickmen."[30]

Holmes had pitched well enough in 1937 to be in demand by various clubs the following year. On May 3 the *Allentown Morning Call* listed "Sonny Holmes, pitcher, who secured his experience with Ed Bolden's Philadelphia Stars and Homestead Grays" as being "among the leading stars" for the Bacharachs.[31] Two days later, the *Atlanta Daily World* reported that Atlanta Black Crackers manager Nish Williams had been "very dissatisfied with the showing of his nine against league opposition" and intended to secure, among others, "'Sonny' Holmes who pitched for the Philadelphia Stars last season."[32]

Despite newspaper forecasts and teams' desires for Holmes's services, he saw limited action in 1938. In his only Negro major-league stint, he appeared in two league games for the NNL2's Washington Black Senators. He started against his former team, the Philadelphia Stars, on June 6 at Elks Field in Chester, Pennsylvania. Holmes went the distance and allowed only five hits, but he surrendered nine walks that resulted in a 6-2 defeat.[33] He also took the loss in the second game of a doubleheader on June 12 that gave him a 0-2 record and a 6.75 ERA with Washington.[34]

The Philadelphia Bacharach Giants became Holmes's fallback team for the remainder of his career. Game articles and box scores show that he pitched for the team sporadically for several more years. His obituary states that he "played for 20 years," which may well be accurate.[35] For a time, when he was not playing baseball, Holmes was working for his uncle, Felix Hall, at Philadelphia's historic Touraine Hotel, as is indicated on his World War II draft registration card from October 1940.

In 1942 Holmes played for one other team besides the Bacharachs, joining the Baltimore Grays of the new and short-lived Negro Major Baseball League. He was reunited with his former Stars teammate Rocky Ellis and sometimes also played in the outfield on days when he was not scheduled to pitch.[36]

Holmes retreated into anonymity during his post-baseball life. At some point – apparently in the early 1980s – he returned to his native town of Brunswick, Georgia, perhaps to be closer to his two remaining siblings. His only surviving brother and former 1930 Harlem Black Sox teammate, Leroy ("Phillie"), who had played numerous years for the Jacksonville Red Caps, died on October 7, 1985, in Atlanta.[37]

Frank "Lefty" Holmes died on December 27, 1987, in Brunswick after a brief, undisclosed illness. His obituary listed the following family members as his closest survivors: his wife, Mary Holmes of Brunswick; a daughter, Helda Stricklyn of Philadelphia; and a sister, Dorothy Wiggins of Jacksonville.[38]

ACKNOWLEDGMENTS

Thanks are due to two fellow Negro League researchers who assisted the author in establishing that Lefty Holmes was indeed Frank Holmes:

1. SABR researcher/author Peggy Gripshover uncovered the fact that Felix Hall, whom Holmes named as both his employer and contact person on his World War II draft registration card, was Holmes's maternal uncle and traced his origins to Georgia; this information provided an accurate locus to search for records of Holmes and his family. Peggy also located an obituary for Frank Holmes, which provided further information that confirmed Holmes's identity.

2. Gary Ashwill of Seamheads.com helped to confirm the suspicion that "Eddie" Holmes (a name that first popped up in press accounts in 1932) was the same person as Frank Holmes. The team for which both "Eddie" and Frank had played in 1931 – the Philadelphia Bacharach Giants – was one and the same. Gary had written a blog entry about that team after discovering a photo that identified all players, including "Frank Holmes, pitcher" (see "July 26, 2017: Philadelphia Bacharach Giants, 1931" at https://agatetype. typepad.com/agate_type/2017/07/philadelphia-bacharach-giants-1931.html). In a serendipitous quid pro quo, this author's research led to information that established that Frank Holmes and Leroy "Phillie" Holmes were brothers and to Leroy's obituary, which along with Frank's obituary provided the correct dates and places of death for both players that can now be found on the Seamheads Negro League Database.

SOURCES

Except where otherwise indicated, all player statistics and team records were taken from Seamheads.com.

Ancestry.com was consulted for US Census information as well as birth, marriage, and death records.

NOTES

1   Randy Dixon, "The Sports Bugle/Dr. Thomas' Experiment Might Be Salvation of Negro Baseball," *Pittsburgh Courier*, May 30, 1942: 16.

2   "Lincolns Twice Conquer Cubans," *Brooklyn Times Union*, July 5, 1929: 16.

3   The 1950 US Census lists the code "S3" for Holmes on the "School completed" line. This code was probably written in error since that would mean that Holmes had completed only a third-grade education. More likely, the census taker intended to record the code "C3," which would have indicated that Holmes had completed three years of college or professional school. (See https://www.census.gov/history/pdf/1950instructions.pdf.)

4   "Lloyd Men Win and Lose Sund'y/Holmes, Relief Mound Man, Came Through in Splendid Form," *New York Amsterdam News*, July 3, 1929: 9.

5   "Cubans Lose at Dexter Park/Lincoln Giants in Batting Spree Against Stars Independence Day," *New York Amsterdam News*, July 10, 1929: 9.

6   "Black Sox Heads [sic] North; Play All the Way Up," *New York Amsterdam News*, June 4, 1930: 17.

7   "Black Sox Heads North; Play All the Way Up."

8   "Black Sox Heads North; Play All the Way Up." This article marks the first time the nickname "Sonny" was used for Frank Holmes in the press. The name would occur occasionally throughout his career, though he was most often referred to as "Lefty" and later was sometimes called "Ducky."

9   "Cuban House of David Beats Winsted Nine, 8-5," *Hartford Courant*, June 20, 1931: 14.

10 Gary Ashwill, "July 26, 2017: Philadelphia Bacharach Giants, 1931," https://agatetype.typepad.com/agate_type/2017/07/philadelphia-bacharach-giants-1931.html, accessed December 19, 2022.

11 Hallie [sic] Harding, "I Think So," *Chicago Defender*, October 3, 1931: 9.

12 "Local Team Faces 2 Foes/League Nine Badly Beaten by Bacharachs in Opening Game," *Lancaster* (Pennsylvania) *New Era*, April 25, 1932: 9. The *New Era* mistakenly reported that Lancaster was beaten "by the Bacharach Giants of Atlantic City" when, in fact, it had been the Philadelphia Bacharach Giants.

13 "Black Sox Get Half of Spoils with Pilots," *Baltimore Sun*, May 9, 1932: 9.

14 "Washington Takes Lead in East-West Race/Detroit, Cubans, Grays Spurt in Battle for Lead," *Pittsburgh Courier*, May 21, 1932: 15.

15 "Black Sox in League Lead/Young Pitchers Shaping Up Nicely with the Fast Baltimore Team," *New York Amsterdam News*, May 25, 1932: 13.

16 "Black Sox Handed Double Setback by Washington," *Baltimore Sun*, June 27, 1932: 11.

17 "All-Stars Beaten by Black Sox Foe/Phila. Clubbers Lost After Dark Battle to Baltimore Clan, 9 to 4," *Philadelphia Inquirer*, July 24, 1932: 39.

18 "All-Star Nine in Even Break/Defeats Black Sox in Opener, 8-2, but Bows in Nightcap, 9-6," *Baltimore Sun*, October 10, 1932: 10.

19 "All-Star Nine in Even Break." Wilson hit two home runs, but the box score does not indicate in which inning he hit his second, nor does the game write-up make mention of it; thus, there is uncertainty as to whether he hit one or both of his home runs off Holmes.

20 "All-Star Nine Beats Black Sox by 13-9," *Baltimore Sun*, October 31, 1932: 10.

21 "Philadelphia Stars Win 2 from Newark," *Philadelphia Tribune*, May 17, 1934.

22 "Phillie All-Stars Beat Nashville," *York* (Pennsylvania) *Daily Record*, June 16, 1934: 5; "Philadelphia Stars Top Nashville Club," *York Dispatch*, June 16, 1934: 7. Oddly, both York newspapers named the Nashville club as the "Colonels" rather than the Elite Giants.

23 "Philadelphia All-Stars Win Four: Capture a Pair Twin Bills and Take 2d Place/Run All Over Strong Cleveland Nine," *Chicago Defender* (National Edition), June 30, 1934: 16.

24 "Philly Batters Win Over Dodgers, 2 to 1," *Trenton Evening Times*, September 21, 1934: 23. Although the game was played in New Jersey, the box score indicates that the Stars played as the home team.

25 "Satchell [sic] Paige's Fire Ball Hurling Fells Stars by 4-2 Count," *Pittsburgh Courier*, October 13, 1934: 14.

26 "Plenty of Pitching Class Here," *Chicago Defender* (National Edition), July 20, 1935: 15. The caption to a photo of the Stars' pitching staff that was included here erroneously gave Holmes' first name as "Sam."

27 Cum Posey, "Cum Posey's Pointed Paragraphs," *Pittsburgh Courier*, April 25, 1936: 14. It is unknown what illness if any Holmes suffered from in 1935.

28 "Bacharach Giants Here Tonight to Battle Allentown Tossers/Local East Penn Leaguers Face Strong Colored Team at Fair Grounds," *Allentown* (Pennsylvania) *Morning Call*, May 12, 1937: 21.

29 "All-Lancaster at Home Today/Strong Bacharach Giants Will Play on Ed Stumpf Field," *Lancaster Sunday News*, June 20, 1937: 11.

30 "All-Lancaster Beaten 7 to 1 by Bacharachs/Atlantic City Club Have Easy Time Topping Locals, 300 Fans Present," *Lancaster Intelligencer Journal*, September 10, 1937: 22. In what was a common error throughout the history of the semipro Philadelphia Bacharach Giants, the newspaper assumed that the team was still its more famous predecessor from Atlantic City.

31 "Locals to Play Colored Stars/Bacharach Giants Here for Twilight Game Tomorrow Night," *Allentown Morning Call*, May 3, 1938: 21. Despite this newspaper's assertion about Holmes's prior experience, there is no evidence that he had ever pitched for the Homestead Grays.

32 "Black Crackers Seek New Pitchers; Add New Infielder to Present Combination," *Atlanta Daily World*, May 5, 1938: 5. Misinformation about Holmes abounded. The *Daily World's* claim that Holmes had pitched for the Philadelphia Stars in 1937 was incorrect. He had last pitched for the Stars in 1935 and had pitched for the Philadelphia Bacharach Giants in 1937.

33 "Negro National League," *Delaware County Daily Times* (Chester, Pennsylvania), June 7, 1938: 10. Only the box score is present; there is no game recap article. The newspaper had run a preview article for the game in its previous day's edition.

34 "Trade Shellackings/Black Senators Beat Shamrocks, 21-4, Then Flop, 10-5," *Washington Evening Star*, June 13, 1938: 14.

35 "Holmes Rites to Be Held Here Tomorrow," *Brunswick* (Georgia) *News*, December 31, 1987: 3.

36 "Daisies Defeat Baltimore Grays," *Philadelphia Inquirer*, May 11, 1942: 25; Randy Dixon, "The Sports Bugle: Dr. Thomas' Experiment Might Be Salvation of Negro Baseball."

37 "Obituary: Leroy "Philly" Holmes," *Atlanta Voice*, October 19-25, 1985: 7.

38 "Holmes Rites to Be Held Here Tomorrow." The obituary claimed incorrectly that Holmes was 83 years old; he was 80 (February 28, 1907, to December 27, 1987).

CLIFFORD IRONS

By Margaret M. Gripshover

Clifford Calvin Irons appeared in only one documented game for the Philadelphia Stars. The game took place in Philadelphia on July 6, 1934, and Irons shared mound duties with another teenager, Bernard Blackwell.[1] Irons was described in a newspaper account of the game as a "first-rate twirler" from Bryn Mawr High School, but he actually attended and played baseball for Haverford High.[2] The Stars and these two young moundsmen defeated the Mitchell Athletic Association of Philadelphia in a nonleague tilt, 6-2.[3] Neither teenage hurler ever appeared in another game for the Stars.

Irons was born in 1913 in Montgomeryville, Pennsylvania, a suburban community about 30 miles north of Philadelphia. His father was a farmer, but shortly after Irons was born, the family moved 20 miles southwest to Haverford. Irons and his family lived on Preston Avenue in a working-class enclave of Haverford, a community that is part of the historically affluent Main Line of Philadelphia. In mid-October of 1918, when Irons was just 5 years old, both his father and an uncle died within days of each other from influenza during the height of the historic pandemic. That same week, influenza claimed the lives of more than 4,500 Philadelphians, and over the course of the pandemic, at least 12,000 died in the Philadelphia area.[4] After the death of his father, Irons' widowed mother split the family in two. Clifford and his brother, Arthur, were eventually sent down the street to live with their maternal grandparents, while his sister, Lillian, lived with their mother.

Despite this family trauma, Irons managed to attend school and compete in sports. He was a member of the predominantly White Haverford High's track team and excelled at the broad jump.[5] At the same time, he was Haverford's star relief pitcher and earned the nickname Whip for his quick delivery and late-inning heroics.[6] In 1932, before he finished high school, Irons had taken on some extracurricular duties as a relief pitcher for a local amateur nine, the Main Line Tigers, a "fast Negro outfit," and "one of the strongest clubs in the eastern part of Pennsylvania."[7] In 1933,

Irons' senior year, Haverford finished as the runner-up to first-place Lower Merion in their suburban prep-league championship.[8] After graduation, he rejoined the Main Line Tigers.

In late June 1934, the week before he pitched for the Stars, Irons was in the lineup for the Tigers for a tilt against the Baltimore Pirates in nearby Bryn Mawr.[9] It is likely that Irons' participation in high-school and suburban baseball leagues caught the attention of Ed Bolden and the Stars and resulted in Irons' recruitment. Irons was 19 years old when he pitched in his one and only game for the Stars.[10] He made the most of his brief foray into Negro League baseball and helped the Stars defeat the Mitchell Athletic Association of Philadelphia, 6-2.[11]

After finishing his cup of coffee with the Stars, Irons continued to play for suburban amateur nines for two more years. In 1935 he played his last baseball for an amateur aggregation, pitching for the Wayne Black Hawks.[12] Unfortunately for Irons, his career on the mound did not end on a high note. In June 1935, Irons and the Black Hawks lost 7-1 to the Royersford Needleworks team in Pottstown.[13] Irons' retirement from baseball came around the same time as his marriage to Goldie Brown, with whom he had at least four children.

Irons lived in the Haverford area throughout the 1940s, working as a laborer and apartment superintendent until approximately 1950, when he relocated his family to North Philadelphia. Irons worked for Owens-Illinois Forest Products Division's corrugated box factory in Bristol Township, northeast of Philadelphia, in Bucks County.[14] He remained with Owens-Illinois for more than 20 years.[15] Irons died in Philadelphia in January 1975 at the age of 61.

Sources

Unless otherwise indicated, all Negro League statistics and records were sourced from Seamheads.com.

Ancestry.com was used to access census, birth, death, marriage, military, immigration, and other genealogical and public records.

NOTES

1   "Philly Stars Garner Two During Week," *Baltimore Afro-American*, July 14, 1934: 19.

2   "Philly Stars Garner Two During Week."

3   "Philly Stars Garner Two During Week."

4   John M. Barry, *The Great Influenza: The Story of the Deadliest Pandemic in History* (New York: Penguin Random House, 2005), 370; Department of Health and Charities of the City of Philadelphia, "Monthly Bulletin," November 1918: 3.

5   "Haverford Easy Winner in Delco Tests at Lansdowne," *Delaware County Daily Times* (Chester, Pennsylvania), April 24, 1933: 12.

6   "Lower Merion Tossers Defeat Norristown Foe to Cart Off Section 1 Laurels," *Philadelphia Inquirer*, June 7, 1933: 18.

7   "Dover Pros Defeat Main Line Tigers," *Philadelphia Inquirer*, August 21, 1932: 41; "Baltimore Pirates in Holiday Bill," *Baltimore Afro-American*, June 30, 1934: 19.

8   "Lower Merion Tossers Defeat Norristown Foe to Cart Off Section 1 Laurels."

9   "Philly Stars Garner Two During Week."

10   "Philly Stars Garner Two During Week."

11   "Philly Stars Garner Two During Week."

12   "Needleworks Leading 7-1 as Rain Halts Tilt," *Pottstown* (Pennsylvania) *Mercury*, June 18, 1935: 5.

13   "Needleworks Leading 7-1 as Rain Halts Tilt."

14   Scoop Lewis, "Buildings on the Rise in Bristol Township," *Bristol* (Pennsylvania) *Daily Courier*, October 16, 1965: 4.

15   "Proudly We Hail," *Bristol Daily Courier*, October 23, 1963: 16.

STEWART "SLIM" JONES

BY FREDERICK C. BUSH

The legend of Slim Jones has loomed large over the history of the Negro Leagues due to his death at the youthful age of 25 in 1938. In truth, by the time of his passing, Jones already had entered the pantheon of baseball's "could have beens" as injury and alcoholism had depleted his pitching ability. His reputation was built upon one glorious season that was never forgotten by the players and fans who witnessed it, a season that has become a part of baseball lore.

Jones was an unproven 20-year-old pitcher with two unremarkable seasons under his belt when he went to Puerto Rico for the 1933-34 winter season. On the island, the 6-foot-6, 185-pound southpaw struck out 210 batters, "the highest total ever recorded in Puerto Rico, [although it] has not been recognized because at that time there were no official leagues, mostly weekly games and tournaments."[1] Jones's unofficial record foreshadowed his breakout in the Negro Leagues, and his 1934 campaign still stands as one of the greatest seasons by any pitcher in any league and era.

Stewart Jones was born on September 16, 1913, in Baltimore to James and Ida (Brown) Jones.[2] At the time of the 1920 census, the family lived in a rented home at 826 South Warner Street in Baltimore's 22nd Ward. James worked as a miller for a grain company and Ida owned and operated a restaurant, while Stewart's sister, Alena, who was 10 years older, worked in a factory. His uncle, Winchester Jones, also lived with the family and worked as a chauffeur.

During the 10-year interval between censuses, Jones's parents divorced. In 1930 Jones was living with his father at 240 Eislen Street, still in Baltimore's 22nd Ward. James Jones now worked as a packer for a shirt manufacturing company to support himself and his son. The 1930 census indicates that Stewart was no longer attending school at that time; however, it lists no employer either. Whatever work he was doing, he also was honing his pitching skills in local semi-pro ball and came to the attention of the Baltimore Black Sox.

In 1932 Jones signed with the Black Sox, a member franchise of the ill-fated East-West League. The circuit had been founded by Homestead Grays owner Cumberland Posey that year and died a "quick death by early July."[3] The Black Sox ended the shortened campaign with a 29-26 record in league play (33-33 overall) and finished in third place behind the first-place Detroit Wolves and the Grays.

Jones made his professional debut on Sunday, May 29, 1932, in the first game of a doubleheader against the league rival Hilldale Daisies at Maryland Park. The *Baltimore Afro-American* provided a report of the new hometown hurler's exploits, noting that "the 20-year-old [sic] youngster, a former sandlotter with the Baltimore Red Sox, made a lasting impression upon the fans by his performance. He toiled four and one-third innings, allowing but one hit, and fanning four."[4] Baltimore mounted a dramatic ninth-inning comeback to pull out a 4-3 victory. Since Jones was

Pitching ace Stewart "Slim" Jones

Graig Kreindler

long gone from the mound by then, the *Afro-American* explained the reason for his early hook: "His peculiar cross fire [*sic*] delivery so puzzled Umpire Brown that that official missed several perfect strikes. Manager [Dick] Lundy, fearful lest Jones become upset, took him out and sent in [Herb] Smith to finish the game."[5]

In playing up Jones as a hometown hero, the *Afro-American* had neglected to mention that he also had walked three men and hit another batter with an errant pitch. During his first year with the Black Sox, Jones appeared in three additional games (two starts) and finished the brief season 0-3 with a 3.96 ERA over 25 innings pitched while striking out 14 hitters and walking 10.

In 1933 the Baltimore club found a new league home in the second iteration of the Negro National League.[6] Financial hardships caused by the Great Depression, along with difficulties in scheduling opponents and the availability of ballparks, created an immense imbalance in the NNL2's schedule. Baltimore played only 31 league games, finishing in fifth place at 13-18, while the league-champion Pittsburgh Crawfords – the rare Negro League team that owned its own ballpark – played a 64-game league slate and finished 41-21-2.

It was the second consecutive year that Jones had played an abbreviated schedule with his hometown nine; thus, there were few highlights. Jones had turned in a fine performance on August 6 in the first game of a doubleheader against the Cuban Stars at Baltimore's Bugle Field. He fanned 10 batters and allowed only four hits while overcoming four walks and three errors behind him in a complete-game 6-4 triumph.[7] At the end of the season, his five wins in NNL2 play tied for the franchise lead with Tom Richardson and Burnalle "Bun" Hayes, his 51 strikeouts led the Sox staff, and his 4.23 ERA was second only to Richardson's 3.44 mark.

Jones was included on the Black Sox roster for the squad's annual postseason series against an all-star team composed of White major- and minor-league players, an honor he had not earned the previous season.[8] He appeared in two games with mixed results. Jones started the first game of a doubleheader on September 17 but lasted only 4⅓ innings as the Sox took an 11-1 drubbing, and he surrendered seven hits, one walk, and five runs while striking out only one batter.[9] On September 24, he entered the first game of a doubleheader in relief of Phil Cockrell and threw 5⅔ innings of shutout ball, allowing two hits, striking out six and walking one, in a game the Sox lost by a 6-4 score.[10]

Jones had shown improvement, but nothing had hinted at the big leap that he was about to take. Nonetheless, Fred "Tex" Burnett, Baltimore's veteran starting catcher, saw potential in Jones and helped to put him on the road to stardom. After Jones's breakout season with the Philadelphia Stars in 1934, the *Brooklyn Times Union* provided the answer to everyone's "Where did he come from?" queries:

> Last summer Tex Burnett, a leading figure in the colored National League, took an interest in Jones and persuaded the then 21-year-old [*sic*] kid's father to permit him to take Stuart [*sic*] to Porto Rico [*sic*] for a winter of development in the fast leagues there.

> Unstable and green at first, Jones slowly began to rid himself of his faults. Tex gave him confidence and overnight Slim changed from a boy to a man. He pitched amazingly well as the season wore on and fanned 210 players before the campaign ended.

> That won him a job with the Philly Stars. ...[11]

The Stars and their emergent southpaw ace were about to take each other to great new heights.

On May 6, 1934, Stars owner "[Ed] Bolden introduced a newcomer to the fans in 'Slim' Jones, lanky 7 foot [*sic*], 20-year-old twirler who pitched six innings and permitted but three men to reach first base" before being relieved by Cockrell.[12] A crowd of 6,000 had witnessed Jones's debut in the City of Brotherly Love as the Stars clobbered the Philadelphia League's Wentz Olney team by a 12-1 margin.

Jones took the mound for the team's NNL2 home opener against the Newark Dodgers on May 12 at Passon Field. Dick Lundy, who had managed the Black Sox during Jones's rookie season, now skippered the Dodgers. If Lundy thought that his team's batters would feast on the inconsistent southpaw he remembered from 1932, he was soon disabused of that notion. Only 5,000 fans "braved a chilly atmosphere," but they saw Jones take a no-hitter into the seventh inning before having to settle for a three-hit, 12-0 whitewashing of the Dodgers.[13]

Eight days later, Jones dueled Satchel Paige and the powerful Crawfords at Greenlee Field in Pittsburgh. The teams split their four-game series, but the Stars bested Paige on Sunday in what could hardly be called a pitchers' duel. Jones pitched the first eight innings, struck out five men, and surrendered five runs, one of which came on a moonshot home run by Josh Gibson.

Paige fanned 11 Philly hitters, and the Crawfords led, 5-3, entering the ninth inning. Suddenly, "a fusillade of bats exploded in front of [Paige], and the great 'Satch' couldn't check the machine-gun batting attack."[14] After the smoke cleared, Philadelphia led, 10-5. Stars pitcher-manager Webster McDonald took the mound and sealed the victory by setting the Smoketown nine's batters down in order.

Jones, the gangly lefty, and Paige, the equally lanky righty, faced each other again a mere three days later at Eagle Park in York, Pennsylvania, their repeated encounters perhaps appearing like battles between baseball-slinging giraffes. This time, the Stars emerged with a 3-0 victory. Both hurlers both went the distance, and each amassed 11 strikeouts, but Jones held the Crawfords to four hits while Paige allowed twice that number, which resulted in Philly's three runs.[15]

Although there were other teams in the NNL2 besides the Stars and Crawfords, the imbalanced league schedule resulted in these two squads facing off repeatedly.[16] On June 11, they clashed at Harrisburg, Pennsylvania, and Jones lost a 1-0 duel to Sam Streeter in which the only run came on Vic Harris's homer. Both pitchers had allowed only six hits in what the *Harrisburg Evening News* called "[o]ne of the classiest baseball games ever staged in this city."[17] Not to be outdone, the *Harrisburg Telegraph*, while noting that Harris had "straightened out one of Mr. Jones' fast balls [sic]" to win the game, also raved: "Mr. Jones, incidentally, had real smoke on that pill. If there was ever a colored prototype of Lefty Grove, it is the said Mr. Jones. Tall, lanky, and with speed that makes the ball resemble a pea going over the plate, it is a fine thing to know that he has remarkable control; if he ever misgauged, he'd knock the opponent into the next county."[18]

On June 23 the Stars swept a doubleheader from the Cleveland Red Sox at Passon Field. Jones struck out nine batters and pitched "splendid ball" in the opener to come out on the winning end of a 1-0 pitching duel with Script Lee.[19] The next day the Stars swept another twin bill from Cleveland and moved into second place in the standings.

The NNL2 used a split-season format, and the Stars fell one spot to finish in third place in the first-half standings. The Chicago American Giants claimed first place and the Crawfords finished second. However, in late July, those two squads were "now battling for second place as the Philadelphia Stars [had] stepped away out in the lead for supremacy of the second half."[20]

As the calendar turned to August, the Stars took both ends of a doubleheader against Chicago to remain in first place.[21] Then, on August 18, Philadelphia swept another doubleheader, this time from Pittsburgh at Greenlee Field, with Jones capturing a 6-3 win in the opener and Paul Carter tossing a 1-0 victory in the nightcap.[22] However, the Crawfords returned the favor at Philadelphia just two days later, notching their own doubleheader sweep, with "Lefty Jones, the Stars' giant southpaw, […] the peak victim of the Crawfords' 14-hit attack," an onslaught that included two Josh Gibson round-trippers that accounted for seven of Pittsburgh's eight runs.[23]

As the Stars, Crawfords, and American Giants continued to jockey for position in the standings, the time arrived for the second annual East-West All-Star game at Chicago's Comiskey Park. A crowd estimated at 25,000 turned out on August 26 to watch the best players in Black baseball compete. Since members of the Stars and Crawfords were both part of the East team, Jones and Paige combined their efforts on this day. Jones started the game, pitched three innings of one-hit shutout ball, and struck out four batters. Harry Kincannon of the Crawfords continued to keep the West off the scoreboard in the fourth and fifth innings and then ceded the hill to Paige. In a classic pitchers' duel, the East's James "Cool Papa" Bell scored the game's only run in the top of the eighth inning. Paige pitched the final four frames, in which he allowed only two hits and struck out five batters.[24]

On September 3 the NNL2's season concluded, and the Stars claimed the second-half title,[25] which meant that they would meet Chicago in a playoff series to determine the league champion. Prior to that clash, Jones and Paige dueled yet once more. On September 9, "[t]he largest crowd to ever witness a baseball doubleheader played by colored teams in New York – estimated by some as over 30,000 – turned out at the Yankee Stadium on Sunday afternoon."[26] In the first game of the four-team slate, Chicago beat the New York Black Yankees, 4-3. It was a good contest, with the Black Yankees creating excitement by scoring three runs over the final two innings. However, it paled in comparison to the second game between the Crawfords and Stars, which became an epic battle that everyone remembered.

After a game for the ages, one reporter lamented that Jones "was cheated by fate of a deserving victory on an unfortunate break in the eighth."[27] The Stars struck early against Paige as they scored a run in the bottom of the first. Jake Stephens drew a leadoff walk, advanced to second on Dewey Creacy's base hit and – after Chaney White whiffed – scored on Jud Wilson's fielder's-choice grounder. Jones made the 1-0 lead stand until the top of the eighth. In that fateful frame, Judy Johnson led off with a single and took second when Stars right fielder Jake Dunn muffed the play.

Pitcher "Slim" Jones won the NNL2 championship-clinching game in 1934. Stewart "Slim" Jones

Center for Negro League Baseball Research

Chester Williams laid down a bunt that Jones fielded, but he threw the ball to first to retire Williams and allowed Johnson to advance to third. Clarence "Spoony" Palm pinch-hit for Ted Page and was walked; Jimmie Crutchfield entered the game as Palm's pinch-runner. Leroy Morney then singled to drive home Johnson with the tying run.

Philadelphia almost pulled out a win in the bottom of the ninth, but "Paige arose to his greatest height in this inning when he filled the bases by walking two pinch hitters and then struck out the last two batters in a row."[28] The game ended in a 1-1 tie as it "had to be called at the end of the ninth inning because it was seven o'clock and so dark the batters would strike at the ball and duck."[29] Jones had allowed only three hits and struck out nine while Paige had surrendered six hits and fanned 12.

Two days later, Chicago and Philadelphia met in Game One of the championship series at Passon Field. Rocky Ellis started for the Stars and held a 3-2 lead when he gave way to Jones at the top of the ninth inning. Jones surrendered two runs to hand the American Giants a 4-3 victory.[30] Games Two and Three were part of a doubleheader at Cole's Park in Chicago on September 16. Jones started Game Two but lost a tough 3-0 ballgame to Chicago's Ted Trent, who stymied the Stars with a four-hitter.[31] Philadelphia salvaged the nightcap by a 5-3 score, but lost Game Four the next day by a 2-1 tally to find itself in a three-games-to-one hole.[32]

Ellis kept the Stars alive with a tough-as-nails 1-0 shutout in Game Five at Passon Field on September 27, and Paul Carter followed with a complete-game four-hitter in a 4-1 triumph on September 29 that knotted the series at three games apiece.[33]

Prior to Game Seven of the championship series, another four-team doubleheader was held at Yankee Stadium on September 30. The sequel did not live up to the original as "[a]ll prospects of a pitching duel [between Paige and Jones] was [sic] ruined at the outset of the first game when Seay, the Stars second baseman, missed a fast roller in the first inning, giving the Crawfords their first score."[34] Oscar Charleston also tallied a run in the first inning for a quick 2-0 Pittsburgh lead. Both teams scored a single run in their respective halves of the seventh inning, and the 3-1 margin stood up as the final score. After the Black Yankees turned the tables on the American Giants and defeated them in the nightcap, it was time for Chicago and Philadelphia to finish their battle for the championship.

Game Seven at Passon Field on October 1 ended in a 4-4 tie when the game had to be called after nine innings because of darkness.[35] The game was re-played the next day, and Jones not only "twirled the Ed Bolden crew to the loop diadem with his speedball and baffling cross-fire to turn in six strikeouts, but he also put the game on the proverbial ice when he blasted in the final run with a sharp single to left in the seventh."[36] He finished the championship clincher with a five-hit, 2-0 triumph.

Few pitchers have experienced a season like the one Jones had in 1934. He pitched to a 20-4 record in NNL2 regular-season play with 164 strikeouts and a minuscule 1.29 ERA over 203 innings of work. He led the league in every major pitching statistic and no one – not even Paige – was close. Yet he never approached that level of success again.

However, before 1934 ended, Jones added one final jewel to his crown against Dizzy and Daffy Dean and their all-star team on October 16 at Philadelphia's Shibe Park. The Dean brothers had accounted for all the St. Louis Cardinals' victories – two apiece – in their seven-game World Series triumph over the Detroit Tigers, and they were cashing in on their fame with a barnstorming tour. Webster McDonald spun an 8-0 shutout for Philadelphia in the first game of the doubleheader as the Dean brothers played the corner outfield spots. Dizzy then pitched the first two innings of the seven-inning nightcap, in which Jones and Philly prevailed by a 4-3 score. Jones struck out eight all-stars as he went the distance for the win.[37]

Jones played winter ball in Puerto Rico again, but there were no reports about his performances in the American press. Upon his return, Jones began the 1935 season appearing to pick up where he had left off the previous year. After the Stars had lost the first game of a twin bill against the Brooklyn Eagles, he hurled his team to a 5-1 triumph in the six-inning nightcap.[38]

In early July, however, it was reported that Jones "has just recovered from a sore arm."[39] His rehabilitation regimen apparently did not satisfy Stars owner Ed Bolden, who "stopped Jones's salary and suspended him from the Stars for his 'failure to attain proper physical condition.'"[40] The second, and more critical, effect that the injury had on Jones was that he turned to alcohol to numb the pain he now experienced.

Jones struggled to a 4-5 record in league games and struck out only 36 batters in 67⅓ innings while his ERA ballooned to an unsightly 5.88. The Stars finished with a 37-31-4 record and failed to make the playoffs.

Jones's last hurrah came in a losing cause on August 11, 1935, in the East-West game at Comiskey Park. Despite his injury, suspension, and poor record, Jones received the nod as the East's starting pitcher for the second consecutive year. He again threw three innings of one-hit, shutout ball, although he struck out only one batter this time. For good measure, he also hit a solo homer in the top of the fourth that increased the East's lead to 3-0. In the end, however, the West's Mule Suttles was the hero of the day as his 11th-inning circuit clout won the game, 11-8.[41]

After Jones's stellar showing in the East-West game, Crawfords owner Gus Greenlee tried to turn back the clock to 1934 by arranging a Paige-Jones tilt as part of a four-team doubleheader at Yankee Stadium on September 22. Paige took $300 from Greenlee for the appearance and then pulled one of his infamous no-shows. After the Nashville Elite Giants had edged the New York Cubans, 4-3, in the opening game, Ernest "Spoon" Carter started in Paige's place for the Crawfords against the Stars. Pittsburgh pounded Philadelphia, 12-2, and knocked Jones out of the box after just one inning of work in which he allowed four runs, thus sending the fans home doubly disappointed.[42]

Subsequently, Jones traveled to Puerto Rico in November for his last season of winter ball. Considering his miserable 1935 season, it might have been wiser for him to rest, as the additional workload probably aggravated his arm injury.

Jones went from bad to worse in 1936 as his record fell to 2-4 in 14 appearances (four starts) and his ERA climbed to 6.96. The Stars finished 33-42-1 in NNL2 play under Webster McDonald, who was replaced as manager by Jud Wilson the following year.

By 1937, Jones was a pitcher in name only. He won his lone mound appearance despite surrendering three runs in 5⅓ innings of work. Wilson used him at first base on the rare occasions when he was healthy enough to play. Jones batted .333 (12-for-36) with seven RBIs, but his contributions were minimal as the Stars struggled to a 30-32-1 record and a third-place finish.

Prior to the 1938 season, there was hope that Jones finally would rebound into his 1934 incarnation. A late-April news article reported:

When Slim Jones visited Bolden in Philadelphia before leaving for training duties in the Southland and to sign his contract, he seemed to be in excellent form. When asked about his outlook for the coming season, Slim definitely went on record that he guarded his health throughout the winter with plenty of rest and is looking forward to a minimum of 25 victories.[43]

The comeback was not meant to be, though, as Jones could not overcome his injury issues. He made seven appearances (one start) and pitched to a 1.42 ERA, but he worked only 12⅔ innings. Wilson again played him at first base, as well as in left field and as a pinch-hitter, but now Jones went 11-for-52 at the plate for a lowly .212 batting average. The Stars improved to 41-32-3 in league play but finished a distant second behind the Grays.

In September *Pittsburgh Courier* columnist Randy Dixon wrote, "Remember when Slim Jones emerged from the obscurity of the Baltimore backlots to become a burning satellite flashing brilliantly across the baseball horizon of 1934?"[44] Plenty of people still remembered, but it seemed long ago, and Jones's career appeared to be at an end.

And then, suddenly, Jones's life ended. A story spread that Jones had "sought an advance on his salary, and when his request was refused, he sold his overcoat to buy a bottle of whiskey and subsequently contracted pneumonia and died shortly afterward."[45] A slight variation of this tale had Jones "freezing to death on the streets of Philadelphia."[46]

Whether Jones sought an advance on his 1939 salary or sold his overcoat to buy whiskey is uncertain, but he neither froze to death nor died of pneumonia. However, there was truth in the assertion that Jones's alcoholism had contributed to his death. He was admitted to Baltimore's Bay View City Hospital on November 14, and was diagnosed with uremia, urinary extravasation, and gangrene of the prostate gland. In sum, his kidneys were failing, and he had numerous infections.[47] Jones's doctor performed a procedure to provide relief, which was likely also a precursor to further surgeries, but his condition was too advanced, and he died on November 19, 1938.

Jones had lived with his father his entire life, and their last home together was at 505 Welcome Alley in Baltimore. James Jones had his son buried in Baltimore's Mt. Calvary Cemetery on November 24, 1938. Ed Bolden delivered Jones's eulogy, and "[a] large number of Quakertown fans attended the rites."[48]

In a 1976 interview, Satchel Paige, a Hall of Famer and living legend, named Slim Jones as one of the three best pitchers he had ever seen, along with Bob Feller and Dizzy Dean.[49]

Acknowledgments

Thanks to Rachel Frazier, reference archivist for the Maryland State Archives, for providing a copy of Stewart Jones's death certificate.

This biography was vetted by Phil Williams, fact-checked by Kevin Larkin, and copyedited by Len Levin.

Sources

Ancestry.com was consulted for public records such as census information and ships' passenger logs.

Negro League player statistics and manager/team records were taken from Seamheads.com, unless otherwise indicated.

Notes

1   William F. McNeil, *Black Baseball Out of Season: Pay for Play Outside of the Negro Leagues* (Jefferson, North Carolina: McFarland & Company, Inc., 2007), 115. The Puerto Rico Winter League's first season was in the winter of 1938-39.

2   Two items bear discussion here: 1) the correct spelling of Jones's first name, and 2) his correct date of birth. Regarding the first item, numerous sources – including the Seamheads Negro League database – spell Jones's first name as Stuart. However, census records, ships' passenger logs, his death certificate, and most contemporary newspaper articles spell his name as Stewart; thus, the author has chosen to use Stewart. (It is also of interest to note that, although Jones grew up in the city, he was known by the nickname "Country" in addition to the much more common moniker Slim). As to the second item, every print and internet source lists Jones's date of birth as May 6, 1913. This author found numerous ships' passenger logs from Jones' trips to Puerto Rico and back: One log listed May 8, 1913, as his birth date while another year's log did indeed have the date as May 6, 1913. However, Jones's death certificate, for which his father provided all personal information, has his birth date as September 16, 1913; considering this documentation and its source, the author has chosen to provide September 16 – rather than May 6 – as Jones's birth date.

3   Lawrence D. Hogan, *Shades of Glory: The Negro Leagues and the Story of African-American Baseball* (Washington: National Geographic, 2006), 240.

4   "Black Sox Take Doubleheader from Hilldale Club/Daisies Drop Two by 1-Run Margin," *Baltimore Afro-American*, June 4, 1932: 14.

5   "Black Sox Take Doubleheader from Hilldale Club."

6   Even today, there is still some confusion about the name for Baltimore's 1933 entry in the Negro National League II. The 1932 Baltimore Black Sox (an East-West League member franchise), the 1933 Baltimore Sox (NNL2 members), and the 1934 Baltimore Black Sox (still in the NNL2) were one continuous organization. However, in 1933 a group headed by James B. Hairstone filed an injunction against Joe Cambria, owner of the 1932 Baltimore Black Sox. Hairstone alleged that he had an organization named the Baltimore Black Sox Baseball and Exhibition Company that had been compelled to forfeit its charter for non-payment of 1930 taxes, and he now wanted to resume his baseball operations and to prevent Cambria from using the Black Sox name (see "Seek to Enjoin Team from Use of 'Black Sox'," *Baltimore Afro-American*, May 27, 1933: 16). Hairstone won his injunction and the rights to the Black Sox name, but Cambria "reported that he had regained the trade name" later in the 1933 season, and his NNL2 squad used the moniker again in the 1934 season (see "Jack Farrell Let Go Upon Larceny Count," *Baltimore Afro-American*, July 14, 1934: 15). The press muddled the situation further by referring to Cambria's NNL2 member team as either the "Black Sox" or the "Sox," depending upon which newspaper

was publishing game write-ups. The resultant confusion created such consternation that Bill Gibson, a columnist for the *Baltimore Afro-American*, blended equal portions of humor, frustration, and sarcasm as he explained in the newspaper's June 17, 1933, edition: "In answer to a half hundred or more inquiries regarding the identity of Baltimore's two professional baseball teams, the pillar explains that the city literally has a pair of Sox. The local entry in the National Association of Baseball Clubs [NNL2] is the Baltimore Sox team, sponsored by Joe Cambria, local sportsman and business man [*sic*]. This club has Bugle Field on the Edison Highway as its home park, and is managed by Jess Hubbard. The Baltimore Black Sox (notice the Black) are not affiliated with any baseball organization and operate at Maryland Park. The club is incorporated with James B. (Harry) Hairstone as president and general manager. The club revives the tradition of the original Black Sox, which passed out of the hands of George Rossiter two seasons ago. So[,] you see, the city has two clubs – the Sox and the Black Sox. You're welcome, I'm sure" (see Bill Gibson, "Hear Me Talkin' To Ya," *Baltimore Afro-American*, June 17, 1933: 17).

7   "Cuban Stars and Baltimore Sox Break Even in 2 Games," *Chicago Defender*, August 12, 1933: 9.

8   "Black Sox Open Series with Double Tomorrow," *Baltimore Sun*, September 24, 1932: 10; "All-Stars Open Annual Series with Sox Today," *Baltimore Sun*, September 17, 1933: 21.

9   "Heffner's Bat Defeats Sox," *Baltimore Sun*, September 18, 1933: 9.

10 "Baltimore Sox Split Pair with All-Stars," *Baltimore Sun*, September 25, 1933: 11. Cockrell had played for the independent Philadelphia Bacharach Giants during the 1933 season but had joined Baltimore for the series against the all-stars.

11 "Colored Ace Made Good in a Hurry," *Brooklyn Times Union*, October 9, 1934: 15.

12 "Phila. Stars Outhit Wentz Olney to Win," *Philadelphia Inquirer*, May 7, 1934: 16.

13 W. Rollo Wilson, "Jones Holds Lundymen to Three Hits; Phila. Stars Win Opener in Big Way," *Pittsburgh Courier*, May 19, 1934: 14.

14 Chester L. Washington, "Crawfords Win 2 Out of 3 from Philly Stars/Hunter Holds Foe to 2 Hits, Wins, 3 to 0," *Pittsburgh Courier*, May 26, 1934: 14. The *Courier's* headline is a bit misleading as the two teams had played the opening game of the series, won by the Stars, on Thursday, May 18; however, that game had been reported in the newspaper's previous edition while the three weekend games were reported in this article.

15 "Philadelphia Stars Triumph/Defeat Pittsburgh Crawfords in Great Pitchers Battle at Eagle Park," *York* (Pennsylvania) *Daily Record*, May 24, 1934: 10.

16 At the conclusion of NNL2 play, each team had played the following number of league games: Pittsburgh Crawfords, 77; Philadelphia Stars, 56; Chicago American Giants, 51; Nashville Elite Giants, 47; Newark Dodgers, 32; Philadelphia Bacharach Giants and Cleveland Red Sox, 25 each; and the Baltimore Black Sox, 13.

17 "Crawfords Take Fast Colored Game Here; Major Clubs Idle/Home Run Sends Philadelphia to Defeat in Duel," *Harrisburg Evening News*, June 12, 1934: 13.

18 "Nobe" Frank, "It Just Occurred to Me," *Harrisburg Telegraph*, June 16, 1934: 6.

19 "Philadelphia All-Stars Win Four/Capture a Pair of Twin Bills and Take 2d Place," *Chicago Defender*, June 30, 1934: 16.

20 "Crawfords to Meet Chicago Champions on Carlisle Field," *Harrisburg Telegraph*, July 26, 1934: 12. Since the Seamheads.com Negro League database was used as the primary source for player statistics, team records, and league standings, it should be noted that the site is in error about the 1934 NNL2 champions. It inadvertently has reversed the first- and second-half champions, listing the Stars as the former and the American Giants as

the latter; however, newspaper articles, such as the one cited here, clearly indicate that the American Giants were the first-half champions.

21 "Philly Beats Chi, Holds League Lead; Nashville Elites Second/Philly All-Stars Stop Chi Twice, Keep Lead," *Pittsburgh Courier*, August 4, 1934: 15.

22 "Crawfords Lose Twice to Stars," *Pittsburgh Press*, August 19, 1934: 14.

23 "Crawfords Twice Trip Phila. Stars," *Philadelphia Inquirer*, August 21, 1934: 26.

24 Dan Burley, "East Shuts Out West in Classic Tilt, 1-0/Satchel Paige Bests Foster in Slab Duel," *Atlanta Daily World*, September 2, 1934: 5.

25 Christopher Hauser, *The Negro Leagues Chronology: Events in Organized Black Baseball, 1920-1948* (Jefferson, North Carolina: McFarland & Company, Inc., 2006), 83.

26 William E. Clark, "30,000 Attend Four-Team Double Header at Yankee Stadium; Black Yanks Lose; Stars-Crawfords Tie," *New York Age*, September 15, 1934: 5.

27 Edgar T. Rouzeau, "New York Wants Baseball/Exciting Games at the Yankee Stadium Bring Out 30,000 Enthusiastic Fans," *New York Amsterdam News*, September 15, 1934: 10.

28 Clark, "30,000 Attend Four-Team Double Header at Yankee Stadium."

29 "30,000 Attend Four-Team Double Header at Yankee Stadium."

30 Hauser, 84.

31 "Giants Lead Philly in World's Series 3 to 1," *Chicago Defender*, September 22, 1934: 16.

32 "Giants Lead Philly in World's Series 3 to 1."

33 "Phila. Stars Triumph," *Philadelphia Inquirer*, September 28, 1934: 22; "Stars Jolt Giants and Tie Up Series," *Philadelphia Inquirer*, September 30, 1934: 51.

34 Edgar T. Rouzeau, "Paige Again Stars at Stadium/Thousands Again Turn Out to Witness Four-Game Double-Header at Stadium," *New York Amsterdam News*, October 6, 1934: 10. The *Amsterdam News* reported the crowd for this sequel doubleheader at 25,000, but the *New York Age* gave a figure of 35,000; see C. Augustus Austin, "35,000 Fans See Black Yankees and Pittsburgh Crawfords Defeat Chicago and Phila. at Stadium, *New York Age*, October 6, 1934: 5.

35 Hauser, 85.

36 "Stars Upset Giants Win National Title/'Slim' Jones Hurls Phila. Negro Team to 2-0 Win Over Chicago Rival," *Philadelphia Inquirer*, October 3, 1934: 22.

37 "Dizzy-Daffy Stars Lose Double Bill/J. Dean Twirls 2 Frames; Paul Plays Afield," *Philadelphia Inquirer*, October 17, 1934: 17.

38 "Brooklyn Eagles Get an Even Break," *Brooklyn Daily Eagle*, May 13, 1935: 12.

39 Lewis K. Dial, "The Sports Dial," *New York Age*, July 6, 1935: 8.

40 Courtney Michelle Smith, *Ed Bolden and Black Baseball in Philadelphia* (Jefferson, North Carolina: McFarland & Company, Inc., 2017), 92.

41 Al Monroe, "Suttles' Home Run Wins for West, 11-8: Blow Comes in 11th with Score Knotted and 2 On," *Chicago Defender*, August 17, 1935: 6.

42 William E. Clark, "15,000 Fans See 4-Team Series at Yankee Stadium Sunday; Crawfords and Elite Gts. Win," *New York Age*, September 28, 1935: 8.

43 "Philly Stars' Chances Up with Jones Back in Form," *New York Amsterdam News*, April 30, 1938: 15.

44 Randy Dixon, "The Sports Bugle," *Pittsburgh Courier*, September 24, 1938: 17.

45   James A. Riley, *The Biographical Encyclopedia of the Negro Baseball Leagues* (New York: Carroll & Graf Publishers, Inc., 1994), 451. Some contemporary newspapers also erroneously reported the cause of death as pneumonia; for one such account, see "Bury Slim Jones, Bolden's Philadelphia Stars' Ace," *Chicago Defender*, December 10, 1938: 9. Yet other outlets gave the cause incorrectly as tuberculosis; see "Bay Parkways Meet Eagles," *Brooklyn Daily Eagle*, May 4, 1939: 21.

46   Thom Loverro, *The Encyclopedia of Negro League Baseball* (New York: Checkmark Books, 2003), 163.

47   As the author of this biography is not a doctor, numerous reliable medical websites – such as the National Institutes of Health – were consulted to determine what Jones's conditions, as well as the surgical procedure he underwent, entailed. The explanation provided in the main text of this article is unsophisticated but accurate.

48   "Phillies Star Pitcher Buried/Services for 'Slim' Jones Conducted in Baltimore," *New York Amsterdam News*, December 3, 1938: 19.

49   Dave Anderson, "Satch Surveys Catfish and Ages," *New York Times*, October 12, 1976: 55.

GRANVILLE LYONS

By Darren Gibson

Rookie Granville Lyons received his first shot in the Negro Leagues in 1931 after Willie Bobo, the starting first baseman for the Nashville Elite Giants, died during winter ball on the West Coast following a night out in Tijuana, Mexico. Three years later, in July 1934, Lyons experienced quite the 11-day stretch in the Negro National League II: going from starting for the Elite Giants to replacing Oscar Charleston at first base for the Pittsburgh Crawfords (for a day anyway) to finally replacing Jud Wilson at first in an exhibition for the Philadelphia Stars.

In theater circles, the phrase "break a leg" is employed to wish a thespian good luck in their debut performance.[1] Unfortunately, Lyons, in his Philadelphia Stars debut, literally broke his right leg on July 19, 1934, in his first and only appearance for the team that season. The first baseman and occasional outfielder and pitcher returned to the Stars in 1935 and eventually completed a 17-year Negro League career as a player and manager.

Granville Henry Lyons Jr. was born on July 16, 1908, in Nashville, Tennessee, to Granville Lyons Sr. (1869-1929), a janitor and porter, and Kittie M. Keeble Lyons, a widowed dressmaker. It was the second marriage for both. Granville Sr. was a divorced boarder and farm laborer who could not read or write as of the 1900 census. He had been involved in a serious automobile accident in 1906, nearly losing his life, while driving a passenger car dubbed a "Jim Crow Car" full of bricks, which was slammed into by a double truck.[2] The couple had another son, Herbert, in 1914; he died in 1920. Young Granville also had a half-sister, Martha, and two half-brothers, Flowers and Ernest, from Kittie's first marriage. Granville Jr. attended school only through the sixth grade.[3]

As a 17-year-old, Granville Jr. married Mable Anderson in September 1925 in Nashville. They welcomed daughter, Seleane, in March 1926, but she died in November 1928. The couple also had a son, named Granville Lyons Jr., born on July 22, 1927, who tragically died a day later. They welcomed a second son, also named Granville Jr., on Christmas Day 1928 and

then had two more daughters, Katie Louise, born in 1933 and Myrtle Doris, born in 1934. Granville and Mable divorced later in the decade, and he later married Arkia (Artie) Lyons.

The local Negro League ball team in Lyons' hometown of Nashville was the Elite Giants, owned by Tom Wilson, a nightclub operator who also owned gas stations and real estate. Wilson had a stadium built for the 1930 season at Trimble Bottom, in the center of Nashville's largest Black community, which had seating for 4,000 and was named for him.[4] After a last-place finish in the Negro National League in 1930, Wilson sent his team, including pitcher Jim "Cannonball" Willis, catcher Poindexter Williams, first baseman Willie Bobo, and outfielder Jack Ridley, out west to play in the California Winter League. After a mid-February 1931 contest against a San Diego squad in which he was hit in the side by a pitch, Bobo and others went across the border to Mexico. While in Tijuana, Bobo "drank some liquor that made him very ill," and died soon after returning to California.[5] The "popular and slugging" Bobo, dubbed the "Black [George] Sisler," had been the Elite Giants' starting first baseman for three years.[6] This tragedy opened the door for Lyons to earn the first-base spot for the Nashville squad.

For 1931, owner Wilson fielded both a Nashville team in the new minors-level Negro Southern League and one in Cleveland, named the Cubs, in the majors-level Negro National League. Wilson moved most of his talented Nashville players, including Willis and Ridley, to the Cleveland franchise, and even signed Satchel Paige.

The rookie Lyons, playing for his hometown squad, collected four hits from the sixth spot as Nashville lost a doubleheader to the NNL's Louisville White Sox in late April.[7] A couple of weeks later, the Elite Giants swept the Knoxville (Tennessee) Giants at home, with the "fielding and hitting of Lyons and [Ewing] Russell of the locals featured [in] Saturday's tilt."[8] By late June, against the Birmingham Black Barons, Lyons was leading off for Nashville.[9]

Nashville won the NSL's first half title, and then beat Birmingham again, on July 27, with "home runs by [Henry] Henderson, a newcomer, and Lyons [being] features of this game."[10] Lyons, a 5-foot-9 lefty thrower and hitter, weighing in at 170 pounds, received the following writeup in the *Nashville Banner* in mid-August: "Granville Lyons took Bobo's place at first when the latter died during the California trip last winter. Home is in Nashville. Only twenty years old [actually 23]. Hitting around .310."[11] By the end of August, Nashville, which won both halves of the NSL season, faced the Monroe Monarchs, the Texas-Louisiana Negro League champions, in a seven-game series for the Dixie Negro championship. Nashville captured the Dixie championship, and then the team headed back to the West Coast for another season of winter ball.[12]

Wilson's NNL-member Cleveland franchise disbanded after the 1931 season, so in 1932 he focused his efforts on his Nashville franchise. The Elite Giants were still members of the NSL, but that circuit had become strong enough that it is today considered to have been a major league for that one season. Lyons attended Nashville's spring training in March,[13] but began the season with the Louisville Black Caps, another NSL member franchise. On July 2 Lyons took the mound and pitched all 13 innings in an 8-7 home loss to the Chicago American Giants, hindered by five Black Cap errors.[14] By late August, Lyons was back with Nashville, and participated in the NSL Championship Series, which was won in seven games by the Chicago American Giants. Lyons went 3-for-6 in the series and, in spite of Nashville's loss of the series, the press noted that, in Game Four, "the fielding of [Hoss] Walker and Lyons for the locals was outstanding."[15]

Lyons started 1933 with the Indianapolis ABCs in the new incarnation of the Negro National League, alongside former Nashville teammates James "Black Bottom" Buford and Percy Bailey. Manager Candy Jim Taylor moved his ABCs franchise to Detroit in mid-May due to low attendance, and the team was renamed the Stars.[16] Lyons was the primary first baseman of the franchise during the season, both in its Indianapolis and Detroit incarnations. In June a *Pittsburgh Courier* article observed that "Lyons' flashy fielding around the first base and timely hitting has established himself."[17] Lyons was Detroit's third leading hitter as of late June, at .311, behind catcher Clarence Palm and outfielder Jim Williams.[18] Lyons is the only player listed as having hit a home run on the

season for the team (he had two), and the offensively-challenged Detroit Stars finished in last place.

In 1934 Lyons returned to Tom Wilson's Nashville Elite Giants, for whom Jim West was now the regular first baseman. However, Lyons did start at first base at Pittsburgh on July 1, batting fifth and collecting three hits and scoring two runs in beating the Crawfords, 10-4, in the opener before losing the nightcap to Satchel Paige, 6-0.[19] He also started for Nashville on July 8 in a 7-1 loss to Philadelphia.[20]

Four days later, Lyons joined the Pittsburgh Crawfords, and started at first base in place of regular starter and manager Oscar Charleston in a doubleheader split with the Philadelphia Stars at Pittsburgh's Eagle Park. Lyons collected four hits in nine at-bats as he batted behind leadoff hitter Cool Papa Bell and in front of Leroy Morney and Josh Gibson.[21]

Obviously impressed by his opponent Lyons' day, Philadelphia Stars owner Ed Bolden secured Lyons for his squad just days later. Lyons debuted for the Stars on July 19 in place of Jud Wilson in a game at 12th and Bigler Streets Park against the semipro South Phillies. Lyons broke his leg sliding into third base and was treated at St. Agnes Hospital. The *Philadelphia Tribune* wrote that Lyons, a "star recruit … newly from Nashville, cracks limb sliding into third."[22] Lyons' popularity had become such that he still finished fourth in voting at first base for the West prior to the annual East-West All Star Game, held in late August at Comiskey Park in Chicago.

Lyons returned to Bolden's Stars in 1935. The *Afro-American*, overlooking his one-game stint with the team in the previous season, reported in spring training that "among the new players (are) Granville Lyons, first baseman, once with the Nashville Elites."[23] He reported to camp in late April for manager and starting pitcher Webster McDonald. However, due to Jud Wilson's incredible season, Lyons also saw time in the outfield. On May 12, Lyons' three-run homer against a new Brooklyn Eagles hurler, 18-year-old Leon Day, accounted for the Stars' only runs in an 8-3 loss at Philadelphia's Passon Field.[24] On May 28, in a game against the Pittsburgh Crawfords, "the finest fielding play of the contest came in the eighth frame when Lyons ran near the right field wall and made a one-handed running catch and then doubled up a Pittsburgh player at first base to end the inning."[25] In mid-June in front of 5,000 at Farmer Stadium in Brooklyn against the Farmers, Lyons played left field in the opener then tossed five relief innings in the nightcap.[26]

Lyons returned home to Nashville for 1936 as the starting first baseman and cleanup hitter for the NSL's Black Vols, a team managed by Hoss Walker that succeeded the Elite Giants as Nashville's Negro professional baseball club.[27] No statistics are available for the season, but infielders Henry Kimbro, James "Black Bottom" Buford, and Red Longley and pitchers Frank McAllister and Johnny Williams all were teammates on the Black Vols.[28] The squad won the first-half championship, which ended on July 4, with one newspaper asserting that "in Lyons, at first base, the Vols have one of the ranking negro players of all times."[29]

In July 1937 Lyons moved across Tennessee to ply his trade with the Memphis Red Sox. He received the fifth-most votes for first base for the West squad in the fifth East-West Game.[30] On August 22 Lyons played for the South All Stars in a 13-5 loss to the North All Stars at Rickwood Field in Birmingham, Alabama. He subbed for Felix Manning, and had two errors in the field while going 0-for 2 at the plate. In his last pitching appearance, on August 30, Lyons, coming over from first base (with Buck O'Neil moving from left to first), took the 11-inning loss against the Cincinnati Tigers.[31] Just as in 1933, Lyons once again was credited as the only player on his team to hit a home run on the season.

Lyons reunited with the Elite Giants for 1938, for at least one game in right field, although Tom Wilson had moved the franchise to Baltimore. The team now had a young catcher in Roy Campanella, along with Henry Kimbro and Biz Mackey among others. It was also reported in the *Louisville Courier Journal* that Lyons played for an Atlanta team during the season; however, no game accounts of his time with a team in that city have been discovered.[32]

The 1940 census listed Granville as a married ballplayer, but he was living in Nashville with his mother, Kittie, his half-sister Martha, and his three children. In April, Lyons re-signed with owner-manager J. Leonard Mitchell's Louisville Black Colonels.[33] By late May, Lyons was nowhere to be found as Mitchell had released several veterans. The next month, Lyons popped up, along with old teammate Ewing Russell, as softball umpires in the Negro Municipal Association in Nashville.[34] Lyons was listed in the Nashville city directory in 1941 as a porter and was living with his new wife, Arkia.

Lyons returned yet again to Wilson's Elite Giants in Baltimore for eight games in 1942, playing left field in a victory on May 11 against the Homestead Grays in which he and Campanella each collected doubles.[35] On May 31 Lyons batted eighth and played first base for Baltimore in their 5-3 victory over the Philadelphia Stars, ending the Stars' nine-game winning streak, in front of 20,000 fans in Yankee Stadium.[36] On June 5 he went 0-for-4 against the Philadelphia Stars, again at Yankee Stadium.[37] By the end of June, George Scales was playing first base for the Elites against the New York Black Yankees in Belmar, New Jersey.[38] Lyons soon was released and was replaced by James "Lefty" Turner.[39]

In late June 1945, Dr. R.B. Jackson, head of the Nashville Black Vols and the new minor Negro Southern League, appointed Lyons to replace Bill Perkins as manager of his team.[40] After less than a month, it was remarked that, in Lyons, the "local man has done an exceptionally fine job handling the team."[41] The Black Vols were leading in the second-half standings as Lyons started Smoky Joe Hall in August against the Atlanta Black Crackers, the first-half winner.[42] However, by early September, Lyons became ill, so second baseman Dusty Owens was tasked to take over as manager.[43] The Black Crackers ended up winning both halves of the NSL.

In 1950 Lyons played for one final team, manning second base for the Owensboro Braves of the Negro Southern League, under manager Rufus Hatten, but the team disbanded halfway through the season. He was listed as a professional ballplayer and living with Arkia in the 1950 census. By 1951, son Granville Jr. had enlisted in the Army and eventually became a corporal. In 1952 the elder Lyons was granted a federal gambling tax stamp from the Internal Revenue Service,[44] acting as an agent for some other professional gambler.

Granville Lyons Jr. died suddenly of unknown causes on April 14, 1953, in Nashville at the age of 44[45] and was buried in Nashville's Greenwood Cemetery. He was survived by his wife, Arkia (Artie), his son, Granville Lyons Jr., daughters Katie McNeil and Myrtle Smith, and his sister Selene.

Sources

In addition to the sources cited in the Notes, the author consulted MyHeritage.com, Seamheads.com, and Baseball-Reference.com

NOTES

1   Mark Robinson, "8 Rules Every Theatre Must Follow – Do You Know All of Them?" Playbill.com, https://www.playbill.com/article/8-rules-every-theatre-person-must-follow-do-you-know-all-of-them-com-373336, July 1, 2019 (retrieved August 8, 2022).

2   "Street Car Crashes into Transportation Car," *Nashville Banner*, October 31, 1906: 11.

3   1940 Census figures: Granville Lyons, Nashville, Tennessee.

4   Euell A. Nielsen, "Nashville/Baltimore Elite Giants (1920-1951)," December 2, 2020, Blackpost.com, https://www.blackpast.org/african-american-history/baltimore-elite-giants-1920-1951.

5   "Bill Bobo, Noted Negro Ball Player, Is Dead," *Sacramento Bee*, February 24, 1931: 16.

6   "Elite Giant First Baseman Dies After a Brief Illness," *Nashville Banner*, February 26, 1931: 20.

7   "Local Negro Ball Club to Engage Louisville," *Nashville Banner*, April 23, 1931: 14.

8   "Elite Giants Play Double Bill Today," *Nashville Tennessean*, May 17, 1931: 11.

9   "Elite Giants Lose to Black Barons, 9 to 8," *Nashville Tennessean*, June 21, 1931: 14.

10   "Elite Giants to Perform in Dell," *Nashville Banner*, July 28, 1931: 11.

11   Tom Anderson, "Nashville's Baseball Champs," *Nashville Banner*, August 14, 1931: 13.

12   "Nashville Negro Ball Team Playing Winter Ball on West Coast," *Nashville Banner*, October 7, 1931: 14.

13   "Giants Drill: Nashville Colored Ball Club Begins Spring Training," *Nashville Banner*, March 29, 1932: 12.

14   "Giants Tip Black Caps in 13 Innings by 8 to 7," *Louisville Courier Journal*, July 3, 1932: 15.

15   "Elites Lose," *Nashville Banner*, September 19, 1932: 8.

16   John L. Clark, "Notes on the Negro National Association," *Pittsburgh Courier*, May 27, 1933: 15.

17   "Detroit Club Gaining Favor of Ball Fans," *Pittsburgh Courier*, June 10, 1933: 14.

18   "'Texas' Burnett Leads Hitters, Summary Shows," *Pittsburgh Courier*, June 24, 1933: 14.

19   "At Pittsburgh, July 1," *Baltimore Afro-American*, July 7, 1934: 17.

20   "Philly Stars Garner Two During Week," *Baltimore Afro American*, July 14, 1934: 18.

21   "Crawfords and All-Stars Split," *York* (Pennsylvania) *Gazette and Daily*, July 13, 1934: 11.

22   "Philly Stars Win 5, Drop 2; Player Breaks Leg," *Philadelphia Tribune*, July 26, 1934: 12.

23   "Bolden's Stars Won't Go South; Prep in Philly," *Baltimore Afro-American*, April 13, 1935: 17.

24   "Day Again Ace for Eagles Nine," *Brooklyn Times Union*, May 13, 1935: 11; "Brooklyn Eagles Get an Even Break," *Brooklyn Daily Eagle*, May 13, 1935: 12.

25   "Philadelphia All-Stars Shut Out Pittsburg Crawfords," *York* (Pennsylvania) *Gazette and Daily*, May 29, 1935: 10.

26   "Farmers Split Twin Bill with Philadelphia Stars," *Brooklyn Times Union*, June 17, 1935: 13.

27   "Black Vols Play Twin Bill Today," *Nashville Tennessean*, May 3, 1936: 14.

28   Dr. Layton Revel, "Forgotten Heroes: Henry Kimbro," Center for Negro League Research, 2019, http://www.cnlbr.org/Portals/0/Hero/Henry_Kimbro%202019-10.pdf

29   "Two Crack Negro Teams to Play," *Moberly* (Missouri) *Monitor-Index*, July 15, 1936: 5.

30   "Interest in Big All-Star Game in Chi Soaring," *Pittsburgh Courier*, July 24, 1937: 18.

31   Howard V. Milliard, "Negroes Give Classy Show," *Decatur* (Illinois) *Daily Review*, August 31, 1937: 8.

32   Victor Perry, "Church League Games Again Postponed," *Louisville Courier Journal*, April 23, 1939: 52.

33   Victor Perry, "Black Colonels Sign Up New Players," *Louisville Courier Journal*, April 8, 1940: 11.

34   "Morocco, Goldblumes Set Softball Pace," *Nashville Banner*, June 5, 1940: 11.

35   Os Figard, "Homestead Grays Weak at Bat as Baltimore Takes Nod, 8-2," *Altoona* (Pennsylvania) *Tribune*, May 12, 1942: 10.

36   "Phila. Stars Lose, Win Streak Halted," *Philadelphia Inquirer*, June 1, 1942: 22.

37   William E. Clark," *New York Age*, June 6, 1942: 11.

38   "Black Yankees Play Baltimore," *Asbury Park* (New Jersey) *Press*, June 29, 1942: 10.

39   "Play Grays in Night Contest," *Baltimore Afro-American*, July 4, 1942: 23.

40   "Black Vols Play Mobile Shippers Here on Fourth," *Nashville Tennessean*, July 1, 1945: 39.

41   "Black Crackers in Dell Friday," *Nashville Tennessean*, July 29, 1945: 42.

42   "Black Vols Host to Crax Tonight," *Nashville Tennessean*, August 3, 1945: 29.

43   "Dusky Dellers and Louisville Tangle Today," *Nashville Tennessean*, September 9, 1945: 52.

44   Davis Gets Gaming Stamp," *Chattanooga Daily Times*, February 1, 1952: 18; "39th Nashvillian on Gaming List," *Nashville Tennessean*, January 31, 1952: 1.

45   "Obituaries: Lyons," *Nashville Tennessean*, April 15, 1953: 25.

BIZ MACKEY

by Chris Rainey

In the summer of 1946, *Pittsburgh Courier* columnist Wendell Smith gave Newark Eagles manager Biz Mackey all the credit for molding "together the best all-around pitching staff in Negro baseball."[1] Assembling talent is one thing, using it wisely and coping with obstacles that arise is a totally different talent. Mackey's ace, Leon Day, opened the season with a no-hitter and led the team in wins. But he struggled with a sore arm and was of little use in the World Series. Mackey used his staff effectively, especially young Rufus Lewis, to capture a championship. His shortstop, Monte Irvin, simply said of Mackey, "As a player, as a manager, and as a personality, he was in a class by himself."[2]

Capturing the Negro League banner in 1946 was the final jewel of Mackey's brilliant career. Generally regarded as the finest defensive catcher in Negro League history, he was no slouch at the plate. The switch-hitter batted .411 in 1922 and .406 in 1930. He captured two World Series crowns in the Negro Leagues, one as a player and one as manager. He also won a championship in his only season in Cuba. In 2006 his life and talent were recognized with his selection to the National Baseball Hall of Fame in Cooperstown.

The journey to the top of his baseball world was not an easy one for Mackey. He was born the son of Texas sharecroppers. The absence of a birth certificate has led to speculation about his birthplace. In the past 30 years various researchers and writers have placed Mackey's birth in Eagle Pass, Texas, as well as Seguin, Kingsbury, Luling, and Eagle Lake, all in Texas.[3] Most current sources (Seamheads.com is a notable exception) accept the Eagle Pass location. Mackey listed his birthplace as Caldwell County (near Luling) on his World War I and World War II draft registrations.[4]

We do know that James Raleigh Mackey was one of six children born to John Dee (known as Dee to family and friends) and Beulah (Wright) Mackey, joining the family on July 27, 1897. His parents had wed in 1886 in Caldwell County and farmed there. In the 1900 census, Beulah listed herself as married but Dee was not living under the same roof. She was remarried in 1903 to

Montgomery Meriwether, a farmer in a neighboring county. The 1910 census lists them in Guadalupe County between Seguin and Kingsbury. This blended family included Meriwether's three daughters along with Beulah's five surviving offspring.

The town of Luling, Texas, claims Mackey as its native son. He was wed there on October 20, 1917, to Ora Lee Dorn.[5] It is uncertain if Mackey and Ora ever had children. Mackey did have a daughter named Narcissus. She was born in 1914 and later married George H. Odoms. They took up residence in Caldwell County and raised at least three children. Her oldest son, Riley Mackey Odoms, had a long and successful football career with the Denver Broncos.[6]

Biz and Ora Lee moved to Dallas, where he played baseball and worked as a laborer in 1918. They separated in 1919 and divorced a few years later. Ora Lee remarried in 1924. She and her husband, Will Elam, lived in California. Late in his life, Mackey reconnected with Ora Lee and she is listed on his death

Catcher "Biz" Mackey, a 24-year veteran of the Negro Leagues.

National Baseball Hall of Fame

certificate as "Informant" and appears to have handled his funeral arrangements.[7]

Mackey received his schooling in nearby Prairie Lea, Texas, through the 10th grade. It was common in rural America for students to take an exam when their schooling ended. They would earn the equivalent of today's high-school diploma with a good performance on the "Common Exam." Mackey met the requirements when he completed the test.

The 1910 census noted that Mackey worked as a farm laborer when not in school. A few years later he took a job as a clerk in a railroad warehouse. At age 16 he reportedly joined his brothers Earnest and Ray playing on the Luling Oilers, the local semipro team. Mackey caught and pitched. Most sources claim he joined the San Antonio Black Aces in 1918. It is more likely that he played for the Dallas Black Giants that season.

Before Mackey earned his nickname, he was known to fans and writers as Riley, Rollie, or Raleigh. He appears in box scores sometimes as Mackey and sometimes by his first name.[8] Based upon that information, it is likely that the Dallas catcher/pitcher in 1918 shown as Riley was in fact Mackey.[9] He opened the 1919 season with the Giants but soon joined the Waco Black Navigators. His time with them was short-lived; he joined five other Waco players in jumping to the San Antonio Black Aces in early June.[10]

The addition of six starters to the Black Aces made them into a juggernaut. League standings showed them with a 45-10 record at the end of the Texas Colored League campaign in 1919. The Waco squad, which had started the season as the strongest team, disbanded shortly after the player defections. Dallas finished with a 51-17 mark and took on San Antonio in a postseason five-game championship.

After tight matches decided by a single run, the series came down to the nightcap of a doubleheader. The Aces sent Walter "Steel Arm" Davis to the mound, but he was pounded for three runs in the first. Mackey took the hill and allowed two more runs the rest of the way. In typical Hollywood fashion, Davis (who moved to center field) came to the plate in the eighth with two men on and lashed a double to give San Antonio a 7-5 victory and the title.

In December the leader of the Black Aces, L.W. Moore, announced his hopes of creating a Colorado-Texas-Oklahoma League. He also announced the signing of two catchers "who will fill the vacancy" created when Riley Mackey became a pitcher exclusively.[11] The new league did not materialize, and the Black Aces remained in the Texas Colored League. Mackey took the hill as planned but when one of the catchers left the team, Mackey was returned to occasional catching duties. He highlighted his return with a 5-for-5 performance against the Black Giants on June 11.

A month later Mackey was enticed to leave Texas. On July 13 he and Aces teammate Henry Blackmon (mistakenly called Blackburn in the box score) debuted for the Negro National League Indianapolis ABC's against the Cuban Stars. Mackey smacked a double in four trips in the 5-2 victory.[12] Behind the plate he "worked in first-class style." When the Cubans' shortstop Matias Rios tried to steal second, "Mackey got the ball there so far ahead of him" that the second baseman walked up the line to tag Rios.[13] Many authors have said Mackey's contract was sold to the ABC's, but an article in the *San Antonio Evening News* mentioned that Aces leadership was contemplating a lawsuit because the players had jumped their contracts.[14]

The ABC's finished in fourth place. Mackey's work at bat and behind the plate earned him a contract for 1921. He wintered in Texas and played ball there before returning to Indiana for spring training in early April. Indianapolis opened the season with two wins over the Cuban Stars, but quickly fell off the pace after that. Mackey was even forced to take the mound and took three losses during the campaign. At the plate he hit .304, tied for the team lead in triples, and punched three home runs.

The ABC's stayed together after the season and did some barnstorming. Mackey played third base late in the year and during the fall. Russell Powell handled the catching during the regular season. In the fall, Mack Eggleston was recruited to catch. The team also welcomed back Oscar Charleston, who had spent the season with St. Louis.

Charleston remained with the ABC's in 1922 and the team finished second, tied with the Monarchs but trailing the Chicago American Giants. Charleston batted .395 and slammed 14 doubles, 9 triples, and 11 home runs. Not to be outdone, Mackey also mashed 14 doubles and hit a robust .411 while playing some shortstop and outfield along with catching.

In 1923 Ed Bolden, owner of the Hilldale Daisies (also called Giants and Darbys), led the formation of the Eastern Colored League (ECOL). A talent war ensued between the ECOL and the NNL that resulted in Mackey being signed by Hilldale. There he joined future Hall of Famers Judy Johnson, Pop Lloyd, and Louis Santop. Mackey was now 25 years old and had reached his full stature of 6 feet tall and probably 210 pounds.

The ECOL season opener was staged before 17,000 fans in Hilldale's new park. Mackey caught and batted fifth in the lineup behind Lloyd. The game was called because of rain in the sixth with Hilldale up 4-2 over the Bacharach Giants.[15] Mackey split the catching duties that season with Santop and spelled the 39-year-old Lloyd at shortstop. He is credited with leading the team in batting and RBIs. Hilldale posted a league-leading 32-17 record.

The nickname "Biz" first started to appear in 1923. Both the *Philadelphia Inquirer* and *Pittsburgh Courier* were using it by the end of the season. Mackey was a friendly, loquacious fellow with a competitive streak. He was known for giving the batter an earful when at the plate, hoping to break their concentration and focus. This "giving them the business" earned him the nickname of "Biz." It should be noted that he was not the first "Biz" Mackey to make the sports pages. A featherweight boxer who twice had world-championship matches against Abe Attell – yes, that Attell of Black Sox infamy – had appeared in headlines for two decades as the catcher grew up.

Hilldale was the dominant ECOL team again in 1924, posting a 47-22 mark. Mackey led the team in batting and handled the pitching staff of Nip Winters, Red Ryan, and Phil Cockrell expertly. The two Black leagues staged a world series after the regular season and the Kansas City Monarchs captured five of the nine games.

After the season Mackey went to Cuba to play for Almendares. He joined Lloyd, Charleston, Wilbur "Bullet" Rogan, and Adolfo Luque on a team that proved to be a juggernaut. The season was ended early because of Almendares' dominance. Mackey batted .309 with a team-leading 11 doubles.[16]

Because the regular season closed early, a post-season series was staged between an all-Cuban team and the "All Yankees" team made up of Negro League players. The All Yankees posted a 5-2-1 record. Mackey faced Cuban pitchers José Méndez and Martín Dihigo in the series and reportedly batted .333. Interestingly, Baseball Commissioner Kenesaw Mountain Landis attended one of the games.[17]

Unlike many of his contemporaries who played winter ball in the Caribbean and Mexico, this was Mackey's sole trip to the islands. He chose to spend his winters playing in the California Winter League, which featured a mix of Black and White teams. Mackey played 18 seasons on the West Coast and eventually made his permanent home in California. He is credited with a .366 batting average and 28 home runs in those seasons.[18]

The Hilldale squad ran away with the title again in 1925, posting a 52-15 record. The players did prove to be human during a week in June when they dropped three to the Harrisburg Giants and then lost a doubleheader to the Baltimore Black Sox. Mackey, who batted cleanup, produced only four hits in the games.[19] Hilldale was knocked out of first place by the losses but regained the lead in mid-July and never looked back.

Hilldale earned a rematch with the Monarchs in an October series. Mackey struggled early in the series. He was 2-for-17 in the first four games and even dropped a ball in a home-plate collision. Baseball takes a team effort and his teammates picked him up as Hilldale captured three of the first four matches. In the final games, in Philadelphia, Mackey's bat came alive and he had three hits, including a home run and double. Hilldale took five of six to capture the crown.[20]

Hilldale returned their core in 1926, and even added John Beckwith but its record dropped to 34-24 and the team finished in third place. In the offseason Mackey joined a barnstorming squad called the Philadelphia Royal Giants. They went to California and played in the winter league, posting a 26-11-1 record to win the crown. The team split up and some players returned to their teams for the regular season.

Mackey, along with Rap Dixon, Andy Cooper, and others, traveled to Japan and played a 48-game tour, the first tour by a Black entourage. The Americans entertained the locals with their brand of baseball, which included a pregame "shadow ball" routine. Years of experience in barnstorming had taught Mackey and his teammates the importance of keeping the local fans interested and entertained. Winning 20-0 would dampen enthusiasm and lessen the gate. It was to their advantage to keep the games close. In doing this they "played to the Japanese sense of honor and dignity."[21]

Mackey established himself as a fan favorite. He launched a massive home run at the new Meiji Shrine Stadium in Tokyo. He fascinated and amazed the crowds with his ability to throw from the crouch. He was quick with a smile and genuine sincerity toward opponents and fans alike. After hitting him with a pitch, a Japanese hurler bowed to apologize, as is the style in the country. Mackey returned the gesture and bowed in return.[22]

Biz returned to Japan for a second tour five years later. On this tour he did some pitching and led the

American contingent with a .388 batting average.[23] The Japanese Baseball League would begin in 1936. Japanese baseball historian Kazuo Sayama credits the Royal Giants and Mackey with hastening the adoption of the game in his country. Babe Ruth's visit in 1934 certainly created a countrywide sensation, but without the groundwork laid by the Negro Leaguers the game would not have reached its level of influence and popularity.

The lengthy tour in 1927 caused Mackey and his mates to miss the first half of the ECOL season. Hilldale was experiencing a poor first half. Joe Lewis handled the catching, but three players were suspended indefinitely in early June because of their indifferent play. Mackey was threatened with a five-year suspension after his return to the United States in early July. The suspension proved to be a hollow threat and he was in the lineup on July 28 for a 5-3 win over the Bacharach Giants.[24]

The Daisies finished third in the second half after being in fifth at the close of the first half. Mackey batted .284. He was recruited by Cum Posey in the fall and traveled with the Homestead Grays on their extensive barnstorming trip.

Hilldale added Oscar Charleston to the roster but dropped out of the league in March 1928. Playing an independent schedule against all comers, the team covered the East with appearances. Mackey found himself playing shortstop on numerous occasions. In

late September he and second baseman Frank Warfield were added to the roster of the Baltimore Black Sox.

Hilldale moved into the American Negro League in 1929 and Mackey returned to the team. He stayed with it through 1931 after they went independent. In 1932 he declined a contract and stayed in California until promoter Lonnie Goodwin left for the Orient with his tour. The team played nine games in Honolulu, then crossed the Pacific to play in Japan. They also had 10 games scheduled in China and 30 in the Philippines.

From 1933 to 1935 Mackey played with the Philadelphia Stars. He was selected by fan vote as the starting catcher in the inaugural East-West All-Star Game, played before 19,000 fans in Comiskey Park in Chicago. He split time with Josh Gibson at catcher in the 11-7 loss by his East team. In 1936 he was traded to the Columbus Elite Giants, but that franchise moved to Washington. Mackey had his first taste as manager when he filled in for Candy Jim Taylor. He also earned a starting spot in the All-Star Game.

The consensus among fans and scholars of the Negro Leagues was that Gibson was the better hitter, but Mackey was by far his defensive superior. Author James Riley said it best: "Considered the master of defense, (Mackey) possessed all the tools necessary behind the plate. ... An expert handler of pitchers, he studied people. ... [H]e was a master at ... framing and funneling pitches. Pitchers recognized his generalship and liked to pitch" to Mackey. His surprising agility for a big man enabled him to play the infield.[25]

In 1937 Mackey took over as Washington manager when Taylor moved on. Mackey was selected by the fans as the manager for the East-West All Star Game. His East squad emerged with a 7-2 victory. He was tipped off about the talent of a teenager named Roy Campanella. Washington signed Campanella for $60 a month and Mackey began the task of turning him into a professional catcher. When Mackey left the Elite Giants, Campanella was ready to step into his shoes. Campanella recalled, "Biz Mackey was the master of defense of all catchers." Campanella always was quick to give Mackey credit for his development.[26]

Mackey was sold to the Newark Eagles in 1939. He took over as manager from Dick Lundy partway through the 1940 season. Despite a growing waistline and aching knees, Mackey continued to be an asset on the field. In 1942 he had a falling-out with the owners, Abe and Effa Manley, over salary and was replaced by Willie Wells.

Mackey returned to his California home. He supported the war effort by working at North American

Hall of Fame catcher Raleigh "Biz" Mackey

Graig Kreindler

John W. Mosley Photograph Collection, Temple University

"Biz" Mackey was a career .330 hitter in 1,118 major Negro Leagues games.

Aviation in Los Angeles and played baseball with the San Francisco Sea Lions. When the Manleys had a dispute with Wells, Mackey returned to Newark in 1945. He continued to play occasionally, mostly at first base.

The Eagles captured the first-half championship in 1946 with a record of 25-9. They weathered some hard times in the second half, including the demise of the team bus which forced players to drive their own cars to games at one point.

Mackey was renowned for his levelheadedness and emotional control on the field throughout his managerial career. He uncharacteristically lost his cool in a game against the Cleveland Buckeyes in late July of 1946 and pulled the Eagles from the field in protest. The Black press took him to task for being unsportsmanlike. Effa Manley came to his defense with a letter to the *Pittsburgh Courier* and the issue blew over.

The Eagles took the second half with a 22-7 mark and met the Kansas City Monarchs in the World Series. Led by Monte Irvin's bat and the pitching of Rufus Lewis, Newark captured the pennant, a triumph that earned each player a diamond ring.

Mackey managed the Eagles again in 1947. The Eagles sold Larry Doby to the Cleveland Indians that year. Mackey recommended moving the youngster from second base to the outfield, which the Indians did. Mackey was named manager of the East squad for the All-Star Game. The game was played on

his 50th birthday and Mackey rewarded himself by pinch-hitting in the eighth inning. He had seen very little action that season, and his waistline had grown to where writer Wendell Smith called him paunchy. His girth did not affect his batting eye; he walked. He immediately replaced himself with Vic Harris.

Mackey retired to California, where he continued to play with the Sea Lions and other teams. Fate has an odd way of impacting our lives. When Mackey made his first trip to Japan, he was intrigued to find a large contingent of Afro-Asians living in Tokyo. He met a young woman of mixed ancestry named Lucille and they became friendly. On later trips to Japan he made it a point to contact her. The pair understandably lost contact during the war.

According to Mackey's great-nephew Ray, Lucille and her family came to the United States in the late 1940s or early 1950s. She and Mackey were reunited in San Francisco. They spent the rest of their lives together. Mackey's reputation in baseball was that of a jovial, trash-talker but in his private life he was very reserved. He bordered on reclusive and did very little to publicize his baseball life.

That changed, for one day at least, on the evening of May 7, 1959. A reported 93,000 fans attended an exhibition game in the Los Angeles Coliseum between the Dodgers and the Yankees. The occasion was to pay tribute to Roy Campanella, the longtime Dodgers catcher, who had been paralyzed in a traffic accident the previous year. In the crowd were Mackey and his nephew Ray. In his thank-you speech to the throng, Campy called for Mackey to join him on the field and made sure that everyone there realized how important Biz had been in his development.[27]

After the Campanella tribute, Mackey lived quietly in Los Angeles and worked as a forklift driver for the Stauffer Chemical Company. In those days before the publication of *Only the Ball Was White*,[28] it was commonplace for a former Negro League player to live in anonymity. Lucille, called "Aunt Lucy" by the family, died a few months before Biz. The family wondered if the loss of the love of his life hastened Mackey's demise. Biz died on September 22, 1965, in Los Angeles. He was buried in that city's Evergreen Cemetery. His death received no coverage in *The Sporting News* nor did it appear in the Necrology of the *1966 Sporting News Official Baseball Guide*. In the 1970s and beyond, Mackey's name would make newspapers as a Negro League player who deserved Hall of Fame consideration. His time to enter Cooperstown finally came in 2006.

Sources

Statistics come from Baseball-Reference.com unless otherwise noted. Standings of teams come from *The Negro League Book* published by SABR in 1994. A big thank-you to Ray Mackey III for his tremendous wealth of information about Biz and the Mackey family. I would also like to extend my gratitude to renowned Negro League historian Larry Lester for his support and guidance in this research. Finally, a tip of the hat to the Allen County Library in Fort Wayne, Indiana, where a researcher named Cristella searched the *Los Angeles Sentinel* for Mackey info.

Notes

1   Wendell Smith, "The Sports Beat," *Pittsburgh Courier*, July 13, 1946: 16.

2   templepress.wordpress.com/2018/01/24/biz-mackey-a-giant-behind-the-plate/.

3   John Holway listed the birthplace as Seguin in his 1988 book *Blackball Stars*; other sources found in Mackey's Hall of Fame file suggest Kingsbury, which is east of Seguin and Luling; in a correspondence from 2000 there was mention of Eagle Lake.

4   ancestry.com/interactive/6482/005152930_01688?pid=16453080&backurl=https://search. Last accessed February 26, 2019. search.ancestry.com/cgi-bin/sse.dll?db=YMDraftCardsWWII&indiv=try&h=17975243. Last accessed March 11, 2019.

5   search.ancestry.com/cgi-bin/sse.dll?dbid=60183&h=66427&indiv=try&o_vc=Record:OtherRecord&rhSource=8842.

6   Brad Gray, "Biz's Big Day," *Austin American-Statesman*, July 31, 2006: 20.

7   Gary Krause, email exchange from February 2000 found in Mackey's Hall of Fame file. Krause was researching Mackey's personal information and corresponding with a Hall of Fame library researcher, Eric Enders.

8   An example would be the box scores in the *Dallas Express* from August 23, 1919: 11, in which he was listed as Riley in the first game and Releigh (*sic*) in game two.

9   "Dallas Black Giants Win," *Dallas Morning News*, August 12, 1918: 7. He was also residing in Dallas in August when he signed up for the draft. See Note 4.

10   Gary Ashwill, "Steel Arm Davis," Agate Type, November 3, 2014. agatetype.typepad.com/agate_type/2014/11/steel-arm-davis.html. Last accessed February 26, 2019.

11   *San Antonio Evening News*, December 13, 1919: 10.

12   "New Players Show Class," *Indianapolis Star*, July 14, 1920: 10.

13   "New Players Show Class."

14   "Suit May be Filed for Taking Players from Black Aces," *San Antonio Evening News*, August 2, 1920: 7.

15   "Hilldale Opens New Park with Victory," *Philadelphia Inquirer*, April 29, 1923: 20.

16   Jorge S. Figueredo, *Cuban Baseball: A Statistical History, 1878-1961* (Jefferson, North Carolina: McFarland, 2003), 157-59.

17   Figueredo, 162.

18   Geri Strecker, "Winter Baseball in California: Separate Opportunities, Equal Talent," *The National Pastime* (SABR, 2011), accessed on February 28, 2019 at sabr.org/research/winter-baseball-california-separate-opportunities-equal-talent.

19   "Harrisburg Sweeps Three-Game Series with Hilldale; Leads Eastern League," *Pittsburgh Courier*, June 27, 1925: 12.

20   Game coverage from the *Pittsburgh Courier* of October 10 and 17.

21   Gary Joseph Cieradkowski, "Biz Mackey: International Man of Clout," Infinite Card Set blog October 2013. Last accessed on February 28, 2019 at infinitecardset.blogspot.com/2013/10/160-biz-mackey-international-man-of.html.

22   Kazuo Sayama and Bill Staples Jr., *Gentle Black Giants: A History of Negro Leaguers in Japan* (Fresno, California: NBRP Press, 2019), 121.

23   William F. McNeil, *Black Baseball Out of Season: Pay for Play Outside the Negro Leagues* (Jefferson, North Carolina: McFarland, 2012), 108.

24   "Mackey's 'Five-Years Suspension' Over, Aids Hilldale in Win Over Seasiders," *Pittsburgh Courier*, July 30, 1927: 16.

25   James A. Riley, *The Biographical Encyclopedia of the Negro Baseball Leagues* (New York: Carroll & Graf Publishers, 1994), 502-03.

26   Gray, "Biz's Big Day."

27   Telephone interviews with Ray Mackey III, March 6 and 11, 2019.

28   Robert Peterson, *Only the Ball Was White* (New York: Oxford University Press, 1992).

WEBSTER MCDONALD

By Leslie Heaphy

I was strictly a submarine pitcher, a lot of junk. I had a good fast one, but I didn't throw it when I didn't have to. With the hard hitters, I'd time them. I'd throw mixed pitches – "56 varieties" they used to call me. And then when I showed them a good fast ball, they weren't ready. I'd say, "See, you weren't ready."[1]

Remembered best for his pitching against White major-league players, Webster McDonald was a star pitcher in the Negro Leagues and independent ball from 1918 through 1946. McDonald began his playing career in 1918 with the local Philadelphia Giants and ended with the Brooklyn Brown Dodgers. He was an underhand submariner who was well-liked and respected by everyone he worked with, and he played and managed for many teams, providing mentorship for new stars and aging veterans. During his career McDonald was part of seven pennant-winning teams, anchoring their pitching staffs and guiding the team strategies. Yet many fans have yet to learn about the pitcher about whom Connie Mack once said, "I'm sorry to say this, but I'd give half my ball club for a man like you."[2]

Born on January 1, 1900, in Glasgow, Delaware, McDonald was one of six children of Charles McDonald, a carpenter from North Carolina, and Georgia native Katie Roundtree, listed in the census as a housewife. He was taken to Philadelphia when he was 3 years old to live with his aunt, Sally Cluster, who worked in a stocking mill; and Philadelphia became his home for the rest of his life.

Growing up in Philadelphia, McDonald played sports on the playgrounds and local ball fields. He got his start in baseball in 1918 with the semipro Philadelphia Giants. The Giants were not the same star-studded team of earlier baseball history but a new club with the same name. Between 1918 and 1924 McDonald played for several local independent teams while trying to break into the pitching staff for the Hilldale Daisies. He got a few starts with Hilldale but never was able to crack their roster. McDonald pitched for the Madison Stars, the Norfolk Stars, and the Philadelphia Giants before signing in 1925 with the new Wilmington Potomacs.

The Potomacs were unable to complete their season in the Eastern Colored League (ECL) and disbanded in July. McDonald pitched in 12 games for Wilmington with a 3-4 record over 48 innings. He got his first victory against the Cuban Stars, winning 6-1 on a two-hitter. A local reporter wrote that he had "showed the fans a brand of baseball that has seldom been seen around these parts."[3] McDonald finally got his big break when he joined the Chicago American Giants late in the 1925 season and stayed until the 1929 season. He ended the

Graig Kreindler

Pitcher Webster McDonald, a 17-year veteran of the Negro Leagues.

1925 season having pitched in 10 games for the Giants, compiling a 6-2 record.[4]

McDonald returned to Chicago in 1926 and pitched to a 10-5 record in 135 innings. He showed the control he became most known for by striking out 80 batters and walking only 31. Hall of Fame first baseman Buck Leonard had the following to say about McDonald's mastery: "He had good control. Whatever your weakness was, he'd throw the ball there."[5] The Giants earned the right to play the Kansas City Monarchs in a nine-game series to take the Negro National League (NNL) title and face the Atlantic City Bacharachs in the World Series. McDonald's only two decisions in the postseason were both losses. One was a 10-0 loss in Game Three of the World Series in which Atlantic City's Claude "Red" Grier threw a no-hitter.[6]

McDonald returned to the Giants in 1927 and had another good year with a 10-5 record in 134⅔ innings. He struck out 68 while walking only 21. One of the best games of his career came on August 15 when he came on in relief and proceeded to pitch seven innings of no-hit ball into the 10th inning, although the Giants ended up losing the game 1-0.[7] The Giants again made the World Series against the team from Atlantic City. McDonald pitched the Giants to one victory, 9-1, over the Bacharachs' Luther "Red" Farrell, but Chicago eventually claimed its second consecutive championship.

In 1928 McDonald started with the Giants but left in May to join the Little Falls Independents, a Minnesota entrant in the Northwestern League. He made the move to Little Falls for a higher paycheck, starting at $350 a month but later claiming to earn as much as $750 a month. McDonald pitched for Little Falls from May through August every season until 1932. Before and after the Little Falls schedule, he picked up games with a number of ballclubs that were willing to pay his salary. McDonald chose to stay in the United States and pitch rather than head south of the border for the offseason, opting to stay close to Philadelphia because of health problems affecting his wife, Frances.[8]

McDonald was often the only Black player in Little Falls. On occasion his catchers were either John Van, a Black man from Kansas, or Sylvester Foreman, a player from the Kansas City Monarchs. He became a popular player with the fans because he helped the team win the Northwestern League title from 1928 through 1931. An article in 1935 claimed that while he was in Little Falls he became the highest paid Black player in the country.[9] One of the players he often

pitched against was John Donaldson, who had recommended McDonald to the Little Falls club. In 1930 he beat Donaldson twice during the season.[10]

McDonald opened the 1929 season with the Homestead Grays, pitching their opening game on May 4. He left the Grays to join Little Falls in May, pitching them to victories over teams such as the Utah Mormons, Detroit Lakes, and McCoy-Nolan Colored Giants. McDonald relied on his control and a sneaky underhanded delivery. He found continued success in 1930, winning games against St. Cloud and the McCoy-Nolan Colored Giants. After the 1930 season ended, McDonald did what he was best known for, joining teams to help them win the playoffs and pitching against major- and minor-league All-Stars. On August 30 in front of an estimated 4,000 fans, McDonald helped Little Falls defeat members of the Minneapolis team of the American Association. McDonald struck out six and walked two en route to a 6-3 win.[11]

McDonald ended the season with two victories over major-league pitcher Eddie Rommel and a team of all-stars. McDonald gained both wins while pitching for the Baltimore Black Sox. He also pitched the Black Sox to a victory over an all-star squad that included three St. Louis Cardinals led by Frankie Frisch.[12]

McDonald pitched for Little Falls, Hilldale, and the Homestead Grays in 1931. He was credited with a 4-0 record with Hilldale. He also claimed a 4-0 record vs. a team of White all-stars from the National and American Leagues, including a triumph over George Earnshaw. The win was a hard-fought 3-2 victory, solidifying McDonald's strong showing against White all-stars.[13] In September, while pitching for Hilldale, McDonald helped his team win a 9-0 shutout over the Cuban Stars. The hitting stars of the game were Chaney White and Rap Dixon.[14]

In 1932 McDonald joined the Washington Pilots of the East-West League, compiling a 5-5 record and taking over as manager after Frank Warfield died during the season. As manager, McDonald led the Pilots to a 7-11 record, leaving them in sixth place for the season. His victories came against teams such as the Fewster Nine and the New York Black Yankees among others.[15]

McDonald's reputation led to Ed Bolden approaching him to be a player-manager for his new Philadelphia Stars (of the Negro National League II) beginning in 1933. A Brooklyn paper referred to him as "Webster McDonald, peerless underhanded twirler."[16] McDonald spent the remainder of his major Negro

League career with the Stars, leading them to the NNL championship in 1934. In 1933 McDonald pitched in 11 games with a 4-3 record. In a series of games against the Philadelphia SPHAs, McDonald continued to be seen as a pitcher who could come in at any point in the game and shut down the opposition.[17]

The 1934 squad that McDonald piloted was filled with star players. Slim Jones led the pitching staff while the hitting was led by Jud Wilson, Chaney White, and Jake Dunn.[18] McDonald helped the Stars to early victories over Wentz-Olney, the Raphaels, and the Camden Nine. His star power was shown in June when the Detroit Cubans advertised in the papers that he would be pitching for them against the Eagles. A crowd of over 4,000 showed up, but, when fans found out they had been duped and McDonald was never on the roster, they left after the second inning.[19] In leading the Stars to the championship in 1934 McDonald beat Satchel Paige and the Homestead Grays, 2-1, during the season and then defeated Chicago's Bill Foster, 5-3, in Game Three of the playoffs. Wilson led the team in hitting with a .358 average while Jones compiled an impressive 20-4 record and then won the final game of the playoffs to give the Stars the title.[20]

The Stars came back in 1935 to finish in fourth place in NNL play. While his team did not fare as well as they had in 1934, McDonald was named as manager for the East in the annual East-West Classic. The East lost, 11-8, on a three-run homer by Mule Suttles.[21] McDonald continued his late-season play against White all-stars, beating the Bushwicks and Dazzy Vance, 6-2, in September.[22]

McDonald returned in 1936 to lead the Stars to a last-place finish and then, in 1937, the Stars rebounded to third place. In 1938 McDonald returned to just playing for the Stars as they finished second to the Homestead Grays. As the Stars dropped back to fifth place in 1939, Jud Wilson took over the main managerial duties. McDonald pitched in only four games in 1940, his final season with the Stars and his last year to play in the Negro Leagues. During each of these seasons, McDonald also continued to shine in exhibition games. For example, in August 1936 in a game against the Black Yankees, McDonald pitched 18 innings in a game that ended in a 3-3 tie, though he collected eight strikeouts and only four walks. A month later he pitched in a benefit game at the Polo Grounds for Sam Langford. McDonald left the game against the Elite Giants in the seventh inning with a 3-3 tie. The Stars, however, went on to lose the game, 7-3.[23]

The Stars began the 1937 season with a newspaper-reported 14-1 record in their spring-training games. Fans were excited for the season, and one reporter wrote about McDonald, "He is known for his under-handed delivery and ability to place the pellet just where he wants it."[24] Sadly the good start only resulted in a third-place finish under Wilson's managing.

Though he had been pitching for 20 years in 1938, newspapers still lauded McDonald for his sneaky underhand delivery. He was called a "submarine artist"[25] and someone with "an uncanny underhand delivery."[26] The Stars finished with their best showing since 1934 with a second-place finish behind the Homestead Grays. McDonald saw fewer games in 1939 but still won against the Bushwicks, the Brooklyn Farmers, and a group of White major leaguers, proving he could still pitch with the best.[27]

As the 1940s began, and through the time of his registration for the draft during World War II, McDonald worked as a helper at the United States Mint in Philadelphia. He continued to play on, and sometimes manage, local ballclubs. In 1942 he was a member of the Philadelphia Daisies, a new independent team managed by Fats Jenkins. He appeared again in 1945 and 1946 in the new Unites States League (USL), the brainchild of former Pittsburgh Crawfords owner Gus Greenlee, that had been commandeered by Branch Rickey. McDonald started 1945 with the Hilldale entry and became the manager of the Brown Dodgers in July 1945 and again in 1946 before ending his career in baseball.

In 1950 McDonald was employed as a freight worker at the US Custom House in Philadelphia. He reported that he spent 26 years working the post office and later as head of the linen department at the Liberty Bell Racetrack.[28]

Webster McDonald died on June 12, 1982, of complications from injuries sustained in a mugging earlier in the year.[29] He is buried in Fairview Cemetery, Philadelphia. In one of his obituaries, Monte Irvin said about McDonald, "He was considered among the best."[30] Pitcher Bill Holland explained McDonald's longevity, saying, "He could pitch an entire week because he didn't use much energy. He pitched underhand and he had a good fastball. Then he had this curveball that comes in low, then breaks up. His curves used to rise and his fastballs would sink. Then he'd slow it up."[31] Jake Stephens said, "When he had one of his good days, there wasn't anybody going to lick him."[32]

Sources

All Negro Leagues baseball data used in this biography comes from Seamheads. com, as of January 8, 2023.

Notes

1 John Holway, *Voices from the Great Black Baseball Leagues*, rev. ed. (New York: DaCapo Press, 1992), 74.

2 John Holway, "Historically Speaking: Webster McDonald," *Black Sports*, May 1974: 55.

3 "Cubans Beat by Potomacs," *Wilmington Morning News*, May 7, 1925: 10.

4 https://www.seamheads.com/NegroLgs/player.php?playerID=mcdon01web; "Potomacs Take Cubans in Camp," *Wilmington Evening Journal*, May 7, 1925: 8.

5 Dr. Layton Revel and Luis Munoz, "Forgotten Heroes: Webster McDonald," Center for Negro Leagues Baseball Research, 2014). http://www.cnlbr.org/Portals/0/Hero/Webster-McDonald.pdf.

6 https://www.seamheads.com/NegroLgs/team.php?yearID=1926&teamID=CAG&tab=pit.

7 https://www.seamheads.com/NegroLgs/player.php?playerID=mcdon01web.

8 https://www.seamheads.com/NegroLgs/player.php?playerID=mcdon01web.

9 "Negro Stars Strong," *York* (Pennsylvania) *Dispatch*, July 16, 1935: 11.

10 http://www.cnlbr.org/Portals/0/Hero/Webster-McDonald.pdf..

11 "Bernie Gets Hit, Rolls Under Fence," *St. Cloud* (Minnesota) *Times*, August 30, 1935: 14.

12 "The Outfield," *Baltimore Evening Sun*, October 10, 1930: 48; "Stars' Hopes Soar with Eddie Rommel Opposing Black Sox," *Baltimore Evening Sun*, October 17, 1930: 47; "Stars are Primed for Seasons' Largest Stand against Sox," *Baltimore Evening Sun*, October 24, 1930: 44; "Colorful Ball Aggregation to Play for All Star Nine," *Baltimore Evening Sun*, October 11, 1930: 10.

13 Revel and Munoz, "Forgotten Heroes: Webster McDonald."

14 "Hilldale Defeats Stars of Cuba," *New York Age*, September 19, 1931: 6.

15 "Washington Pilots Win Two from Chick Fewster's Kings Team," *Brooklyn Citizen*, July 11, 1932: 6; "Kings Club Finds Pilot Nine Tough," *Brooklyn Times Union*, July 11, 1932: 11; "Manager Will Pitch," *Washington Evening Star*, September 6, 1932: 27.

16 "Philly Stars Strong in OF Players," *Brooklyn Times Union*, September 9, 1933: 13.

17 "Sphas Hammer Out Victory over Stars," *Philadelphia Inquirer*, July 15, 1933: 16; "Bolden's Stars Trip Sphas Under Lights," *Philadelphia Inquirer*, September 1, 1933: 16.

18 https://www.seamheads.com/NegroLgs/player.php?playerID=mcdon01web.

19 "Detroit Cubans Play Eagles in First Home Tilt Tonight," *St. Cloud Times*, June 12, 1934: 10; "Fans Walk out of Park after 2nd Inning," *St. Cloud Times*, June 13, 1934: 14.

20 https://www.seamheads.com/NegroLgs/team.php?yearID=1934&teamID=PS&tab=pit.

21 "Pick M'Donald to Manage East All-Star Team," *Chicago Tribune*, August 5, 1933: 16.

22 William J. Granger, "Philly Stars Beat D. Vance as Bushwicks Break Even," *Brooklyn Citizen*, September 16, 1935: 10.

23 "Philly Stars Play 18-Inning Game," *Brooklyn Daily Eagle*, August 27, 1936: 22; "Crawfords Win in Polo Grounds Benefit for Old Sam Langford," *New York Age*, September 26, 1936: 9.

24 "Ed Bolden's Phila. Stars to Oppose Landreth Nine," *Bristol* (Virginia) *Daily Courier*, May 4, 1937: 6. This was the newspaper that reported the 14-1 record.

25 "Braves to Tackle Philadelphia Nine," *Asbury Park* (New Jersey) *Press*, July 21, 1938: 17.

26 "Pirates to Play Philly All-Stars," *Long Beach* (New Jersey) *Daily Record*, June 3, 1938: 8.

27 John Holway, *Black Sports*, 54; "Heavy Hitting Locals Topple Famous Rivals," *Delaware County Daily Times* (Chester, Pennsylvania), May 6, 1939: 15; "Stars Hit Hard Behind Miller's Fine Work," *Delaware County Daily Times*, June 29, 1939: 24; "Philadelphia Colored Stars Play Here Tonight," *Bristol Daily Courier*, May 24, 1939: 4; "Philadelphia Stars Hand Bushwicks First Double Defeat of the Season," *Brooklyn Citizen*, August 7, 1939: 6.

28 Holway, *Voices*, 86.

29 "Webster McDonald, Negro League Pitcher," *New York Times*, June 15, 1982: B6.

30 "Webster McDonald," *Time*, June 15, 1982. In the Webster McDonald file at the National Baseball Hall of Fame Library, Cooperstown, New York.

31 Holway, *Black Sports*, 54.

32 Revel and Munoz.

DICK SEAY

By Alan Cohen

*"Nobody's a better second baseman
than Dick."*
– Satchel Paige, 1941[1]

*"This is not a tale of home runs and
batting averages, for Dick Seay's bat was
largely dormant. He was primarily known as
a glove man, a leader, and a mentor during
his career that spanned the years 1926
through 1947.*
*"Dick Seay was my idol. He and I used to
talk a lot because I had a lot of confidence
in him. I used to ask 'bout pointers playing
second base, and he and I were very good
friends. He really was a nice person."*
– Birmingham Black Barons All-Star
second baseman Tommy Sampson, 2000[2]

*"He told me some of the things about
second base, what to watch out for because
those fellows would try to hurt you."*
– Mahlon Duckett (New York Black
Yankees teammate in 1941), 1998[3]

And in addition to baseball, he also played a pretty good game of basketball.

Richard William Seay was born on November 30, 1904,[4] in West New York, New Jersey, to George and Agnes Johnson Seay. He was the fourth of five children; his older siblings were Beatrice, Gladys, and George Jr., while younger sister Harriet was born three years after Dick.

Unlike most Black ballplayers of his time, Seay grew up in a predominantly White community. His father was employed by the railroad. Seay as a teenager played with the Pennsylvania Redcaps. Among his teammates was Charlie "Chino" Smith, who went on to play with the Brooklyn Royal Giants and New York Lincoln Giants.

Seay first played professionally in 1926, splitting his time between the Newark Stars and the Baltimore Black Sox. Both teams were members of the Eastern Colored League, but much of the competition was in barnstorming events against nonleague opponents. On May 6 Newark won both games of a doubleheader against the Jamaica Cardinals. In the opener, Seay went 2-for-5 in a 17-4 win, and in the nightcap, he went 3-for-5 in a 12-8 triumph.[5] He joined the Black Sox in late June and was with the Black Sox when they fell to Hilldale, 5-4, on August 26; he had one hit in the game.[6] At season's end, the Black Sox took on Bethlehem Steel in a game for the mythical Baltimore city championship and split two games. Seay was the center of controversy in the first game when he was hit by a pitch in the fourth inning. Pitcher Costello of Bethlehem Steel got into a heated discussion with umpire Spencer, striking the arbiter, and was ejected from the game. The Black Sox scored four times in

Graig Kreindler

Second baseman Dick Seay

the inning en route to a 6-3 win. Bethlehem won the second game, 5-2.[7]

In 1927, the infielder, who stood 5-feet-7 and weighed 162 pounds, was with the Brooklyn Royal Giants and played shortstop. The next season, he traveled to Montreal, where manager George "Chappie" Johnson converted him into a second baseman.

Seay returned to the Brooklyn Royal Giants in 1929 and starred at second base. The Royal Giants barnstormed that season and often played against White semipro teams in the New York metropolitan area.

On April 14, against his former Baltimore teammates, the right-handed-hitting player had two hits, including a triple in an opening-game loss.[8] On May 12, in a doubleheader against the semipro Bay Parkways, he handled 12 chances flawlessly as the Royal Giants split with the Bay Parkways, who featured a very young Hy Greenberg at first base. In the opener, Dick "Cannonball" Redding defeated the Bay Parkways, 16-5. Greenberg, who went 5-for-7 with a pair of doubles, had a key hit in the second game as the Bay Parkways won, 7-4.[9] Late in 1930, Hank Greenberg played his first game with the Detroit Tigers.

A frequent opponent of Seay's teams during his career was a well-known semipro squad, the Brooklyn Bushwicks, an aggregation that included several men who had played in the major leagues. When Seay was with the Royal Giants in 1929, they faced the Bushwicks on September 29 in a doubleheader at Dexter Park in Queens. In the opener, won by the Bushwicks, Seay converted a double play, and in the second game he doubled in a run as the two teams split the twin bill.[10]

By this point in his life, Seay actually had received as much publicity for his exploits on the basketball court as he had for his play around second base. He had first played basketball with the Lewis Big Five team in the Jersey City area.[11] Prior to a game in December 1926, when he was playing for the Y.M.D. Alumni, the *Pittsburgh Courier* remarked that he "has never lost a ball on a dribble."[12]

The next time the *Courier* caught up with him, "Tricky Dick" was described as "smooth, clean-cut, and fast as lightning" as he scored a team-high 10 points during his St. Christopher squad's victory over the Capitol team, 55-21, in a game at Asbury Park on December 5, 1927.[13] His team, described as a "well-drilled red and black machine," played in the Eastern League of Associated Basketball Clubs.[14] They extended their record to 5-0 with a one-sided 45-14 rout of the Montclair Y and a 36-35 overtime win against the

Vandals in February.[15] By late 1928, Seay was suiting up with the Rockland Athletic Club,[16] but he also continued to play for St. Christopher and accompanied the team to Philadelphia for a game against the Tribune Big Five. Although his team came out on the short end, Seay, playing at forward, scored 12 points in the 28-24 loss.[17]

In 1932, Seay was reunited with his baseball mentor, Chappie Johnson, on the basketball court. He was a member of Chappie Johnson's Colored Stars, and they played all comers – White and Black. Showmanship was a big part of the game for the Colored Stars and their showman was Jack Livingston.[18] Talent was also in ample supply and after the game on January 9, the *Rochester Democrat and Chronicle* wrote, "[T]hese athletes seem able to do everything in the court game, and their smart tactics fooled the Centrals time and again."[19]

Seay had continued to play baseball for the Royal Giants through 1931. During this period, the team remained unaffiliated with any league, but he had the opportunity to play at Yankee Stadium on July 12 in a doubleheader against the Harlem Stars. In front of a small crowd of 1,500, the Stars swept the doubleheader from the Royal Giants, 7-2 and 4-3. In the opener Cannonball Redding, now 41 years old, was the losing pitcher.[20]

In 1932, following a minor controversy, Seay joined the Baltimore Black Sox, now a member franchise of the East-West League. Prior to the season, the two-sport specialist had become a two-team specialist, signing with both the Newark and Baltimore entries in the East-West League. After the dust settled, his contract was awarded to Baltimore and he paid a fine for his transgression.[21] He batted .288 with Baltimore that season as they finished in third place in the league's only year of operation. Once the 1932 season was over, Seay returned to the hardwood and played for Courteers of the Colored House of David.[22]

Seay remained with Baltimore when the team joined the new Negro National League II in 1933. The team finished fifth in the NNL2, and after the season Seay opted to skip basketball and find warmer weather. In the winter of 1933-34, he traveled to Puerto Rico and played with the Ramirez All-Stars.

Seay signed on with the Philadelphia Stars at the beginning of the 1934 season. Although he was known primarily for his glove work, he opened the season with a flourish against the Newark Dodgers on May 12, when he had three hits in the Stars' 12-0 victory.[23] The next day, on the road against the same team, he had a pair of hits in a 5-4 win in the first game of a double-header. He also had a hit as the Stars won the second game, 4-1.[24] Seay doubled and scored in a 5-2 loss to the powerhouse Pittsburgh Crawfords on May 22.[25] Despite many clutch hits, he wound up batting only .184 (42-for-228 with seven extra-base hits) during the regular season.

Seay's glove was very much in evidence in a 1-0 shutout loss to the Crawfords in Harrisburg, Pennsylvania, on June 11. His eighth-inning stop of a ball hit by Oscar Charleston got the crowd's attention, and the local newspaper called the play "about the most sensational stop ever seen on the Island" where the ballpark was located.[26]

In the balloting for the annual East-West Game, Seay (5,287 votes) finished second in the polling to the Crawfords' Chester Williams (5,394 votes).[27] Seay was on the East roster for the game in Chicago, but he did not play as Williams manned the keystone sack for the entire nine innings in the East's 1-0 victory.

The 1934 Stars were on fire. Starting on July 4, they won their first eight games in the second half of the season and, surprisingly, Seay's bat was a big part of the equation during this winning streak. On July 4, in a doubleheader sweep of the Nashville Elite Giants in Philadelphia, he had two hits in the 7-1 morning win. In the Stars' 9-2 afternoon triumph, Seay's fourth-inning walk forced in the second of his team's nine runs.[28] On August 4 at Chester, Pennsylvania, Seay contributed two hits as the Stars blasted the Baltimore Black Sox, 19-14.[29] The next day in Philadelphia, the Stars swept a doubleheader from the Black Yankees and Seay had a single in the second game as the Stars won 7-3.[30]

The Stars finished as second-half champions in the NNL and took on the first-half winner, the Chicago American Giants, in a championship series at the end of the season. The series went eight games (one game ended in a tie), and the Stars came out on top. Seay's key contribution was a squeeze bunt in Game Six at Philadelphia that proved pivotal as the Stars tied the series at three games apiece. Otherwise, he went only 2-for-21.

Seay remained with Philadelphia for the 1935 season. He brought his average for the season up to .257 and was again named to the East squad for the annual East-West All-Star Game at Chicago's Comiskey Park on August 11 after leading the balloting for his position with 13,019 votes. In the game, he went 1-for-3 before leaving for a pinch-hitter, as his East team (members of the Philadelphia Stars, Brooklyn

Eagles, New York Cubans, and Newark Dodgers) was beaten 11-8 by the West squad (members of the Homestead Grays, Pittsburgh Crawfords, Chicago American Giants, and Columbus Elite Giants).

Prior to the 1936 season, Seay was traded to the Pittsburgh Crawfords for Bert Hunter and Curtis "Popeye" Harris.[31] He joined a team that had won the NNL2 championship in 1935 and fielded five future Hall of Fame players (Josh Gibson, Judy Johnson, Cool Papa Bell, Oscar Charleston, and Satchel Paige). The 1936 Crawfords repeated as league champions, making it two out of three seasons in which Dick Seay was on a championship team.

In 1937 Seay joined the Newark Eagles and teamed with Mule Suttles, Willie Wells, and Ray Dandridge to form the premier infield in the league. Collectively they were known as the "Million Dollar Infield." In spite of their star power, the Eagles finished second to the Homestead Grays in the NNL2 that year.

In 1938 Seay remained with the Eagles. Their record dropped below .500 and they finished in fifth place. During the 1938-1939 Puerto Rico Winter League season, he played for Humacao and flashed some speed as he stole 33 bases.

In Newark's 1939 season, with Seay bringing his average above .200 for the first time in three years and Monte Irvin taking over at third base, the Eagles

Slick-fielding second baseman Dick Seay, a veteran of 19 seasons.

moved up to second place. In the offseason, Seay managed the Santurce club in the 1939-1940 Puerto Rico Winter League season. His club included Ed Stone of the Newark Eagles, Josh Gibson of the Homestead Grays, and pitcher Bill Byrd of the Baltimore Elite Giants.[32]

In 1940, Seay split his time between two teams, finishing the season with the New York Black Yankees. His most productive time was with the Newark Eagles, with whom he started the season. He appeared in 26 games for the Eagles and had nine extra-base hits, his most-ever in a season. One of those extra-base hits, an RBI double, came against the Homestead Grays at Griffith Stadium on June 16 and keyed a two-run rally that tied the game in the top of the ninth inning; unfortunately for Seay and the Eagles, the Grays came back to win, 7-6, with a run in the bottom of the ninth.[33] Seay found the short right-field porch at Newark's Ruppert Stadium to his liking and hit three home runs, two of them coming in a game against the New York Cubans on June 27 that the Eagles won, 9-2.[34] He was selected to start the East-West Game for the second time and scored two runs in an 11-0 East victory on August 18. The gloveman had five putouts and six assists, and initiated the game-ending double play.[35]

Weeks before the 1940 East-West Game, the 35-year-old infielder had been released by the Eagles[36] and latched on with the Black Yankees, his first game with them being on August 11.[37] With New York, he got into five league games over the remainder of the regular season.

In 1941, Seay was still with the Black Yankees and was selected as an East All-Star again. Later in life, he indicated that his biggest thrill in baseball was playing in front of 50,000 fans in the 1941 East-West Game.[38] He was 36 years old during the 1941 season, but spectators still marveled at how well he played second base. Fay Young raved in the Chicago Defender, "(Felton) Snow and Seay robbed West batters of hits, both pulling down two line drives with one-handed stabs." Seay remarked, "[P]laying in front of such an audience was great, but playing with such baseball headliners as Satchel Paige, Roy Campanella, and Monte Irvin topped everything."[39]

After having been with contending teams during his time with the Stars and Eagles, Seay was a member of a perennial also-ran with the Black Yankees. In 1941 the team was 21-32 against Negro League competition, but there were occasional highlights. Seay was joined by his former Eagles teammate Mule Suttles, and they both played a role in a come-from-behind win

on Memorial Day at Yankee Stadium as an estimated 22,000 fans looked on. The Black Yankees trailed the Newark Eagles 5-3 going into the bottom of the ninth inning. With one out and one on, Suttles singled and was removed for a pinch-runner. By the time Seay came to bat, the score was 5-5 and Henry Kimbro was on first base with two outs. Kimbro took off for second base, and Seay's hard grounder to the hole between shortstop and third base could not be handled. Seay was credited with a single, and the winning run was in scoring position. Moments later, Harry Williams drove home the winning run in a 6-5 game.[40]

Seay was the type of player who, even without a base hit, could impact the outcome of a game. He was back at Yankee Stadium on July 20, 1941, as the Black Yankees played the Philadelphia Stars in the second game of a four-team doubleheader. In the opener, the Kansas City Monarchs, with Satchel Paige on the mound, had defeated the New York Cubans, as 27,000 spectators cheered for Negro baseball's biggest drawing card. In the second game, the Black Yankees took an early lead as Seay reached first base on an error, took second on a sacrifice, and scored on a single by Suttles. After Philadelphia had tied the game with an unearned run in the top of the sixth inning, the Black Yankees came back. Seay ignited the rally when he walked, again moved to second on a sacrifice, and scored the lead run on a single by Jim Starks. Starks came around to score the Black Yankees' final run in a 3-1 win.[41]

In 1942 Seay once more was among the top vote getters in balloting for the East-West Game, trailing only Ray Dandridge, but his season was cut short when he was called to military service on July 29, 1942. In his last game before leaving for the Army, he went 3-for-4 with two doubles as the Black Yankees defeated the Chicago American Giants at Yankee Stadium, 8-0.[42]

Seay missed parts of four seasons before returning to the Black Yankees in 1945. He was stationed at Bangor, Maine, for much of his time in the Army and played on the Dow Field Bombers baseball team there.[43] He also played basketball with the camp's team.

Although his official discharge did not come through until August 19, 1945,[44] Seay appeared with the Black Yankees in a game on July 8. He played in eight NNL2 games with the Black Yankees after his military stint ended, and he had 8 hits in 31 at-bats as the team finished the season in last place.

Seay returned to the Black Yankees in 1946. Once again, they finished in last place and Seay had 12 hits and a .218 batting average in 19 league games. His best game was on August 24, when he had three hits in a 7-5 loss to the Philadelphia Stars.

Seay's last season as a player was with the Black Yankees in 1947. In 1948 he managed the San Juan Stars, the Puerto Rican Winter League champions, as they barnstormed in the United States.

After Seay's playing days were over, he continued to travel to Puerto Rico and coached for Santurce in the Puerto Rican Winter League. His tenure there lasted 15 years, and he coached the likes of Willie Mays, Roberto Clemente, and Orlando Cepeda. Once he completed his tenure in Puerto Rico, he was a coach for the Jersey City team in the Atlantic Collegiate baseball league from 1967 through 1970, serving under manager Johnny Kucks.

Seay appears to have been married during his playing days (circa 1941), but, by the time of the 1950 census, he was divorced. He later entered into a second marriage, to Vivian Jones, on October 30, 1959.[45]

Dick Seay died in Jersey City, New Jersey, on April 6, 1981. According to the *New York Times*, he was survived by two nieces and three nephews.[46] No spouses or children were listed in the obituary.

Sources

In addition to the sources shown in the Notes, the author used Seamheads.com, Retrosheet.org, and the following:

Holway, John B. *Black Giants* (Springfield, Virginia: Lord Fairfax Press, 2010), 112-122.

Notes

1   Bob Considine, "On the Line," *Washington Post*, July 22, 1941: 18.

2   Brent Kelley, *The Negro Leagues Revisited: Conversations with 66 More Baseball Heroes* (Jefferson, North Carolina: McFarland and Company, 2000), 125.

3   Brent Kelley, *Voices from the Negro Leagues: Conversations with 52 Baseball Standouts* (Jefferson, North Carolina: McFarland and Company, 1998), 95.

4   According to his Hall of Fame player questionnaire and Baseball Reference, Seay was born on November 30, 1904. Per his draft card, he was born on November 30, 1905. Per the 1905 New Jersey state census, he was born in 1904.

5   "Newark Stars Capture Both Ends of a Twin Bill at Jamaica Oval Sunday," *New York Amsterdam News*, May 12, 1926: 6.

6   "Hilldale Nine Wins in Tenth," *Pittsburgh Courier*, September 4, 1926: 14.

7   "Balto. Black Sox Tie Bethlehem Steel for City Crown," *Baltimore Afro-American*, September 18, 1926: A9.

8   "Fans Brave Cold to See Sox Win," *Baltimore Afro-American*, April 20, 1929: 15.

9   "Royals Divide with Parkways," *Brooklyn Daily Times*, May 13, 1929: 3A.

10   "Royals Get Split with Bushwicks," *Brooklyn Daily Times*, September 30, 1929: 2-A.

11   "Lewis Big Five," *Pittsburgh Courier*, November 14, 1925: 14.

12   Thomas W. Young, "Y.M.D. Alumni and Omega Psi Phis in Big Game," *Pittsburgh Courier*, December 18, 1926: 2: 7.

13   "Vandals and St. Christopher Fives Out in Front in Eastern Floor Loop," *Pittsburgh Courier*, December 17, 1927: 2: 5.

14   "Vandals and St. Christopher Fives Out in Front in Eastern Floor Loop."

15   "St. Christopher Defeats Vandals in Fast Game,' and "St. Christopher Five Defeats Montclair Y," *New York Age*, February 18, 1928: 6.

16   "New Quintet Formed," *Pittsburgh Courier*, October 13, 1928: 2:5.

17   "Tribune Five Defeats St. Christopher," *New York Age*, December 27, 1930: 6.

18   "No Letup in Sight for Centrals: Harlem Quintet Will Furnish Hard Work for Purple and Gold," *Rochester Democrat and Chronicle*, January 5, 1932: 17.

19   "'Room to Roam' Gives Stars of Harlem Chance to Show Wares," *Rochester Democrat and Chronicle*, January 15, 1932: 26.

20   "Harlem Stars Take Doubleheader from the Brooklyn Royal Giants," *New York Age*, July 18, 1931: 6.

21   "Dick Seay Feels League Lash," *Pittsburgh Courier*, May 21, 1932: 2: 4.

22   "Saunders, 205 lb. Center, Leads Husky Negro Cagers Against St. John's Five," *Binghamton Press*, December 1, 1932: 22.

23   W. Rollo Wilson, "Jones Holds Lundymen to Three Hits; Phila. Stars Win Opener in Big Way," *Pittsburgh Courier*, May 19, 1934: Section 2: 4, and "Phila. Stars Victors in Colored Opening," *Philadelphia Inquirer*, May 13, 1934: S-3.

24   "Philadelphia Stars Win Two from Newark," *Philadelphia Tribune*, May 17, 1934: 12.

25   "Crawfords Win Again," *Pittsburgh Post-Gazette*, May 23, 1934: 16.

26   "Home Run Sends Philadelphia to Defeat in Duel," *Harrisburg* (Pennsylvania) *Evening News*, June 12, 1934: 13.

27   Complete balloting shown in *Pittsburgh Courier*, August 25, 1934: 2-5.

28   "Boldens Whip Nashville," *Chicago Defender*, July 14, 1934: 16.

29   "Balto. Black Sox Lose to Stars," *Philadelphia Tribune*, August 9, 1934: 12.

30   "Philly Stars Slap Yankees Twice," *Philadelphia Tribune*, August 9, 1934: 12.

31   Lewis E. Dial, "League Heads Row in Meetings," *New York Age*, March 14, 1936: 8.

32   "Josh Gibson to Autograph Six Baseballs at Black Yank Reception for His Female Fans," *New York Amsterdam News*, September 23, 1939: 14.

33   "Grays Divide Double-Header with Newark," *Washington Post*, June 17, 1940: 18.

34   "Newark and Cuban Stars Divide Doubleheader," *New York Age*, July 6, 1940: 5.

35   Play by play information available on Retrosheet.org.

36   "Revamped Eagles Take 3 in a Row," *Baltimore Afro-American*, July 27, 1940: 21.

37   "Eagles Nip Elites, Yanks Top Stars," *Baltimore Afro-American*, August 17, 1940: 20.

38   Player questionnaire from the National Baseball Hall of Fame and Museum A. Bartlett Giamatti Research Center.

39   "Only Baseball's Color Line Closed Big Leagues to Seay," *Jersey Journal* (Jersey City), April 8, 1981: 42s.

40   The articles in the *Chicago Defender* and *New York Amsterdam Star News* were inconsistent (neither had box scores), and the rendering herein is based on a composite of the accounts. Maurice Dancer, "Yanks Defeat Newark; Cubans Trounce Elites," *Chicago Defender*, June 7, 1941: 23, credited Seay with the tying RBI; Dan Burley, "Black Yankees Trip Newark, 6-5 in Ninth Inning," *New York Amsterdam Star News*, June 7, 1941: 18, credited Kimbro with the tying RBI.

41   William E. Clark, "27,000 See K.C. Monarchs Down Cubans; Black Yanks Beat Philly," *New York Age*, July 26, 1941: 11; Maurice Dancer, "27,500 See Kansas City and Paige Defeat Cubans: Satchel Holds Islanders to Three Hits in 5 Innings; Black Yanks Down Phils," *Chicago Defender*, July 26, 1941:

23; "Monarchs Turn Back Cubans; Yanks Beat Stars," *Norfolk* (Virginia) *Journal and Guide,* July 26, 1941: 12.

42   "Yanks Top Chicago; Cubans Best Barons," *Norfolk New Journal and Guide,* August 1, 1942: A-15.

43   Ben Toomey, "Sportlets," *Waterville* (Maine) *Morning Sentinel*, May 1, 1945: 2.

44   "Black Yanks Well Heeled for Dexter," *Brooklyn Daily Eagle*, August 24, 1945: 12.

45   Player questionnaire from the National Baseball Hall of Fame.

46   "Dick Seay, 2d Baseman, Black Baseball All-Star," *New York Times*, April 10, 1981: B6.

JAKE STEPHENS

By Bob LeMoine

*"You were a good man to have on
a team. You kept the spirits up.
You were the life of the party."*
Ted Page, to Jake Stephens [1]

Jake Stephens may have been the greatest defensive shortstop of all time. He was on par with Modern Era defensive shortstops like Mark Belanger and Ozzie Smith, but they had the advantage of television highlight reels. Stephens, called "The Wizard of York," after his Pennsylvania hometown, had none of those benefits since he toiled in the Negro Leagues from 1921 to 1937. A little guy at 5-feet-6 and 135 pounds, the crafty Stephens was called "the diminutive Rabbit Maranville of colored baseball" by Chester Washington in the *Pittsburgh Courier*, and "one of the dandiest little shortstops ever to wear a glove" by the *York Dispatch*. The *Chicago Defender* called him the "human jumping jack." [2] He was known as a great bunter and "spectacular" fielder with a "whiplash arm" who was "greased lightning on the basepaths." [3] His name was often misspelled "Stevens" in the local papers and his birth name, Paul, gave way to Jake. "You know how I got the name Jake?" Stephens told a sportswriter. "Those big guys from the city figured I was from a hick town, so they used to call me Country Jake. It stuck." [4]

Stephens also stuck, earning his reputation as a "wonder shortstop" whom the *Courier* dubbed the "jackrabbit of York." [5] "Fans get a great kick out of seeing Jake Stevens," wrote the *Altoona Mirror* in 1930. "He covers so much ground in the infield that he is what is called a triple threat man in football. One minute he gobbles up a scorcher over towards third base. On the next he is in deep short and again he may be found over near second base. Few ground balls get past him." [6] If Stephens had learned to hit the curveball, as he himself confessed, he might have been a more recognized name in Negro League history. "He couldn't hit a bull in the ass," Sam Bankhead joked. "But he could field!" [7]

Paul Eugene Stephens was born on February 10, 1900, in Pleasureville, an unincorporated community in Springettsbury Township in York County, Pennsylvania, to William Henry and Minnie (Bear) Stephens. [8] The 1900 census was conducted when Paul was just a few weeks old. William was working as a laborer in a chain works to provide for his family, which included older brothers, William (known as Harry) and John. At the 1910 census, William Henry was working at the Frey Brothers Coal Yard and the family was living in a rented house at 706 King Street. That area of East York was called Bullfrog Alley, a low-lying, swampy area that attracted the croaking creatures. Willow trees were plenteous, and many residents made their living as basket makers. Germans populated the area, as did those labeled "gypsies" for their junk peddling, horse trading, and bootleg whiskey. [9] "Let's put it this way," Stephens said, "you stayed in your own neighborhood, about three or four blocks." Stephens claimed he developed a strong throwing arm from the snowballs he threw to protect other children crossing the alley. [10]

Young Paul was often dropped off with neighbors who essentially raised him. "I went to church with them every Sunday," he remembered, "and there wasn't any such thing as a color line. I guess I was 14 or 15 before I *realized* I was a Negro." [11]

Stephens witnessed many tragedies in his young life. His little sister, Flora, died before her second birthday in 1904. His mother died two years later, at the age of 29. In 1917 his brother Harry died when his wagon was struck by a freight train. [12]

On his World War I draft card, Stephens listed his occupation as a self-employed peddler working out of the family home at 667 Edison Street. In the meantime, he also learned baseball on the sandlots of his hometown. In 1918 he played for at least two teams in Pleasureville, Twelfth Ward and the Colored Giants. [13] In 1919 he played on the local Smith Athletic Colored club, one of four in the York Twilight League. He had the best fielding percentage (.910) of all league shortstops, and his brother John led the league in batting. Smith AC finished 4-8 in league play and 22-12 overall. [14]

In 1920 the Stephens brothers played for another all-Black team in York, the Ajax Colored Giants. "P. Stevens, the acrobatic shortstop of the Ajax, is playing a bang-up game again this season," wrote the *Daily Record,* which hailed him as a "flashy fielder and a good hitter."[15] Ajax played the Midvale Steel workers team in a game Stephens recalled in his own two-edition column in the *Philadelphia Tribune* in 1926. Ajax held a 4-3 lead with one out and the bases loaded with Midvale up. "The stands were in an uproar," Stephens wrote. "It seemed to us that all the mill hands in the world were up there yelling for our scalps." The pitcher, full of nerves, threw three straight balls. His fourth pitch was a "mile high" but the batter didn't want to walk so he swung. "I caught a glimpse of a white streak flashing through the pitcher's box," Stephens wrote, "and I hurled myself forward, my gloved hand outstretched." Stephens came up with the ball and stepped on second to end the game. The mill workers swarmed the field and hoisted Stephens on their

Shortstop Jake Stephens

shoulders. "I wouldn't have changed places for any man alive," he said.[16] Feeling cocky about his skills, Stephens joined the Pleasureville team the next week as they played Glen Rock for the county championship. His error cost Pleasureville the championship. "It was a great lesson (in humility)," Stephens wrote, "and I reckon it carries over into every other walk of life."[17]

In 1921 Stephens joined the professional Hilldale club of Darby, Pennsylvania, a small, mostly Black suburb of Philadelphia. He sent a series of anonymous letters to team owner Ed Bolden, boasting of the talents of *this* young shortstop. Bolden was oblivious, but the fake letters drew his attention to the real skills of Stephens. He impressed Bolden at a tryout and became a candidate for starting shortstop.[18]

Hilldale began as an amateur youth club in 1910, became semipro, then turned professional in 1917. Bolden was "a tireless and brash promoter," wrote Michael Haupert, and "one of the greatest hustlers in the history of the Negro Leagues." He was responsible for putting Hilldale on the map. Bolden was a master publicist and drew lucrative exhibitions to Darby Field (Hilldale Park) against well-known Eastern Black or White teams.[19] Bolden also had a strict set of rules, Stephens recalled. "Only gentlemen got on the team – gambling and women chasing were out."[20]

There were 30 Black baseball teams in the Philadelphia area by 1920, with Hilldale the top drawing card, especially for weeknight games. Bolden capitalized on the mass migration of African Americans fleeing deteriorating circumstances in the South who sought Philadelphia's manufacturing jobs in the post-World War I years. Bolden had a tempestuous relationship with Rube Foster, founder of the Negro National League in 1920. Bolden and other Eastern club owners considered forming a rival league. Foster prohibited NNL clubs from playing Hilldale and other Eastern independent clubs like the Bacharach Giants, Lincoln Giants, and Brooklyn Royal Giants. The NNL was a success in 1920 and Bolden decided to join with Foster, paying $1,000 for Hilldale to become an associate member of the NNL.[21]

Stephens made the club and remained with Hilldale for most of the decade. His name (Stevens) appears in many box scores, but player-manager Bill Francis played the majority of league games at short. In July 1921 Bolden acquired another defensive stalwart, future Hall of Famer Judy Johnson, who occupied third base. Hilldale had an amazingly strong infield. In a July 30 contest against the Indianapolis ABCs,

Gary Ashwill

"Stevens and J. Johnson cut off scores with plays that seemed impossible," praised the *Philadelphia Inquirer*.[22]

Hilldale dominated the 1921 season, finishing 107-40, according to the *Philadelphia Tribune*, counting all exhibitions and other various games with amateur clubs. Hilldale was 28-18-1 among major Eastern independent clubs.[23] "The twelfth year has rolled around," the *Tribune* wrote of Hilldale, "and finds Ed Bolden president of a thriving corporation and one of the best baseball managers east, west, north or south."[24] Stephens played in just six league games and broke his leg in August.[25]

In early 1922 Bolden and other NNL owners soured on their association with Foster. Bolden lost revenue since Hilldale could not play teams outlawed by Foster. He wanted to leave the NNL and get his $1,000 back, but Foster threatened to raid his team if he did so. Bolden relented and faced more financial losses from a Western trip and when Western clubs refused to travel to Darby. Hilldale fell to 20-26-2 against Eastern clubs.[26] Stephens played just a few league games. He was just 22 and in the shadow of veteran stars Louis Santop, Otto Briggs, Chaney White, Toussaint Allen, and Phil Cockrell.[27]

Bolden resigned from the NNL at the end of 1922 and Foster refused to issue a refund. Bolden formed the Eastern Colored League, which included Hilldale and the Baltimore Black Sox, Brooklyn Royal Giants, Lincoln Giants, Cuban Stars, and Atlantic City Bacharachs. "The formation of the Eastern Colored League," wrote Neil Lanctot, "was an inevitable reaction to Foster's domination of the Midwest, revealing conclusively that Black baseball had grown beyond the control of one man."[28] While the ECL was being formed, Paul (Jake) and his brother John (known as Frank) Stephens helped establish an all-Black team known as the York Colored Giants or the Monarch Giants. Frank played for this club in 1923 after two seasons with the Indianapolis ABCs of the NNL.[29]

Stephens was demoted to a backup role as Bolden signed one of the all-time greats of the Negro Leagues, John Henry "Pop" Lloyd, as player-manager. Pop could still hit, but at 39 he had lost more than just one step in his fielding. "They brought him over to replace me," Stephens said, "but the old man couldn't do it. He was washed up. He could hit that ball, but you've got to cover territory." Lloyd was later released.[30] They needed Stephens' glove. He was "the smallest man on the club and the best glove man I know," said teammate Script Lee. "If the ball hopped bad, he'd hop

with it."[31] Hilldale easily won the ECL pennant with a 37-21-1 record. They won five games against two groups of barnstormers from Connie Mack's (White) Philadelphia Athletics, but Stephens didn't factor in the series.[32]

Stephens spent the first half of the 1924 season with Dan McClellan's Philadelphia Colored Giants, a Black minor-league barnstorming club. "We played up in New England," remembered teammate Webster McDonald. "When Hilldale needed somebody, they'd call us. We covered the waterfront up there, all down east, Nova Scotia, New Brunswick, Maine."[33] Stephens needed more experience and McClelland's tutelage paid dividends when he returned to Hilldale at the end of July. "The methods of Dan, the Ancient, got results," wrote W. Rollo Wilson in the *Pittsburgh Courier*. "He stuck Steve in and told him to go to it. Steve knew that he was to play day after day no matter how many errors he made or how few hits he garnered. It had its effect. The kid's confidence was established, his nerve was strengthened and here he is saving games for Hilldale."[34] When he returned, Stephens became the regular shortstop and joined second baseman Frank Warfield in a "stalwart defense," which lasted through 1928 despite the fact that the two didn't get along.[35]

Stephens's return was cut short on September 14; he was carried off the field with a sprained ankle after sliding into second base. Stephens missed most of the rest of the season as Hilldale (47-26) won another ECL pennant. Stephens batted .183 over 28 games. With many NNL clubs struggling financially, Foster realized an ECL-NNL Colored World Series would be a boost to the game. Hilldale played the Kansas City Monarchs. Stephens, still noticeably limping, started only Game Seven of the best-of-nine series and left in pain after three innings. Kansas City won the series five games to four, with one tie.[36]

Stephens was Hilldale's starting shortstop in 1925, batting .217 in 54 games. Hilldale again dominated the ECL, finishing 53-18-1. They faced the Monarchs (59-23-2) in a rematch for the Colored World Series. Stephens batted .250 (5-for-20) and Hilldale prevailed, five games to one. In a postseason banquet for the champions, Stephens joined Script Lee, George Carr, and Clint Thomas in a "Hilldale Quartet."[37]

The 1925-26 seasons were financial disappointments for most NNL and ECL clubs. Attendance and ticket prices couldn't keep pace with expenses. Issues with umpiring, scheduling, statistical tracking, and poor administration plagued the ECL in 1926. In the

NNL, Foster's physical and mental health declined, and he was admitted to an institution. The winner of three straight ECL pennants, Hilldale finished second to the Atlantic Bacharach Giants in 1926. Stephens batted a solid .271 in 66 games.[38]

In 1927 Hilldale fell to fifth place (38-48-1) and Stephens batted .234 in 82 games. But his defense still garnered attention. "Although he was charged with two errors," the *Courier* reported in a June game against the Cuban Stars, "Stevens brought the fans to their feet time and again in accepting 10 of his 12 chances."[39]

Bolden, like Foster, suffered a breakdown and resigned from both the ECL and Hilldale. He was away for several months. When he returned to Hilldale in early 1928, he announced he was pulling the team out of the ECL, the league he had created, after losing $18,000. The ECL itself would soon collapse. Hilldale finished 35-28-1 as an independent club, and Stephens batted a meager .152 in 54 games.

Many Negro League players were able to survive financially by playing winter league ball in California, Puerto Rico, and Cuba (where a player could make $400-$500 per month). Stephens played in Puerto Rico in the winter of 1926-27. The following year he joined the Philadelphia Royal Giants in the California Winter League, batting .250 in 14 games. He spent the 1928-29 winter in Cuba.[40] "We were playing in Cuba one winter," remembered Clint Thomas, "and Jake had trouble hitting the curveball. So, when pitchers started curveballing him, he sent himself a wire saying his father had died and he had to go home." Jake pulled the same trick in California. "I used to tease him, wondering how his father could have died twice."[41]

In 1929 Bolden formed the American Negro League (ANL) with Hilldale and five other clubs. Stephens had a falling-out with Hilldale management and his days were numbered. "They started me with $150 a month," he recalled in 1979, "and after eight years I was making $200. But I knew I was worth more than that. I was a halfway decent shortstop, and I knew I could get a job with another club. We had the best Negro ball team in America, and I knew they could afford it. I told them if they didn't pay me more money, I would go back to York County and farm."[42] Stephens was involved in a blockbuster trade with the Homestead Grays of the ANL. The Grays sent the legendary slugger Martín Dihigo and pitcher George Britt to Hilldale for Stephens and infielder Walter Cannady.[43] The excitement of the trade was soon gone, however, as for unknown reasons Stephens deserted the Grays in early May. The issue had to have been related to his relationship with Grays manager Cumberland Posey, who suspended Stephens. Posey traded Stephens *back* to Hilldale and reacquired Britt. "As this is written," Wilson of the *Courier* noted in his July 13 column, "Stevens is still out, and wires and letters have failed to bring him to the Hilldale club."[44] Stephens played in just 15 games.

It was a short reunion with Hilldale, as the survival of the franchise was in doubt when the ANL folded. Stephens, Oscar Charleston, and Judy Johnson all defected to the Grays, now an independent club. "Posey in agreeing to bury the hatchet and use the player whose desertion probably cost him the gonfalon in the Eastern League last year," wrote the *Courier*, "shows that he's trying hard to provide a real winner."[45] Combined with George Scales, a solid veteran second baseman, the Grays infield "looms as one of the best in Negro baseball," the same newspaper noted. "Charleston, Scales and Johnson are three of the best all-around infielders in the game and Stevens is generally considered to be about the classiest fielding shortstop in the East."[46] One of the greatest pitching duels of all time occurred in Kansas City on August 2 as the Grays' Smokey Joe Williams faced Chet Brewer of the Monarchs. Williams fanned 27 batters in a 1-0, 12-inning win while Brewer fanned 19. The game was on the line in the bottom of the eighth with a runner at second and a blooper hit to center. Stephens "went back and made a spectacular catch to rob the Monarchs of a probable victory," enthused the *Courier*.[47]

The club finished the season 45-15-1 and defeated the Lincoln Giants in a 10-game postseason tournament, declaring itself the best in the East. Stephens was "in splendid form for the series," wrote the *New York Age*.[48] He batted .271 in 55 games and was considered the best defensive shortstop in the Negro Leagues.[49]

After success with the Grays, Stephens and Judy Johnson were persuaded to return to Hilldale for a few games to close the season. Johnson remained with Hilldale, becoming their manager for two seasons as the club was rebranded the Hilldale Daisies under new ownership.[50] The NNL folded after the 1931 season. Stephens re-signed with the Grays for $350 a month. "I hated to go to bed at night," he said, "afraid I was going to miss something. You know, the country boy in the big city. Depression? I didn't know what the Depression was. I lived high off the hog. You could get a haircut for 35 cents, a shave for 15 and a pack of cigarettes for a dime then."[51]

Days before leaving for spring training in 1931, Stephens suffered a freak mishap at home when he fell down the stairs and broke two ribs. He missed several weeks.[52] He was limited to a reserve role, batting .250 in 17 games while also battling a stomach ailment.[53]

Stephens returned as the starting shortstop for the Grays, who belonged to Posey's new East-West League in 1932. He had his best year at the plate, batting .327 in 28 games. With the East-West League struggling to survive, the Detroit club was merged with Homestead, creating an abundance of players. Stephens was traded to the Pittsburgh Crawfords, where he rejoined Judy Johnson (Hilldale had folded). Stephens batted .193 in 46 games.[54]

Stephens and several teammates moved east in 1933. "A gang of us then jumped the Crawfords," Stephens recalled in 1963, "and joined up with Eddie Gottlieb to form the Philadelphia Stars."[55] Gottlieb was a White Philadelphia booking agent who is more remembered for his legacy in basketball. He had a 50 percent share in the Stars and provided the financial backing for the franchise. He brought Ed Bolden back into professional baseball to handle the administrative tasks of the club. Gottlieb and Bolden attended a meeting of the new Negro National League (known as Negro National League 2) formed by Gus Greenlee. Bolden again had issues with the cost of belonging to a league and kept the Stars independent in 1933. He found financial success booking exhibition games against White teams and even marketed his club as Hilldale, renting Hilldale Park to attract patrons in Philadelphia.[56]

Bolden signed former Hilldale players, including Stephens, Biz Mackey, Chaney White, and Eggie Dallard, and other stars such as Jud Wilson and Dick Lundy. "We had a cracking good team," Stephens said. "What a gang!"[57] The independent club in 1933 had a successful 22-13 run with Stephens as the starting second baseman, batting .310 in 28 games. "'Steve' thrilled the fans here again," wrote the *Courier*, "by his sparkling and peppery playing."[58] Manager Webster McDonald said, "Stephens and (Dick) Seay were the best double play combination in baseball. I called them 'the acrobats.' Stephens was fast, aggressive. He could jump like a cat."[59] The Stars benefited from new laws allowing Sunday ball, more economic optimism, and the prevalence of night games. By 1934, both Greenlee, seeing monetary potential in the Philadelphia market, and Bolden, with his new Passon

Field and increased attendance, put their differences aside and the Stars joined the NNL2.

Stephens, often batting leadoff for the Stars, batted .264 (on-base percentage of .325) and "still play[ed] one of the best games at shortstop and [was] considered by many as one of the leading infielders in colored ranks," wrote the *York Gazette and Daily*.[60] He finished second in voting for the starting shortstop for the East in the East-West Game, losing to Dick Lundy 5,515 to 4,840. "Both shortstops have been playing a whale of a game," wrote the *Courier*, "and the letters coming in from the fans indicated that Lundy's ability to hit harder than 'Steve,' although no more consistently, gave the Newark manager a margin."[61] The Stars defeated the Chicago American Giants four games to three (with one tie) to win the NNL2 championship, their only title. Stephens called Bolden the greatest all-time manager in the Negro Leagues. "Ed knew all the answers on how to get the best out of a winning combination," Stephens said.[62]

On January 7, 1935, Stephens wed Vivian Segrow, the daughter of Andrew and Ida (Carroll) Segrow. The Segrows were residents of New Orleans, where Andrew worked as a ship steward.

Jake spent 1935 with the Stars, batting .242 in 40 games. He was voted the top shortstop (14,028) for the East in the East-West all-star game on August 11 at Comiskey Park in Chicago before a crowd of 25,000.[63] He singled off Ray Brown to lead off the game, moved to second on a passed ball, reached third on an error, and scored on Dihigo's single. The West won a thriller, 11-8, on a walk-off home run by Mule Suttles. Stephens had some fun in the Windy City that night and went back to his hotel at 2:00 A.M. "half juiced up," he said. He bothered his often-irritable roommate, Jud Wilson, who grabbed little Jake and held him by one leg out the window, 16 stories up. Stephens had little memory of the event the next morning. The two were lifelong friends despite the very odd story. "A very sincere man," Stephens said of Wilson. "But when he put that uniform on, he played for keeps. He was a little like me, he hated umpires."[64]

Stephens left the Stars to play for the New York Black Yankees in his final seasons of 1936-37. The Black Yankees were loaded with veteran players, most of them north of 30 years old, including Jake, who was 36 in 1936. The well-traveled Walter Cannady (34) manned second base and with Stephens "loom[ed] as the best double-play combination in the league," according to the *Courier*.[65] Stephens was called the "sparkplug" of the club by the *New York Age*. The team finished 22-16-1 in the NNL2, second to the Crawfords. Stephens batted .212 in 31 games but had not lost his argumentative nature. In a game against the New York Cubans, he "tried to get (Neck) Stanley's goat," wrote the *Age*, "by accusing Stanley of cutting the ball. Umpire (Mo) Harris took his arguments seriously and then Stevens began helping his argument out by cutting a few balls himself. Every time he asked to see a ball, he would dig his long fingernails into the ball and cut the cover himself."[66]

By the spring of 1937, Stephens was not "in condition to play regularly," wrote the *Brooklyn Times-Union*. "His job is coaching now."[67] He batted a strong .284 in 24 games for the sub-500 team but was hampered by a twisted ankle. He and several other players were fined by Greenlee for unruly conduct against umpires. "If patrons want to see fist-fights," the commissioner stated, "they'll go to prize fights. But I believe patrons of the Negro League want to see baseball."[68]

In 1943 Stephens was asked by the *Pittsburgh Courier* for his all-time Negro League all-star team. Many of them were his former teammates: Mackey (C), Wilson (1B), Warfield (2B), Judy Johnson (3B), Vic Harris (LF), Charleston (CF), Rap Dixon (RF), and pitchers Willie Foster, Nip Winters, and Bill Holland. The other two players were Dobie Moore (SS) and Rats Henderson (P). Notably absent, even from Stephens' list of his second team, was Satchel Paige, who received only an honorable mention. One writer recalled Stephens once saying Paige was "the most overrated player ever God put breath into."[69]

Stephens finished his career as a .236 hitter. He often batted leadoff, however, so one has to wonder about his accredited .307 on-base-percentage. Stephens found creative ways to get on base. "Our uniform shirts were puffy," he said, "and when I would go to the plate, I would pull part of the shirt from under the back of my belt, and it would stick out slightly. The pitchers worked me closely and I pulled back to avoid being hit. I twisted my body so the ball would hit the shirt. I got free rides to first."[70]

"I knew Father Time was catching up with me," he recalled in 1979. "I knew I was washed up. Nobody has to tell you that. When you can't do the things you used to do, it's time to quit. So I folded up my tent and headed back to York." The exhausting travel had much to do with it. "We would play seven games over a weekend," he remembered, "say a twi-night in Pittsburgh on Friday, then an afternoon game in Baltimore, a twi-nighter there on Saturday, and a doubleheader in New York on Sunday. It was just too much, and we went everywhere by bus."[71]

Stephens opened a café in York upon retiring but sold it after a couple of years. At the time of the 1940 census, Jake and Vivian (still spelled "Stevens") were renting a house for $25 a week at 410 East King Street in York. Jake worked at the Department of Revenue and made $1,600 in 1939. He developed a messenger service that he ran for 12 years until it "got so big I couldn't handle it anymore," he said. It is laughable, considering the misspellings of his last name over the years, that the enumerator collecting data for the 1950 census wrote "Stevens" and crossed it out and wrote "Stephens." Someone finally got it right. Stephens worked as an "analyzer" for the State of Pennsylvania in the Bureau of Motor Vehicles. He officially retired at age 67, then took a part-time job as a deputy sheriff at the county courthouse and also worked as a notary public.[72]

Stephens was active in local and state politics. He served as the county chairman of the Republican Bureau of Negro Affairs and was secretary for the Republican Negro State Council. In 1939 Stephens spoke out against communism and Nazism. In 1944 he conducted a survey of African American soldiers in Pennsylvania and found their strong support for the Thomas Dewey-John Bricker Republican ticket, which was defeated by Franklin D. Roosevelt's fourth term as president. In 1947 Stephens considered a run for mayor of York but later withdrew.[73] In 1952 he was outspoken against the Democrats selecting Alabama Senator John Sparkman as Adlai Stevenson's running mate. Stephens called Sparkman, known for his pro-segregationist and anti-civil rights policies, "an insult to the Negroes of this country. A man so antagonistic to colored people should not be placed in such a high position of responsibility."[74] Stephens supported the eventual winning Republican ticket of Dwight Eisenhower and Richard Nixon.

Stephens was inducted into the York Sports Hall of Fame in 1977. He threw out the ceremonial first pitch at Baltimore's Memorial Stadium on York Night when the Orioles faced the Royals on August 16, 1979.[75]

Jake Stephens died on February 5, 1981, just shy of his 81st birthday. He was buried at Mount Zion Cemetery. He and Vivian had divorced in 1963, and he had remarried a White woman named Grace who bore him his only son in his late 60s, Paul E. Stephens Jr. Jake and Grace also were divorced a year before Jake's death.[76]

In 2017 SABR members in Pennsylvania sparked a grass-roots fundraising campaign for a new plaque to recognize Stephens, whose gravestone had no such recognition. "The 'Wizard of York,'" the inscription, written by Negro Leagues historian Larry Lester reads, "was black baseball's greatest fielding shortstop. Outstanding on the basepaths and considered an excellent bunter." "A lot of guys compare him to Ozzie Smith," Ted Knorr said of baseball's other "wizard." "I compare him to Mark Belanger of the Orioles. Belanger was on five pennant-winning clubs and won many Gold Gloves. Jake Stephens was on four or five championship teams in the Negro Leagues, and he'd have as many Gold Gloves as Belanger if they had the award."[77]

Sources

Special thanks to Ted Knorr and Ike Rollins for assistance in writing this biography. In addition to the sources in the Notes, the author was assisted by the following:

Baseball-reference.com

Familysearch.org

"John S. Stephens," York (Pennsylvania Daily Record, March 4, 1991: 10.

Seamheads.com

"Sports Hall of Fame Names Three," York Daily Record, January 13, 1977: 15.

York County Historical Society

Notes

1   John B. Holway, "Country Jake: Paul 'Jake' Stephens," in Black Diamonds: Life in the Negro Leagues from the Men Who Lived It" (New York: Stadium Books, 1991), 1.

2   Cited in Holway, Black Diamonds, 1.

3   Chester L. Washington, "Ches' Sez: Adding Color to Baseball," Pittsburgh Courier, March 7, 1936: 15.

4   "Paul Stevens – York Shortstop Was Ranked with the Best," York Dispatch, February 12, 1963: 16.

5   "Yancey to Play With Darby, Say," Pittsburgh Courier, March 21, 1931: 15; "Charl'ston Johnson, Stevens Sign," Pittsburgh Courier, February 14, 1931: 14; W. Rollo Wilson, "Sport Shots," Pittsburgh Courier, February 15, 1930: 15.

6   "Homestead Grays Promise Real Battle Against Works," Altoona Mirror, August 15, 1930: 19.

7   Holway, Black Diamonds, 1.

8   Alternate spellings are Baer and Bair.

9   June Lloyd, "The Basket Makers of York's Bullfrog Alley," York Daily Record, July 8, 2019. Retrieved May 31, 2022. ydr.com/story/opinion/2019/07/08/basket-makers-yorks-bullfrog-alley/1674955001; June Lloyd, "York Had Its Own Unique Gypsy Community," York Daily Record, September 9, 2019. Retrieved May 31, 2022. ydr.com/story/opinion/2019/09/09/york-had-its-own-unique-gypsy-community/2264973001; Lori Snyder, "Baseball Historians Pull Back Curtain on Wizard of York." Fox43. Retrieved May 25, 2022. fox43.com/article/news/local/contests/baseball-historians-pull-back-curtain-on-wizard-of-york/521-7af2a238-15e2-43ae-8851-0f0324dc60fc.

10   Holway, Black Diamonds, 4.

11   Holway, Black Diamonds, 4.

12   "Died," York Gazette, April 26, 1904: 1; "Deaths and Burials," York Dispatch, August 11, 1906: 7; "Negro Killed by Train," York Dispatch, August 17, 1917: 2; "Knocked Down by Horse," York Dispatch, May 13, 1918: 6.

13   Dave Gulden, "'Country Jake' Stephens," York Sunday News, February 7, 1999: C1; The Twelfth Ward was the section of York where Stephens lived (667 Edison Street), based on the 1910 census; "Twelfth Ward Suffer at Wrightsville," York Gazette, June 17, 1918: 6; "Colored Giants Lose to 12th Ward," York Daily Record, September 9, 1918: 7.

14   "Form City League for Twilight Ball," York Daily Record, June 18, 1918: 7; "Official Averages of Twilight League," York Daily Record, October 31, 1919: 7; "Colored Athletics Made a Fine Record," York Daily Record, September 29, 1919: 7.

15   "Fast Colored Ball Club Organized," York Daily Record, April 23, 1920: 9; "Twilight League Starts Play Tonight," York Daily Record, May 24, 1920: 3; "Dope for Twilight League Fandom," York Daily Record, June 18, 1920: 10; "Stevens May Join Hilldale," York Daily Record, April 19, 1921: 7.

16   Paul Stevens [sic], "Did Success Ever Go to Your Head? 'It Once Went to Mine,' Says Stevens," Philadelphia Tribune, January 30, 1926.

17   "'It Took a Glaring Error to Knock the Conceit Out of Me,' Says Paul Stevens," Philadelphia Tribune, February 6, 1926.

18   "Opening Game at Hilldale Base Ball Park, Saturday, April 30," Philadelphia Tribune, April 23, 1921: 7.

19   Michael Haupert, "Hilldale (Daisies) Club Team Ownership History," SABR Team Ownership History Project. Retrieved May 15, 2022. sabr.org/bioproj/topic/hilldale-daisies-team-ownership-history.

20   "Paul Stevens – York Shortstop, Was Ranked with the Best," =

21   Haupert; Neil Lanctot, Fair Dealing & Clean Playing: The Hilldale Club and the Development of Black Professional Baseball, 1910-1932 (Syracuse: University of Syracuse Press, 2007), 58, 84-87, 127.

22   "Hilldale Bows to ABC in Thirteenth," Philadelphia Inquirer, July 31, 1921: 21.

23   From Baseball-reference.com and Seamheads.com respectively. Lanctot writes that Hilldale won 75 percent of its games against White teams (68-23-2) and had a 37-18-1 record against Black teams for a total record of 105-41-3. See Lanctot, Fair Dealing & Clean Playing, 63, 232.

24   "Hilldale Continues to Win as Biggest Season of Baseball Slowly Ends," Philadelphia Tribune, November 5, 1921: 7.

25   "Hilldale's Injured List," Philadelphia Tribune, August 20, 1921: 7.

26   Haupert; Lanctot, 91-92, 232.

27   "Hilldale Club Meets Allentown Pros Today," Allentown (Pennsylvania) Morning Call, July 9, 1922: 13.

28   Lanctot, 94.

29   "York to Have Fast Colored Ball Team," York Daily Record, March 5, 1923: 7.

30   "John Henry Lloyd Deposed as Captain of Hilldale Team," New York Age, September 29, 1923: 6.

31   Holway, Black Diamonds, 1.

32   Lanctot (p. 102) suggests the 32-17 record, which is used by the Baseball Hall of Fame. See Cassidy Lent, "The Hilldale ECL Champions," baseballhall.org/discover/short-stops/hilldale-giants, retrieved June 1, 2022; Lanctot, 104.

33   John Holway, *Voices from the Great Black Baseball Leagues*, Revised edition. (New York: Da Capo Press, 1992), 76.

34   "Paul Stevens Back with Hilldale Club," *York Daily Record*, July 25, 1924: 8; W. Rollo Wilson, "Eastern Snapshots," *Pittsburgh Courier*, August 9, 1924: 7; Lanctot, 109.

35   "Lincoln Giants Humbled by Hilldale Lads, 9 to 2," *Pittsburgh Courier*, May 28, 1927: 17.

36   "Hilldale Beaten, But Comes Back," *Philadelphia Inquirer*, September 15, 1924: 18; Larry Lester, *Baseball's First Colored World Series* (Jefferson, North Carolina: McFarland & Co., 2006), 106, 153-154; Lanctot, 109-110.

37   Lanctot, 140-141.

38   Lanctot, 142, 146.

39   "'Nip' Zips 'Em, Hilldale Is Ahead," *Pittsburgh Courier*, June 4, 1927: 16.

40   "Macks Coming Here," *York Dispatch*, March 12, 1927: 12; Gary Ashwill, "Negro Leaguers in Puerto Rico," Agate Type blog. Retrieved May 29, 2022. agatetype.typepad.com/agate_type/2017/01/negro-leaguers-in-puerto-rico. html; William McNeil, *The California Winter League: America's First Integrated Professional Baseball League*. (Jefferson, North Carolina: McFarland, 2002), 127; Rollo Wilson, "Sport Shots," *Pittsburgh Courier*, January 5, 1929: 13.

41   Holway, *Black Diamonds*, 2.

42   Curt W. Nix, "Orioles' 'York Night' Honors Jake Stephens," *York Daily Record*, August 15, 1979: 1B.

43   W. Rollo Wilson, "Sport Shots," *Pittsburgh Courier*, January 5, 1929: 13; W. Rollo Wilson, "Grays and Hilldale Figure in Big Trade," *Pittsburgh Courier*, March 9, 1929: 13.

44   "Grays Open Series With Hilldale Foe," *Pittsburgh Press*, May 17, 1929: 51; "Britt Returns to Hilldale in Trade; Second Half Schedule Released," *Pittsburgh Courier*, July 6, 1929: 17; W. Rollo Wilson, "Sport Shots," *Pittsburgh Courier*, July 13, 1929: 16.

45   William G. Nunn, "The 1930 Edition of the Grays," *Pittsburgh Courier*, March 22, 1930: 15.

46   "Big Shakeup in Grays' Ranks," *Pittsburgh Courier*, February 22, 1930: 15.

47   "Smokey Joe Scores 27 Strikeouts," *Pittsburgh Courier*, August 9, 1930: 15.

48   "Homestead Grays Win Title as Champions of the East in 10 Games With Lincolns," *New York Age*, October 4, 1930: 6.

49   W. Rollo Wilson, "Sport Shots," *Pittsburgh Courier*, September 20, 1930: 14.

50   "Camden Club Plays Hilldale 2 Scraps," *Camden* (New Jersey) *Courier-Post*, September 27, 1930: 16; "Hilldale Club Braces to Win Windup Fray, 5-2," *Morning Post* (Camden, New Jersey), October 13, 1930: 12.

51   "Grays '31 Infield Problems Solved," *Pittsburgh* Courier, February 14, 1931: 14; Nix, "Orioles' 'York Night' Honors Jake Stephens."

52   "Ball Player Injured," *York Dispatch*, March 14, 1931: 11; "Yancey to Play With Darby, Say," *Pittsburgh Courier*, March 21, 1931: 15.

53   W. Rollo Wilson, "Sports Shots," *Pittsburgh Courier*, November 12, 1931: 14.

54   "Grays, Detroit to Merge; League Shifts Loom," *Pittsburgh Courier*, June 11, 1932: 15; "Rejuvenated Crawfords Crawfords and Grays to Clash," *Pittsburgh Courier*, June 18, 1932: 15.

55   "Paul Stevens – York Shortstop,"

56   Haupert; Lanctot, 222-223.

57   "Paul Stevens – York Shortstop,"

58   "Smiling Steve," *Pittsburgh Courier*, June 10, 1933: 15.

59   Holway, *Voices*, 83.

60   "Philadelphia Stars Face Birmingham Foe at Eagle Park Friday," *York Gazette and Daily*, August 16, 1934: 10.

61   "Willie Foster, Brown, Satchell [sic] Paige, Jones Lead East-West Poll," *Pittsburgh Courier*, August 25, 1934: 14.

62   Chester L. Washington, "The Scintillating Stevens Selects an All-Time All-Star Team," *Pittsburgh Courier*, January 30, 1943: 17.

63   "The East," *Pittsburgh Courier*, August 10, 1935: 15.

64   There are several accounts of this story. These details were taken from John Holway's *Blackball Stars: Negro League Pioneers*. (New York: Carroll & Graf, 1988), 203; Holway, *Blackball Stars*, 214.

65   W.R. Wilson, "National Sport Shots," *Pittsburgh Courier*, August 22, 1936: 14.

66   William E. Clark, "Black Yanks & Cubans Split Twin Bill Before Big Crowd," *New York Age*, July 11, 1936: 9.

67   Irwin N. Rosee, "Bushwicks Seek Ex-Big Leaguer to Bolster Club," *Brooklyn Times-Union*, April 27, 1937: 12.

68   "Black Yanks Point to Injured Players in Explaining Slump," *Pittsburgh Courier*, June 23, 1937: 17; "Greenlee Cracks Whip on Unruly Players; Charleston, Stevens, Wilson, Burnett Fined," *Pittsburgh Courier*, June 19, 1937: 16.

69   W.M. Lee Smallwood, "Column Rekindles Memories of Negro League Star," *York Daily Record*, August 26, 2007: B4.

70   Harry McLaughlin, "Yorker Played With Some of the Greats in Negro League," *York Dispatch*, April 19, 1996: 2.

71   Nix, "Orioles' 'York Night' Honors Jake Stephens,"

72   "Paul Stevens – York Shortstop"; Nix, 2B.

73   "Bureau of Negro Affairs Meeting," *York Daily Record*, May 14, 1938: 7; "Franklin Republicans Hear Paul Stevens," *York Dispatch*, October 26, 1939: 28; "Negro Soldiers Are Voting for Dewey," *York Dispatch*, November 1, 1944: 18; "Paul E. Stephens Enters Republican Mayoral Contest," *York Dispatch*, July 15, 1947: 18; "Snyder Unopposed for Renomination," *York Dispatch*, July 22, 1947: 18; "John Sparkman: A Featured Biography," United States Senate. Retrieved May 7, 2022. senate.gov/senators/FeaturedBios/Featured_Bio_SparkmanJohn.htm.

74   "Sparkman Is Target Among Negro Voters," *York Dispatch*, November 1, 1952: 22.

75   "Sports Hall of Fame Names Three," *York Daily Record*, January 13, 1977: 15; Smallwood, "Column Rekindles Memories"; "Local Sports Figure Dies," *York Dispatch*, February 7, 1981: 30; Larry Shapiro, "KC Spoils 'York Night,'" *York Daily Record*, August 17, 1979: 1B.

76   "Legal," *York Gazette and Daily*, July 18, 1963:39; *York Daily Record*, January 31, 1980: 15.

77   Snyder, "Baseball Historians Pull Back Curtain on Wizard of York."

PETE WASHINGTON

BY BILL JOHNSON

Negro Leagues encyclopedist/historian James A. Riley summarized outfielder Pete Washington's skill set as one of a "very fast outfielder with exceptional range afield ... got a great jump on the ball and was one of the best defensive outfielders in the East during the '20s and '30s. However, his offensive punch was not equal to his glovework, and he usually batted in the lower half of the batting order throughout. ..."[1] The description of Washington, while technically accurate, is a bit misleading. The fielding excellence he displayed while roaming left and center fields for various teams in the 1920s and 1930s was undeniable, but at the peak of his career Washington performed in the top half of the American Negro League in OPS+. He hit 10 home runs in their shorter seasons twice and posted a lifetime .270/.341/.407 slash line over his career.

In one of the best games of his career, in 1934 and just two years before his retirement from baseball, his grand slam off George Britt contributed to a season-opening Philadelphia Stars win over Dick Lundy's Newark Dodgers. At only 5-feet-9 and 160 pounds, Washington did not look like a right-handed power hitter, but he fused his generally reliable – if not always spectacular – offense with his often-brilliant defense to craft a solid 13-year career in professional baseball. His career included stops in the Eastern Colored Leagues and the short-lived American-Negro and East-West Leagues, before finally culminating in a championship with Philadelphia in the second Negro National League.

Peter Smith Washington was born on June 25, 1903, to Joseph and Fannie Smith Washington in Albany, Georgia. Washington had an elder stepbrother, Jerry, and older sisters Ella and Eureka, as well as younger sisters Josie and Lucy and brothers Charlie and Joseph [called Hercules]. Albany is one of the larger communities in southwest Georgia. While predominantly agricultural, the city has spawned athletic talent over the

Centerfielder Pete Washington

Gary Ashwill

years ranging from football Hall of Fame fullback Marion Motley to more modern stars like Ray Knight. Leesburg, barely 10 miles north, is the home of former San Francisco Giants catcher and 2012 National League Most Valuable Player, Gerald "Buster" Posey.

Peter's father, Joe Washington was a lineman for an emerging telephone company. While little is known about Pete's scholastic career, he did work as a delivery person for a local tailor shop in 1920.[2] In 1921 Washington's mother, Fannie, died. The following year, Pete and Lillie Washington were married. Both were just 19 years old, but the next year they welcomed a daughter, Fannie, named after her grandmother. That year Pete signed to play baseball with the Washington Potomacs of the East Coast League.[3] Washington's manager, future Hall of Famer Ben Taylor, a gifted player in his own right and a cerebral baseball coach, evidently sanded some of the rough edges off the 20-year-old's game. By midseason the young player was starting in the outfield.

In 1924 Washington started 47 games in left field, and notched 50 hits in 198 plate appearances. The next season the team moved to Wilmington, Delaware, but it folded soon thereafter, forcing Washington to play out the rest of the year with the New York Lincoln Giants. There is no record of his playing in 1926, but in 1927 he joined the Baltimore Black Sox as full-time center fielder. Riley noted that, in August, he and several other players were involved in a serious automobile accident, but Washington emerged with only a few scrapes.[4] Despite the brush with disaster, Washington was obviously not seriously hurt, as he hit .288 and slugged at a .498 clip for the season. That slugging average included 10 home runs, and his OPS+ finished at what became a career-high 124.

The 1928 season marked another campaign in which Washington's OPS+ exceeded the league average (107), and in 1929 he batted .315 with 10 more homers to help pace Baltimore to the American Negro League title in that circuit's only year of existence. At the age of 27, Washington was playing at what proved to be the apex of his ability.

That winter, according to the US Census, Pete, Lillie, and Fannie returned to Albany while he worked as a porter in a local department store. Lillie took in laundry for the extra income, which was helpful when she gave birth to their second daughter, Decoursey, later that year. At some point not identified, either at birth or in infancy, Decoursey contracted polio. The disease claimed her life 21 years later.

Washington's overall performance on the field declined over that summer of 1930. His glove and his legs kept him in the starting lineup in center field, but his batting average dropped to .255 and his OPS+ to 81. After two more seasons with the Black Sox, he signed on with the then-independent Philadelphia Stars in 1933. In 1934 the Stars joined the new, second iteration of the Negro National League, and they won the inaugural title in a controversial seven-game series against the Chicago American Giants.

The 1934 season started well for Washington. In an April game, the *Pittsburgh Courier* reported, he started in center field and scored two runs in Philadelphia's 9-3 win over a local club squad.[5] In May he contributed to wins over the Newark Dodgers[6] and the Pittsburgh Crawfords (a team with an aging Oscar Charleston, Josh Gibson, and Jimmie Crutchfield) as the starting right fielder.[7] Against the Dodgers, Washington hit a fourth-inning grand slam completely out of Passon Field in Philadelphia. He also doubled in two runs, for a total of six RBIs in the game.[8] In the opening game of a late June doubleheader against the Cleveland Red Sox, Washington drove in the game-winning run when he doubled home Jud Wilson in the bottom of the ninth inning.[9]

While Washington was clearly aging, his power at the plate still emerged on occasion. On July 9 he homered against Newark in a 15-4 Stars win, and in August he drove in a pair of runs against a squad called Kearney Lumber. On August 6, against Ed Gottlieb's Philadelphia League All Stars, Washington stole home for the only Stars' run of the exhibition.[10] Early in August, final voting put him in second place to James "Cool Papa" Bell for the starting center-field slot in the second East-West All Star Game.[11]

On August 26 Washington hammered his final homer of the year, a solo shot against the Nashville Elite Giants that proved to be the difference in the 4-3 Philadelphia win.[12] At the end of September, on the 29th and in front of roughly 3,000 spectators at Passon Field, Washington contributed two hits and a run in the Stars' 4-1 win over the American Giants. The latter team was talent-laden, with Turkey Stearnes leading off and followed in succession by the intimidating trio of Ted "Double Duty" Radcliffe, Mule Suttles, and Willie "El Diablo" Wells, but Philadelphia prevailed.[13] That championship series marked the end of what was Washington's only championship season in the Negro National League, and the second of his career. Washington closed out his 1934 campaign with an RBI double against the mighty Pittsburgh Crawfords on October 7 in Washington, D.C.[14]

The next year, 1935, Washington was relegated to a reserve role, and he logged only two extra-base hits in stints with both the Stars and the New York Black Yankees. In 1936 he appeared in only three games with the Brooklyn Royal Giants, and while he picked up six hits and two walks in only 14 plate appearances, he was not offered a contract for 1937. Pete Washington's big-league career included 585 games and 2,330 plate appearances. He had 546 hits and 50 home runs in amassing a lifetime .270/.341/.407 slash line, and a lifetime OPS+ of 96. In all, it was not a bad offensive career for a player known mostly for his defense.

By 1940, Washington was living in Baltimore and working odd jobs to eke out a living. His entry in the 1940 census identified him as a widower, but a separate page in the census recorded Lillie, Fannie, and Decoursey as living in Tallahassee, Florida, roughly 90 miles south of Albany. Lillie, working as a private maid, was also listed as a widow. Clearly both were alive, yet each self-identified as widowed. There is no existing explanation, although it appears that the couple may have separated but not divorced.

In 1941 Washington returned to Philadelphia and worked as a stevedore for the Southern Steamship Company. In 1942 he left that job to enlist in the US Army. Entering the Army at Camp Butner, in North Carolina, on Halloween, 1942, Washington served with the 922nd Air Base Security Battalion before his discharge six months later.[15] Six weeks after his release from the Army, Washington's father died in Albany.

Washington remained in Philadelphia after his wartime service. In 1946 daughter Fannie married James Alexander of New Jersey and they later gave Pete two grandchildren. In 1948 Decoursey had a daughter, a third grandchild, with Israel Green, also from Albany, Georgia. It is possible that Lillie had passed away, and Fannie went to live near her father while Decoursey stayed with the extended family in the South.

In 1950 Washington applied for a wartime pension and was awarded $60 per month. That, combined with the money he made working in a Philadelphia restaurant, appears to have been his only forms of subsistence for the remainder of his life. On September 4, 1962, at the age of 59, Pete Washington was pronounced dead on arrival at Graduate Hospital in Philadelphia. The cause of death was identified as hypertensive arteriosclerotic heart disease.[16] On September 11 he was buried in Beverly, New Jersey.

Pete Washington was an excellent baseball player, started on championship teams in both Baltimore and Philadelphia, and enjoyed a well-deserved reputation for defensive excellence on the diamond over his 13-year professional career. While such comparisons are at best estimates only, the website baseball-reference.com lists Jackie Jensen, who had an excellent run of seasons with the Boston Red Sox from 1954 to 1959, as a comparable player to Washington.

Washington was a husband, a father, and a grandfather as well as a ballplayer, but his life still ended in the relative anonymity shared by so many of his Black contemporaries. His life is, for that reason alone, one that is worth remembering.

SOURCES

The statistical data was culled from seamheads.com, and the secondary comparative information from baseball-reference.com.

NOTES

1   James A. Riley, "Pete Washington," *The Biographical Encyclopedia of the Negro Baseball Leagues* (New York: Carroll & Graf, 2002), 280.

2   United States Census, 1920. Georgia/Dougherty County/Albany/District 0061.

3   "Silks Win Decisive Victory Over Potomacs, Scoring All Their Runs in Two Innings," *Shamokin* (Pennsylvania) *News-Dispatch*, August 20, 1923: 3.

4   Riley, 280.

5   "Bolden's Stars Flare, Blot Out Raphael Team," *Pittsburgh Courier*, April 21, 1934: 14.

6   Rollo Wilson, "Jones Holds Lundymen to Three Hits; Phila. Stars Win Opener in Big Way," *Pittsburgh Courier*, May 19, 1934: 14.

7   "Stars Beat Crawfords," *Pittsburgh Post-Gazette*, May 19, 1934: 14.

8   "Stars Topple Newark for Inaugural 12-0 Win," *Philadelphia Tribune*, May 17, 1934.

9   "Phila. Stars Beat Cleveland Four Straight," *Philadelphia Tribune*, June 28, 1934: 12.

10 "Philly Stars Slap Yankees Twice," *Philadelphia Tribune*, August 9, 1934: 12.

11 "Final Standing: The East," *Pittsburgh Courier*, August 25, 1934: 15.

12 "Stars Clip Nashville Gts.," *Philadelphia Tribune*, August 30, 1934: 12.

13 "Philadelphia Stars 4, Chicago American Giants 1" Online: https://www.retrosheet.org/NegroLeagues/boxesetc/NgLg/B09290PH51934.htm.

14 "Craws, Grays Win Against Stars, Yanks," *Baltimore Afro-American*, October 13, 1934: 21.

15 "Peter S. Washington Application for World War II Compensation," *Commonwealth of Pennsylvania form No. 1*, April 26, 1950.

16 Commonwealth of Pennsylvania Department of Health, Medical Examiner's Certificate of Death; file 089562-62, registered number 17424, issued September 11, 1962.

CHANEY WHITE

By Frederick C. Bush

Outfielder Chaney White had a 17-year career in the Negro major leagues from 1920 through 1936. During that time, he was a member of numerous championship teams that included squads in various Negro Leagues, the Cuban Winter League, the Florida Hotel League, and the California Winter League. In 1934, at age 40, he was still a major contributor to his last championship squad, the Philadelphia Stars of the Negro National League II. Chaney, whom a World War I draft registrar described as "tall" and "stout" – he was listed as 5-feet-10 and 196 pounds during his playing days – compiled Negro League career totals that included a .312 batting average, a .375 on-base percentage, and 1,057 hits in 887 games against league or top-caliber independent opponents. Additionally, he batted .347 in three seasons in Cuba[1] and .316 in two seasons in the California Winter League.[2] His accomplishments were more than enough for him to make it onto the preliminary ballot of the National Baseball Hall of Fame's 2006 Special Committee on

Left fielder Chaney White

National Baseball Hall of Fame

the Negro Leagues, although he was not selected for enshrinement.

Chaney Leonard White was born on April 15, 1894, in Longview, Texas, the ninth of Alfred and Minda White's 11 children.[3] Alfred was a farm laborer while Minda tended to the home and children. At the time of the 1900 US Census, the White family was living in rural Kaufman County, Texas. By 1910 the family had moved to the town of Terrell, also in Kaufman County, which is 98 miles west of Longview and 32 miles east of Dallas.

Kaufman County was an unlikely place for the family to settle as it was extremely inhospitable to African American residents. In fact, on July 16, 1892 – slightly less than two years before Chaney White's birth – the White citizens of Elmo, six miles east of Terrell, adopted several resolutions "[w]ith a view of discouraging the immigration of negroes into the settlement and removing the obnoxious citizens of color already in the precinct."[4] One of the resolutions expressed the concern that "[n]egro immigrants are pouring in upon us with an increase of ratio, which, if not stopped, will result in ruin to our schools and society. ..."[5] Amid such virulent racism, it was only a matter of time before the White family moved to Dallas, a city with no less segregation but with a much larger Black community in which they could feel more at home. The 1920 Census shows that Alfred and Minda White, along with their youngest daughter, Lottie, and granddaughter, Beulah Evans, lived on Golden Gate Avenue in the Western Heights section of Dallas. However, after Alfred's death, Minda moved back to Terrell, and the 1940 Census shows she was living there with her daughter Lizzie (White) Johnson.

As for Chaney, nothing is known about his youth or how he first came to play baseball. What is definite is that he was playing professionally by 1917 (and perhaps earlier) as his World War I draft registration card from that year lists his profession as "Ball player" and his employer as Enos Whittaker, owner of the Dallas Black Giants. The Dallas team was a member franchise of the Texas Colored League, and White was in fast company on the 1917 squad that included fellow future stars like Dave Brown, Jim Brown, and Oliver "Ghost" Marcell. White's early career was interrupted when Uncle Sam came calling. He served in the US Army in World War I, and was discharged on August 9, 1919.

At the outset of the 1920 season, the *Dallas Express*, which had been "made the official organ of the Texas Colored League," reported that "Johnson Hill and Chaney White, one fleet-footed out fielder [*sic*] are slated to be sold to Detroit."[6] White was not sold to Detroit, but, in an April 10 news article, was reported to be a member of the Fort Worth Black Panthers as that team prepared to face the Black Giants.[7] The same article noted, "Lewis Lofton [*sic*], better known as 'San Top' a former Texas Leaguer and ex-Royal Giant was in Dallas Monday ... This year San Top will be a member of the famous Hilldale Club of Philadelphia."[8]

San Top was Fort Worth-born Louis Santop Loftin, a catcher who was inducted into the Hall of Fame in 2006, and he stayed around his hometown long enough to play the early months of the season with Chaney and the Black Panthers. The box score from the April 11 matchup between the Dallas and Fort Worth teams shows that White started in left field and batted leadoff (his speed garnered him the nickname Reindeer) and that he went 2-for-4 with a double, a triple, and three runs scored in a 13-3 triumph for Fort Worth. "Sand Top" [*sic*] was Fort Worth's starting catcher and had a 2-for-3 day at the plate with a double and two runs scored.[9]

White made such a great impression on Santop that the catcher, who also served as a scout/recruiter for Hilldale, took him north to Philadelphia when he left Texas to rejoin Ed Bolden's Hilldale Club.[10] White's widow, Helena, confirmed this sequence of events 20 years after his death, relating, "My husband told me that 'Sandtop' brought him to Philadelphia from Texas. Now, 'Sandtop' was one of the greatest Negro catchers that there ever was. I guess that was in about 1920 or 21. I'm not sure. That's how my husband broke into baseball."[11] Since White had already been playing professionally, it is more accurate to state that his journey to the Northeast is how he set out on the road to stardom and a Hall of Fame-caliber career.

Santop and White joined Hilldale in July 1920, but White scuffled in his first season up North. There was no organized Negro League in the Northeast at that time, so Hilldale played against fellow top Black independent squads and faced off against many White semipro teams and even occasional White

major-league aggregations. Although White fared well enough against the semipros,[12] in 14 games against the top Black clubs, he batted only .160 (8-for-50) and had a .222 on-base percentage. In three games (all losses) against White major leaguers, he batted .091 (1-for-11). Hilldale had a 9-9-2 record against its fellow Eastern Independent clubs, while the Brooklyn Royal Giants (13-7-2) and Atlantic City Bacharach Giants (22-16-2) played superior ball. Hilldale played as far into the fall as possible, and, on October 16, defeated a semipro team from Upland, Pennsylvania, for what the *Philadelphia Inquirer* identified as "the championship of Delaware County."[13] White had two hits, stole two bases, and scored a run in Hilldale's 3-2 triumph.

Both White and the Hilldale Club made dramatic improvements in 1921, so that the team could boast of more than a mere county championship. White became the team's starting left fielder and in 40 games against top Black teams, he batted .300 for the first time as he rapped out 45 hits in 150 at-bats. Hilldale finished with a 28-18-1 record that gave the squad a .609 winning percentage. Hilldale's closest competition, the Atlantic City Bacharach Giants, played a far greater number of games and compiled 16 more victories, but the team's 44-36-2 mark resulted in only a .550 winning percentage. Thus, Hilldale claimed superiority over its six top competitors in the East for the season.

The 1922 season brought about different results, however. For one thing, there were four new top-caliber Black clubs in the East, a circumstance that caused a bidding war for available players. Apart from Phil Cockrell, Hilldale's pitching staff was thin and posted an 85 ERA+, denoting that – as a staff – they were 15 percent below the average of all Eastern teams. White remained Hilldale's starting left fielder, but his batting average dipped to .285, though he was still a productive player. His team's record fell to 20-26-2 against the other Black independent clubs, and the Richmond Giants ruled with a 31-17-3 ledger.

At the season's conclusion, Bolden called a meeting with several of his fellow team owners, and the group founded the Eastern Colored League that was to begin play in 1923. Now, the Eastern clubs truly had a championship to play for, and the new circuit also provided competition for Rube Foster's Western loop, the Negro National League. In fact, from 1924 to 1927, the champions of the two leagues were to clash in the Negro World Series for supremacy over all Black baseball.

Prior to the 1923 season, Bolden cleaned house to assemble an improved squad that might make Hilldale the ECL's first champion. He released several players who had filled only minor roles or whose performance had declined in 1922. White fell into the latter category and, though he had certainly not performed poorly, he found himself looking for new employment. He did not have to wait long for a new team to come calling, as the press soon reported that the Atlantic City Bacharach Giants, an ECL member franchise, had "grabbed Chaney White, the crack outfielder."[14] Both Hilldale and Atlantic City participated in two Negro World Series before the ECL's demise during the 1928 season; however, only Hilldale, in 1925, emerged triumphant from Black baseball's championship tilts between its Eastern and Western circuits.

The Bacharachs finished in fourth place in the ECL's 1923 inaugural campaign, but White contributed the sterling defense for which he was known and a .304 batting average in 47 league games played. In 1924, when Atlantic City again finished fourth, White was batting .344 in 21 ECL games before he abruptly switched teams to the Washington Potomacs, another ECL member. The reason for White's move is unknown; in fact, there is uncertainty as to whether he jumped teams or was released by Atlantic City because of a series of minor injuries he was reported to have suffered during the first half of the season.[15] In any case, White manned center field and batted .288 in 19 games for the seventh-place Potomacs, which gave him a cumulative .318 batting average for the season. That year, White's former team, Hilldale, lost the first Negro World Series, five games to four, to the NNL's Kansas City Monarchs.

In 1925 the owner of the Potomacs, George Robinson, moved the franchise to Wilmington, Delaware, in the hope that his team would fare better financially. White moved from Washington to Wilmington with the club and from center to right field on the diamond. He smashed the ball to the tune of a .377 batting average in 32 games played, but the Potomacs fared miserably and finished 10-21-2 in a half-season. On July 23, with the franchise's bottom line still bleeding red, it was announced, "George Robinson, sole owner of the Wilmington Potomacs, has quit. The Eastern officials have been notified by him that he is out of the game and that his players are now at liberty to sign with any other outfit."[16] Oddly, White was signed by his previous employer, the Atlantic City Bacharach Giants.

Back in New Jersey, White played 30 games in left field and batted .328 (for a .353 cumulative BA) for a Bacharachs team that finished in fourth place for the third consecutive year. Meanwhile, Hilldale became the first ECL team to be crowned king of Black baseball as it defeated the Monarchs, five games to one, in a rematch of the previous season's Negro World Series. Soon, the Bacharachs were to take their shot at the title.

Dick Lundy took over Atlantic City's managerial reins in 1926 and piloted a squad with an excellent pitching staff (117 ERA+), led by Rats Henderson and Claude Grier, to the ECL title.[17] The Bacharachs faced the Chicago American Giants in a World Series that was to go to a maximum of nine games, if necessary, but 11 games were played as Games One and Four ended in ties. Grier threw a no-hitter in Game Three, a 10-0 drubbing of Chicago. After Atlantic City won Game Eight, 3-0, with White's three-run triple providing the winning margin, the team had a four-games to two lead. The Baseball Fates, however, decreed that Chicago was to pull off a miracle, and the American Giants won the next three games to capture the Series. Future Hall of Famer Willie "Bill" Foster, Rube's younger brother, stymied the Bacharachs in a tightly contested finale, 1-0. As for White, he had hit .283 in 56 games during the regular season; however, despite his Game Eight heroics, he batted only .231 in the World Series.

Lundy and his team were determined to defend their ECL title in 1927 and to have another shot at a Negro World Series championship. The ECL had adopted the split-season format for the first time, which created the possibility that there might be a league championship series to play to determine the loop's World Series representative. The Bacharachs avoided such a scenario by winning both halves of the season. In fact, the squad overcame all obstacles thrown its way, including financial instability – the team's parent corporation entered bankruptcy proceedings in April – and being temporarily thrown out of its home venue, Bacharach Park, in mid-June.[18]

White patrolled center field and batted .328 with a .398 on-base percentage while leading the ECL in hits (115), runs scored (79), and games played (89). Lundy, Oliver Marcell, and Clarence Smith also hit over .300 to pace Atlantic City's offensive attack, and the pitching staff, led now by Luther "Red" Farrell, alongside Henderson and Jesse "Mountain" Hubbard, was as strong as the previous year (107 ERA+). The Bacharachs breezed to a return engagement against the same foe, the Chicago American Giants, in the World Series.

This time around, Chicago took a commanding lead by capturing the first four games, none of which was even close; the American Giants won 6-2, 11-1, 7-0, and 9-1. Amazingly, an Atlantic City pitcher again hurled a no-hitter, but this time it gave the team only its first triumph in the Series. Farrell tossed seven no-hit innings in Game Five, although five walks and four errors resulted in a slim 3-2 victory; the game was shortened by nightfall but it nonetheless counted as a win and gave the Bacharachs continued life. A Bacharachs pitcher throwing a no-hitter was not the only event that harkened back to the 1926 Series. After Game Six ended in a tie, Atlantic City won the next two games to make it a 4-3 series; however, Willie Foster again prevailed for Chicago in Game Nine and handed Atlantic City its second consecutive World Series loss. White struggled mightily against Chicago's pitching staff and batted only .152 in the Series.

Despite White's postseason struggles, he was now hitting his stride as a star player. First, he played for the Royal Poinciana squad in the Florida Hotel League. (He had been a member of the Breakers team in 1925.) Then he participated in his first winter league outside of the United States as he ventured to Cuba, where he joined the Almendares team during the 1927-28 winter season. White led his team with a .363 batting average, but it did not prevent the squad from finishing last. Things got so bad that "[w]hen Habana devastated Almendares 18 to 4 on January 21, the Blues withdrew from the league in shame and the season was terminated after one last victory of the [Habana] Reds over Cuba."[19]

White returned to Atlantic City for the 1928 season and continued his run of stellar center field defense and powerhouse hitting. His batting average climbed to .371 and led the team, and his .424 on-base percentage contributed to his leading the league in runs (54) for the second consecutive year. White's performance had not gone unnoticed, and, in June, the *Pittsburgh Courier* extolled his abilities:

One can't mention the great outfielders of all time and leave out the name of Chaney White. ...

There is no team in the country which could not bench a man in order to make room for this Texas speedboy who has burned up the base paths and the back lawn grass with his fleetness since he came North and East seven or eight years ago.

Observers rate him the peer of Oscar Charleston in the middle garden, and certainly he does everything as well as the Hoosier hustler. ...[20]

Not only the press, but also White's peers, had taken notice. His rare combination of size and speed led one opponent to declare that he was "built like King Kong but runs like Jesse Owens."[21] Added to that combination was a "hard-nosed approach" to the game that "earned him a reputation as a 'dirty' ballplayer, and he made no distinction about who was on the receiving end of his flashing spikes."[22] His rough and rugged personality on the diamond "contrasted with his demeanor off the field, where he was quiet and slow-talking, with a girlish laugh ... and was described as a gentleman and a scholar."[23]

As big a star as White had become, neither he nor his teammates could do anything more to solve the Bacharachs' financial dilemma other than to play their best baseball. Finances were an issue for every ECL team, and the league disbanded in June. White remained with the Bacharachs, which played out the season as an independent club.

In the winter, White returned to Cuba and played for Cienfuegos. Although he was part of a different team, it was a season of déjà vu. White hit the cover off the ball at a .394 clip, but Cienfuegos and Cuba withdrew from the league after Almendares had taken a 10½-game lead in the standings. Cienfuegos finished in last place.[24]

The 1929 season marked White's last year with Atlantic City. The franchise folded after the season. The Bacharachs were now members of the new American Negro League, which included five teams from the ECL along with the Homestead Grays; the ill-fated league also disbanded at the conclusion of its only season. Once again White played outstanding ball and batted .346, but the Bacharachs went backward and finished in fifth place ahead of only the Cuban Stars East team. White summarized the Bacharachs' struggles that year succinctly, when he explained, "When we're hitting the pitchers are going bad. When the pitchers [*sic*] settin' 'em down we're not hitting."[25]

In September White played a few games for Hilldale and then joined Danny McClellan's All-Stars for a brief tour of exhibition games; the only available box scores show him with a 4-for-7 batting line for a .571 average in two games. Next, he traveled south for his last round of winter ball in Florida. White was the hero of the championship game "when his base hit drove in ... the winning run and captured the 'league' title for the Royal Poinciana squad."[26] Afterward, he went to Cuba, where he again played for Cienfuegos, for what also became his last winter season on the island. Cienfuegos' fortunes were completely reversed, and, while White batted a more modest .310, the team captured the championship by 6½ games over second-place Santa Clara.[27]

Upon his return stateside, White briefly roamed the outfield for the Homestead Grays[28] before he once again joined the Hilldale Club in May. Hilldale played as an independent team in 1930 and struggled mightily. In spite of talent including White and catcher Biz Mackey, and a pitching staff that included Cockrell, Hubbard, and Webster McDonald, the team managed only an 8-30-1 record.

Like the Potomacs and the Bacharachs before, the Hilldale franchise experienced serious financial problems in 1930, and White left the team in July to rejoin the Homestead Grays, for whom he batted .348 in 45 games as the team finished 45-15-1, the best record of all the Eastern Independent Clubs. In the season's most notable game, White smashed a 12th-inning, game-winning RBI double against the Kansas City Monarchs at Muehlebach Field on August 1 to end a remarkable pitchers' duel. The Monarchs' Chet Brewer went the distance and struck out 19 Grays batters, but Homestead's starting pitcher, Smokey Joe Williams, outdid him by fanning 27 Monarchs as he completed the shutout.[29]

When the time for winter league play arrived, White headed west to California – rather than returning to Cuba – to play in what was the only integrated league in the United States at that time. The 1930-31 winter season in the Golden State was an unusual one as "there were two competing integrated winter leagues, the 'official' California Winter League, whose Negro league entry played out of White Sox Park, and whose primary competition was Pirrone's All-Stars, and the 'other' Winter League, whose Negro league team played out of Wrigley Field."[30] White was a member of the Philadelphia Royal Giants that played at Wrigley Field, where they dominated the competition. Statistics for the league are incomplete, but available information shows that White played center field and batted .328 in 16 games for the Royal Giants while the team compiled a 28-2-1 record.[31]

In 1931 John Drew took over the ownership of the Hilldale Club, and he signed many of the team's former stars, including White, to try to resurrect the once great and proud franchise. The team again played an independent schedule but performed much better than it had in 1930, finishing with the best record of the Eastern Independents at 38-14-1. Mackey led the squad in hitting with a .362 batting average while White slumped a bit to .296, fifth among the team's starting batters. At the end of the year, White headed West to play his last season of winter league ball in California. The league was back to normal – only one circuit consisting of four teams – and White and the Philadelphia Royal Giants again dominated the competition. Available articles and box scores show that White batted .294 in seven games while the Royal Giants won 20 games and lost only 2.[32]

The following season, Hilldale joined the new East-West League that was formed by Grays owner Cumberland Posey. The league consisted of eight full-fledged member franchises and two associate members, but it was doomed to financial failure from the outset. On March 31 Drew announced that he was "slashing the team budget to $2,200 per month," which spurred immediate player defections by numerous stars, including Mackey, Rap Dixon, and Martin Dihigo.[33] Player-manager Judy Johnson defected to the Pittsburgh Crawfords in June, adding another nail to the team's coffin. White made his move in July when he signed with the Baltimore Black Sox, which finished in first place in the EWL's brief season. White had hit only .257 in 29 games with Hilldale, but he was rejuvenated in Baltimore and improved to .358 in 15 games with the Black Sox to give him a cumulative .292 batting average for the season.

In 1933 Ed Bolden formed a new team called the Philadelphia Stars and, unsurprisingly, filled the squad's roster with many of his former Hilldale players, including White. The Stars played as an independent team that year and finished with a 22-13 record against other top Black clubs in the East. At 39 years old, White still started in left field but batted only .265 in 28 games.

The Stars gained admission to the Negro National League II in 1934. The new league also had been founded the previous year after a one-year gap since Rube Foster's first NNL had folded at the conclusion of the 1931 season. Now entering his 40s, White showed he still had one last burst of energy left in his baseball tank. He played in 67 NNL2 games in which he batted .302, led the team in runs scored (52), and was second in hits (77) to Jud Wilson; Wilson was the only other starter to bat over .300 (.358) and had 78 hits. Outside of White and Wilson, the Stars were no offensive juggernaut, so they relied on their stellar pitching staff. Philadelphia's primary starters for league games – Slim Jones, Rocky Ellis, Webster McDonald, and Frank "Lefty" Holmes – all had seasons in which they were well above the league average in ERA+. The Stars were locked in a three-way battle with the Chicago American Giants and intrastate-rival Pittsburgh Crawfords for supremacy in the NNL2. Chicago claimed the league's first-half title, but the Stars prevailed in the second half.

White and his new team, the Stars, now faced his old Bacharachs nemesis, the Chicago American Giants, in a playoff series to decide the NNL2 champion. On September 11, the two teams met for Game One at Passon Field in Philadelphia. Ellis started for the Stars and held a 3-2 lead when he gave way to Jones at the top of the ninth inning, but Jones surrendered two runs to hand the American Giants a 4-3 victory.[34] Games Two and Three were part of a doubleheader at Cole's Park in Chicago on September 16. Jones started Game Two but lost a tough 3-0 game to Chicago's Ted Trent, who stymied the Stars with a four-hitter.[35] Philadelphia salvaged the nightcap by a 5-3 score, but lost Game Four the next day by a 2-1 tally to find itself in a three-games-to-one hole.[36]

The series now moved back to Passon Field for the final three games. Ellis kept the Stars alive with a tough-as-nails 1-0 shutout in Game Five on September 27, and Paul Carter followed with a complete-game four-hitter in a 4-1 triumph on September 29 that knotted the series at three games apiece.[37] Game Seven, on October 1, ended in a 4-4 tie when the game had to be called after nine innings because of darkness.[38] The game was replayed the next day, and Jones not only "twirled the Ed Bolden crew to the loop diadem with his speedball and baffling cross-fire to turn in six strikeouts, but he also put the game on the proverbial ice when he blasted in the final run with a sharp single to left in the seventh."[39] He finished the championship clincher with a five-hit, 2-0 triumph. White, who had played a big role in helping the Stars to reach the championship series, played in only two of the games but batted .286 with a double and an RBI; he also stole a base, showing that he still had his speed as well as his bat.

White returned to the Stars in 1935, and the team was expected to contend for a second consecutive championship. An article in the *Chicago Defender* declared that the Stars' pitching staff was "rated with the best in baseball."[40] Philadelphia's offense was vastly improved, but the vaunted pitching staff's ERA climbed from 2.61 in 1934 to 5.28 in 1935 and

the team finished in fourth place in the NNL2 with 37-31-4 record. After one last hurrah in 1934, White again began to show signs of age as he batted .287 for the season in 55 league games; it was a respectable mark but placed him only sixth among the batters in Philadelphia's starting lineup.

The Stars did not re-sign White for the 1936 season, but the New York Cubans, another NNL2 franchise, decided to see how much he had left to contribute. The Cubans used White primarily as a backup outfielder,[41] and he batted .308 in 17 league games. Despite his production when given an opportunity, the Cubans released White in late July. He signed with the Brooklyn Royal Giants, where he again saw limited duty, and then retired quietly at the end of the season.[42]

At some point in the early 1940s – most likely in 1943[43] – White married Helena Louise Pringle and started a family in Philadelphia. White worked as a bartender while his wife raised the children and tended to their home. Their first son, Leonard, was born in 1944. Their second son, Darryl, died of pneumonia just 11 days after his birth in December 1947. Chaney and Helena overcame this tragedy and had two additional children, daughters Chanette and Beverly.[44] Chaney White died of acute renal failure on February 23, 1967, and was buried at Mount Lawn Cemetery in Sharon Hill, Pennsylvania. Helena outlived Chaney by 38 years, and she became a Philadelphia institution herself as a health-care union activist.[45]

In a 1987 interview Helena gave about her husband, she showed both his gentlemanly side and how he had remained involved with baseball even though he had not been an active participant in any way. She related that "[h]e used to give the ballplayers, the younger fellows who came in to play with the Stars, a place to stay if they spent all their money. We had a large rooming house[,] so we used to keep them during the summer. If they'd spent their money, he would buy them a bus ticket so they could get back home."[46] She also noted that White "[w]as never bitter about only being able to play in the Negro Leagues, though. He was glad when Jackie Robinson broke in. He said that now the younger men would have a chance to do what they couldn't do."[47]

At the conclusion of her interview, Helena added about Chaney White, "My husband was a center fielder. Different people I've talked to said that he was one of the greatest that they had at the time. ... They were just too late in giving the black ballplayers their share."[48] Considering White's statistics, longevity, and championships won, perhaps he will yet have a share in the National Baseball Hall of Fame with his own plaque.

SOURCES

Except where otherwise indicated, Negro League player statistics and team records were taken from Seamheads.com.

All Cuban Winter League player statistics and team records were taken from the two books by Jorge S. Figueredo that are cited in the Notes. In some instances, there are minor variations between Figueredo's statistics and the CWL statistics found on Seamheads.com.

Ancestry.com was consulted for US Census information as well as birth, marriage, military, and death records.

McNary, Kyle, *Black Baseball: A History of African-Americans & the National Game* (New York: Sterling Publishing Co., Inc., 2003).

Revel, Dr. Layton. "Forgotten Heroes: Chaney White," Center for Negro League Baseball Research, http://www.cnlbr.org/Portals/0/Hero/429409%20Chaney%20White%20Serie.pdf, accessed January 4, 2023. (Dr. Revel's extensive research also includes statistics for as many exhibition games as he could locate in newspapers, which differentiates his career totals for White from the statistics found on Seamheads.com's Negro League database that include only games against teams of Negro major-league caliber. This author has chosen to use the statistics from Seamheads since the quality of semipro teams and other exhibition opponents varied dramatically; however, it must be conceded that Dr. Revel's findings give a more complete picture of White's career statistics and especially highlight the great number of games he played beyond league contests.)

NOTES

1   Jorge S. Figueredo, *Who's Who in Cuban Baseball, 1878-1961* (Jefferson, North Carolina: McFarland & Company, Inc., 2003), 360-61.

2   William F. McNeil, *The California Winter League: America's First Integrated Professional Baseball League* (Jefferson, North Carolina: McFarland & Company, Inc., 2002), 263.

3   Two items regarding White's birth information and genealogy must be addressed. 1) White always cited 1894 as his birth year; however, his death certificate, for which his wife provided information, lists 1895; since White always provided 1894 and all other official records list the same, it appears to be the correct year. 2) As a child, White's name was never listed as Chaney in any US Census but rather was given as some misspelled version ("Lenton" or "Lenard") of his middle name Leonard – it is possible that his family called him by his middle name; as an adult, by the time of the 1950 Census, his name was rendered as "Chaney L White." Considering the misspellings of his name and the inconsistencies about his birth year between the 1900 and 1910 Censuses (the latter of which still lists "Lenard" in proper birth order among the children in the house but gives the wildly incorrect birth year of 1909), White's death certificate, which indicates that his mother had the uncommon first name Minda, was vital in determining that this author had discovered the correct White family; although her name was also misspelled as "Lindia" or "Menda" at times, in other instances it was correctly rendered as "Minda."

4   "Color Line at Elmo/A Movement on Foot to Rid That Community of Worthless Negroes/Thrifty White Laborers Are Desired," *San Saba County* (Texas) *News*, July 22, 1892: 2.

5   "Color Line at Elmo."

6   J. Alba Austin, "Local Happenings/Everything Fit to Print," *Dallas Express*, March 27, 1920: 9.

7   J.A. Austin, "Baseball," *Dallas Express*, April 10, 1920: 11.

8   J.A. Austin, "Baseball."

9   "Baseball," *Dallas Express*, April 17, 1920: 3.

10   Santop also took pitcher Cornelius "Connie" Rector – another Black Panther and ex-Black Giant – along with White to join the Hilldale Club. For evidence of Rector's play for both Fort Worth and Hilldale, see: J.A. Austin, "Baseball," and Frank H. Ryan, "Hilldale Beats Paterson Stars in Great Finish," *Camden Courier-Post*," September 2, 1920: 19.

11   Renee V. Lucas, "Her Husband Was a Center Fielder in Negro League/Helena White, 67," *Philadelphia Daily News*, February 3, 1987: 35. Seamheads.com shows that White played in 17 games for Hilldale in 1920; thus, Helena White was correct when she initially stated that 1920 was his first season in Philadelphia.

12   See, for instance: "Hilldale Colored Club Trounces Harlan, 11 to 3," *Wilmington* (Delaware) *Morning News*, August 24, 1920: 8, and Frank H. Ryan, "Hilldale Beats Paterson Stars in Great Finish."

13   "Hilldale Beats Upland Before 7000 Rooters," *Philadelphia Inquirer*, October 17, 1920: 22.

14   "Bushwicks in Double Header Sunday," *Brooklyn Standard Union*, April 27, 1923: 19.

15   Dr. Layton Revel, "Forgotten Heroes: Chaney White," Center for Negro League Baseball Research, http://www.cnlbr.org/Portals/0/Hero/429409%20Chaney%20White%20Serie.pdf, 14, accessed January 4, 2023.

16   "Wilmington Potomacs Throw Up the Sponge/Robinson Gives Up; Players Go," *Pittsburgh Courier*, July 25, 1925: 13.

17   As of January 2023, Seamheads shows Hilldale with a 53-33-2 (.616) record and Atlantic City at 43-28-1 (.606), which would lead a person to believe that Hilldale should have been the ECL champion in 1926. An imbalanced schedule, poor reporting, and various other circumstances resulted in Atlantic City claiming the ECL title that year. For explanations about how the Bacharachs became the champion, see: James Overmyer, *Black Ball and the Boardwalk: The Bacharach Giants of Atlantic City, 1916-1929* (Jefferson, North Carolina: McFarland & Company, Inc., 2014), 144-46, and Revel, "Forgotten Heroes: Chaney White," 17.

18   Overmyer, 161.

19   Jorge S. Figueredo, *Cuban Baseball: A Statistical History, 1878-1960* (Jefferson, North Carolina: McFarland & Company, Inc., 2003), 174-77.

20   "A Warrior Bold," *Pittsburgh Courier*, June 23, 1928: 16.

21   James A. Riley, *The Biographical Encyclopedia of the Negro Baseball Leagues* (New York: Carroll & Graf Publishers, Inc., 1994), 833-34.

22   Riley, 834.

23   Riley, 834.

24   Figueredo, *Cuban Baseball*, 177-81.

25   Overmyer, 182.

26   Revel, 38.

27   Figueredo, *Cuban Baseball*, 182-83.

28   "Grays Defeat Saints by 4 to 1 Margin," *Chicago Defender* (National Edition), April 26, 1930: 9.

29   "Grays Win 1-0 as 'Smokey Joe' Fans 27 K.C. Players," *Chicago Defender* (National Edition), August 9, 1930: 8.

30   McNeil, 143.

31   McNeil, 152-53.

32   McNeil, 156.

33   Revel, 30-31.

34   Christopher Hauser, *The Negro Leagues Chronology: Events in Organized Black Baseball, 1920-1948* (Jefferson, North Carolina: McFarland & Company, Inc., 2006), 84.

35   "Giants Lead Philly in World's Series 3 to 1," *Chicago Defender*, September 22, 1934: 16.

36   "Giants Lead Philly in World's Series 3 to 1."

37   "Phila. Stars Triumph," *Philadelphia Inquirer*, September 28, 1934: 22; "Stars Jolt Giants and Tie Up Series," *Philadelphia Inquirer*, September 30, 1934: 51.

38   Hauser, 85.

39   "Stars Upset Giants Win National Title/'Slim' Jones Hurls Phila. Negro Team to 2-0 Win Over Chicago Rival," *Philadelphia Inquirer*, October 3, 1934: 22.

40   "Plenty of Pitching Class Here," *Chicago Defender* (National Edition), July 20, 1935: 15. The caption to a photo of the Stars' pitching staff that was included here erroneously gave Holmes's first name as "Sam."

41   Revel, 36.

42   Revel, 37.

43   White appears still to have been single in 1942. He listed a friend as his contact person on his World War II draft registration card that year, and his first son, Leonard, was born in 1944; thus, 1943 makes sense as the year of his and Helena's marriage (although the year remains uncertain).

44   Yvonne Latty, "Deaths: Helena Pringle-White, Ex-Union Activist," *Philadelphia Daily News*, January 5, 2005: 22. The obituary states that Helena White was also survived by an adopted daughter, Clarice Pierce, but does not indicate whether Clarice was adopted by both Whites or by Helena alone after Chaney White was dead.

45   Latty.

46   Lucas.

47   Lucas.

48   Lucas.

JUD WILSON

By Joseph Gerard

Jud Wilson was one of the greatest hitters in the history of Negro League baseball, known for his fierce hitting style as well as his explosive temper and his penchant for brawling with both players and umpires. He stood only 5-feet-8 inches tall but weighed a solid 195 pounds, with broad shoulders, a small waist and tiny calves that left him bowlegged and pigeon-toed. He was a slashing left-handed hitter who often drove the ball to the opposite field. Wilson played for 23 seasons, from 1922 through 1945, beginning with the Baltimore Black Sox before moving on to the Homestead Grays, Pittsburgh Crawfords, and Philadelphia Stars. He finished with a lifetime batting average of .351 that was the fifth highest in Negro league history, and batted over .300 in 16 seasons and over .400 four times.[1] He spent six seasons in the Cuban Winter League and compiled an average there of .372. On July 30, 2006,

Hall of Fame first baseman Jud "Boojum" Wilson

Graig Kreindler

Wilson was posthumously elected to the National Baseball Hall of Fame.

Ernest Judson "Jud" Wilson was born on February 29, 1896, in Remington, Virginia.[2] For many years his birthdate was listed as February 28, 1899, as indicated in a letter from his widow, Betty, to the National Baseball Hall of Fame in April 1972, but at some point it was revised to February 28, 1894, which is engraved on his plaque at the Hall of Fame and on his tombstone. Wilson's World War II draft registration card lists February 29, 1893, which is an invalid date. The earliest source – the 1900 census – lists February 1896. As Wilson himself put it, "These fellows in our league lie too much about their ages."[3]

The first mention of Wilson's early life was his induction into the U.S. Army on June 29, 1918. He served in World War I as a corporal in Company D of the 417th Service Battalion. After his discharge from the Army, he settled in Washington, D.C., and played semipro baseball on the sandlots of his Foggy Bottom neighborhood. It was there that he was discovered in 1922 by Scrappy Brown, shortstop of an independent Negro team, the Baltimore Black Sox. Brown encouraged Wilson to return with him to Baltimore for a tryout, and Wilson passed the test, only to leave the team two weeks later when he became disenchanted with Baltimore. Brown tracked Wilson down in Foggy Bottom and persuaded him to return, only to have his protégé skip the team again. Finally, on his third foray to Baltimore, Wilson remained with the Black Sox.

It did not take long for Wilson to make his presence known. His teammates quickly tagged him with the nickname "Boojum," for the sound his line drives made when they smashed into outfield walls. The independent 1922 Black Sox – founded in 1916 by white businessman George Rossiter, a restaurateur, and his partner, George Spedden – finished the season with a 49-12 record, and Wilson is credited with a batting average of .467.

The Black Sox joined the fledgling Eastern Colored League in 1923. The league was formed when the Hilldale Club of Philadelphia and the Bacharach

Giants of Atlantic City splintered from the Negro National League to form their own circuit. Wilson hit for an average of .338 but Baltimore finished last in the six-team league with a 19-30 record. They bounced back to finish a strong second the following year, with a mark of 51-35. Wilson hit .385 and compiled a hitting streak of 24 straight games.

In 1925 the Black Sox posted a winning percentage of .678, finishing at 61-29, but still could not overtake the Hilldale Club (sometimes known as the Daisies), which was led by future Hall of Fame inductees Judy Johnson and Biz Mackey. Wilson finished ninth in the league in hitting with an average of .354.

After the 1925 season, Wilson made his first venture out of the country, traveling to Cuba to play for the Habana Leones of the Cuban Winter League. He made his mark in his first season in Cuba by leading the league with a batting average of .430, and by hitting a rare home run over the right-field wall at Almendares Park, a distance of more than 400 feet, in the last season before the park was destroyed by a hurricane. In doing so, Wilson joined Cristóbal Torriente, Oscar Charleston, Alejandro Oms, and Esteban Montalvo as the only men ever to do so, earning himself the nickname El Jorocon – The Bull – in the process.

Back in Baltimore in 1926, Wilson hit .347, but the Black Sox slipped to 23-36, leaving them 30½ games behind the Bacharach Giants, who finished with an extraordinary record of 63-15. Wilson returned to Cuba that winter but saw limited action, hitting .333 in only 54 at-bats. The following year, 1927, he was at his peak. He hit .403 for the Black Sox, who once again finished far behind the repeat pennant winners from Atlantic City. Wilson followed this with one of the greatest performances seen up to that time in Cuba, leading the league in hitting (.424), triples (7), and runs (36), only to be upstaged by his own teammate, Martín Dihigo, who not only hit .415 but pitched five complete games, winning four of them and the league MVP award in the process, as Habana easily captured the pennant.

In 1928 the Eastern Colored League, beset by the constant disagreements and financial difficulties of its club owners, disbanded in June, with two of its teams, the Philadelphia Stars and the Cuban Stars, lasting only three weeks. Many of the teams continued to play each other and other independent Negro clubs, and Wilson is credited with a .399 batting average for the Black Sox in 42 games. He returned to Cuba that winter and finished second in batting (with a .397 average) behind Habana teammate Oms, and in runs and

home runs behind Cool Papa Bell. Habana decimated the competition by winning 14 of its first 16 games, and by the time they had raced ahead to a ten-game lead, two of the other three teams – Cuba and Cienfuegos – had bowed out of the competition altogether.

The American Negro League was formed in 1929 by five carryovers from the Eastern Colored League – the Bacharach Giants, the Cuban Stars, the Hilldale Giants, the Lincoln Giants (of New York), and the Black Sox. The popular and renowned independent Homestead Grays, as well as a new incarnation of the Harrisburg Giants, were added in an attempt to bolster the league's structure.

The circuit debuted with a split-season format, but the Black Sox made that aspect moot by winning both halves of the season, doing away with the need for a playoff to determine the champion. The Black Sox were bolstered by a realignment of talent in the league, and featured what came to be known in the black press as "The Million Dollar Infield," of Wilson at first, Frank Warfield at second, manager Dick Lundy at shortstop, and Oliver Marcelle at third, so named for what they would have been worth had they been white players.

Wilson hit .344 in 1929, and in a testament to his stature as a ballplayer, a rumor unfolded that Baltimore was entertaining a trade of Wilson to the Homestead Grays for both the esteemed Dihigo and the talented John Beckwith, perhaps the only man with a reputation for meanness that exceeded even that of Wilson. The trade never took place.

That fall Wilson played in several documented exhibitions against white teams that included major-league players. Wilson went 2-for-4 against pitcher Ed Rommel of the Philadelphia Athletics in an 8-3 victory over the world champions. In a game against the St. Louis Browns, Wilson hit a home run and a double against pitcher Johnny Ogden in a 5-2 win.

Wilson returned to Cuba only days before the stock market crash that would imperil the existence of the Negro leagues. He hit .363, second to Oms, who hit .380. The Leones had a reversal of fortunes, slipping all the way to last place as Cienfuegos won the pennant, mostly on the basis of defeating the Habana club in 15 out of 20 games.

Despite improved newspaper coverage and great play on the field, the American Negro League did not reorganize in 1930. The Black Sox soldiered on as an independent team, and were credited with a 21-16 record, with Wilson hitting for an average of .372. In an October doubleheader against a team of barnstorming major leaguers, he got three hits against New York Yankees pitcher Roy Sherid in game one and went 1-for-2 with two stolen bases in the nightcap against Big Jim Weaver of the Cubs.

In 1931 Wilson joined the independent Homestead Grays, who traveled the country taking on all comers, teams in the Negro National League as well as white semipro clubs, and were credited with an extraordinary record of 186-17. Joining Wilson were Oscar Charleston, Josh Gibson, Smokey Joe Williams, Vic Harris, Double Duty Radcliffe, and Ted Page. On a team of hard-nosed fighters, Wilson brooked no nonsense. Page recalled that the team pulled up to a black rooming house in Zanesville, Ohio, after a game. The landlady filled the bath with hot water, and the men lined up – behind Wilson, who was first. "I was second," said Page. "I was his roommate. Nobody fooled with Jud Wilson."[4]

As a result of the Great Depression, there were no operative Negro leagues left after the demise of the Negro National League in March of 1932. By that time, Cum Posey, the owner of the Grays, was facing a stern challenge from the Pittsburgh Crawfords, an upstart youth club that had been garnering attention for years. At times Posey would help the Crawfords out with money for uniforms and equipment, but always with an ulterior motive in mind. He finally lured the Crawfords' top player, Josh Gibson, to the Grays, but it was too late. By 1932 businessman, restaurateur, and numbers racketeer Gus Greenlee had built the Crawfords into a formidable club, replacing local semipro talent with the finest professional players he could attract.

The Crawfords began the 1932 season with spring training in Hot Springs, Arkansas, and then barnstormed across the South against the best competition they could find. They arrived in Pittsburgh on April 29 to open Greenlee Field, the spectacular new ballpark their owner had built for his team.

Posey hoped to turn back the Crawfords' tide by filling the void left by the demise of the previous Negro leagues. He started his own circuit, the East-West League, which was the first attempt to include both Eastern and Midwestern cities in a black baseball league. The league could not overcome the dismal economic conditions; by late May, Posey was forced to capitulate to the Crawfords, having already lost many of his premier players to Greenlee, including John Gibson, Oscar Charleston, and Cool Papa Bell. Wilson had begun the season as player-manager of the Grays, but he too defected to their crosstown rivals.

Despite inviting the Crawfords to join his circuit, Posey was forced to shut down the East-West League before June.

The Crawfords' roster resembled that of the 1931 Grays in many ways, with the notable inclusion of the great Satchel Paige. In October they played a series against Casey Stengel's major-league All-Stars, winning five of the seven games. The Crawfords also played an exhibition game against a team featuring Babe Didrikson, the female Olympic champion, who often pitched for barnstorming male teams as a gate attraction. "We told Jud to take it easy on her," remembered manager Vic Harris. Wilson proceeded to smash a line drive past Didrikson's head. "She don't have no business out there," he said upon returning to the bench. Harris took him out of the game. "He used to like to win," said Harris.[5]

In 1933 Wilson jumped the Crawfords to join the Philadelphia Stars, a new team formed by Ed Bolden with the financial backing of white promoter Ed Gottlieb. Bolden was the force behind the old Hilldale club and the founder of the ill-fated Eastern Colored League. The Stars were independent in their inaugural season despite Greenlee's establishment of a new Negro National League, which had a tempestuous unveiling that saw only three clubs make it to the finish line. Bolden believed the Stars would be more profitable barnstorming against the strong semipro teams on the Eastern Seaboard, most of them composed of white players. Wilson had an auspicious debut for the Stars, batting .372/.456/.555, and he was voted by readers of the *Chicago Defender* and *Pittsburgh Courier* to be the starting third baseman for the East squad in the first Negro league East-West All-Star Game, held on September 10 at Comiskey Park in Chicago. Despite inclement weather, a crowd of just under 20,000 attended, and the game quickly became one of the most important annual events in black sports. With one out in the second inning, Wilson got the first hit in the All-Star Game's history, and he drove in two runs in the fifth inning with a single.

The most renowned example of Wilson's temper took place after the game; his best friend and roommate, Jake Stephens, returned inebriated to the hotel room where Wilson had been sleeping, and made more noise than his friend was disposed to tolerate at that moment. "He got mad, grabbed ahold of my leg and held me out the window 16 stories above the street," said Stephens. "I yelled 'Oh please, Willie, don't drop me.' Then I started kicking. I was kicking his arm with my free leg. So he shifted hands on me, just like that, from one hand to the other, 16 floors above the street."[6]

The Philadelphia Stars joined the Negro National League in 1934, and while the circuit remained solvent, it was still subject to the instabilities of a startup league, exacerbated by poor administration and a lack of resolve on the part of league management to rein in the scheduling whims of team owners. Under these less-than-ideal circumstances, the Stars were awarded the second-half pennant and the right to face the first-half winners, the Chicago American Giants, for the league championship in a best-of-seven series.

The first four games were well played and cast the teams in a positive light, but things went unaccountably downhill from that point on. First, interest in the series was lost as Game Five was delayed for 10 days to allow the Stars to play various exhibition games, including the second game of a lucrative, four-team Negro doubleheader at Yankee Stadium in which Wilson collected four hits including a home run. When the series resumed, Game Six featured one of the more blatant examples of Wilson's flagrant disregard of authority. After disagreeing with one of umpire Burt Gholston's decisions, Wilson apparently struck the umpire, but was somehow allowed to remain in the game, despite the protests of Chicago's manager, Dave Malarcher.

Commissioner Rollo Wilson met with both sides before the seventh game, and heard evidence from Gholston that he intended to eject Wilson until the player threatened to get him after the game. Once again, money trumped principle in a league matter, as the commissioner caved in to pressure applied by Bolden, who threatened to boycott the remaining games if Wilson was banned. Wilson played in Game Seven, which ended in a 4-4 tie due to a curfew. Finally, the series ended when the Stars won the final game by 2-0, a result that had to withstand another protest by Chicago.

Wilson hit .360/.436/.500 for the year. He drove in Cool Papa Bell from second base with an infield single to give the East a 1-0 win in that year's All-Star Game in front of a crowd of 25,000 at Comiskey Park. "When Bell stole second and Wilson of the Philadelphia Stars singled to break up a six-pitcher duel, you should have heard the mob, they forgot themselves temporarily. Who knows that they had not seen the greatest ball game ever played," wrote Nat Trammell.[7]

Wilson continued to play for the Stars from 1935 through 1939, and he played the 1935-36 season in Cuba, which was to be his last. He was voted to the East All-Star Game again in 1935, and had two more hits, finishing with a career average of .455 in the event. He hit .344/.380/.566 with 10 home runs in 1935, but the Stars entered a period of decline both on the field and at the box office. As receipts dwindled, Bolden could no longer afford to send his team south to train each spring, which cost him considerable income from the exhibitions he typically scheduled as his squad worked their way north, and made it more difficult for players to round into prime physical shape for the season.

Under these circumstances, it is not difficult to explain Bolden's decision to have Wilson assume managerial responsibilities in 1937. He saved a salary, and he knew that his fiery star was a fierce competitor who expected the very best from himself and his teammates. Wilson suffered a broken rib in late June of 1937 when the Stars' bus overturned outside of Pittsburgh on a trip to Cleveland. It was one of the few times in his career that Wilson would not attempt to play through injury.

Jake Stephens recalled a time when pitcher Jim Wilson, who threw very hard, beaned Wilson with a fastball. The ball ricocheted off Wilson's skull into the screen behind home plate. "It would have killed anyone else," Stephens said.[8] Wilson crowded the plate and was often hit by pitches, including one in 1926 that broke his elbow. Rumored to be out for the season, he returned to play after only two weeks. Wilson was not known to be a graceful fielder either, and he suffered numerous injuries by knocking down groundballs with his body. It became an effective strategy, however; he had such a strong arm that he could recover in time to retrieve the ball and still throw out the runner.

Wilson held the position of manager until he was relieved of his duties by Bolden in favor of Jake Dunn midway through the 1939 campaign. That did not prevent him from hitting .373 for the season. Cum Posey still coveted Wilson's services, and in 1940 brought him back to the Grays, then based in Washington, D.C. Wilson joined Gibson, Bell, and Buck Leonard, giving the Grays four Hall of Famers in their lineup. Wilson produced a two-out, two-run single that won the 1940 pennant for the Grays, and he was mobbed on the field by the 30,000 spectators. He played more sparingly during his time with the Grays, but contributed to six straight Negro National League championships, from 1940 through 1945. In the winter of 1944, he made his only foray to Puerto Rico to play in the island's Winter League, where he hit .404.

Many of his contemporaries lauded Wilson as one of the greatest hitters of his time. Josh Gibson said Wilson was the greatest hitter he had ever seen, and Radcliffe said that Wilson was even better than Gibson himself: "Boojum was a better hitter than Josh. He didn't hit as many home runs, but he hit so many doubles and singles."[9] Satchel Paige once said that the two toughest hitters he ever faced were Chino Smith and Jud Wilson. Wilson recalled hitting against Paige: "He just tried to blur that ball by you. I timed his blinding stuff and just raked him for base hits."[10] Teammate Ted Page said that Wilson hit Lefty Grove "like Grove came off the sandlots."[11] In 1928 Wilson got two singles and a double off Grove in Baltimore, and in his one season in the California Winter League (in which he hit .469 and .385 against major leaguers) Vic Harris reported that Wilson took two pitches from Grove before lining the third between the pitcher's legs into center field, at which point Grove threw his glove down and left the mound. Pitcher Script Lee said

Infielder Jud Wilson, a 24-year veteran of the Negro Leagues.

National Baseball Hall of Fame

Wilson hit one home run that was longer than any he had seen off the bats of Babe Ruth or Jimmie Foxx. In 26 barnstorming games against major-league pitchers, Wilson hit .353.

Wilson may have been even better had he been able to control his temper. He is remembered for his aggressive nature and fondness for fighting. While generally under control off the field, Wilson often lost it between the white lines. "When he saw an umpire," said Stephens, "he became a maniac. There was never a meaner, nastier man than Boojum when he put his uniform on."[12] In an era noted for rough play and a lack of respect for arbiters, Wilson often set the standard for bad behavior. He once lifted umpire (and former player) Phil Cockrell off the ground by the skin on his chest and would not let him down until teammate Crush Holloway brandished a bat on behalf of the victim. On another occasion, Wilson was wrongfully accused of hitting an umpire and exploded when tossed from the game. It took three policemen to subdue him with their nightsticks and haul him to jail. At Bushwick Park in Brooklyn, he once chased another umpire out to center field waving his bat.

Players were scared of Wilson as well. Clint Thomas said, "He'd kill you. He was dangerous! He was never out. The pitcher never throwed a strike. All ball players were scared of him."[13] Chino Smith, a tough cookie himself, once felt Wilson's wrath firsthand. He slid hard into third, and Wilson picked him up and threw him 15 feet into the air. "You better go about your business, boy," said Wilson. "I'll break every bone in your body."[14]

Despite these examples to the contrary, Stephens and other contemporaries experienced a gentle, good-natured side to Wilson's personality. "He was good-hearted," said Judy Johnson. "He would do anything in the world for you."[15] "Jud was a kind-hearted individual," said Ted Page. "He would give you the shirt off his back. The writers made him into a villain."[16] "He loved me. I could do anything with him," said Stephens.[17]

In the last few years before he retired from baseball, Wilson began to act erratically. Buck Leonard recalled a game at Griffith Stadium that had to be interrupted because Wilson was drawing small circles in the dirt at third base with his fingers. At times he did the same with his bat while hitting, and it would take several players to snap him out of his trance. On another occasion, Wilson was on a ferry to Chester, Pennsylvania, when he began to remove his clothing and had to be restrained.

After retiring from baseball, Wilson worked on a road crew building the Whitehurst Freeway in Washington, and his last job was as a janitor. He lived in Washington with his wife, Betty, whom he had married in February of 1923 after visiting her in rural Virginia, often by crossing a stream on a log. "Jud was all man," she said. "He was a man of few words, but when he said those words, he meant them."[18]

Eventually the incidents Wilson experienced worsened into epileptic seizures, which may have been brought on by an auto accident, the frequent pitches to the head, or the beatings he received fighting. His condition deteriorated, and he had to be institutionalized. Toward the end of his life, he had ceased to be able to remember most people, but brightened up when told about his old friend Jake Stephens.

Jud Wilson died on June 27, 1963, from a heart attack. He was buried in Arlington National Cemetery in Virginia. On July 30, 2006, he was elected to the National Baseball Hall of Fame along with 16 other former Negro league players and executives, having received more than 75 percent of the votes of a committee of baseball historians assembled to consider a roster of 94 nominees. His great-niece and only living relative, Sha'Ron Taylor, accepted the award. She remembered that her grandmother told her that Wilson would take her onto the field at Griffith Stadium after games.

It is of course unfortunate that Jud Wilson was never able to play major-league baseball, but his record indicates that he would have been more than up to the challenge. Unlike some Negro league players, Wilson supported integration but did not believe it would be forthcoming. "It's too big a job for the people who are now trying to put it over," he said in 1939. "It will have to be a universal movement, and that will never be … because the big-league game, as it is now, is overrun with Southern blood. These fellows would have to stop at the same hotels, eat in the same dining rooms and sleep in the same train compartments with the colored players. There'd be trouble for sure."[19]

By the time integration finally came, it was too late for Wilson, but that did not minimize his remarkable achievements on the field. "Wilson was one of our great players," said Cool Papa Bell. "He was mean. Ballplayers are like that a whole lot. As soon as they walk out on that field, they want to win. Well, he was that type of guy. Good fellow, but he just got so much heart and soul in this ball game."[20]

ACKNOWLEDGMENTS

This original biography of Jud Wilson was updated by Gary Belleville in July 2021.

SOURCES

In addition to the sources cited in the Notes, the author consulted a number of other sources including:

Holway, John, *The Complete Book of Baseball's Negro Leagues* (Winter Park, Florida: Hastings House, 2001).

McNeill, William F., *Black Baseball Out of Season: Pay for Play Outside of the Negro Leagues* (Jefferson, North Carolina: McFarland & Co, 2007).

Riley, James A., *The Biographical Encyclopedia of the Negro Baseball Leagues* (New York: Carroll & Graf Publishers, 1994).

Lanctot, Neil, *The Rise and Ruin of a Black Institution* (Philadelphia: University of Pennsylvania Press, 2008)

Porter, David L., *Biographical Dictionary of American Sports: Baseball* (Westport, Connecticut: Greenwood Publishing Group, Inc, 2000).

Sheinin, Dave, "D.C.'s 'Boojum' Gets His Day in Hall of Fame," *Washington Post,* July 31, 2006.

Ancestry.com, Baseball-reference.com, Seamheads.com

Baseball Hall of Fame Library, player file for Ernest "Jud" Wilson

NOTES

1   Unfortunately, official uniform statistics for the Negro Leagues do not exist. The author relied on the work published by Seamheads.com, Baseball-Reference.com, and historian John Holway to cover the extent of Wilson's career. While these sources sometimes diverge (usually as a result of how non-league games are treated), they are a reliable and invaluable resource.

2   Email from renowned Negro Leagues historian Gary Ashwill to Gary Belleville on July 7, 2021.

3   Sam Lacy, "Sepia Stars Only Lukewarm Toward Campaign to Break Down Baseball Barriers," *Baltimore Afro-American,* August 12, 1939.

4   John Holway, "One of the Greatest Hitters to Ever Swing a Bat: Jud (Boojum) Wilson," *The Sun Magazine,* June 24, 1979.

5   Holway, "One of the Greatest Hitters to Ever Swing a Bat: Jud (Boojum) Wilson."

6   Holway, "One of the Greatest Hitters to Ever Swing a Bat: Jud (Boojum) Wilson."

7   Nat Trammell, "Baseball Classic – East vs. West," *Colored Baseball and Sports Monthly,* October 1934.

8   Holway, "One of the Greatest Hitters to Ever Swing a Bat: Jud (Boojum) Wilson."

9   John Holway, *Blackball Stars: Negro League Pioneers* (New York: Carroll & Graf Publishers, 1992), 200.

10   Holway, "One of the Greatest Hitters to Ever Swing a Bat: Jud (Boojum) Wilson."

11   Holway, *Blackball Stars,* 201.

12   Holway, *Blackball Stars,* 201.

13   Holway, *Blackball Stars,* 201.

14   Holway, *Blackball Stars,* 203.

15   Holway, *Blackball Stars,* 202.

16   Holway, *Blackball Stars,* 202.

17   Holway, *Blackball Stars,* 209.

18   Holway, *Blackball Stars,* 204.

19   Lacy, "Sepia Stars Only Lukewarm Toward Campaign to Break Down Baseball Barriers."

20   Holway, *Blackball Stars,* 214.

ARMON STOVALL

BY RICHARD BOGOVICH

It would not have been surprising if Armon Stovall had wished his only brush with fame had been as batboy for the champion 1934 Philadelphia Stars. Instead, 18 years later, he was the subject of a brief news item printed coast to coast over many months because his strong attraction to a certain model of powerful automobile had landed him in trouble more than once. In contrast, his legal victory about 20 years later, in a ruling by a Coast Guard vice admiral, may have received no media attention.

Armon Stovall was born on July 28, 1919, in Newark, New Jersey, to Armon Stovall Sr. and Marie (Paul) Stovall.[1] Though this date of birth is confirmed in New Jersey birth records, he was not listed with his parents when they were visited for the census in January of 1920 as they were living with Henry and Anne De Mund, his uncle and aunt.[2] In the 1930 census, he was the only child listed, though his father apparently was remarried to a woman named Theresa by then.[3]

In mid-August of 1934, the *Baltimore Afro-American* noted that the younger Armon had been serving as batboy for the Philadelphia Stars but was days away from returning to New York City to live with his aunt, Mrs. De Mund. For one year he had been living with another aunt, Mrs. Florence Crawley, in Philadelphia's Germantown neighborhood. This news item was not on the sports pages; thus, the paper offered no further insights into his time with the ballclub.[4]

Alas, the former batboy was presumably the Armon Stovall listed in the 1940 census as imprisoned at Rikers Island jail in New York City and who was 20 years old, Black, and born in New Jersey. When the former batboy completed a military registration card on January 3, 1941, he was once again living with his aunt Florence (and unemployed). His middle name was reported on that card as Benedict. He stood 5-feet-7-inches tall and weighed 137 pounds, though later government documents listed him as 5-feet-5.

His obituary said he was survived by a son named Boyd Scarberry. That could have been the Boyd Scarberry who was born on February 1, 1943, and who died in the same city as Stovall just six years after. However, Scarberry's obituary identified a different father, also with the surname Scarberry, and a federal document identified Boyd as White.[5]

International travel records show Stovall serving as a seaman on several ships from October 1944 to mid-1946, between East Coast cities and such places as Liverpool, England, the Mediterranean island of Malta, and Naples, Italy. During the summer of 1946 he arrived in Galveston, Texas, from Naples. Late that same year he was convicted in Texas of burglary and sentenced to two to five years in prison.[6]

Stovall was released by early 1950 and likely was the Armand Stovall who was among several employees of a New York City nightclub who were held up at gunpoint on January 23 of that year.[7] It was definitely the former batboy who broke into a car dealership in Connecticut two months later and stole a model valued at a hefty $3,525.[8] He was sentenced to spend one to six years at the Osborne State Prison Farm and by May of 1952 he had thus picked up the nickname "Cadillac." At that point, he and another prisoner escaped and walked seven miles along nearby railroad tracks to Springfield, Massachusetts. When they passed an automobile showroom, they decided to take a Cadillac, which they drove toward New York City. They did not resist arrest as they were surrounded at East Hartford. The police succeeded much more quickly than in 1950, when Stovall had remained at large for more than a week.[9]

Stovall's latest arrest led to his nationwide brush with fame, when his saga was condensed to a single sentence that was printed in newspapers over many months, including in Canada: "Armond [*sic*] (Cadillac) Stovall, whose fondness for high-powered automobiles landed him in a prison farm, escaped but was caught three hours later, driving a stolen Cadillac."[10] About two weeks after this news item started spreading via wire services, the two perpetrators were each sentenced to an additional term of four to eight years.[11]

By the early 1960s, Stovall's life entered a long period of stability. Around 1959 he settled in San Francisco, where he lived for 30 years. He married Constance Tyler in March of 1968, back in New Jersey. They were married for 26 years, until his death. At some point Stovall became "a Seafarers Union steward [and] a member of the "U.S. Merchant Marines and Seafarers Union (International)."[12]

In 1966 Stovall had another run-in with authorities, but he had to be satisfied with the ultimate ruling on the matter, even though it came many months later. While serving on the *SS San Juan* in March of 1966, he was charged with marijuana possession at sea, and then was charged again when the vessel docked six days later at Port Elizabeth, New Jersey. It took more than three years for the resulting legal process to unfold, and on May 13, 1969, an examiner of the US Coast Guard revoked Stovall's seaman's documents. At one point in the process, on August 12, 1968, Stovall's attorney was excused and the sailor acted on his own behalf. A major scheduling complication occurred that year because Stovall was serving on the *SS President Jackson* during a round-the-world voyage.[13]

Stovall's seaman's documents were reinstated in March of 1971 when the 1969 revocation order was vacated and the original charges were dismissed, in the *Armon Stovall vs. U.S.* decision by Coast Guard Vice Admiral Thomas R. Sargent III. Sargent did not blame Stovall for all of the process delays, thought it was plausible that Stovall had not been properly notified along the way, and considered the incomplete record of proceedings to be "embarrassing" for the Coast Guard. Near the end of his written opinion, Sargent's expression of sympathy for Stovall included evidence he had submitted which indicated that, over the course of the year after his marijuana possession, he had served on four other ships on seven voyages without additional misconduct. "I am mindful of the fact that Appellant [Stovall] does not appear innocent of inducing errors in this case," Sargent concluded. "But to prolong this case further because of procedural errors made by Coast Guard personnel, even if induced by Appellant's own wiles, would appear to be harassment."[14]

Stovall relocated from San Francisco to Reno, Nevada, around 1989 and died there on May 25, 1994. He was survived by his son, Boyd, and his wife, Constance. He was to be cremated; no funeral was scheduled at the time of his obituary.[15] All told, his life might not have been a particularly remarkable one, but it had its moments. Still, it is natural to wonder how different Stovall's adulthood might have been if he had spent a few more years befriending members of the Philadelphia Stars.

NOTES

1   "Armon Stovall," *Reno* (Nevada) *Gazette-Journal*, May 28, 1994: 2C. Common misspellings of his first name included Armond and Armand.

2   See New Jersey birth records for 1901-1929, accessible via familysearch.org.

3   In Newark's 1937 city directory, his father's wife was also identified as Theresa, making it seem unlikely that the 1930 census listed Mrs. Stovall's first name incorrectly.

4   Joseph A. NcNeal [sic, McNeal], "Germantown," *Baltimore Afro-American*, August 18, 1934: 16. Mrs. De Mund's first name was spelled differently elsewhere, such as in the 1915 New Jersey census, in which she was called "Ann." After suffering "a slight stroke on Christmas morning" of 1933 she was called "Anna" in "Newark, N.J.," *Pittsburgh Courier*, January 20, 1934: 4. The latter also mentioned Florence Crawley. One reason Stovall resumed living with her in the early 1940s could have been his other aunt's uneven recovery from that stroke in late 1933.

5   "Boyd Leon Scarberry," *Reno Gazette-Journal*, December 17, 2000: 19C. See also Note 1 and the US Social Security Applications and Claims Index, 1936-2007, accessible via genealogical websites.

6   Texas Convict and Conduct Registers, 1875-1954, accessible via ancestry.com.

7   John Martin, "Hold Up a Night Club at Noon, Grab $0.00," *New York Daily News,* January 24, 1950: 5.

8   "It Happened in Connecticut," *Hartford Courant,* April 13, 1950: 3.

9   "Stovall's Love for Fine Cars Betrays Him," *Hartford Courant*, May 4, 1952: 2; "Court Shows Leniency for Good Record," *Hartford Courant*, June 7, 1950: 5.

10   For example, see "Likes That Car," *Montreal Star*, June 12, 1952: 23. For a much later instance, see "Likes That Car," *Huron County Tribune* (Bad Axe, Michigan), January 30, 1953: 2.

11   "Two Escapees Sentenced to 4 to 8 Years," *Hartford Courant*, June 25, 1952: 2.

12   See Note 1, and the New Jersey Marriage Index, 1901-2016, accessible via genealogical websites.

13   See Note 1 and the *Armon Stovall vs. U.S.* decision, March 2, 1971, accessible at https://media.defense.gov/2017/Dec/27/2001861245/-1/-1/0/1834%20-%20Stovall.pdf.

14   *Armon Stovall vs. U.S.*

15   See Note 1.

EDWARD W. BOLDEN

By Michael Haupert

Before he became a giant in the annals of Black base-ball history, Ed Bolden was a domestic servant and a clerk in the Philadelphia post office. He stood a scant 5-feet-7 and weighed less than 150 pounds, but his diminutive stature belied a forceful presence. By the time he retired from his post-office job in 1946, he was an accomplished baseball executive and a 42-year veteran of the US Post Office. The latter was not a glamorous career, but it was prestigious for a Black man in the early twentieth century. In addition to his "day job," Bolden found time to make a mark on the baseball world as an owner, officer in three different professional leagues,[1] and one of the great innovators in the history of professional baseball.

Edward W. Bolden was born in Concordville, Pennsylvania, about 20 miles west of Philadelphia, on January 17, 1881. A search of census records turns up no clear indication of what sort of occupations his parents may have had. When he was young, the

Philadelphia Stars owner Ed Bolden

public domain

family moved to Darby, an African American enclave of 6,300 people five miles southwest of Philadelphia, where he attended the local public schools.[2] His baseball career began in 1910 as a humble volunteer scorekeeper for a local amateur team managed by 19-year-old Austin Thompson. The Hilldale Daisies, as they were known, began by playing other amateur squads in the Philadelphia area, but they soon out-grow both their competitive and geographic boundar-ies. While Thompson started Hilldale on the road to prominence, he was not around to see the club reach it.

At 19, Thompson was barely older than the play-ers on his team. The 29-year-old Bolden was more mature (he had a wife, Nellie, and a 3-year-old daugh-ter, Hilda), had more business experience (six years with the post office), and, as time would prove, pos-sessed superior marketing skills.[3] The combination of Thompson's youth and Bolden's experience led to a change in leadership. With Bolden at the helm, Hilldale grew from a local amateur organization into a professional powerhouse, flourishing financially through the 1920s before finally succumbing to the Great Depression. During his two decades in charge, Bolden built some of the best Black ballclubs in the East. From 1923 to 1928 he also headed the Eastern Colored League (ECL), of which Hilldale was a char-ter member.[4] All the while, Bolden retained his full-time position at the post office.

Bolden was a tireless and brash promoter, who was unafraid to play the race card. He successfully mar-keted the fact that Hilldale was Black-owned, which played a role in the team's ability to land top-qual-ity talent and schedule attractive opponents. It also made him a local hero of sorts in Darby. But while he promoted Hilldale as a "race institution," he was not afraid to do business with White men when he found it to be profitable. Segregation of any form was not profitable, argued Bolden, "only where the color-line fades and cooperation instituted are our business ad-vances gratified."[5]

Despite his willingness to deal with businessmen regardless of color, Bolden remained devoted to Black businesses and causes. He was a member of several Black organizations, including the Elks, Masons, Shriners, and the Citizens Republican Club. He donated generously to Black causes and regularly took part in benefits and charity events, both individually and through the ballclub.

Bolden earned a reputation as a clean, upstanding owner with little tolerance for rowdiness or umpire-baiting. He advocated "clean ball" and gentlemanly behavior on the field and expected the same from the fans in the stands. Once, during the 1916 season, he went so far as to press charges against patrons of his own park for rowdy behavior. This incident led to his employment of security guards at home games to ensure the safety and comfort of the players, umpires, and fans.[6]

Ed Bolden's greatest stroke of marketing genius may have been the construction in 1914 of a ballpark at 9th and Cedar Avenue, known as Darby Field or Hilldale Park. Unlike National and American League teams, which could borrow or self-finance the construction of a ballpark, Hilldale had to make annual improvements out of its operating budget. As a result, their park was a modest and continual work in progress.[7] It was a wooden ballpark with a seating capacity of only a few thousand, which grew over time as additional bleachers were added. The location of the park was convenient for the team's fan base, but Bolden was not content with that. He assured that the park would also be easy to reach by arranging with the local streetcar company to have a line run straight to his ballpark, adding extra cars during games.[8]

Bolden's success drew the attention of White New York booking agent Nat Strong, who coveted Hilldale for his booking agency. When Bolden rebuffed his advances, Strong threatened to drive him out of business by locating a competing team across the street from Darby Field. Bolden responded promptly and publicly to this threat by taking out an ad in the *Philadelphia Tribune* to state his case:

> The race people of Philadelphia and vicinity are proud to proclaim Hilldale the biggest thing in the baseball world owned, fostered, and controlled by race men. ... We are proud to be in a position to give Darby citizens the most beautiful park in Delaware County, a team that is second to none and playing the best attractions available. To affiliate ourselves with other than race men would be a

mark against our name that could never be eradicated.[9]

Bolden's public-relations coup and his skills at signing top talent defused Strong's threat and contributed to the rise of Hilldale to the top of the Eastern colored circuits. His refusal to play second fiddle to White baseball men won him praise and admiration. Years later, his reversal of this practice was to cost him in the court of public opinion.

Hilldale was particularly innovative in marketing and in their pursuit of complementary sources of income. They sold the standard peanuts and soft drinks from the first days and added ice cream and cigarettes in 1917. Enticing customers with cold drinks was one way to attract fans on a sweltering summer afternoon in Philadelphia. Another clever marketing approach was used to get around the Sunday blue laws by admitting fans to the ballpark free, provided they purchased a program. The programs were generally profitable for the club, since they sold advertising to cover the printing costs.[10] This ruse frequently ran afoul of local law enforcement, but became a moot point when Hilldale began to lease a ballpark across the river in New Jersey in 1920.

In December of 1920, Hilldale joined Rube Foster's Negro National League (NNL) as an associate member for a $1,000 deposit. The membership provided protection from player raids by other league members. The following year Bolden made one of his most lucrative investments, purchasing the contract of future Hall of Famer Judy Johnson from the Madison Stars for $100.[11] Johnson became a fixture in the Hilldale lineup for the next decade, leading the team with a .341 average during the 1924 colored World Series and managing the team in 1931 and 1932. He later worked in the front office for Bolden's second professional team, the Philadelphia Stars.

By 1922 Bolden was no longer satisfied with his membership in the NNL. While he was protected from player raids, he had lost lucrative dates against Eastern clubs on Foster's outlaw list. Foster forbade NNL members to play outlawed teams in an effort to punish them for their refusal to recognize NNL contracts. He felt that by denying these outlaws lucrative dates against the high-quality teams of the NNL, he would punish them at the box office. Unfortunately for Hilldale, the NNL teams suffered as well.

The travel costs associated with league play were another sore point for Bolden. During the 1921 and 1922 seasons, only four Western teams came to

THE STARS SHONE ON PHILADELPHIA

Hilldale for games, and Hilldale's Western trip in 1922 was a financial loss. The cost of transportation, food, and lodging were more than Hilldale's share of the gate.

Hilldale resigned from the NNL after the 1922 season. Foster refused to refund Hilldale's league deposit, and Bolden retaliated by forming a rival league, the Mutual Association of Eastern Colored Baseball Clubs, popularly known as the Eastern Colored League (ECL), to begin play in 1923. Unlike the NNL, which was governed by Foster, the ECL had no president, but was run by a commission composed of one representative from each club. Bolden was elected chairman of the commission.[12]

The formation of the league set off a public-relations war with Foster and the other members of the NNL. Foster's chief criticism was that some of the owners of ECL teams were White. Of particular concern to Foster was Bolden's inclusion of Nat Strong as a league member. From Bolden's perspective, Strong's tight control of the New York market made it necessary to do business with him, especially since Sunday ball was still prohibited in Philadelphia but not New York. Bolden countered that most of the NNL teams rented parks from White owners and rent on these parks ran to 25 percent of gross receipts. In contrast, many of the ECL parks were controlled by Black owners.

Foster's NNL and Bolden's ECL maintained frosty relations throughout the 1923 season and into 1924. But in September, the two executives met in New York and put their differences aside, agreeing to stage a colored World Series and "respect the sanctity of their inter-relationship" between the two leagues.[13] Reading between the lines, this meant they were willing to put their personal feud aside to make money. This agreement became the groundwork for more substantial cooperation between the leagues.

After the Series, Bolden and Foster set about normalizing relations between the NNL and the ECL. In December they signed a National Agreement that divided geographic territory between the two leagues, standardized player contracts, and formally inserted a reserve clause into player contracts.[14] By mimicking the organizational structure of the White major leagues, Bolden and Foster felt they would provide the stability necessary to ensure the financial success of the two Black leagues.

The heavy toll of presiding over a team and a league while at the same time holding down a full-time job eventually took a toll on Bolden's personal life and his postal career. He suffered a nervous breakdown as the 1927 season came to a close, leading to his resignation from both his league and team leadership positions.

In February of 1928 Bolden began his comeback when he was reelected secretary-treasurer of the ECL. The following month he regained the presidency of Hilldale. One week later he announced that Hilldale had withdrawn from the ECL. Though he had founded the league and had just recently rejoined its executive ranks, he no longer found membership profitable and abandoned it. He estimated that the team lost $18,000 in 1927 and could do better as an independent team.

Just one year later, Bolden changed his mind again about league membership. He assembled five of the six original ECL franchises and formed the American Negro League (ANL) in time for the 1929 season. He learned from some of his past mistakes and did some things differently when constructing the new league. For one thing, the league was more welcoming to the press, which it invited to league meetings, something the ECL never did. It helped that Bolden appointed Rollo Wilson, a respected reporter in the Black press, as league secretary. Despite his best efforts, the league lasted only one season.

The 1929 season marked the last flush year for Hilldale. Jobs were disappearing and the economy was plunging into what would become the Great Depression, wreaking financial havoc on Black baseball. Bolden's solution was to dissolve the Hilldale corporation in 1930. He quietly made plans for a new team he planned to organize with the financial backing of White promoter Harry Passon. The rest of Hilldale's board had other ideas, however. They blocked his attempt and bought him out of the corporation. Ed Bolden was no longer a part of the legacy he had created in Hilldale. John Drew, a Black politician who earned his fortune operating a successful bus line in Philadelphia, took over and ran the club until it collapsed midway through the 1932 season.

In August of 1930, Bolden was threatened with a demotion by the post office for falling efficiency ratings, likely a result of his time-consuming involvement with baseball. He appealed on the strength of his past work record and benefited from the support of his congressman, James Wolfenden, in his successful petition to retain his position.

Bolden returned to professional baseball in 1932 with the Philadelphia Stars. His return was controversial because he partnered with White booking agent Eddie Gottlieb, who had the connections and capital necessary to run a baseball team. Gottlieb received a 50 percent share of the team in return for providing

158

most of the financial backing. Bolden continued to handle the bulk of the administrative tasks. So many exhibition games were booked that by midseason 1932, the Stars had played against only two league teams.

It was a logical move for Bolden to partner with Gottlieb, who had a stranglehold on baseball bookings in the Philadelphia area and had close ties to Nat Strong, who similarly dominated the New York market. While it was a sound financial arrangement on paper, partnering with a White man went against Bolden's history as a "race man" and risked alienating Black fans. Bolden asserted that in the Depression economy it was necessary to trade race for sound finances, which were hard to come by in the Black community.

After the problems the ECL had surviving in league baseball, which was dependent primarily on Black fans, Bolden was reluctant to commit to a league with his Stars team. He preferred a simple working agreement among teams that would honor player contracts but not require a lot of unprofitable league games. Bolden pointed out that the Stars made most of their money on exhibitions against White teams and lost money when they committed to league games. He and Gottlieb attended a meeting of the newly formed Negro National League II (NNL2)[15] in March of 1933, but the Stars did not join the league. Bolden promoted the Stars, who played as an independent team that year, as "Hilldale" and rented Hilldale Park on occasion. Instead of salaries, the players were paid a share of the gate receipts.[16]

The repeal of Pennsylvania's blue laws in 1933, the greater availability of lights, and the more optimistic economic outlook of 1934 made Bolden reconsider his opposition to joining Gus Greenlee's NNL2. Greenlee wanted Bolden's Stars in the league to provide a team in the Philadelphia market, and the Stars rejoined league ball, becoming a member of the NNL for the 1934 season. Before playing a game, Bolden began to throw his weight around regarding league matters.

Bolden was a well-known and respected magnate in the Black baseball world, and he used that cachet to prevent Harry Passon from entering the Philadelphia market. He was the lone holdout when Passon attempted to join the league and move his Bacharach Giants to Philadelphia. Though the other five league owners supported both the Giants and Baltimore Black Sox as new entrants, Bolden was able to convince them that Philadelphia was not a big enough market for two teams, and Baltimore was an inferior market for even

Center for Negro League Baseball Research.

Ed Bolden (in suit) with his 1917 Hilldale team

one. As a result, the league played the first half-season that year with only six teams.[17] Halfway through the season, after several home sellouts, Bolden relented, and the Giants and Black Sox joined the league for the second half of the season.

The press loved Bolden. They praised him for his regular and timely reporting of game results to their newspapers and regularly inserted his name into their stories and headlines, variously referring to the team as Bolden's Stars, the Boldenmen, the Boldenboys, the Boldens, and the Bolden team.[18] And Bolden and Passon quickly made good with each other when Bolden agreed to rent Passon Field for the season.

As much as the press loved him, his co-owners did not. Bolden fell back on his old habits by skipping league games for lucrative exhibition dates. He was particularly guilty of ignoring expensive Western road trips in favor of home-field tilts against traveling barnstorming teams.[19] He played exhibition games with Dizzy and Paul Dean donning Stars uniforms. He played games with players on donkeys, against the House of David, the Zulu Jungle Giants – replete with grass skirts – and just about any Black or White squad that would come to town.

The inaugural season in the NNL2 was a good one for the Stars. They drew well, playing to capacity crowds estimated at 5,000 or more on several occasions, and they frequently drew more than 4,000. On occasion they played multiteam doubleheaders in National or American League ballparks to crowds estimated at 20,000 or more.[20] They captured the second-half pennant and faced the Chicago American Giants in the NNL2 Championship Series. They won the series four games to three, including one tie, but it was several weeks before their flag was official. The Giants protested Game Five of the series, played under the lights in Philadelphia, citing a league rule that prohibited night games during the championship series. They were also upset about the way the Stars treated the umpires in several games. The protests were eventually overruled, but the resulting chaos left a bitter taste in Bolden's mouth.

The 1935 season did not go as well for the Stars. The deteriorating financial climate renewed Bolden's skepticism about league baseball, especially during the depressed economy. The team did not draw as well as it had in 1934 and Bolden questioned remaining with the league, noting the loss of lucrative White exhibition dates to long, unprofitable Western road trips mandated by the league schedule. That attitude changed, however, when Gus Greenlee resigned as

league president in the spring of 1936 and Bolden was elected to replace him. As president, Bolden felt he could turn the league around by employing the same principles he had used when guiding the ECL a decade earlier.

It was not to be. Bolden's authority, much like Greenlee's, was thwarted by uncooperative owners. Unfortunately for Bolden, they followed his earlier lead and eschewed league games for more profitable exhibition tilts. Bolden canceled the 1936 championship series between the Elites and the Crawfords after one game when several players from the participating teams found lucrative opportunities with barnstorming teams. Bolden defended his action by arguing that an unprofitable championship was worse than none at all. This was an unpopular move, however, and his tenure as league president was short. In January of 1937, less than a year after taking office, he was ousted, and Gus Greenlee resumed control.

The end of the Depression did not make life any easier for Black baseball owners. The World War II years posed a different set of obstacles, such as rationing, which curtailed the ability to travel. Bolden continued to innovate in order to balance the budget. He recognized that the attendance of prominent Black leaders reinforced baseball's legitimacy and served as an additional attraction at the ballpark, so he cultivated their patronage and support by providing passes to representatives of all the major local Black institutions. He also recruited respected Black men and women to throw out ceremonial first pitches.

Despite the challenges posed by World War II, Black baseball thrived in the 1940s, as crowds grew, salaries rose, and teams more frequently played in major-league parks. Player rowdiness, however, was a stain on the otherwise improving fortunes of Black baseball. Even Bolden, who had earned a reputation in his first ownership stint as a "fair dealing and clean playing" man and encouraged his Hilldale players to act like gentlemen, turned a blind eye toward the antics of two of his managers, Jud Wilson and Goose Curry, whose reputations for umpire-baiting were well known around the league.

After the war, integrated baseball took center stage. Despite its obvious threat to the existence of Black baseball, Bolden supported integration and pledged to work with his players to gain access if the White major leagues came calling. He believed that integration would make the Black leagues stronger because it would result in better efforts from the players who now saw greater opportunities. History proved otherwise, but Bolden did not live to see it.

The Philadelphia Stars sold the contract of Roy Partlow to Brooklyn Dodgers general manager Branch Rickey on May 14, 1946, for $1,000. Though a small sum by National League standards, it was considered a symbolic victory for Black clubs, whose owners hoped that it would establish a precedent for the recognition of their player contracts by "major-league" clubs. There was no promise that Partlow would be given a legitimate shot at earning a roster spot, but Bolden was optimistic.[21]

As it turned out, the recognition of Negro League contracts by National or American League teams proved to be spotty. Raids by those clubs and the drain of young talent to the White minor leagues were major factors leading to the amalgamation of the Negro American League and the NNL2 after the 1948 season. Despite the higher travel costs involved with the merger, Bolden was among those who felt it was a necessary step to ensure continued bookings and offer protection from player raids by Black and White teams alike. It was, instead, the beginning of the end for the Negro Leagues.

Bolden was not around to witness the twilight of Black baseball. He died in Darby on September 27, 1950, after suffering a stroke. He outlived his wife, Nellie, by two years. He was survived by two brothers, Norris and Walter, and his daughter, Hilda Bolden Shorter, a pediatrician, to whom he left his share of the Stars. She retained her share of the team until it folded after the 1952 season. Hilda did not take active interest in the team, though, and left the daily management to Eddie Gottlieb. Oscar Charleston took over player personnel duties. Bolden's death ended an era in race baseball and the attempt on the part of its pioneers and successors to elevate it to a big-time level.

Gottlieb eventually folded the Stars, announcing the dissolution of the franchise in March of 1953. He briefly walked that announcement back, changing his decision to a sale of the franchise. However, when he failed to find a buyer, he released all players from their contracts in April, ending Black baseball in Philadelphia.

SOURCES

In addition to the sources cited in the Notes, the author consulted a number of other publications, including the following:

Baseball-reference.com

Cash-Thompson Archives, African American Museum, Philadelphia, Pennsylvania

Clark, Dick, and Larry Lester, eds. *The Negro Leagues Book* (Cleveland: SABR, 1994)

Coley, Harvey. "Bolden Was a Negro League Pioneer," Ed Bolden file, National Baseball Hall of Fame Library

Haupert, Michael. "Ed Bolden," Society for American Baseball Research Baseball Biography Project, http://sabr.org/bioproj/person/84ab3bca, (Fall 2012a)

Lanctot, Neil. *Negro League Baseball* (Philadelphia: University of Pennsylvania Press, 2004).

Newman, Roberta J., and Joel Nathan Rosen. *Black Baseball Black Business* (Jackson: University Press of Mississippi, 2014)

Pollock, Alan J., and James A. Riley, eds. *Barnstorming to Heaven: Syd Pollock and His Great Black Teams* (Tuscaloosa: University of Alabama Press, 2006)

Riley, James A. *The Biographical Encyclopedia of the Negro Baseball Leagues* (New York: Carroll & Graf, 1994)

Smith, Courtney Michelle. *Ed Bolden and Black Baseball in Philadelphia* (Jefferson, North Carolina: McFarland & Co.), 2017

White, Sol. *History of Colored Base Ball* (Lincoln: University of Nebraska Press, 1995)

NOTES

1 The Eastern Colored League, the American Negro League, and the second Negro National League.

2 Michael E. Lomax, *Black Baseball Entrepreneurs 1902-1931* (Syracuse, New York: Syracuse University Press, 2014), 188.

3 For a discussion of his imaginative marketing skills, see Michael Haupert and Ken Winter, "The Old Fellows and the Colonels: Innovation and Survival in Integrated Baseball," *Black Ball* 1, no. 1 (spring 2008): 79-92.

4 He later added brief stints as chairman of the board of the American Negro League, and president of the second Negro National League to his executive résumé.

5 Neil Lanctot, *Fair Dealing and Clean Playing: The Hilldale Club and the Development of Black Professional Baseball, 1910-1932* (Jefferson, North Carolina: McFarland & Co., 1994), 66.

6 Lawrence D. Hogan, *Shades of Glory* (Washington: National Geographic, 2006), 142.

7 For example, in 1915 the Hilldale ledger, found in the Cash-Thompson archives, records $117.73 spent on lumber for grandstand, building permit, carpentry work, nails, wire for outfield fence and backstop, and paint. In 1917 an additional $754.29 was allocated for lumber, labor, and hardware, for further expansion of the grandstand.

8 Haupert and Winter, 2008

9 Hogan, 67.

10 Cash-Thompson archives.

11 Johnson was not the only Hall of Famer to play for Hilldale. At one time or another, Martin Dihigo, Louis Santop, Biz Mackey, and Oscar Charleston all donned the Hilldale flannels. In addition, Smokey Joe Williams joined the team for a series of exhibition contests after the 1917 season.

12 Michael Haupert, "Ed Bolden: Black Baseball's Great Modernist," *Black Ball* 5, no. 2 (Fall 2012): 61-72.

13 Lanctot 1994, 110.

14 Lanctot 1994, 130.

15 This was a new NNL, formed by Gus Greenlee, not the same NNL Rube Foster had formed.

16 Haupert 2012 and Haupert and Winter 2008 for a fuller discussion of Hilldale's finances.

17 *Pittsburgh Courier*, February 17, 1934: A4; *Baltimore Afro-American*, February 17, 1934: 19; *Pittsburgh Courier*, February 24, 1934: A4; *Baltimore Afro-American*, August 25, 1934: 18.

18 See *Pittsburgh Courier*, April 14, 1934: A4; *Philadelphia Tribune*, June 7, 1934: 12; *Baltimore Afro-American*, June 9, 1934: 16; *Chicago Defender*, June 30, 1934: 16; *Norfolk New Journal and Guide*, June 30, 1934: 13; *Philadelphia Inquirer*, July 11, 1934: 21; *Philadelphia Tribune*, July 12, 1934: 12.

19 *Baltimore Afro-American*, July 21, 1934: 19; *Baltimore Afro-American*, August 25, 1934: 18.

20 Various issues of the *Pittsburgh Courier, Philadelphia Tribune, Chicago Defender, Baltimore Afro-American, Philadelphia Inquirer,* and *Atlanta Daily World.*

21 Partlow was released by the Dodgers without ever making the team and returned to Philadelphia to finish out his career.

EDDIE GOTTLIEB

By Rebecca T. Alpert

Eddie Gottlieb was primarily known as the organizer of the SPHAS basketball team, an acronym for the South Philadelphia Hebrew Association, where the team got its start. The SPHAS were among the premier semiprofessional basketball teams in the country in the 1920s to 1940s – competing with the top teams such as the Harlem Rens and the Original Celtics. The SPHAS were Gottlieb's first love and central preoccupation. Gottlieb was not only the founder, a player, and the coach of the SPHAS, but was also a founder of the Basketball Association of America (the precursor to the NBA) and subsequently the coach, general manager, and owner of the Philadelphia Warriors. Beginning in 1946, and until 10 days before his death in 1979, he made the entire schedule for the BAA/NBA each year based on his unparalleled math skills and memory, as efficient and effective as the computer that replaced him. His contributions earned him a place in the Basketball Hall of Fame in 1972. The outstanding NBA rookie each year is awarded the Eddie Gottlieb trophy.

Although Gottlieb is best known for his role in basketball, he also made important contributions to Black baseball. As the main East Coast booking agent and scheduler, officer of the National Negro League, co-owner with Ed Bolden of the Philadelphia Stars, and a member of the committee that chose the first Negro League athletes for baseball's Hall of Fame, Gotty, or the Mogul, or Mr. Basketball as he was known, was a major influence in the professional development and popularity of the Negro Leagues in the 1940s.

Isadore Gottlieb was born in Kyiv, Ukraine (then a part of the tsarist Russian Empire), on September 15, 1898. His family – his father, Morris; his mother, Lena; and his older sister, Bella – migrated in 1902 to New York, where his father ran a candy store. They moved to Philadelphia when Isadore was 10 years old. There his father worked as a presser before he died a few years later. The family spoke Yiddish at home, and Izzy Gottlieb listed Yiddish as his native tongue on census records into early adulthood. As a teenager,

Gottlieb, like many children of immigrants, changed his name to the more American sounding Edward.

Ed Gottlieb got involved in sports at a young age. Baseball was his first love. He was quoted in his obituary as saying: "We lived in NYC and I would hitch rides on the back of ice truck to watch the NY Giants play at the Polo Grounds. I was an average player. Two things were wrong with me as a catcher. I couldn't hit very well and I couldn't throw very well, but I was an A-1 receiver."[1]

He continued with his athletic interests at South Philadelphia "Southern" High School, playing varsity basketball and semiprofessional baseball on the weekends. A historical marker at the site commemorates his importance to his South Philly neighborhood.[2]

Eddie Gottlieb in 1958. The Stars' co-owner is better known as a member of the Basketball Hall of Fame

After high school, Gottlieb went to the School of Pedagogy (later affiliated with Temple University) and then briefly taught junior high school physical education while also working as a clerk at a wallpaper store.[3] However, his real passion was playing and coaching basketball. Along with teammates and friends from South Philly High, Harry Passon and Hugh Black, he organized a semipro basketball team under the auspices of the local YMHA (Young Men's Hebrew Association). When the arrangements did not work out, the three attached themselves to a social club, the South Philadelphia Hebrew Association, after which they named their team the SPHAs. The name stuck even after that arrangement ended as well.

In 1920, in search of better uniforms and equipment for their basketball team, Gottlieb, Passon, and Black opened their own sporting-goods store, PGB Sports, in downtown Philadelphia. It was through the store that Gottlieb first made connections to Negro League baseball. As early as 1921, one of his best customers was Ed Bolden, proprietor of the Hilldale Daisies, the era's standout Black team in the East.[4] Gottlieb also continued to play baseball himself. He was the catcher and manager of the Philadelphia SPHAS – or Hebrews, as they were often called –composed of players who were also on his basketball team of the same name. They frequently played against Black teams in Philadelphia, often against Hilldale, but they also traveled to New York to play Negro League teams like the Lincoln Giants and the New York Black Yankees.[5]

Gottlieb and Black sold their interest in the sporting-goods business to Passon a few years later.[6] Gottlieb then focused on sports promotion and started a booking agency in an office above the store.[7] He became the leading booking agent for all Philadelphia sports, Black and White. Gottlieb explained that he became a promoter by accident. On a whim, he got in touch with Nat Strong, who owned the most powerful booking agency on the East Coast, asking him to send the House of David, a popular traveling team of White players from Michigan that wore long beards (as was the custom of the Messianic Christian community that sponsored them), to play another amateur White team Gottlieb managed, the Philadelphia Elks. Strong told Gottlieb he would send the House of David if Gottlieb arranged four games for them in Philadelphia. According to Gottlieb, "I lined up four games and became a promoter." One of the teams that played against the House of David was Bolden's Hilldale club.[8]

By the early 1930s Ed Gottlieb had become the premier booking agent in Philadelphia. Ed Bolden had relinquished ownership of the Hilldale Daisies but wanted to return to baseball. With Gottlieb's financial assistance, he organized a new team, the Philadelphia Stars. The Bolden-Gottlieb partnership lasted until Bolden's death in 1950. Webster McDonald, who pitched for and later managed the Stars, remembered Bolden and Gottlieb as "two partners, one colored, one white."[9] Bolden, who had worked in prior years with Nat Strong, knew very well that Gottlieb's affiliation with Strong would make it possible to get good dates for games in New York and New England as well as in Philadelphia. With Gottlieb's financial backing and connections to the Nat Strong Booking Agency and Bolden's baseball expertise, the Stars quickly became the top Black baseball attraction in Philadelphia.[10]

In 1933 Gus Greenlee formed a new Negro National League (NNL2) and wanted the Stars to join. Bolden was skeptical. To persuade Gottlieb, Greenlee requested that he book a match between the baseball SPHAS and the Crawfords, whose roster included future Hall of Famers Oscar Charleston, Judy Johnson, Josh Gibson, and Satchel Paige. The SPHAS lineup included several Jewish players from the basketball team and some (White) ringers. The Crawfords won, 5-2, and the *Pittsburgh Courier* called it an "upset."[11] Bolden was still not persuaded, and the Stars played independently for a year. They joined Gus Greenlee's league in 1934 and promptly won the NNL2 championship against the Chicago American Giants; it was the only time they won the title.

Gottlieb assiduously avoided calling attention to himself as the owner of the Philadelphia Stars and worked behind the scenes. He practiced the art of skillful scheduling, keeping their travel burdens lighter than those of many other teams. The Stars rarely toured in the South, avoiding many of the horrendous experiences of Jim Crow that other teams endured. He also was responsible for making sure that the Stars got select dates at the ballpark he leased at Penmar Park, and later at Philadelphia's major-league venue, Shibe Park, when he got the rights to book Black teams there in 1943.[12] The players saw him only occasionally at games but regularly when he paid them. They were aware of his power as a promoter on the local scene. "Everybody knew him," said Stanley Glenn, a catcher with the Stars. "If you wanted a game, you had to go through Eddie. If you didn't, you didn't play."[13] Some of the Stars characterized him as fair but not generous. Yet Webster Mc Donald, who played for the

Stars from 1933 to 1940, remembered Gottlieb as more of a "hands on" owner who kept him up late at night talking strategy and who occasionally provided bonuses for good play.[14] Gottlieb believed he was providing good work for a number of men who would otherwise be "bell hopping or mopping floors." He also noted that in the early days the players were paid poorly (often on percentage rather than salary) and worked in bad conditions, but in later years that improved as the owners, like himself, began to make some money and were able to be more generous.[15] When Bolden died in 1950, he left the team to his daughter, Dr. Hilda Bolden. Ed Gottlieb continued his business responsibilities with the team until its demise. His efforts to sell the franchise in the winter of 1953 proved futile, and he disbanded the team in April of 1953.[16]

Gottlieb had already been booking games for the Stars as well as for the other Negro National League teams when they traveled east of Pittsburgh. The new league, like its 1920s predecessor, Rube Foster's original Negro National League, did not want to deal with Nat Strong's booking agency, but had no choice if they wanted to play White semipro teams on the East Coast. Nat Strong's unexpected death in 1935 created an opportunity to improve the conditions for Black baseball in New York, and an opportunity for Ed Gottlieb to extend his reach. Although the owners discussed hiring a new booking agent after Strong's death, Gottlieb retained the position. He continued to work in affiliation with Strong's agency and with Strong's successor, William Leuschner. Together with Max Rosner, the Jewish owner of the popular White semipro Brooklyn Bushwicks, they exercised a great deal of power over bookings in New York and access to ballparks there that would cause conflicts in the years to come.

Greenlee's Pittsburgh rival, Cum Posey, worried that Gottlieb and Leuschner would soon encroach on his territory in western Pennsylvania and suggested that the league's problems were directly related to the power that Leuschner and Gottlieb exercised. Posey emerged as a frequent critic of Gottlieb's power and scheduling activities throughout their years of association in the Negro National League, often accusing Gottlieb of lacking concern for the welfare of the league and being interested only in having teams he booked make money.[17] But Posey was also interested in turning a profit, and he and Gottlieb became strategic allies in later years.[18]

To counter Gottlieb and Bolden's power in the NNL2, Posey recruited Harry Passon's Bacharachs to join the league. In 1931 Harry Passon had started his own Black baseball team. He called them the Bacharach Giants to capitalize on the name recognition of the successful and popular team that had played in Ed Bolden's Eastern Colored League in the 1920s. Passon's Bacharachs were based in Philadelphia and played at the field he leased, which came to be known as Passon Field. In 1933, as interest in the team grew, Passon made improvements to the field, adding a grandstand, clubhouse, and lights. The Stars also played most of their home games at Passon Field (and often against the Bacharachs) from 1933 to 1935 before relocating to Penmar Park.

Passon was enthusiastic about bringing his team into organized play. He applied for league membership and attended several organizational meetings, but the other owners rejected his application, bowing to the interests of Bolden and Gottlieb, who did not want two league teams in Philadelphia. Passon, who still worked closely with Gottlieb at the sporting-goods store and other promotional activities, was surprised by their opposition. Cum Posey saw this as a personal defeat. He expressed his disappointment with the decision, contending that so long as the clubs did not play in Philadelphia on the same date, the Bacharachs, who could draw on the road, would be an important attraction for the league.[19] Posey got his way eventually, and the Bacharachs were accepted. But Passon could not compete with Bolden and Gottlieb. By the time the league owners met in the winter of 1935, Passon had decided to quit.[20]

Gottlieb's multiple roles – as owner of the Stars, booking agent for the league, and head of his own booking agency – gave him a lot of power in the NNL2. His relationship to the other owners was complicated. They valued his contributions and believed that he was an asset to the league, and they relied on him to keep proper records. Gottlieb was also given the task of assigning umpires and served with two other owners on an arbitration committee. He even held league office as recording secretary.[21] Gottlieb often hosted league meetings at his Philadelphia offices and worked to get the league on firmer financial footing, improve relationships with the press, and raise the standards of umpiring.[22]

But he was at the same time viewed as a White Jewish outsider who, like his (non-Jewish) predecessor Nat Strong, sought his own financial gain at the expense of the league. Gottlieb became the center of a controversy over power that saw NNL2 owners ultimately divided into pro- and anti-Gottlieb factions.

In 1939 Tom Wilson, the NNL2 president and owner of the Baltimore Elite Giants, awarded Gottlieb the task of negotiating with the New York Yankees to use Yankee Stadium for Sunday doubleheaders, replacing Gus Greenlee, who was no longer affiliated with the league. Greenlee's original plan had called for all the league's teams to be showcased in New York, and Gottlieb was eager to follow through. He believed that the success of these ventures (especially when Satchel Paige was pitching) encouraged other owners of major-league ballparks to offer reasonable rents, to the benefit of all the NNL2 teams. Gottlieb also believed that showcasing stars like Paige was the key to promoting Black baseball to White audiences.[23]

Gottlieb put together a deal with Yankees general manager Ed Barrow for five Negro League doubleheaders at Yankee Stadium for 1939. The arrangement saved the league $12,500 in rental fees. For his work, Gottlieb received a 10 percent booking fee. The owners had all agreed to Gottlieb taking the percentage when he took on the Yankee Stadium promotion, and Gus Greenlee had taken 10 percent booking fees when he had negotiated the contract originally. Gottlieb, as promoter, put up all the advance money, and the clubs involved gained over $16,000 in profits. For his work, Gottlieb received a total of $1,100.[24]

Gottlieb and Leuschner realized profits of less than $2,400 each year, and their contract required that they give a quarter of their earnings back to the league. Their agencies were useful for the league because they had full-time offices that could handle all the work involved in scheduling and booking for all six NNL2 teams, an expense that the other teams could not afford. According to Cum Posey, Gottlieb and Leuschner were "experienced and fair" and their work necessary to the functioning of the league.[25]

But the New York owners – James Semler of the Black Yankees, Abe and Effa Manley of the Newark Eagles, and Alex Pompez of the New York Cubans – did not like the fact that Gottlieb was awarded the contract. Semler, Pompez, and the Manleys saw Gottlieb's booking of Yankee Stadium as an incursion into their territory, for which they should have been compensated or brought in as partners. They, not Gottlieb, should get the 10 percent booking fee. Supported by Wilson and Cum Posey, Gottlieb fought back, arguing that the New York owners "were in the same position as a patient who applies for medical aid and then curses out the doctor when he charges him a sum for curing him."[26] At the winter meetings in 1940, they banded together to fight the reelection of Gottlieb's main supporter, Tom Wilson, as president of the league.

The owners' issues with making sure Negro League baseball was a Black business and not run by White men simmered under the surface of some of the accusations against Gottlieb. Gottlieb was a carpetbagger, "bringing his white staff over to Harlem every time a league promotion is held at Yankee Stadium, packing his Black bags full of coin and scooting back to Philly."[27] He was charged with paternalism; "pulling the strings" and turning Posey, Wilson, and Bolden into his puppets. It was common knowledge that Gottlieb exercised power in the league because of his position as team owner, league booking agent, and proprietor of one of the most powerful sports promotion agencies in the country, but there was one additional factor that explained his dominance: Gottlieb gained leverage over the owners by lending money to them and providing credit for equipment purchased from Passon's Sporting Goods store. Cum Posey assumed that was the basis of Gottlieb's support and advised him "Don't lend in 1941, then see the friends you will be able to keep."[28] Jewish economic power, always suspect, interjected into a struggling Black business would make a simple quarrel over money into an issue of race.[29]

For some sportswriters, this was also an opportunity to air their problems with Gottlieb as the owner of the Stars. Sportswriter Ed Harris lamented in the *Philadelphia Tribune* that Gottlieb's ownership was hurting the local team because the other owners did not want to do business with him. Gottlieb was also responsible for the poor conditions at the Stars' home field, Penmar Park, which he leased and ran.[30] The former home field of the Pennsylvania Railroad team, the park was in a predominantly Jewish neighborhood, but convenient to public transportation. But it was also close to the train tracks, and therefore noisy and often covered with soot from the trains. Press box accommodations were poor, and Gottlieb employed White staff there, including young Jewish boys from the neighborhood. Concerns were also raised about the power Gottlieb wielded over promotions in Philadelphia. Gottlieb, "genial and suave," had, over the years, put himself in the position of booking so many facilities in the area that a team could not play without going through his agency. His connections with Strong's agency in New York strengthened his hold on any team that wanted to play in lucrative venues in the Northeast.[31]

Ultimately, the problem was settled by compromise. At the next league meeting, Wilson was confirmed as president, as Pompez abstained from voting, giving Wilson's side a majority. Gottlieb was reprimanded and removed as recording secretary but allowed to keep the Yankee Stadium promotions for one more year. For the sake of harmony, Gottlieb agreed to relinquish the Yankee Stadium promotions after 1940 to New York Black Yankees owner Jim Semler, who was also granted permission to book one game for the Black Yankees and New York Cubans in that venue in the coming season. With Gottlieb doing the booking, the Manleys chose not to play in Yankee Stadium in 1940 in protest. Peace was declared. Effa Manley, when asked whether she opposed White ownership, replied, "Certainly not. Some white owners are the best of men. I even admire Gottlieb's business ability. He would be all right if the chairman [Wilson] could handle him. He needs to be whipped into line." Gottlieb, the talented businessman, was welcome to help, and the Black owners were ready to take advantage of his skills, but Manley believed that Gottlieb had too much power and did not want him to control the league. What on the surface was a small matter over a small amount of money became a symbolic question of Gottlieb's place as a White man as the most powerful force in the NNL2.[32]

While Gottlieb was a major force in Negro League baseball and spent much of his time booking venues for every sport (and some well-known entertainers), his central preoccupation remained basketball. According to Doug Stark, Gottlieb's focus as a manager and coach was always teamwork, fundamentals, and winning. He was known as a great analyst of the game with a steel-trap memory and a head for numbers.[33] Gottlieb's first major involvement in professional (and semipro) basketball was the Philadelphia SPHAs. Between 1917 and 1946 the SPHAs won 12 championships in different leagues. Gottlieb founded the team with Passon and Black in 1917. Though he played in the early years, his real talents were managerial and organizational. He handled all the scheduling and coaching until 1946 and remained the owner until 1949, when he sold the franchise to a group in Utica, New York. Since they weren't interested in fielding the team itself, Gottlieb worked with his friend Abe Saperstein, owner of the Harlem Globetrotters, to make the SPHAs one of the regular touring teams that played in exhibition games against the Globetrotters. They traveled around the world, and Gottlieb often joined them on those trips. They played to vast audiences around the United States, often as a warm-up to NBA games where the Globetrotters were the main draw.[34]

Gottlieb moved on from the SPHAs in 1946 because he became a founding member of the Basketball Association of America. He was a key player in the BAA merger with the National Basketball League to become the National Basketball Association in 1949. Along with the owner, Pete Tyrell, he started the Philadelphia Warriors, adopting the name that the SPHAs used from 1926 to 1929. In the 1946-47 season the Warriors won their only championship with Gottlieb as coach. He purchased the club in 1952, remained the coach through the 1953 season, and continued to serve as general manager until he sold the team in 1962. As coach he came under attack from the Black press for his failure to draft African American players, which NBA teams began to do in 1950, while the Warriors remained all-White. The *Pittsburgh Courier* had this to say about Gottlieb:

> Local fans have bitterly criticized Gottlieb for never having signed any Negro stars to play with the Warriors. They have felt, and justly, that since he had long been connected with Negro baseball he would realize the advantage and good-will to be obtained by such an act. Eddie, however, remained callous to all criticism.[35]

Although he claimed that he was waiting to find the right talent, it is likely that Gottlieb did not want to break up the monopoly the Harlem Globetrotters had on premier Black players, since they continued to be the main gate attraction when they played before select NBA games; for Gottlieb, the gate mattered above all. Jackie Moore was the first African American to play for the Warriors, in 1955, before the Philadelphia Phillies integrated in 1957, but Gottlieb also had bigger plans.

As an influential member of the NBA rules committee, he came up with the idea of the territorial draft, and it benefited the Warriors greatly. It was a rule designed to give a team the opportunity to claim a local high-school or college player. That was how the Warriors were able to sign Overbrook High School talent Wilt Chamberlain in 1959. Although they had to wait for him for three years, including time at the University of Kansas and a tour with the Harlem Globetrotters before he became a Warrior, he was the superstar Gottlieb was waiting for, who changed the game of basketball with his extraordinary skills and magnificent style and made the Warriors highly competitive.

In 1962 Gottlieb sold the Warriors to a company in San Francisco, though he continued to work for the team as general manager until 1964. He remained involved in the business side of the NBA, primarily as schedule maker and as a major influence on the Rules Committee, up until his death in December 1979.

Gottlieb's whole life was sports, and his closest friends were basketball associates, including Harvey Pollack and Dave Zinkoff. He never married and left no descendants. He lived most of his life with his mother and his developmentally disabled sister and cared for both until their deaths. The family was active in the Jewish community, and Gottlieb contributed generously to Jewish institutions. He is buried in Har Nebo cemetery in northeast Philadelphia.[36]

SOURCES

Rich Westcott wrote the definitive biography of Eddie Gottlieb, *The Mogul: Eddie Gottlieb, Philadelphia Sports Legend and Pro Basketball Pioneer* (Philadelphia: Temple University Press, 2008).

Also see Douglas Stark, *The SPHAs: The Life and Times of Basketball's Greatest Jewish Team* (Philadelphia: Temple University Press, 2011), which details Gottlieb's role with his team, and Rebecca Alpert, *Out of Left Field: Jews and Black Baseball* (New York: Oxford University Press, 2011), which describes Gottlieb's role in the Negro Leagues. This article is adapted from that work.

NOTES

1   Frank Deford, "Eddie Is the Mogul," *Sports Illustrated*, January 22, 1968. Original quotation from Deford paraphrased in "Eddie Gottlieb Dies; A Pioneer in the N.B.A.," *New York Times*, December 8, 1979.

2   Jeff Gamage, "Mr. Basketball Eddie Gottlieb Memorialized," *Philadelphia Inquirer*, May 21, 2014, written when the state erected a historical marker in his memory.

3   Deford.

4   Rich Westcott, *The Mogul: Eddie Gottlieb, Philadelphia Sports Legend and Pro Basketball Pioneer* (Philadelphia: Temple University Press, 2008), 26; *Philadelphia Evening Bulletin*, June 1, 1929, from Ed Gottlieb Files, Special Collections Research Center (SCRC), Temple University.

5   "Giants Defeat Then Tie the Philly Hebrews," *Baltimore Afro-American*, May 16, 1925: 8; Sam Leaden Bernstein, telephone interview with author, October 15, 2008; *New York Age*, August 1, 1925; Jim Goldfarb, "Harlem's Team: The New York Lincoln Giants," in *Afro-Americans in New York Life and History* 26.2 (2002).

6   Rebecca Alpert, "Harry Passon: Philadelphia Baseball Entrepreneur," in Morris Levine, ed., *The National Pastime: From Swampoodle to South Philly* (Phoenix: Society for American Baseball Research, 2013), 68 n.4.

7   Gottlieb kept his offices above Passon's store at 507 Market until 1944 when he moved the office to 1537 Chestnut Street. Letter from Ed Gottlieb to Effa Manley, January 24, 1944, Newark Eagles Papers.

8   Westcott, *Mogul*, 67; *Philadelphia Record*, September 24, 1939, in Gottlieb Files, SCRC. A news report describes the annual pilgrimage of the House of David to Philadelphia. "House of David Nine Loses to Hilldale 10-4," *Chicago Defender*, July 7, 1928: 8.

9   Interview with Webster McDonald in John Holway, *Voices from the Great Black Baseball Leagues*. rev. ed. (New York: Da Capo Press, 1992), 82.

10   Neil Lanctot, *Negro League Baseball: The Rise and Ruin of a Black Institution* (Philadelphia: University of Pennsylvania Press, 2004), 30.

11   "Pittsburgh Crawfords Top Eddie Gottlieb's SPHAS in Close Tilt on P.R.R Field," *Pittsburgh Courier*, July 8, 1933: A5.

12   Neil Lanctot, "Baseball: Negro Leagues" in *The Encyclopedia of Greater Philadelphia*, https://philadelphiaencyclopedia.org/essays/baseball-negro-leagues, accessed July 22, 2022.

13   Westcott, *Mogul*, 94.

14   Holway, 84-85.

15   Interview with Ed Gottlieb in Art Rust, *"Get that N*** Off the Field!"*: *A Sparkling, Informal History of the Black Man in Baseball* (New York: Delacorte Press, 1976), 54.

16   Courtney M. Smith, *Ed Bolden and Black Baseball in Philadelphia* (Jefferson, North Carolina: McFarland and Company, 2017), 155-156.

17   Cum Posey, "Cum Posey Reviews Ups and Downs," *Pittsburgh Courier*, September 30, 1933: 15; "Cum Posey's Pointed Paragraphs," *Pittsburgh Courier*, March 2, 1935: A4.

18   Lanctot, *Negro League Baseball*, 111.

19   "Blacksox, Grays Not Included," *Pittsburgh Courier*, February 17, 1934: A4; Cum Posey, "Posey's Pointed Paragraphs," *Pittsburgh Courier*, March 3, 1934: A5.

20   William Jones, "Sidelights on League Meeting," *Baltimore Afro-American*, March 16, 1935: 21.

21   Courtney M. Smith, 108.

22   Cum Posey, "Posey's Points," *Pittsburgh Courier*, January 22, 1938: 16; letter from Effa Manley to Ed Gottlieb, May 23,1939, NEP; 1938 memo to "All Owners of NNL Clubs" from Tom Wilson, n.d., Newark Eagles Papers.

23   Gottlieb recalled in the interview with Frank Deford in *Sports Illustrated* 34 years later, regarding his first effort to showcase Paige in 1934: "That was the first four-team doubleheader in Yankee Stadium. We came in with the Pittsburgh Crawfords in the first game against the Philadelphia Stars, and in the second game it was the New York Black Yankees against the Chicago American Giants. It rained the whole night before the game and really didn't stop until just before the first game started, but we had 25,000 there, and the concessions were treemendous [*sic*]. Slim Jones – he died of pneumonia when he was still very young – he was pitching for the Stars. Oh, he was fast! And we had Satchel pitching for the Crawfords. It was a 1-1 tie, so we called it in the 10th inning with the idea in mind that we could repeat the whole damn game a few weeks later, which we did. And you know, we got just about the same gate all over, even though, just like the first time, it rained right up until the game started." https://vault.si.com/vault/1968/01/22/eddie-is-the-mogul, accessed July 30, 2022.

24   "Nat'l Amerik Loops Seek Peace," *Pittsburgh Courier*, February 4, 1939: 17; Rust, *Get That N*** Off the Field!*, 54.

25   Cum Posey, "Posey's Points," *Pittsburgh Courier*, February 24, 1940: 16.

26   "N.N.L. Meeting Ends in Deadlock," *Pittsburgh Courier*, February 10, 1940: 16.

27   "Reports on Sports by Daniel," *New York Amsterdam News*, February 24, 1940: 18.

28   Cum Posey, "Posey's Points," *Pittsburgh Courier*, January 4, 1941: 16.

29   Rebecca T. Alpert, "Racial Attitudes Towards Jews in the 'Negro Leagues': The Case of Effa Manley," in *Annual Review of the USC Casden Institute for the Study of the Jewish Role in America Life* volume 12 (2014), 9-42.

30   Ed Harris, "Happy Days Are Here Again," *Philadelphia Tribune*, February 15, 1940: 11.

31   Ed Harris, "How Did He Get In?" *Philadelphia Tribune*, April 11,1940: 11.

32   Harry Webber, "Strife Breaks Out Again in NNL Baseball Ranks," *Baltimore Afro-American*, April 27, 1940: 19.

33   Douglas Stark, *The SPHAs: The Life and Times of Basketball's Greatest Jewish Team* (Philadelphia: Temple University Press, 2011), 16-19.

34   Stark, *SPHAs*, 207-211.

35   "Saperstein Buys Stock in Warriors," *Pittsburgh Courier*, May 24, 1952: 26.

36   https://www.findagrave.com/memorial/13720851/edward-gottlieb, accessed July 21, 2022.

PASSON FIELD[1]

By Rebecca T. Alpert

The first half of the twentieth century featured the proliferation of amateur and professional sports teams, including baseball, softball, football, basketball, soccer, and hockey. Baseball, Black and White, was far and away the most popular, and flourished in the city of Philadelphia beginning in the mid-nineteenth century. Philadelphia was home to hundreds of baseball teams.

Amateur, semipro, and professional games were played at several dozen ballparks and athletic fields throughout the city, mostly by men and boys but also by women.[2] Some of the parks and fields were in the burgeoning neighborhood of West Philadelphia. Beginning at the turn of the last century, the population of West Philadelphia tripled in number as it became home to new immigrants from Southern and Eastern Europe, primarily Italians and Jews. As part of the Great Migration, Southern Blacks also began to make "West Philly" their home during this time.[3] Among these groups were many sports enthusiasts. One of those West Philadelphia spaces where they came to watch games was Passon Field, at 48th and Spruce Streets. It was there that the 1934 championship series between the Philadelphia Stars and the Chicago American Giants took place. The park was known as Passon Field from 1929 to 1942 but was called by many other names before and after.[4]

Beginning in 1923 the athletic field at the northwest corner of 48th and Spruce Streets received attention in the Black and White press. It was occasionally referred to as Lit Brothers Field or Elks Field, but most often it was just called the athletic field at 48th and Spruce, or simply 48th and Spruce and occasionally Spruce Field.[5] The 1927 Bromley atlas of Philadelphia map of the block between Spruce and Locust and 48th and 49th Streets shows a small apartment complex, Chatham Court, at the corner of 49th and Locust. The rest of the block is an open space, with the name Eli K. Price printed across it.[6] Price (1797-1884) was a Pennsylvania state senator and a prominent Philadelphia lawyer and civic leader. He

Passon Field has been renamed Pollock Field and is still in use by West Philadelphia High School sports teams.

Courtesy of Lynn Alpert

purchased many parcels of land in West Philadelphia that were passed down through his estate.[7] 48th and Spruce was one of those properties, purchased in 1852. The estate maintained ownership until 1948, when Price's great-grandchildren, as trustees, sold it to the City of Philadelphia's Department of Recreation for use as a public playground and recreation center for $259,000.[8] The property was used by the School District of Philadelphia starting in 1950 and it became the home field of West Philadelphia High School's Speedboys football team, while it continued for many years to be used as a public playground and recreation center.[9]

The *Philadelphia Inquirer* first mentions the field in 1923, calling it the athletic field at 48th and Spruce, and describes it as a site for high-school games.[10] Between 1923 and 1929 the Black press reported frequently on games played, mostly by semipro Black teams playing against White teams. The *Inquirer* featured stories about games played by the (White) Lit Brothers team, made up primarily of employees from that department store, against Black teams including Ed Bolden's Hilldale Daisies at "Forty-eighth and Spruce" in 1925.[11] The Lit boys, as they were known, also played "at their home field" against the Black Wilmington Potomacs that year.[12] In 1926 the local Black weekly, the *Philadelphia Tribune,* reported that the Newton Coal Athletic Association team had exclusive use of Lit Brothers' Field.[13] In 1927 the (White) Philadelphia Elks, managed by sports promoter and booking agent Ed Gottlieb (1898-1979), called 48th and Spruce home.[14]

In 1928 Hilldale played several games at Spruce Field or Elks Park as it was also called in the press.[15] After July 4, the Daisies played their Thursday home games there, although they scheduled a lucrative meeting with the House of David in Darby, the park they generally called home, which had a larger capacity.[16] The Homestead Grays came to town to play Hilldale at Passon Field at the end of the season. The Pennsylvania Giants also called Elks Park their home field on Tuesdays and Fridays.[17]

By the end of the 1928 season, it was obvious to Harry Passon (1897-1954) that this field had become a popular place to play semipro baseball games, especially for Black teams that were growing both in number and in popularity as the Black population in that area also grew, and he came up with a plan to lease the field and rename it Passon Field. Passon was the owner of the leading sporting goods store in Philadelphia. The store, originally known as PGB

Sporting Goods, opened in 1920. It was the joint project of Passon, Ed Gottlieb, and Hughie Black, hence the name featuring their initials. Passon (and his brothers) played baseball and basketball in their youth, but Harry soon realized that his main interest and personal strength was in the business side of sports. He bought out Gottlieb and Black, renamed the store Passon's Sporting Goods, and employed family members to help him run the store, which supplied high quality equipment and uniforms to local teams. But the store at 507 Market Street not only sold goods – it also became the hub of the Philadelphia sports world. It was the home for the Passon Athletic Association and all the Passon clubs the Association sponsored – baseball, basketball, boxing, track and field, and soccer. Ed Gottlieb, former business partner and then leading promoter and booking agent, and owner of the Philadelphia SPHAS teams, maintained his agency in the building until 1944. Gottlieb was responsible for most of the bookings in the greater Philadelphia area, and later extended his reach more broadly in the Northeast corridor.[18] The store, and Gottlieb's adjacent office, were where anyone involved in sports in Philadelphia came to meet, buy equipment, make deals, and schedule games.

Passon leased the field at 48th and Spruce from the Price estate. There were many reasons he decided to do this. The field would become a regular source of income from scheduling fees from the games held there that would be arranged and promoted by Ed Gottlieb. Making sure the arena would be known as Passon Field created a real opportunity to advertise the Passon brand, which was becoming a household word in the Philadelphia sports community.[19] Since the short-staffed weekly newspapers usually printed whatever information promoters and managers sent them to fill their sports pages, Passon made sure the new name was well advertised. 48th and Spruce officially became Passon Field in April 1929 when the *Tribune* announced that the Homestead Grays, Baltimore Black Sox, and Bacharach Giants would be playing there that summer.[20] The (White) Passon club team that the store sponsored also played its home games there.[21]

The grounds needed improvements. By May, Passon had added 1,500 new seats in hopes of making the location an even more popular attraction for Black and White audiences.[22] In August the *Pittsburgh Courier*'s W. Rollo Wilson wrote that "the largest crowd ever at Passon Field" came to see the illustrious Homestead Grays.[23] In his new role as proprietor of the field, Passon got involved in the legal struggle against the 1794 Pennsylvania blue law that prohibited the playing of baseball on Sundays.[24] He and other team owners in Philadelphia understood that not being able to play on Sundays, when people had time to attend games, was causing a serious loss of revenue and opportunity. Most other states had abolished blue laws, or never enforced their centuries-old laws. The law in Pennsylvania was particularly irksome, as it specifically prohibited playing games on the Christian Sabbath. Connie Mack's Philadelphia Athletics team made the first major challenge to the law in 1926. The Athletics lost a long legal battle, and Sunday baseball remained prohibited.

The *Tribune* regularly protested the prohibition[25] as did teams and their owners who understood baseball as a leisure activity that in no way dishonored the Sabbath and were enraged by the hypocrisy of the state permitting other leisure activities, like miniature golf, while baseball was targeted. On Sunday, September 1, 1929, the (White) Passon club played a game against the Negro League star Louis Santop's Broncos at Passon Field in defiance of the law. Both managers (Santop and Malcolm McGowan) were arrested and fined. They paid the $10 fine and the incident received only scant attention.[26] The following August, however, another Passon Field challenge to the Sunday laws became national news. This time two White teams, the Passons and the North Penn Athletic Club, held a contest on August 3, 1930. The two managers (Malcolm McGowan and Edward Sherman) went into the stands to pass the hat, which Passon believed challenged the commercial aspect of the Sunday law. Three policemen arrested the managers and the umpire (Todd Voorhees) and charged them with disorderly conduct. This time they refused to pay the fines and they were sentenced to 30 days in jail. Passon and his lawyer, Michael Saxe, also filed a complaint against the arresting officers, claiming they were in violation of another old Pennsylvania law that prohibited police from making arrests on the Sabbath without a warrant. The local newspapers, Black and White, followed the story closely. Although the defendants were initially found guilty, a sympathetic appeals judge, Edwin O. Lewis, overturned the judgment, ruling:

"The evidence produced before us as to the conduct of the baseball game on August 3 does not establish that disorderly conduct amounting to a breach of the peace was committed by all or any one of the defendants. Their arrest on Sunday without a warrant was therefore unlawful, the whole proceeding being without effect and void."[27]

Lewis's extensive and well-publicized ruling[28] also supported legalizing Sunday baseball as an opportunity to reduce crime. However, the ruling only supported amateur Sunday baseball in nonresidential areas. He allowed the teams to take up a collection in the stands, but not if it was a "subterfuge" for paid admission. He further stipulated that since Passon Field was in a residential area and near a hospital, apartment house, and a miniature golf course, baseball games on Sunday would be considered a disturbance of the peace even if acceptable on other days. Police could therefore stop games and disperse Sunday crowds at Passon Field, but not make arrests without a warrant.[29]

By drawing attention to the law and clarifying its scope, Passon made an important contribution to the effort to keep the law in the news. Using the courts to overturn the law, as Connie Mack discovered before him, would not be a successful strategy. However, both efforts drew public attention to the need to change the law and encouraged the governor and the legislature to act. It would take a major legislative battle and ultimately a public referendum for Sunday baseball (at least between the hours of 2 and 6 P.M.) to become legal in 1934.

At the beginning of the 1930 season, the *Tribune* reported that plans were underway for Ed Bolden (1881-1950), who was no longer involved with the Hilldale team that he had built and managed, to start a new team, the Hillsdales, and that they would make Passon Field their home park. He shipped the team's equipment he had stored in Darby to 48th and Spruce.[30] An article in the *Chicago Defender* called Passon's "rebuilt park … one of the best semipro diamonds in this city" and a logical place for Bolden to start over since the Hilldale team had been playing there regularly the year before.[31] The *Baltimore Afro-American* claimed that Ed Gottlieb had been hired as the business manager.[32] But when Bolden learned that the Lincoln Giants also planned to make Passon Field their home base that year,[33] fearing that there would be too much local competition and hence insufficient revenue, he changed his mind about fielding the team for that season. Dick Sun reported in the *Tribune* that another reason this plan never materialized was that most of Hilldale's players stayed with the Darby team, and Randy Dixon maintained that it was Bolden's reliance on the "Nordic" support of Gottlieb and Passon that made Bolden's efforts less appealing to the players and fans.[34]

Although Bolden's plan to develop a new team with Gottlieb and Passon's help did not come to pass, rumors continued to surface in the winter of 1931 about Bolden's new team. Speculation was that it would be operated by former Hilldale star John Henry "Pop" Lloyd and sponsored by "the Passon interests."[35] Perhaps inspired by these possibilities, Passon decided to field his own independent Black team, which he called the Bacharach Giants after the Eastern Colored League team that had been playing in Atlantic City (and occasionally at Passon Field) but that had folded in 1929 due to financial difficulties. Passon had installed arc lights to his newly refurbished field, and they would play there on Monday evenings, traveling on Wednesdays and Saturdays. He hired former Hilldale star Otto Briggs as the manager, and other former Hilldale greats, including Turkey Stearnes and Pop Lloyd, also joined the team.[36] They did well in 1931 and 1932, when they played against topflight opponents including the Pittsburgh Crawfords, Homestead Grays, and New York Black Yankees.[37]

After their strong season in 1932, Passon planned to field the "Bees" (as they came to be known) again in 1933. Given their success, Passon made more improvements to his field, adding a grandstand, clubhouse, and a more sophisticated lighting system.[38] Malcolm McGowan, the Bacharachs' general manager, commented in the *Tribune*:

"After the improvements are finished the park aside from being the most convenient one, will be the most beautiful one in the city. The admission prices are going to be in reach of everyone even a small girl or boy will be able to get in."[39]

Ed Bolden, meanwhile, started a new independent Black team, the Philadelphia Stars. Instead of working with Passon as had been rumored, Bolden enlisted Ed Gottlieb to run the business side of the Stars. Bolden and Gottlieb would own the Stars together, with Gottlieb remaining the financial power and silent partner, until Bolden's death in 1950, when Gottlieb took control, with Bolden's daughter Hilda becoming the nominal owner. For the 1933 season Bolden and Gottlieb made the newly refurbished Passon Field the Stars' home, and it remained home field for the Bacharachs as well. The *Tribune* highlighted the Stars' practices at Passon Field before the season began.[40] The Bacharachs and Stars were the top two Black teams in the area, and played their games against each other at Passon Field, including a five-game series in June. (The Stars took three out of the five games.)[41] The Black press built it up as a rivalry, probably at Bolden and Gottlieb's urging, to encourage fan interest.[42] In addition to games against each other, both teams

played against Passon's White team.[43] Both teams also held contests against Gottlieb's White Jewish team, the SPHAS, as well as popular traveling teams that Gottlieb booked, like the House of David.[44] At the end of the season the Stars also played against teams from the newly formed Negro National League, but those contests were held at Penmar Park and the Hilldale Stadium, not Passon Field.[45] It therefore did not come as a surprise in February of 1934 that Ed Bolden announced that the Stars would have a new home field the following season, Penmar Park, located at 44th and Parkside, owned and operated by the Pennsylvania Railroad.[46]

The winter of 1934 proved to be eventful. As a result of Connie Mack and Harry Passon's earlier efforts and with other sports magnates putting additional pressure on the governor and legislature, a voter referendum was passed that finally allowed Sunday afternoon baseball in Philadelphia, creating new possibilities for games at Passon Field.[47] Although in February Bolden had stated publicly that the Stars would be playing elsewhere, in March he announced that the Stars would, in fact, play all their Saturday night and Sunday home games at Passon Field. At Bolden's urging, Passon agreed to add 4,000 seats, renovate the field, and upgrade the lighting for night games.[48]

This turn of events was surprising given the tensions between Bolden and Passon over the entry of the Stars and Bacharachs into the Negro National League. Gus Greenlee's new league was started in 1933, but neither Philadelphia team was interested in applying for membership at that time despite Greenlee's invitation to the Stars that Bolden turned down, citing his difficult experiences with league play when he operated the Hilldale team.[49] But Bolden was persuaded by the new circumstances available in 1934: Sunday afternoon games in Philadelphia, Passon's upgrading of the lighting and capacity at Passon Field (and better lighting in many parks), and the overall economic climate that seemed to be improving, finally, after the 1929 stock market crash, all of which would encourage better attendance at games and improve the financial viability of league play.[50]

Passon was also eager for his Bacharachs to join the league. He was interested in putting his players on salary rather than using the "co-op system" that had proved difficult to manage in prior years, and that he believed to be unfair to the players.[51] But Bolden and presumably Gottlieb were not enthusiastic about including the Bacharachs. He told Gus Greenlee and the other team owners that the Stars would not join the league if the Bacharachs were included. The reason he gave publicly was that he did not believe Philadelphia could support two league teams economically, a reason he had given in 1930 when he folded his new Hillsdale team at the beginning of the season. Several of the other owners argued that the competition would be good for the league, and Cum Posey, owner of the Homestead Grays, noted that it would work if they didn't play in Philadelphia on the same day.[52] Bolden and Gottlieb, however, were looking to elevate the Stars and did not want the Bacharachs cutting into their profit margin or public attention. Passon graciously withdrew his application for full membership, although *Tribune* reporter Randy Dixon described Passon as "shocked."[53] Since Gottlieb was in business with both Passon and Bolden, the hard position Bolden and Gottlieb took on membership, and their interest in playing in other venues surely must have distressed Passon. Ultimately, the Bacharachs would be welcomed by the league as associate members for the first half of the season,[54] and would become full members in the second half.

The Passon Field Negro National League season began on May 12, 1934, a game between Ed Bolden's Philadelphia Stars and Dick Lundy's Newark Dodgers. League Commissioner and sportswriter W. Rollo Wilson described Lundy in his "Sports Shots" column in the *Pittsburgh Courier* as "baseball's greatest shortstop" and lauded the new league for its quality.[55] There was a celebratory opening ceremony with the Octavius V. Catto Band playing and Commissioner Robert Nelson of the Pennsylvania State Athletic Commission tossing the first ball. The advertisement in the *Tribune* noted the 4,000 new seats and admission prices of 25 cents for those seats and 35 cents for the newly refurbished grandstand.[56] The Stars won, 12-0, behind the pitching of Stewart "Slim" Jones, who would be their star and main attraction in this banner year for the team. Some 5,000 fans were in attendance and appreciated the new features of the field.[57]

The first half of the season ended in early July. The Stars were in second place. The Bacharachs had done well in league competition and Bolden did not raise objections when they became full members.[58] To keep enthusiasm high for the second half, the Bacharachs and Stars initiated a competition, a five-game series at Passon Field to determine the city championship. A "well-known downtown sportsman" (probably Passon himself) donated a trophy for the winners, and the *Tribune* reported that Bolden and Passon made a

wager on the games, with Gottlieb as the "stakeholder."[59] The Stars won four out of five games, with Slim Jones the winning pitcher in two of the contests.[60]

The second half of the season went well for the Stars, but not for the Bacharachs. Passon Field also experienced some difficulties. Racial tensions were rising in the neighborhood.[61] In August Passon hired an attendant to keep the peace and collect balls that a "gang of hoodlums" hanging out near left field all summer had been taking. The attendant was beaten by the "gang." When a detective from the local precinct who was attending the game pursued them, he too was hit, but managed to apprehend two of the alleged assailants.[62] This situation caused Passon to consider ending night games at the field. Passon was also criticized by visiting league teams for the low admission prices, and he was persuaded to make admission prices comparable to those in other cities, raising Sunday prices from 40 to 55 cents.[63]

While the Bacharachs faded (and would not rejoin league play in years that followed), the Stars were the NNL winners of the second half and went on to play in a championship series against the first-half winners, the Chicago American Giants. The Stars' four home games were played at Passon Field to crowds that numbered from 2,000 to 5,000. They lost the first game at home. Three were planned but could not take place because of inclement weather.[64] They won only one of three games in Chicago.[65] The series was then interrupted by a series of exhibition games, held at Yankee Stadium, with 25,000 spectators. In a doubleheader, the Giants beat the New York Black Yankees and the Stars tied the Pittsburgh Crawfords.[66] The large size of the mixed-race crowd was probably the result of Satchel Paige pitching for the Crawfords. Slim Jones held his own against Paige for the Stars. The championship series could not compete with the money to be made in New York.[67]

Ed Gottlieb claimed responsibility for the interruption of the series. As Gottlieb recalled in a later interview:

"That was the first four-team doubleheader in Yankee Stadium. We came in with the Pittsburgh

Crawfords in the first game against the Philadelphia Stars, and in the second game it was the New York Black Yankees against the Chicago American Giants. It rained the whole night before the game and really didn't stop until just before the first game started, but we had 25,000 there, and the concessions were tree-mendous [sic]. Slim Jones – he died of pneumonia when he was still very young – he was pitching for the Stars. Oh, he was fast! And we had Satchel pitching for the Crawfords. It was a 1-1 tie, so we called it in the 10th inning with the idea in mind that we could repeat the whole damn game a few weeks later, which we did. And you know, we got just about the same gate all over, even though, just like the first time, it rained right up until the game started."[68]

The Stars went on to win the last games at Passon Field when play was resumed. They had to play four games because what would have been the seventh and final game could not be completed before the 6 P.M. curfew required by the revised Sunday blue law. The series was also marred by violence, not by "rowdy fans" but by players physically attacking umpires and each other; clearly the outcome mattered to them. Slim Jones won the eighth game with both his pitching and hitting, but since they were playing on a weekday because of the attenuated game seven, the crowd was only 2,000 and the series gathered little press.[69]

After that year Bolden and Gottlieb would no longer make Passon Field their home ballpark. Gottlieb took out a lease at Penmar Park at 44th and Parkside in 1935, which boasted more seating accompanied by much soot and dust as the result of its location near the Pennsylvania Railroad roundhouse.[70] The Stars did continue to play some games at Passon Field in 1935.[71] In the first half of the 1936 season they played regularly at Passon Field on Sundays.[72]

In July of 1936, Passon Field's stands were condemned, and no baseball games were played there for the rest of the season.[73] That fall football, soccer, and boxing matches were held there,[74] and baseball games started again in 1937 although few were noted in the press.[75] Unlike Gottlieb, who stayed busy promoting the NNL and the Stars, Passon had lost interest in the goings on at the field and often failed to inform the *Tribune* about what was happening there. The Bacharachs and the White Passon team (often called the "storeboys"), under the guidance of Malcolm McGowan, continued to play independent semipro ball, often against Negro League teams. In 1937 Passon's employee at the store and former Negro League player Tom Dixon was the Bacharach manager

who discovered 15-year-old Roy Campanella. Campy played with the Bacharachs in May and June that year. There is no record of his playing at Passon Field during his time with the Bacharachs.[76]

In 1937 Passon Field again gained notoriety when world heavyweight champion Joe Louis brought his softball team, the Brown Bombers, to play against Chickie Passon's (White) Philadelphia All-Stars in a game arranged by Harry Passon. The crowd was estimated by police at 20,000, obviously beyond the capacity of the field. When Louis arrived for batting practice and hit a few balls out of the park, the enthusiastic crowd stormed the field, and the newly rebuilt grandstand collapsed, injuring five people. The game was played the next day at Municipal Stadium.[77]

The *Philadelphia Inquirer*'s regular coverage of games at Passon Field, which included baseball teams from industrial leagues, softball, high-school football, and soccer, continued through the 1939 season. In 1941 the "old" Passon Field was only mentioned as the location for parades for British War Relief. In 1942 the stands had been torn down and the field was vacant, although a 1942 land-use map still calls the area Passon Field.[78] The students at neighboring West Philadelphia High School, whose baseball and football Speedboys teams had played there in years past, requested that the School District buy the land for their school.[79] Before that would come to pass, in 1943 the Price estate permitted the field to be repurposed as 200 World War II Victory Gardens.[80] A *Philadelphia Evening Bulletin* photograph from March 1944 had this caption: "Some 200 gardens measuring 25 by 25 feet are laid out across this tract (formerly Passon Field) for victory gardens."[81] The field at 48th and Spruce was Passon Field no more. The Price estate attempted to sell the field for commercial use in 1947, but the City Council would not rezone the property because the Welfare and Recreation Department had other plans for it.[82]

In 1948 the Price estate sold the field to the City of Philadelphia's Department of Recreation. In 1950 the School District obtained the title. From then on it would be known as the West Philadelphia High School Athletic Field. In addition to the Speedboys, many high-school and amateur football, soccer, and baseball teams played their games there and it was the location for track and field meets as well. The Recreation Department continued to use it as a community center and a playground that was open for the public during summers in the 1960s.[83]

In 2002 the field was renamed Pollock Field in honor of the West Philadelphia High School alumnus and Alumni Association head Joseph L. Pollock. Pollock, who graduated in 1940, grew up poor in West Philadelphia and credited West Philly High with enabling him to get a good education and ultimately a good life. It is likely that he was among those students and recent alums who petitioned to turn Passon Field into his school's athletic field in 1942.[84] In 2014 the field received an upgrade with new lighting,[85] and the West Philadelphia High School Speedboys (and Speedgirls) football, soccer, and lacrosse teams continue to use the field. Although the baseball team no longer plays there, their presence is commemorated in a "Speedboy" mural.[86]

NOTES

1   Sections adapted from Rebecca T. Alpert, "Harry Passon: Philadelphia Baseball Entrepreneur," in Morris Levine, ed., *National Pastime: From Swampoodle to South Philly* (Phoenix: SABR, 2013), 64-68. I also relied on John L. Puckett, "A Storied Athletic Venue in West Philadelphia: From Passon Field to Pollock Field" https://collaborativehistory.gse.upenn.edu/stories/storied-athletic-venue-west-philadelphia-passon-field-pollock-field West Philadelphia Collaborative History website, accessed July 1, 2022; Courtney M. Smith, *Ed Bolden and Black Baseball in Philadelphia* (Jefferson North Carolina: McFarland & Company, 2016), and Neil Lanctot, *Negro League Baseball: The Rise and Ruin of a Black Institution* (Philadelphia: University of Pennsylvania Press, 2004), as well as the ProQuest Historical Newspaper Digital Collection. I am grateful to Lynn Alpert, who helped with research and photography.

2   Philip Lowry, *Green Cathedrals: The Ultimate Celebration of All 271 Major League and Negro League Ballparks Past and Present* (Reading, Massachusetts: Addison-Wesley Publishing, 1992).

3   See Douglas Ewbank, "Migration and Immigration," West Philadelphia Collaborative History website, https://collaborativehistory.gse.upenn.edu/stories/migration-and-immigration, accessed July 24, 2022.

4   From 1923 to 1929 the field was known as Elks Field, Lit Brothers Field, or Spruce Field. From 1929 to 1942 it was called Passon Field. From 1943 to 1945 it served as a World War II Victory Garden. From 1950 to 2001 it was known as the West Philadelphia High School Athletic Field. In 2002 it was renamed Pollock Field to honor a celebrated alumnus. Throughout its history it has often been referred to simply as "48th and Spruce."

5   The Lit Brothers department store's team often played there, as did the team known as the Philadelphia Elks that was managed by Ed Gottlieb. I found no reference to any legal or special relationship either to the department store or to the team. It could have been called Elks after the fraternal organization, which wanted an Elks Field in every town where there was a chapter. "Elks Start Big Move to Start Playgrounds," *Washington Post*, June 6, 1922: 8.

6   George W. Bromley and Walter S. Bromley, "Atlas of the City of Philadelphia, wards 24, 27, 34, 40, 44 & 46, West Philadelphia, from actual surveys and official plans," published by G.W. Bromley, Philadelphia, 1927, plate 24; Free Library of Philadelphia Digital Map Collection.

7   Eli K. Price was also described as a "speculator in West Philadelphia real estate." https://collaborativehistory.gse.upenn.edu/media/eli-k-price.

8   Price family papers (Collection 4163), Historical Society of Pennsylvania, Box 27, folders 6-7. The finding aid for the collection details the family history. http://www2.hsp.org/collections/manuscripts/p/Price4163.html, accessed August 5, 2022.

9   *Ordinances of the City of Philadelphia from January 1 to December 31, 1948* (Philadelphia: Dunlap Printing Company, 1949), 220-221. The ordinance refers to the property as a playground and recreation center. The trustees (J. Sergeant Price, Philip Price, and E. Gwen Martin) were cultural leaders in Philadelphia.

10   The *Philadelphia Inquirer*, May 24, 1923: 21, called it Lit Brothers Field when describing one high-school game that was played there, but most of that summer the field was referred to as 48th and Spruce in reference to games played there.

11   "Washington's Double Wins for Hilldale," *Philadelphia Inquirer,* July 18, 1925: 11 .

12   "Hampton Causes Potomacs Downfall," *Baltimore Afro-American*, May 2, 1925: A14.

13   "Newton Team Gets Lit Brothers Field," *Philadelphia Tribune*, April 17, 1926: 10.

14   "Elks Down Wilmington Potomacs By 5-3 Score," *Philadelphia Tribune*, September 15, 1927: 10. Other teams also called 48th and Spruce home in 1927, including the Philadelphia White Socks. There were 2,000 fans at their opening game. The field was booked by W.A. Ringold, who could be reached at 4513 Wallace Street, or by phone, Baring 8687, if a team wanted to book a game. "White Sox Open Season With Victory," *Philadelphia Tribune*, May 19, 1927: 11. See also Rich Westcott, *The Mogul: Eddie Gottlieb, Philadelphia Sports Legend and Pro Basketball Pioneer* (Philadelphia: Temple University Press, 2008), 67.

15   "Hilldale Secures Local Grounds," *Philadelphia Tribune*, March 22,1928: 11. Rollo Wilson, "Sports Shots," *Pittsburgh Courier*, April 7, 1928: A4.

16   "Hilldale Club Battles House of David," *Philadelphia Tribune*, June 28, 1928: 11.

17   "Homestead Grays to Meet Daisies Here," *Philadelphia Tribune,* September 6, 1928: 11. "Pennsy Giants See Games in Balto.," *Baltimore Afro-American*, June 30, 1928: 12.

18   Gottlieb kept his offices above Passon's store at 507 Market until 1944, when he moved the office to 1537 Chestnut Street. Letter from Ed Gottlieb to Effa Manley, January 24, 1944, Newark Eagles Papers.

19   There were at least two other fields that Passon named "Passon Field," one in the Germantown section at Chelten and Magnolia ("SPHAS Turn Back Hilldale Foemen," *Philadelphia Inquirer Public Ledger*, May 27, 1925: 25) and another in the Northeast at Kensington and Torresdale Avenue ("North Catholic Blanks Mastbaum at Soccer," *Philadelphia Inquirer*, November 6, 1940: 34).

20   "Prof. Leslie Pinckney Hill to Throw Out First Ball," *Philadelphia Tribune*, April 18, 1929: 11.

21   "Atlanta Giants in Win Over Passons," *Philadelphia Tribune*, May 23, 1929: 10.

22   "Hilldale Clan All Set for Baltimore," *Philadelphia Tribune*, May 2, 1929: 10.

23   Rollo Wilson, "Sport Shots," *Pittsburgh Courier*, August 3, 1929: A5.

24   John A. Lucas, "The Unholy Experiment – Professional Baseball's Struggle Against Pennsylvania Sunday Blue Laws 1926-1934," in *Pennsylvania History: A Journal of Mid-Atlantic Studies*, 38:2 (April 1971), 163-175.

25   See for example, "Blue Sunday Laws," *Philadelphia Tribune*, July 25, 1929: 16.

26   "Broncos Leading by One Run When Police Break Up Game," *Philadelphia Tribune*, September 5,1929: 10.

27   "Free Donations at Sunday Games Upheld by Lewis," *Philadelphia Inquirer*, August 23, 1930: 1.

28 Three Sentenced for Sunday Ball Game in Philly," *Syracuse Herald*, August 5, 1930; "3 Men Get 30 Days for Sunday Ball," *Philadelphia Evening Bulletin*, August 4, 1930.

29 "Free Donations at Sunday Games Upheld by Lewis, "*Philadelphia Inquirer*, August 23, 1930: 3.

30 "Ed Bolden to Organize New Ball Outfit," *Philadelphia Tribune*, April 10, 1930: 10.

31 "Ed Bolden Is Head of New Ball Outfit," *Chicago Defender*, April 19, 1930: 8.

32 "Name Briggs Leader," *Baltimore Afro-American*, April 19, 1930: 14.

33 "Lincoln Giants Open as Philly Home Team," *Philadelphia Tribune*, May 15, 1930: 10.

34 Dick Sun, "Bolden Gesture Fades," and Randy Dixon, "Sport Sidelights," *Philadelphia Tribune*, April 24, 1930: 11.

35 Randy Dixon, "Money Man Aligns with Hilldale Team," *Philadelphia Tribune*, February 26, 1931: 10. The following section is adapted from Alpert, "Harry Passon," *The National Pastime.*

36 "New Bacharach Giants Test Mettle with Camden Sunday," *Philadelphia Tribune*, June 18, 1931: 10.

37 "Bacharachs Execute Triple Play," *Philadelphia Tribune*, May 19, 1932: 11; "Bacharachs String of Eight Victories Snapped," *Philadelphia Tribune*, July 7, 1932: 11; "Bacharachs Meet Acid Test in Game with Crawfords," *Philadelphia Tribune*, August 25, 1932: 9.

38 "Quaker Team to Open Soon," *New York Amsterdam News*, April 5, 1933: 9.

39 "Bacharachs to Keep Stars for Coming Season," *Philadelphia Tribune*, April 6, 1933: 11.

40 Smith, *Ed Bolden*, 70; "Daily Practice Sessions for Phila. Stars," *Philadelphia Tribune*, April 13, 1933: 11.

41 "Bolden's Stars and Bacharachs Start Five Game Series," *Philadelphia Tribune*, June 22, 1933: 11. Smith, *Ed Bolden*, 73.

42 "Boldenmen at Passon's Wed." *Philadelphia Tribune*, August 17, 1933: 10; "Bacharachs and Boldenmen Settle Dispute Saturday," *Philadelphia Tribune*, August 24, 1933: 10; "Passon Nine to Meet Bacharachs and Boldenmen," *Philadelphia Tribune*, August 31, 1933: 10.

43 "Negro Clubs to Oppose Passon '9,'" *Philadelphia Tribune*, July 13, 1933: 12.

44 "Bolden's Nine Trims Bearded Clan by 5 to 1," *Chicago Defender*, May 13, 1933: 9; "Passon Outfit Set to Check Bolden's Stars," *Philadelphia Tribune*, July 6, 1933: 10.

45 "Boldenmen Succumb to Smoky City Nine," *Philadelphia Tribune*, September 7, 1933: 11.

46 "Ed Bolden Announces New Base Ball Plans," *Philadelphia Tribune*, February 1, 1934: 11.

47 Lucas, "Unholy Experiment."

48 "Bolden's Team to Play All Games at New Passon Field," *Chicago Defender*, March 24, 1934: A5.

49 Lanctot, *Negro League Baseball*, 27-28.

50 Lanctot, *Negro League Baseball*, 27-28.

51 Rollo Wilson, "Sports Shots," *Pittsburgh Courier*, December 9, 1933: A4.

52 Cum Posey, "Cum Posey's Pointed Paragraphs," *Pittsburgh Courier,* March 3, 1934: A5.

53 Randy Dixon, "Baseball Magnates Convene in Parley," *Philadephia Tribune*, February 15, 1934: 10; "Blacksox, Grays Not Included," *Pittsburgh Courier*, February 17, 1934: A4.

54 Randy Dixon, "Wilson Named Landis of Negro Baseball," *Philadelphia Tribune*, March 15, 1934.

55 W. Rollo Wilson, "Sports Shots," *Pittsburgh Courier*, May 12, 1934: A4.

56 "Display ad 21," *Philadelphia Tribune*, May 10, 1934: 20.

57 "Stars Topple Newark 12-0," *Philadelphia Tribune*, May 17, 1934: 12; W. Rollo Wilson, "Phila Stars Win Opener," *Pittsburgh Courier*, May 19, 1934: 14.

58 *Pittsburgh Courier*, July 7, 1934: A5.

59 "Bacharachs and Stars to Play Series," *Philadelphia Tribune*, July 26, 1934: 12.

60 "Stars Drub Bees," *Philadelphia Tribune*, August 2, 1934: 12; "Stars Down Passon," *Philadelphia Tribune*, August 16, 1934: 12.

61 Smith, *Ed Bolden,* 80.

62 "Crack Detective Is Hurt," *Baltimore Afro-American*, August 18, 1934: 19.

63 "Craws-Yanks Play Tonite; Stars Sunday," *Philadelphia Tribune*, September 20, 1934: 11.

64 "Chicago Stops Stars in Playoff Start," *Philadelphia Tribune*, September 13, 1934: 14.

65 "McDonald Wins," *Philadelphia Tribune*, September 20, 1934: 11.

66 Ed Harris, "Points and Errors," *Philadelphia Tribune*, September 13, 1934: 14.

67 Ed Harris, "Jones and Paige Duel to 1-1 Tie," *Philadelphia Tribune*, September 13, 1934: 14.

68 Frank Deford, "Eddie Is the Mogul," *Sports Illustrated*, https://vault.si.com/vault/1968/01/22/eddie-is-the-mogul, accessed July 30, 2022.

69 Ed Harris, "Stars Clip Giant for 2 Runs," *Philadelphia Tribune*, October 4, 1934: 11. The headline read "Jones Hurls Boldens to Championship."

70 Lanctot, *Negro League Baseball*, 201.

71 "Stars Tag Brooklyn," *Philadelphia Tribune*, May16, 1935: 11; "Evans Hurls Mates to Win," *Philadelphia Tribune*, May 23, 1935: 11; "Stars Drop Two Games," *Philadelphia Tribune*, June 27, 1935: 12; "Casey Breaks Leg," *Philadelphia Tribune,* July 18, 1935: 11; "Bill Yancey Honored at Career Peak," *Philadelphia Tribune,* August 22, 1935: 9.

72 "Phila. Stars Start Practice," *Philadelphia Tribune*, April 16, 1936: 12.

73 Ed Harris, "The Gossip Post!!!," *Philadelphia Tribune*, July 23, 1936: 10.

74 "Wilmot Lions Tackle Lincoln," *Philadelphia Tribune*, November 12, 1936: 11.

75 "Display Ad 13," *Philadelphia Tribune*, June 17, 1937: 12. This advertisement for a Newark Eagles-Washington Elite Giants game was an exception.

76 Neil Lanctot, *Campy: The Two Lives of Roy Campanella* (New York: Simon and Schuster, 2011), 21-26. In June Campanella signed with the NNL's Washington Elite Giants and began to work with his new mentor, Biz Mackey.

77 "Fourteen Hurt in Crash of Two Grandstands," *Philadelphia Inquirer Public Ledger,* September 21, 1937: 2; "Five Hurt Treated at Louis Ball Game" *Philadelphia Tribune*, September 23, 1937: 3; "Fans Nearly Mob Joe Louis in Baltimore," *Baltimore Afro-American,* September 25, 1937: 24; "Joe Louis Mobbed by Crowd of 30,000 in Philly," *Pittsburgh Courier*, September 25, 1937: 1; "Louis Fans Wreck Stands," *Cleveland Call and Post*, September 30, 1937: 10.

78 Philadelphia Land Use Map, 1942, Plate 4A-1 (Land-Use Zoning Project 18313, Plans and Registry Division, Bureau of Engineering Surveys and Zoning, Department of Public Works, Federal Works Progress Administration for Pennsylvania, Free Library of Philadelphia Digital

Map Collection)https://www.philageohistory.org/tiles/viewer/, Accessed August 10, 2022.

79 "West Phila. Students Petition to Take Over Passon Field," *Philadelphia Inquirer Public Ledger*, March 18, 1942: 35.

80 "Corn Grows High in Phila. Too," *Philadelphia Inquirer*, July 11, 1943: 68.

81 "Row on Row," *Philadelphia Evening Bulletin*, March 21, 1944. George D. McDowell Evening Bulletin Photographs Collection, SCRC, Temple University. https://digital.library.temple.edu/digital/search/searchterm/passon%20field/order/nosort accessed July 20, 2022.

82 Price Family Papers, Box 27, Folder 7.

83 "Playgrounds Open on July 1," *Philadelphia Tribune*, June 18, 1963: 15; "Eighty-three Playgrounds Will Open on July 6," *Philadelphia Tribune*, June13, 1964: 9; "School Playgrounds to Open July 1," *Philadelphia Tribune,* July 1, 1969: 5.

84 Gayle Ronan Sims, "Joseph L. Pollock, 82, W. Phila. High Booster," *Philadelphia Inquirer*, April 9, 2004.

85 Aaron Carter, "Speedboys Are Stars Under the Lights," *Philadelphia Inquirer,* September 7, 2004. https://www.inquirer.com/philly/sports/high_school/pennsylvania/20140907_Speedboys_are_stars_under_the_lights.html. Accessed October 18, 2022.

86 In the early 2020s the field was upgraded with new equipment. There was a new football coach, and local alumni provided concession stands. The coach was unaware that the field had been renamed Pollock Field, and no marker to indicate the name was visible. ("Koach Bubb," Personal interview with author, August 11, 2022).

1934 PHILADELPHIA STARS TIMELINE

By Bill Nowlin

The year began with a January 13 meeting of the leaders of the Negro National League 2[1] in Pittsburgh, home city of the 1933 champion Pittsburgh Crawfords. The Craws had won by the thinnest of margins – a half-game: they were 41-21-2 in league play, followed by the Chicago American Giants at 41-22-1.[2] The Homestead Grays played .500 ball (14-14) and are shown in third place. The Nashville Elite Giants won five more games than the Grays but at 19-22-1 finished with a .463 winning percentage, their 42 league games being 50% more than the Grays' 28 games and reflecting the unbalanced nature of NNL2 baseball at the time.

Whether there even would be a league was somewhat up in the air.

The 1933 Philadelphia Stars were a first-year independent (non-league) club with a 22-13 record, under manager Dick Lundy, with their home games played both at Passon Field, Philadelphia, and at Hilldale Park in nearby Darby, Pennsylvania.

The Pittsburgh meeting was to be held in the second-floor dining room of the Crawford Grill. Invited as well were representatives of several other teams, to discuss matters of mutual interest. Among those invited by Gus Greenlee, owner of the Crawfords, were Tom Wilson of Nashville, but also non-league leaders of Black baseball such as Ed Bolden of the Stars, Joe Cambria of Baltimore, John Henry Lloyd of Atlantic City, Tenny Blount of Detroit, and J. L. Wilkinson of Kansas City.[3] Chicago, Cincinnati, Cleveland, Newark, and New York team executives were also invited, and advance word of the gathering indicated that representatives from clubs in Dayton, Indianapolis, Columbus, and Akron were expected to attend.

One of the goals was simply to foster cooperation. As sports columnist W. Rollo Wilson explained, "Even the optimistic Gus realizes that any league including all of those towns listed would be too unwieldy and transportation costs would be prohibitive. His thought is to effect certain cooperative, principles, whether the clubs be in leagues or playing independently.

These apply to player problems, salaries and booking arrangements."[4]

The meeting was poorly attended. Cum Posey reported that only Nashville and Pittsburgh were represented among the league clubs. Prentice Byrd from Cleveland also came. But Greenlee reported that Philadelphia, Baltimore, Newark, and the Bacharachs would have clubs – and ballparks in which to play.

Greenlee sent out another set of invitations for a meeting to be held on February 10 in Philadelphia. Which clubs might constitute a league in 1934 remained unclear.[5] Akron, Columbus, Detroit, and the Homestead Grays had all "relinquished membership."[6] Wilson wrote, "there will be several plans advanced and a way may be found – possibly by the amalgamation of the various ideas – to have either a league or a mutual association of some sort."[7]

In the meantime, Ed Bolden of the Philadelphia Stars made a number of moves. He replaced manager Dick Lundy with pitcher Webster McDonald, referred to by more than one newspaper as "the gentleman of colored baseball."[8] Bolden said home games would be played in Philadelphia at the YMCA park at 44th and Parkside and not in Darby.

McDonald had previously managed the Washington Pilotsof the East-West League in the second half of 1932, after Frank Warfield's heart attack and July 24 death in midseason. McDonald pitched for the Stars in 1933.

Two players from the 1933 Philadelphia Stars team had also died – third baseman Tom Finley (d. September 5, age 30) and first baseman Eggie Dallard (d. November 26, age 34).

The February meeting at the Citizens' Republican Club was a success. It was agreed to launch a Negro National Association which would embrace six clubs: the Chicago American Giants, Pittsburgh Crawfords, Philadelphia Stars, Newark Dodgers, Nashville Elite Giants, and a team from Cleveland that became known as the Cleveland Red Sox. The inclusion of Chicago was something of a surprise because it had been thought – and reported – that owner R.A. Cole might be going a different way. The New York Black Yankees were said to have "aligned themselves as an associate member" while "Baltimore interests, not represented at the parley, sent word that they are okay to be counted in."[9]

In addition to bringing in McDonald as manager, the Stars said they had signed Jud Wilson, Chaney White, Biz Mackey, Jake Stephens, Cliff Carter, and Rap Dixon, and were talking with Jake Dunn and Dick Seay.[10] All but Carter and Dixon played with the Stars during the 1934 season.

There was an unexpected development at the meeting. Originally, it had appeared that two clubs from Philadelphia would joining the league, but that seemed economically untenable to Ed Bolden, and so Harry Passon of the Bacharach Giants – rather than perhaps create enemies – "withdrew his application and wished unlimited success to those remaining."[11] As events transpired, the Bacharachs joined the league in midseason.

As an aside, columnist Rollo Wilson said that he believed Philadelphia could support two teams. Given that there were to only be three games a week, and one team would be on the road as long as the teams were contenders, the market could support three games a week.[12] Cum Posey outlined a number of the considerations, feeling Chicago was too far west, but that Philadelphia could support two teams.[13]

That Sunday baseball had just become legal in Philadelphia made a big difference. Pennsylvania was the last state to prohibit baseball on Sundays. The state legislature finally approved it in 1933; voters validated the decision in a referendum, 87% voting in favor.[14]

On February 19, Bolden brought Phil Cockrell to the offices of the *Tribune*, where he signed to pitch for the Stars in 1934.[15]

A further meeting was called for March 10 in Philadelphia. Applications from Baltimore, the Homestead Grays, and the Bacharachs were to be voted upon. Newspaperman W. Rollo Wilson was named commissioner of the new league, with Greenlee as chairman of the board and Tom Wilson of Nashville as vice-chairman.[16] Six teams were designated league members: Chicago, Cleveland, Nashville, Newark, Philadelphia Stars, and Pittsburgh Crawfords. Baltimore was voted in as a full member, but immediately asked their membership be suspended until they could determine if they could obtain enough good players. The New York Black Yankees were told they would be welcome as an associate member if they accepted and abided by the rules of the organization.

Teams in Birmingham and Memphis, the Homestead Grays, and the Bacharach Giants were all designated associate members. It was the goal to form a working relationship with the Southern League.[17] A schedule was drafted, with the first half to run from May 12 to July 4, and the second half to then run until September 9. The winners of each half were to face each other in playoffs.

There was considerable turnover in league teams from 1933 to 1934, enough that this was considered a new league by the newspapers of the day. Teams which were new to the league in 1934 included the Newark Dodgers, Cleveland Red Sox, the Bacharachs (known as the Philadelphia Bacharachs that year, playing their home games at Passon Field), and the Philadelphia Stars, also playing at Passon Field.[18]

Wilson's first ruling as commissioner was to award third baseman Dewey Creacy to the Stars. Creacy had signed with the Stars but led Cleveland to believe he would be willing to serve them as manager. Wilson censured him and warned him that any such similar conduct in the future would result in his suspension.[19]

In April, Wilson wrote an amusing column in which he interviewed his "alter ego" – the commissioner – in which, among other things, the commissioner revealed his salary only ran from May 1 to October 1 and that "Nothing was said about an expense account and I'll probably be owing myself money when the season ends."[20]

On March 18, Ed Bolden announced that the Stars would play all their home league games at Passon Field, at 48th and Spruce, rather than at the YMCA park as previously planned. Some 4,000 new seats were to be installed and other improvements made.[21]

The initial first-half schedule was initially set as follows:

May 12 – Newark at Philadelphia Stars

May 13 – Philadelphia Stars at Newark

May 15 - Newark at Philadelphia Stars (night game)

May 19, 20, and 21 – Philadelphia Stars at Pittsburgh Crawfords

May 25 and 26 – Homestead Grays at Philadelphia Stars

May 30 – Pittsburgh Crawfords at Philadelphia Stars

June 2, 3, and 5 – Chicago at Philadelphia Stars

June 9 – Nashville at Philadelphia Stars

June 16 – Philadelphia Stars at Homestead Grays

June 17 and 18 – Philadelphia Stars at Cleveland

June 23 - Bacharachs at Philadelphia Stars

June 24 - Philadelphia Stars at Newark

June 25 – Philadelphia Stars at Bacharachs

June 30, July 1 and 2 – Homestead Grays at Philadelphia Stars (the July 1 and 2 dates were listed as tentative)

July 4 – Nashville at Philadelphia Stars

Of the 23 games listed, one can immediately see that six of them were against Homestead, a non-league team. Eleven were home games.[22]

Several of the players who would appear with the Stars during the 1934 season played in a game at Hilldale Park on April 1, playing as the "Mackey All-Stars." Despite being out-hit six hits to three, they beat a team dubbed the Zulu Jungle Giants, 3-2, the latter "decked out in warpaint, grass skirts, and head dress [which] created the impression that they are a bunch of Murphys, O'Briens, and Smiths in disguise."[23] The game was one of the first legal baseball games played on a Sunday in Pennsylvania.

Just to confuse things a bit, an independent team was organized, based in Philadelphia, calling themselves the Birmingham Black Crackers.[24]

PRESEASON GAMES

There were a few preseason games.

On April 8, the Stars beat a team of White ballplayers, the Wentz-Olney team, 10-4, in a game played at Front and Chew Streets in Philadelphia. The Stars scored twice in the top of the first. Their opponents scored once. At the end of three, it was 3-3. In the sixth inning, Joe Juliano took over pitching for Mush Higgins and "the colored batters…bit off seven runs in rapid succession."[25] The Stars used four pitchers; Webster McDonald got the win. Mickey Casey had three hits, while Dick Seay, Jake Dunn, and Dewey Creacy each had two.

The April 12 *Tribune* informed readers that infielder Jud Wilson had been appointed team captain of the Stars.[26]

On the 15th, the Stars played Raphael, the reigning Philadelphia League champions, in another game where one big inning made all the difference. The Stars had a 4-3 lead through seven innings, but then scored five runs in the top of the eighth to put the game away. Casey had another three-hit day, two of them doubles. The game at 58th and Elmwood drew 3,000.[27]

As the players were getting in some activity, the league was still organizing. There was a special meeting called to consider Baltimore's application to join, neither Cambria nor any other team representative showed up. They were thus rejected. This was hardly surprising, in that the team had lost a staggering number of players to other teams, or to death.[28]

So was Nat Strong's application on behalf of the New York Black Yankees. The players from both teams were considered to be fair game ("free agents") for league teams. It was determined how player signings would be deemed valid. There was some tinkering with scheduling, and agreement on how to employ and utilize umpires. Not that one would expect otherwise, but Commissioner Wilson drew a headline by banning rowdyism.[29]

The Stars played a doubleheader in Newark on April 22, winning both games from the Meadowbrook Club, 11-5 and 13-1. Dunn, Seay, and Chaney White all homered in the first game.[30]

Rap Dixon was not going to be able to play for the Stars. *Tribune* sports editor Randy Dixon said he had "contracted a peculiar stomach ailment upon his recent return from Puerto Rica (sic) that causes acute pain when he attempts to as much as walk." He was hospitalized and believed perhaps be lost for the season.[31] Two other players who had seen action in Puerto Rico were Stars pitchers Rocky Ellis and Slim Jones. Rollo Wilson said they were the two best pitchers on the island over the winter.[32]

The game on April 29 drew 4,000, the largest crowd to date. The Stars beat the South Phillies, 4-1, with all four runs coming in the top of the eighth. It had been a tight contest, with the South Phillies scoring their one run in the bottom of the sixth. The first batter up in the eighth was Stars reliever Slim Jones, who singled. The next two batters struck out – Stephens and Seay – but then the floodgates were burst open. Chaney White singled, Jones running to third base. Jud Wilson drew a walk, loading the bases. Mickey Casey pinch-hit for Dunn; he singled, driving in two. Mackey then singled, again driving in a pair.[33]

On May 5, Stars right-hander Paul Carter had a perfect game going into the seventh inning pitching against the Westville (New Jersey) Villagers. Left fielder Shorty Thompson singled with one out. Only one of the Westville players reached base, on a two-out

Commissioner Rollo Wilson Bans Rowdyism In Baseball

Pittsburgh Courier, *April 21, 1934: A5.*

fielding error in the eighth by Dick Seay. The Stars had eight base hits, three of them by shortstop Jake Stephens.[34]

When it came time to open the season, there were a number of scheduling problems which included, among other things, the canceling of the opening series between the Cleveland Red Sox and the Homestead Grays, a non-league game – so the Cleveland team decided to stay in New Orleans. Two players signed to Crawfords contacts turned up on other teams, one of them as the manager, and Double Duty Radcliffe (who was supposed to play with Nashville) instead started playing with an "outlaw team" out west.[35]

The last game before the regular season was on May 11 at the Gittane Memorial Field in Vineland, New Jersey, about 40 miles south of Philadelphia. About 400 saw the Wene Chix host the Stars. The "Bolden All-Stars" were perhaps just going through the motions at first, as they were held scoreless through the first four innings, but then the "colored lads bombarded base blows all over the field." Pitching for the Stars were Webster McDonald and "Charleston" – presumably Porter Charleston, who pitched for them in 1933 and 1934. The final score was 5-1. Jake Stephens had both a double and a triple.[36]

1934 REGULAR SEASON

May 12, 1934: Philadelphia Stars 12, Newark Dodgers 0, at Passon Field, Philadelphia

The Opening Day game was on a Saturday afternoon at Passon Field. Left-hander Slim Jones threw a three-hitter and shut out the visiting Newark Dodgers, 12-0.

The opening ceremonies included the Octavius V. Catto Elks Club band and a first pitch thrown by one of Pennsylvania's three Athletic Commissioners. The game drew some 5,000.

Neither team scored for the first three innings. In the bottom of the fourth, Stars batters got to Newark starter George Britt, a right-hander. Leadoff batter and right fielder Jake Dunn doubled down the third-base line. Catcher Mickey Casey walked. Third baseman Dewey Creacy was called out for interference, the umpire declaring that he had "jumped into a pitched ball."[37] Center fielder Pete Washington doubled to left field, driving in Dunn and Casey.

In the fourth, the Stars scored six more runs. Second baseman Dick Seay singled. Left fielder Chaney White doubled. Jud Wilson, the Stars' first baseman, looked at four pitches off the plate and drew a walk. Dunn flied out to center field, but Paul Arnold dropped the ball, and Seay scored as White ran to third. He tagged and scored when Casey flied out to center, this time Arnold catching the ball. Creacy singled, loading the bases with two outs. Washington hit a grand slam to left field, out of the park and into Locust Street beyond. Arthur White relieved Britt and got the final out.

In the eighth, the "Boldenmen" scored four more runs. Shortstop Jake Stephens walked. Seay struck out, but then both Chaney White and Casey drew walks, too. Dunn hit what was thought an easy fly ball to right field, but Bert Johnson lost the ball in the sun and it went for a triple, clearing the bases. Casey singled Dunn home.

The Dodgers were held hitless through six innings, the no-hitter finally spoiled on Bert Johnson's seventh-inning single over second base. With two outs in the ninth, the Dodgers loaded the bases on a walk to pinch-hitter Goldie Cephus (in his only plate appearance of the season), and singles by shortstop/manager Dick Lundy and another by Johnson, but Cephas was "cut down at the plate, by a mighty throw from Dunn."

Seay had three base hits and Dunn had two, but Pete Washington's six RBIs on his double and a grand slam were the biggest blows. The Stars defense played error-free ball. Newark committed six errors.

Three umpires worked the game, two of them former ballplayers: Judy Gans umpired first base and Ben Taylor worked at third.

May 13, 1934: Philadelphia Stars 5, Newark Dodgers 4 (first game); Philadelphia Stars 4, Newark Dodgers 1 (second game), at General Electric Field, Bloomfield, New Jersey

The two teams traveled to Newark area to open the season there. Commissioner Rollo Wilson threw out the first pitch before this Sunday doubleheader which attracted another 5,000 fans. He bounced the ball in the dirt in front of the plate.[38] The Stars swept. They scored once in the top of the first inning off right-hander Bob Evans, added three runs in the fifth, and a fifth run in the sixth. Lefty Holmes worked eight-plus innings for the Stars – and contributed three base hits at the plate. Seay had two hits. Holmes gave up one run in the second, one in the fourth, and two more in the seventh, as Newark made it a one-run game. In the ninth, the Dodgers started to threaten. Philadelphia manager Webster McDonald turned to Slim Jones

– though he had just thrown a complete game the day before – and Jones secured the win for Holmes.[39]

"Webster McDonald has fashioned a great team which has no apparent weakness and they should be somewhere around the top when the season ends." Such was a comment from columnist Rollo Wilson, written after the first three games.[40]

May 18, 1934: Philadelphia Stars 4, Pittsburgh Crawfords 2, at Greenlee Field, Pittsburgh

Officially the "opening game of the colored league season," the hosting Pittsburgh Crawfords gave the ball to veteran right-hander William Bell. Starting for the Philadelphia Stars was rookie righty Rocky Ellis. It was a night game at Greenlee Field. Both pitchers held the other side scoreless for the first three innings. The Crawfords scored first, one run in the bottom of the fourth. Bell didn't let the Stars score for the first seven innings. The Crawfords added a second run in the bottom of the seventh, taking a 2-0 lead. Lacking any game story, we don't know how the runs scored, but one can see that Ellis only allowed four base hits, all of them singles.[41] The Stars burst forth with four runs in the top of the eighth. Left fielder Chaney White homered, but we don't know how many runs his homer produced. The only other extra-base hit in the game was a double by first baseman Jud Wilson.

The four-run outburst was the final one in the game, resulting in a 4-2 Stars win. The only error in the games was by Stars shortstop Jake Stephens. The number of walks issued by either pitcher is not indicated, but we do know that Ellis struck out three and Bell struck out five. The brief story in the *Post-Gazette* said that "formal opening exercises" would take place the following afternoon.

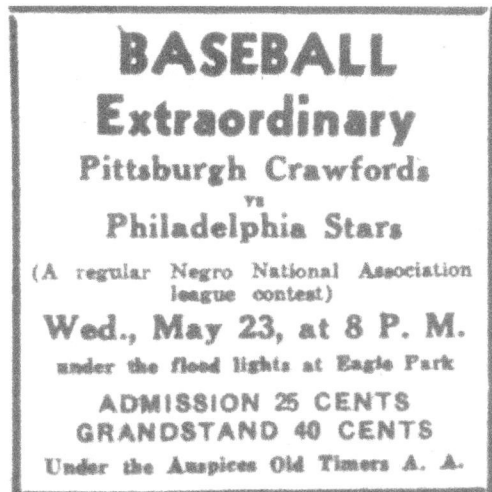

York Daily Record *(York, Pennsylvania), May 18, 1934: 10.*

May 19, 1934: Pittsburgh Crawfords 3, Philadelphia Stars 0, at Greenlee Field, Pittsburgh

The Stars got blanked in Pittsburgh, righty Bert Hunter throwing a two-hit shutout. Pittsburgh Mayor William McNair threw out the first pitch before a crowd of 3,000 to 6,000 (accounts differ) at the Crawfords' home opener.

Lefty Holmes pitched for Philadelphia. He only allowed four hits, but lost.

In the bottom of the fourth inning, center fielder Cool Papa Bell walked. Fellow outfielder Vic Harris, playing left field, sacrificed him to second. Bell scored on a ball that got away from Stars catcher Mickey Casey. In the bottom of the sixth, the game still 1-0 at the time, Crawfords manager/first baseman Oscar Charleston came to bat with a man on base and homered "high and wide over the centerfield fence."[42] Harris doubled in the game and Chester Williams tripled.

The only two hits by Stars batters were a single by Mickey Casey and a double by Jud Wilson. One writer credited Bell for "beautiful running catches in the outfield…as he snatched liners that looked like sure-fire hits."[43]

May 20, 1934: Philadelphia Stars 10, Pittsburgh Crawfords 5, at Greenlee Field, Pittsburgh

The Sunday afternoon game saw a big seven-run Stars rally in the top of the ninth snatch a win away from the Crawfords. The Stars started out on top with a three-run top of the first off Satchel Paige. Slim Jones pitched for Philadelphia, allowing two runs in the fourth, one in the fifth, and – breaking what was then a 3-3 tie – two more in the bottom of the seventh. Josh Gibson homered at some point. Paige had settled down and didn't allow a run from the seventh through the eighth, but suddenly "a fusillade of bats exploded in front of him" in the Stars' top of the ninth and "the great 'Satch' couldn't check the machine-gun batting attack."[44] He stated the course, but at the expense of seven runs, catapulting Philadelphia to a 10-5 lead.

Webster McDonald, the "submarine shark," relieved Jones in the ninth, and the score held.

May 21, 1934: Pittsburgh Crawfords 7, Philadelphia Stars 5, at Greenlee Field, Pittsburgh

A Monday night game saw Charleston homer again, as the Crawfords piled up seven runs in just the first two innings. In the top of the fifth, the Stars scored four times on two base hits and two errors. They added a fifth run in the ninth, but Pittsburgh's starting pitcher, lefty Leroy Matlock, shut them down before they could do any further damage. Working for the Stars was "Sir Phil Cockrell," who, once he had survived the onslaught at the start, held the Craws scoreless their final six frames. Jud Wilson had three hits for Philadelphia, while Pittsburgh got two hits apiece from Charleston, Cool Papa Bell, and shortstop Chester Williams.[45]

May 22, 1934: Pittsburgh Crawfords 5, Philadelphia Stars 2, at Greenlee Field, Pittsburgh

The coverage of this game in the *Pittsburgh Courier* read, in full: "A well-pitched game by Bell brought a 5-2 victory to the Crawfords in their encounter with the Philly All-Stars at Greenlee Field, Tuesday. Williams, Charleston and Wilson and Seay shown for their respective teams."[46] Presumably "shone" was the word intended. William Bell was the Pittsburgh starter. Shortstop Chester Williams and first baseman Oscar Charleston were the two Crawfords who featured; Williams both tripled and homered. Charleston homered as well. Jud Wilson (1B) and Dick Seay (2B) each doubled for the Stars, as did Biz Mackey, who was one of three pinch-hitters in the ninth, driven in by the second pinch-hitter, Lefty Holmes. Webster McDonald pitched for Philadelphia. Both pitchers walked one and both struck out three. The Crawfords outhit the Stars, though, 12 hits to 7.[47]

May 23, 1934: Philadelphia Stars 3, Pittsburgh Crawfords 0, at Eagle Park, York

The Old-Timers A.A. hosted a night game in York between the Stars and Crawfords, with the Stars coming out on top on a four-hit shutout by Slim Jones, their "lanky portsider speedball artist."[48] Opposing Jones was Satchel Paige, who allowed eight hits but had kept it a 1-0 game through seven innings. That one run scored in the top of the first inning when leadoff batter Paul "Jake" Stephens (who hailed from York) "beat out an infield hit, was advanced by Creacy and scored by Wilson, the colored Babe Ruth, who cracked a single to right." Jones walked three, threw a wild pitch, and saw both Josh Gibson and Judy Johnson steal a base; Paige didn't walk a man or allow any other such misadventures. The Stars' second run came in the top of the eighth when center fielder Pete

Washington "dropped one on the pike for the circuit" and their third run in the ninth when Jud Wilson doubled, followed by Biz Mackey's single. Before his home run, Washington had also doubled. Both pitchers struck out 11 opponents.

"WHAT HAPPENED IN PENNANT RACE? WE GUESS, MAKE YOURS" – HEADLINE, CHICAGO DEFENDER[49]

It is not just later historians who struggled to learn about Negro League baseball in 1934. The *Chicago Defender*, hometown newspaper to the Chicago American Giants, couldn't find out what was happening, either, in the early days of the league. In the May 26 paper, the newspaper wrote, in its entirety, "The *Chicago Defender* is anxious to know what has actually happened in this so-called baseball league. From Pittsburgh comes a wire showing Philadelphia leading with four wins and two loses (sic), Chicago second with five wins and three loses, Crawfords next with four wins and three loses, Nashville trailing with one win in four games played and Newark in the cellar with no wins and three loses. Since there is no report on the Philadelphia-Crawfords games excepting Sunday's postponement we conclude that the Craws whipped the Bolden nine twice while losing one game. The Craws won two games here in Chicago and must not have counted the Nashville series since Nashville is credited with only the three defeats in Chicago and the one victory."

GAMES THAT MAY OR MAY NOT HAVE BEEN PLAYED

Trying to pin down what games the Stars played, or didn't play, is difficult. The *Chicago Defender* clearly found it difficult at the time. Throughout the course of reading through this timeline, one will find any number of games which were apparently planned – sometimes an evening game was announced in that very morning's newspaper – but for which we can find no evidence indicating that the game ever occurred. This could be true for established daily newspapers such as the *Asbury Park Press*, founded in 1879. A substantial five-paragraph article in the issue of September 7, for instance, announced a game for that very evening and provided the location (Memorial Field, Belmar) as well as the time ("promptly at 9 o'clock.")

The article noted the prior matchup between the two ballclubs on July 28, providing some details about the game. (As it happens, the Stars hosted the Chicago American Giants at Passon Field on July 28, sweeping both games. Did they actually play three games that day, two in Philadelphia and one in Belmar? The two communities are about 75 miles apart, making that unlikely.)

The newspaper said the final score was 3-2, with Belmar scoring the tying and go-ahead runs in the ninth inning. The *Press* reported that Ed Bolden had declared that Paul Carter would pitch in the September 7 game. An array of player names for each team fleshed out the article. It was definitely the Philadelphia Stars team.[50]

The day before, the September 6 *Evening Post* of Camden, New Jersey had announced a game for that evening, datelined Woodstown, New Jersey. The game was to be between the local Woodstown Aviators and the Philadelphia Stars, at 8:45, and Aviators manager Hop Gohegan had reportedly "made plans to handle the largest crowd of the years."[51] Was Gohegan and his team standing around with a big crowd on hand awaiting a team that never arrived? Did the game get played, but fail to be reported? We don't know.

How many games did the Philadelphia Stars actually play in 1934? We don't know that, either. Naturally, they played a good number of non-league exhibition games – as both the games against Woodstown and Belmar would have been (and may have been). But one does wonder about the November 7 article in the *Houston Chronicle* announcing a "post-season series" between the Austin Black Senators and the Philadelphia Stars planned for November 10 and 11 at West End Park, Houston. The article declared the Stars as "Negro National League champions" and added, "The Stars compiled a record of 130 victories, 24 defeats and nine ties during the past season."[52] Had they really already played 163 games?

They did play those November games and maybe – or maybe not – another game or two on November 12. See below.

May 24, 1934: Philadelphia Stars 12, Stonehurst Hills 0, at unknown location

Stonehurst is a populated place located within the Township of Upper Darby, a minor civil division (MCD) of Delaware County.

Due to a "last minute change," the May 25 Belmar Braves game planned for Memorial Park in Belmar, New Jersey against the Baltimore Black Sox was changed and the 9:00 P.M. game was to be against the Stars, "weather permitting."[53] Weather apparently did not permit.

May 26, 1934: Homestead Grays 5, Philadelphia Stars 4 (11 innings), at Passon Field, Philadelphia

Rocky Ellis started the game for McDonald and the Stars. He held the Grays scoreless through three innings, while watching his team run up a 3-0 lead off the Grays' Joe Strong with one run in the first and two more in the third. The Grays bounced back with three of their own in the top of the fourth, and took a one-run lead after adding a fourth run in the sixth inning. Center fielder Pete Washington hit a solo home run in the bottom of the sixth and it was tied, 4-4.

When the Grays started to mount a threat in the seventh, McDonald had Lefty Holmes relieve Ellis and the threat was squelched. Neither team scored in the seventh through the 10th, but in the top of the 11th inning, Homestead first baseman Buck Leonard homered off Holmes. The homer held and Homestead won, 5-4.[54]

In other news in the June 2 *Afro-American*, Satchel Paige was reportedly detained by the Chicago police. Under contract to the Crawfords, he was reportedly about to leave for Bismarck, North Dakota. Crawfords owner Greenlee had no comment at the time.[55]

May 27, 1934: Homestead Grays 4, Philadelphia Stars 3 (first game); Philadelphia Stars 4, Homestead Grays 3 (second game), at Passon Field, Philadelphia.

The Grays and Stars split a doubleheader, each team winning by identical 4-3 scores in front of an overflow crowd. Both games were won in the ninth inning. The first game featured Webster McDonald starting for the Stars and Harry Salmon for the Grays. Jake Stephens singled, stole second, was sacrificed to third by Creacy, and came home on Chaney White's infield out. A similar sequence saw the Grays tie it up in the top of the second – a single, stolen base, third base on an error by Stephens, and a sacrifice fly to center by Neil Robinson. The Stars went one up on Casey's single, stolen base, and a following single but the Grays scored twice in the fifth to take a 3-2 lead on a ball hit by Salmon which Washington misplayed in center field. In the eighth, the Stars tied it up again. Stephens laid down a "running bunt" for a single, stole second, and scored on a hit-and-run sacrifice by Creacy. In the top of the ninth, Homestead shortstop Harry Williams doubled. Buck Leonard grounded to Seay. The Grays' "J. Williams" (we're not sure who that was) hit a hard shot to McDonald and the ball caromed off his foot, deflected to Seay, who threw home. Judy Gans was the plate umpire. He called Williams out, but when it was pointed out to him that Casey had dropped the ball, he reversed his decision and the Grays went up by a run, 4-3. An intentional walk and a single put two more on base, but Dunn's throw from right field to the plate erased Williams trying to score on the single. Slim Jones relieved McDonald and struck out the one batter he faced, pinch-hitter Louis Dula. The Stars failed to score, though Holmes – batting for Dunn – led off with a single to left and stole second. Seay rolled one back to Salmon. Biz Mackey pinch-hit but popped up to third baseman Jimmy Binder, and Salmon struck out Jones.[56]

In the second game, Phil Cockrell started for the Stars facing Ray Brown of the Grays. Homestead scored first, a pair of runs in top of the third. The Stars matched that an inning later, in the bottom of the fourth. The Grays edged ahead by one run in the sixth, but Philadelphia promptly matched that in their half of the inning. The score stood 3-3 after seven. Slim Jones had come into the game, relieving in the eighth and struck out six batters. The score stood 3-3 heading into the bottom of the ninth. The first two Philadelphia batters got on, and Jones came up to be and "did a Frank Merriwell and won the game."[57] He hit a tie-breaking, game-winning single.[58]

May 27, 1934: Philadelphia Stars 8, Hightstown 3, at Windsor Airport Field, Trenton, New Jersey

It seems the Stars played three on Sunday the 27th. They played two games in Philadelphia on Sunday the 27th, but the game story appeared in the May 28 *Trenton Evening Times* and referred to the game as "last night." The game between Hightstown nine and Bolden's "All-Stars" had been announced on May 22, for 8:45 PM on Sunday night. Trenton is approximately 30 miles from Philadelphia.

In coverage of the August 23 game between these same two teams, there had been reference to an earlier game and SABR researcher Bob Golon turned up this one.

Paul Carter pitched for the Stars and held Hightstown to five hits and three runs, one in the fourth inning and two in the bottom of the ninth. Though striking out nine times, the Stars had 11 hits, including an eighth-inning home run by Washington and a double by Seay. They also collected six bases on balls. They scored three runs in the third inning and five in the eighth.[59]

DETAILS OF NEGRO LEAGUES GAMES

That more details of Negro Leagues games are not available to historians is due to a number of reasons, some evident on the surface, such as the fact that in catering to, and serving, a minority population, publications were often weekly, limited in advertising dollars, and thus the number of pages and available staff. Some ballclubs were better about documentation than others. Bill Gibson, writing in Baltimore's *Afro-American*, credited Bolden for being one of the better team executives in this regard: "A bouquet of posies to Edward, the Bolden, who, whether his team wins or loses, always has reports of the games of the Philadelphia Stars on the writer's desk each Monday ayem…Stinkweed to those managers who send in reports only when their team wins, and even then, fail to remember that the other team had stars, too." He added, "Stinkweed to the reports who try to palm off week-old-and-more-than-that copy on the press services in the guise of NEWS."[60]

That said, we yet still lack information about many games, even of the Stars, because newspapers didn't always devote the space and because there was perhaps no other adequate repository (a league office, local libraries, etc.) that preserved the data.

May 30, 1934: Pittsburgh Crawfords 3, Philadelphia Stars 0 (first game); Pittsburgh Crawfords 3, Philadelphia Stars 2 (second game), at Passon Field

An "overflow crowd" attended what was described as a morning game and an afternoon game. The Crawfords came out on top in both. They shut out the Stars in the morning, with William Bell holding the Stars to just three hits – one apiece by Seay, White, and Wilson. Slim Jones was touched for nine base hits, and three runs – two in the fourth and another in the sixth.[61]

The Craws got to Lefty Holmes in the second game for two runs in the top of the first. He walked Cool Papa Bell, induced Vic Harris to hit one back to him, but then saw Oscar Charleston double, scoring Bell. On the very next pitch, Charleston stole home, sliding under Mickey Casey's tag. In the sixth inning, the Craws got their third run when Chester Williams drew a base on balls, stole second base, and then scored on a single by shortstop Leroy Morney.[62]

On June 1, there was to have been a game against the Belmar Braves at Memorial Park, perhaps a makeup of the game planned for May 25. This game, however, may have been canceled.[63]

June 2, 1934: Chicago American Giants 11, Philadelphia Stars 2 (first game), Chicago American Giants 6, Philadelphia Stars 2 (second game), at Passon Field

The Chicago American Giants dislodged the Stars from first place on Saturday, June 2. At least 5,000 fans "packed every inch of space" at Passon Field.[64] The first game saw Phil Cockrell oppose Chicago's Willie Foster (Rube Foster's brother.) Foster gave up seven scattered base hits. Cockrell was hit harder – Chicago shortstop Willie Wells alone collected five hits (a triple, two doubles, and two singles).

In the second game, Paul Carter started for Philadelphia but was knocked out in the third inning, scoring five runs in that frame alone. The big hit of the inning came when Turkey Stearnes hit a "boundary belt" with two mates aboard. Webster McDonald relieved Carter and didn't allow another run, but the Stars were once more limited to two runs.

June 3, 1934: Meadowbrook Club 15, Philadelphia Stars 14 (first game); Philadelphia Stars 7, Meadowbrook Club 6 (second game, seven innings), at Newark. New Jersey

After being swept in back-to-back doubleheaders by league rivals Pittsburgh and Chicago, it was perhaps a bit humiliating to score 14 runs against a local team at Newark – but lose. They won the second game against the Meadowbrook Club, but then only barely, by one run.

The first game saw each team produce 17 base hits. Leadoff batter Jake Stephens reached base six times in six plate appearance – a double, three singles, and two bases on balls. Dick Seay homered and so did Dewey Creacy. A former infielder of the Philadelphia Phillies, named in the *Tribune* as Carl Knothe, homered twice in the first game.[65] The Stars scored three runs in the eighth and three more in the ninth, taking a 14-11 lead, only to see Meadowbrook come back with four runs in the bottom of the ninth. It appears as though Jones, Ellis, and Carter all pitched in the game.

In the second game, the Stars scored twice in the first inning, only to see Meadowbrook score three times in the bottom of the first. A five-run fifth which featured home runs by Pete Washington, Chaney

White, and Dick Seay gave Philadelphia the lead. Meadowbrook got two in the sixth and one more in the final seventh inning. coming up just one run short. Holmes and Jones pitched for the Stars.

June 5, 1934: Philadelphia Stars 6, Chicago American Giants 2, at Passon Field

One of the reasons the Stars may have underperformed in the doubleheader sweeps by the Pittsburgh and Chicago was a mention of "Seay, Creacy, and Wilson, the injured members of the Stars" during coverage of this June 5 night game which drew 3,000. They were said to be "back in form and cavorting about the diamond as good as new."[66] Lefty Jones walked four Giants, but allowed them only three hits. They scored one run in the second and one in the sixth. For Philadelphia, Jud Wilson had three base hits all by himself. His teammates collected five more hits. Facing Willie Cornelius, the Stars scored one in the first and three more in the fourth, Ted Trent relieving Cornelius in the fourth. The Stars added single runs in the sixth and eighth.[67]

June 8, 1934: Philadelphia Stars 9, Passons 1, at Passon Field

The Stars took on the semipro Passons in a Friday night game. It was only the second loss of the season for the strong Passons squad, a White team, but Holmes struck out 13 of them and allowed just five hits. The Stars assembled five hits and a walk in the third inning, scoring six runs. Chaney homered and they added another pair in the fourth. He also had a double and single, among the Stars' 10 hits.[68]

June 9, 1934: Philadelphia Stars 5, Nashville Elite Giants 1 (first game); Philadelphia Stars 3, Nashville Elite Giants 0 (second game), at Passon Field

The teams played two nine-inning games, with the Stars winning them both and thereby moving in to second place in NNL standings. Slim Jones struck out 10 and allowed but six hits in the first game. He had two base hits himself, as did Dunn, between them accounting for four of the Stars' eight hits. The Philadelphians scored one in the second inning and two in the third, then (after Nashville got its lone run in the top of the eighth) added two more insurance runs.[69]

Rocky Ellis pitched the second game, holding Nashville to four hits. The Stars scored twice in the first inning when Stephens and Creacy singled off Jim Willis, both tagging and moving up a base on Chaney White's deep fly to right field. Jud Wilson singled to drive both in. White singled and Mickey Casey doubled in the sixth for the other Stars run.[70]

June 10, 1934: Pittsburgh Crawfords 12, Philadelphia Stars 4, at Griffith Stadium, Washington D.C.

It was "one monstrous rally" that made the difference in this game – the Crawfords scored 10 runs in the sixth inning. Phil Cockrell had started for the Stars, but after five innings and with a 3-1 lead, he was replaced by Lefty Holmes. Holmes didn't have it.

Leadoff batter Jake Stephens walked to kick off the game, advanced to second on a single by Dewey Creacy, and scored while the Crawfords were pulling off a double play on a grounder hit by Chaney White. The Stars got two more in the of the third when Cockrell tripled. He scored when Stephens hit a ball that was too hot for shortstop Chester Williams. Stephens then stole second when White hit another ball to Williams, resulted in another error. The Craws got one run in the third and one in the fourth, but blew the game open in the sixth. After Holmes had let in the first four, Paul Carter took over with two runners on base. They scored and before the inning was over, 10 runs in all had come across.[71] The Stars did assemble 12 base hits (Casey, Washington, and Seay each singled for one more in the eighth), and Jud Wilson had three of them, but they came up eight runs short.

June 11, 1934: Philadelphia Stars 1, Pittsburgh Crawfords 0, at Island Park, Harrisburg, Pennsylvania

The two teams matched up again on Monday, in Harrisburg in a game dubbed "one of the classiest baseball games ever staged in this city."[72] It was an NNL game that drew 800 to Island Park. Slim Jones was pitching for the Stars and allowed just one run – a fifth-inning leadoff home run by left fielder Vic Harris "parked...over the right-field fence." Two singles followed, but no more scoring. Each team was held to six hits. The Crawfords' Sam Streeter won a 1-0 shutout. Rocky Ellis worked the final three innings for the Stars. The play of the game was made by Dick Seay, who robbed Oscar Charleston of a base hit in the eighth inning, a "sizzler," when "Seary (sic) sprinted over near second base and made a seemingly impossible backhand stop and tossed Oscar out at first.

The play drew a tremendous ovation."[73] The paper declared it "about the most sensational stop ever seen in the island."

June 15, 1934: Philadelphia Stars 5, Nashville Elite Giants 4, at Eagle Park, York, Pennsylvania

In a two-sentence story which ran in Baltimore's *Afro-American*, we don't learn the names of the starting pitchers or any details regarding the scoring for this Friday night game, only that the Stars were able to "eke out" a 5-4 win and that "Extra base raps by Jud Wilson, Creasy (sic), and Chaney White in the pinches accounted for the victory in Philadelphia." The game was not played in Philadelphia, as the paper's dateline made clear. It was in York.[74] And the York newspapers shed much more light on the game – though both papers named the Nashville team as the "Colonels."[75]

The pitching matchup was 21-year-old righty Bob Griffith for Nashville and "Sonny" (Lefty) Holmes for the Stars. The Stars only got eight hits off Griffith (two of them by Holmes) while Nashville got 10 (four by Sam Bankhead), but Holmes struck out 15 batters to Griffin's three. The lead see-sawed back and forth, the Stars taking the lead in the first on catcher Mickey Casey's two-run single. Nashville tied it in the third, but Philadelphia struck right back, Casey driving in one more run. Nashville scored twice in the top of the fifth, to take a 4-3 lead. The Stars went ahead for good in the seventh. Holmes "beat out a slow grounder to third and Stevens (sic) bunted through the box and all hands were safe."[76] The two executed a double steal. Holmes scored on Creacy's sacrifice fly to right field and Stephens scored on a passed ball.

June 16, 1934: Homestead Grays 3, Philadelphia Stars 0 (first game); Homestead Grays 7, Philadelphia Stars 4 (second game), at Greenlee Field, Pittsburgh

The Grays swept the Stars again, this time in Pittsburgh in a twi-night doubleheader with a 4:00 PM start. Ted Strong shut out the Stars in the first allowing, only five hits (two by Seay, one of them a

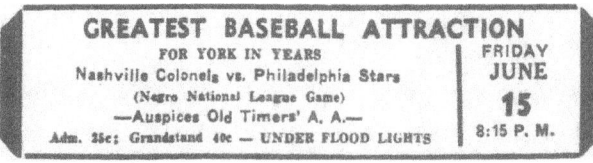

Gazette and Daily *(York, Pennsylvania), June 15, 1934: 10.*

double.) Rocky Ellis pitched for Philadelphia, touched for two runs in the fifth and a third one in bottom of the seventh. Ellis walked a couple of batters and struck out three. Strong struck out six and seems to have walked no one. Only a line score has been found for the second game. It shows someone named Brown pitching for the Grays and Paul Carter pitching for the Stars. The Grays scored two runs in the bottom of the first. After Philadelphia scored once in the top of the sixth, the Grays responded with a five-run bottom of the sixth, which put the game away.[77]

June 17, 1934: Philadelphia Stars 7, Cleveland Red Sox 2 (first game); Philadelphia Stars 1, Cleveland Red Sox 0 (second game), at League Park, Cleveland

The Sunday doubleheader drew only 2,000 ("one of the smallest crowds ever seen at League Park," per the *Courier*), "But the attendance was soon forgotten as thrilling plays were executed. Hard hit balls, difficult catches, accurate throws and close plays were all rewarded with applause through the stands."[78] All nice, but no details were reported in the newspaper. Fortunately, the *Chicago Defender* provided a couple of boxscores and four sentences. Oddly, one of the sentences said "Both of the Red Sox hurlers did brilliant work" but added that the Stars were "too great for them" and had "hammered" them for 21 base hits – 12 in the first game and nine in the second game.[79]

The first game saw right-hander Holsey Scranton Scriptus "Script" Lee pitch against Slim Jones. The Stars got single runs in the second and third, and then had a big four-run fifth. Cleveland scored one in the bottom of the fifth and another in the seventh – after Philadelphia had added a seventh run. Biz Mackey had a single, a double, and a home run over the right-field wall. He had two RBIs. Jones allowed four hits, two singles and two doubles, and he struck out 10.

The second game ran the full nine innings, in a time of 1:40. Webster McDonald allowed Cleveland just four hits. Bill Byrd allowed nine, but just the one run in the top of the seventh, driven in by Jud Wilson with one of his two hits.

June 18, 1934 – a planned game between the Stars and the Cleveland Red Sox at League Park in Akron, Ohio, was called off due to wet rounds.[80]

STANDINGS

The *Afro-American* ran league standings in the June 23 paper, up to but not including games on June 18. They read:

Chicago American Giants	10	5	.666
Pittsburgh Crawfords	13	8	.619
Newark Dodgers	6	5	.545
Nashville Elite Giants	8	8	.500
Philadelphia Stars	8	9	.470
Cleveland Red Sox	2	13	.133

There was commentary suggesting that "the dopesters" believed Chicago had the best chance to cop first-half honors. That didn't look too difficult to guess. Of the Stars, the paper said, "The Philadelphia Stars are too deep in the cellar to make the landing – their remaining games being with Nashville and Cleveland."[81]

June 23, 1934: Philadelphia Stars 1, Cleveland Red Sox 0 (first game); Philadelphia Stars 11, Cleveland Red Sox 3 (second game), at Passon Field

The first game was a rematch of the Slim Jones vs. Script Lee game on June 17, but one in which both pitchers excelled. Neither allowed a run through the first eight innings. Both pitchers allowed four base hits. Biz Mackey was superb behind the plate, throwing out four Red Sox baserunners. The only run of the game came with one out in the bottom of the ninth. Jud Wilson walked, then stole second while pinch-hitter Mickey Casey came in to hit for Jake Dunn. Casey was walked intentionally. Pete Washington hit the second pitch he saw down the third-base line, scoring Wilson and winning the game.[82]

The second game saw Webster McDonald start for the Stars and Johnnie Bob Dixon for Cleveland. The Stars scored two in the third inning and one in the fourth, but then Dixon "blew up" in the sixth inning, loading the bases and then giving up a grand slam

PHILLY STARS EXTEND STREAK

Afro-American, *June 23, 1934: 18.*

to Chaney White.[83] The drive cleared the center-field fence. Left-hander Sleeky Reese relieved. He gave up three runs in the eighth inning. The Stars led 11-0 after eight innings, but the chance of back-to-back shutouts went by the boards when Cleveland put three runs across in the top of the ninth.

June 24, 1934: Philadelphia Stars 2, Cleveland Red Sox 1 (first game); Philadelphia Stars 9, Cleveland Red Sox 0 (second game), at Passon Field

Back-to-back doubleheader sweeps of Cleveland "boosted the City of Brotherly Love team into second place in the National League," wrote Chester Washington.[84] The first game featured Rocky Ellis allowing six base hits, the same number allowed by Bill Byrd. The Stars scored once in the second and once in the third, the Red Sox only scored once, in the top of the eighth.

The second game pitted Lefty Holmes against Cleveland's Sleeky Reese. Holmes shut out the Red Sox, touched up for only two base hits. Reese was relieved by Roy Roberts, the two combining to grant 15 base hits. Stephens, White, and Wilson all had three-hit games. Holmes had two hits himself, as did Washington. The Stars scored once in the third, once in the fourth, and five times in the sixth. They added a final two runs in the eighth. The *Chicago Defender* said the wins put the Stars in second place.[85]

June 25, 1934: Philadelphia Stars 16, Germantown Artisans 6, at 18th and Olney Avenue, Philadelphia

A pitcher named Richardson started for the Stars and immediately got whacked for four runs, thanks to a grand slam by Germantown catcher Joe Brown. The Stars got one back in the first and two more in the second, but when the Artisans (a White team) began to produce once more in the third inning, Phil Cockrell relieved Richardson. The Artisans failed to score again. The Stars piled up the runs, scoring three in the third, two in the fifth, three in the sixth, and five in the seventh. Creacy, Casey, and Dunn each had four hits. The game was halted after eight innings.[86]

June 26, 1934: Philadelphia Stars 6, Scanlon C. C. 4, at Jackson and Sanger Streets, Philadelphia

Paul Carter pitched and Mickey Casey caught in a game that drew 3,000 – a reminder at how important

these non-league games could be to team finances. It was a good game, too, error free for both teams and only resolved in the later innings. Scanlon actually outhit the Stars by a significant margin, 12-7, but Carter threw a considerable number of strikeouts, perhaps as many as 12 (the number of putouts accorded Casey.) The Stars scored twice in the first, but Scanlon matched that in the bottom of the second. Neither team scored for the next four innings. The Stars took a 3-2 lead in the top of the seventh, added two more in the eighth, and then a sixth run in the top of the ninth. Scanlon got a pair of runs in the bottom of the ninth, but came up two runs short.[87]

June 27, 1934: Philadelphia Stars 9, Stonehurst A.A. 7

Where this game was played is unclear. The score was provided in the July 7 *Afro-American*, along with information that it was called before the full nine innings because of darkness.[88]

See also May 24 for another Stonehurst Hills game

June 28, 1934: Philadelphia Stars 1, New York Black Yankees 0, at Passon Field

The Thursday night game was a pitchers' duel between Slim Jones for the Stars and Bill Holland for the New York Black Yankees. Jones gave up but four base hits, Holland only three. Neither team scored a run for the first six innings of the game, played before "one of the largest crowds ever to witness a night game" at the park. In the bottom of the seventh, Chaney White led off with a double to right-center field. Manager George Scales had Holland intentionally walk Jud Wilson. Casey hit the ball and Wilson was forced at second base, but Chaney tore around third base and streaked for home, sliding in safely with what proved to the only run of the game.[89]

June 30, 1934: Philadelphia Stars 6, Homestead Grays 2 (first game); Philadelphia Stars 1, Homestead Grays (tie, second game), at Passon Field

Webster McDonald pitched the first game on Saturday, giving up nine hits but just two runs – one each in the eighth and ninth. The Stars had just one more hit, but scored twice in the first inning, once in the third, and three times in the fifth. Two of the fifth-inning runs came on Jud Wilson's two-run homer with Creacy aboard. John Strong started for the Grays, relieved by James Evans, who was in turn relieved by

Philadelphia All-Stars Win Four

CAPTURE A PAIR TWIN BILLS AND TAKE 2D PLACE

Chicago Defender, *June 30, 1934: 16.*

George Cheatham. This was a pitching staff working under strain of overuse. They were said to be "shot."[90]

The second game pitted Lefty Holmes against Louis Dula, who was apparently not one of the pitchers that had been overworked. Both pitched well, Dula giving up eight hits but just one sixth-inning run. The Grays scored first, one run off in the fourth inning, but Holmes only allowed three hits in the game. The score was 1-1 after nine innings, but did not go into extra innings "because of Homestead's evening engagement with another team."[91] The Grays had planned a night game in Phillipsburg.[92]

At the end of the month, Dan Burley of the *Atlanta Daily World* offered his selections for an all-star baseball team, with up to two players from each team. The only one of the Philadelphia Stars among the 20 players listed was Dewey Creacy at third base. Pittsburgh's Judy Johnson was the other third baseman named.[93]

As July began, the *Philadelphia Tribune* ran an article explaining that Negro National Association membership would expand from six teams to eight for the second of the league season. The Philadelphia Bacharach Giants, owned by Harry Passon, had been "associate members" but "asked for and was given full membership."[94] Likewise, the Baltimore Black Sox were added as a full member. The Homestead Grays remained an associate member. Grays owner, Cum Posey, had not applied for full membership, "content to fill in his independent schedule with league games." Posey had kept his team busy. A report in the July 7 *Courier* said that "the club has played over 70 games already and looks it. Even the uniforms have suffered."[95]

Boxing promoter Jack Farrell was the owner of the Baltimore team and he hired Rap Dixon as manager. The team was to have as its nucleus players from the Washington Pilots and were to play their first game on July 8 against Nashville.[96]

The second-half schedule was adopted.[97]

July 1, 1934: Philadelphia Stars 10, Homestead Grays 9, at Passon Field

Back from their "evening engagement," the Grays played their fourth game in two days. Rocky Ellis started for the Stars. He was hammered for four runs in the top of the first. The Grays got two more runs in the second inning. Webster McDonald relieved Ellis at some point and Slim Jones pitched as well. The Stars battled back, again facing Strong, who had been knocked out of the first game on Saturday. They scored two runs in the second inning, one in the third, two more in the fourth on a homer by Creacy, and then took an 8-6 lead with three runs in the fifth. Dula took over for Strong.

The Grays tied the game, with two runs in the top of the ninth on a home run by right fielder Jim Williams. This game did go into extra innings, and Homestead scored a go-ahead run in the 10th, taking a 9-8 lead despite giving up one out when Tex Burnett having batted out of order. The run came in when catcher Casey fired a high pickoff throw to Seay at second base and baserunner Jimmy Binder scored on the error. Lefty Williams took over from Dula, but the Stars got singles from Wilson and Casey, watched two fly balls go for out, but then Jake Dunn won the game with a two-run triple.[98]

There were two games planned but the first game took more than three hours to play, and with a 6:00 curfew, it seemed unlikely to get even in the minimum five innings so the second game was scrubbed.

July 2, 1934: Bartram 11, Philadelphia Stars 10, at 65th and Dicks Avenue, Philadelphia

The local Bartram team from the Philadelphia League attracted 3,500 to a game at the ballpark at 65th and Dicks, beating Bolden's Stars, 11-10, in an eight-inning game, even though the Stars out-hit Bartram, 16 hits to 13. Each team used three pitchers. The Stars employed a man named Coleman –first name unknown, perhaps a pitcher loaned them – and then Paul Carter and Slim Jones. The Stars held a 3-1 lead after two innings, but saw Bartram score four in the fourth, two in the sixth on center fielder Jimmy Brown's two-run homer, and four in the seventh. They tried to recover, with a five-run seventh inning and two more in the eighth, but came up one run short in the eight-inning game.[99]

SECOND HALF OF THE 1934 SEASON

The first half of the season ended with the Chicago American Giants in first place, with the Pittsburgh Crawfords in second place, and the Philadelphia Stars just one game behind the Crawfords. Newark was 6-5, in fourth place. Every club in the league – Chicago,

Pittsburgh, Philadelphia, Newark, Cleveland, and Nashville – "surpassed all attendance records for the past two years."[100]

Dan Burley offered some outspoken criticism of the league. "What we can't understand," he wrote, "is how Newark and the Philadelphia Stars could be members of a league, when they never came West to play. Why did the Crawfords and the American Giants hog the spotlight on the Giant's schedule here in Chicago? Why didn't the fans get a chance to see Newark and the Stars in the supposed to be 'first half'?"[101] Rather than a balanced schedule, he said the whole thing seemed to be a series of "gentlemen's agreements" that maximized short-term profit at the expense of building a true league.

A SCHEDULING DEBACLE

Though Baltimore had been granted full membership, the Stars never played in Baltimore in 1934. There was a game announced for July 15, the Stars against Baltimore at Bugle Field. Ed Bolden had been against the Black Sox being admitted, because he didn't think the city would be a good enough one for league baseball. Rap Dixon, Black Sox manager, said that William Force had booked the game "without the knowledge of the management of the Black Sox." There was some financial advantage to Force, and to Bugle Field's owner, Joe Cambria. But the Black Sox management canceled the announced game and instead played the Crawfords at Harrisburg.[102]

July 4, 1934: Philadelphia Stars 7, Nashville Elite Giants 1 (first game); Philadelphia Stars 9, Nashville Elite Giants 2 (second game), at Passon Field

"A pair of easy wins," wrote the *Chicago Defender*.[103] Rocky Ellis threw a five-hitter in the morning game, allowing just one run in the top of the first inning and no more. The Stars scored twice in the bottom of the first and never looked back. They added another run in the fifth, one more in the sixth, and three in the eighth. Every batter in the Stars lineup had at least one hit; Washington and Seay had two.

In the afternoon game, the only two Stars who did not get hits were Washington and Seay, but when Seay came up with the bases loaded in the fourth, he drew a walk to earn himself a run batted in. Pitcher Slim Jones drew a walk, too, and Stephens hit a sacrifice fly to right field. The three runs gave Philadelphia a 4-0 lead. After Nashville scored once in the top of the

fifth, the Stars responded with three more runs in the fifth and two in the sixth, putting the game well out of sight.

July 5, 1934: Philadelphia Stars 1, New York Black Yankees 0, at Passon Field

This was not only a low-scoring error-free one-run night game, but there were only seven hits in the game, three by the Stars (two by Chaney White and one by Slim Jones) and four by the Black Yankees (two each by right fielder Clyde Spearman and first baseman Dave Thomas). The lone run scored off New York pitcher Bill Holland in the bottom of the seventh. White led off with a double to right-center field. Jud Wilson was walked intentionally. Mickey Casey had apparently come into the game for Mackey at some point, and he hit into a force play, Wilson out at second base – but White managed to run all the way from second and score, sliding into home plate.[104]

July 6, 1934: Philadelphia Stars 6, Mitchell A.A. 2, at 24th and Passayunk Avenue, Philadelphia (afternoon game)

The Stars played two games against amateur or local semipro clubs on July 6, a day game against Mitchell A. A. Pitching for the Stars were two men named Blackwell and Irons, perhaps loaned them by the other team. Between them, they only allowed seven hits and two first-inning runs. The Stars scored twice in the first twice, in the third, and twice in the fifth. The game lasted eight innings.[105] Irons appears to have been named Cliff Irons, as there is a reference to him in the July 19 *Tribune*.[106]

July 6, 1934: Passon 5, Philadelphia Stars 2, location unknown (evening game)

In a game played under the lights, Cockrell was hit for five runs – two in the fourth and three in the sixth. McDonald relieved him in the seventh, after Aneal Brooks (who had recently come over from Cleveland) had pinch-hit in vain. Each team had nine hits. Passon was the home team and the *Tribune* said the "store-boys' hurlers proved the undoing" of the Stars.[107]

July 7, 1934: New York Black Yankees 7, Philadelphia Stars 3, at Hinchliffe Stadium, Paterson, New Jersey

The pitchers were left-hander Neck Stanley of the New York Black Yankees against Webster McDonald of the Philadelphia Stars. In the top of the first, the

Philly Stars Take Two From Grays

Afro-American, *July 7, 1934: 16.*

Stars put two on the board. Jake Stephens walked, moved to second on Creacy's single, and scored on White's single. Wilson walked and the bases were loaded and still no one out. Aneal Brooks hit an in-field roller for an out, but Creacy scored from third. Stanley buckled down and struck out Dunn, then got Washington to ground out. The Stars scored only once more, one run in the eighth. White singled, Brooks doubled, White stopping at third – but then scoring on a passed ball.

Third baseman John Beckwith was the star of the game for the Black Yankees. With the score still 2-0, Stars, the New Yorkers scored five runs in the bottom of the fourth. Their first hit of the game off McDonald was a single by Clint Thomas. Walter Cannady's hit-and-run single resulted in men on first and third. Beckwith doubled to left-center, driving in one. Dave Thomas drove in two with a double of his own. Then George Scales doubled and Bill Yancey singled. There were six successive hits before the first out was record, the first run coming in on Stanley's groundout. Beckwith hit solo home runs to left-center in the fifth and the eighth.[108]

July 1, 1934: Bartram 11, Philadelphia Stars 10, location unknown

Pitching for the Stars, though perhaps not trying their hardest, were Coleman, Carter, and Jones. Who Coleman might have been is unknown, perhaps another pitcher loaned them. The Stars held a 3-1 lead after two innings, but saw Bartram score four in the fourth, two in the sixth, and four in the seventh. They tried to recover, with a five-run seventh inning and two more in the eighth, but came up one run short in the eight-inning game. [109]

July 9, 1934: Philadelphia Stars 15, Newark Dodgers 4, at General Electric Field, Bloomfield, New Jersey

In a seven-inning twilight game at the Newark Dodgers' home park – often known as Sprague Field – the Stars bludgeoned the Dodgers, 15-4. The first blow was Jud Wilson's three-run homer in the top of the first inning. Pete Washington also homered, later in the game.

Rocky Ellis pitched for Philadelphia, allowing the four runs on six hits – one run in the first, one in the fourth, and two in the sixth on a homer by Newark catcher John Hayes.

The Stars added two more in their half of the fourth, three in the fifth, and seven runs in the top of the seventh. Every batter in their lineup got at least one hit, and catcher Ameal Brooks let the parade with three. The Dodgers used three pitchers – George Britt lasted five, relieved by Ray Clark and then Bob Evans.[110]

July 10, 1934: Philadelphia Stars 4, Pittsburgh Crawfords 3 (first game); Philadelphia All-Stars 7, Philadelphia Stars 4 (second game, seven innings), at Baker Bowl, Philadelphia

The team played two games on July 10. The first game was, according to the July 12 *Philadelphia Tribune*, played "at the Phillies field."[111] "Johnson" won the game for the Stars. Who was Johnson? No other details about the game were available. Fortunately, the *Inquirer* elected to report on the game, and it turns out the Stars pitcher was Slim Jones. We learn that the Stars booked 12 hits to nine for the Craws, who started Sam Streeter with Bret Hunter taking over. Both teams scored a run in the first and both teams scored a run in the fifth. The difference in the game had come in the third inning, when Pittsburgh scored one but Philadelphia scored two. Jake Stephens was 4-for-4 in the game, all singles. Dewey Creacy had a three-hit game, and Jud Wilson has two hits. Jesse Williams had three of the nine Crawfords hits.[112]

The second game was Stars vs. Stars – the Philadelphia Stars vs. the Philadelphia All-Stars, described as "a picked aggregation of All-Stars selected from the premier white teams of the city."[113] The *Tribune* said "Holmes and McDonald were unable to hold back the All-Star barrage."[114] The All-Stars, drawn from various teams in the Philadelphia League, included four different pitchers, three of them from Wentz-Olney, and outfielder Wes Slater from Nicetown, who was leading that league in hitting. The All-Stars only had four more hits, 12-8 in number, but they played error-free while the NNL team committed three. The All-Stars scored three runs in the top of the first and four more in the third inning. The Stars got two in the third and their other two in the seventh.[115]

July 12, 1934: Pittsburgh Crawfords 7, Philadelphia Stars 4 (first game); Philadelphia

Stars 7, Pittsburgh Crawfords 6 (second game), at Eagle Park, York, Pennsylvania

The pair of night games drew 1,500. The first game was tied 3-3 after five innings. The Crawfords scored once in the first, while the Stars had made their three runs in the top of the third. Pittsburgh evened it up, scoring once in the fourth, and once in the fifth. In the bottom of the sixth, they put the game away with four runs off Lefty Holmes. Winning pitcher for Pittsburgh was Harry Kincannon. After the third inning, he pitched hitless baseball until the ninth, when Philadelphia made one more run.

The Stars outhit the Craws, 11-10, in the second game. Both Chaney White and Jake Dunn had three-hit games. It was a bit of a see-saw game. The Stars took a 1-0 lead in the second. Tied 1-1 after the third, the Stars scored three runs in the top of the fourth. The Crawfords responded with two. With a run in the fifth, Philadelphia took a 5-3 lead, but Pittsburgh scored three and took a 6-5 edge. The Stars tied it with one in the seventh and took a 7-6 lead in the eighth. Neither team scored in the ninth.

The field may have been a rough one. There were a lot of errors in the games: the stars committed four in the first game and two in the second, while the Crawfords made three and four, respectively.[116]

July 13, 1934: Philadelphia Stars 4, Kearney Lumber 2, at unknown location

Cliff Irons appears again, one week later to the day, pitching a Friday game against Kearney Lumber. The game was evidently a financial success, drawing a reported 2,000.[117]

July 14, 1934: Philadelphia Stars 2, Pittsburgh Crawfords 1 (first game); Philadelphia Stars 9, Pittsburgh Crawfords 4 (second game), at Passon Field

The first game was "a humdinger, a regular pitchers' battle."[118] The game pitted Satchel Paige against Webster McDonald.[119] Both pitchers were perfect through three innings. It was scoreless through four, but the Stars took a 1-0 lead when Casey led off the fifth with a double to right field and was knocked in on Dunn's double to the wall in right that followed. The Crawfords lost an opportunity in the sixth when Paige hit a high bounding ball back toward McDonald. It hopped over his head and Seay was unable to get a grip on it. Rollo Wilson asked, "Meanwhile, where was Paige?" He hadn't run and had walked back

toward the bench. Manager Oscar Charleston was "disgusted" and angry enough that he pulled Paige and had Harry Kincannon pitch the rest of the game.

The Crawfords tied it in the eighth. Judy Johnson singled. Vic Harris singled and Johnson raced to third, but Harris got erased in a rundown between first and second. Chester Williams hit a ball hard, which deflected off Creacy at third base to Stephens at short in time to throw out Williams, but Johnson managed to score when Casey dropped the throw to the plate from first baseman Wilson. In the ninth inning, Chaney White doubled to left field. Two walks followed, Wilson and Dunn getting free passes to load the bases. Lefty Holmes pinch-hit for Pete Washington and hit a fly ball deep enough to left field to enable White to tag and score the winning run on a very close play.

The second game was a "corking" game, too, said the *Tribune*. In the *Courier*, Rollo Wilson said that it was "loosely played" and that the Crawfords had adopted "a beaten attitude almost from the first." Slim Jones and William Bell were the pitchers. Ameal Brooks caught his first game for the Stars, and was the star on offense with a three-run homer in the third that went "into 48th Street" and an RBI double in the seventh.[120]

July 15, 1934: Philadelphia Stars 4, Pittsburgh Crawfords 2 (first game); Philadelphia Stars 1, Pittsburgh Crawfords 0 (second game, 5 innings), at Island Park, Harrisburg, Pennsylvania

The first game of this Sunday doubleheader pitted Pittsburgh's Bert Hunter against Philadelphia's Paul Carter. The game was in Harrisburg, and considered a home game for the Crawfords. The Stars got one run in the first, surrendered two in the fifth, then re-took the lead for good with three runs in the top of the eighth. The Crawfords got 10 hits (four by Cool Papa Bell) to the Stars' seven.[121] Some 2,800 reportedly took in the games.

The Star scored first on Jud Wilson's first-inning sacrifice fly after Stephens walked and White singled. In the fifth, Carter gave up singles to Hunter and Cool Papa Bell. They both advanced 90 feet on a groundout, and then both scored on Oscar Charleston's double down the right-field line. In the top of the eight, the Stars got three runs on one hit. Wilson walked. Casey doubled. Dunn grounded to second base, but the throw

PHILLY STARS BEAT CRAWS, TAKE LEAGUE LEAD

Pittsburgh Courier, *July 21, 1934: A4.*

was to the plate and it went wild, with both baserunners scoring. Dunn took second. Washington reached on catcher Josh Gibson's error, Dunn going to third, from where he scored on a wild pitch.[122]

Satchel Paige pitched for the Crawfords in the second game, and "Ducky" Holmes for the Stars. Paige had trouble with the Stars; he had pitched eight games against them in 1933 and to this point in 1934 and not won any of them. Paige pitched well, only allowing three hits. Holmes allowed two through the first five innings. The Stars scored once in the first inning when Chaney White singled and Jud Wilson doubled. That was the only run either team scored for five innings. This game was, it seems, deemed a home game for Philadelphia.

The *Pittsburgh Courier* and Baltimore's *Afro-American* report different scores for the second game. The *Courier* said it was a 1-1 deadlock, and that it had been 1-0 through five. In the top of the sixth, Charleston tripled off Holmes and then a pinch-runner, Crutchfield, scored on a wild pitch. The game was called after the conclusion of the sixth, due to the Sunday 6 PM curfew law.[123] The "special to the AFRO" noted Charleston's triple and the wild pitch, but clearly stated that the sixth inning had not been completed and thus "the score reverted to the fifth inning."[124] The *Afro-American* account provides far more details, and lacks the internal inconsistency of the *Courier* boxscore and thus appears more credible. The *Tribune*, however, showed it as a 1-1 tie, agreed on the curfew, in the text and boxscore, with the Crawfords scoring in the sixth.[125]

July 16: There was a game advertised for the Stadium in Hagerstown, Maryland on Monday night, July 16, between the Pittsburgh Crawfords and the Philadelphia Stars, but there is no indication the game was ever played.[126]

July 18, 1934: Philadelphia Stars 6, Hightstown 2, at Windsor Airport Field, Hightstown, New Jersey

The game was reported in the July 26 issue of the *Tribune*. All it said was that the Stars had traveled to Hightstown and that "a barrage of singles in the seventh did the trick."[127] Fortunately, the *Trenton Evening Times* covered the game. Slim Jones pitched for the Stars, while Jack Barlow's semipro Hightstown club had Eddie Lautenbacher and Joe Stryker in relief after the seventh. Hightstown took a 2-0 lead in the bottom of the first. The "crack colored combine" (the Stars)

didn't score for the first six innings, but they scored four times in the seventh and twice more in the top of the ninth. Jones struck out 10 and walked three. The "sepia stars" prevailed, 6-2.[128]

July 19, 1934: Philadelphia Stars 6, South Phillies 6 (tie), at 12th and Bigler, Philadelphia

Granville Lyons "playing his first game for the Bolden team, broke his leg sliding in to third base." The article's subhead said that Lyons was "newly from Nashville." He had been with the Elite Giants earlier in 1934. Carter took over pitching for the Stars. [129]

July 20, 1934 (day): Philadelphia Stars 7, Kensington 3, at Passon Field (likely)

Carter pitched again. Both he and Seay "collected two runs each."[130]

July 20, 1934 (evening): Philadelphia Stars 8, Passons 1, at Passon Field

We think the score was 8-1. The brief note in the *Tribune* actually said that they "demolished the store boys with 12 base blows, scoring 8 hits to Passon's 1."[131] That sounds like 12 hits and eight runs, but we can't be sure. McDonald was the winning pitcher.

July 22, 1934: Philadelphia Stars 3, New York Black Yankees 2 (first game); New York Black Yankees 7, Philadelphia Stars 1 (second game), at Passon Field

The games were played before what the *Tribune* said was the largest crowd of the season to date. Slim Jones dominated in the first game, allowing but four hits. Frank Blake pitched for New York and allowed just six. Both teams scored one run in the first inning. The two runs that made the difference came in the bottom of the fourth. Jake Dunn singled. He took second on Washington's groundout, third to first. Jake Stephens singled and drove in Dunn. He advanced somehow – it's unclear how – and scored when the next batter, Jones, executed a hit-and-run. The Black Yankees got another run in the top of the fifth but that was the last run either team scored.

Ellis pitched the second game for the Stars but he was out-pitched by Neck Stanley, who limited Philadelphia to just four hits. New York got nine. They scored two in the second, three, in the third, and two more in the seventh. Shortstop Bill Yancey hit a two-run homer.[132] The game was called in the eighth due to the Sunday curfew.

Over the course of the four games, each pitcher got one base hit.[133]

July 23, 1934: Philadelphia Stars 13, Homestead Grays 3, at Passon Field

The big hit of the game was a seventh-inning grand slam by Jud Wilson, hit over the center-field fence. Webster McDonald struck out 11. The game was called after eight innings because of an 11:15 P.M curfew.[134] Pitching for Homestead was Ray Brown.[135]

The July 26 *Tribune* foreshadowed a five-game series between the Bacharach Giants and the Philly Stars to begin on the 29th for the "city championship." Both teams used Passon Field as their home park.[136]

July 26, 1934: Philadelphia Stars 3, Nicetown 3 (tie, eight innings), at 12th and Luzerne Streets

A pitcher named Walsh did a good job for Nicetown while the Stars used three pitchers in the game: Holmes, Jones, and Ellis. The game was called after eight innings due to darkness.[137] Nicetown is a neighborhood in north Philadelphia.

July 28, 1934: Philadelphia Stars 3, Chicago American Giants 2 (first game); Philadelphia Stars 9, Chicago American Giants 3 (second game), at Passon Field.

Philly Stars Snatch Two From Chicago

Afro-American, *August 4, 1934: 18.*

Ace (Ted) Trent only allowed the Stars two hits in Sunday's first game – but one was a two-run homer by Jud Wilson in the bottom of the fourth inning. Chaney White was on base at the time. Pete Washington had the other hit. Stars pitchers McDonald and Jones combined to hold Chicago to two runs on nine hits.

The second game pitted Rocky Ellis against Willie Foster, who was relieved by Percy Bailey. Chicago scored one in the top of the first, but the Stars came back with two and two more in the fourth, and would have scored more but for four double plays, one in each of the first four frames. Philadelphia added one more run in the fifth, and then exploded for four in

the bottom of the eighth. Ellis held the Giants to solo runs in the first, sixth, and eighth. Of the nine Stars hits, two apiece were had by Creacy, White, Dunn, and Miles.[138]

July 29, 1934: Philadelphia Stars 7, Philadelphia Bacharach Giants 0 (first game); Philadelphia Stars 9, Philadelphia Bacharach Giants 7 (second game), at Passon Field

Slim Jones threw a one-hitter in the first game. The only player to get a hit off him was second baseman Obie Lackey, who doubled. Jones struck out nine and only faced two more than the minimum, 29 batters in all.

Luther Farrell, starting for the Bees (the Bacharachs), was knocked out of the box in the very first inning, as the Stars scored four runs. Sonny Collins took his place. That didn't discourage the visitors, however, and they scored four of their own in the top of the second. When it was their turn to bat again, the Stars put up another four in the bottom of the inning. This couldn't go on forever, and didn't. The stars added one in the fifth, the Bees added one in the sixth and then two more in the seventh. Holmes got the win for the Stars.[139]

July 30, 1934: Philadelphia Stars 5, Passon 2, at Passon Field

As a tag on the end of a reasonably detailed story about the July 29 doubleheader, the *Tribune* also reported a game on "Monday night," which would make it July 30. It said that Stars pitcher Webster McDonald "wilted in the late sessions and got kicked for two runs" but the Stars won easily enough, 5-2.[140] The *Philadelphia Inquirer* offered more information, reporting that 2,000 fans turned out for the game, and that the Passon team outhit the Stars, eight hits to seven, and that Passon pitcher Babe Mitchell struck out six while only walking two, but committed three errors. The two teams were tied, 1-1 when, in the top of the sixth, the "rotund first baseman" Jud Wilson "pocked a homeric swat" to right field. The Stars scored two runs and added one more in each of the seventh and eighth innings. Passon's other run came in the bottom of the eighth off the "underhanded star" McDonald.[141]

July 30, 1934: Philadelphia Stars 3, Chester Stars 1, at Sixth and Yarnall, Chester, Pennsylvania

The July 31 *Chester Times* reported another night game on the very same date. It drew as many as 6,000 people, "the largest mob that ever witnessed a game in that vicinity."[142] Bolden's Stars played the Chester Stars, said to be a new assemblage drawn from the best of local semipro ranks. Percy Hall pitched for Chester and Phil Cockrell for the Philadelphia Stars. It was an eight-inning game. The visitors scored one run each in the first, fourth, and sixth innings. Chester scored its lone run in the bottom of the seventh. Philadelphia outhit Chester, nine hits to four. Dick Seay had three of the nine hits. Pete Washington had two, including the only extra-base hit for the visitors.

After a pair of first-inning two-out walks, Jake Dunn singled to right-center. The throw home would have had White out, but pitcher Hall cut off the throw. In the fourth, Washington singled. Seay's bunt was mishandled and both runners were safe, Washington on third, from where he scored on Ameal Brooks's sacrifice fly to center. In the sixth, Washington doubled on a hit to right-center. Seay singled to right and drove him home.

The article concluded that "fielding stole the limelight from hitting and pitching. It was the great play of Stevens, Seay and Cockrell himself, that pulled the veteran out of many tight squeezes."

July 31, 1934: Wentz-Olney 3, Philadelphia Stars 2, at unknown location

Wentz-Olney got a win, after two blowouts losses earlier in 1934. The score was 3-2, and Phil Cockrell was the loser, clearly lacking run support.[143]

August 3, 1934: Philadelphia Stars 9, Kearney Lumber 2, at Passon Field

Holmes pitched this night game. Seay and Washington got two hits and two runs apiece.[144]

August 4, 1934: Philadelphia Stars 19, Baltimore Black Sox 14, at River Field, Chester, Pennsylvania

A Negro National League game played in Chester drew 4,000 and saw 33 runs scored. The "Boldenmen" had 17 base hits and the Black Sox had 16. Paul Carter started for the Stars, but was knocked out in the fourth inning. Phil Cockrell finished. For Baltimore, it was

Philadelphia Stars Win Three, 19-14, 4-2 and 7-3
**Philadelphia Stars
Retain Top Position**

Atlanta Daily World, *August 13, 1934: 5.*

left-hander Melvin "Half Pint" Allen, Bun Hayes, and Bud Mitchell on the mound. Every batter on both teams collected one hit – except for the trio of Baltimore pitchers, none of whom hit safely.

The two big innings for Philadelphia were the first inning, when they scored six runs, and the sixth inning, when they scored eight. Half of the runs scored in the sixth came when Jud Wilson hit a grand slam.[145] The Black Sox had three four-run innings – the third, fourth, and seventh.

August 5, 1934: Philadelphia Stars 4, New York Black Yankees 2 (first game); Philadelphia Stars 7, New York Black Yankees 3 (second game, seven innings), at Passon Field

Slim Jones won the first game, though he gave up 11 base hits to the seven surrendered by New York Black Yankees pitcher Ace Trent. The Stars scored once in the first inning and once in the fourth. The New Yorkers scored a pair in the top of the sixth, tying it up. Jones won the game for himself with his bat, hitting a solo home run over the right-field fence in the bottom of the seventh, and then worked a scoreless eighth and ninth, his teammates adding an insurance run in the bottom of the eighth.[146]

In the second game, Webster McDonald allowed three runs on five hits. Holland and Stanley pitched for New York. Wilson and Brooks both had a two-hit game. Dunn, Washington, and Seay each had one. New York scored all three runs in the top of the second inning, but the Stars immediately one-upped them, with four runs, adding two more in the third and a seventh run in the sixth.[147]

August 6, 1934: Philadelphia Stars 1, Ed Gottlieb's Philadelphia League All Stars 1 (tie), at Passon Field

This Monday night game was something of a rematch of the July 10 game against a picked team of All-Stars. In the third inning, Pete Washington walked, advanced on Seay's single to right. After two outs, he was on third base. Creacy walked. And Washington stole home with the only run of the game through the first eight innings. Ellis pitched for the Stars. A brief rally in the ninth inning resulted in a 1-1 tie.[148]

August 8, 1934: Philadelphia Stars 8, House of David 4, at Phillies Park; House of David 1, Philadelphia Stars 0 ("donkey ball" game, one inning), at Phillies Park

Played under floodlights, the Stars beat the House of David team, with Rocky Ellis pitching. The Stars scored first, two in the second, then saw the House of David tie it with a pair in the fourth. Taking a 4-2 lead, in the sixth, the Stars quickly got one back – and then added five runs in the seventh. Jud Wilson had two hits, one a double. The *Tribune* said that Casey had three hits.[149]

There was also a game of "donkey ball," courtesy of "eleven honest-to-God Texas burros." The spectacle drew 5,000 to Phillies Park. The *Afro-American* described the action: "The Philly Stars, not used to riding the donkeys, had a hard time getting their balky animals started, but the bearded baseballers, more accustomed to the unique sport that is sweeping the country with popular favor, got a run across the plate to win, 1-0, and gain a break in the 'double-header.'" All players other than the pitcher and catcher were mounted on donkeyback. A special "indoor ball' was used. "The batsman hits, then mounts and attempts to reach first ahead of the ball. Sometimes he does. More often he never gets 10 feet away from the plate." With an exhibition of "pepper ball" mixed in, the whole evening was entertaining, which the paper said was "side-splitting" and something approaching a three-ring circus.[150]

The *Tribune* added a bit, telling readers that Stephens – "ordinarily a daredevil" hesitated to get on donkeyback. "Biz Mackey set the fans in hysterics as he tried to coax his mount down to first base against the wishes of said animal. Not even the Stars who turned out en masse could get the beasts to perambulate down the line," while the House of David's "bearded baseballers, more used to the critters, ambled around the bases like U.S. cavalrymen."[151]

A REMINDER REGARDING SEGREGATION

Ed R. Harris, the sports editor of the *Philadelphia Tribune* devoted part of his August 16 column to 18-year-old Johnny Taylor from Hartford, Connecticut. He wrote:

"While sitting in the press box at Passon Field striving to forget, by the power of mind over matter, the noxious fumes of the murderous cigars Ed Bolden smokes, I started dreaming. I wondered would I ever see colored boys playing in the big baseball leagues. I thought of Johnny Taylor, a young New England chap who has a pitching record so excellent that it is little short of unbelievable. Just to mention one or two items. Taylor has struck out as many as twenty-five men in succession to come back in a latter game and strike out

seventeen. His work is consistent and is common for him to strike out ten or twelve men per game. And he backs up his pitching ability by his rugged handling of the ash. His fame has gone all over New England and down into New York where the management of the New York Yankees heard about this marvel. The powers sent out a scout to look hm up and to get him to sign a contract. All went well until the scout found that he was a colored boy. Sic sempre."[152]

August 11, 1934: Philadelphia Stars 8, Philadelphia Bacharach Giants 0 (first game); Philadelphia Stars 3, Passons 2 (second game), at Passon Field.

Only the first game of this twin bill was a league game; the second was another game against the White semipro club, the Passons (or, s the typesetter in the *Chicago Defender* rendered it, the Passion Club.) It was Slim Jones on the mound in the official league game, against Lefty Luther Farrell, an 8-0 shutout reported as the Stars' ninth win in a row and one which extended their lead in the season's second half. The Stars scored the only run they needed in the first inning, but added three runs in the fourth inning, two more in the fifth, and another two in the seventh. The Stars got 15 base hits. Washington and Wilson each collected three hits; Stephens, Casey, and Dunn each had two. The only batter to go hitless was Dunn.[153] Webster McDonald threw the game and Passon got to him for two runs in bottom of the first inning, but that's all they got. McDonald reached on an error in the third, Stephens singled, McDonald running to third. Wilson singled to center field and both baserunners scored. In the fifth inning, Stephens reached base, got to second, and scored on White's single through the shortstop hole.[154]

SEGREGATION IN AMERICAN LEGION BASEBALL

The 1934 American Legion junior baseball tournament was held in Gastonia, North Carolina. When manager Sidney Davis arrived at the local hotel booked for his team from Springfield, Massachusetts, he learned that Ernest Taliaferro – the team's star pitcher and outfielder – was to be refused accommodations. The hotel blamed North Carolina state law, which it said prohibited it from accepting a "colored guest." Davis withdrew the team from the tournament.[155] A local family offered to house Taliaferro, but Davis would not bend. Two of the six teams in the tournament -- the Legion teams from Cumberland,

Maryland and Tampa, Florida both announced their refusal to play with Taliaferro on the field. Chuck Wilson, the national head of the American Legion, said that Taliaferro could play, and tried to convince Davis to stay, but it was not within his power to overrule local law.[156] When the team arrived back in Springfield, 1,000 supporters turned out to welcome them home.

August 17, 1934: Philadelphia Stars 17, Birmingham Barons 3, at Eagle Park, York, Pennsylvania

The "last all-colored attraction of the season to be sponsored by the Old Timers' Athletic Association" drew the smallest crowd of the season to Eagle Park. Birmingham scored three runs on five hits in the top of the first off Lefty Holmes, but Holmes only allowed five more hits and no more runs for the rest of the game. The Stars scored seven runs in the bottom of the third, two more in the sixth, five in the seventh, and three in the eighth.

Jake Stephens was a York resident and, according to the local newspaper, "York's only entry in the colored ranks of professional baseball." He shared star billing with catcher Mickey Casey, who had been 5-for-5 (all singles) at the plate. Shortstop Stephens (and the leadoff batter) was 4-for-6 and "gave a wonderful exhibition of fielding {as he] roamed to all corners of the infield pulling down hard hit ground balls and tossing his man out at first with apparent ease. His one-handed pickup and throw in the late innings was the gem play of the evening."[157]

August 18, 1934: Philadelphia Stars 6, Pittsburgh Crawfords 3 (first game, 10 innings); Philadelphia Stars 1, Pittsburgh Crawfords 0 (second game, six innings), at Greenlee Field, Pittsburgh

The Crawfords hosted the Stars for back-to-back doubleheaders on Saturday the 18th and Sunday the 19th, getting swept on the 18th but coming back to sweep the Stars on the 19th. They then swept the Stars again on the 20th, this time in Philadelphia.

The first game was a 10-inning affair that saw the Stars score two in the second and add another run in

Philly Stars Add to League Lead

WIN 9 STRAIGHT TO STAY AT TOP IN FLAG BATTLE

Chicago Defender, *August 18, 1934: 16.*

the third. The Crawfords promptly matched that, scoring three times in the bottom of the third. "Submarine" McDonald started for Philadelphia and Leroy Matlock for Pittsburgh. The game then rolled on with neither team scoring in any of the next six innings. At some point, William Bell relieved Matlock and Slim Jones relieved McDonald. Philadelphia scored three runs in the top of the 10th. Pittsburgh had Clarence Palm bat for Vic Harris, and then Ted Page run for Palm. Curtis Harris pinch-hit for shortstop Leroy Morney. It was in vain; Jones held the Crawfords scoreless, and the Stars won, 6-3.[158]

The second game was curtailed after six innings. We lack a game story, or a detailed boxscore. A basic boxscore in the *Afro-American* shows the pitchers to have been Bert Hunter for the Crawfords and Paul Carter for the Stars. Hunter allowed two base hits and Carter allowed three. There was only one run – scored by the Stars in the top of the fourth inning. It's not clear how it scored, but we see that Jake Dunn is credited for the run scored and the man who followed him in the order – Pete Washington – had one of the two base hits. There was one Pittsburgh error. Walks are not shown. It is possible that Dunn reached via base on balls, or the error, and that Washington drove him in.[159]

August 19, 1934: Pittsburgh Crawfords 6, Philadelphia Stars 4 (first game); Pittsburgh Crawfords 4, Philadelphia Stars 1 (second game), at Greenlee Field, Pittsburgh

Satchel Paige and Rocky Ellis squared off in the first game of the Sunday doubleheader. The Stars got to Paige early, building up a 3-0 lead with one run on the first and two in the third. Then the Crawfords buckled down. The offense scored two runs in the bottom of the third, two runs in the fourth, and two more runs in the fifth, giving them a 6-3 lead. Paige only allowed one more run, in the eighth. The Craws out-hit the Stars, nine hits to six. There were three triples in the game – one by Jud Wilson, and one each by the Crawfords' Vic Harris and Paige. Oscar Charleston had two RBIs. Ellis struck out four, but Paige struck out 10.[160]

In the second game, William Bell pitched for Pittsburgh and Phil Cockrell for Philadelphia. Both the *Courier* and Baltimore's *Afro-American* had only a basic boxscore for the second game, but the *Chicago Defender* had a more complete one. The Crawfords scored one run in the first, two more in the second, and the Stars scored just one run, in the seventh. Vic Harris doubled twice, while pitcher Bell drove in two of his team's four runs. It is an odd feature of the day that the three above-named newspapers all showed Pittsburgh scoring a fourth run in the ninth inning, when they already held a 3-1 lead. Had both teams traveled to Philadelphia to play the Sunday games? The next morning's *Pittsburgh Post-Gazette*, in its two sentences of coverage, made clear the game was at Greenlee Field and showed the fourth run scoring in the bottom of the eighth. One suspects a compositor's error was responsible for the way the run was rendered in the other three newspapers, all drawing on one common source.[161]

August 20, 1934: Pittsburgh Crawfords 8, Philadelphia Stars 2 (first game); Pittsburgh Crawfords 4, Philadelphia Stars 3 (second game), at Baker Bowl

Josh Gibson was the story in the first game, with two home runs over the right-field barrier at Phillies Field and a five-hit game with three RBIs. One way or another he was involved with seven of the eight Crawfords runs. It was Jones' worst day of the season, giving up 14 base hits. Pittsburgh scored three runs in the first and never looked back, adding single runs in the third, fourth, and seventh, and then a final pair in the top of the ninth. Henry Kincannon allowed seven hits and limited the Stars to solo runs in the fourth and seventh. Stephens, White, and Casey each had two hits in the game.

The second game was Webster McDonald against Roosevelt Davis. The Stars outhit the Crawfords, 10-8, but came up one run short. Pittsburgh scored once in the third, which the Stars matched in the fourth. The Craws added two in the sixth, and a fourth run in the seventh. In the bottom of the eighth, catcher Aneal Brooks hit a two-run homer to right field, driving in Jud Wilson ahead of him. The *Inquirer* said the Stars protested the use of Davis because he had been a pitcher for Cleveland but the game proceeded and Davis got the win.[162]

At some point this week, the Stars were beaten, 8-7, by the Philadelphia Angels, and by Stonehurst, 4-3.[163]

August 23, 1934: Newark Dodgers 4, Philadelphia Stars 3, at Windsor Airport Field, Trenton, New Jersey

The game had been planned as between the Hightstown semipro club and the Newark Dodgers, but the Hightstown team was "being revamped…[and]

subject to some volcanic changes," so the Stars were invited to play in their stead.[164]

Alonzo Bailey and Bob Evans pitched for Newark; Lefty Holmes pitched for the Stars. The Dodgers scored once in the top of the first, then fell behind as the Stars scored one in the fourth and one in the fifth, but pulled out in front with a three-run top of the eighth. Ray Dandridge led all with a three-hit game. Newark collected 10 hits; Philadelphia eight (with Dunn and White each having two hits.)

August 24, 1934: Philadelphia Stars 6. Holmesburg 2, at Leon & Decatur, Holmesburg neighborhood of Philadelphia

Cliff Irons pitched for the Stars. Dewey Creacy and Jimmy Miles each had a pair of hits. Someone named Grundel pitched for Holmesburg of the Quaker City league. Everyone in the Stars lineup had at least one hit, except for Irons.[165]

August 24, 1934: Philadelphia Stars 7, Passon 0, at Passon Field (night game)

In a seven-inning game played under the arc lights, Paul Carter shut out the Passon team, 7-0, allowing seven scattered base hits. Jake Stephens scored three runs in the game. Chaney White hit a three-run homer in the fifth inning, scoring Creacy and Miles, and two other hits besides. The Stars scored once in the first, five more in the top of sixth, and one final run in the seventh.[166]

August 25, 1934: Philadelphia Stars 5, Birmingham Black Barons 4 (first game); Philadelphia Stars 9, Birmingham Black Barons 8 (second game), at Passon Field

The non-league Birmingham Black Barons outhit the Stars in both games, 10-7 and 12-8, but the Stars edged the visitors in both games by one run in each. Phil Cockrell pitched the first game. Columbus Vance pitched for Birmingham. Philadelphia scored first, with two runs in the second, lost the lead when Birmingham scored three times in the third inning, but regained it by adding another two runs in the fifth. The Stars added a fifth run in the bottom of the seventh. When Birmingham scored their fourth run – but no more – in the top of the ninth, the game was over and the Stars won, 5-4.

In the second game, Jones and Collins pitched for the Barons. Someone named Williams was said to have pitched for Philadelphia. Who that may have been is unclear. He got through the fist inning, but gave up one run in the second, two in the third, and a fourth run in the top of the fourth. The Stars began to respond with one run in the bottom of the fourth, one in the fifth, and one in the sixth. It was 4-3, Barons, but they scored four more runs in the top of the seventh, driving Williams from the game (Webster McDonald relieved). The Stars banged out five runs in the bottom of the seventh, tying the game 8-8. They scored a final ninth run in the eighth, and held on to win.[167]

August 26, 1934: Philadelphia Stars 4, Nashville Elite Giants 3 (first game); Philadelphia Stars 8, Nashville Elite Giants 2 (second game), at Passon Field

Both teams were playing without some of their top players – the Stars, for instance, were without Jones, Seay, and Wilson, who had gone to Chicago's Comiskey Park for the East-West Game. Four players from the Giants were unavailable for the same reason. The pitching matchup was McDonald for Philadelphia and "Cannonball" Jim Wilson for Nashville. Neither team scored in the first two innings but the Stars scored all four of their runs in the bottom of the third. The first of the four was a solo home run over the left-field wall by Pete Washington. Nashville scored once in the fourth and once in the fifth, then mounted a final rally in the top of the ninth. Catcher Tommie Dukes got on, and came home on a double by Lloyd Scott. Percy Miller pinch-hit but lined to Biz Mackey at first base for the final out of the game. Both teams had eight base hits.[168] The *Chester Times* reported the ending as coming on a bases-loaded double play.[169]

In the second game, the Stars scored three in the first and three in the second. That drove starter Percy Miller from the mound. Lefty Holmes pitched for Philadelphia. Bob Griffith relieved him. The Stars out-hit the Elite Giants, 11-9. The only Star without a hit was second baseman Richard Harris. they scored two more runs in the bottom of the fifth. Nashville's two runs came in the eighth.[170]

August 27, 1934: Philadelphia Stars 8, Nashville Elite Giants 2, at Passon Field

This game, a night game, was only mentioned in passing in the August 30 *Tribune,* but fortunately the *Inquirer* offered a boxscore and a few lines. Carter pitched for the home team and gave up two first-inning runs. He held Nashville to seven hits. Jim Willis pitched for Nashville. He gave up three hits in the first,

two in the second, and one each in the third, fourth, and sixth. Jake Dunn was 3-for-5 off him. The box-score shows Rocky Ellis playing second base. The *Inquirer* says Stephens and Casey each had a pair of hits, but the boxscore says it was Stephens and Ellis. It was a busy day for the infield; Mackey was credited with 17 putouts at first base.[171]

One wonders if a number of fans turned up at a different game. The very morning of this game, the *News Journal* of Wilmington, Delaware ran a story saying that "two clubs of the National Negro League, the Philadelphia Stars and the Birmingham Barons, will play at Pennsy Filed tonight. The game is scheduled for 5:30 o'clock."[172] There is no evidence that this anticipated game was ever played.

August 29, 1934: Philadelphia Stars 6, Narberth 1, at Narberth, Pennsylvania

The team from the Borough of Narberth (Montgomery County) on the western outskirts of Philadelphia was the "leader of the Main Line League," an independent baseball league based in Philadelphia. The Stars scored two runs each in the first, fourth, and seventh innings (it was a seven-inning games) while Slim Jones held the Narberth team to one second-inning run.[173]

August 30, 1934: Philadelphia Stars 13, Palmyra 1, at unspecified location

It was apparently the second night game for the borough of Palymra in Pennsylvania's Lebanon County. The local nine played in the South Anthracite loop but the Stars "swamped the boro tossers to the tine of 13-1."[174]

The *Chester Times* had announced a game for 5:30 that evening at Elks Park between the Stars and the Baltimore Black Sox.[175] Chester and Palmyra are just under 100 miles apart.

September 1, 1934: Philadelphia Stars 2, Chicago American Giants 1 (first game); Philadelphia Stars 1, Chicago American Giants 1 (tie, seven innings), at Passon Field

These games were given short shrift in the *Philadelphia Tribune.* The article did say the "fans got plenty of thrills." The second game was mentioned in one sentence: "The second game the Stars came from behind to knot the score 1-1."[176] The *Chicago Defender* offered more under an eight-column headline: GIANTS LOST TO PHILLY; THEN TIE, 1-1."[177]

THE STARS SHONE ON PHILADELPHIA

Both games were low-scoring affairs. In the first game, lefty Slim Jones faced Willie Cornelius, pitching for Chicago. Jones gave up six hits; only catcher Larry Brown got more than one. Cornelius gave up eight (three of them to right fielder Jake Dunn). One of the Stars' hits was in the second inning, by Jones, who singled to left field for the first run of the game, driving in Dunn.[178] Jones struck out eight. The Giants committed three errors. The other Stars run was scored in the third inning. Creacy singled and – somehow or other – later scored.

Chicago outhit Philadelphia in the seven-inning second game, seven hits to four. Neither team scored for the first five innings. Ellis pitched for the host team. Chicago brought out "a whole flock of pitchers" – Malarcher, Lillard, Foster, and Bailey – in just the seven innings. Chicago scored the first run, in the top of the sixth. In the bottom of the seventh, their backs against the wall, the Stars pushed across the tying run, scored by Dunn. The Stars used two pinch-hitters in the seventh.

The box score shows not a single putout being made at first base by the Stars; Chicago had nine of them at first. Six outs were recorded by Stars outfielders.

September 2, 1934: Raphael 4, Philadelphia Stars 3 (first game); Philadelphia Stars 4, Raphael 2 (second game), at Passon Field

Matching up once more, as they had in early April, the Stars played the Raphael club of the Philadelphia League. Raphael played well, very much in both games, winning the first and within striking distance throughout the second. Former Boston Red Sox infielder Bill Narleski played for Raphael and had a 5-for-8 day.

Webster McDonald pitched the first game. The Stars scored twice in the sixth inning to tie it, but Raphael got two in the bottom of the eighth, and then held off a rally in the ninth during which the Stars employed three pinch-hitters and scored one run, but came up one run short. Holmes pitched the second game.[179] Wilson's homer in the eighth inning of the second game was the game-winner.[180]

September 3, 1934: New Orleans Crescents 8, Philadelphia Stars 3 (first game, 10 innings); Philadelphia Stars 4, New Orleans Crescents 1 (second game)

The first game was a Monday morning game, played on Labor Day. Phil Cockrell started for the Stars and pitched into the eighth. The Stars scored single runs in the third, fourth, and fifth, but the Crescents came back with two runs in the eighth, and tied it in the ninth, Jones relieving Cockrell to get the final out. Jones hurt his arm, however, as one run scored. Rocky Ellis had to come in cold to pitch the 10th. He was hammered for four more runs, which the Stars could not match.

Ellis pitched the full second game, holding New Orleans to just one run, and that coming only in the top of the ninth.[181] Because the two teams had played just two games and split evenly, the New Orleans newspaper later described the Crescent Stars as the only team against which the Stars did not hold an edge.[182] In October, however, the Stars reportedly won four straight games against New Orleans.[183]

September 5, 1934: Philadelphia Stars 7, Royersford Needleworks 1, at Pottstown, Pennsylvania

The visiting Philadelphia Stars scored one in the first, got four in the third, and added single runs in the seventh and eighth. The local team bunched together three doubles in the seventh inning for its lone run. Jake Dunn had three hits, while Mackey, Washington, and right fielder Jimmy Miles had two apiece. Pitching for the Stars was "Yokly" – presumably Laymon Yokely, who normally played for the Philadelphia Bacharach Giants in 1934, but may have sat in with Bolden's Stars for this game. He was 0-for-4. On the mound, he struck out six.[184]

The September 8 issue of the *Chicago Tribune* said the Stars were "winners of the second half championship of the Negro National League."[185]

September 9, 1934: Pittsburgh Crawfords 1, Philadelphia Stars 1 (tie, nine innings), at Yankee Stadium, New York

The Crawfords-Stars game was the second game of a four-team doubleheader at Yankee Stadium that drew 20,000 to 30,000 spectators.[186] In the first game, the Chicago American Giants beat the New York Black Yankees, 4-3, with a pair of runs in the third and another pair in the fourth, and then holding on as the New York team scored two in the eighth and one in the ninth.

The second game saw Slim Jones pitching for the Stars and Satchel Paige for the Crawfords. The Stars scored their only run in the first inning when Jake Stephens walked and advanced to third on Creacy's hit-and-run single. Chaney White struck out. Creacy stole second. Jud Wilson grounded to third base; Judy Johnson's play was to first base and Stephens scored. The Crawfords got their run in the eighth on a double by Johnson (the *Courier* said it was a single, and that Johnson took second on Dunn's error, but no error is ascribed to Dunn in the box score), a sacrifice by Chester Williams, and a single by Leroy Morney.[187]

Jones allowed but three hits; Paige allowed six. The box score shows no walks charged to Jones, but Paige walked three. The *Tribune* account indicates that Jones had a perfect game through six innings, until Oscar Charleston singled. Jones struck out nine and Paige struck out 12. Two of Paige's strikeouts were key to keeping the game a tie. In the bottom the ninth inning, the Stars came to bat. Accounts differ as to who did what, but all agree that the Stars loaded the bases with just one out. The *New York Amsterdam News* says that, after Chaney White grounded out, Jud Wilson hit a ball that struck the mound near Paige's feet and went to second baseman Chester Williams, who threw toward first. The throw hit Wilson after he had crossed the bag, and caromed toward the stands.[188] It was ruled a single and then an error. Biz Mackey walked, loading the bases. Casey pinch-hit for Dunn, and he drew a walk as well. (The *Courier* says it was intentional.) McDonald pinch-hit for Washington, and Paige struck him out on three called strikes. Then Ameal Brooks pinch-hit for Seay and Paige struck him out, too, all three strikes swinging. The game was then called after nine on account of darkness.[189]

Those who watched this day's doubleheader had the opportunity to see quite an array of baseball talent. Eleven future members of the National Baseball Hall of Fame played on this one day: Cool Papa Bell, Oscar Charleston, Bill "Willie" Foster, Josh Gibson, Judy Johnson, Biz Mackey, Satchel Paige, Turkey Stearnes, Mule Suttles, Willie Wells, and Jud Wilson.

September 10, 1934: Kensington 2, Philadelphia Stars 1, at D and Tioga Streets, Philadelphia

The Stars kept playing as they prepared for the playoffs. This game was an abbreviated six-inning game between a club called Kensington and featuring a pitcher called Wild Bill Durham. Holmes pitched for the Stars and struck out seven while only allowing three hits and walking three, but gave up solo runs in the first and second inning. Holmes got one of the five hits off Wild Bill. There were no errors for either team.[190]

SOME REFLECTIONS ON THE SEASON THAT HAD BEEN

The *Philadelphia Tribune*'s Ed R. Harris offered a column in the September 13 paper that looked back on the season and offered a perspective worth noting. He highlighted the September 9 doubleheader at Yankee Stadium for drawing such a huge crowd and a level of play "that was fit for the big time leagues."[191]

He noted that some – such as Cum Posey – had criticized the league as dominated by three figures: Gus Greenlee of the Crawfords, Bob Coles [*sic*] of the Chicago American Giants, and Ed Bolden of the Stars. Harris suggested he subscribed a bit to the idea that "half a league is better than no league" and made allowances for this being the startup year. He did add, regarding scheduling problems, "It is an unfortunate circumstance that colored baseball cannot entirely support itself by inter-league competition. Therein lies one of the major difficulties that the league has had to battle. Booking of independent teams is necessary for any semi-pro team to exist and in many cases these bookings have only been scheduled at the cost of already booked league games, which had to be canceled. When the day comes that the colored teams are supported enough by colored fans that a straight league schedule can be maintained, it will be a great one in the annals of Negro baseball." He naturally enthused over the turnout for the East-West Game in Chicago and the four-team doubleheader at Yankee Stadium.

W. Rollo Wilson offered his thoughts after the regular season and before the playoffs. He made it sound as though everyone just about broke even, but no more, writing, "Few, if any, clubs made any money; the losses of other clubs were surprisingly small."[192] The East-West game was, however, a spectacular success. As commissioner of the league, he was optimistic about the year to come though recognizing that there were bound to be changes in ownership and changes in cities represented in the league. He expressed his congratulations to everyone who "did their best to keep the machinery oiled and functioning, who lived up to – as best they could – their obligations and duties." And for bearing with him even when sometimes his decisions went against them. He said most of the umpires were good, but that a better umpiring arrangement was needed.

He then presented his selections for an all-league club, in effect an all-star team. Because the Homestead Grays were associate members only, he left them out but said that he ranked their first baseman, Buck Leonard, as the best player he saw all year.

He named Josh Gibson and Larry Brown as the best catchers, but singled out Paul Casey of the Stars as the "hardest-working maskman in the league and deserving honorable mention," in large part because Biz Mackey had not been able to perform and Casey had to take on extra work with good backup.

For pitchers, he named Paige (Crawfords), Trent and Foster (Chicago), McDonald and Jones (Stars), Porter (Nashville), and Evans (Newark).

First base: Jud Wilson (Stars). He noted the Crawfords' Oscar Charleston had been hampered by a leg injury.

Second base: Hughes of Nashville, with Ches Williams of the Crawfords and Dick Seay of the Stars following.

Shortstop: Willie Wells, of the Chicago American Giants; his hitting giving him the edge over Lundy of Newark and Stephens of the Stars.

Third base: Creacy, Stars. No one else was even mentioned.

Left field: Vic Harris (Crawfords), his fielding giving him the edge over Nashville's Parker and Philadelphia's Chaney White. White was noted as a more consistent hitter.

Center field: Cool Papa Bell (Crawfords), again with fielding giving him an edge over Turkey Stearnes.

Right field: Jake Dunn of the Stars.

Wilson also named a few utility players and several who did "creditable work" (the two Stars being pitchers Holmes and Ellis).[193]

THE PLAYOFFS

September 11, 1934: Chicago American Giants 4, Philadelphia Stars 3, at Passon Field (Game One of the NNL playoffs)

The Giants had scored first, once in the top of the first, matched by a run by the Stars in the bottom of the second. The Giants took a 2-1 lead in the seventh, only to find the Stars score twice and grab their first lead of the game. In the eighth, Chicago scored one more run.

The ninth inning was the crucial one. The game was tied, 3-3, Rocky Ellis pitching for the Stars and Willie Foster for the Giants. Dewey Creacy threw wildly and Giants catcher Larry Brown was not only safe but got to second base. Mule Suttles singled to right field, and Brown scored the go-ahead run. The Stars loaded the bases in the bottom of the ninth, with two outs. Biz Mackey came to bat. But, the *Tribune* wrote, "the best the 'Big Boy' could do was to bingle

one weakly to second base to make the third out and end the game."[194]

Two other games that the two teams planned to play in Philadelphia were both rained out and the series shifted to Chicago.

September 16, 1934: Chicago American Giants 3, Philadelphia Stars 0 (first game); Philadelphia Stars 5, Chicago American Giants 3 (second game), at Cole's Park, Chicago (Games Two and Three of the NNL playoffs)

The Chicago American Giants took a two-games-to-none lead in the championship series with a 3-0 four-hit shutout by Ted Trent in the first game of the Sunday, September 16, doubleheader, and then lost the day's second game, 5-3. Slim Jones faced Trent in the first game, and neither team scored for the first five innings, but the Giants got to Jones for two runs in the sixth on a Jack Marshall single, a triple to left-center by Turkey Stearnes, and a single by Alex Radcliffe. They added an insurance run in the bottom of the eighth on a two-out double by Trent and a single by Stearnes.[195] Pete Washington had two of the Stars' four hits. Jones struck out seven; Trent struck out eight.

The second game pitted hurler Willie Foster for the Giants against Webster McDonald for the Stars. It was the Stars who got on the board first, with one run in the third inning on two singles, a walk, and an error, but the Giants took the lead with a three-run bottom of the third, on four hits. Philadelphia tied it with two runs in the fourth inning on a double by Jake Dunn and a triple to center field by Pete Washington, who scored on a wild pitch. They took the lead with two more in the top of the fifth on one hit – thanks to a single, a sacrifice, a walk, a long fly ball, and another wild pitch, by Foster. The game went the full nine innings, but there was no further scoring.[196] The games drew a relatively small crowd of about 2,000.

September 17, 1934: Chicago American Giants 2, Philadelphia Stars 1, at Cole's Park, Chicago (Game Four of the NNL playoffs)

The Giants took a solid three-games-to-one lead in the playoffs with a 2-1 win in Game Four, played on Monday afternoon in Chicago. Willie Cornelius pitched for the Giants and Rocky Ellis for Philadelphia. Cornelius allowed five hits, Ellis four. Both pitchers threw complete games. Neither team scored for the first five innings. In the bottom of the sixth, the Giants bunched three of their four hits. Either

Alex Radcliffe or Mule Suttles singled.[197] Willie Wells followed with a double and Jack Marshall singled. Two runs counted. In the top of the seventh, Jud Wilson doubled for Philadelphia and Biz Mackey singled, producing one run for the Stars. The *Chicago Defender* account says the run actually scored on two passed balls. In any event, only one run came across. There was no more scoring in the game.

September 20, 1934: Philadelphia Stars 2, Newark Dodgers 1, at Windsor Airport Field, Trenton, New Jersey

The Stars, beaten in a one-run game on August 23, faced the Newark Dodgers again and turned the tables. The pitching matchup was the same, with Evans and Bailey pitching for the Dodgers. As in the earlier game, Holmes handled pitching duties for the Stars, and allowed just four hits and one second-inning run. That run gave the Dodgers a lead until the Stars tied it in the fifth, and then won it in the ninth. The box score noted that there was no one out when the winning run scored, suggesting that the Stars were playing as the home team.

The Trenton paper said, "By winning, the Philadelphians gained the right to meet the House of David at the same field Sunday night at 8:30."[198] Though perhaps they had that right, a doubleheader in their home park against the New York Black Yankees was apparently more attractive. See September 23.

September 22, 1934 – a 3:30 P.M. game at East Orange, New Jersey, was announced between the Stars and the East Orange BBC, to be played at East Orange Oval. This is another game announced, but for which we have yet to find evidence that it was played.[199]

September 23, 1934: Philadelphia Stars 4, New York Black Yankees 1 (first game); Philadelphia Stars 4, New York Black Yankees 3 (second game, seven innings), at Passon Field

Keeping in fighting trim, the Stars took on the New York Black Yankees for two games this Sunday, drawing 3,000 fans. Jones threw a two-hitter in the first game, striking out nine. Clint Thomas singled and Carl Beckwith doubled. That was it. They got their one run in the fifth. Neck Stanley pitched for New York. The Stars got 10 hits, including three by White (one a double) and two by Creacy.

The opposing pitchers in the second game were Paul Carter for Philadelphia and Frank Blake for New York. The visitors scored three runs in the top of the first. The Stars scored once, then added a second run in the bottom of the fifth. In the seventh, the 6 P.M. curfew was looming. Mickey Casey doubled leading off for the Stars. He advanced to third on a fielder's choice, Rocky Ellis batting for Carter and reaching first, the defense more concerned with preventing Casey from scoring on the play. Seay singled and Casey scored, tying it, 3-3. Creacy popped up to second base, but Jud Wilson singled in Ellis with the winning run.

In the seven innings, Carter struck out eight.[200]

September 27, 1934: Philadelphia Stars 1, Chicago American Giants 0, at Passon Field, Game Five of the NNL playoffs

This was a true pitchers' duel, pitting Philadelphia's Rocky Ellis against Chicago's Willie Foster. There was a total of one run scored in the game. For the first seven innings, both pitchers held their opponents scoreless. Each pitcher struck out nine. Neither team made an error, but there may have been a bit of pitching inside – Foster hit two Stars with pitches and Ellis hit three Giants. Chicago outhit Philadelphia, eight to five. The Stars drew more bases on balls – five to the three the Giants got off Ellis. Each team had two doubles. Both teams left 13 runners on base – but only one ever scored. In the bottom of the eighth, Brooks got on base and Dick Seay singled to drive him in. Ellis pitched a scoreless top of the ninth and the home team Stars had their second win in the playoffs.

September 28, 1934: Philadelphia Stars 5, New York Black Yankees 3, at Memorial Park, Belmar, New Jersey

There finally was a game played at Belmar. The Black Yankees behind the pitching of Frank Blake allowed nine hits, while Holmes gave up 10, but the Tars came out on top. Neither team scored in the first three innings. Each team scored once in the fourth. The three runs the Stars scored in the top of the sixth made the difference.[201]

September 29, 1934: Philadelphia Stars 4, Chicago American Giants 1, at Passon Field, Game Six of the NNL playoffs

The Stars won the game, evening the series at three wins each. Both pitchers went the distance. Paul Carter was the winning pitcher; Ted Trent bore the loss. The Giants scored first with one run in the top of the third – their only run, a solo home run by center fielder Turkey Stearnes. It was one of only four base hits off Carter. The Stars scored twice in the fourth and twice more in the fifth. In the fourth, there were three extra-bases hits – a double by Ameal Brooks to lead off, and a double by Pete Washington that drove Brooks home. Washington had to hold while the next two batters made outs, but then Creacy tripled to left. In the fifth, Biz Mackey homered to right. Dunn singled and later scored when Brooks singled. The Stars had 10 hits in the game.

There were a couple of "sorry incidents" in the game that prompted a column in the *Philadelphia Tribune*. During an argument with first-base umpire Bert Gholston, the Stars' Jud Wilson "laid violent hands" on the umpire and the two had to be separated. In the eighth inning, Stars catcher Ameal Brooks "laid his hands against [plate umpire John] Craig's face and pushed him away."[202] Neither player was ejected, and author Ed R. Harris – the sports editor of the *Tribune* – chastised the umpires for "trying to be good sports" rather than upholding the integrity of the game. The players were wrong in allowing their personal anger perhaps get them thrown out of a championship game, and thus letting down their teammates and the fans that came to see baseball. Harris strongly felt both players should have been tossed and perhaps further disciplined.[203]

September 30, 1934: Pittsburgh Crawfords 3, Philadelphia Stars 1 (game one of four-team doubleheader), at Yankee Stadium, New York

With a move that would be almost inconceivable today, on Sunday, September 30, the Philadelphia Stars and Chicago American Giants both took a day off from the NNL playoffs and participated in a four-team doubleheader played at Yankee Stadium – between Game Six and Game Seven of the playoffs. They didn't play each other – the Stars played the Pittsburgh Crawfords and the Giants played the New York Black Yankees. As an event staged to garner attention for the league, and bring in additional revenue, it was very successful, attracting 25,000 paying customers. There is no question that it was intended to achieve maximum publicity. Commissioner Wilson threw out the ceremonial first ball to celebrated dancer and entertainer Bill "Bojangles" Robinson, known as the "Mayor of Harlem."[204]

The first game featured Satchel Paige against Slim Jones. In the bottom of the first, the Crawfords scored two runs off Jones. With one out, Vic Harris singled.

Oscar Charleston walked. Josh Gibson hit a ball that Dick Seay misplayed at second base, Harris scoring and Charleston taking third. Judy Johnson lifted a high foul ball between first and second, caught for the second out by Stars catcher Johnny Hayes, but no one covered the plate and Charleston ran home.

Paige held Philadelphia scoreless until the seventh inning, when he surrendered one run. Dewey Creacy led off with a single and stole second. Biz Mackey drove him in with a double, a hard-hit ball that went over third base and bounced into the box seats beyond. The Crawfords matched that with a run on singles by Johnson and Jimmie Crutchfield and a run-producing sacrifice by Leroy Morney.[205]

In the day's second game, the New York Black Yankees played a game called after six innings due to darkness, the home team overcoming a 2-0 deficit with three runs in the bottom of the sixth to take the lead, and the game. After a leadoff walk, there followed two hard-hit doubles (one of them sounded catchable save for the darkening) that tied the game. A "downhearted" Ted Radcliffe then walked two to load the bases, and then walked in another that ended the game.[206]

October 1, 1934: Chicago American Giants 4, Philadelphia Stars 4 (tie), at Passon Field, Game Seven of the NNL playoffs

This was the seventh game in the best-of-seven series; the winner would become Negro National League champion for 1934. Rocky Ellis took the mound for the Stars. Willie Cornelius pitched for Dave Malarcher's American Giants. Ellis was hit for three runs in the top of the third, the first runs of the game. He'd given up two hits and walked three in 2⅓ innings. He also committed an error. McDonald pulled him and he himself finished both the inning and the game. The Stars got one run in the bottom of the third on doubles by McDonald and Jud Wilson. Neither team scored in the fourth or fifth, but the Stars got one more run in the sixth, on a triple by Wilson and a single by Mackey to bring themselves within a run, 3-2.

Willie Foster pitched the seventh for Chicago and kept the Stars at bay, though he did put two runners on – one with a hit and one with a walk. Philadelphia scored twice in the bottom of the eighth, taking a 4-3 lead. Ted Trent had taken over from Foster, and gave up a two-base hit to Creacy, hit Wilson, and walked Mackey. Dunn singled in Creacy. After Casey made an out, Brooks walked, forcing in the second run.

The Giants scored the tying run in the top of the ninth and it was 4-4. The Stars did not score. The game did not go into extra innings and finished as a tie game, with another game to be played the following night.[207]

October 2, 1934: Philadelphia Stars 2, Chicago American Giants 0, at Passon Field, Game Eight of the NNL playoffs

Slim Jones pitched for Philadelphia and he threw a shutout. Willie Cornelius started for Chicago and worked the first six innings. Ted Trent worked the final two. They each gave up one run.

Both Jones and Cornelius retired the side in order in the first inning. One reached for the Giants in the second on an error by Creacy. One reached for the Stars in the second: Jake Dunn walked. Neither team scored in the third either, though Jones gave up a double to Willie Wells and Alex Radcliffe reached on an error. Cornelius saw the leadoff man reach, erased by a double play. He then gave up two singles before he worked his way out of the threat.

The first three American Giants got singles in the top of the fourth, but after the second one, Jones picked off the lead runner for the first out. He escaped unscathed. In the bottom of the fourth, the Stars got on the board. Mackey led off with a single, taking second on a groundout and scoring on Casey's single.

Neither team scored in the fifth or sixth, despite Cornelius walking two Stars. Double plays rescued both pitchers, Jud Wilson grounding into one in the bottom of the fifth and Suttles grounding into one in the top of the sixth.

In the top of the seventh, a leadoff walk was followed by another yet double play – fortunate because Melvin Powell then got a two-base hit. Wilson Redus pinch-hit for Cornelius, and Jones struck him out. In the bottom of the seventh, with Trent now pitching for Chicago, Pete Washington led off with a single. After Seay flied out to right, Jones himself singled to left field, and Washington scored all the way from first base, giving the Stars an insurance run. Jones took second base on the throw in but was stranded there, on two outfield flies.

Neither team did anything in the eighth, but Chicago mounted a threat in the top of the ninth. First

PHILLY STARS WORLD'S CHAMPS?

TAKE 3 STRAIGHT FROM GIANTS
BUT 1 DEFEAT IS BEING PROTESTED

Chicago Defender, *October 2, 1934: 17.*

up was Suttles, who doubled. Ted Radcliffe pinch-hit for first baseman Joe Scott and he singled, Suttles stopping at third. For the second time in the game, Suttles was picked off – this time picked off third. Larry Brown struck out. Dave Malarcher pinch-hit for Jack Marshall and he flied out to Dunn in right field. The game was over, a 2-0 win for Slim Jones, and the league championship belonged to the Philadelphia Stars.

Or did it?

The Defender noted that the Giants had jumped out to a three-games-to-one lead but that "Bolden's Stars, their backs to the wall, rallied and took one game played Thursday night and a twin bill Saturday to cinch the crown." The newspaper said, "The American Giants blew sky high here in the East. They played ragged ball and in addition appeared to be frightened from the first game right through to the final. They truly did not play like champions."

However, according to the *Chicago Defender*, "league rules provide that no championship game shall be played at night."[208]

The Chicago American Giants protested the Thursday night game.

Even a few weeks later, Wilson declared, "You may put the whole business down as spite work. Coles is still sore because I did not rule in his favor in the playoff."[209] Cum Posey wrote that Wilson "has not yet given a decision" but he did choose not to run again as commissioner.[210]

The protest was ultimately "refused" rather than denied, Wilson's argument being that (these were not his words but those in the newspaper) "the conduct of the umpires in the game in question was unjustifiable, but at the same time rules that he, being a spectator, had no authority to overrule them on that particular game."[211] There was some thought that the Stars might elect not to be in the league again in 1935.[212]

WRAPPING UP THE 1934 SEASON

The *Philadelphia Tribune*'s Ed R. Harris offered a summary of the season, writing in part: "Now that the pennant of the National Association championship lies in the collective arms of Ed Bolden's Philadelphia Stars, the league closes its season. The first season that organized colored baseball has stuck together through a campaign. There's been plenty of hard words said, misdeeds done and unwise moves made. But still the league is to be congratulated."[213]

Even the *Philadelphia Inquirer* took note of the Stars' success, singling out Slim Jones for accolades.

"More than one member of Bolden's Philadelphia Stars, colored champions, is good enough for the major league lawn," the *Inquirer* wrote, adding, "That 20-year-old giant sidewinder, Slim Jones, would have every scout in the majors following him if he were white."[214]

Harris saw storm clouds on the horizon, though, plenty of them. "There are clubs dropping out, other clubs demanding concessions and the more fearful predict that the league will not reopen next year. A foretaste of what is in the wind occurred last Monday when the moguls of the Philadelphia and Chicago gathered before Commissioner Wilson to debate of the protest made by Dave Malarcher of the Giants. Dave protested the retaining of Jud Wilson in the Saturday game after he had struck Umpire Gohlson [*sic*]. The Commissioner was for keeping Wilson out of Monday's game but Ed Bolden said if such a move was made the Stars would not play if '50 or 50,000 people were in the park.' Harris wrote. "It is my hope that the Association will function next year – it's what colored baseball needs and its initial season has done much towards making the game a profitable enterprise for owner, player and fan alike."[215]

Malarcher's protest was adjudicated and Commissioner Wilson ruled, in his words: "The conduct of the umpires was unjustifiable but at the same time rules that he, being a spectator, had no authority to overrule them on that particular game. Any action to punish the arbiters for indefensible conduct must be in the future on their efficiency, or lack of it, shown in the past."[216]

POST-POSTSEASON GAMES

October 6, 1934: Pittsburgh Crawfords 4, Philadelphia Stars 2, at Passon Field.

In a night game in Philadelphia, the champion Stars were perhaps understandably "decidedly off-form, suffering a let-down after the strain of the title series with the Chicago American Giants."[217] Satchel Paige struck out 12 or 13 Stars (the game story and box score differ) and walked two. Lefty Holmes pitched for Philadelphia; he walked five Crawfords batters. Each team managed seven hits. A major difference in the game was six errors by the home team while the Crawfords made none. The Stars scored one in the first inning and one in the ninth. The Crawfords got three in the second and one more in the fourth.

October 7, 1934: Pittsburgh Crawfords 6, Philadelphia Stars 1, at Griffith Stadium, Washington

In a doubleheader, the Crawfords took on the Stars and the Homestead Grays took on the New York Black Yankees. Five thousand came to see the games. Both Pittsburgh teams prevailed. The Grays beat the Yankees, 5-3, in a darkness-shortened seven-inning second game.

The first game featured Leroy Matlock pitching against Webster McDonald, the Crawfords being the "home" team. The Craws scored first, with one run in the bottom of the second on singles by Judy Johnson and Curtis Harris. It was the only run either team scored through four. In the top of the fifth, Dunn walked. Catcher Johnny Hayes sacrificed Dunn to second, and he took third on what was either a passed ball or a wild pitch. Pete Washington then doubled down the line in left field. The Stars managed only two other hits off Matlock in the whole game, singles by Jud Wilson and Dick Seay.

In the seventh, the Crawfords broke the 1-1 tie by adding three runs. McDonald hit Ted Page with a pitch. Matlock walked. Slim Jones relieved McDonald. Vic Harris drew a walk, loading the bases. Rap Dixon hit a sacrifice fly to right field for the first run, and Oscar Charleston singled over the shortstop to drive in two more. In the eighth Johnson singled, Bill Perkins doubled, and Curtis Harris dropped a Texas Leaguer into center field, driving in both runners, in part thanks to a poor throw from catcher Hayes to Seay at second.[218]

October 13, 1934: Philadelphia Stars 8, Dizzy Deans All Stars 0; Philadelphia Stars 4, Philadelphia All-Stars 3 (7 innings), at Shibe Park, Philadelphia

The *New York Amsterdam News*'s Romeo L. Dougherty was not impressed with the effort put forth by the Deans, dubbing an effort put forth against the Black Yankees at Dexter Park a "travesty" and writing, "When thousands had hoped that they would see one of the Deans in real action against some of our clubs, the result at hand shows that it was a circus which Barnum and Bailey could just as well have palmed off on the ever willing suckers."[219] In the game against the Stars, Dizzy pitched all of two innings – holding the Stars scoreless – but then departed, and the Stars jumped on his replacement and won, 8-0. It was far from a true exhibition of what two of the top pitchers in White baseball could do against the championship team in Black baseball.

The Deans played with the Philadelphia All-Stars, another team made up of White major- and minor-league players.

October 14, 1934: New York Black Yankees 3, Philadelphia Stars 2 (first game, 10 innings); New York Black Yankees 4, Philadelphia Stars 3 (second game), location uncertain

Apparently home games for the Black Yankees, these two one-run games helped the New Yorkers batters balance the scales against the Stars. The first game had been tied 1-1 through nine innings. The Stars scored once in the top of the 10th but was resolved in the bottom of the 10th by John Beckwith "hitting the ball over the fence."[220] There was no information other than the score provided regarding the second game. One of the games – but we don't know which – was pitched by Bill Holland for New York. We don't know who pitched for Philadelphia.

October 20, 1934: On this Saturday night, before the Stars left for a tour to play in some Southern states, they were feted at a banquet at the O. V. Catto Elks Lodge in Philadelphia, treated to some wrestling and boxing matches, then a dinner with music, and the players presented gold baseball emblems.[221]

October 21, 1934 – a Sunday DH vs New York Black Yankees, at Catholic Protectory, at East Tremont Avenue and Unionport Road was previewed in the October 20 *New York Amsterdam News*. Whether the game was played is uncertain.

Later in October, the Stars returned to New Orleans. The *York Dispatch*, Jake Stephens's hometown newspaper (which called him by his first name Paul and spelled his last name as Stevens), reported that after beating the Chicago American Giants, "they went south and played New Orleans, the southern champions, and defeated New Orleans in four straight games, giving Captain Stevens' team full claim to the title of colored champions of the United. States." The Stars were said to be planning to travel to Mexico to play, but Stevens was said to be unsure whether or not he would join them.[222]

October 27, 1934: Philadelphia Stars 2, Crescent Stars 0, at Crescent Park, New Orleans

The two teams had met in Philadelphia on Labor Day. Now they played each other again in New Orleans. The *Philadelphia Tribune* reported that the first of the games was a 2-0 win for pitcher Paul Carter on October 27. Carter struck out seven and benefited from RBI singles by Jud Wilson and Biz Mackey.[223]

October 28, 1934: Philadelphia Stars 10, Crescent Stars 0; Philadelphia Stars 4, Crescent Stars 2, at Crescent Park, New Orleans

In a Sunday doubleheader, Slim Jones struck out 13 of the Crescent Stars while shutting out the host team in the first game. His teammates scored 10 runs, with three RBIs apiece by Jud Wilson and Jake Dunn. Rocky Ellis pitched the second game, holding the Crescent team to three base hits. Both Wilson and Leroy Morney (who had played with the Pittsburgh Crawfords during the regular season) homered for Philadelphia.[224]

What they did in the intervening days is unclear. But two weeks later the Stars played a pair of games in Austin, Texas.

November 11, 1934: Philadelphia Stars 8, Austin Black Senators 1; Austin Black Senators 3, Philadelphia Stars 2, at West End Park, Houston

We don't truly know when the season ended. The last scores we found were for this Sunday doubleheader in Houston indicating a split, but with no further details regarding pitchers, players, etc. There were two different brief bits in the Austin newspaper, on adjacent pages, both saying that a 1:30 P.M. doubleheader would be played at Sam Houston Stadium, Austin, that very day.[225] Was it? It was not reported in the *Statesman*.

Sources and acknowledgments

Special thanks to Gary Ashwill, Rich Bogovich, Rick Bush, Alan Cohen, Bob Golon, Larry Lester, Brian Michael, and Rich Puerzer, all of whom contributed valuable information.

Brian Michael in particular offered a wealth of newspaper clippings. He was assisted in some of his work by Ashleigh Hume and Adam Yeager.

Thanks to Bruce R. Bardarik of the Paterson Free Public Library and Beth Zak-Cohen, reference librarian, New Jersey Room, Newark.

NOTES

1   The actual name of the league on such legal documents as there may have been is unclear, but we have called it the Negro National League, or NNL2 here, even though there are a large number of newspapers which called it the Negro National Association or by other names. After the regular season was over, the league's commissioner, W. Rollo Wilson, referred to it as the National Negro Association of Professional Baseball Clubs. See W. Rollo Wilson, "Curtain Falling on Season," *Pittsburgh Courier*, September 15, 1934: 14. The secretary of the league, John L. Clark, was presented in the *Courier* with a byline and title reading "Secretary, Natl. Assn. of Negro Baseball Clubs." See John L. Clark, "1934 Season Considered Successful; Baseball Highlights Recalled," *Pittsburgh Courier*, January 5, 1935: 14. Two weeks later, Ches Washington called it the National Association of Negro Baseball Clubs." See "Sez Ches," *Pittsburgh Courier*, January 19, 1935: 15.

2   All league statistics are as presented by Seamheads, unless otherwise indicated.

3   "Negro National League Moguls to Meet Here," *Pittsburgh Courier*, January 6, 1934: A4.

4   W. Rollo Wilson, "Sport Shots: Baseball's First Powwow This Saturday," *Pittsburgh Courier*, January 13, 1934: B4. Wilson added, "More and more the owners are coming to recognize the necessity of limiting their league clubs to a reasonable distance apart. There should be a Southern, Western and Eastern league. Present rumors are that a western group will merge with some of the southern clubs under the lead of J.L. Wilkinson. The Dixie clubs, however, maintain that they will retain their present body." That was the Southern League.

5   "Sound Second Call for Baseball Meet," *Baltimore Afro-American*, January 27, 1934: 18.

6   "Baseball Men Meet in Philly," *Baltimore Afro-American*, February 10, 1934: 12. The various considerations of a number of different clubs are discussed in "Baseball Owners En Route to Philly Pow-wow," *Pittsburgh Courier*, February 10, 1934: A5.

7   W. Rollo Wilson, "Sport Shots: About Baseball's Heroes Then and Now," *Pittsburgh Courier*, February 10, 1934: A4.

8   See, for instance, "McDonald Manages Philadelphia Stars," *New York Amsterdam News*, January 31, 1934: 7, and Randy Dixon, "Ed Bolden Announces New Base Ball Plans," *Philadelphia Tribune*, February 1, 1934. Dixon called him the "gentleman of Negro baseball."

9   Randy Dixon, "Baseball Magnates Convene in Parley Here," *Philadelphia Tribune*, February 15, 1934.

10   "Baseball Magnates Convene in Parley Here."

11   "Blacksox, Grays Not Included; Seek 7th Club," *Pittsburgh Courier*, February 17, 1934: A4.

12   W. Rollo Wilson, "Sport Shots"; Fans Want an Open Game," *Pittsburgh Courier*, February 24, 1934: A4.

13   "Cum Posey's Pointed Paragraphs," *Pittsburgh Courier*, March 3, 1934: A5.

14   Albert J. Menendez, "The Battle for Sunday Baseball," *Liberty*, September/October 2007. https://www.libertymagazine.org/article/the-battle-for-sunday-baseball. Accessed August 1, 2021. For a full study of "The Major Leagues' Struggle to Play Baseball on the Lord's Day, 1876-1934," see Charlie Bevis, *Sunday Baseball* (Jefferson, North Carolina: McFarland, 2003).

15   W. Ardee, "Phil Cockrell to Twirl for Phila. Stars," *Philadelphia Tribune*, February 22, 1934.

16   Randy Dixon, "Newspaperman Accepts Job as Baseball Commissioner; Sweeping Reforms Are Made," *Philadelphia Tribune*, March 15, 1934.

17   Randy Dixon, "Wilson Made 'Judge Landis' of New Negro Baseball League," *New York Amsterdam News*, March 17, 1934: 10.

18   The Bacharach Giants had been based in Atlantic City and played there from 1916 through 1929. The team played independent baseball until 1942, with 1934 being the only year after 1929 that they played league ball.

19   Randy Dixon, "Creacy with Stars; Big Cage Frays on Tab," *Philadelphia Tribune*, March 22, 1934.

20   W. Rollo Wilson, "Baseball Head Quizzed by 'Alter Ego,' Declines to Have Press Battles with Angry 'Magnates,'" *Pittsburgh Courier*, April 14, 1934: A4.

21   "Creacy with Stars; Big Cage Frays on Tab." For more on Passon, see Rebecca Alpert, "Harry Passon: Philadelphia Baseball Entrepreneur," in *The National Pastime*, Society for American Baseball Research, 2013.

22   "First Half of Schedule for the N.N.A. for 1934," *New York Amsterdam News*, March 24, 1934: 10.

23   "Zulus Bow to All Stars by 3 to 2 Count," *Philadelphia Tribune*, April 5, 1934. The Zulu players included names such as Tanganyika, Kalahari, Tahooli, Zanzibab, and Wampoo. Nyasses was almost certainly Peanuts Nyasses. See also "Bizz Mackey's All-Stars Beat Zulu Jungle Giants," *Pittsburgh Courier*, April 7, 1934: 14.

24   "Birmingham Black Crackers to Field First Class Nine With Philly as Home Base," *Philadelphia Tribune*, April 5, 1934: 10.

25   "Philly Stars Win, 10-3," *Baltimore Afro-American*, April 14, 1934: 18. The most detailed account of the game is "Bolden Stars Swamp W. Olney in First Game," *Pittsburgh Courier*, April 14, 1934: A4.

26   "Jud Wilson Named Phila. Stars Capt.,'" *Philadelphia Tribune*, April 12, 1934.

27   "Stars Bunch Hits to Stop Raphael, 9-3," *Philadelphia Tribune*, April 19, 1934: 10.

28   The losses the Baltimore team had borne are detailed in Bill Gibson, "Hear Me Talkin' to Ya," *Baltimore Afro-American*, May 12, 1934: 18.

29   "Commissioner Rollo Wilson Bans Rowdyism in Baseball," *Pittsburgh Courier*, April 21, 1934: A5.

30   "Bolden's Stars Win 2 from Newark," *Philadelphia Tribune*, April 26, 1934: 12. The headline in the *Afro-American* indicated four more homers in the night game. "Philly Stars Slam Out 7 Homers in Twin Bill," *Baltimore Afro-American*, April 28, 1934: 19.

31   Randy Dixon, "Randy Says," *Philadelphia Tribune*, April 12, 1934. The May 5 *Baltimore Afro-American* featured a photo of Rap Dixon, with the news that he was still confined to a Philadelphia hospital and had been released. "Released by Philly Stars," *Baltimore Afro-American*, May 5, 1934: 19.

32   W. Rollo Wilson, "Sport Shots: Here's Your Old Col Again," *Pittsburgh Courier*, May 5, 1934: A4.

33   "Bolden Stars Rally in Eighth," *Philadelphia Tribune*, May 3, 1934: 10.

34   "Westville Drops Pair over Weekend," Camden (New Jersey) *Courier-Post*, May 7, 1934: 16.

35   Rome L. Dougherty, "Four Clubs to Open National Negro League Season May 12," *New York Amsterdam News*, May 17, 1934: 10.

36   "Colored Stars Easily Beat Chix," *Vineland* (New Jersey) *Daily Journal*, May 12, 1934: 8.

37   Opening Day game information primarily comes from a detailed account in the *Philadelphia Tribune*. See "Stars Topple Newark for Inaugural 12-0 Win," *Philadelphia Tribune*, May 17, 1934. See also W. Rollo Wilson, "Jones Holds Lundymen to Three Hits; Phila. Stars Win Opener in Big Way," *Pittsburgh Courier*, May 19, 1934: 14.

38 W. Rollo Wilson, "Sport Shots: Saw Loop Openers," *Pittsburgh Courier*, May 24, 1934: A4.

39 "Philadelphia Stars Win 2 From Newark," *Philadelphia Tribune*, May 17, 1934.

40 "Sport Shots: Saw Loop Openers."

41 This is based on the box score and two-sentence game account. "Stars Beat Crawfords," *Pittsburgh Post-Gazette*, May 19, 1934.

42 Chester L. Washington, "Crawfords Win 2 out of 3 from Philly Stars," *Pittsburgh Courier*, May 26, 1934: A4.

43 "Mayor Is Tosser at Opener," *Atlanta Daily World*, May 25, 1934: 5.

44 "Crawfords Win 2 out of 3 from Philly Stars."

45 "Crawfords Win 2 out of 3 from Philly Stars." See also "Sez Ches," *Pittsburgh Courier*, May 26, 1934: A5.

46 "Craws Win Finale," *Pittsburgh Courier*, May 26, 1934: A5.

47 "Crawfords Win Again," *Pittsburgh Post-Gazette*, May 23, 1934: 16.

48 "Philadelphia Stars Triumph," *York* (Pennsylvania) *Daily Record*, May 24, 1934: 10. All quotations in this game summary come from this article. The paper misspelled both Satchel Paige's surname and that of Stephens. Washington's home run was hit out of the park, presumably right down the line in either left or right field, where it was 305 feet to the fence, rather than to straightaway right field at 395 feet. Washington batted right-handed. Park dimensions are from Philip J. Lowry, ed., *Green Cathedrals* (Phoenix: SABR, 2019), 312.

49 "What Happened in Pennant Race? We Guess, Make Yours," *Chicago Defender*, May 26, 1934: 16.

50 "Braves Tackle Bolden's Nine," *Asbury Park* (New Jersey) *Press*, September 7, 1934: 13.

51 "Woodstown Aviators to Meet Phila., Stars," *Camden* (New Jersey) *Evening Post*, September 6, 1934: 16.

52 "Negro Ball Teams to Play Series Here Saturday, Sunday," *Houston Chronicle*, November 7, 1934: 25. A little more than a week earlier, the *New Orleans Times-Picayune* had reported the same totals. "Crescent Stars and Philly Nine to Clash Today," *Times-Picayune*, October 28, 1934: 57.

53 "Belmar Braves Play Tonight," *Asbury Park Press*, May 25, 1934: 25.

54 "Philly Stars Drop Brace to Grays," *Baltimore Afro-American*, June 2, 1934: 17.

55 "Chicago Police Reported Holding Crawford Pitcher," *Baltimore Afro-American*, June 2, 1934: 17.

56 W. Rollo Wilson, "Philly All-Star Win Second Game on Sunday, Bow in First to Posey's Club," *Pittsburgh Courier*, June 2, 1934: A6. There is a discrepancy between Wilson's account of the game and the less fulsome one that appeared in the *Philadelphia Tribune*, which said that Jones had relieved in the eighth (perhaps after McDonald was struck in the foot) and was charged with the loss.

57 "Grays Topple Stars," *Philadelphia Tribune*, May 31, 1934: 12. Frank Merriwell was a fictional character popular in the first three decades of the twentieth century, portrayed as an exceptionally clean-cut Yale man who always triumphed over odds stacked against him.

58 See also W. Rollo Wilson, "Philly All-Star Win Second Game on Sunday, Bow in First to Posey's Club."

59 "Philly All-Stars Nip Hightstown," *Trenton Evening Times*, May 28, 1934: 17.

60 Bill Gibson, "Hear Me Talkin' to Ya," *Baltimore Afro-American*, June 9, 1934: 16.

61 "Phila. Stars Lose to Crawford Foe," *Philadelphia Inquirer*, May 31, 1934: 20. The *Inquirer* offered a box score, showing the number of runs per inning, but the June 7 *Tribune* (which said the first game was 5-0) did not.

62 "Crawfords Take Two," *Philadelphia Tribune*, June 7, 1934: 12.

63 "Two Games for Al Mamaux Team Today," *Red Bank* (New Jersey) *Daily Register*, May 30, 1934: 18.

64 "Chi Adds Two More," *Philadelphia Tribune*, June 7, 1934: 12.

65 "Stars Divide Twin Bill After Losing Four in Row," *Philadelphia Tribune*, June 7, 1934: 12. Whether "Carl Knothe" was Fritz Knothe or his brother George Knothe is not known; both had been infielders with the Phillies, though George played in only six games compared with Fritz's 41.

66 "Passons, Chi Giants Taken Over by Stars," *Philadelphia Tribune*, June 14, 1934: 12.

67 "Stars Drop Giants from First Place," *Pittsburgh Courier*, June 16, 1934: A4.

68 "Passons, Chi Giants Taken Over By Stars."

69 "Stars in Second Place After Whipping Nashville," *Philadelphia Tribune*, June 14, 1934: 12.

70 "Phila Stars Cop Two from Nashville Nine," *Philadelphia Inquirer*, June 10, 1934: S5.

71 Details of Pittsburgh's scoring may be found in an article by A. Mantel Carter, under the incorrect headline "Craws Down Philly Stars in D.C., 12-2," *Baltimore Afro-American*, June 16, 1934: 17.

72 "Home Run Sends Philadelphia to Defeat in Duel," *Harrisburg* (Pennsylvania) *Evening News*, June 12, 1934: 13.

73 "Home Run Sends Philadelphia to Defeat in Duel." Harris's first name was rendered as Verne.

74 "Philly Stars Extend Streak," *Baltimore Afro-American*, June 23, 1934: 18.

75 "Phillie All-Stars Beat Nashville," *York Gazette and Daily*, June 16, 1934: 5; "Philadelphia Stars Top Nashville Club," *York Dispatch*, June 16, 1934: 7.

76 "Phillie All-Stars Beat Nashville."

77 "Grays Beat Philly; Meet Barons Saturday," *Pittsburgh Courier*, June 23, 1934: A4

78 John L. Clark, "Wylie Avenue, Pittsburgh," *Pittsburgh Courier*, June 23, 1934: 5.

79 Emmett H. Armstead, "Philadelphia Beats Cleveland," *Chicago Defender*, June 23, 1934: 17.

80 *Akron Beacon Journal*, June 19, 1934: 21.

81 The logic regarding the Stars was more difficult to follow. "Chicago May Cop League Honors," *Baltimore Afro-American*, June 23, 1934: 18.

82 "Phila. Stars Beat Cleveland Four Straight," *Philadelphia Tribune*, June 28, 1934: 12.

83 "Philadelphia Stars Win Double Bill," *Philadelphia Inquirer*, June 24, 1934: 8.

84 "Sez 'Ches,'" *Pittsburgh Courier*, June 30, 1934: A5.

85 "Philadelphia All-Stars Win Four," *Chicago Defender*, June 30, 1934: 16.

86 The pitcher may have been Tom Richardson, who is listed on Seamheads as pitching one game for the 1934 Bacharachs and in one 1934 game for the Baltimore Black Sox. For game data, see "Stars Trip Artisans in Frantic Fuss," *Philadelphia Tribune*, June 28, 1934: 12. The ethnicity of the Artisans as White was indicated in "Philly Stars Take Two from Grays," *Baltimore Afro-American*, July 7, 1934: 18.

87 "Bolden Stars Win," *Philadelphia Inquirer*, June 27, 1934: 19.

88 "Philly Stars Take Two from Grays."

89 "Philly Stars Take Two from Grays."

90   "'Shot' Pitching Staff Falls Before Bats of Stars in Two Defeats," *Pittsburgh Courier*, July 7, 1934: A4.

91   "Bolden Boys Trip Grays, 10-9, 6-2; Tie 1," *Philadelphia Tribune*, July 5, 1934.

92   Phillipsburg, New Jersey, was an hour and a half from Philadelphia, a more likely destination than Phillipsburg, Pennsylvania, which was 3½ hours' distance.

93   Dan Burley, "Dan Burley Lists 'Greats' of Negro Athletic World," *Atlanta Daily World*, June 28, 1934: 5. Burley also named players from track and field, boxing, and tennis.

94   "Bees and Black Sox Join National League," *Philadelphia Tribune*, July 5, 1934: 12. See also John L. Clark, "Baltimore, Bacharachs Get Berth in League," *Chicago Defender*, July 14, 1934: 17.

95   "'Shot' Pitching Staff Falls Before Bats of Stars in Two Defeats."

96   "Black Sox Secure League Franchise," *Baltimore Afro-American*, July 7, 1934: 19. The same edition of the newspaper had another article centered on the Black Sox. See Bill Gibson, "Hear Me Talkin' to Ya," *Afro-American*, July 7, 1934: 19.

97   The schedule was printed in the *Baltimore Afro-American* on July 7, 1934, on page 19.

98   See both "Bolden Boys Trip Grays, 10-9, 6-2; Tie 1" and "'Shot' Pitching Staff Falls Before Bats of Stars in Two Defeats."

99   "Stars Whip Craws, Then Lose to All-Stars by 7-4 Score," *Philadelphia Tribune*, July 12, 1934: 12; "Bartram Topples Philadelphia Stars," *Philadelphia Inquirer*, July 3, 1934: 16.

100   Romeo L. Dougherty, "Sports," *New York Amsterdam News*, July 14, 1934: 10.

101   Dan Burley, "Writer Sees Baseball League as Misnomer," *Baltimore Afro-American*, July 21, 1934: 19.

102   More complete details, including more of Dixon's statement, are available at "Sox Boss Tells Why No More Games Were Played in Baltimore," *Baltimore Afro-American*, August 25, 1934: 18.

103   "Boldens Whip Nashville," *Chicago Defender*, July 14, 1934: 16.

104   "Philly Stars Take Two from Craws." *Baltimore Afro-American*, July 7, 1934: 18.

105   "Stars Whip Craws, Then Lose to All-Stars by 7-4 Score."

106   "Stars Slap Craws 3 Out of 4 Games," *Philadelphia Tribune*, July 19, 1934: 12.

107   "Stars Whip Craws, Then Lose to All-Stars by 7-4 Score."

108   "Beckwith's Two Homers and Double Figure in 7-5 Win," *Paterson* (New Jersey) *Morning Call*, July 9, 1934: 19.

109   "Stars Whip Craws, Then Lose to All-Stars by 7-4 Score."

110   "Philadelphia Stars Beat Dodgers, 15-4," *Newark Evening News*, July 10, 1934: 27.

111   "Stars Whip Craws, Then Lose to All-Stars by 7-4 Score."

112   "Ed Bolden's Stars Divide Twin Bill," *Philadelphia Inquirer*, July 11, 1934: 21.

113   "Stars Whip Craws, Then Lose to All-Stars by 7-4 Score."

114   "Stars Whip Craws, Then Lose to All-Stars by 7-4 Score."

115   "Ed Bolden's Stars Divide Twin Bill."

116   "Crawfords and All-Stars Split," *York Gazette and Daily,* July 13, 1934: 11.

117   "Stars Slap Craws 3 Out of 4 Games."

118   "Stars Slap Craws 3 Out of 4 Games."

119   W. Rollo Wilson, "Boldenmen Trip 'Craws' Twice to Take Top Rung of League Flag Ladder," *Pittsburgh Courier*, July 21, 1934: A4.

120   "Boldenmen Trip 'Craws' Twice to Take Top Rung of League Flag Ladder."

121   "Stars Win and Tie in Harrisburg," *Pittsburgh Courier*, July 21, 1934: A4. The *Courier* box score showed seven hits, but the *Baltimore Afro-American* but the *Courier* mistotaled them as six.

122   "Philly Stars Take Two from Craws," *Baltimore Afro-American*, July 21, 1934: 19.

123   "Stars Win and Tie in Harrisburg."

124   "Philly Stars Take Two from Grays," *Baltimore Afro-American*, July 7, 1934: 18.

125   "Stars Slap Craws 3 Out of 4 Games."

126   The advertisement ran in the *Hagerstown Daily Mail* on July 12, 1934, on page 11.

127   "Philly Stars Win 5, Drop 2; Player Breaks Leg," *Philadelphia Tribune*, July 26, 1934: 12.

128   "Bolden All-Stars Beat Hightstown," *Trenton Evening Times*, July 19, 1934: 19.

129   "Philly Stars Win 5, Drop 2; Player Breaks Leg."

130   "Philly Stars Win 5, Drop 2; Player Breaks Leg."

131   "Philly Stars Win 5, Drop 2; Player Breaks Leg."

132   "Philly Stars Break Even in Twin Bill with Yankees," *Afro-American*, July 28, 1934: 18.

133   "Philly Stars Win 5, Drop 2; Player Breaks Leg."

134   "Philly Stars Win 5, Drop 2; Player Breaks Leg."

135   "Philly Stars Rout Homestead Grays," *Baltimore Afro-American*, July 28, 1934: 19.

136   "Bacharachs and Stars to Play Series for City Championship," *Philadelphia Tribune*, July 26,1934.

137   "Stars Drub Bees in City Series Start; Boldenboys Take Two Games," *Philadelphia Tribune*, August 2, 1934: 12.

138   "Philly Stars Snatch Two from Chicago," *Baltimore Afro-American*, August 4, 1934: 18.

139   "Stars Drub Bees in City Series Start; Boldenboys Take Two Games."

140   "Stars Drub Bees in City Series Start; Boldenboys Take Two Games."

141   "Phila. Stars Down Passon A.A. Tossers," *Philadelphia Inquirer*, July 31, 1934: 10.

142   "Bolden's Stars Beat Chester, 3 to 1," *Chester* (Pennsylvania) *Times*, July 31, 1934: 10.

143   "Stars Drub Bees in City Series Start; Boldenboys Take Two Games."

144   "Philly Stars Slap Yankees Twice," *Philadelphia Tribune*, August 9, 1934: 12.

145   The *Atlanta Daily World* story says it was the seventh that was the eight-run inning, but the *Philadelphia Tribune* box score (the Atlanta paper had no box score) shows it was the sixth, the inning in which Wilson hit the grand slam. The box score shows two runs added in the seventh and ninth innings. See "Philadelphia Stars Win Three, 19-14, 4-2 and 7-3," *Atlanta Daily World*, August 13, 1934: 5; "Balto. Black Sox Lose to Stars," *Philadelphia Tribune*, August 9, 1934: 12.

146   "Philly Drubs Yanks, Sox," *Chicago Defender*, August 11, 1934: 16.

147   "Philly Stars Slap Yankees Twice."

148   "Philly Stars Slap Yankees Twice."

149   "Philly Stars Slap Yankees Twice."

150   "5,000 Philly Fans Roar at New Fangled Baseball," *Baltimore Afro-American*, August 11, 1934: 18.

151   "Philly Stars Slap Yankees Twice."

152   Ed R. Harris, "Points and Errors," *Philadelphia Tribune*. August 16, 1934. For more on Taylor, see Jon Daly, "Johnny Taylor," SABR BioProject, https://sabr.org/bioproj/person/johnny-taylor/.

153   "Philly Stars Add to League Lead," *Chicago Defender*, August 18, 1934: 16.

154   "Philly Stars Take Pair from Bacharachs," *Baltimore Afro-American*, August 18, 1934: 18.

155   "Colored Player Barred, Coach Quits Tourney," *Philadelphia Tribune*, August 30, 1934. The *Tribune* misspelled Taliaferro's surname and Coach Harris's first name in its article.

156   "Springfield Legion Baseball Nine Voluntarily Withdraws from Eastern Title Tourney," *Springfield* (Massachusetts) *Republican*, August 23, 1934: 1, 13. The Legion team from Charlotte said they would have

no problem playing Springfield. Taliaferro lived in Western Massachusetts until his death in 1967.

157   "Philadelphia Stars Humble Birmingham," *York Gazette and Daily*, August 18, 1934: 10.

158   "Craws Win 4 out of 6 from Philly," *Pittsburgh Courier*, August 25, 1934: A4.

159   "Crawfords, Stars Even in 4 Games," *Baltimore Afro-American*, August 25, 1934: 18.

160   "Crawfords Split Series with Philly," *Chicago Defender*, August 25, 1934: 16.

161   "Crawfords Win Two," *Pittsburgh Post-Gazette*, August 20, 1934: 11.

162   "Crawfords Twice Trip Phila. Stars," *Philadelphia Inquirer*, August 21, 1934: 26.

163   "Stars Top Nashville, Birmingham Tossers," *Baltimore Afro-American*, September 1, 1934: 19.

164   "Newark Dodgers Win Over All-Stars, 4-3," *Trenton Evening Times*, August 24, 1934: 17. The *Evening Times* mistakenly rendered the Stars as All-Stars. It said that Hightstown had beaten the Philadelphia team earlier in the year.

165   "Phila. Stars Clip Holmesburg Nine," *Philadelphia Inquirer*, August 25, 1934: 24.

166   "Stars Clip Nashville Gts.," *Philadelphia Tribune*, August 30, 1934: 12. See also *Philadelphia Inquirer*, August 25, 1934: 14.

167   "Stars Top Nashville, Birmingham Tossers." See also accounts in "Phila. Stars Land Twin Bill Victory," *Philadelphia Inquirer*, August 26, 1934: S7.

168   "Stars Clip Nashville Gts." See also "Phila. Stars Twice Down Nashville Foes," *Philadelphia Inquirer*, August 27, 1934: 16.

169   "Nashville Meets All-Stars Tonite," *Chester Times*, August 27, 1934: 11.

170   "Stars Clip Nashville Gts."

171   "Phila. Stars Trip Nashville Giants," *Philadelphia Inquirer*, August 28, 1934: 14.

172   "Pennsy Field Game," *Wilmington* (Delaware) *News Journal*, August 27, 1934: 16.

173   "Phila. Stars Beat Narberth Tossers," *Philadelphia Inquirer*, August 30, 1934: 16.

174   "Palmyra Bows 13-1," *Lebanon* (Pennsylvania) *Daily News, and the Lebanon Daily Times*, September 1, 1934: 4.

175   *Chester Times*, August 30, 1934: 11.

176   "Crescents Tie with Phila. Stars."

177   "Giants Lose to Philly; Then Tie, 1-1," *Chicago Defender*, September 8, 1934: 17.

178   This information came from the *Tribune*.

179   "Raphael Divides Twin Bill With Stars, Losing Second After Winning First," *Philadelphia Inquirer*, September 3, 1934: 11.

180   "Crescents Tie with Phila. Stars."

181   "Crescents Tie with Phila. Stars," *Philadelphia Tribune*, September 6, 1934: 9.

182   "Crescent Stars and Philly Nine to Clash Today," *New Orleans Times-Picayune*, October 28, 1934: 57.

183   "Paul Stevens Captain of Championship Nine," *York Dispatch*, November 6, 1934: 13.

184   "Negro Team Beats Needleworks, 7-1," *Pottstown* (Pennsylvania) *Mercury*, September 6, 1934: 5.

185   "American Giants to Play in Negro World Series Today," *Chicago Tribune*, September 8, 1934: 21.

186   Newspaper accounts differ, even within the same article (the *Philadelphia Tribune* article said 30,000 in the headline and 25,000 in the text.) See also "Black Yankees Lose, 4-3, Before 20,000," *New York Times*, September 10, 1934: 21. The games were a benefit for the Col. Charles Young American Legion post, in memory of two soldiers. See Bessye J. Bearden, "Giants, Trent Win All-Star Ball Game," *Chicago Defender*, September 15, 1934: A5. Estimates are that as many as 5,000 were turned away – not because the seats were filled to capacity, but because many more turned out for the game than had been expected, and as few as four ticket windows and gates were open. See, among other accounts, Romeo L. Dougherty, "Sports," *New York Amsterdam News*, September 22, 1934: 10. Dougherty says they expected 5,000, not as many as 30,000.

187   Chester L. Washington, "Craws, Phillies in 1-1 Tie; Chi Beats N.Y., 4-3," *Pittsburgh Courier*, September 15, 1934: A4.

188   W. Rollo Wilson, "Sport Shots: Big Moments in Baseball," *Pittsburgh Courier*, September 22, 1934: A4.

189   The most complete accounts of this game are Washington's in the *Courier* and Edgar T. Rouzeau, "New York Wants Baseball," *New York Amsterdam News*, September 15, 1934: 10. It is marred a bit, though, by unfamiliarity with player names – Biz Mackey was called Biff Mackay. Webster McDonald was called McDowell, and the Crawfords' first baseman Charleston appeared in the box score as Gholston, presumably confused with veteran umpire Bert Gholston, one of three who worked the game. (Gholston worked first base.) The *Tribune* account, written by Harris, differed in that it said White singled to lead off, and never accounted for the first out. Further, it is contradicted by its own box score, which shows Brooks (and not McDonald) pinch-hitting for Seay.

190   "Kensington Nips Phila. Stars, 2-1," *Philadelphia Inquirer*, September 11, 1934: 28.

191   Ed R. Harris, "Points and Errors," *Philadelphia Tribune*, September 13, 1934.

192   W. Rollo Wilson, "Baseball's Curtain Falling on Season," *Pittsburgh Courier*, September 15, 1934: A4.

193   Wilson, "Baseball's Curtain Falling on Season."

194   "Chicago Stops Stars in Playoff Start," *Philadelphia Tribune*, September 13, 1934: 14.

195   "Ted Trent Twirls Beautiful Game," *Atlanta Daily World*, September 24, 1934: 5.

196   "Ted Trent Twirls Beautiful Game" and "Giants, Stars Break Even in Double Header," *Chicago Tribune*, September 17, 1934: 23.

197   The *Chicago Defender* said it was Radcliffe. The *Chicago Tribune* said it was Suttles. See "Giants Lead Philly in World's Series, 3-1, *Chicago*

Defender, September 22, 1934: 16, and "American Giants Take 3 to 1 Lead in World Series," *Chicago Tribune*, September 18, 1934: 23.

198   "Philly Batters Win Over Dodgers, 2 to 1," *Trenton Evening Times*, September 21, 1934: 23.

199   "East Orange to Meet Philly Colored Team," *Bridgewater* (New Jersey) *Courier-News*, September 21, 1934: 21.

200   "Jones, Carter Reverse Yanks," *Philadelphia Tribune*, September 27, 1934: 11.

201   "Black Yanks Bow to All-Stars, 5-3," *Asbury Park Press*, September 29, 1934: 10.

202   Ed R. Harris, "To Be or Not to Be," *Philadelphia Tribune*, October 4, 1934.

203   Harris, "To Be or Not to Be."

204   For one article preceding the event, see "Commissioner to Toss Ball," *New York Amsterdam News*, September 29, 1934: 10.

205   Edgar T. Rouzeau, "Paige Again Starts at Stadium," *New York Amsterdam News*, October 6, 1934: 10.

206   "Paige Again Starts at Stadium."

207   "Chicago Giants Tie Stars in Series Tilt," *Philadelphia Inquirer*, October 2, 1934, 19; "Boldens Get 2 Runs to Tie Payoff Tiff," *Philadelphia Tribune*, October 4, 1934: 11, 14.

208   "Philly Stars World Champs?" *Chicago Defender*, October 6, 1934: 17.

209   Ed R. Harris, "Coles Refuses to Pay League Salaries Due," *Philadelphia Tribune*, November 8, 1934.

210   Cum Posey, "Posey and Wilson Air Views on National League Controversy," *Pittsburgh Courier*, November 10, 1934: A4.

211   "Baseball Commission Explains Its Attitude," *New York Amsterdam News*, December 1, 1934: 11.

212   See, for instance, Romeo L. Dougherty, "Sports," *New York Amsterdam News*, December 15, 1934: 11.

213   Ed R. Harris, "… and Bright Stars," *Philadelphia Tribune*, October 11, 1934.

214   James C. Isaminger, "Tips from the Sport Ticker," *Philadelphia Inquirer*, October 21, 1934.

215   Harris, "… and Bright Stars."

216   "Commissioner Wilson Refuses Chi Protest," *Pittsburgh Courier*. December 1, 1934: 14.

217   "Satchel Paige's Fire Ball Hurling Fells Stars by 4 to 2 Count," *Pittsburgh Courier*, October 13, 1934: A4.

218   "Craws, Grays Win Against Stars, Yanks," *Baltimore Afro-American*, October 13, 1934: 21.

219   Romeo L. Dougherty, "Barnum and Bailey Had Nothing On Those Dean Boys from the Cardinals," *New York Amsterdam News*, October 27, 1934: 10.

220   "Stars Again Meet Yanks," *New York Amsterdam News*, October 20, 1934: 10.

221   "Fete Baseball Champs at Banquet," *Philadelphia Tribune*, October 25, 1934.

222   "Paul Stevens Captain of Championship Nine," *York Dispatch*, November 6, 1934: 13.

223   "Philly Stars Beat La. Team Three Straight," *Philadelphia Tribune*, November 8, 1934: 11.

224   "Philly Stars Beat La. Team Three Straight."

225   "Negroes Play Today," *Austin* (Texas) *American-Statesman*, November 12, 1934: 6; "Black Senator Split," *Austin American-Statesman*, November 12, 1934: 7.

THE HOTTEST SHOW IN TOWN: SATCHEL PAIGE MOWS 'EM DOWN IN NEGRO LEAGUES EAST-WEST ALL-STAR GAME

AUGUST 26, 1934: EAST ALL-STARS 1, WEST ALL-STARS 0, AT COMISKEY PARK, CHICAGO

BY WILL OSGOOD

The summer of 1934 was one of the hottest on record in Chicago. Although the heat was nothing out of the ordinary for Negro League All-Stars like Alex Radcliff and Satchel Paige, who both grew up in Mobile, Alabama, it was still fortunate for them, and for the fans attending the matchup of the best that Black baseball had to offer that season, that the temperatures cooled slightly from the record-setting 105 degrees of July 24 and the 100 degrees of August 8. August 26 was, as one observer put it, "one of those perfect baseball days. Not a cloud in the sky to mar the perfect azure-blue of the heavens."[1]

What the weather may have lacked in heat, the annual East-West All-Star Game, played at Comiskey Park, made up for. It was a hotly contested game.

Although it was an exhibition, both teams wanted nothing more than to win. The 1934 edition of the classic turned out to be a pitchers' duel if ever there was one. The East team won, 1-0, on a run that crossed the plate in the next-to-last inning.

Until then, the West pitching had been excellent. Ted Trent started and allowed two hits while striking out three batters. He was helped by top-notch defense, with Sammy Hughes and Willie Wells making great plays in the infield. Chet Brewer pitched the middle three innings, yielding two hits and striking out a pair of batters including Oscar Charleston, who struck out twice in the game. Willie Foster entered the game in the seventh inning and allowed a two-out single to Chester Williams, who was stranded when Paige grounded out to shortstop.

Cool Papa Bell, one of six Pittsburgh Crawfords to start the game, scored the game's only run in the top half of the eighth inning. Bell was known throughout the Negro Leagues as an excellent baserunner. According to Ted "Double Duty" Radcliffe, Bell was "so fast, he'd run out of sight."[2] (Double Duty was the brother of Alex Radcliff, who started at third base for the West team.)[3] Bell was also an on-base artist extraordinaire, who knew how to work pitch counts when necessary to reach first base. His pesky ways got only more annoying for opposing pitchers, catchers, and managers once he got on base, and that was most certainly the case in the eighth inning of this game. Facing hometown pitcher Foster of the Chicago American Giants, Bell worked the count to 3-and-1 and then took first on a base on balls. It was the only walk Foster issued in three innings of mound work.

Pittsburgh Crawfords catcher Bill Perkins, pinch-hitting for Jimmie Crutchfield, was up next. Bell used his legendary speed to steal second base on a swinging strikeout by Perkins. Pittsburgh first baseman Oscar Charleston then hit a soft liner to first baseman Mule Suttles for the second out. Philadelphia Stars third baseman Jud Wilson, "one of the game's most dangerous hitters," was down in the count 0-and-2 when he "hit a looping single over second. It was a hit, but [shortstop] Willie Wells and [second baseman Sammy] Hughes both went for it."[4] With two outs, Bell had been off on contact. Both Wells and Hughes "broke the ball down, but it rolled a few feet away."[5]

The *New York Amsterdam News* described the hit as a "fast grounder through the pitcher's box out into short center field."[6] As both middle infielders went for the ball, "Wells got in front of it" but "Hughes crashed into him and Bell scampered about third to score."[7]

Josh Gibson was up next and he singled, but the throw from right fielder Sam Bankhead was relayed home and caught Wilson as he tried to score a second run.

In the bottom of the ninth, Paige stuck out Turkey Stearnes and, after a single by Suttles, the game ended on a double play as Williams grabbed a liner by Red Parnell and doubled off pinch-runner Malvin Powell at first base.

Paige, who had entered the game with none out in the sixth inning and a runner on second base, struck out five batters. He prevented the West from scoring in the four innings he pitched and was the pitcher of record when the winning run was scored. As the third and final pitcher (following starter Ted Trent and Chet Brewer) used by West manager Dave Malarcher, Foster took the loss in the contest.[8]

Wilson's Philadelphia Stars went on to win the 1934 Negro National League II championship by defeating the Chicago American Giants in a playoff series; it was the only championship in franchise history. For the moment, however, the big news was that Wilson had played the role of hero in a game that had included stars like Wells, Charleston, Stearnes, and Josh Gibson. Wilson had been second in vote-getting among East position players, and he was such a strong hitter that East manager Dick Lundy had batted him in the cleanup spot for the East. If anyone was likely to drive in the only run in a 1-0 game, Wilson was the one who was the most probable. As it turned out, he had his opportunity and made the most of it.

In addition to Wilson, credit for the East's victory was also due to the sterling efforts of the three pitchers used by Lundy (who doubled as the starting shortstop). Philadelphia's Slim Jones was the starter. His day got off to an inauspicious start as he walked the leadoff hitter, Wells, and then balked him to second. Wells was thrown out trying to steal third as Alex Radcliff struck out.[9] Jones struck out Stearnes to end the inning and then pitched two more innings in which he allowed just one additional baserunner. He struck out four West All-Stars in his three innings on the hill.

However, there were some anxious moments in the second inning. After Suttles opened the inning with a single, Parnell reached base on an error when second baseman Williams's throw was mishandled at first base by Charleston. After Bankhead struck out, the runners advanced to second and third on a wild pitch. Suttles tried to score on Larry Brown's groundball to third base, but Jud Wilson's timely throw home to catcher Gibson prevented the run from scoring. Hughes grounded out to Wilson to end the threat.

After Jones retired the side in order in the third inning, he was relieved by Pittsburgh Crawfords right-hander Harry "Tin Can" Kincannon. The curveball artist was not as sharp for the East squad as his predecessor or his successor. In two innings of relief, he gave up four hits but continued to keep the West team with a zero in the run column as he bridged the gap to the most dominant Negro Leagues pitcher of the era, Leroy "Satchel" Paige. Mule Suttles was thrown out at home after tripling in the fourth inning. Right fielder Crutchfield grabbed a fly ball hit by Parnell and executed a perfect throw to end the inning.

Pitching in this contest against the best Negro Leagues competition he could face, Paige powered through the West lineup with his blazing, heavy fastball for four shutout innings to record the win for the East squad. He used his fastball, curveball, changeup, and even occasional knuckleball to confuse West hitters and keep them off balance.

According to both Bell and Double Duty Radcliffe, Paige threw his fastball as hard as anyone in the Negro Leagues. Radcliffe had caught him when they were teammates with the Crawfords in 1932. He recalled a doubleheader in New York in which he caught Paige in game one, and then took the mound himself in the second game. Both pitched shutouts.

Asked if Paige threw hard, Radcliffe said, "When I had to catch Satchel, I'd go to the store to get a wrap." He asserted that "Nobody who ever lived threw harder than Satchel. Closest was Bob Gibson. Satchel could throw so hard, looked like the ball disappeared."[10]

In addition to the players who were key figures in the East's victory, the 1934 East-West All-Star Game featured much of the best talent the Negro Leagues ever produced. In the midst of that talent, some individual standouts, who did not necessarily affect the final outcome of the game, were Pittsburgh second baseman Chester Williams for the East and Chicago first baseman Mule Suttles for the West, who collected three hits apiece.

For the 30,000 fans in attendance, the second annual East-West Game did not disappoint.[11] They got every bit of their money's worth as they watched the East avenge an 11-7 loss in the inaugural East-West All-Star Game from the year before. In the *Pittsburgh Courier's* September 1 edition, columnist William G. Nunn raved, "Today's game was more than a masterpiece! It was more than a classic! It was really and truly a diamond epic!"[12]

SOURCES

This article was amended by Alan Cohen and Bill Nowlin in 2023 and fact-checked by Carl Riechers. Thanks to Alan Cohen and Tom Thress of Retrosheet. In addition to the sources cited in the Notes, the authors consulted Retrosheet.org and the following:

"East-West All Star Game: Summaries," http://www.cnlbr.org/Portals/0/RL/East-West%20All%20Star%20Game%20Summaries%202019-10.pdf

Lester, Larry. *Black Baseball's National Showcase: The East-West All-Star Game 1933-1962*, Expanded Version (Kansas City: Noir Tech Research, 2020), 40-59.

Mandel, Ken, MLB.com. *Slim Pitcher: Jones Dominated Negro League Baseball for a Short Time*. mlb.mlb.com/mlb/history/mlb_negro_leagues_profile.jsp?player=jones_stuart.

Monroe, Al. "East Beats West in 1-0 Thriller," *Chicago Defender*, September 1, 1934: 16.

Thorn, John, *Black Ball, Part 2*. "Our Game," ourgame.mlblogs.com/black-ball-part-2-1dcade51cdf6.

Washington, Chester. "Says Ches: 25,000 Thrilled at East-West Spectacle," *Pittsburgh Courier*, September 1, 1934: A5.

"Bat Boys Responsible for East Team's 1-0 Victory," *Chicago Defender*, September 1, 1934: 15.

"East All-Star Team Wins, 1-0, Before 25,000," *Chicago Tribune*, August 27, 1934: 21.

NOTES

1   William G. Nunn, "As 'Speedball' Satchell [*sic*] Paige Ambled into the East-West Game and Simply Stole the Show," *Pittsburgh Courier*, September 1, 1934: A4.

2   Ted "Double Duty" Radcliffe, interviewed by Fay Vincent, Society for American Baseball Research, July 5, 2002. oralhistory.sabr.org/interviews/radcliffe-ted-double-duty-2002/.

3   Alex Radcliff's surname was sometimes rendered as Radcliffe.

4   Nunn.

5   Nunn.

6   "East Defeats West in Game at Chicago," *New York Amsterdam News*, September 1, 1934: 10.

7   Dan Burley (Associated Negro Press), "East Shuts Out West in Classic Title, 1-0," *Atlanta Daily World*, September 2, 1934: 5.

8   For a box score of the game, see Al Monroe, "East Beats West in 1-0 Thriller," *Chicago Defender*, September 1, 1934: 16.

9   Julius J. Adams, "Adams Gives a Detailed Story of East's Victory," *Chicago Defender*, September 1, 1934: 17.

10 Ted "Double Duty" Radcliffe interview.

11 Estimates of crowd size ranged from 20,000 to 30,000. Nunn wrote that more than 4,000 of those in attendance were White.

12 Nunn.

SATCHEL PAIGE AND SLIM JONES THROW HEAD-TO-HEAD PITCHING GEMS

SEPTEMBER 9, 1934: PITTSBURGH CRAWFORDS 1, PHILADELPHIA STARS 1, AT YANKEE STADIUM, NEW YORK

BY JAMES OVERMYER

Of the more than 200 Negro League games played at Yankee Stadium in the 1930s and '40s, one of the most memorable was a pitching duel between Satchel Paige and Stewart "Slim" Jones in September 1934 that ended not with a victory, but in a 1-1 tie. Black baseball's fans could have been excused for thinking this was a matchup that would continue to thrill them for many seasons. But Fate – not the low-grade sort that influences bad-hop grounders and fly balls lost in the sun, but the kind that actually affects men's lives – stepped in to ensure that this exciting face-off wouldn't be repeated in future years.

Black major-league teams first played at Yankee Stadium in 1930. After two years of no action in the depths of the Depression, Negro League ball returned in 1934, courtesy of William A. "Gus" Greenlee, owner of the Negro National League's Pittsburgh Crawfords and president of the Negro National League. A natural entrepreneur, Greenlee took responsibility for obtaining the Stadium for Black games when the New York Yankees were on the road.

The four-team doubleheader set up for Sunday, September 9, 1934, was a fundraiser for Harlem's Colonel Charles Young American Legion Post. The Chicago American Giants beat the New York Black Yankees, 4-3, in the first game. Greenlee's Crawfords, for whom Paige pitched, and the Philadelphia Stars, Jones's team, would match up in the second game.

The most-quoted attendance estimate in the newspapers covering the doubleheader was 30,000 fans. This was far better than the numbers that same afternoon for the National League's Brooklyn Dodgers at Ebbets Field (12,000) and New York Giants across the East River at the Polo Grounds (20,000). Such was the drawing power of the already-famous Paige.

His opponent, Slim Jones, a left-hander who at 6-feet-6 and 185 pounds lived up to his nickname, was at age 21 only in his third professional season. But he, like the 28-year-old Paige, already was a star.

Paige, reliably stellar (when not suffering from arm trouble), had a great season in 1934, with a 13-3 won-lost record and a 1.54 ERA. Jones, however, surpassed him – and everyone else. He logged a 20-4 record (in only 22 starts and eight relief appearances), with a 1.24 ERA. Jones's Society for American Baseball Research biographer, Frederick C. Bush, declared that "his 1934 campaign still stands as one of the greatest seasons by any pitcher in any league and era."[1]

The Crawfords and Stars were among the class of the Negro National League in 1934. Philadelphia, with a .684 won-lost percentage, won the league championship. The Crawfords had a .635 winning percentage, the second best in the league. The lineups at Yankee Stadium listed seven future members of the Hall of Fame – Paige, center fielder James "Cool Papa" Bell, first baseman (and manager) Oscar Charleston, catcher Josh Gibson, and third baseman Judy Johnson for Pittsburgh and first baseman Jud Wilson and catcher Raleigh "Biz" Mackey for Philadelphia.

But, even with all those feared bats in the lineups, this was a pitchers' game. Slim dominated the first two-thirds of the contest before fading just a little toward the end. Satchel was in and out of jams until the late innings, but it was noted that he "always seemed to have something in reserve for the pinches."[2] Satch, in fact, got into hot water in the bottom of the first when he walked the Stars' leadoff hitter, shortstop Jake Stephens, who immediately went to third on a hit-and-run single by third baseman Dewey Creacy, and scored one out later on Wilson's groundout.

Meanwhile, for 6⅔ innings Jones was untouchable, with a perfect game until Charleston singled in the seventh. In the third and fourth innings, he struck out four Crawfords in a row, including Bell, Charleston, and Gibson.

Pittsburgh finally reached Jones for its sole run in the top of the eighth, aided by Jones's mental miscue. Judy Johnson opened the inning with a double, which sportswriters implied could have been held to a single if right fielder Jake Dunn had pounced on it a little more quickly.[3]

The *New York Daily News*'s Edgar T. Rouzeau wrote that Slim then "grew nervous," and when second baseman Chester Williams laid down an easy-to-field bunt, he automatically chose to throw him out at first, ignoring a chance to hold Johnson at second or catch him going to third. Jones then walked pinch-hitter Clarence "Spoony" Palm and gave up a single to shortstop Leroy Morney to let in Pittsburgh's run.[4]

The game was tied after 8½ innings, but it was getting dark. The announced starting time for the first game was 1:30 P.M., and there had been four hours of actual baseball played, plus time between the two games. Sunset that day was at 7:17 P.M., and Black sportscaster Jocko Maxwell, who was there, reported that "the shades of night were falling fast."[5]

But the game wasn't over, and the Stars nearly won it, except for Paige again rising to the occasion. With one out in the bottom of the ninth, Jud Wilson hit a sharp grounder back to the box that bounded off Satchel's leg and toward Williams at second. Williams's desperation throw to first was too late to nip Wilson, and it was wild and carried to the grandstand. The 38-year-old Wilson was no speedster, but he was extremely competitive, and he made it to third.

Biz Mackey was the next hitter, and Paige walked him after going to a full count. Philadelphia manager Webster McDonald then ran out a trio of left-handed pinch-hitters, including himself, to try to get the platoon advantage in the gathering dusk that must have favored a pitcher like Paige. Satchel intentionally walked the first one, Mickey Casey, to set up a force at any base. The move worked. McDonald went down on called strikes, and Ameal Brooks swung heartily at Paige's offerings but didn't hit any of them. Then the umpires called the game for darkness.

Brooks's strikeout was Paige's 12th. He walked three batters and gave up six hits. Jones struck out nine, gave up three hits, and walked one. Maxwell, in a year-end article for the *Age*, picked the game as his biggest sports thrill of the year. Veteran sportswriter W. Rollo Wilson of the *Pittsburgh Courier* wrote in 1943 that the game was his biggest thrill, period.[6]

Right after the game, popular music lyricist Andy Razaf, a devout baseball fan, penned a poem "To Judge Landis," arguing that the doubleheader showed what White baseball was missing. The final stanza read:

It's time you and your crowd woke up

In this new and enlightened age

Oh, by the way, your 'Schoolboy Rowe'

Should see these pitchers, Jones and Page [*sic*].[7]

Paige and Jones had a rematch at Yankee Stadium on September 30. Again, both pitchers starred, although this time the Crawfords won, 3-1. The two hurlers had opposed each other twice in May, games that the Stars had won. They had appeared as teammates on August 26 for the East All Stars at the annual Negro Leagues East-West Game. Jones pitched three shutout innings as the East starter, and Paige got the win with four shutout frames at the end of the contest when the East scored the game's only run in the eighth. So as the 1934 season came to an end, the chances of many more exciting Paige-Jones matchups in future seasons seemed bright.

But while Satchel pitched for decades longer and became more and more famous, 1934 was Slim Jones's last good season. He started off well in 1935, but developed trouble with his left shoulder, as well as with Stars owner Edward Bolden, who became concerned that Jones was abusing alcohol to deal with the arm pain.[8] When the season was over, Slim had compiled a subpar 4-5 won-lost record and a worse 5.88 ERA. After that his days as a Negro League starter were basically over. He hung with the Stars through 1938, but McDonald and his successor as manager, Jud Wilson, were mostly inclined to use him in relief, or as an occasional first baseman and outfielder.

In the fall of 1938, back in his hometown of Baltimore, Slim became gravely ill. He died in Bay View Hospital on November 19, at only 25 years of age. Bush, his biographer, cut through a lot of incorrect information about Jones's death, and concluded from his research that Slim's kidneys had failed. Jones was gone, but not forgotten by his opponent of that 1934 faceoff at Yankee Stadium. Paige told an interviewer 42 years later that Slim was one of the three best pitchers he had ever seen, along with Bob Feller and Dizzy Dean.[9]

SOURCES

Negro League player statistics were not always reliably and completely compiled at the time the games were actually played. But efforts have been made in recent years to use box scores and game stories to retroactively compile annual stats. The team won-lost records and pitching statistics cited here are from the Seamheads. com Negro Leagues Database, as of December 2021. The database is considered the most complete of the efforts to re-create Negro League statistics, but it is an ongoing project, and the numbers cited here may change in the future.

The author also relied on information from Baseball-Reference.com and Retrosheet.org.

https://retrosheet.org/NegroLeagues/boxesetc/1934/B09092PH51934.htm

NOTES

1   Frederick C. Bush, "Slim Jones," SABR Baseball Biography Project, https://sabr.org/bioproj/person/slim-jones/.

2   Bessye J. Bearden, "Giants, Trent Win All-Star Ball Game," *Chicago Defender*, September 15, 1934: A5.

3   Edgar T. Rouzeau, "Chi Giants Top Black Yanks, 4-3; Crawfords, Stars Tie, 1-1," *New York Daily News*, September 10, 1934: 171; Bearden, "Giants, Trent Win All-Star Ball Game."

4   Rouzeau, "Chi Giants Top Black Yanks, 4-3; Crawfords, Stars Tie 1-1."

5   Display advertisement for "The Stars of Colored Baseball in a Four (4) Team Double Header," *New York Amsterdam News*, September 1, 1934: 10; "Daily Almanac," *New York Daily News*, September 9, 1934: 2; Jocko Maxwell, "Sports Biggest Thrill in 1934," *New York Age,* December 29, 1934: 7.

6   Maxwell, "Sports Biggest Thrill in 1934"; W. Rollo Wilson, "My Greatest Thrill!: Sportswriter Gets Biggest Thrill from 1-1 Game," *Pittsburgh Courier*, July 3, 1943: 19.

7   Andy Razaf, "To Judge Landis," *New York Amsterdam News*, September 15, 1934: 10.

8   Courtney Michelle Smith, *Ed Bolden and Black Baseball in Philadelphia*, (Jefferson, North Carolina: McFarland & Co., 2017), 107.

9   Bush, "Slim Jones."

DIZZY & DAFFY ALL-STARS LOSE DOUBLE BILL

October 16, 1934: Philadelphia Stars 8, Dizzy Dean All-Stars 0 (first game); Philadelphia Stars 4, Dizzy Dean All-Stars 3 (second game), at Shibe Park, Philadelphia

By Thomas Kern

The 1934 season was an exceptional one for Dizzy Dean. At the young age of 24, he was a 30-game winner with a 2.66 ERA for the St. Louis Cardinals. He appeared in the first of four straight All-Star Games, won Games One and Seven to lead his team to a World Series victory over the Detroit Tigers, and finished as the National League MVP. Jump-started by his early success, Dean became the darling of baseball for the rest of his career. Alongside his early prominence came his penchant for offseason barnstorming, which was a way to make a few extra dollars and to enjoy the limelight of an adoring public.

Dean also continued the tradition established by White ballplayers from earlier years to find opportunities to go head-to-head with Black players, something that was not possible during the regular season due to the so-called "gentlemen's agreement" among White owners that unofficially barred Black players from the White leagues. Despite being frowned upon by Commissioner Kenesaw Landis and team owners, in part because of their fear of offseason injury to players and embarrassment when White teams lost games during interracial play, barnstorming remained a constant in the 1920s and '30s. Dean merely picked up the baton from others who came before him. His first recorded barnstorming appearances were in 1933 in the Midwest. They were organized by Kansas City Monarchs owner J.L. Wilkinson, who assembled a Monarchs-laden team and a few imports – most notably Satchel Paige – to play against Dean, his brother Paul, and a collection of White major leaguers including Lloyd Waner and Pepper Martin. The resulting tour drew large crowds – Black and White – as well as headlines and a paycheck that cemented in Dean's mind the value of these offseason games.[1]

In 1934 Dean was all in for another postseason barnstorming tour. In fact, in the years ahead, rarely an offseason went by when Dizzy did not lead a touring team around the country to play all comers, Black nines among them. The 1934 outing was again organized by Wilkinson whose three-week "Dizzy and Daffy Tour" would take on both White semipro teams and Black teams in the East and Midwest.

Chicago Defender columnist Al Monroe raised the stakes by writing, in light of the Cardinals' World Series championship, "Truly I cannot see how any team can call itself champion of the world that hasn't batted against Satchel Paige. … And I am wondering if 'Schoolboy' Rowe and the Dean brothers can gloat over their strikeout records and world series [sic] wins over teams that failed to include Josh Gibson, Turkey Stearnes, Jud Wilson, Oscar Charleston, and others in their line up."[2] Starting in Oklahoma City on October 10, the touring squad played in the Midwest against a mostly Monarchs team after which the Dean brothers flew to Philadelphia for a Tuesday, October 16, doubleheader against the Philadelphia Stars at Shibe Park, the home of the Philadelphia Athletics.[3]

As was the case in all the venues where the Dean brothers played, they joined an amalgam of local semipros that was sometimes bolstered by the addition of one or more AL or NL players. Their competition in Philadelphia was organized by Philadelphia Stars owner Ed Bolden, whose team had just finished a stellar season in which they captured the Negro National League 2 championship with a memorable 4-3 series victory over the Chicago American Giants, the Midwest Negro League powerhouse. Exactly two weeks after their Game Eight victory on October 2, the Stars were ready to play Dean and his aggregation.

The Tuesday doubleheader on what was described as a fair, partly cloudy day in Philadelphia drew 9,000 fans, Black and White. The Stars played their best lineup in both games led by their two best pitchers, Webster McDonald and Slim Jones. In the first game, Jake Stephens led off at short, followed by Dewey Creacy at third, Jud Wilson in right, Biz Mackey at first, Jake Dunn in left, Johnny Hayes catching, Pete Washington in center, Dick Seay at second, and McDonald pitching. Game two had an unchanged lineup except for Mickey Casey catching and Jones on the mound.[4]

The Dean brothers were on their own with only the all-stars of the Philadelphia semipro league filling out their scorecard, but they knew that was what their barnstorming tour was about. Baseball historian William McNeil wrote, "[T]he games weren't exactly played on a level playing field … since Diz and his brother Paul often teamed up with a bunch of local players to play against the powerful Kansas City Monarchs lineup [or other Negro League teams]. But they packed them in wherever they went."[5] Thus, in retrospect, the Philadelphia Stars' sweep of the Deans' team was not a surprise, although interestingly, Dizzy and Paul's cameo appearances in the games drew criticism from the local papers.

In game one, the Stars shellacked Dizzy's side, 8-0. James C. Isaminger of the *Philadelphia Inquirer* wrote, "Dizzy and Daffy Dean did their chores at Shibe Park yesterday afternoon in a doubleheader, but it was nothing of which the Dean dynasty will be proud."[6] Webster McDonald blanked Dean's team, giving up only four hits. Biz Mackey and Jud Wilson excelled for the Stars, each driving in three runs. The Dean brothers played the outfield, Paul in right field long enough to get two at-bats, Dizzy in left field for six innings. The game lasted a little under two hours.

Dizzy started game two for his team, pitching two innings and allowing no runs on three hits. Spearheaded by Jud Wilson's three-run homer, the Stars scored all four of their runs in the third inning off Dean's replacement, Joe Schmidt. Dean's locals scored one run in the fifth inning and two in the seventh, but the game was called because of darkness, giving Bolden's team a 4-3 win and a series sweep. Slim Jones, a 20-game winner in 1934 and the victor in the deciding game of the championship series against the Chicago American Giants, pitched all seven innings for the Stars, giving up seven hits in addition to the three runs. Reportedly, Paul Dean had a sore arm that precluded him from pitching in either of the games.[7]

The doubleheader win by the Stars was icing on the cake to an outstanding season. And despite the losses, Dizzy did not have much to complain about either. After the game on the way to New York City for their next contest, he learned he had been named MVP of the National League. And, as Isaminger reported:

> The Deans are in the money up to their necks. Last night they went to Atlantic City where they were to receive $1,000 for appearing in a softball game and not even playing. Tonight, they will pitch for the Bushwicks in Brooklyn. They will get a guarantee there and were informed yesterday that every reserved seat had been sold.[8]

In addition to showcasing their talents against at least some White major-league competition, the relationship, at least between Negro League ballplayers and Dizzy, was amicable. According to McNeil, "Dizzy Dean was a regular guy as far as the Negro League ballplayers were concerned, but his brother Paul was a quieter individual who didn't mix in easily."[9] Thanks to Monarchs owner Wilkinson's negotiations in setting up the tour, the Black teams got a share of the gate to make their play worthwhile, although not the same percentage that the Dean brothers garnered.

In New York the next day, the Dean brothers put a more formidable team on the field by joining the fabled semipro Brooklyn Bushwicks and Cardinals teammate Joe Medwick to play a mediocre New York Black Yankees squad. Nonetheless, the Black Yankees still defeated the Deans.[10] The Dizzy and Daffy tour continued westward and by the end of the month, Dean's various local squads finished 4-13-1, losing consistently to the Negro League teams they played.

SOURCES

Unless otherwise noted, all statistics referenced are from Seamheads.com.

NOTES

1   Timothy M. Gay, *Satch, Dizzy & Rapid Robert: The Wild Saga of Interracial Baseball Before Jackie Robinson* (New York: Simon & Schuster, 2010), 50-53.

2   Gay, 71, as referenced from the *Chicago Defender*, October 6, 1934.

3   Gay, 89.

4   James C. Isaminger, "Dizzy Daffy Stars Lose Double Bill, J. Dean Twirls Two Frames, Paul plays Afield," *Philadelphia Inquirer*, October 17, 1934: 17.

5   William F. McNeil, *Black Baseball Out of Season: Pay for Play Outside of the Negro Leagues* (Jefferson, North Carolina: McFarland & Co, 2007), 101.

6   Isaminger, 17.

7   Isaminger, 17.

8   Isaminger, 19.

9   McNeil, 101.

10 Gay, 92.

THE 1934 NEGRO NATIONAL LEAGUE CHAMPIONSHIP SERIES: PHILADELPHIA STARS VS. CHICAGO AMERICAN GIANTS

By Richard J. Puerzer

The 1934 Negro National League Championship Series between the Philadelphia Stars and the Chicago American Giants was a closely contested, contentious nailbiter of a series. Not only did the Series go the full seven games, but the seventh game resulted in a tie that forced an eighth game to decide the series. The American Giants were also known as Cole's American Giants, named after Robert A. Cole, who owned the team from 1932 to 1935. Managed by Dave Malarcher, the American Giants won the first half of the season in the Negro National League. The Stars, managed by Webster McDonald, who was also an important part of the pitching staff, won the season's second half. Thus, the championship was to be determined by the first-half winner taking on the second-half champion in a best-of-seven series.

The American Giants featured a number of star players, including future Hall of Famers Willie Wells at shortstop, Turkey Stearnes in center field, Mule Suttles at first base, and Willie Foster on the mound. The Stars' lineup included two future Hall of Famers in Biz Mackey at first base and catcher, and Jud Wilson in left field and first base. The Stars' 21-year-old pitching phenom, Slim Jones, had a stellar 1934 season. The 6-foot-6 left-hander won 20 games, posted an ERA of 1.29 in league games, and started the East-West All-Star Game for the East team.

The week before the Championship Series was scheduled to start, the Stars and American Giants faced off in a doubleheader on Friday, September 7, in Philadelphia. The Stars won the first game, 2-1, behind the pitching of Slim Jones. The second game was tied at 1-1 when it was halted after seven innings because of darkness.[1] These tight, low-scoring games portended the style of play that was to be found in the coming series.

The Championship Series was to begin in Philadelphia with a doubleheader on Saturday, September 8, but the games were rained out. Both teams did play on Sunday, September 9, at Yankee Stadium; however, they did not play each other. In the first game of a four-team doubleheader, the American Giants took on the New York Black Yankees. Chicago starter Ted Trent pitched a complete game and Turkey Stearnes homered in the 4-3 victory for the American Giants. In the second game, the Stars faced off against the Pittsburgh Crawfords. The game featured a marquee pitching matchup of Slim Jones dueling with Satchel Paige. The Stars scored a run in the first, and Jones had a no-hitter through six innings before he allowed a run to score in the seventh. The game remained knotted at 1-1 into the ninth inning. In the bottom of the ninth, the Stars loaded the bases with no outs. Satchel Paige rose to the occasion, however, and struck out the next three batters. The tied game was then called because of darkness. Jones struck out nine Crawfords batters while Paige punched out 12 Stars in what became a legendary game in Negro League baseball history. An estimated 25,000 to 30,000 fans attended the games at Yankee Stadium that day.[2]

Game One: September 11, 1934, Chicago American Giants 4, Philadelphia Stars 3, at Passon Field, Philadelphia

The Series finally started on Tuesday, September 11, at Passon Field, the home park for the Stars. Veteran lefty Willie Foster started the game for the American Giants against Stars hurler Rocky Ellis. While a number of newspapers covered the game, and a line score and box score were published in the *Philadelphia Inquirer*, few details about the action in the game are available aside from what occurred in the ninth inning. What is known is that the American Giants scored a run in the top of the first and the Stars tallied once in the bottom of the second. There was no more scoring until the seventh, when the American Giants scored a run in the top of the inning and the Stars scored two in the bottom of the frame. The American Giants scored again in the eighth to tie the game, 3-3.

In the ninth, Slim Jones entered the game in relief of Ellis. American Giants catcher Larry Brown batted the ball to Stars third baseman Dewey Creacy, who made a wild throw that allowed Brown to reach second base. Mule Suttles then singled to deep right field, scoring Brown and giving the American Giants the lead. In the bottom of the ninth, the Stars had their chance. They loaded the bases, but with two outs Foster got Mackey to hit an easy groundball to second base to end the game. Foster allowed eight hits but walked only one and struck out 11 in earning the complete-game win. The series was to continue with a doubleheader at Passon Field two days later, on Thursday, September 13, but those games were again rained out, and the series moved on to Chicago.[3]

Chicago	1	0	0	0	0	0	1	1	1		4	6	2
Philadelphia	0	1	0	0	0	0	2	0	0		3	8	1

Game Two: September 16, 1934 (Game One of a doubleheader), Chicago American Giants 3, Philadelphia Stars 0, at Cole's Park, Chicago

Games Two and Three of the Series were played as a Sunday doubleheader at Cole's Park, the home field of the Chicago American Giants. About 2,000 fans attended the games on the cold and windy day. Starting for the Stars was their ace, Slim Jones. The starting pitcher for the American Giants was Ted Trent who, as his mound opponent had done for the East team, had started for the West team in that season's East-West All-Star Game.

The two pitchers held true to form, keeping the game scoreless until the sixth, when the American Giants put together a rally. Chicago's second baseman, Jack Marshall, led off the inning with a single. Trent struck out, bringing up the top of the order and slugger Turkey Stearnes, who tripled to left-center and drove in Marshall for the game's first run. American Giants third sacker Alex Radcliffe followed with a single that plated Stearnes, but that was the end of the scoring in the inning. In the eighth, the American Giants tallied another run when, with two outs, Trent doubled and Stearnes singled to knock him in. The American Giants cruised to an easy 3-0 victory as Trent held the Stars to four hits and four walks while striking out eight.

Philadelphia	0	0	0	0	0	0	0	0	0		0	4	0
Chicago	0	0	0	0	0	2	0	1	x		3	7	1

Game Three: September 16, 1934 (Game Two of a doubleheader), Philadelphia Stars 5, Chicago American Giants 3, at Cole's Park, Chicago

Game Three featured a pitching matchup of Willie Foster, making his second start of the Series for the American Giants, against Stars pitcher-manager Webster McDonald. The 34-year-old McDonald had played for the American Giants from 1925 to 1929, and was now in his second season with the Stars. He threw with a submarine motion and featured a variety of pitches in his repertoire.

The Stars scored first, scratching out a run in the top of the third on two singles, a walk, and an error. In the bottom of the third, the American Giants answered with four singles, a fly out, and a fielder's choice that resulted in three runs. The Stars tied it in the top of the fourth when shortstop Jake Dunn doubled and was driven home on Jack Marshall's triple; Marshall then scored from third on a wild pitch. In the fifth, Willie Cornelius came in to relieve Foster, but he allowed two runs to score that gave the Stars a two-run lead. Cornelius was effective for the remainder of the game, but the Stars and McDonald held on to win 5-3. With the split of the doubleheader, the American Giants now led the series two games to one.[4]

Philadelphia	0	0	1	2	2	0	0	0	0		5	7	0
Chicago	0	0	3	0	0	0	0	0	0		3	6	2

Game Four: September 17, 1934, Chicago American Giants 2, Philadelphia Stars 1, at Cole's Park, Chicago

Game Four of the Championship Series was played on Monday, September 17 at Cole's Park. Willie Cornelius started the game for the American Giants despite his four-inning relief stint the day before. Rocky Ellis was the starter for the Stars, following up on his strong start in Game One. This game featured remarkable pitching from both hurlers and was scoreless through five innings. In the sixth, the American Giants put together a rally, scoring two runs. The *Chicago Tribune* reported that Mule Suttles started the rally off with a single, Willie Wells followed with a double, and Jack Marshall singled them home. However, the *Chicago Defender* wrote that the rally consisted of an Alex Radcliffe single followed by doubles by Willie Wells and John Hines. Regardless of the specifics, the rally gave Chicago a 2-0 lead. In the top of the seventh, the Stars broke out, with Jud Wilson doubling and scoring on Biz Mackey's single. However, the Stars could not add any additional runs, and the American Giants held on to win the game, 2-1. Cornelius pitched a complete game, showing no fatigue from having pitched four innings the previous day. The American Giants now had a seemingly commanding three-games-to-one lead in the series.[5]

| Philadelphia | 0 | 0 | 0 | 0 | 0 | 0 | 1 | 0 | 0 | | 1 | 5 | 0 |
| Chicago | 0 | 0 | 0 | 0 | 0 | 2 | 0 | 0 | 0 | | 2 | 4 | 3 |

Game Five: September 27, 1934, Philadelphia Stars 1, Chicago American Giants 0, at Passon Field, Philadelphia

The Series now returned to Philadelphia. Although it was originally announced that Game Five would be played on Thursday, September 20, it did not take place until Thursday, September 27. During the break in the series, the Stars played a doubleheader against the New York Black Yankees at Passon Field on Sunday, September 23. Before a crowd of 3,000, the Stars won the first game, 4-1, behind the stellar pitching of Slim Jones, and the team was victorious again in the second game, winning 4-3.[6] During this interim, it was also reported that Stars owner Ed Bolden was in a nearly fatal automobile accident on Saturday, September 22. Bolden suffered cuts and abrasions on his face and right leg in the accident.[7]

The Stars and American Giants finally played each other again in a game that started at 8:30 P.M. on Thursday, September 27. Bleacher seats sold for 30 cents, while grandstand seats were 40 cents. Willie Foster started the game for Chicago and Rocky Ellis started for the Stars; each was making his third start of the Series. The game was a pitchers' duel and remained scoreless until the bottom of the eighth. With two out and two men on, Stars second sacker Dick Seay singled to score catcher Ameal Brooks, giving the Stars the sole run scored in the game. Foster was the hard-luck loser despite pitching a five-hit complete game. Ellis also scattered five hits in his hard-earned shutout victory. The Championship Series now stood at three games to two in favor of the American Giants.[8]

| Chicago | 0 | 0 | 0 | 0 | 0 | 0 | 0 | 0 | 0 | | 0 | 8 | 0 |
| Philadelphia | 0 | 0 | 0 | 0 | 0 | 0 | 0 | 1 | x | | 1 | 5 | 0 |

Game Six: September 29, 1934, Philadelphia Stars 4, Chicago American Giants 1, at Passon Field, Philadelphia

Before Game Six, the Stars played and defeated the New York Black Yankees, 5-3, on Friday, September 28, in a 9:00 P.M. tilt in Belmar, New Jersey.[9] On Saturday, September 29, at 2:30 P.M., Game Six of the Championship Series was played before 3,000 fans at Passon Field. Ted Trent toed the slab for the American Giants, and his counterpart was Paul Carter of the Stars, who was making his first appearance in the Series. Stars ace Slim Jones did not get the start, most likely because he was scheduled to face Satchel Paige at Yankee Stadium the next day in a repeat of the Stars-Crawfords/American Giants-Black Yankees doubleheader that had been so successful a few weeks earlier.

The American Giants struck first in the game when in the third inning, Turkey Stearnes slugged a solo home run to give the Chicagoans a 1-0 lead. In the bottom of the fourth, the Stars rallied as Ameal Brooks hit a leadoff double and Pete Washington followed with another double to bring him home. After Carter and second baseman Dick Seay made outs, third baseman Dewey Creacy smacked a triple to left field that drove in Washington for a 2-1 Philadelphia lead before the inning ended on Jud Wilson's fly out.

The Stars rallied once more in the fifth. Biz Mackey led off the inning with a home run over the right-field fence. Next, shortstop Jake Dunn singled and scored on a base hit by Brooks to increase the Stars' lead to 4-1. Carter pitched well for the remainder of the game and neither team scored again as the Stars claimed the victory. The Stars had come back from being down three games to one to tie the Championship Series at three games apiece.

Unfortunately, two incidents marred the game and began the contentiousness that ultimately marked the remainder of the Series. In the second inning, Stars right fielder Mickey Casey reached first and advanced to second when American Giants pitcher Ted Trent misplayed the ball. Umpire Bert Gholston ruled that Casey had to return to first. An argument ensued, and in the heat of the discussion, Jud Wilson of the Stars punched Gholston. To everyone's amazement, Wilson was not ejected from the game after order had been restored. Then, in the seventh inning, American Giants first baseman Joe Scott was awarded first base on catcher's interference. Stars catcher Ameal Brooks took exception to the call and shoved home-plate umpire John Craig in the face. A second dispute resulted and, again, the transgressor – this time Brooks – was allowed to remain in the game. As a result of these two plays and the Stars' victory, American Giants manager Dave Malarcher protested the game by submitting a letter that detailed his protest to Negro National League Commissioner Rollo Wilson, who had attended the game.

A meeting was quickly scheduled for Sunday, September 30, between Stars owner Ed Bolden, American Giants owner Robert Cole, and Commissioner Wilson. Bolden reportedly threatened to pull his team from the Series if Wilson and Brooks were not allowed to play for the Stars. Malarcher's protest was rejected, and the result of the game stood, with the Series now tied at three games apiece.[10] In a follow-up editorial, *Philadelphia Tribune* reporter Ed Harris expressed his displeasure with the actions of the players, but also conveyed disappointment with the inaction of the umpires. He commented, "Unhappy precedents were set, out-and-out diamond lawlessness perpetrated and overlooked, and the National Association took a kick in the pants."[11]

| Chicago | 0 | 0 | 1 | 0 | 0 | 0 | 0 | 0 | 0 | 1 | 4 | 3 |
| Philadelphia | 0 | 0 | 0 | 2 | 2 | 0 | 0 | 0 | x | 4 | 10 | 2 |

Game Seven: October 1, 1934, Chicago American Giants 4, Philadelphia Stars 4, at Passon Field, Philadelphia

Before Game Seven, the American Giants and Stars made their way back to Yankee Stadium on Sunday, September 30, to repeat the doubleheader matchup of a few weeks prior. The doubleheader featured a rematch of Satchel Paige and the Crawfords against Sim Jones and the Stars, as well a second contest between the American Giants and Black Yankees. As the attendance for the event again was approximately 25,000, it laid plain why Slim Jones had skipped his turn to pitch in the Championship Series, which had been drawing only 2,000 to 5,000 fans per game. In the first game of the doubleheader, the fans were treated to a close game in which the Crawfords prevailed, 3-1, and Paige got the better of Jones. In the nightcap, the Black Yankees defeated the American Giants 3-2 in a game that was called due to darkness after six innings. It is notable that Ted "Double Duty" Radcliffe, who did not pitch at all in the Series, took the mound for the American Giants in this game.[12]

The teams returned to Philadelphia to play the seventh and deciding game of the Championship Series on the evening of Monday, October 1, in front of approximately 5,000 fans, the biggest crowd of the series. The pitching matchup was a repeat of Game Four, with Rocky Ellis going for the Stars against Willie Cornelius for the American Giants. Early in the game, there was another rhubarb between a player and an umpire. In the second inning, Mule Suttles took umbrage when home-plate umpire Bert Gholston called him out on strikes. Suttles hit Gholston with his bat and was promptly ejected from the game. Order was eventually restored, and Wilson "Frog" Redus replaced Suttles in the Chicago lineup.

In the top of the third inning, the American Giants got the scoring started. With one out, Cornelius walked, bringing up the top of the order. Willie Wells singled and Alex Radcliffe hit a ball that both pitcher Ellis and second baseman Seay muffed, allowing Cornelius to score. Turkey Stearnes singled to score Radcliffe and Joe Scott's hit drove in Stearnes to give the American Giants three runs in the inning. Stars manager Webster McDonald brought himself in to replace Ellis on the mound. McDonald struck out Redus and induced a groundball out from Marshall to close out the inning.

The Stars got a run back in the bottom of the inning. McDonald led off with a double. After two outs, Jud Wilson doubled to drive in McDonald. There was no more scoring until the bottom of the sixth inning, when Wilson tripled and was driven home by a Biz Mackey base hit that cut the American Giants' lead to 3-2. Willie Foster relieved Cornelius in the seventh and pitched a scoreless inning. In the top of the eighth, the American Giants added to their lead when Turkey Stearnes, who had reached base on a single, came home on another base hit by Joe Scott.

Ted Trent entered the game to start the eighth in relief of Foster and immediately got into trouble. Dewey Creacy led off with a double, Wilson was hit by a pitch, and Mackey walked to load the bases with no outs. Jake Dunn's single drove in Creacy and kept the bags loaded. Mickey Casey flied out for the first out, and the runners did not advance. Brooks then drew a base on balls to score Wilson, and the game was tied, 4-4. Trent was able to get out of the inning without further damage by striking out Pete Washington and getting McDonald to fly out.

Neither team scored in the ninth inning, and the game was then called a tie. It is unclear why the game was called after nine innings. It was played under the lights of Passon Field, and neither a curfew nor an agreement not to go beyond nine innings was mentioned in the press. Regardless, it was determined that the deciding game of the Series would be played the next day.[13]

Chicago	0	0	3	0	0	0	0	1	0		4	7	1
Philadelphia	0	0	1	0	0	1	0	2	0		4	8	1

Game Eight: October 2, 1934, Philadelphia Stars 2, Chicago American Giants 0, at Passon Field, Philadelphia

The eighth and final game in the Championship Series was played on Tuesday afternoon, October 2. Between 2,000 and 4,000 fans (the number varied in different newspapers) were on hand. After having started and having pitched six innings the night before, Willie Cornelius again was the starter for the American Giants while the Stars sent their ace, Slim Jones, to the hill. Jones was going on two days of rest after having pitched at Yankee Stadium on Sunday.

This game was as contentious as the previous two, with both teams lodging protests. In the top of the first, the American Giants went down one-two-three and protested the strikeout call of Turkey Stearnes made by home-plate umpire James Crump that ended the inning.

There was no scoring until the Stars batted in the bottom of the fourth. Biz Mackey led off with a single and advanced to second on a groundout by Jake Dunn. Right fielder Mickey Casey followed with a single that brought Mackey home and gave the Stars a 1-0 lead. Jones continued to cruise on the mound, allowing a double to Willie Wells in the third, a single to Turkey Stearnes in the sixth, and a double to Melvin Powell in the seventh.

The top of the seventh brought a protest from the Stars. The American Giants brought in Frog Redus as a pinch-hitter. Redus had also played the day before for the American Giants, but the Stars now argued that he was under contract with the Cleveland Red Sox and was thus ineligible to play for Chicago in this series. The umpires ruled that Redus was allowed to remain in the game. In the bottom of the seventh, Pete Washington led off with a single. Following a fly out by Dick Seay, Jones came to bat and smacked a sharp single to left field that scored Washington and extended the Stars' lead to 2-0.

In the ninth inning, the American Giants attempted to make one final rally. Mule Suttles led off with a double. Ted Radcliffe, pinch-hitting for Joe Scott, singled and advanced Suttles to third base. However, while Larry Brown was batting, Jones picked Suttles off third base, then struck out Brown. With two outs, in a bittersweet moment, American Giants manager Dave Malarcher entered the game as a pinch-hitter for Jack Marshall. The 39-year-old Malarcher had appeared in only two games during the regular season and was making what was to be his last professional appearance on a ballfield. Malarcher popped out to end the game. The Stars won 2-0 and were champions of the Negro National League.[14]

Chicago	0	0	0	0	0	0	0	0	0		0	8	1
Philadelphia	0	0	0	1	0	0	1	0	x		2	6	2

SERIES POSTSCRIPT

The American Giants played very well in the series. Three of their four losses were by two runs or less. They were led at the plate by Turkey Stearnes, who is credited with 11 hits, four stolen bases, his team's only home run, and a slash line of .458/.480/.708. For the Stars, Biz Mackey led the offense with seven hits, the Stars' only home run, and a slash line of .368/.429/.632. On the mound, Slim Jones pitched a shutout in the finale to cap his magnificent season.

The controversies in the final three games of the Series stained the Stars' victory in the eyes of many fans, players, and reporters. American Giants manager Dave Malarcher was especially disturbed by the way the Series was handled by the umpires and by Commissioner Wilson, and he criticized the commissioner and his lack of action in the Series in a letter to the *Chicago Defender*. "Gentleman" Dave Malarcher then retired from baseball after an accomplished career on the field as both a player and a manager.[15]

The Stars did not hesitate to celebrate their victory and held a banquet at the Octavius Catto Elks Lodge on Saturday, October 20. Gold baseball emblems were presented to each of the players, victory speeches were made, and entertainment was provided in the forms of boxing matches, wrestling competitions, and singing performances that accompanied the dinner.[16] Although the team looked very strong for the future, the 1934 Negro National League title was to be the Stars' only championship.

SOURCES

In addition to the sources cited in the Notes, the author consulted:

Clark, Dick, and Larry Lester, eds., *The Negro Leagues Book* (Cleveland: Society for American Baseball Research, 1994).

Riley, James A. *The Biographical Encyclopedia of the Negro Baseball Leagues* (New York: Carroll & Graf Publishers, Inc., 1994).

Smith, Courtney Michelle. *Ed Bolden and Black Baseball in Philadelphia* (Jefferson, North Carolina: McFarland & Company, 2017).

Unless otherwise noted, Seamheads.com was used for all Negro League player statistics.

NOTES

1 "Giants Lose to Philly; Then Tie 1-1," *Chicago Defender*, September 8, 1934: 17.

2 "30,000 in Yankee Stadium See Youthful Hurlers in Thrilling Pitchers Battle," *Philadelphia Tribune*, September 13, 1934: 14; "30,000 Attend Four-Team Doubleheader at Yankee Stadium; Black Yanks Lose; Stars-Crawfords Tie," *New York Age*, September 15, 1934: 5.

3 For Game One the following references were used: "Chi Giants Trip Stars in Opener," *Philadelphia Inquirer*, September 12, 1934: 24; "Chicago Stops Stars in Playoff Start," *Philadelphia Tribune*, September 13, 1934: 14.

4 For Games Two and Three the following references were used: "Giants Split with Philly Stars in Chicago Clash," *Baltimore Afro-American*, September 22, 1934: 21; "Giants Split Series with Phillies in League Play Off," *California Eagle*, September 28, 1934: 7; "Giants Lead Philly In World Series, 3-1," *Chicago Defender*, September 22, 1934: 16; "Stars Win 1, Drop 2 in Chicago," *Philadelphia Tribune*, September 20, 1934: 11. Note that a box score is not available for Game Three.

5 For Game Four the following references were used: "Giants Lead Philly in World Series, 3-1," *Chicago Defender*, September 22, 1934: 16; "Out with Injury," *Chicago Defender*, September 22, 1934: 17; "Stars Win 1, Drop 2 in Chicago," *Philadelphia Tribune*, September 20, 1934: 11; "American Giants Take 3 to 1 Lead in World Series," *Chicago Tribune*, September 18, 1934: 23; "American Giants Top Phila. Stars," *Philadelphia Inquirer*, September 18, 1934: 20. Note that a box score is not available for Game Four.

6 "Jones, Carter Reverse Yanks," *Philadelphia Tribune*, September 27, 1934: 11.

7 "Ed Bolden Hurt in Auto Accident," *Philadelphia Tribune*, September 27, 1934: 14.

8 For Game Five the following references were used: "Chi Giants Resume Series with Stars," *Philadelphia Inquirer*, September 27, 1934: 19; "Stars-Giants Play Tonight," *Philadelphia Tribune*, September 27, 1934: 11; "Phila. Stars Triumph," *Philadelphia Inquirer*, September 28, 1934: 22; "Stars Tie Series in Stiff Tiff," *Philadelphia Tribune*, October 4, 1934: 14.

9 "Baseball Tonight," *Asbury Park* (New Jersey) *Press*, September 28, 1934: 14; "Black Yanks Bow to All-Stars, 5-3," *Asbury Park Press*, September 29, 1934: 10.

10 For Game Six the following references were used: "Phila. Club Gains Third Win, 4-1, Over Chicago in Negro Playoff," *Philadelphia Inquirer*, September 30, 1934: 51; "Stars Tie Series in Stiff Tiff," *Philadelphia Tribune*, October 4, 1934: 14.

11 Ed R. Harris, "To Be or Not to Be," *Philadelphia Tribune*, October 4, 1934: 11.

12 Ed R. Harris, "Paige Tops Jones to Win Before 25,000," *Philadelphia Tribune*, October 4, 1934: 11.

13 For Game Seven the following references were used: "Chicago Giants Tie Stars in Series Tilt," *Philadelphia Inquirer*, October 2, 1934: 19; "Boldens Get 2 Runs to Tie Payoff Tiff," *Philadelphia Tribune*, October 4, 1934: 11 and 14.

14 For Game Eight the following references were used: "Stars Upset Giants Win National Title," *Philadelphia Inquirer*, October 3, 1934: 22; Ed R. Harris, "Stars Clip Giants for Two Runs to Clinch Title," *Philadelphia Tribune*, October 4, 1934: 11; "Philly Stars World Champs?" *Chicago Defender*, October 6, 1934: 17.

15 Dave Malarcher, "Chicago Hits Ruling by Baseball Head on Protest," *Chicago Defender*, January 19, 1935: 17; "Malarcher, Ideal Leader, Quits Baseball for Good," *Chicago Defender*, February 16, 1935: 17.

16 "Fete Baseball Champs at Banquet," *Philadelphia Tribune*, October 25, 1934: 12; E.A. Festus, "O.V. Catto Elk News," *Philadelphia Tribune*, October 25, 1934: 8.

THREE STRIKES AND YOU'RE NOT OUT: THE TROUBLE WITH UMPIRES

By Courtney Michelle Smith

In 1934 Ed Bolden's Philadelphia Stars baseball team capped off the best season of its existence when the squad defeated the Chicago American Giants and won the Negro National League II (NNL2) title. For Ed Bolden, the victory marked the second time he had led a team to a championship; previously, his Hilldale Daisies had defeated the Kansas City Monarchs in the Negro League World Series in 1925. For the Stars franchise, however, the victory over the Chicago American Giants came amid a spate of controversy that damaged the sport's reputation. Several games during the series featured ugly fights between players and umpires on the diamond. NNL2 Commissioner W. Rollo Wilson, a newspaper columnist who had a relationship with Bolden, faced allegations that he favored the Stars in the punishments he dealt to players involved in those fights. Wilson's actions likely cost him his job and spurred other changes to the NNL2's leadership early in the 1935 season.

The on-field fights and related controversies that marred the Stars' 1934 NNL2 championship had deep roots in the history of Black professional baseball. Some of those roots had a direct connection to the Stars through Bolden, whose name was part of the team's full, official name. During the 1920s, the frequency of attacks upon umpires led leagues like the Eastern Colored League (ECL) and American Negro League (ANL) to pass strict laws governing players' on-field behavior. Bolden, who had formed both of those circuits, served as the leagues' president when those policies were enacted. The ANL, however, neglected to enforce its laws, and the attacks upon umpires continued unabated. Bolden added more fuel to the controversy by using White umpires at a time when Black newspapers were calling for more Black umpires, thereby opening himself up to allegations of prejudice from the *Philadelphia Tribune.*

Overall, the attacks upon umpires that marred the Stars' 1934 title were a symptom of a much larger problem within Black professional baseball. The absence of reserve clauses in player contracts meant that Bolden and other owners regularly tried to poach talent from one another's rosters. That lack of discipline among the owners had a trickle-down effect upon the players as they, too, paid little attention to their contracts and "jumped" them for better offers from teams both inside and outside of the United States. Additionally, the precarious financial state of many all-Black baseball teams made owners reluctant to penalize their top players and to focus instead on getting as much revenue as possible from gate receipts. The attacks upon umpires, therefore, were an unsolvable problem for Bolden and other owners because they depended upon players to attract crowds and to generate gate receipts. Ultimately, the issues with umpires contributed to the atmosphere of instability that characterized Black professional baseball in the twentieth century.

Ten years before the Stars captured the NNL2 championship, the issue of player conduct against umpires was a topic of discussion for Bolden and other owners in the ECL. Similar to other Negro Leagues, the ECL operated under different rules than the ones governing the two leagues in what was then called major-league baseball, the National and American Leagues. In those latter two leagues, the selection of umpire crews did not fall to the individual teams. Instead, the selection of umpire crews happened at the league level. In the ECL and other Negro Leagues, however, responsibility for selecting umpire crews belonged to the individual teams, specifically to the home team. For that reason, allegations of umpire bias against road teams happened frequently in the Negro Leagues. Many games also suffered delays due to on-field confrontations between players and the umpires. To reduce those delays and to dissuade players from striking umpires, Bolden and the ECL owners enacted new policies in 1924 that designated a field captain or player-manager as the only people empowered to resolve disputes with umpires. Additionally, the new policies instituted fines against players who baited umpires into confrontations; such players were subject to fines of $100 and ejection from the game. The players were not the only ones who faced new rules in 1924 – the umpires also worked under new rules because Bolden and the other ECL owners wanted to project an image of professionalism. Even though the home teams continued to select umpire crews, the crews were called upon to act in unbiased ways and to use discretion when ejecting unruly players from contests. At the same time, the rules also pushed umpires to act promptly when dealing with unruly players and to eject such players. Umpires who failed to adhere to the ECL's somewhat vague rules faced expulsion from the league.[1]

Issues surrounding umpires at Negro League games often focused on the race of the umpires who were tasked with managing the behavior of Black players. As the leader of the ECL, Bolden found himself at the center of this issue. Prior to the 1924 World Series featuring the Kansas City Monarchs and Bolden's Hilldale club, a National Commission was formed that consisted of Bolden, Andrew "Rube" Foster of the original Negro National League (NNL1), and other NNL1 and ECL officials. The National Commission had the task of planning the coming World Series, the first for two Negro Leagues; Bolden and others on the commission chose White umpires for the World Series contest. In response, the *Pittsburgh Courier* published criticism that lamented the lack of Black umpires and the message it sent about Black players.[2] W. Rollo Wilson, who published regular columns in the *Courier*, used his forum to issue a reminder about an earlier proposition to change how the leagues selected umpire crews. According to Wilson, the proposition called for "NEGRO umpires, paid by the league, rotated among the cities of the league."[3] As Wilson reasoned, if "colored men can play baseball they can umpire baseball games and should be given the chance to do so."[4]

In the 1925 season, the issues surrounding umpires at Negro League games came to the fore. Bolden and the ECL tried to remedy the situation by hiring rotating umpire crews, thereby ending the practice of home teams selecting their own crews. To manage this new responsibility, the ECL hired a White man, Bill Dallas; his hire prompted the *Philadelphia Tribune* to publish a cartoon depicting the ECL as an Uncle Tom. In turn, Bolden authored a response, carried by the *Tribune*, in which he defended the hiring of Dallas and praised him as competent, fair, and experienced. The hiring of Dallas had little effect upon ECL games as many

contests continued to face delays due to player-umpire confrontations. The NNL1 experienced similar issues, and Foster responded by releasing most of the league's umpires and using the sports pages of the *Pittsburgh Courier* to castigate the poor work of the umpires who had been dismissed. Overall, the ugliness on the sports pages reflected the ugliness on the field of many Negro League games. In one instance, during a game between Hilldale and the Harrisburg Giants, fights broke out both on the field and in the stands. In his columns, Wilson tracked umpire behavior at games that led to allegations of bias and incompetence. At the Hilldale-Harrisburg game, for example, umpires took a break to get some water, and the break appeared to help the Hilldale pitcher. The umpires, furthermore, did nothing when a player threw dirt to protest a call. The disruptions on the field and the lack of a cohesive or effective response threatened to turn fans away from games and to mar the reputation of the Negro Leagues to the general public.[5]

Bolden, Foster, and newspaper columnists were not the only ones who used the sports pages to defend their actions or to air their grievances about umpires. Bert Gholston, one of the Black NNL1 umpires Foster fired, used the sports pages on two different occasions. The first came in the *Pittsburgh Courier* before his dismissal from the NNL when he co-authored a letter with another umpire in which they asked for patience and for more balanced coverage from newspapers. The second occasion came in the *Philadelphia Tribune* after his dismissal; in that article, Gholston asserted that the race of the umpires played a key role in the on-field confrontations. According to Gholston, several NNL1 teams planned attacks on Black umpires and openly refused to respect Black umpires' calls.[6] Gholston and other Black umpires had the support of Wilson, who proclaimed in one of his columns "EASTERN LEAGUE UMPIRES HAVE NO MORE AUTHORITY THAN A KU KLUXER WOULD HAVE AT A BANQUET OF THE 'HELL FIGHTERS!' IN HARLEM!"[7] Wilson did not blame the individual umpires; on the contrary, he blamed the leagues for not supporting competent umpires and hinted that league officials pushed umpires to favor the home teams.[8]

On the heels of that ugliness, the ECL abandoned its policy to hire rotating umpire crews for league games and reinstated the policy that allowed home teams to hire the umpire crews. Unsurprisingly, on-field confrontations and allegations of bias continued unabated. Bolden was once again involved, both as the

ECL's president and as the owner of Hilldale. In one of Hilldale's games, pitcher Phil Cockrell punched an umpire after the arbiter changed his mind on a call. The fight on the field eventually involved local police, one of whom hit Cockrell on the back of his head as he left the field. Bolden enforced the league's rules by fining Cockrell $100 and suspending him for five games. Bolden's actions, however, did little to alleviate the problem or to deflect criticism about the ways the leagues managed relations between players and umpires.[9]

The troubles with umpires followed Bolden three years later when he formed the ANL, his second attempt to form an Eastern league of Black baseball teams. Bolden again served as league president and again tried to implement strict measures to dissuade players from attacking umpires. Under his direction, the ANL team owners agreed to a system of rotating umpire crews. They also agreed to laws mandating fines and suspensions for players who attacked umpires, engaged in on-field fights, or delayed games by arguing with umpires over disputed calls. Bolden and other owners, however, lacked the willpower to enforce their own rules. Games at Hilldale's home ballpark and other ballparks throughout the ANL continued to feature fights and delays over disputed calls.[10] Even more troubling for Bolden, he faced acute criticism from the *Philadelphia Tribune* for his decision to use White umpires. One sharply worded editorial alleged that using White umpires to manage the behavior of Black baseball players fed into racial stereotypes and hindered attempts to promote equal opportunities for Black Americans. The writers asked very pointed and uncomfortable questions of Bolden and the rest of Hilldale's management:

> Are we still slaves? Is it possible that colored baseball players are so dumb that they will resent one of their own race umpiring their game? Or is it that the management of Hilldale is so steeped in racial inferiority that it has no faith in Negroes?[11]

In the next edition of the *Philadelphia Tribune*, the newspaper's editors reinforced their commitment to seeing Black umpires at Hilldale's games. The editorial appeared to be a response to a letter that supported Bolden's use of White umpires. The letter's author questioned whether Black players respected Black umpires enough to respect their decisions. To counter that allegation, the editorial writers offered evidence of Black players treating Black umpires with respect.

Additionally, they once again raised the argument that Bolden and the rest of Hilldale's management used White umpires due to a sense of racial inferiority. As had been the case in the first editorial, the second editorial alluded to slavery to prove its point about Hilldale's racial sensibilities and sarcastically thanked God that "ball players are no longer slaves. They do not think that everything white is perfect and everything black is evil."[12]

The controversies over umpires and pointed allegations toward Bolden presaged his unhappy exit from Hilldale in 1930. They also showed that Bolden had an ugly history regarding umpires when his new team, the Stars, faced the Chicago American Giants in the 1934 NNL2 championship series. Like its predecessor, the NNL1 in the 1920s, the new NNL2, founded in 1933, still had not resolved issues concerning the hiring of umpire crews and the on-field behavior of players who disputed umpires' calls. Those lingering issues spilled out during the series and tarnished the Stars' accomplishments.

On-field disputes regarding umpires' calls helped to turn the planned seven-game series between the Stars and the American Giants into an eight-game series. The series began at Passon Field in West Philadelphia and then shifted to Chicago for Games Two through Four. After four games, the Chicago American Giants had a commanding lead in the series and seemed poised to capture the title.

The Stars, however, made a comeback by winning Games Five and Six to tie the series. American Giants field manager Dave Malarcher formally protested the Stars' victory in Game Six to the NNL commissioner, W. Rollo Wilson. Malarcher pointed out that the umpires had allowed two Stars players, third baseman Jud Wilson and catcher Ameal Brooks, to remain in the game after both players had assaulted the umpires.

While Rollo Wilson considered the protest, Bolden pleaded with him not to suspend either Jud Wilson or Brooks for the pivotal Game Seven. To pressure Wilson, Bolden threatened to pull the Stars from the series; Wilson relented and did not issue any punishments.

Understandably, Wilson's decision incensed Chicago American Giants owner Robert Cole. The problems compounded in Game Seven when the umpires ejected an American Giants player after he assaulted an umpire, thereby opening themselves to allegations of bias toward the home-team Stars. A fight on the field, along with Pennsylvania's blue law mandating an early curfew for games played on Sundays, caused the game to end in a tie and necessitated an eighth game. Amid further disputes, the Stars won Game Eight and took the series.[13]

Sportswriters in the *Philadelphia Tribune* did not hold back their withering contempt for the 1934 NNL2 championship series. Ed Harris covered the series extensively and decried the fact that "two sorry incidents" in Game Six set "[u]nhappy precedents" and fomented "out-and-out diamond lawlessness."[14] He regarded the actions by players Wilson and Brooks as "illegal" and "unfair to their teammates and to the fans that came to the game."[15] Harris further criticized Wilson and Brooks for forgetting "it was a championship game, that their services were valuable to the teams, [and] that spectators had paid to see a baseball game and not a court-room debate or a prize fight."[16] He both expressed sympathy for and criticized the umpires in Game Six. While acknowledging that umpires' decisions almost always attract criticism, Harris chastised them for not ejecting Wilson and Brooks. According to Harris, their actions set "unfortunate precedents" and gave Malacher ammunition for filing a protest with the league commissioner.[17]

The ugly 1934 series featuring the Stars and the American Giants marked the culmination of a decade of controversies regarding umpires and player conduct on the field. Much of the blame for what happened in 1934 belonged to Bolden and other owners who never figured out a realistic system for managing umpire crews. They also lacked the willpower to consistently enforce rules governing player behavior and allowed the problem to fester. The controversies about umpires bled into questions about race and whether latent racial prejudice factored into both the hiring of White umpires and the physical attacks on Black umpires.

A few months after the series ended, NNL2 owners replaced Wilson with a new commissioner, but the new commissioner and owners still failed to create a culture of accountability for on-field behavior. That lack of accountability came to the forefront a few years later when a spate of contract-jumping plagued the NNL2 and is Western counterpart, the Negro American League (NAL). Many of the top players in the Negro Leagues – including Satchel Paige and Josh Gibson – left their teams in the middle of the season and accepted more lucrative offers to play outside the United States. President Rafael Trujillo of the Dominican Republic, seeking to consolidate his political power, saw a successful baseball team as a great way to cement his position. Black players already were popular in the Caribbean because of winter league baseball, and they often earned more money playing in the Dominican Republic and other leagues in that region. The contract jumping caught Bolden and other owners flat-footed, and they responded with tough language that was not supported by tough actions. They welcomed back the contract jumpers, and the problem continued until World War II reduced those opportunities.[18]

Overall, the umpire-related controversies that defined the Stars' 1934 title had deep roots in Negro League history. The controversies were not a one-time event; on the contrary, they were part of a recurring story that stirred up passions and demonstrated the shortcomings of certain aspects of the Negro Leagues' operations. Black sportswriters who supported the leagues understandably expressed dismay and scorn at the on-field disputes that delayed games and seemingly had no resolution. The controversies also touched upon racial issues and contributed to Bolden's temporary exile from Black professional baseball in 1930. Sadly, the Stars never won, or even seriously contended for, another title after the 1934 season. The cloud of controversies and accusations that haunted the series prevented the team and Bolden from fully reveling in their accomplishments.

NOTES

1   "Status of Umpires Discussed at Meet of Commissioners," *Philadelphia Tribune*, April 19, 1924.

2   "Final Arrangements and Complete Details Are Made for East-West Baseball Classic," *Pittsburgh Courier*, September 20, 1924; "The Sportive Realm," *Pittsburgh Courier*, November 1, 1924.

3   W. Rollo Wilson, "Eastern Snapshots," *Pittsburgh Courier*, November 22, 1924.

4   Wilson, "Eastern Snapshots," *Pittsburgh Courier*, November 22, 1924.

5   "White Newspaperman Is Picked by Eastern League as Supervisor of Umpires," *Pittsburgh Courier*, March 28, 1925; "Hilldale Manager Takes Exception to Howe Cartoon," *Philadelphia Tribune*, April 4, 1925; J.M. Howe, "Sport Sidelights," *Philadelphia Tribune*, August 1, 1925; Wilson, "Eastern Snapshots," *Pittsburgh Courier*, August 1, 1925.

6   "Comes to Bat in Behalf of Umpires," *Pittsburgh Courier*, July 18, 1925; "Umpires Not Given Support Says Gholston," *Philadelphia Tribune*, September 5, 1925.

7   Wilson, "Eastern Snapshots," *Pittsburgh Courier*, September 12, 1925. The Hell Fighters (popularly known as the Hell Fighters of Harlem) were a famous Black regiment in the US Army in World War I.

8   Wilson, "Eastern Snapshots," *Pittsburgh Courier*, September 12, 1925.

9   "Near Riot at Shore When Cops Beat Cockrell; Bacharachs Win Game 1-0," *Philadelphia Tribune*, August 14, 1926; "Diamond Dust," *Philadelphia Tribune*, August 14, 1926; William G. Nunn, "Diamond Dope," *Pittsburgh Courier*, August 14, 1926; Wilson, "Eastern Snapshots," *Pittsburgh Courier*, August 21, 1926.

10   "Eastern League Formed, Grays Join," *Pittsburgh Courier*, January 19, 1929; Wilson, "American Negro League Flays Barnstorming; Reserves

Named," *Pittsburgh Courier,* March 2. 1929; "A.N. League Makes Laws," *Pittsburgh Courier,* June 8, 1929; "Possibility of New Baseball League to Replace Defunct Eastern Circuit Looms in Conclave Here Next Month," *Philadelphia Tribune,* January 3, 1929; "System of Rotating Umps Agreed by Baseball Magnates at Parley Here," *Philadelphia Tribune,* February 28, 1929; Neil Lanctot, *Negro League Baseball: The Rise and Ruin of a Black Institution* (Philadelphia: University of Pennsylvania Press, 2004), 192-193.

11   "Negro Umps at Hilldale," *Philadelphia Tribune,* August 1, 1929.

12   "Hilldale Again," *Philadelphia Tribune,* August 8, 1929.

13   "McDonald Wins 5-3 Sat.; Jones and Ellis Drop Games 3-0, 2-1," *Philadelphia Tribune,* September 20, 1934; Ed Harris, "To Be or Not to Be," *Philadelphia Tribune,* October 4, 1934; Harris, "… And Bright Stars," *Philadelphia Tribune,* October 11, 1934.

14   Harris, "To Be or Not to Be," *Philadelphia Tribune,* October 4, 1934.

15   Harris, "To Be or Not to Be," *Philadelphia Tribune,* October 4, 1934.

16   Harris, "To Be or Not to Be," *Philadelphia Tribune,* October 4, 1934.

17   Harris, "To Be or Not to Be," *Philadelphia Tribune,* October 4, 1934.

18   Courtney Michelle Smith, *Ed Bolden and Black Baseball in Philadelphia* (Jefferson, North Carolina: McFarland, 2017), 101-105.

CONTRIBUTORS

Rebecca T. Alpert is professor of religion emerita at Temple University in Philadelphia. She grew up in Brooklyn, rooting for the Dodgers, Mets, and Yankees. She received her PhD in religion at Temple University and her rabbinical training at the Reconstructionist Rabbinical College in Wyncote, Pennsylvania, where she transferred her loyalties to the Philadelphia Phillies.

She has published extensively for academic and general audiences on twentieth-century American Jewish history and culture with a focus on baseball. Her major work in the field, *Out of Left Field: Jews and Black Baseball*, was published by Oxford University Press in June 2011.

Her writings about baseball and race include "Jackie Robinson as a Jewish Icon," in *Shofar: The Journal of Interdisciplinary Jewish Studies* 26:2 (Winter 2008); "A Reason to Vote along Racial Lines," Oxford University Press weblog, August 2011; "Goose Tatum: The King of Showmen," Oxford University Press weblog, August 2011; "Buster Haywood and the Jews of Black Baseball," in Leonard Greenspoon, ed., *Jews in the Gym: Judaism, Sports and Athletics* (West Lafayette, Indiana: Purdue University Press, 2012); and "African-American Attitudes Towards Jews in the 'Negro Leagues': The Case of Effa Manley," in *Annual Review of the USC Casden Institute for the Study of the Jewish Role in America Life* (2014).

Her essay "Harry Passon: Philadelphia Baseball Entrepreneur" in *The National Pastime* (SABR, 2013), led to her writing in this volume.

Richard Bogovich's new book in 2022 was *Frank Grant: The Life of a Black Baseball Pioneer*. For McFarland & Co. he'd previously written *Kid Nichols: A Biography of the Hall of Fame Pitcher* and *The Who: A Who's Who*. He has contributed to such SABR books as *When the Monarchs Reigned: Kansas City's 1942 Negro League Champions* and *The Newark Eagles Take Flight: The Story of the 1946 Negro League Champions*. He works for the Wendland Utz law firm in Rochester, Minnesota.

Frederick C. "Rick" Bush has written articles for over two dozen SABR books, the Biography Project, and the Games Project. The current volume about the 1934 Philadelphia Stars is the sixth SABR book about the Negro Leagues that he has co-edited with Bill Nowlin; a previous book, *When the Monarchs Reigned: Kansas City's 1942 Negro League Champions* (2021), received the 2022 Robert Peterson Recognition Award. Rick lives with his wife, Michelle, their three sons – Michael, Andrew, and Daniel – and their border collie, Bailey, in the Houston metro area. He has been an educator for almost 30 years, the past 19 of which have been spent teaching English at Wharton County Junior College's satellite campus in Sugar Land, which is home to the Astros' Triple-A franchise.

Alan Cohen chairs the BioProject fact-checking committee, serves as vice president-treasurer of the Connecticut Smoky Joe Wood Chapter, and is a data-caster (MiLB first pitch stringer) for the Hartford Yard Goats of the Double-A Eastern League. His biographies, game stories, and essays have appeared in more than 65 SABR publications. He is a proud contributor to SABR books on the Negro Leagues including *Bittersweet Goodbye*, *Pride of Smoketown*, and *When the Monarchs Reigned*. His story "Josh Gibson Blazes a Trail" appeared in the Fall 2020 issue of the *Baseball Research Journal*. He is currently involved with the Retrosheet project on Negro League Games. He has four children, nine grandchildren, and one great-grandchild and resides in Connecticut with wife Frances, their cats, Ava and Zoe, and their dog, Buddy.

Joseph Gerard has been a lifelong Pittsburgh Pirates fan. He grew up hating the Yankees despite being born and raised in Newark, New Jersey – his biggest regret in life is that he was only 2 years old in 1960. Because of Roberto Clemente, he developed an interest in Latin-American baseball history and has contributed biographies of several Latin players to SABR's BioProject. He lives in New York City with his wife, Ann Marie, and their two children, Henry and Sophie.

Darren Gibson spent his Little League, Colt League, and high-school years in Lakewood, California, playing alongside multiple athletes who eventually made "The Show," but his baseball highlight was getting a "call-back" during walk-on try-outs at UCLA in the fall of 1988. Darren has been an avid baseball simulation player for decades, coached baseball and softball for his four children, and he still "bleeds Dodger blue." He has written over 35 SABR baseball-player biographies, and is currently a math teacher, coach, and high-school football official in Aliso Viejo, California.

Margaret M. "Peggy" Gripshover is a professor of geography at Western Kentucky University. She earned her PhD in Geography at the University of Tennessee and her MS and BS degrees in geography from Marshall University. She has been a SABR member since 2006 and combines her love of baseball with her geographic research on race, ethnicity, urbanization, horse racing, and cultural landscapes. Peggy has published articles in the *Baseball Research Journal* and contributed a chapter on "Wrigleyville" for *Northsiders: Essays on the History and Culture of the Chicago Cubs*, edited by Gerald R. Wood and Andy Hazucha (McFarland, 2008). She has written biographies for *Bittersweet Goodbye: The Black Barons, the Grays, and the 1948 Negro League World Series* (SABR 2017); *The Newark Eagles Take Flight: The Story of the 1946 Negro League Champions* (SABR 2019); *Pride of Smoketown: The 1935 Pittsburgh Crawfords* (SABR 2020); *When the Monarchs Reigned: Kansas City's 1942 Negro League Champions* (SABR 2021); and *The First Negro League Champion: The 1920 Chicago American Giants* (SABR 2022), all edited by Frederick C. Bush and Bill Nowlin. She is a native of Cincinnati and a lifelong Reds fan. She lives in Bowling Green, Kentucky, with her husband, Thomas L. Bell.

Michael Haupert is a professor of economics at the University of Wisconsin-La Crosse. He has been a member of SABR since 1985 and is co-chair of the SABR Business of Baseball Committee. He has published many articles and made numerous presentations on the business of baseball.

Leslie Heaphy is an associate professor of history at Kent State University at Stark. She has written or edited six books as well as numerous articles and book chapters on the Negro Leagues, women's baseball, and the New York Mets. She is the vice president of SABR and the president of the board for the International Women's Baseball Center.

Paul Hofmann has been a SABR member since 2002. He has contributed to more than 25 SABR publications and co-edited *The 1883 Philadelphia Athletics: American Association Champions*. Paul is currently the assistant vice president for international affairs at the University of Louisville and teaches in the College of Management at National Changhua University of Education in Taiwan. A native of Detroit, Paul is an avid baseball card collector and a lifelong Detroit Tigers fan. He resides in Lakeville, Minnesota.

Jay Hurd is a librarian, retired from Harvard University, and a museum educator. A member of the Society for American Baseball Research for more than 20 years, he contributes to the SABR Baseball Biography Project and presents on baseball-related topics including the Negro Leagues, baseball literature for children and young adults, and women in baseball. A longtime fan of the Boston Red Sox, Jay relocated from Medford, Massachusetts, to Bristol, Rhode Island in 2016. He continues to research baseball in Rhode Island, with special attention given to Lizzie Murphy, from Warren, Rhode Island, who played professional baseball exclusively on men's teams. He was interviewed on Lizzie Murphy by Rhode Island PBS.

Bill Johnson has contributed over 40 articles to SABR's BioProject and has presented papers at the 2011 Cooperstown Symposium on Baseball and American Culture, the 2017 Jerry Malloy Negro League Conference, and the inaugural Southern Negro League Conference. He has published a biography of Hal Trosky (McFarland and Co., 2017) and most recently an article about Negro American League All-Star Art "Superman" Pennington in the journal *Black Ball*. Bill and his wife, Chris, reside in Georgia.

Thomas E. Kern was born and raised in Southwest Pennsylvania. Listening to the mellifluous voices of Bob Prince and Jim Woods in his youth, how could one not become a lifelong Pirates fan? He now lives in Silver Spring, Maryland, and sees the Nationals and Orioles as often as possible. He is a SABR member dating back to the mid-1980s. With a love and appreciation for Negro League baseball, he has written SABR bios of Leon Day, John Henry Lloyd, Willie Foster, Judy Johnson, Turkey Stearnes, Hilton Smith, Louis Santop, Andy Cooper, and Buck Ewing. Tom's day job is in the field of transportation technology.

Bob LeMoine is a high-school librarian and adjunct professor at White Mountains Community College and Emporia State University. He lives in New Hampshire and has contributed to several SABR projects. Bob is the author of *When the Babe Went Back to Boston: Babe Ruth, Judge Fuchs, and the Hapless 1935 Boston Braves* (McFarland & Co., 2023).

Len Levin is a longtime newspaper editor in New England, now retired. He lives in Providence with his wife, Linda, and an overachieving orange cat. He now (Len, not the cat) is the grammarian for the Rhode Island Supreme Court and edits its decisions. He also copy-edits many SABR books, including this one. He is just down the interstate from Fenway Park, where he has spent many happy hours.

Bill Nowlin has written or edited over 100 books, mostly about baseball but with several related to the music business. He was one of three founders of Rounder Records, which released more than 3,000 albums of folk and related music. A native of Boston and a Red Sox fan, he – like Len Levin – enjoys spending time at his second home, Fenway Park.

Will Osgood is a former sports journalist who wrote for *Bleacher Report, FanSided,* and *Cover 32.* He graduated from San Diego State University in 2010 with a degree in communication while minoring in religious studies. Will is a diehard Cubs fan who cannot make up his mind on whether he loves the city of Chicago or New Orleans more.

James Overmyer writes and lectures on baseball history, primarily African American. He is author of *Queen of the Negro Leagues: Effa Manley and the Newark Eagles; Black Ball and the Boardwalk: The Bacharach Giants of Atlantic City, 1916-1929;* and *Cum Posey of the Homestead Grays: A Biography of the Negro Leagues Owner and Hall of Famer.*

Richard J. Puerzer is the chairperson of the department of engineering at Hofstra University. His writing on baseball has appeared in several SABR books, including *Bittersweet Goodbye: The Black Barons, The Grays, and the 1948 Negro League World Series* (2017) and *Pride of Smoketown: The 1935 Pittsburgh Crawfords* (2020), as well as in *Nine: A Journal of Baseball History and Culture; Black Ball; The National Pastime; The Cooperstown Symposium on Baseball and American Culture proceedings; Zisk;* and *Spitball.* He and his wife, Clare, have four children, Casey, Aaron, Josh, and Addie.

Chris Rainey (1951-2020) was a SABR member since the late 1970s when he helped Eugene Murdock transcribe interviews of former players. In 2008 he wrapped up a 35-year teaching/coaching career in Yellow Springs, Ohio, and used some of his newfound spare time to write more than 80 player biographies for SABR books and the BioProject website.

Carl Riechers retired from United Parcel Service in 2012 after 35 years of service. With more free time, he became a SABR member. Born and raised in the suburbs of St. Louis, he became a big fan of the Cardinals. He and his wife, Janet, have three children and he is the proud grandpa of two.

Courtney Michelle Smith is a professor and chair of the history and political science department at Cabrini University in Radnor, Pennsylvania. She is a lifelong fan of the Philadelphia Phillies and the rest of Philadelphia's sports teams. She is the author of *Ed Bolden and Black Baseball in Philadelphia* and *Jackie Robinson: A Life in American History.* Her work also appeared in *From Shibe Park to Connie Mack Stadium: Great Games in Philadelphia's Lost Ballpark* and *Sports in Philadelphia.* Aside from baseball, her research interests include Philadelphia history, Pennsylvania history, and American political history. She spends her free time rooting for the Phillies, Eagles, Sixers, Flyers, and Union.

Jeb Stewart is a lawyer in Birmingham, Alabama, whose favorite pastime has always been taking his sons, Nolan and Ryan, and his wife, Stephanie, to the Rickwood Classic each year. He has been a SABR member since 2012 and is co-president of the Rickwood Field SABR Chapter. He is an executive committee member on the board of the Friends of Rickwood Field and is a regular contributor to the *Rickwood Times.* He also edits the Friends' quarterly newsletter, "Rickwood Tales." He has written several biographies for SABR's Baseball Biography Project.

Upon realizing that he couldn't hit the curveball, **Mike Whiteman** turned to reading and writing about the national pastime. He is a regular contributor to the Yankee-themed blog *Start Spreading the News* and has contributed to six SABR book projects. He enjoys summers on his porch in Lancaster, Pennsylvania listening to baseball on the radio. His home team includes his wife, Nichole, and their two daughters.

Dave Wilkie grew up a third-generation San Francisco Giants fan in Western Canada idolizing Willie McCovey, Vida Blue, and Jack Clark. His obsession with Negro League baseball can be traced to a 1983 mail-order purchase of the book *The All-Time All-Stars of Black Baseball,* by SABR member James A. Riley. He has written SABR biographies of Negro League greats Sam Bankhead, Johnny Davis, Chester Williams, Cool Papa Bell, Frank Duncan, and Judy Gans. Dave lives in Richmond, Virginia, with his son, Monte, and is currently working on his first book.

The SABR Digital Library

Available wherever books are sold

Friends of SABR

You can become a Friend of SABR by giving as little as $10 per month or by making a one-time gift of $1,000 or more. When you do so, you will be inducted into a community of passionate baseball fans dedicated to supporting SABR's work.

Friends of SABR receive the following benefits:
- ✓ Annual Friends of SABR Commemorative Lapel Pin
- ✓ Recognition in This Week in SABR, SABR.org, and the SABR Annual Report
- ✓ Access to the SABR Annual Convention VIP donor event
- ✓ Invitations to exclusive Friends of SABR events

SABR On-Deck Circle - $10/month, $30/month, $50/month
Get in the SABR On-Deck Circle, and help SABR become the essential community for the world of baseball. Your support will build capacity around all things SABR, including publications, website content, podcast development, and community growth.

A monthly gift is deducted from your bank account or charged to a credit card until you tell us to stop. No more email, mail, or phone reminders.

 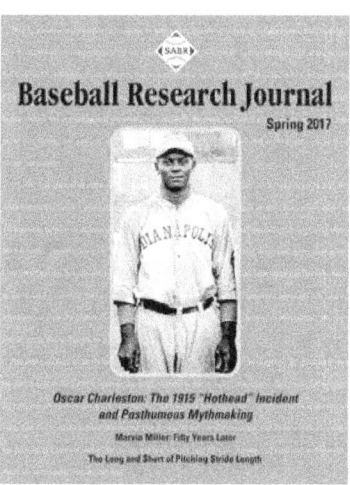 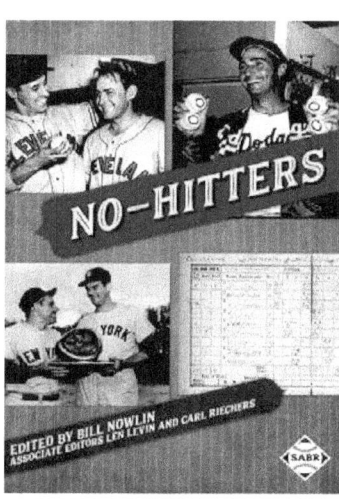

Join the SABR On-Deck Circle

Payment Info: _____Visa _____Mastercard

Name on Card: _____

Card #: _____

Exp. Date: _____ Security Code: _____

Signature: _____

- ○ $10/month
- ○ $30/month
- ○ $50/month
- ○ Other amount _____

Go to sabr.org/donate to make your gift online

Society for American Baseball Research

Cronkite School at ASU
555 N. Central Ave. #416, Phoenix, AZ 85004
602.496.1460 (phone)
SABR.org

Become a SABR member today!

If you're interested in baseball — writing about it, reading about it, talking about it — there's a place for you in the Society for American Baseball Research.

SABR memberships are available on annual, multi-year, or monthly subscription basis. Annual and monthly subscription memberships auto-renew for your convenience. Young Professional memberships are for ages 30 and under. Senior memberships are for ages 65 and older. Student memberships are available to currently enrolled middle/high school or full-time college/university students. Monthly subscription members receive SABR publications electronically and are eligible for SABR event discounts after 12 months.

Here's a list of some of the key benefits you'll receive as a SABR member:

- Receive two editions (spring and fall) of the *Baseball Research Journal*, our flagship publication
- Receive expanded e-book edition of *The National Pastime*, our annual convention journal
- 8-10 new e-books published by the SABR Digital Library, all FREE to members
- "This Week in SABR" e-newsletter, sent to members every Friday
- Join dozens of research committees, from Statistical Analysis to Women in Baseball.
- Join one of 70+ regional chapters in the U.S., Canada, Latin America, and abroad
- Participate in online discussion groups
- Ask and answer baseball research questions on the SABR-L e-mail listserv
- Complete archives of *The Sporting News* dating back to 1886 and other research resources
- Promote your research in "This Week in SABR"
- Diamond Dollars Case Competition
- Yoseloff Scholarships

- Discounts on SABR national conferences, including the SABR National Convention, the SABR Analytics Conference, Jerry Malloy Negro League Conference, Frederick Ivor-Campbell 19th Century Conference, and the Arizona Fall League Experience
- Publish your research in peer-reviewed SABR journals
- Collaborate with SABR researchers and experts
- Contribute to Baseball Biography Project or the SABR Games Project
- List your new book in the SABR Bookshelf
- Lead a SABR research committee or chapter
- Networking opportunities at SABR Analytics Conference
- Meet baseball authors and historians at SABR events and chapter meetings
- 50% discounts on paperback versions of SABR e-books
- Discounts with other partners in the baseball community
- SABR research awards

We hope you'll join the most passionate international community of baseball fans at SABR! Check us out online at SABR.org/join.

- - - ✄ -

SABR MEMBERSHIP FORM

	Standard	Senior	Young Pro.	Student
Annual:	❏ $65	❏ $45	❏ $45	❏ $25
3 Year:	❏ $175	❏ $129	❏ $129	
5 Year:	❏ $249			
Monthly:	❏ $6.95	❏ $4.95	❏ $4.95	

(International members wishing to be mailed the Baseball Research Journal should add $10/yr for Canada/Mexico or $19/yr for overseas locations.)

Participate in Our Donor Program!

Support the preservation of baseball research. Designate your gift toward:

❏ General Fund   ❏ Endowment Fund   ❏ Research Resources   ❏ _____
❏ I want to maximize the impact of my gift: do not send any donor premiums
❏ I would like this gift to remain anonymous.

Note: Any donation not designated will be placed in the General Fund.
SABR is a 501 (c) (3) not-for-profit organization & donations are tax-deductible to the extent allowed by law.

Name _____

E-mail* _____

Address _____

City _____ ST _____ ZIP _____

Phone _____ Birthday _____

* Your e-mail address on file ensures you will receive the most recent SABR news.

Dues $_____

Donation $_____

Amount Enclosed $_____

Do you work for a matching grant corporation? Call (602) 496-1460 for details.

If you wish to pay by credit card, please contact the SABR office at (602) 496-1460 or sign up securely online at SABR.org/join. We accept Visa, Mastercard & Discover.

Do you wish to receive the *Baseball Research Journal* electronically? ❏ Yes   ❏ No
Our e-books are available in PDF, Kindle, or EPUB (iBooks, iPad, Nook) formats.

Mail to: SABR, Cronkite School at ASU, 555 N. Central Ave. #416, Phoenix, AZ 85004

10/19

www.ingramcontent.com/pod-product-compliance
Lightning Source LLC
Chambersburg PA
CBHW080954120626
46546CB00010B/2893